John Locke (1632–1704) is a central figure in the history of thought, and in liberal doctrine especially. This is the first major study of his thought to bring a range of his wider views to bear upon his political theory.

Every political theorist has a vision, a view about the basic features of life and society, as well as a technique which mediates this into propositions about politics. Locke's vision spanned questions concerning Christian worship, ethics, political economy, medicine, the human understanding, revealed theology and education. This study shows how the character of these wider concerns informed *Two Treatises of Government*, especially in respect of a view of divine teleology, and situated a distinctive view of politics which treated the state and the church in parallel terms. Locke's political theory suggested the revision or replacement of many prevailing positions. It also indicates the indivisibility of thought, for in its turn it contributed to the further development of his vision. By connecting his wider interests with his political thought, this volume offers the first intergrated study of the mind of John Locke.

The mind of John Locke

The mind of John Locke

A study of political theory in its intellectual setting

Ian Harris

CAMBRIDGE
UNIVERSITY PRESS

Published by the Press Syndicate of the University of Cambridge
The Pitt Building, Trumpington Street, Cambridge CB2 1RP
40 West 20th Street, New York, NY 10011-4211 USA
10 Stamford Road, Oakleigh, Melbourne 3166, Australia

© Cambridge University Press 1994

First published 1994
Reprinted 1995

Printed in Great Britain by Athenæum Press Ltd, Gateshead, Tyne & Wear

A catalogue record for this book is available from the British Library

Library of Congress cataloguing in publication data

Harris, Ian.
The mind of John Locke: a study of political theory in its intellectual
setting / Ian Harris.
        p.   cm.
Includes bibliographical references and indexes.
ISBN 0 521 35603 2 (hardback)
1. Locke, John, 1632–1704 – Contributions in political science.
JC153.L87H37   1994
320.5′12′092–dc20   93-2917   CIP

ISBN 0 521 35603 2 hardback

TYPESET BY DATIX INTERNATIONAL LIMITED, BUNGAY, SUFFOLK

Parentibus optimis
has primitias
D.D.D.
auctor

Contents

	page
Preface	xi
Acknowledgements	xii
A note on citations	xiv
Introduction	1
Chapter 1	17
Chapter 2	44
Chapter 3	78
Chapter 4	108
Chapter 5	127
Chapter 6	160
Chapter 7	192
Chapter 8	252
Chapter 9	280
Chapter 10	290
Conclusion	319
Notes	331
Bibliography	392
Index of persons	421
Index of subjects	426

Preface

John Locke was a thinker of great range and power. His mind spanned questions concerning the church, ethics, political economy, medicine, the human understanding and education. The object of this study is to show how the character of these concerns informed his political theory, and also how in its turn the latter affected his subsequent views. Locke's political thought at once embodied the power of a wider vision and contributed to its further development.

The subject matter affords ample occasion for the present study. It also suggests that a distinct manner of writing about political theory is appropriate here, one which does justice to substantive continuities of thought across the conventional boundaries of discourse. Locke's political thought figures as the product of a wider vision of existence. Of course, it is not that alone: in particular, it embodies a technique through which general views were mediated into propositions of a specifically political relevance. This study, then, concerns both vision and technique in order to understand the character and relations of Locke's political thought.

Its treatment is restricted to matters fundamental to this task: a wider project would no doubt embrace much besides. But it is true in another and a more important sense that there is always much to add, and there is no place more appropriate than a study of a developing mind to remark that books are evidence of a writer's footprints rather than his destination.

Middlesbrough,
29th August, 1992

Acknowledgements

To compile a list of acknowledgements properly would be to write part of one's own biography, and, interesting though this might be to the writer, the reader may prefer to know who and what helped to make this particular book. What follows, accordingly, is incomplete but not the less for that an expression of gratitude. John Dunn, besides advising and encouraging, has read every draft of my writings about Locke, and but for his support at a crucial juncture the results, had there been any, would have been much poorer. Maurice Cowling has been generous in many ways. Richard Tuck's help has not been the less thoughtful for being apparently casual. The direction the present book has taken owes a good deal to the candid probings, both written and spoken, of Michael Ayers, and to his intellectual tolerance too. Tom Pink read the penultimate draft and improved it with a number of constructive suggestions. But none of these is responsible for any errors or omissions which may remain in the text. The same is true of those who have discussed Lockean matters with me, read preceding pieces of mine or who have directed me to information I might otherwise have missed, not least because they may not recognise the results their interventions produced: Hans Aarsleff, John Day, Peter Glazebrook, Robert Heuston, Tim Hochstrasser, John Hoffman, Mark Knights, Paul Langford, John Rogers, Henry Schankula, Quentin Skinner, Sandy Stewart, Ian Tipton, John Walsh, David Wootton, Keith Wrightson, Jean Yolton and John Yolton. William Davies has been a most considerate, as well as a very patient editor on behalf of Cambridge University Press. A debt infinitely greater than all of these combined, which is difficult to state and which I can never repay, is recorded very inadequately in the dedication.

The present work is the outcome of a process which has involved many other sorts of activity and whose destination, as planned originally, would have been quite different. Accordingly a great many institutional debts have been incurred in producing it, and an acknowledgement here stands for something besides support for this book. First in time came a state research studentship, administered by the British Academy, and augmented both by generous subventions from the I.C.I. Educational Trust and by the munificent patronage of a scholarship on Dr Lightfoot's foundation under the old regulations. The Master and Fellows of Jesus College, Cambridge, by electing me to a research fellowship, allowed this and much else to be begun. The University of Leicester provided conditions under which it has been possible to further it. Travel grants necessary to undertake research have been provided by Peterhouse and Jesus College, Cambridge, the Prince Consort and Thirlwall, and Worts Funds of Cambridge University, the I.C.I. Educational Trust and the Research Board of the University of Leicester. A good deal of the research embodied here drew upon the patience of librarians as well as the resources of libraries: thanks are due to the staff of the Bodleian Library, Oxford (especially Duke Humfrey's Reading Room), Cambridge University Library (especially the Rare Books Room), the Library of St John's College, Cambridge, the British Library, Middlesbrough libraries (especially the reference library), the Pierpont Morgan Library, New York, the Houghton Library of Harvard University, the Beinecke Library of Yale University, the Newberry Library, Chicago, the Henry E. Huntington Library, Somerset County Record Office, the Public Record Office and Leicester University Library (especially the Inter-Library Loan department). The Old Library at Jesus College, Cambridge has a special place as a constantly accessible collection of seventeenth-century works. For permission to quote manuscript material, thanks are due to the Keeper of Western Manuscripts at the Bodleian Library and to the directors of the British Library, the Houghton Library, the Beinecke Library and the Pierpont Morgan Library and to the Master and Fellows of St John's College, Cambridge.

A note on citations

1 *Citations in the Text*

The titles by which Locke's works (and others) are cited in the text derive from usage common to scholars rather than to bibliographical exactness. For this there are several reasons. Firstly, many seventeenth-century titles furnish sufficient material for a modern preface, and it would be cumbersome (as well as needless) to reproduce them in full. Thus, instead of referring to *Two Treatises of Government: In the Former, The False Principles and Foundation of Sir Robert Filmer, And His Followers, Are Detected and Overthrown. The Latter is an ESSAY concerning The True Original, Extent, and End of Civil-Government.*, we content ourselves with writing about *Two Treatises of Government* or even *Two Treatises*, and in a like way to Locke's *Essay concerning . . . Civil-Government*. Secondly, several of the writings examined here were not published by Locke himself, and the titles given to them by their modern editors do not always accord with the manuscripts. It would be a pedantic extravagance to refer to them by their manuscript titles when they are already familiar by other names. Thirdly, there is one case where the usage of scholars is perhaps less scholarly than it ought to be, for they refer to Locke's *First Treatise* and *Second Treatise*, and so suggest that the two parts of *Two Treatises of Government* are separate enterprises rather than 'Book One' and 'Book Two' (as Locke called them) of a single volume. The prevalence of this usage makes it useless to attempt a better replacement, and so (as in so many cases) people must condone what they cannot approve.

2 *References*

The notes and references are gathered after the text but before the bibliography. They are given according to the unlovely but economical Harvard form. Two sorts of exemption have been made. Firstly, Locke's works have been cited by short title, so that the reader can see immediately which texts are being adduced. Secondly, a few classical works, which have no real publication date and whose appearances here would be unaffected by citing critical editions, are cited by their titles (Thus: Plato *Republic* rather than Plato (n.d.)).

The bibliography contains fuller versions of the titles of Locke's writings along with publication details, as well as listing manuscript sources consulted. The list of other works, both primary and secondary, gives references for works *cited* rather than providing a rather more comprehensive list of works *read*.

3 *Dates*

All dates are given according to the Old Style, except that the year is reckoned as beginning on 1 January.

Introduction

To write about *The Mind of John Locke* may strike the reader as a large undertaking, but it is not so daunting as it sounds. For the dictionaries understand by mind the direction or tendency of someone's thoughts. This corresponds to the modest volume in the reader's hand, which sets out to illustrate the direction of Locke's thought, referred especially to his political theory. Its objective is, firstly, to show how the character of Locke's political thought is intelligible in terms of his views and assumptions about other subjects, remote as some of these may seem at first sight, and, secondly, to indicate how his thought subsequent to his *Treatises of Government* and *Epistola de Tolerantia* bear the impress of his political position. It thus treats his political theory as a central item in his thought as a whole. The volume is modest, for its concern with direction implies neither a comprehensive study of Locke's development nor a treatment of every aspect of his thought nor even a full examination of each matter it does include. It addresses only those parts of Locke's thought which are connected immediately with his political theory and thus are connected with one another.

I

Every political theory involves two complementary but essentially distinguishable elements. There is, firstly, the author's view about the basic features of life and society, about what is and what is not fundamental to existence. Let us call this the theorist's vision. There is, secondly, the theorist's technique, the apparatus by which he or she turns the vision into a work about politics.

The vision need not be restricted to matters internal to political organisation and behaviour. Indeed it is hard to see that it could be limited in this way. Whether we understand politics in terms of government or as an aspect of human conduct, much the larger part of life is distinct from it. Morals, religion, education, philosophy, the natural sciences, and art, besides many others, have their claims. It is

1

these which compose a thinker's general vision, and if a view of politics is part of this, it is *only* a part. To understand it properly, then, is to understand the larger vision of the thinker.

Without this understanding, it is probable that the theorist's technique will be misunderstood or, at the least, situated misleadingly. Technique is the means of achieving a purpose and a thinker's purpose does not derive from political affairs alone. The theorist forms it from an attitude to these affairs which is informed by his or her prepossessions – prepossessions that embody a much wider vision (which may, or may not, include a prior general view of politics). Pamphleteers and polemicists may have only a view of affairs, but if so their purpose does not suggest the claim to general significance implied in theoretical writing.

Amidst the numerous particular strengths of scholarly writing about Locke, there is one general weakness. His vision has not been studied with the attention that it demands. To offer an account of that vision implies a sense of Locke's principal works and their connections with each other. Even if the study of Locke's vision is referred to a particular subject, as it is here, this is not a slight task for the scale and diversity of Locke's writing challenge comparison with most. Neither has the trend of scholarship pointed towards a treatment of this sort.

The general direction of the historiography of Locke's politics, for instance, relates to two very partial attempts at characterising his position. The earlier of the two, Leo Strauss', suggested that Locke's professed concern with God and a duty-based morality was a front – deceiving the reader and possibly Locke himself about the real character of his views; these were in fact extremely close to those of Hobbes. The other, C.B. Macpherson's, characterised Locke's real concern as the development of exclusive property rights at the expense of older views of society. These attempts[1] shared an encyclopedic inattention to most of Locke's articulated positions in the second of his *Treatises* and a similar posture towards his concerns beyond that text (unless these could be turned to use in supporting the interpreter's view of it.[2]) The succeeding historiography, whose most distinguished examples in effect supersede rather than merely answer Strauss and Macpherson,[3] escaped their assumptions and indicated that to understand Locke's political posture implies a clear sense of his theological suppositions.[4] The centrality of that position is evident, in that the recent strain of writing which conceives Locke as a figure radical or subversive in relation to aspects of his day (and so continues the tendency, though by no means the specific destination of the earlier historiography) takes serious account of it.[5] But by one of those effects so frequent in academic writing, the works which

2

escape from the conclusions of the earlier historiography have continued to focus attention upon the *Essay concerning . . . Civil-Government*. The focus, of course, is not exclusive: yet it remains true that Locke's other writings receive mention from those who write about his political theory by way of elucidating this central text.[6]

In an obvious sense this concentration is quite proper: attending to Locke's principal treatment of civil government is obviously appropriate. But at the same time it leaves aside the evident fact that this work is one part of Locke's political theory: his writings on toleration belong to it too. Relatively little attention has been paid to these.[7] That little does not concern itself with the question which putting Locke's *Epistola* beside his *Treatises* raises: namely how these parts of his political theory relate to each other.

The pattern of historiography for Locke's writings on the human understanding is similar, in that it displays a broadening of attention within the bounds of a single work. The doyen and exemplar of writing upon *An Essay concerning Human Understanding* for many years was James Gibson's large work.[8] This concentrated upon Locke's treatment of ideas and knowledge in a way which effectively ignored his concern with ethics and its place in his view of the mind.[9] Richard Aaron's work broadened its focus to address both Locke's morals and his politics, but did so in a way that separated them from his philosophical concerns.[10] It is only recently that Locke's moral philosophy has been given a central place in the historiography of *An Essay*[11]. Again, that work remains the focus of the overwhelming bulk of work about Locke's philosophy.[12]

Thus the principal foci of scholarly writing about Locke have been his *Essay concerning . . . Civil-Government* and *An Essay concerning Human Understanding*. These two foci have been conceived separately, on the whole, and attempts to connect the two have aimed to show how certain concepts in the latter elucidate aspects of the former.[13] Locke's other writings, of course, have not been forgotten and scholarly works about them endeavour not to leave them isolated from the two spotlights of attention.[14]

None of this is to say that Locke's vision has been entirely neglected. The accent which lies upon his theology in writing about his politics ensures otherwise, whilst several editions of his works and the publication of his correspondence cast much light upon his various concerns.[15] Yet if one were to examine the literature about Locke[16] one would find that the two essays on civil government and the understanding absorb by far the greatests amount of scholarly energy. In an obvious sense this is as it should be, and it is no part of the present writer's purpose to diminish the importance of these two works. It is rather to suggest that Locke's political theory benefits from a more determined attention to his wider work.

We may say, firstly, that many matters are simply absent (or nearly so) from the scholar's agenda. Toleration, as we have noted, is surely part of political theory and toleration is certainly the subject of a large part of Locke's writing. Again, Locke presumably meant his *First Treatise* to bear some close relation to his second when he put them between a single set of covers. In the midst of a concern with the theology in Locke's politics the question of what secular elements they may contain goes unasked, just as by contrast the significance of theological assumptions in his philosophy requires attention. These latter questions remind us that to broaden the focus of our attention is to begin enquiries that relate Locke's different works to each other, and so we obtain a sense of his vision.

We can say, secondly, that to answer questions like these will draw attention to points which are important to understanding Locke's political theory, but which have been overlooked through too exclusive a concentration on the *Essay concerning . . . Civil-Government*. One example would be that Locke's relation to Hobbes comes into relief: he did address Hobbes, though at an earlier point than has been supposed, and the way in which he did so was significant for his own political position.[17] Again, Locke's view of toleration had important implications for his view of the state. Another central example is that *Two Treatises* display a logical interconnection of a highly significant kind: the first specified a teleology which is vital to the arguments of the second.[18] That teleology, moreover, was situated by Locke's preceding views on medicine, political economy and, especially, the human understanding. These examples could be multiplied, as the reader will see, and can be complemented by cases illustrating how political commitments were important for Locke's subsequent thought. For the moment, there is a more general reflection.

A thinker's vision, precisely because it is a vision, is continuous: its parts connect with each other. No doubt if our interest in with some specific part of the vision, we shall direct our attention principally to it and to those of the other parts that are most germane to it: but it is not prudent to forget the significance of these. For by understanding the vision we are better placed to understand the purpose to which a specific technique answers. To give an example in terms which are concrete (but, it is to be hoped, not sufficiently concrete to suppress curiosity), it will be seen that the character of the theological postulates in Locke's vision led him to treat the state as a secular organisation.

4

That treatment is reflected in his political purpose, which was broader than has been supposed. Locke's aim was not confined to civil government, but involved a wider reassessment of the state, the church and their relations to each other.

We will see also, that vision and technique are interdependent. For instance, this reassessment of church and state proceeded in the light of Locke's assumptions about the human understanding, so that vision informed technique, and also involved a view of agency and responsibility with important implications for his wider views, so that technique reacted upon vision. Thus, where Locke commenced with theological postulates that were not unusual and perhaps unexamined we find that by the end of his life the place of Adam, whether in linguistics, political order or revealed theology has been strikingly revised. But these remarks are anticipations of the book that follows: perhaps a word about how visions are composed is in order.

II

Intellectual relations are such that an idea in one area of thought often affects the ideas held in others, superficially distinct from the first though they may be. Ideas, like people, are rarely without relations. More specifically, it frequently happens in the work of distinguished thinkers that a series of ideas span a wide intellectual area to form a pattern of thought. Because the ideas embodied in it agree, together they provide a connected view of many, apparently diverse, questions. Indeed the intellectual range they cover often spans several of those fields which are conventionally distinguished in academic study. This coverage often strengthens the plausibility of each part, for whilst these ideas need not be logically implicated their connection offers a picture, if not of the world, then of a good part of it.

Those relations are possible because ideas, at least those outside of the more austere parts of logic and mathematics, are neither so utterly univocal nor so self-contained as to exclude a wide range of connections. Ideas, firstly, are likely to admit of a number of interpretations, as anyone who has ever given even the slightest thought to a term like 'freedom' is bound to admit. For that reason, secondly, each is capable, under different interpretations, of joining in company with a variety of other ideas. 'Nature' refers in Rousseau's hands to a more or less primitive condition, whilst for Burke it means the consummation of civilisation. The student of the history of thought is more frequently struck by the ingenuity with which these possibilities are exploited than by ideas that are confined to only one reference.

5

Neither should we suppose that ideas respect rigid boundaries. A concept, or a group of concepts, may pattern a thinker's view of an area which may seem very remote from the one where it was first formulated. Malthus' view of competition for survival, formulated with respect to human societies, struck Darwin as a powerful device to explain natural evolution. Again, a concept may make its mark in areas, apparently quite diverse and separate, within the thought of a single writer. Adam Smith's moral philosophy and his political economy alike reflect his assumptions about inequality in society and those assumptions, indeed, lend to those two departments a common direction.

Thus families of ideas are formed in a thinker's mind. The vision which they compose may come together in many ways. For instance, an idea interpreted in a given way will colour his or her view not of one subject alone, but of two or perhaps more, and so display a series of concepts, forming together a distinct understanding. For example, a reaction against the totalitarian view that society should embody a single, consistent and exclusive set of values embodies itself within the work of Isaiah Berlin not only in a highly distinctive interpretation of liberty, which would exclude the legitimate imposition of such a monolithic scheme, but also in an understanding of values as inconsistent with one another, which renders a univocal ethical scheme impossible. Besides which Berlin has developed, albeit in a manner more aphoristic than explanatory, an account of European intellectual history since the 1730s, which situates his account of values and focusses on figures superficially so disparate as Vico, Herder, Hamann and Montesquieu (not to mention Machiavelli).[19] It will be seen that whilst none of these three concerns logically demands either of the others, together they produce a distinctive mapping of a broad range of conceptual concerns.

We should not suppose that because a concept appears in one family it cannot be found in another. Just as a given understanding of a concept may be possible because that concept admits of more than one reading, so the existence of the family does not exclude the use of the same concept as part of quite a different ensemble by another thinker. The notion that mankind is sociable has quite different bearings in Grotius and Kant because where the former treats conflict as a derogation from social existence, the latter assumes that conflict originates from sociability. Sometimes, too, different thinkers may use the same understanding of a idea for quite different purposes, whether by combining it with a different set of ideas or merely by directing it towards another subject matter. Where Blackstone had supposed that law was command in order to relate God and the human legislator analogically, Bentham used the same supposition to argue that the common law did not really qualify as law and, treating theology sceptically, to insinuate that God was not really a legislator.

The capital point is that a family of ideas offer a *connected* vision of reality. The connection can take many forms. It may be merely that the views held by an author in one area within a department of thought are dovetailed into another, as Hobbes' account of divine law is accommodated to his view of sovereignty. It may be something more extensive, as where Pareto's sociology and his economics both suggest a world in which inequalities are legitimate and ineradicable. It may be that there is throughout a large and diverse body of writing the development of one or two propositions, as we find with Durkheim, or a sort of intellectual game of tag in which the solution to one problem generates a further difficulty, which we find in the works of Rousseau. There is the case too where ideas on disparate subjects are united by a single style and direction of argument, as in Mill's later writings, or the quite different case where unity derives from a search for arguments to support and situate a single dominant assumption, which we encounter in Rawls. Not least there is the deliberate project of making all departments of thought answer to one intellectual signature, characteristic of Hegel. No doubt many other modes of connection can be envisaged, and it would be fruitless to limit them categorically. At any rate these relations, however created, have been amongst the most salient features of intellectual life, and are overlooked only because that life is organised nowadays according to the demands of delimited professions.

These matters concern the genesis and development of ideas, rather than their validity. It is true, no doubt, that all of the ideas mentioned are ones that have admitted of a reasoned idiom and, in that sense, they may be described as rational. Rational discourse, however, is not a sufficient condition for truth, though it may be a necessary one.

A family of ideas, then, may constitute a grouping of ideas, each understood in a way that relates it to at least one of the others and which together provide a distinctive vision of the conceptual map. We shall see how Locke's vision came to be formed, but first it may be worth making some general points about vision in political argument.

III

We need not suppose that the bodies of thought we distinguish customarily are always substantively discontinuous. It is true, certainly, that some writers devote themselves entirely to work which lies within one body and that their ideas manifest a familial relationship which does not extend beyond it. But it is true also that we find frequently that these boundaries are effectively discounted by other writers, whose ideas pattern a wider range of concerns.

The subjects that bear upon human conduct tend especially to invite this treatment. It is quite difficult to form a satisfying picture of them which draws ideas from only one genre. If we were to begin by categorising Weber's typology of traditional, charismatic and bureaucratic domination as political sociology, we would find it difficult to confine his related concern with rationality within the same category, still less the connection of the latter with his view of religion. Certainly a picture of one aspect is likely to adumbrate a view of others.

Of the subjects that bear upon human conduct, politics is worthy of especial note because it is, in its nature, a composite. One of the characteristic habits of the more important thinkers is to pattern a number of conceptual fields in a way which they take to be coherent: hence the fascination of history of thought and its irreducibility to a single set of ideas. But it is true of politics especially that it *cannot* be isolated successfully from the other aspects of human conduct. To think about politics is to have not merely a technique but also sense of those many aspects of life and thought which affect political positions or are themselves the subject of political decision. The exception, perhaps, is where behaviour may be conceived in mathematical terms, but this concerns only a very small area of political life. The questions which most often interest political thinkers have wider reference.

In considering significant political thinkers, then, we are bound to encounter ideas with relations that extend beyond political organisation and behaviour. Political theory is informed by considerations that lie beyond it, if we suppose that reflection has categories that are sharply distinct. By a like token, political theory will have implications for other areas within a thinker's mind. For instance, this study of Locke will show how his political theory, which itself includes his view of toleration, is informed by his arguments and assumptions about the social order, religious practice, ethics, theology, political economy and the human understanding. It will show, too, how his political theory related to his mature view of the human understanding, as well as bearing upon his view of the church, education and revealed theology.

IV

Political argument, the result of technique's work upon vision, provokes at least two questions. They are, *how does it work?* and *how does it come to be formed?*

The first question presents itself because the very point of translating a vision into a specific form in one way rather than another is to lead the reader (and perhaps the writer) to conceive matters in one way rather than another, and this is primarily a matter of argument. This purpose depends upon a theorist's ability to combine ideas in a given way. He or she may draw or adapt some of these ideas from others' work, some from their own vision and some may be devised for the occasion. To understand how the thinker executes this purpose, we must examine the ideas that compose the text and ask how they are related to each other.

To do justice to a writer's purpose, then, implies looking not merely at a few words or phrases from a given text but on taking into consideration its whole direction and its background in its author's vision. For the work may bespeak an overall design and reflect a wider view and to neglect these is to risk misinterpreting the pattern of thought before us. It is true that life is short and that books about books ought to be shorter, but before we write them we must assure ourselves at least that the principal constituents in a text have been related to each other or, if we suppose a work to be defective or to have a divided aim, understood to be separate from one another. Whether or not all the results of this enquiry are presented in print, its findings should inform our understanding of any work. In short, the terms on which a piece *works* need to be considered.

Complementary to this question is an enquiry into how a given family of ideas comes to be formed. Whilst it is probably not fruitful to catalogue exclusively the many ways in which this can happen, a question that can be answered properly only by examining evidence, one or two points *about* the process are worth making.

The first concerns the contingency of the terms on which visions and purposes are formed. If we were to take a section at virtually any point in the history of thought, we would find that any thinker, except perhaps one very badly informed, had before him or her a range of ideas or interpretations of ideas on a given spread of subjects that admitted of choice amongst those ideas, even assuming in that thinker no independent power of intellectual construction. Neither is it likely that so many of the patterns into which those ideas had been assembled before he or she considered them would be so obviously defective in their logic that only one of them would be intellectually respectable: if it were so, then the history of thought would have been a great deal simpler than in fact it is. To compose a family of ideas of one's own, then, may imply a degree of choice, and to do so in the face of a range of intellectual possibilities implies something by way of purpose.

How that purpose is constituted is another question, and one to which a great many answers are possible. We cannot always assume fixity of opinion from the word go. Each person imbibes opinions, but these can be augmented, revised or sloughed off. There are vast ranges of thought from which to choose and many reasons for choosing. Sometimes practical considerations may be necessary for a mind to assume a determinate shape in the presence of intellectual diversity. But to be categorical here is to pre-empt enquiry.

The second is that usually an historical account is the most appropriate way to understand the shape of a family of ideas. The ideas and their connections, of course, will be capable of being expressed in propositional form and so are intelligible if their terms are understood. But understanding *why* just those connections are formed is a rather different matter. Everything we have noted so far suggests that this not the product of rational inference alone. Certainly the ideas with which a theorist is working must admit of some connection: but the nature of the connection may not be inferential – it may be that a given idea protects another from a possible line of criticism, for instance. More generally, understanding why a thinker moves in a given direction may depend upon understanding the preceding trajectory of their thought. The examples could be multiplied, but the contingent element in the formation of families of ideas points to the historical mode of understanding.

Just because our business is to display connections and their formation, the character as well as the relations amongst ideas must be carefully considered. The character of the connections in hand cannot be understood without delineating both the ideas and how they are connected. It is necessary, too, that the properties of arguments be studied critically. This is not to say that thinkers need be subject to criticism for having the misfortune not to belong to a different school of thought or to a more 'knowing' epoch. Rather it suggests that understanding arguments implies understanding their deficiencies, especially their deficiencies for the purpose their author had in mind, for these are surely as much part of them as any other feature. For instance difficulties or omissions in one area of thought may be a condition of a thinker's intellectual development in another. There is, in other words, a style of criticism which, working with a light hand, illuminates and explains rather than besmirches and destroys. Delineation and criticism are both tools of explanation.

To pay due attention to the formation and character of a family of ideas, then, is to look at two matters. One is the connection of the ideas that a thinker or thinkers come to link together, seeking for these wherever they are found and whatever they are. The second is the historical activity of observing how such a family came to be formed, whether by looking at the scene an author enters, or the progress of his or her mind; the problems, whether intellectual or practical, that confront him or her; and the way in which a pattern of thought develops, changes and extends itself under his or her hand. Involved throughout is the delineation of ideas, the arguments into which thinkers arrange them and the ensemble which results.

V

This study presents the political theory of John Locke as part of a continuous sequence of thought, by which it was moulded and which, in its turn, it moulded. Amidst the diversity of Locke's concerns we may see the formation and development of a vision, its mediation into a technique, and the effects of political reflection upon Locke's vision. Whilst the present study aspires neither to be exhaustive nor to assert that every aspect of Locke's thought was moulded by the considerations set out here, it is probable that his writings as a whole could be described in terms congruent with the ones employed here. But it might try the patience of the public to write a volume three or four times the size of this one.

With that thought in mind, it may be worthwhile turning briefly to some assumptions current in Locke's day that are structural to his thought. His contemporaries for the most part assumed that existence was structured by a series of superiorities. By a superiority is meant a relation between two individuals in which one, the superior, directs the other, who is his or her (usually his) inferior in some salient respect. The relation subsisted because the inferior was dependent on the superior, whether because incapable of self-direction or because deficient in some other important requisite that the superior could supply but he or she could not. In return for the benefit or benefits which the superior provided, the inferior was meant to perform appropriate services for the superior. These usually included some variety of obedience, though other forms of return were possible. The word authority conveys to the modern mind the notion of direction, but perhaps not the dependence involved here.

Superiorities took a great many forms, but it is worth attending to four in particular, the superiorities of heads of households, political governors, ecclesiastics and God. In one way or another these four structured society. The authority of heads of households directed many of the salient aspects of social and economic life, whilst political governors maintained order in society. The clergy had a twofold importance. Firstly, they were the purveyors of Christian doctrine, whose significance in a social context lay in explaining the character of the order that households and governors presented. It would be hard to underestimate the significance of the pulpit in an age of mass illiteracy, especially as the clergy also exerted a degree of control over education and the press, and often succeeded in making church attendance socially desirable.[20] Anticlericalism was a tribute to the pervasiveness, though not the completeness, of their influence. That influence lay not least in being the ministers of God.

God was the greatest superior of all, for His supereminent attributes of power and wisdom implied the dependence upon Him of every human being and indeed of the world as a whole. His directions to mankind and His ordering of existence as a whole were central facts of life in Locke's day. The implications of this were manifold, and in understanding some of them we must make a distinction.

Religion is not identical with theology. The former denotes an activity, whose forms are as various as the form of public worship, moral conduct or private contemplation but which, at any rate, is a mode of practice. Theology is the theoretical explanation of religious practice on the basis of propositions about a deity. It too may assume several forms, of which the most salient in Christian countries have been revealed and natural theology. Revealed theology concerns itself with explaining the events of the Bible and further devising doctrines of salvation and related matters that bear a relation to these prior explanations. Natural theology concerns itself with what can be discovered about God's being, attributes and activities without drawing upon revelation.

Theology in this case was turned to explain not only certain aspects of religion but also many other features of existence. It was of the first importance to the thought of the day that the highest authority was supposed to be a being to whom *intentions* could be attributed. Whilst theologians assumed that to discourse about God's character was to use metaphors, they concurred in attributing to Him goodness, wisdom and power. His possession of power meant that He could have an impact upon existence: and because His power was held to be omnipotence that impact would be in every sense formative. On these terms God's will would explain a great deal and theology, therefore, would be an archetypal mode of thought.

This was true not least because the seventeenth century made use of theology in a way that attributed a wide locus to God's intentions. His directions were disclosed not only through the medium of scripture but often too through nature. This natural theology involved a point of great importance, namely that the faculties naturally belonging to mankind, especially reason, were the means to discover God's intentions.

Locke assumed that theology was important to explanation. That is to say that explanation, to be valid, had to show that it squared with God's intentions – either that it derived from them or was compatible with them. This is as true of Hobbes or Montaigne as of others in their age: their special character was to interpret God and His intentions in a way others had overlooked. The great breach with this model was the work of the next century when God was ushered out of reasoned explanation by Hume and Kant. But for the seventeenth century we should emphasise that the idea of God was explanatory.

It was a matter not merely of explanation but also of consistency. At the same time that writers deployed theological explanations, no one supposed that God had declared views about everything. In worship, for instance, He was supposed to have prescribed certain practices: but even here there were many things about which He had not pronounced and which were, in this sense, indifferent. The point about such matters was that they must be consistent with the views that *were* attributed to God. This was not in every case a very constricting requirement.

For the conclusions theological explanation were never monolithic. The ideas involved were as liable to interpretation as any others. Though theology, done properly, is a difficult discipline, requiring the synthesis of philosophical reflection and hypothesised facts, its materials lend themselves rather easily to the projects of theorists. In both Testaments, which are large works of many moods, specific narrative predominates over general propositions. This leaves a wide latitude for reasoned reflection upon the content of revelation, besides a still wider ambit for reason to attribute intentions to God not recorded in revelation. The theology of Locke's age, whether revealed or natural, therefore, admitted a variety of explanations supporting a range of opinions.

Theological explanation, then, was both central and permeable. It is hard to conceive a lot of seventeenth-century writing without it, but at the same time it admitted a variety of uses. In this connection we should attend less to the private beliefs of writers than to the fact that theology offered an idiom to them, an idiom capable of bearing many messages. It would not be right to assume that theology always dominated thought in general – rather it was an integral part of thought. Whilst the evidence of Locke's private journals does not allow us to doubt his theism, we should attend to the explanatory uses to which he put theology in his various works and how it answered to his purposes, as well as how it sometimes guided them.

For whatever the particular cast of the individual thinker, common theological assumptions imparted a special character to the thought of the day. We shall see their presence in Locke's view of politics and of the human understanding. More generally, we may say that God was conceived not merely as creator and preserver of mankind, but as setting purposes fundamental to human life. After all, what were taken to be divine directions could not be ignored: as Locke himself put it, 'the Authority of God in his Precepts cannot be questioned.'[21] Partly this was a matter of teleology – the destiny of mankind conceived in terms of God's purposes – and of the explanation of duty, but partly too a matter of the turn which theological assumptions gave to how life was to be lived. Some of God's purposes concerned only terrestrial existence. But theology also suggested that there was another life. This suggested a twofold task for mankind: to live on certain terms in this life and to find their way to Heaven.

This brings us to the second significance of the clergy. We have seen that the church was a means of explanation, explicating a view of the social order and impressing it upon the laity. On the other hand, we find in Locke's early life a series of problems connected with the church's relation to terrestrial existence, which in effect indicated that clerical pretensions might interfere with the conduct of civil life and that the intellectual character of theological explanations, as well as the standing of the church in relation to civil government, required revision. It is from Locke's response to these matters and from the difficulties and elisions in his manner of responding that his vision takes it rise: and it is to these that we should turn now.

The opening five chapters of this work show Locke traversing matters arising from the church, theology, toleration, ethics and the human understanding as well as from medicine and political economy. Through this process he formulated his vision. The march of events and Locke's relation to them played their part, as well as intellectual dexterity (or its lack initially). Political thought had its part to play, if we understand it to include toleration (for to say that an attitude towards politics is only part of a vision is not to say that it is not part of forming that vision). The sixth and seventh chapters show Locke mediating his vision into a technique. His technique lay in combining items from his vision, from the repertoire of other thinkers and from his own invention.[22] The theoretical purpose which his technique served was to provide complementary views of the state and the church. His views about the human understanding and about God's purposes were important for this project, along with many of his other assumptions and conclusions. The closing three chapters illustrate the effects of Locke's political position upon some of his subsequent works. To see how all this happens, let us begin with Locke's England.

Chapter 1

In a sense the incidents of a life of thought are accidents. The mind gets to work on problems presented to it by events, whether practical or intellectual, and employs the cerebral resources, whether mental capacities or acquired learning, which its possessor happens to command. The most powerful thinkers use these resources in ways that weave a pattern of ideas explaining large portions of conceptual life; the less impressive thinkers illustrate the fashion of their day. But whatever their intellectual destiny, thinkers are situated in a world of practice. This may not be the subject of their work, though in some cases it is; in every case they assume its presence, a presence usually articulated in a body of practical thought.

Central to Locke's England was the notion and presence of superiority. Everyone had a superior. The servant had a master and the child parents. The parent too found his or her superior in the magistrate. Magistrates were themselves formed into a hierarchy, rising from the most humble justice of the peace to the monarch himself. The monarch too had a superior, for above all stood God.

What was the character of this order? To say that a scene displays order, putting the matter at its most general, is to indicate that its components are related to one another according to some pattern. This in itself suggests, though it need not imply, that the objectives of some agent or agents has been attained. Indeed the order for which people look in society is not *any* pattern but a pattern that leads to a particular result, an organisation of social life that promotes certain goals.

The intention was God's, at least according to the terms in which the fifth commandment was understood. The terms of the commandment were 'Honour thy Father and thy Mother'. Whilst in its literal signification this established the subordination of children to parents, it bore a wider reference in the thought of the day. The Presbyterian *Larger Catechism* observed that by 'father' and 'mother' in the fifth commandment 'are meant not only natural parents but all superiors in age and gifts, and especially such as by God's ordinance are over us in places of authority, whether in family, church, or commonwealth'. The *Book of Common Prayer* prescribed similarly not only that parents be honoured and obeyed but also a duty 'to honour and obey the King and all that are put in authority under him; to submit myself to all governors, teachers, spiritual pastors, and masters'. Just as this understanding spanned a denominational divide, so it was found alike in Samuel Crooke, the Somersetshire minister who baptised Locke, and in Gabriel Towerson, Fellow of All Souls'.[1]

Thus society should be hierarchical. God's ordinance marked out a series of superiors and, correlatively, their inferiors.

This notion of a difference in status of persons implied, amongst other things, that direction should come from the superior, whilst the inferior should obey. Hence '*Command* and *obedience* are the *body* and *soule* of *humane societie*'. It implied, too, that there was a disparity of attributes between superior and inferior which made sense of one being set over the other. Hence we find Fortescue asking what was order 'but a disposition of equal and unequal entities, assigning each its proper place? And what is the proper station of a superior but the condition and degree by which a superior is set over an inferior? And what is the station of an inferior but the condition and degree whereby he is placed under the superior in the order of the universe?'[2] In what did the disparity consist?

To put the matter another way, why was it rational for inferiors to obey? No doubt they had a variety of motives – for on the whole they did obey – but the reality which the theory presupposed was dependence. A superior was one who, whether by personal capacity or acquired attribute, had what the inferior lacked and needed. Thus God was mankind's superior in that His capacities made possible functions vital for the human race but beyond its own powers. The notion of dependence was pervasive. In Henry King's words, there was 'nothing so much sets out the Vniverse as *Order*, to see how subordinate causes depend of their Superiours': to put the matter specifically, 'all were not borne to be rich, nor all to be wise, nor all to teach, nor all to rule, but some for *Disciples*, some for *Masters*, some for the *Throne*, some for the *Mill*, some for *Seruants*, some for *Lords*'.[3]

Generally speaking, superiority was understood in terms of the attributes, whether natural or acquired, that fitted one person to direct another for his or her benefit. Thus, for instance, intelligence (in the contemporary idiom, wisdom) and power figured prominently, but so did wealth, social standing and age. The catalogue was diverse, for so are the forms of advantage which one person has over another.[4]

From the superior's greater intelligence and wherewithal it could be inferred that he (or, more rarely, she) had a responsibility to direct and sustain his inferiors. The language of Sir John Cheke embodied both direction and support: 'we see that the sheepe will obeie the shepheard, and the neat be ruled by the neathered, and the horsse will know his keeper, and the dog will be in aw of his maister, and euerie one of them feed there, and of that, as his keeper and ruler dooth appoint him & goeth from thence, and that, as he is forbidden by his ruler'. James I supposed that 'the king is bound to take care for all his subiects' in respect of their 'nourishing, education, and vertuous gouernment'. This responsible direction applied not just to their terrestrial concerns but also to their spiritual ones too: James considered himself responsible for his subjects' religious welfare ('they for whose soules I must answere to GOD') and, more generally, the Church could claim to instruct the laity.[5]

All this presupposed inferiors stood at a level of intellectual attainment too low to direct *themselves* with success towards right or profitable conduct. It is unsurprising that writers were fond of describing the relations of superior and inferior in terms of a father's care for his children. This habit, it should be noted, is not identical with a patriarchal *explanation* of political superiority, though it could be incorporated into the same family of ideas.[6] The essential matter was the restricted powers for self-guidance of the inferior. It scarcely need be remarked that a different assessment of the latter's understanding would imply a significant reassessment of order in the community.[7]

The result of this order was supposed to be unity. For if inferiors obeyed superiors and superiors themselves fell obediently into a hierarchy, then human behaviour collectively would fall into a single pattern. Conversely, on these assumptions, an absence of hierarchy involved social incoherence. Hence, as James instructed his elder son, 'paritie [is] the mother of confusion, and enemie to Vnitie, which is the mother of order'.[8] So much for thought: what were its implications for practice?

Such a hierarchical order may seem redolent of feudalism. The whole scheme, perhaps, has a medieval sound to it and as such may seem out of place in the seventeenth century. Indeed parts of it can be explained in quasi-feudal terms, as we shall see. For the moment we should turn to see how it served important functions in organising and explaining the activities of the community. For its effect was to orientate a pre-industrial community. The household order, which subordinated servants, children, women and young men to the head of a family was closely connected with the running of the rural economy. The elevated status of the magistrate reflected assumptions about human behaviour. Most significantly God figured as the explanation of this entire order and as such was integral to it.

These matters were of general significance to Locke's England. They are illustrated in the present chapter largely from the Somersetshire community into which our subject was born, where he spent the first fifteen years of his life and which he revisited in search of peace into his thirties.[9] This reference is not meant to suggest that the locus of his early experience was unique, but merely to show, on a manageable scale, how the theory of superiority was embodied in practice. Neither is it meant to suggest that his youth was decisive for the development of those ideas we identify as distinctively Lockean, but rather to illustrate the structure of order which he assumed. For embedded in his works are ideas which correspond to a way of life and a way of viewing it, both of which were exemplified in his part of the West country. It is to that order and its explanation that we should turn.

Locke's early world was characterised by an economic situation and a social organisation which yielded institutions and practices to sustain the economy. In that sense we may say that his society had features which were rational in relation to its economy. This way of life was accompanied by a way of talking about it which was, in essence, explanatory. That was Christian discourse. The preacher explained that certain types of conduct were to be preferred and that certain of the facts of West country life were estimable. His account distinguished them as morally imperative because they were in accord with the views of an authority from whom there was no appeal, namely God. Explanation was complemented by enactment, for civil magistracy enforced the conclusions of this social and moral order.

I

Nature, in Locke's opinion, was not a bountiful mother. Unaltered by human activity it would provide little for the support of human life, for 'Nature and the Earth furnished only the almost worthless Materials'.[10] But mankind's work could transform nature dramatically, because labour, for instance, '*puts the greatest part of Value on Land*'.[11] Thus people could turn nature to their use, for value in this context meant what was 'useful to the Life of Man'. Locke was keen we should not underestimate the degree to which it was man who made nature serve his ends. 'I think it will be but a very modest Computation to say, that of the *Products* of the Earth useful to the Life of Man 9/10 are the *effects of labour*,' he observed and added, 'nay, if we will rightly estimate things as they come to our use, and cast up the several Expences about them, what in them is purely owing to *Nature*, and what to *labour*, we shall find, that in most of them 99/100 are wholly to be put on the account of *labour*'.[12] This view of nature reflects the economy of Locke's native locality.

What was for 'our use'? Locke listed amongst 'the ordinary provisions of Life' 'food, rayment, and delight' or 'Meat, Drink and Cloathing'.[13] We can follow a more specific formulation, of 'Bread, Wine and Cloth'[14] to the leading industry of Somerset: for as Locke declared early in his career, 'clothing is not born with us'.[15] The transformation most characteristic of his county was turning a sheep's fleece into cloth and Nicholas Locke, our subject's grandfather, was one of Somerset's clothiers.

The physical character of the land itself might suggest that pastoral farming take priority over arable. The climate, topography and soils of the South-West pointed to livestock.[16] This was true in particular of Locke's immediate locality. Pensford, where he was brought up, lay near the Mendip hills and its soil compared unfavourably with the Somerset Levels. Somerset's main arable crop was wheat and Pensford would have to find a living in other ways.[17] This was found in dairying, cattle-grazing and sheep-keeping. These products no doubt found a ready market, for, lying North of the Mendips, Pensford was placed well to serve Bristol.[18]

Sheep provided the means of supporting a large population. Somerset was the third or fourth most populous county in England, with perhaps 196,000 people in 1642.[19] Pensford's diversified economy drew on other sources, but textiles were traditionally prominent. In the mid fourteenth century one to two thousand broadcloths were made annually and Pensford's textiles were still significant in Leland's time.[20] Certainly contemporary observation related cloth-making to livelihood. Justices of the Peace from four hundreds in the North-East of the county wrote of a country in 'a great part . . . forest and woodlands, and the rest very barren for corn' whose people were 'for the most part occupied about the trade of cloth-making' and suggested 'that by reason of the trade of cloth-making, and the increase of people working about that trade, there have been very many cottages erected . . . for them to work in, which have no means of living but about that trade'.[21] The population of the county cannot be referred to cloth-making alone, particularly in the South and West of the county (the vale of Taunton Dene was called by one observer 'the paradise of England') and the circumstances of the North could lend themselves to livestock other than sheep (for instance supplying dairy products to Bristol), but we can hardly doubt the importance of the cloth trade to Somerset or, indeed, to the country as a whole. The sheep population of England and Wales was in the region of 12,000,000 by the late seventeenth

21

century and in the middle of the preceding century had been estimated at about 8,400,000.[22] The market for wool rose on the whole: the dues of Blackwell Hall (the country's biggest cloth market) show a three-fold increase from the 1570s to the early eighteenth century.[23] Somerset enjoyed its share: only Devon, Yorkshire and London were assessed for more ship money.[24] Textiles constituted the most significant national industry at the beginning of Locke's century and the West country its most important base, arguably because of the superior quality of its wool and the fine broadcloth it manufactured.[25] This brings us to the process of transforming fleeces into cloth.

Making cloth was a complex and lengthy process of several stages, each of which comprised several activities. Before these could begin the wool itself had to be treated, whether by combing (for long, coarse wool) or carding, which the shorter, fine wool characteristic of the West country[26] suited. From this state the wool was subjected to a series of operations to change it into a fabric and fix it as such, notwithstanding its constant tendency to disintegrate towards its natural state. The manufacture itself was a technically difficult task, requiring ingenuity, determination and many hands – as Sir William Petty (himself the son of a clothier) put it 'so nice a business'. After it was made it had to be finished to a standard fit for sale.[27] At the end of the day the wool had been altered radically from its natural state, virtually useless to man, to the means of protecting him from the rigours of the North European climate.

Thus created cloth provided a livelihood for many. Its obvious usefulness secured it a ready market. This was as well, for the process involved many hands. An estimate of 1702 suggested that to process a pack of wool from the raw state to finished cloth took sixty-three people. An alternative way of reckoning would be by the number of looms involved. According to one estimate the West country mustered 1,222 looms or thereabouts in 1620 and, assuming that in normal times each loom gave work, either part or full time, to about sixteen people, this implies 19,552 involved to a greater or lesser degree with textiles[28] Whatever the exact figures the number of hands needed for the process must have been relatively high, for the degree of mechanisation was low. There were some opportunities for technological changes in carding,[29] but on the whole innovations appear to have been few: for the period from 1617 to 1700 only 12 per cent of patents relate to textiles in any way and a heavy concentration of these, before 1760, were in finishing rather than the main production processes.[30] Cloth-making remained labour intensive in Locke's day and it makes sense that he should have noted 'how much *labour makes the far greatest part of the value of things*, we enjoy in this World'[31] and insisted that prosperity depended 'upon the number and industry of your people'.[32]

The industry of the people was needed particularly in Locke's youth, for depression overtook the textile trade from the 1620s. That decade saw a shortage of fine home-grown wool.[33] This difficulty was escaped partly by an exercise in economic adaptation. The shortage in raw materials was met by the mixing of English wool with fine wool imported from Spain, yielding the cloth called Spanish medley.[34] This had established itself by the 1630s and kept its place for the rest of the century.[35] Somerset was well placed to adapt, for as early as 1606 there had been some use of Spanish wool.[36] Adaptation was a matter of economic survival. Margins were cut sharply. The situation was compounded by the fact that cloth-making was often located in wood-pasture areas, so that land for other agricultural purposes might be short, and by the large population which textiles encouraged. Clearly economic rationality, whether in importing wool or seeking it from hitherto unexploited sources outside the west country or importing the expertise of foreign artisans, was in order.[37]

Locke's immediate locality, of course, also dealt in other products. Nearby at Wrington, where he was born in 1632, the father of his mother Agnes, Edmund Keene, was a tanner. His uncle, Peter Locke, closer still at Bishop Sutton, tried his hand at the same trade. Leather-working was a process of transformation for which the area's woodlands and cattle provided the raw materials.[38] Brewing was feasible for the same reasons. Devon and Somerset were strong in cider-apples and their inhabitants took advantage of the fact. Peter Locke was amongst them and another uncle, Edward Locke, set up as brewer in Bristol.[39] Drink was certainly one of 'the ordinary provisions of Life' John Locke knew, for when his father came to die he bequeathed to his eldest son 'my *Brewing Brasse Furnace*'.[40] Locke's lands, naturally, included an orchard.[41] He might have appreciated the joke when Shaftesbury wrote of the Bishop of Bath and Wells 'whose stronge Beere is the onely spirituall thing any Somersetshire Gentleman knows'.[42] But, more seriously, Locke stressed the difference between what 'unassisted Nature furnishes us with' and the end product 'which our industry and pains prepare for us'.[43] Human artifice suited North-East Somerset. By 1670, possibly earlier, there were artificial grasses.[44] Locke's very language seems to apply to his homeland. Much of the common land enclosed in Somerset seems to have been waste and some years later he wrote that 'Land that is left wholly to Nature, that hath no improvement of Pasturage, Tillage or Planting, is called, as indeed it is, *wast*.' His ideas, also, accommodated the facts of the situation, for his account of the succession of private property to common dwelt on the increase in yields it gave: 'for I aske,' he wrote, 'whether in the wild woods and uncultivated wast of America left to Nature, without any improvement, tillage or husbandry, a thousand acres will yeild the needy and wretched inhabitants as many conveniencies of life as ten acres of equally fertile land doe in Devonshire where they are well cultivated?'[45]

The economic circumstances into which Locke was born dictated that industry was needed for prosperity. Nature in herself gave little beyond the materials of subsistence, if that much: the rest was given by human work. Pensford and its vicinity was no 'paradise of England'. The textile depression of Locke's early years must have accented that fact. The conditions of life left their impress upon him. They were also related intimately to the social organisation of his early world.

II

The economy of England, like that of every country before the coming of the machine, had an intimate dependence on manpower. An economy so closely reliant on intensive labour was, *eo ipso*, central to the organisation of the community. Where so much work by so many hands went to sustain life, toil pervaded the social order. The medium in which economy and society corresponded, since the characteristic industries of Somerset were founded on a domestic basis, was the order of the household. The organisation of life to economic ends, of course, was not attractive to everyone; but it was strong enough, as we shall see, to inform some of Locke's ideas.

We know that Locke's father had brewing equipment in his house. The domestic basis of the textile trade is attested more generally. Both carding and spinning, for instance, were carried out as cottage industries.[46] These processes, which were central to cloth-making, were capable of being split up into simple stages requiring no elaborate training; the technology was sufficiently simple and inexpensive to be found in the ordinary worker's cottage; the raw materials were sufficiently inexpensive to be entrusted to out-workers. Thus, where necessity required, women and children could be drawn into production as well as men, so that textiles could occupy the whole household. The arrangements for putting-out were more fully developed in the West country industry than elsewhere and in the country generally it has been estimated that the spare hours of at least a quarter of the cottage-farming population of England were spent in making woollens.[47] Other parts of textile production, however, required centralised manufacture.

24

The evidence which attests the prosperity of West country clothiers – such as owning their own fulling-mills or organising their own warping – testifies also to their factory-like methods.[48] It underlines, again, the importance of organising people's habits to productive ends, for it reminds us not only of the trade's labour intensiveness but also the large numbers involved. Either way, whether trade was grounded at home or in a separate workplace, economic efficiency required that people be directed to their place in the scheme of production, and this implies a superior, whether the head of the household or the master tradesman, and obedience to him.

We can infer that this organisation was effective, for England seems to have outstripped its rivals by its superior labour productivity.[49] The perceived need for production was perhaps reflected in one of England's fits of moral self-criticism, as when George Herbert apostrophised 'O England! full of sinne but most of sloth' and declared idleness to be 'the great and nationall sin'.[50] There was a local version of the same doctrine. Samuel Crooke, who was the rector of Wrington, wrote 'A Short Prayer for the Morning'. This requested of God that we 'never be a burden unto humane societie, nor a blemish unto humane societie, nor a blemish unto the profession of Christianitie, by idlenesse, or inordinate living'. As the prayer figured in a work written for the 'instruction of the younger sort', we see that the merit of work was taught early in Locke's Somerset.[51]

Yet the mention of idleness reminds us that virtues imply vices. A society based on the household might be countered to some extent by habits and practices which sapped its order. The masterless, the vagrant, the bastard and the pleasures of the alehouse in their different ways all countered habits of industry. A household society required everyone to have a master or parents. The records of seventeenth-century courts are punctuated with orders to masterless individuals to put themselves into service.[52] Preventative steps could be taken, as Locke recollected at the end of his life, when he made provision for apprenticing poor children in Pensford.[53] One example of masterless-ness, namely vagrancy, was particularly prominent. For the general flow of migration reached a particular destination in areas with opportunities for employment, like textile areas.[54] No doubt some migrants were driven by economic dislocation, but most of them appeared to have escaped from covenanted service. They were viewed as examples of idleness and even immorality: certainly they did not fit into household order.[55] Still less did children for whom no father could be found, for a society governed by an authority which was usually male would identify individuals by paternity. It seems to have been supposed in the West country that the sexual opportunities provided by popular festivals and celebrations were to blame for this breach of familial order.[56] Somersetshire JPs seem to have been particularly worried, issuing a series of orders against church ales – revels of 'feasting, dancing, and strenuous exercises' in aid of parish finances – from 1594 onwards. In 1628 and again in 1632 there was a general order covering Somerset, Devon and Dorset.[57] That popular entertainment had its social dangers was clear to the Lockes: at Pensford fair in 1656 Edward Locke, then petty constable, was 'much ill-treated' when he tried to keep order.[58] Whilst revels were an occasional if pointed occurrence the alehouse was a constant presence. It offered an escape from superiors into the arms of oblivion or, viewed from the opposite angle, 'here are you deprived of the obedience of your sons, of the duty of your servants'. Concern that drink attracted people to the detriment of 'their parents' and masters' service' seems to have been particularly pointed in the cloth-making area during the depression, but it was an ever-present concern: and some of the revellers who beat up Edward Locke came from the local inn.[59]

All the same there were strong pressures towards conformity. Breaches of accepted standards of familial conduct were restrained by a variety of unofficial sanctions.[60] For despite the pressures of the economy a sense of communal identity could survive; for instance, whilst the population turnover in a parish might be as high as 50 per cent over ten years, mobility often fell within a short range, normally under twenty miles and often under ten, and even a majority of vagrants, whose horizon was wider than most, often travelled less than fifty miles from their place of origin.[61] Few people could travel far enough to escape their reputation. When the charivari was used to shame people who violated their community's standards it would have been effective.[62] One could generalise from this: Samuel Crooke observed that many people were restrained 'from notorious crimes, by feare of shame and punishment, desire of honour and reward' and Locke was attracted to the view that people were moved by a desire for approval, incorporating it into his own educational writings: 'Esteem and Disgrace are, of all others, the most powerful Incentives to the Mind, when once it is brought to relish them,' he wrote, adding that 'if you can once get into Children a Love of Credit, and an Apprehension of Shame and Disgrace, you have put into them the true Principle, which will constantly work.'[63]

If there were sanctions we have still to ask to what code of conduct they answered, as in Locke's phrase, which added that 'the true Principle ... will ... incline them to the right'. In a moment we shall turn to the kind of ethics which the young Locke knew, but first it will be as well to turn to the psychology underlying morality, what he called 'the great Principle and Foundation of all Vertue and Worth'. This lay in following the dictates of reason rather than pleasure where they disagreed, 'That a Man is able to *deny himself* his own Desires, cross his own Inclinations, and purely follow what Reason directs as best, tho' the Appetite lean the other way.'[64] This doctrine had obvious relevance to an economy in which diligence was necessary to uphold prosperity, whether directly in hard work or at one remove in shunning the alehouse, and so was pointed out by reason. But desire might lead to over-indulgence at the inn or elsewhere undermining the basis of society. The preference for the reasonable course over the alternatives, which Locke's background implies, makes it easy to see why he could say that 'it seems plain to me, that the Principle of all Vertue and Excellency lies in a Power of denying our selves the Satisfaction of our own Desires, where Reason does not authorize them' and supposed that a child not brought up in this way 'is in danger never to be good for any thing'.[65] The idea is unlikely to have been a subsequent inspiration, for Locke's account of bringing up a child reasonably corresponds to the way his father had treated him. The child was to be held in awe of parental authority until it was capable of acting according to reason.[66] Not the least of his later distaste for Sir Robert Filmer's higher view of patriarchy lay in its exceeding this measure of power.[67] His preference for reason was deep grained.

One of the means to the end of prosperity lay in the market. West country products were often for consumption elsewhere, whether sending cloth to Blackwell Hall or, as from North Somerset, dairy products to Bristol. The raw materials for industry could be bought in, as with Spanish wool. Extensive exchange, whether in materials or money, was an obvious fact of life. Locke was content to treat its workings as a fair regulation of price.[68] The market, however, was balanced to some extent by justice to the poor through charity, whether by Wrington parish spending slightly more on them than on its eucharist or by Locke's own bequest to the poor of Pensford.[69] Certainly equity was needful in the market itself, for the community depended on exchange for its livelihood. Hence, as dependent on the market, society was dependent on contracts and other forms of promising. It is hardly surprising that Samuel Crooke expressed a dislike of vain oaths. Locke thought that 'good faith . . . agreements . . . oaths . . . are the bonds of human society'.[70] Hence, as we shall see, those whose oaths he considered unreliable, like Roman Catholics or atheists, or who refused them altogether, like Quakers, were the objects of his sustained dislike.

These considerations bring us to the moral explanation for the habits and practices of Locke's society, namely religion. Christianity would have an appeal to his locality. Pensford and Wrington fell into what has been called a 'cheese' area, one where dairying and the rest from continual tillage afforded by cloth-making gave people time to think on other things with a contemplative spirit, as John Aubrey reflected: 'That, and the Bible, and ease – for it is now all upon dairy-grassing and clothing – set their wits a-running and reforming.'[71] It is time to see how Christianity explained the facts Locke experienced in his early life.

III

The significance of Christianity in Locke's early world was two-fold. It explained, firstly, that rational conduct had moral authority and, secondly, it made sense of the conditions on which life was lived or, if we care to speak more generally, of the world and its contents. Its character was of course more complex than these two points alone would suggest, for their explanatory power derived from being part of a more general scheme. The scheme was Christian theology, which treated mankind always in relation to God's purposes for it. Thus, for instance, the explanation of moral conduct assumed that God was the author of moral rules and that following those rules, if accompanied by a proper sense of man's dependence on God, might lead to eternal felicity for him. In short the analysis of conduct assumed the aspect of moral theology, an aspect woven into many of the theoretical arguments which the incidents of Locke's life led him to develop, as indeed they would appear in the life of any believer.

The most commanding figure amongst the Christians in Locke's background was Samuel Crooke, whom we have met already as rector of Wrington and as the minister who baptised Locke. Crooke's surviving sermons and books are mainly about Christian morality. The frequency of his preaching – he was described as 'a daily orator' – and the intelligibility of its content, for when dealing with 'vulgar auditories' he used 'to pitch upon that sense of scripture which is most genuine, and not to distract hearers by mentioning various readings and judgements' because that was 'rather savouring of ostentation, than tending to instruction' – were matched by his evident popularity.[72] Locke, who was born in the house next to the gates of his church, is unlikely to have escaped Crooke's doctrine, for he took pains to remember and indeed adapt the wisdom of *Proverbs* 22.6, 'Traine up [or *Catechise*] a Child in the way he should goe: and when he is old he will not depart from it.' That counsel was followed by the man who thought 'the Minds of Children as easily turned this or that way, as Water it self' and supposed that 'the little. . .Impressions on our tender Infancies, have very important and lasting Consequences'.[73] The content of Crooke's preaching and catechising is preserved in his popular *The Guide unto True Blessednesse* and his simplified version of it for young people, *A Briefe Direction to true happinesse*.[74] From these, and other sources current in Locke's lifetime, we can see the account of Christianity he met.

Christian morality was conventionally understood to reside primarily in the Second Table of the Decalogue. The First Table (the first four Commandments) outlined our duty to God and the Second our duty towards mankind, or as Crooke said *'dutie* to God' and 'dutie to our *neighbor'*.[75] These six Commandments provided an account of right conduct which coincided with the dictates of rational conduct. But how could these six yield positive rather than negative duties? Their contents, literally stated, are prohibitive, except for the fifth. Crooke, however, laid down an interpretative principle which made them yield prescriptive guidance. He suggested not only 'that where any *dutie is enjoyned,* as in the affirmative Commandements, the contrariest *sinne* is *forbidden'*, but also that 'where any *sinne* is *forbidden,* as in the negative, the contrarie *dutie* is required'.[76] What were these duties? It will be convenient to begin with the sixth Commandment.

This required us to preserve our neighbour as ourself. In general terms it meant 'that the *life* and *person* of man be, by man, not impeached, but preserved'. To speak more specifically it intended that each person should preserve himself (and the steps he should take were specified in plain terms, even including '*Sober* and *wholsome dyet*, with helpe of Phisicke, when neede is, *preventing* unnecessary dangers &c') and that he should also have the same concern for his neighbour, 'Love of him, as of our selves'. Or again, in the more concrete language Crooke used in the junior version, the sixth commandment both forbade 'everie *hurt, done, threatened,* or *intended,* to the *soule,* or *bodie,* either of *our selves,* or of our neighbours' and required 'that we *love* & *cherish,* both the *soule,* and *bodie,* of our *neighbour,* as we *would,* and *ought* to doe, our *owne'*.[77] Crooke, in short, took it to comprise the same message as the golden rule: thou shalt love thy neighbour as thyself. That rule is often taken to summarise the Second Table and we can see how the latter's other precepts can be understood to conduce to the end of preservation.

The economic and social order of Somerset, we may recollect, supported a considerable population thanks to a system of industry dependent on the discipline of household order. It was underpinned, in other words, by the direction of superiors, whether parents in the household or masters in the workplace. As we would expect, the fifth Commandment gave an explanation of their authority, for it prescribed 'that *inferiors reverence,* and obey *their superiors'*. To what ends should superiors direct the community's energies? Since without property there would be no preservation, the eighth Commandment excluded any diminution of the community's wealth and, considered in a positive sense, required its increase, both prohibiting 'the *hindering,* or *abusing, of our owne wealth,* or of the wealth *of our neighbour'* and prescribing 'that we *preserve,* and *further,* both *our owne* wealth, and *our neighbours,* by all *lawfull courses* and *honest dealing'*. The poor, of course, had to be preserved out of others' wealth and Crooke's view of the tenth Commandment accommodated them, demanding nothing '*contrary* to the rule of *charitie,* and the good of our neighbour' and charity might obviously take the form of 'Almes'. The seventh Commandment, prohibiting adultery and recommending purity, obviously warranted the restrictions of household order, just as the ninth, forbidding lying and equivocation and recommending truth-telling, would validate honest dealing in the market.[78] In short the Second Table provided a moral explanation for the rational practices preserving Somersetshire life.

Thus scripture produced moral authority for what had been found to be rational. From this position it was a small step to talk of man's power of reasoning as a means of identifying good and evil. This meant that it could be assumed that rational conduct would coincide with conduct that was morally authoritative though, of course, not all rational conduct would concern matters of interest to morality: but one could say that rational conduct could not be wrong. People, in this sense, had a faculty which distinguished good and evil, just as they had a will to choose between them. Thus Crooke could write of reason and will comprising 'the reasonable soul' which 'is the *Lords candle'* and in which 'there are two faculties; the one discovering and discerning between good and evil; the other chusing and refusing; the one being the minde, the other the will'.[79] That a faculty or power of reason is meant, rather than an innate knowledge of duty, is clear from this language.

It is clear also in a phrase occasionally taken to suggest innatism, that of the law written in the heart: for whilst the phrase by itself might be read that way, its usage tells a different story. The 'heart' included both mind and will, for it embraced not 'a mere speculation' but knowledge or belief that moved the will to action: hence Crooke observed that 'by the *Heart* we must understand. . .the *Soule* of Man, especially the *Will*, chusing and affecting'. It figured in describing how God might dispose a man's faculties to accept truths, as when John Winthrop described his decision to leave for the New World as an occasion 'when God intendes a man to worke' and so 'he setts a Byas on his heart so as tho' he be tumbled this way and that yet his Bias still drawes him to that side, and there he restes at last'. Thomas Hooker spoke of the heart being led to a proposition, for a heart subdued to God 'either lies right, or will come right, it will come to that bent of the Rule that is revealed'. This language speaks of God's purpose coordinating intellect and will so that, at the very least, a man becomes convinced of the truth of what is put to him. But it does not specify *how* it is put to him; indeed it tells us nothing about that and requires us to look elsewhere to determine how a man's mind is informed. Thomas Shepard explained the events leading to his conversion through God's using one of his five senses: listening to John Preston preach, 'the Lord so bored my ears as that I understood what he spake and the secrets of my soul were laid upon before me. . .as if one had told him of all that ever I did, of all the turning and deceits of my heart, insomuch as that I thought he was the most searching preacher in the world'.[80] Since 'heart' suggests the *effective* reception of an idea, regardless of the mode of transmission, we need not suppose, for instance, that many years after Locke decried innatism he capitulated to it: when he wrote of Cain, 'he cries out, *Every one that findeth me, shall slay me*; so plain was it writ in the Hearts of all Mankind', he used a phrase to underline the liveliness of Cain's belief, for '*Cain* was so fully convinced' of his own iniquity.[81] So we should attend not to an innatism which Crooke's belief that reasoning distinguished good from evil precludes, but to the agreement of reasoning with scripture, when he wrote of 'the *morall* law, or law of *nature*, engraven by God himselfe, first in the heart of man in his creation, after in *tables* of stone, in the *daies* of Moses. . .commonly called the *Decalogue*'.[82] For God's disposing man to exercise his reason and to act on it makes sense of the phrase 'where nature ends, reason and morality (the improvement of reason) begin; adding a new luster, and, as it were, temper to nature'.[83] In this sense we might speak of the Second Table corresponding to a code of conduct discovered through reason ('*morall* law') and, since the reason which disclosed it and the will which led to its performance were part of man's nature, we might call it natural law.[84] There may be certain difficulties with the notion of natural law, as Locke discovered subsequently, but at any rate the way in which reason and scripture can recommend the same conduct is evident.

Christianity also explained the human situation, beginning with the very fact of existence. It did so, naturally enough, in terms of God's intentions. All things, Samuel Crooke thought, should serve God's glory. In this he was not alone. According to *Proverbs* 16.4 'the Lord hath made all things for himself'. 'God has made all things for himself,' noted Sir Thomas Browne, 'and it is impossible hee should make them for any other end than his owne glory; it is all he can receive, and all that is without himselfe.' The point that creation, whether of the world or its inhabitants, was for God's glory ('the principal end of our Creation') was reiterated by a multitude of writers.[85] But what exactly did it mean? How could God, who was perfect in Himself, require glorification? The answer lies in the meaning imported into 'glory'. God's glory consisted not in the adoration of His creatures, but in the exercise of His benevolence in giving them life and therewith the possibility of happiness; as Benjamin Whichcote, who for a time held a Somersetshire living, wrote, 'God does all for his *own Glory*, by communicating good out of himself; *not* by looking for any thing from his Creatures: our duty is not for His sake: our duty is Our Perfection and Happiness.' Ralph Cudworth, the son of another Somerset incumbent, indicated the agreement of God's glory and His benevolence in similar terms. 'The *reason* why God made the World, was from his own *Overflowing* and *Communicative Goodness*,' he wrote, 'that there might be other Beings also *Happy* besides him, and enjoy themselves. Nor does this at all clash, with God's making of the world, for his own *Glory* and *Honour*,' because, ' . . . God did not make the World, merely to ostentate his *Skill* and *Power*; but to communicate his Goodness, which is chiefly and properly his *Glory*, as the *Light* and *Splendor* of the Sun, is the *Glory of it*'.[86] So God intended the happiness of his creatures and, we may add, human happiness in particular. For the major beneficiary of God's kindness was mankind.

Mankind was placed at the highest point a worldly creature could attain. Height, in this sense, was relative to God. For instance angels, who were supposed to resemble God more closely because lacking sensual attributes, were placed above man: but of the creatures of the earth man most resembled Him. The *imago dei* which mankind possessed at the creation was assessed variously by different writers, but it was widely held that it included domination over lower animals. Man fitted this position because by possessing the power of reasoning, as the lower animals did not or did not significantly, he resembled God. It was appropriate that as the highest of creatures on earth he should enjoy there some part of the authority which God enjoyed everywhere: as Locke noted at the beginning of *An Essay concerning Human Understanding* 'it is the *Understanding* that sets Man above the rest of sensible Beings, and gives him all the Advantage and Dominion, which he has over them'. The *imago* might also be found in the immortality, perfect understanding and so on, which man, when first created, possessed. Crooke noted it in a reasonable and immortal soul, true wisdom and holiness and dominion over the creatures.[87] God, naturally enough, desired the multiplication of such a creature or, in Milton's words 'Knew it not good for Man to be alone' and so created woman, 'Thy likeness', 'exactly to thy hearts desire'. Locke's God 'made Man such a Creature, that . . . it was not good for him to be alone'. The point could be generalised beyond Eve to recommend the increase of the human race, for in Donne's words 'God loves not singularity' or, in those of Petty, 'the first command of God was to encrease and multiply'.[88]

Mankind, created thus, was happy. Its happiness consisted not merely in the abundance of Eden, but in following the will of God. It was supposed that God had so constructed matters that righteousness would have as a consequence happiness. For instance Samuel Crooke's Adam, with the 'abilitie for perfect obedience' which his reasonable soul (understanding and will) supposed, would find that his obedience, whether of outward conduct in tilling and dressing the Garden or of inward disposition in worshipping God, would bring blessedness in the continuance of his immortality. 'If wee be at peace with God,' Richard Sibbes observed, 'all other peace will follow'; and for Cudworth, 'Happinesse is nothing but that inward sweet delight, that will arise from a Harmonious agreement between our wills and Gods will.'[89] But man soon violated the conditions on which happiness was to be had.

The Fall followed from man's overlooking his dependent character. Man depended on God for his happiness. God required him to manifest love, prescribing love as a divine characteristic man should manifest: human love was the counterpart of that celestial benevolence that had created him. It was, as Milton put it, 'as a fire sent from Heaven to be ever kept alive upon the altar of our hearts, [to] be the first principle of all godly and vertuous actions in men'; and whether manifested in Adam's prelapsarian affection for Eve or in the frame of mind prescribed by the golden rule it was meant to recommend a disposition issuing in good conduct towards others as we have seen in the Crookean interpretation of the Second Table. Love 'seeketh not her own' and 'drives a man out of himselfe'.[90] But if love directed towards the benefit of others, it had its opposite, pride, which put the self first and so undermined the social and celestial order. Pride 'hates Superiors . . . scornes Inferiors . . . owns no equalls' and so appeared when anyone 'setteth up himselfe instead of God'.[91] Thus, observed Bishop Lake of Bath and Wells, the fallen angels had 'fixt their Eyes, and setled their Affection vpon themselues, that modell of Diuine being, which they had in themselues, and ouer-valuing their own worth, deemed themselues to be their own Soueraigne Good'. Lucifer and Adam alike fell because 'puffed up' with pride: 'it was by reason of this *Self-will*, that Adam fell in Paradise; that those glorious Angels, those *Morning-starres*, kept not their first station'.[92] Thus Lucifer and Adam alike erred.

It was hardly surprising that this disobedience should be punished: Adam and Eve lost both ease and life, ejected from the plenty of Eden and forfeited their natural immortality (being separated from the Tree of Life). Adam's guilt indicated that the government of man by reason was less than complete and since the *imago dei* thus was not faithfully reflected the animals appropriately became less submissive. The loss of Eden and an authority over creatures which had now to be worked at implied an end to happiness on earth, just as the loss of immortality entailed it in a deeper sense, and a beginning to labour: God inflicted, in the words of Jeremy Taylor, 'the evils of a troublesome mortal life. For Adam did not die that day, but Adam began to be miserable that day, to live upon hard labour, to eat fruits from an accursed field, till he should return to the earth from whence he was taken.'[93] But at any rate it remained true that God willed man to multiply, subdue the earth and have dominion over animals. To take up the 'great and primary Blessing' of *Genesis*, as John Locke quoted it, '*And God blessed them, and God said unto them, be Fruitful and Multiply and Replenish the Earth and subdue it, and have Dominion over the Fish of the Sea, and over the Fowl of the Air, and over every living thing that moveth upon the Earth.*'[94] Only now people had to work at it. Thus the story of man's position in the creation and his Fall explained the human condition as it might be found in seventeenth-century life, for example in Locke's Somerset. There the increase of mankind, recommended by *Genesis*, was supported by labour, made necessary by postlapsarian conditions, through exploiting sheep and other livestock or by farming of other kinds, at any rate by subduing the earth and by exercising dominion over animals as the Bible approved.

Yet this explanation raised the question of how the human condition might be improved. If a Christian account explained what was rational conduct for man after the Fall and showed how the facts of his life had arisen, so uncongenial to happiness, might one not ask whether it could show how his happiness might be regained? It could, and did so by connecting the two branches we have seen, rational conduct and the nature of fallen life. Man was supposed to desire happiness. The satisfaction of his desire constituted an end, indeed an end so commanding that it could not be ignored. The Fall meant that the means to it had to be somewhat wider than good conduct and so, as we shall see, came to involve a rational reliance not only on works but faith also.

Mankind's desire for happiness, which was axiomatic to this explanation, could be adduced conveniently from Aristotle. 'The naturall Philosopher in his inquest of Happines laieth this ground,' noted Crooke, 'that *All things desire that which, either in trueth, or in opinion, is good for them*'; and he added, 'and that onely is good, which tendeth unto the onely good, the uttermost end and perfection of their severall natures'. Crooke meant that men desired (and indeed should desire) happiness in this life and the next, 'that, being to live a while in this world, and for ever in another, they may bee, both heere and heereafter *truly blessed*'.[95] The means to that 'onely good' prescribed before the Fall was conformity with God's will. The code prescribed had taken the form of conduct, as we saw in Adam's duty to worship God and tend the Garden and, of course, refraining from the Tree. These precepts, though disclosed by God's statement rather than discovered by reasoning, were rational in the sense that happiness was contingent on following them; they were means to an end, even though we might think of their connection with the end simply as something arranged. At any rate reason dictated that they should be obeyed. But the very fact of the Fall suggested that perpetually rational conduct was too much for people.

Whilst reason indicated that the desire for happiness pointed to obedience to God, other desires or passions might prove too strong for reason's prompting. For if man was like the angels in possessing reason he was so merely as the highest of earthly creatures and like them possessed inclinations towards pleasure. Lower creatures, lacking reason, were given up solely to the prompting of desire: but man, possessing reason, had the capacity to consider his desires, single out the most powerful and seek the means to satisfy it: or, as Locke put it, 'purely follow what Reason dictates is best'. Man's strongest desire was for happiness and God had arranged the means to it in good conduct.

The point was that

> in a body, which doth freely yeeld
> His partes to reasons rule obedient,
> And letteth her that ought the scepter weeld,
> All happy peace and goodly gouernment
> Is setled there in sure establishment.

Where reason was disobeyed, however, the body became

> fowle and indecent,
> Distempred through misrule and passions bace:
> It growes a Monster, and incontinent
> Doth loose his dignitie and natiue grace.[96]

This happened when Adam succumbed to temptation, symbolising the fact that man was always liable to forsake reason's conclusions for self-indulgence.

It followed that something more than the regime of good conduct, which man was unlikely to keep satisfactorily, was needed if he was to escape his postlapsarian state. Thus God's reminding the Israelites of the paths of rational conduct and promising immortality once more in return for obedience, when he revealed the Decalogue to Moses, was unlikely to be completely within human grasp. It was imaginable that man might keep the outward conduct prescribed there, but inward dispositions also were needed to satisfy the law. Man might achieve external conformity, because moved by the incentives of honour and shame; but, as we saw with Adam, inwardly he was less likely to manifest the loving disposition required. Thus, whilst the temporal benefits of rational conduct might accrue, man would fail to keep the whole law and so fail to earn salvation. The Christian God, fortunately, looked benevolently on the human condition.

The rules which were set for man, whether the Decalogue or the law of nature (that body of precepts whose content was disclosed by reason and, which was assumed to be congruent with the Second Table), were conditions for conduct. Anyone who followed the rules prescribed would obtain happiness. The rules, in other words, were the substance of a covenant of works: if we suppose here some contractual form, one who fulfils the conditions prescribed has earned salvation. But few, if any, were likely to do so. Yet if man could hardly earn happiness God would condescend to offer a covenant of grace. The concept of grace denoted, if that is not too precise a word, divine aid to achieve what was required of man but of which he was incapable or usually so: in Herbert's expressive phrase 'grace fills up uneven nature'. It marked the end to which nature should move and so grace and nature were complementary: '*Nature* it selfe in the last resolution is of *Grace*; for God gave that' or 'Nature is many wayes a step-mother to grace.' A covenant of grace implied an offer from God to man which would permit him to achieve the end desired. It offered the means to happiness. To speak specifically it suggested that faith in God and His promises, particularly of salvation on new conditions, would win pardon for man's defects of disposition and performance.[97] According to the particular interpretation Crooke put on this covenant, to believe in this very offer of pardon was 'that speciall act of faith' God required of people, 'whereby wee *give credit* unto the report of the word and spirit of Christ touching our salvation in *particular*'.[98] So under the covenant of grace people could achieve blessedness despite their shortcomings, if only they believed that God would forgive them. That covenant, understood in general terms, offered accommodation to the fallen on terms which they could meet and so gave them grace.

Crooke's particular interpretation was conditioned by his choice of view about the effects of the Fall on man. For whilst there were certain points which followed uncontroversially from it, such as man's being subject to death because separated from the Tree of Life or that the *imago dei* was reflected imperfectly in a creature whose government by reason was uncertain, others were less straightforward. For instance it was held commonly that Adam and Eve sinned not only in their own persons but as representatives of mankind – that they stood 'by Gods appointment, not as singular persons onely, but also as *heads of mankind* & we all tooke parte with them, both *in this fall*; and in the *wofull* effect thereof' – and so could be described as subject to original sin. This generated a logical difficulty. Sin would be defined obviously as '*swerving from the law of* God'. How could this definition be made to fit the case of original sin? It did not apply straightforwardly, for if mankind was represented it was hardly in breach of the law in its own person; and the difficulty was apparent enough, for Crooke described his definition of such a breach as '*actuall sinne*'. The answer was to suggest that the consequences of the Fall involved mankind without exception in actual sin, as by positing consequences that disabled man from doing good. Crooke suggested that everyone suffered not only a loss of wisdom and holiness but also a gain, if it could be so termed, of concupiscence, i.e., an utter disability to do good and a proneness to all manner of evil. This generous addition required in its turn some mode of transmission, which was found in the assumption that children begotten in a state of concupiscence would partake of it. Adam and Eve were in that state when they fell, since at '*enmitie*' to the good and prone to '*all evill*' and so, as universal parents, transmitted it to the world: Crooke at length described this original corruption as 'an hereditary disease'.[99] So people were disabled from doing good by their nature, though the extent of that disability was as yet undetermined. Mankind's limit was found in a lack of goodness sufficient to earn salvation: in particular it could act externally as required (and so incidentally support civil society), 'for though all are alike *disposed* vnto all manner of evill, having in their corrupt nature the *seedes* of every sinne, yet doth God, for the good of humane societie, *restraine* many from notorious crimes, by feare of shame and punishment, desire of honour and reward &c.' so that they could achieve 'unto many actions profitable for *humane societie*, and for the *outward* service of God'.[100] Whilst people were capable of rational morality, as in upholding the Decalogue, it was impossible that they should act from a loving disposition: and so they could never fulfil the whole law properly. For this grace was necessary in a form which would alter man's inward nature and this was found in the action of the Holy Spirit in implanting faith in God's benevolence – the '*first effect* of the spirit of Christ disposing us to *cleave* to him' – and so the covenant of grace dwelt on divine benevolence to the individual in implanting the love of God, which he could never have attained for himself.[101] We need not read too narrow an exclusivism into this doctrine. The election which it implies could be recognised, Crooke thought, by 'the word *preachd*, and *Sacraments* duely administered', so that the wide audience of Crooke's appropriately unremitting preaching and lectures, so far as it coincided with the communicants of his church, could be recognised as godly: and to spend £4 10s on bread and wine in a single year suggests a frequent or a large communion.[102] But it does describe a particular account of the nature of the Fall and therewith the covenant of grace and some related matters.

Such was the style of Christian explanation favoured in Locke's locality. Its three aspects of a rational morality, an account of the human condition and a remedy for it in a covenant of grace are all apparent in his own mature works. The lectures he wrote when a young don at Christ Church, Oxford, which we know as *Essays on the Law of Nature*, embodied an explanation of the moral character of rational conduct. None, Locke thought, overlooked his desire for self-preservation. Man needed to cooperate with others in order to achieve that end and so, as it happened, needed to enter society.[103] It followed that the conduct needed to preserve society was also rational. Locke supposed that society depended on justice (justice he described as the maintainer of trust, which was specified to be the bond of society) so that the practice of justice conduced to what he summed up as 'in a word, happiness' and of course for Locke it was axiomatic that 'the end and aime of all men' was 'happynesse alone'.[104] This order was not only rational but also moral, because God could be identified as a superior and so entitled to issue laws. Further the rational and the scriptural coincided, as one might expect. If just dealing was supposed to be the bond of society, the criteria of what was just, i.e., the specification of man's duty, corresponded to the Decalogue. Man was to worship God and to act out of love towards his neighbour. He was to obey superiors, refrain from theft and murder, tell the truth and keep his promises and feed the hungry. In short, Locke supposed that God willed man to glorify Him, whether by worship or by the maintenance of society, so that the rational and the moral coincided in content.[105] If the lineaments of the Two Tables are visible, as in the reference to what man owed to God and to his neighbour, as we shall see, they are even clearer in Locke's *Two Treatises* where (as in Crooke's account of the sixth Commandment) a duty of self-preservation and a duty to preserve all offer a foundation for civil society;[106] but here it was obvious enough in Locke's insistence that natural law required not merely external performances but also certain dispositions, which turned out to include reverence for God and the love of our neighbour.[107] Of the human condition, with its need to labour and its dominion over the earth and animals, we shall hear more in the *Treatises*, but man's postlapsarian character was plain when Locke's *Essays* stressed man's propensity to vice, notwithstanding the view of the future author of *An Essay concerning Human Understanding* that we should conduct ourselves according to reason: few men, he wrote, conducted themselves by reason. How could they achieve the 'height of virtue and happiness'?[108] When Locke came to consider this question in *The Reasonableness of Christianity* he framed his answer in terms of a law of works, which 'to the Apostle's time, no one of *Adam's* issue had kept', which fortunately God complemented with a law of faith, which required 'every one to believe what God requires him to believe, as a condition of the Covenant he makes with him'. That covenant, of course was 'an Act of Grace'[109] and the general pattern of the covenant theology of Locke's youth is obvious, though as a man he developed a somewhat different view of the Fall. But certainly these themes of moral theology which were available to the young Locke figure quite remarkably in his mature works and are treated there in broadly the same way. Indeed, as we shall see, they function as assumptions from which some of his more distinctive views were developed.

The church figured as as instrument of discipline as well as the bearer of an explanation: Nicholas Locke knew what he was doing in bequeathing money for the maintenance of the weekly Bible lecture. In particular the church courts provided a means for satisfying parochial disquiet, particularly towards sexual offences, and, conversely, for clearing one's reputation against adverse opinion. In other words they served to help protect the concerns of society and, it seems, determined their own business only to a limited extent.[110] The power of the pulpit itself was apparent and in time one of Locke's particular worries about Filmer was that *'the Pulpit . . . publickly owned his Doctrine, and made it the Currant Divinity of the Times'*: 'the Drum Ecclesiastick' was a powerful instrument.[111] This lay in the future as yet and it is perhaps time to turn to the more general instrument of order, civil magistracy.

IV

The magistrate, thought Samuel Crooke, should rule over the members of the church.[112] To what end? we may ask. His function was to regulate society so that moral conduct would be observed. This was not merely a moral function, for as we have seen the practice of virtue was supposed to be rational in that it sustained society. Its enforcement was in this light natural enough. Hence in 1667 we find Locke making the precise point that 'the magistrate commands not the practice of vertues because they are vertuous . . . but because they are the advantages of man with man, and most of them the strong ties and bonds of society, which cannot be loosened without shattering the whole frame'.[113] Thus the civil magistrate's task of upholding society complemented the economic, social and religious aspects of Locke's society.

The magistrate's work would be necessary because postlapsarian men for the most part lacked that loving disposition towards others that would have made them do good spontaneously. Now the whole tenor of rational morality was that virtue upheld society: God, as Locke put it, had joined virtue and public happiness together 'by an inseparable connetion' and made the practice of virtue 'necessary to the preservation of Society'. So how was virtuous conduct to be induced in default of a proper disposition? Instead of answering to love, mankind was governed by external constraints, such as honour or shame. Coercion would have seemed a natural supplement to this way of thinking and we ought not to consider the processes of law as contrasted with those of the community.[114] The enforcement of morals, whether by opinion or law, may seem odd to a more modern view, for which compulsion removes the moral value of actions, since these in turn are supposed to proceed from an unconstrained will. Yet in the light of this Christian estimate of man, according to which the will would work only by constraint, the choice was merely between types of constraint. As a charge to a grand jury in the 1690s phrased the matter, man was 'an unruly disobedient creature whom the light of nature, the laws and dictates of his own conscience, cannot make honest or civilised'. Coercion was thus worthwhile for rational ends: as Locke wrote late in life, 'punishments and severities thus applied, we are sure, are both practicable, just and useful.'[115] So the civil magistrate worked to sustain society.

He worked to this end by providing a single source of direction. That is to say people were not allowed to pursue the diverse ends on which their passions fastened when undirected by reason. It was common to liken a person under the government of the passions to a loss of calm, as with Milton's fallen Adam and Eve, who

> sate them down to weep, not onely Tear
> Raind at thir Eyes, but high Winds worse within
> Began to rise, high Passions, Anger, Hate,
> Mistrust, Suspicion, Discord, and shook sore
> Thir inward State of Mind, calme Region once
> And full of Peace, now tost and turbulent.

This clearly contrasted with government by reason, which composed the passions. Even so the magistrate's action would compose the 'tost and turbulent' relations between people. For he enforced what sustained society and so partook of reason. We find the point implied in the common likening of the magistrate to the head and society to the body, for the seat of reason was supposed to be the head.[116] This idea, though superficially obscure, clarifies the role of magistracy.

By the magistrate's rational direction it was possible to speak of a multitude of individuals being united in one body, as in the words of the young Locke 'men unite with each other as in one body'. Characteristic of this idea is a certain conceptual difficulty in distinguishing state and society, for the magisterial function of enforcing reasonable conduct united people into a single body in the first place. Hobbes wrote of a state in which there was an authority to 'conforme the wills of particular men unto unity, and concord' as a '*City*, or civill society' or again of 'the multitude united in one person' as 'a COMMONWEALTH, in Latin CIVITAS'. Locke, in mature years, called a chapter of his *Second Treatise* 'Of Political or Civil Society' and thought that because men constituted for themselves '*one Community* or Government, they are thereby presently incorporated, and make *one Body Politick*'.[117] Thus the magistrate provided the constitutive moment of civil society, embodying it out of a multitude. He provided, in particular, an enforcement of the rational conduct which was necessary to society. Thus it was natural to write of civil society as

41

'animated, held together, and set to work' by law or, with the young Locke, to think of the magistrate's power to enforce law as integral to *res publica*.[118]

Again the end of the magistrate's work, whether in enforcing the rational morality of the Second Table or natural law or in making positive laws to further its ends as circumstances required, lay, by definition, in the common good. That phrase, so opaque in many contexts, in this set of notions stands plainly for what sustains society, as prescribed by the morality which was also reason. The magistrate enforced morality and this was the common good, because moral conduct was the means of supporting society.[119]

The magistrate's work was known to Locke at its most basic level, because his father seems to have been a clerk to some local Justices of the Peace.[120] The duties of the JP, into whose hands fell the execution of day to day business in the localities, seem to have been arduous. In the notebook of Locke's father we find a miscellany of enforcement, united by upholding the social order: bastardy orders, recognisances for the drink trade, providing overseers for the poor, assessing contributions for a hospital, and, more picturesquely, issuing a licence to sell butter. Drink, in particular, seems to have interested Locke the lawyer. The alehouses of the Mendips seemed a resort for thieves and vagrants and a particular object of enmity for the local bench. The alehouse no doubt had a social function as a lubricant of business; but the business was sometimes criminal and frequently disorderly, so that regulation was in order: in 1647 we find a Western Circuit assize order suppressing all the alehouses of one Somersetshire hundred, 'except those recommended by the minister, churchwardens and principal inhabitants of any place'.[121] The work of magistracy, of course, included constraining people to act in some ways well as stopping them in others: for instance, magistrates could require the repair of the bridges, so obviously necessary to the economic infrastructure.[122]

At a more exalted level the Assizes had a similar aim. Their interests differ in emphasis from those John Locke senior recorded. The settlement of paupers seems to have bulked largest, reflecting no doubt the depression in the county. Bastardy and vagrancy came next amongst moral concerns with alehouses making a relatively poor fourth. But a glance at the cases will confirm that their contents were sometimes interconnected. The third place overall amongst the matters we have discussed, after bastardy and the poor, was occupied by the immediately economic interest of bridge and highway repair. Whatever the difference in the distribution of business the Assizes reflected the same frame of mind as we see in the elder Locke's memoranda.[123]

That frame of mind corresponded to the Christian explanation of man's condition, which provided in its turn a way of looking at the social and economic nature of the county. The character of Locke's part of Somerset, viewed in this way, displayed a series of complementary aspects in economy, society, religion and magistracy. Their complementary character can be seen reflected in various of Locke's own views.

Locke's thought did not disown the values his society assumed rather, as we have seen, it embodied many of them. His views, we know, were wider in scope than the social order of England and included a broad range of explanatory concerns. Some of Locke's explanations, as we shall see, would differ from those accepted in his youth. For instance, his views on Christian doctrine differed widely in some particulars from Samuel Crooke's. But these differences concerned explanation: they did not concern the values inherent in the social order or in Christian ethics. Neither did they question God's superiority, but, instead, made powerful use of it.

To understand the explanations Locke developed and indeed to understand the question he faced we need to consider not only the character of his county and country, but also their fortunes. In the years 1633 to 1660, coinciding with Locke's youth and early manhood, there occurred a series of events which seemed to demand a solution of a kind we find in Locke's earliest significant writings.

These writings concerned the conditions on which the magistrate should uphold the order of civil society, particularly in relation to ecclesiastical life. For if the Christian Church was the major instrument in explaining the social order and an important force in upholding it, then the problems of Christian society must be central to the fortunes of civil society. The ecclesiastical was part of the political. It is unsurprising that much of Locke's political theory should concern the relations of ecclesiastical and civil government. Locke's early life coincided with a series of threats to the civil order into which he was born, many of them from ecclesiastical sources. For in his youth the ecclesiastical lost its traditional synchronisation with the civil order. These threats focussed his attention on the fundamentals of his society, not least in their political aspect, and so explained his point of entry into theoretical writing. To understand the content of his views we must turn our attention to the content of those writings, his *Two Tracts of Government*. Thence we may see the beginning of the trajectory of Lockean thought.

Chapter 2

The problem which first engaged Locke's attention lay with the relations of church and state, specifically the relation between the authority of the civil government in what are called things indifferent and the claims of the Christian believer's conscience.[1] Viewed in a technical way this was a fairly well-defined problem, but when considered in its ramifications it was a single aspect of a more general question, a question about authority in England. Integral to the frame of mind prevalent at Locke's birth was authority, as we have seen. The superior's role was to direct and the inferior's to obey. God above all others directed mankind through His laws and raised up some to guide the rest. But His was perhaps the sole superiority relating to politics whose standing was not questioned during Locke's lifetime. In particular the authority of the church and its connection with the state came under question.

The problems internal to the English state were three: public finance, political authority and ecclesiastical affairs. They are easier to distinguish in the understanding than to separate in practice. They mark the history of the seventeenth century with inescapable frequency and very often went together. Insofar as problems are ever solved, these were dealt with in the decade after 1688, when they achieved settlements that endured, albeit with internal changes, for the next century.[2] For our purpose the important point is that in the discourse of explanation they involved questions about the nature and limits of political authority.

The problem, to put the matter very generally, was that superiority and dependence did not coincide at the upper levels of political life. That is to say, the bearer of the highest political authority could not rely on those who were his juridical inferiors being in a posture of dependence – a posture likely to make them ready to follow him. The monarch could not rely upon the unreserved and unquestioning obedience of the Lords and Commons in parliament, because in at least one vital particular he was dependent on them rather than they on him.

The finances of the state were fundamental to this matter. The

English polity preserved feudal forms until 1660. These were inadequate to the requirements of contemporary government. The financial resources of the monarchy consisted in the royal demesne, and in various devices such as wardships and monopolies, which permitted the monarch to raise the royal income.[3] These reflected only a small percentage of the nation's wealth, which was founded upon land, manufacture and commerce. Hence whilst the monarch was at the apex of political hierarchy, the national assets lay largely in the hands of others, the nobility, gentry and merchants. So long as these groups and the monarchy were of one mind the differing locations of authority and wealth mattered little; and, broadly speaking, they had a common sense of hierarchy. There was one way amongst others in which they differed quite often. That was when royal policy required the monarchy to dip deeply into the subject's funds.

The monarchy's own resources were probably inadequate to its task. Whilst the internal government of the country was relatively inexpensive – being conducted by magistrates who were often unpaid and who were backed by an apparatus for enforcement that was locally rather than centrally funded for the most part – its external relations were more costly. War had become sufficiently sophisticated to be expensive. The result was that military and naval enterprise were usually accompanied by royal debt. Monarchs unable to pay out of their own resources – which were not always sufficient to peace-time requirements, not least because of inflation in the earlier part of the century – had therefore to appeal to their subjects. The feudal apparatus for doing so – whether through levies, aids, benevolences or wardship – was helpful but not sufficient. For the political history of England from the Conquest had been a story in which the feudal resources of the monarch had been first drained and then jealously limited by the subject. The avenues which the monarchy had explored energetically from the thirteenth century had been twofold: borrowing and parliamentary taxation. Borrowing was useful (especially if the borrower was eager for honours, vulnerable to pressure or a foreigner) but not nearly adequate to expenditure. Parliamentary taxation had therefore to be sought: monarchs had to persuade the Lords and Commons to underwrite the government.

This was a delicate task. By tradition the two Houses of Parliament, especially the Commons, were entitled to correlate supply with a redress of their grievances. In economically difficult times (as times always seem to be) not the least of their grievances was having to vote taxation, especially as the warlike initiatives of the monarchy were frequently unsuccessful.[4] Their grievances tended to become criticism of the monarch or, euphemistically, his advisers, for executive policy proceeded from him personally – the executive character of monarchy was signalled by the theorists' referring to the ruler as 'magistrate'. Taxation meant the inroads into the subjects' resources and so *property* became a matter of some concern. In this sense the action of the government and the subject's property stood in tension.

Questions of finance occasioned constitutional debate. The Commons, approached for extraordinary finance, expressed their scepticism about the methods by which government had been conducted. They sought to scrutinise or even supervise expenditure, and so made it more or less explicit that the monarch was not free to act as he wished. This programme was expressed less in terms of constitutional demands, since hierarchy was to be respected, but rather in terms of the subject's rights over his or her property. The response of royal apologists lay not least with arguing that this property was properly at the king's disposal, and therefore that he did not need parliametary consent to claim it. Naturally this met with objections, especially when it involved taxation without parliamentary consent. The intellectual difference grew more sophisticated and more radical on both sides, just as the dispute itself became more heated over time.[5] But whatever its specific form it was essentially a matter of the limits to the locus of political authority: and so of powers of government and by correlation of the subject's *liberty*.

The history of the English monarchy in the seventeenth century thus exhibits a steady alternation (and some spectacular oscillations). The monarch's ability to act without parliamentary pressure depended on avoiding over-expenditure, avoiding especially an adventurous foreign policy. So long as royal policy was fiscally prudent the monarch enjoyed relative independence from parliament: prodigality made him dependent. These swings made relevant a concern for the liberty and property of the subject and raised questions about the extent and location of governmental authority. It is noteworthy, for instance, that the three episodes of governmental upset during the reign of Charles II – 1667, 1673 and the years after 1678 – coincided with failure abroad and financial straits at home. But it was not authority in civil society alone that was under scrutiny.

Since the church functioned not least as an arm of civil order, it had a political as well as a purely ecclesiastical aspect. In the first instance this did not concern its political role: before the forties most people who articulated views assumed that there should be a single church upheld by the state.[6] It concerned the character of that church, especially the character of its worship and ecclesiastical government.[7] Not the least problem was the change from the Jacobean church, capacious in matters of doctrine and worship, to the aggressive pretensions of Archbishop Laud, a change with political resonance since Laud's followers included apologists for royal authority.[8] The terms of the question changed when Charles I's policies in church and state alike gave some an unhappy sense that the benefits conferred by one royal superior at least were dubious and so moved the country along a path to civil war.[9] The breakdown of ecclesiastical discipline that followed the onset of the conflict permitted a proliferation of religious sects. From the fifties their diversity and numbers made it evident that belief about the church would not reduce easily to one type. The question became, what sort of church would the state patronise and what would be its attitude to other forms of worship? In other words, what was the proper character of ecclesiastical authority? Whatever the answer, its dimensions were likely to reflect the lay conviction that the church's function was to support civil order and that the ecclesiastical positions that threatened this order were unacceptable.[10]

These general problems assumed a particular shape during Locke's youth. Events encouraged new explanations. The disputes about the church, the challenge to monarchical authority and the remakings of government which succeeded it all generated conceptual change. These changes were not insulated, for the disturbance to civil life disposed people to question most things. As Aubrey observed from the middle years of the century people became disposed to accept intellectual change, which previously had been their last desire. 'In those times, to have had an inventive and equiring Witt, was accounted Affectation,' he wrote. But 'about the yeare 1649' the case altered, for previously "twas held a strange presumption for a Man to attempt an Innovation in Learnings; and not to be good Manners, to be more knowing than his Neighbours and Forefathers'. Late in life Locke himself called his age 'quick-sighted'.[11] The sceptical attitude to inherited explanations we find in Locke's works reflects this temper. But it was authority especially that was subject to question. 'The great subject of debate, difference, exagitation, and contrivement in the late commotions,' wrote Edward Gee

that which the most stir hath been about is the matter of Authority. Divers other things, indeed, have (scarce any thing but hath) been in dispute with some, or other. No principle so plain, no right so manifest, but some have been to stand up in question or contradiction of it. But in all the controversies that have risen, there is nothing (to my observation) that hath been so universally, really and continuedly insisted on as this matter of Power.[12]

Locke reflected the experience of the period, for his writings concern themselves often as not with questions of authority – whether of God or the government, the church or the human understanding. Even when authority is not his subject, his manner of writing bespeaks the same temper, for Locke's style is nearly always explanatory and a concern with explanation is the natural pendant to relentless questioning.

Events common to Somerset and Oxford, common indeed to the whole country, directed his attention first to one concern especially, the relations of church and state. Of all ecclesiastical matters this had been the most contentious. In Gee's words again, 'the thing which- . . . hath abidden most contention (the most both for the multitude, and vehemency of contenders) and which hath been still held up, and disceptations have been continuedly . . . renewed about it, is the matter of Church Order, and Ecclesiastical Power.'[13] Certainly when Locke first addressed the subject in 1660 there were questions both intellectual and practical remaining to be settled.

I

Locke's earliest extended writings, the works known to posterity as *Two Tracts on Government*, argued that the civil government – to use his own term, the civil magistrate – was entitled to regulate ecclesiastical affairs. They argued, specifically, that the magistrate had authority to govern the church in things indifferent, meaning those parts of religious worship for which God had not Himself laid down regulations. We should consider first the state of mind informing the work before attending to the particular form it took; and so we should turn to the events of Locke's early life. *Two Tracts* focussed on the problem for authority in civil society, particularly civil government, posed by groups who claimed a religious status. There arose, in other words, religious positions which seemed at variance with those which warranted the order of life into which Locke was born. Or, to use Locke's own coloured language, there had been 'no design so wicked which hath not worn the vizor of religion, nor rebellion which hath not been so kind to itself as to assume the specious name of reformation, proclaiming a design either to supply the defects or correct the errors of religion,' so that 'none ever went about to ruin the *state* but with pretence to build the *temple*'. This was not Locke's view alone: according to William Sancroft religious opinion 'is the common skreen of private design'.[14] Let us see how events up to 1660 might inform this point of view.

Locke's words suggest that some ecclesiastics had left their proper office, which in the relevant respect was to sustain civil society, and instead preferred other designs. Events, beginning in the West country in 1633 but with implications for the whole country, might lend themselves to this interpretation: that ecclesiastical pretensions were accompanied by threats to civil society, whether to the authority of the civil magistrate or to the moral values he upheld. This came first when Laudian assertiveness was accompanied by Charles I's probing of the localities and continued with the events of the forties and fifties, especially the rise of religious radicalism.

'As for myself,' Locke declared in 1660, 'I no sooner perceived myself in the *world* but I found myself in a storm, which hath lasted almost hitherto.'[15] He was born on 29 August 1632. Within twelve months the affair of Somerset church ales had manifested itself. Magistrates had long regulated these revels in order to enforce good conduct. The order of Baron Denham at the county assizes in March 1632 was the latest in a long series. The great novelty lay in the sharp reaction of Bishop Laud of London, who had been – recently though transiently – bishop of Bath and Wells. Laud complained to the king that the judge's injunction, which addressed the clergy, was an invasion of the diocesan's authority. Charles agreed and both Denham and Chief Justice Richardson were charged strictly to revoke all prohibitions of church ales on the Lent circuit of 1633. Once in Somerset, however, Richardson signified clearly that the ban should stand. Indeed in response to a personal order from Charles to proceed Richardson used the assizes of August 1633 to expound the other view. Before the county's JPs he recapitulated the need for magisterial regulation and its long history; and his revocation of Denham's order stressed its substantial validity:

Which former Order being warranted by so many Presidents [sic.], Judge Richardson said hee conceived hee had no power absolutely to reverse; but being commanded to do it . . . he did as much as in him lay revoke it: but yet doubted not, that if the Justices of Peace would truely informe His Majesty of the grounds of the former order, His Majesty would give Order to revive it

and accompanied his point with some derogatory remarks about bishops. After Richardson returned from circuit he faced a Council in which Laud, now archbishop of Canterbury, was prominent. When the Chief Justice left the Council Chamber 'very dejectedly with tears in his eyes', 'the Earle of Derset seeing him in such a sad condition, and demaunding him how he did, he answered, "Very ill my Lord for I am like to bee choked with the Archbishops Lawnsleeves."' From the viewpoint of moral order in Somerset, however close Richardson had come to tailoring the letter of the law to its spirit, this was the victory of an ecclesiastic over civil magistracy and the values it defended.

This point was underlined when Laud exploited his victory to reissue the Book of Sports in October of the same year. James I, happening to be in Lancashire in 1617, had been informed of that county's longstanding suppression of church ales; which, some courtiers intimated, was a grievance for the common folk. James' declaration to the local JPs, allowing revels, had been extended to the whole kingdom in 1618. The Book of Sports was a modest statement of which recreations were acceptable on Sundays after divine service and, as such, a warrant for church ales so long as order was preserved. Laud meant that the Book of Sports, reedited to give a more powerful endorsement of church ales, should serve to define those activities acceptable to ecclesiastical authority. Whether or no church ales were a serious threat to civil order this act was bound to offend some: for it could appear to overturn authority in society. For at least one observer it encouraged inferiors to show 'high contempt' for their superiors: 'the common vulgar against the magistrate and minister, servants against their masters, children against their parents, and wanton wives against their husbands'.[16] Ecclesiastical authority might seem to encroach on the civil magistrate's sphere and so on the moral order in a deleterious way.

This impression was soon reinforced. Laudian church practices, however innocent they might seem in themselves, would become objectionable if they accompanied unequivocally unacceptable innovations. The Laudian restriction on preaching and Bible lectures was scarcely acceptable. To the archbishop and his ally William Peirs of Bath and Wells the restriction of the pulpit to parochial incumbents in their own parishes and the regulation of even their frequency of preaching doubtless seemed a proper exertion of episcopal authority: but in a largely illiterate society, where the spoken word was paramount, it was the pulpit which explained the moral directives of social authority, and restriction of its use must have looked objectionable. The use of the church courts to enforce the Laudian view and so indirectly to quieten the message which underwrote civil magistracy told the same story. It is hardly surprising then that the Laudian institutions of altars, organs, surplices, kneeling at sacrament, bowing at the name of Jesus and making the sign of the cross in baptism should become suspect to some incumbents, and indeed to their congregations.[17] John Locke the elder found himself asking whether bowing to the altar or at the name of Jesus were 'lawfull' or 'pious' and if a minister could properly administer the sacrament to 'one not kneelinge'.[18] One obvious response was to wonder too, as the elder Locke wondered, whether in the election of ministers 'the voice of the people be requird', that is whether to dispense with bishops, at least of Laudian powers, and institute Presbyterianism. When the enforcement of episcopal authority collapsed in the forties there was a vigorous attempt to establish Presbyterian classes in North Somerset (contrasting with the desultory conventicle of 1605 at Wrington, which had pre-occupied itself with drinking).[19]

Peirs' attempt to mould his diocese to the Laudian specification would not have become more attractive for being associated with inroads against property. Property, after all, was a base of social authority and was validated by the Christian explanations we have seen. Nearly sixty-eight per cent of patrons in the diocese were private individuals, a higher proportion than in many counties, and no doubt a proprietorial attitude was common. Certainly when Peirs attempted to insert his son into a living in the gift of the Popham family, they declared that his action 'tendeth to the preduce of the inheritance of your Peticioner and all temporal Patrons who by this example are like to be deprived of their right of patronage'. Peirs' success – and his reply to the Pophams that 'this proposall is not fayre' – must have seemed a further instance of the ecclesiastic overstepping the limits of his proper authority. Alexander Popham was, in a more informal sense, the patron of the elder Locke and the case would be known to our subject.[20]

A case which no property owner could ignore was ship money. Taxation in the earlier part of the thirties had seemed worthy of note to the elder Locke. Somerset had objected to an earlier levy in 1627. No county proved more resistant to ship money. Whilst its earlier instalments were largely paid they were accompanied by loud complaints; and of the eight thousand pounds demanded by the writ of November 1639 ninety-six per cent was not paid. The previous exactions were unwelcome, for the broadcloth regions, to name no others, were probably somewhat overpopulated and had scarcely recovered from depression. Such was the suspicion of the new drain on property that increases in the cost of living were attributed to it. According to the nineteen gentlemen of the grand jury at the Bath assizes of July 1638 farmers were supposed to have to sell at high prices to meet the tax, so that

Corne and other provision is growne to an excessive rate, which wee doe conceave not to be occasioned soe much by scarcity and want. . .as by other accidents, namely one principall one is the great and heavy taxacions by new invented wayes

and the threat to property, in short, was unacceptable. We need hardly underline the prominence of property and the magistrate's duty to *protect* it in Locke's *Two Treatises*.[21]

Property was an ecumenical programme. The choice between king and parliament was a more difficult one. A man's option depended on any number of considerations. But whatever his choice the consequences of this rupture for the county were apparent. They included not only challenges to liberty and property quite as obvious as those of Laud and Charles I but also the growth of some religious claims which were a great deal more of a challenge to the order of society than Laudianism could ever have seemed.

No area in England suffered more than the west country and the neighbouring Welsh border and Severn Valley, where much of the most intensive campaigning occurred. Murder made a striking entry in the county assizes. At a less dramatic, but economically important level, there were persistent problems with bridges and their repair. Somerset records show plenty of cases of girls consorting with soldiers from both sides. Pensford suffered its fair share of troubles, even putting aside Captain Locke's short and inglorious career in a parliamentary regiment. In September 1645 after the fall of Bristol, Fairfax withdrew his army, in order to avoid the plague, and billeted it for three weeks on Pensford. In 1648 the elder Locke noted contributions to Fairfax's funds, under the title 'ransoms'. By March 1649 the assizes at Taunton recorded that Pensford's poor relief had become defective. The consequences of conflict were only too apparent.[22]

Even after the civil war there were difficulties not only with property but liberty also. The latter was compromised by the effective centralisation of power implied in the war effort, and property, similarly, by war taxation. During the war these had dampened ardour on the royalist side; afterwards it was the turn of their opponents to be dissatisfied with the rule of the army and the taxation needed to support men in arms.[23] The phenomenon characteristic of this mood had declared itself during the war, namely action for the sake of local ends only. That is to say people were willing to defend themselves (and so preserve their property) and thus to act independently of central guidance (preserving their liberty). Captain Locke had been Alexander Popham's agent in collecting 'loans' for military purposes restricted to the locality as early as June 1642 and had brought in 'large sums' (thus perhaps he earned Popham's good offices in finding a place for his son at Westminster School five years later). At a later date the Clubmen, with their desire to see off intruding outsiders, displayed a belligerent neutralism.[24] A return to conditions more favourable to the tenor of ordinary life was obviously desirable.

The pretensions of certain religious groups, in particular, pointed that moral. For whilst one intrusive persuasion had met a rebuff, its removal, along with the church courts, allowed other views to flourish. Some of these seemed very different from that Christianity which explained the moral character of rational practices. Ranters, Baptists, Quakers and Fifth Monarchy men appeared, to differing degrees, to offer accounts of religion which were mistaken and incongruent with the order of society.

These groups employed a particular interpretation of how people came to be saved. It was commonly assumed that man, subject to passions which might divert him from the conclusions of reason, would not find it easy and might find it impossible to attain a proper faith in God. God would therefore persuade such as He cared to save by direct action, namely by striking conviction into them through the Holy Spirit. This persuasion, being divinely provided, required no authenication from man and it was customary to say that it was not subject to the judgement of reason. Calvin, for instance, maintained that the *testimonium internum spiritus sancti* was stronger than all proof. According to Samuel Petto 'the Spirit . . . irresistibly striketh the soule into such cleare, firme, and strong apprehensions and perswasions' and therefore did not employ reasoning, it 'witnesseth not in a Discursive way, by deducing Conclusions from premises'. Likewise John Owen, who was dean of Christ Church when Locke went up to Oxford, found that 'the true Nature of Saving Illumination consists in this, that it gives the Mind . . . a direct intuitive insight and prospect into Spiritual Things'.[25] This type of view need in itself have no particular implications for the relation of Christianity to the social order. Its proponents assumed that the Holy Spirit would persuade people to a belief in the Bible and it was 'a known and received maxim that the Gospel clashes against no righteous ordinance of man'; indeed the action of the Holy Spirit was conceived in terms of reason, for 'it alters the judgement by presenting greater reasons'. The trouble was that some people decided that the Holy Spirit might have novel truths to tell, which God might also be supposed to have decided were of greater authority than what the scripture and reason had announced: and so transcend the order of society. As William Sydenham remarked 'that which sticks most with me, is the nearness of this opinion to that which is a most glorious truth, that the spirit is personally in us.'[26] What did they have to say?

Sometimes the views advanced were just transparently self-interested, as when a Somerset man told the woman he hoped to seduce that 'there was no punishment for any man', for 'after this life there was no punishment because there was neither heaven nor hell'.

Often, however, there was a more highly developed theory to support what would otherwise have seemed unreasonable conduct. For instance, there was the doctrine of antinomianism. This suggested that God could justify people without regard to their conduct. This is one interpretation of the indispensability of faith for salvation, albeit incompatible with a Christianity which lends moral authority to the social order, but not previously a popular one. Before the civil war it had been 'but the fancy of solitary vicars musing to themselves'. In the later forties the Baptists took up the idea, albeit only as an idea, for they practised a literal obedience to scripture. The Ranters, on the other hand, considered that scripture was a dead letter to the regenerate and adopted moral practices which contradicted the ordinary account of it, announcing that alcoholic self-indulgence, free love and extensive swearing were compatible with salvation. One Somerset Ranter, John Robins, decided that he was God and permitted his followers to exchange spouses. Obviously all this was as repugnant to accepted religion as to the order of society.[27]

The most notable account of the Holy Spirit, however, came from the Quakers. George Fox maintained the usual view of the Holy Spirit, recounting that 'I did not see by the help of man nor by the letter . . . but I saw . . . in the light of the Lord Jesus Christ and by his immediate Spirit and power' and, accordingly, that it was 'not the letter, nor the writing of the Scripture, but the ingrafted Word' that was 'able to save . . . soules'. He added in the ordinary way that this was not 'a naturall light' but on 'ye contrary . . . divine and spirituall from Christ' and so one could infer that its authenticity was beyond doubt and above the canons of scriptural interpretation and reason: 'these divine inward revelations . . . are not to be subjected to the test either of the outward testimony of the Scriptures or of the natural reason of man'. Thus the spirit was *'true, unerring and infallible'*. But he exploited the possibility that the Holy Spirit would work in novel ways, claiming that 'the eternal glorious power of Christ' communicated to him was 'the same eternal power of God . . . that afterwards shook the nations, priests, professors, and people'. Some of his followers claimed that their inward regeneration would be succeeded by social reorganisation. In the words of one group 'Conscience was above the scriptures; and the scriptures ought to be tried by it, and not that by the scriptures'. Clearly these theories might admit of views and of conduct with a very different content from the rational morality of Samuel Crooke.[28]

The supremacy of conscience over scripture, and therefore over reason and the social order, was a theoretical point; but it was soon applied to practice. Quakers scorned the honouring of superiors, substituting 'thee' and 'thou' for 'you' and 'yours' as a 'fearful cut to proud flesh and self-honour'. Since obedience to superiors was connected with productivity it was not long before a Somerset grand jury was demanding action against 'persons known by the name of Quakers, living often in idleness'. By extension it might be thought they were against property, as when Fuller remarked that 'such as now introduce Thou and Thee will (if they can) expel Mine and Thine, dissolving all property into confusion'. Their rejection of tithes suggested that they were against all the church represented. Their rejection of oaths would confirm that impression. Here was a form of religion which transcended mere worship and whose doctrine opposed rather than upheld the order of society: Quaker 'principles and practices' seemed 'diametrically opposed both to magistracy and ministry'. All this proceeded from their view of the Spirit and conscience; and truly here was 'The World turn'd upside down'.[29]

The Quakers posed a threat to the social order whose potential was in plain fact never realised; the implications of their thought threatened an upheaval which did not occur. Yet the potential seemed present, particularly in certain parts of the country. The Quakers were especially strong in Bristol, as well as in London and certain rural areas. They made their presence felt in Oxford from 1654. Not only their views and habits but also their numbers caused disquiet: at the Restoration they were between thirty and forty thousand, and perhaps as many as sixty. Certainly they were regarded as a nuisance in Bristol from 1654 onwards, where their presence had set the garrison (which was sympathetic) against the city government and divided the government against itself. At Bristol, too, came the movement's most dramatic manifestation. In 1656 James Nayler, who bore a passable facial likeness to the common representation of Christ, projected a more substantial identity when he entered the city to the hosannas of his followers, in imitation of the Messiah's entry into Jerusalem. This might be supposed to follow from the Quaker attitude to the spirit: 'this error, of making the light within the only rule,' wrote William Grigge, 'would make them cast off Scripture, Ordinances, Ministry, and look upon themselves godified, and to say what this Blasphemer saith, I am Christ'. Nayler, so it seemed to a sceptical witness of his examination at Westminster in November, asserted 'that Christ being the same to day and for ever what honour was given to him at Jerusalem might be given to him where and in whomsoever he is manifested from god'. The witness was John Locke.[30]

Locke thought Quakerism embodied rather less than the truth. It provided, he noted as late as 1675, 'a great instance' of 'how little truth

& reason oporates upon mankinde'. If the doctrine was untrue it might be nonsense (as Locke said 'noething but a sceane of mirth'); if it was unreasonable then, by the linkage of reason and the common good, as contrasted with passion and selfishness, it might also be self-interested: and to Locke Nayler and his followers seemed both. Selfishness, of course, was linked to an undue desire for independence which, as with Milton's Satan, meant a desire to rule. Fox's observation that 'he that sanctifieth and they that are sanctified, are of one, and the Saints are all one in the Father and the Son', once placed in the light of Nayler's lording it over others, might be better redescribed as 'a liberty for men at pleasure to adopt themselves children of God, and from thence to assume a title to inheritance here and proclaim themselves heirs of the world'. The Quaker supersession of reason was absurd and a touch sinister to Locke's way of thinking.[31]

There was, no doubt, a theoretical reply to these pretensions. The credentials of the supposed action of the spirit might be questioned, as in Locke's chapter on faith and reason in his *Essay concerning Human Understanding*. Locke, of course, accommodated faith, which he defined as 'Assent to any Proposition, . . . made out . . . upon the credit of the Proposer, as coming from GOD, in some extraordinary way of Communication.' But he took care that the extraordinary should not contradict what was known through 'the natural ways of Knowledge'. Propositions established through reason, he argued, were certain, whilst those known from revelation were probable. Hence it could not be rational to accept the latter if it contradicted the former. Whilst this did nothing to discredit the Bible, whose precepts were seen to agree with reason, it debarred the acceptance of supposed revelations which would upset the conclusions of reason, and so the scriptural and social order. His target was made even more explicit in his chapter 'Of Enthusiasm', added in 1700. Enthusiasm suggested a 'laying by Reason' to 'set up Revelation without it'. The consequences of this were obvious, for without reason passion alone would rule, 'men being most forwardly obedient to the impulses they receive from themselves'. Lest anyone doubt his meaning Locke alluded to the enthusiast's illumination as the 'light within', an obvious reminder of the Quakers' inner light. On the contrary, true revelations would agree with reason: for 'God when he makes the Prophet does not unmake the Man.' Faith, in short, 'cannot be afforded to any thing, but upon good Reason'. Thus the pretensions of those who claimed the Holy Spirit could never upset either scripture or reason.[32] However all this, as yet, lay in the future and the development of a theory was postponed to the demands of practice.

For whilst the Quakers presented a disagreeable potential the Fifth Monarchy men projected violent action. They believed in the rule of the saints on earth, fulfilling the prophecies of Daniel. They countenanced force as their means, for they supposed that all true authority came directly from God and that all other institutions, which were thus merely 'carnal', should be destroyed. They were not a negligible group, having twelve or thirteen members in Barebone's Parliament, and from time to time supposed that they should act out their theories, as in 1653. In January 1661 one Venner, with about fifty followers, tried to set up in the streets of London the Fifth Monarchy. He and others were hanged, but here clearly was an active attempt to proclaim the adoptive children of God as the heirs of the world. As Locke remarked 'it may well be feared by any that will but consider the *conscientious* disorders amongst us that the several bands of *Saints* would not want their *Venners* to animate and lead them on in the *work of the Lord*'.[33] A practical response was needed to meet a conscientious-ness which, it seemed, undermined the proper ends of religion.

II

The obvious step to quieten the enthusiasts was to reassert the civil magistrate's power, specifically in the form of restraining any religiously inspired manifestations which threatened the order of civil society. After all, if both Quakers and Fifth Monarchists denied that the magistrate had any proper business with them, agreeably to their view of the supremacy of conscience over external rules, the point was clear enough. As William Grigge put it there had been 'an opposing and undermining of those great Ordinances of god, a right Magistracy and Ministry, who in a civil and ecclesiastical way do, or would carry on Government in Church and Commonwealth'. The magistrates of Bristol were keen to act, complaining that they were 'destitute of a law to bound and restrain' Quakers. When the instructions came they remarked that 'we have waited long for some directions to this purpose'. As one man told the same body in 1658, 'magistrates should not bee as Jupiters log, which by lying still, and doing nothing, made the frogs bold with it'.[34]

The natural complement to this view was that other denominations, though divided on other points, would unite in upholding scripture, reason and the social order. Presbyterianism had been the natural response to Laudianism; and Independency had accommodated those who disliked even its measure of central direction. But Presbyterian, Independent and Anglican of all hues could find points of agreement.

By the later 1650s it was clear that the attempt to provide effective church discipline through Presbyterian classes had failed: in Somerset only one approached real efficacy. Most of the parish clergy, whatever the opinions of more elevated clerics, appear to have been satisfied with the Jacobean pattern of church discipline and with the Book of Common Prayer. Whilst it was perhaps unclear what form of church polity would be established and what the limits of comprehension within it and toleration outside of it would be, Independents joined with Presbyterians in an 'utter dislike and abhorrence of a Universal Toleration'. A rising compounded of royalists and Presbyterians in 1659 claimed as its warrant the need to defend religion and property against the Quakers. If the reunion of the churches could be achieved the regulation of the enthusiasts would be attractive.[35]

Who was to provide the regulation? The question was less one of personalities or parties than of finding someone who could achieve an effective enforcement of the values which had been threatened in the preceding decades. In Somerset the county seems to have been unitedly for 'liberty and property', an ecumenical programme and one whose contents had seemed threatened at one time or another by every government from Charles I's to Cromwell's. After Cromwell's death it was unclear who would secure order. The Rump, despite rejecting universal toleration and ignoring a Quaker petition of fifteen thousand signatures for the abolition of tithes, failed quite to please the Presbyterians ('whose number', wrote the French ambassador, 'far exceeds that of all the other Sectaries put together') because they freed Nayler and recruited Quakers into the army. At the end of July 1659 a disturbance convinced the worshippers of Carfax Church near Oxford that 'anabaptists and quakers were come to cut their throats'. As for Devon and Somerset, the news sheets reported that 'Anabaptists and Quakers were joyned together to cut the Throats of all the Ministers and Magistrates in those parts', whilst Ralph Farmer asked querelously 'is not contempt of *Magistracy* and *Ministry* grown to an *insupportable* height?'. By November Locke's 'Oh for a Pilot that would steare the tossed Ship of state to the haven of happinesse' would have been echoed by others.

It began to seem that the best means to the end of 'happinesse' or peace was the restoration of the monarchy. By the beginning of 1660, according to Lucy Hutchison, the Presbyterians preached for it 'and began openly to desire the king; not for good will to him, but only for destruction of all the fanatics'. About the same time Ralph Josselin wrote of 'the nacion looking more to Charles Stuart, out of love to themselves not him'. John Fell had observed that 'without trusting some one or other, the Nation is certainly destroyed, and no person in the world, besides the King, is in a capacity to avert the impendent ruin'. Locke saluted Charles II as *conservator pacis*, just as he had earlier apostrophised Cromwell in the same terms. 'I no sooner perceived myself in the *world* but I found myself in a storm, which hath lasted almost hitherto', we may recollect him writing; he added, 'and therefore cannot but entertain the approaches of a calm with the greatest joy and satisfaction'. His opinion of the Stuarts' potential for this end was to change, but for the moment his desire for peace brought him to agree with the common point of view.[36]

Locke expressed his joy and satisfaction at the beginning of the earlier of his two tracts on behalf of the civil government's authority in ecclesiastical affairs. The trajectory of events in his early manhood pointed to that conclusion as the way to defend the complementary relation of faith, reason and civil life. It was an obvious response to the facts of the situation. The formula that Samuel Rutherford had used about the Presbyterians applied equally to other parties: they had tried to set up a 'state opposite to a state'.[37] The obvious response was to assert the authority of the civil government over the church.

Obvious though it was, the form that it assumed was not satisfactory. Locke wished to assert the government's authority over ecclesiastical practices: which fitted the fact that ecclesiastical pretensions to self-direction had been problematical. The arguments Locke advanced, whilst bent on his primary aim of defending civil society against undue religious inroads, did not achieve their end without cost. The cost was to find that two components in the conceptual array that Locke inherited could conflict. Civil peace and the following of a conscience pleasing to God might be at odds.

What was more, Locke's treatment of the church did nothing to explain the relation of revelation, the object believed in, to reason. Locke needed to stabilise the relations of revelation, supposititious or genuine, to reason because the achievement of his primary aim depended on showing that the conclusions of reason could not be ignored. So Locke's *Two Tracts* presented an incomplete case.

To intellectual difficulty and omission was added practical discomfort. For the terms of political practice changed into a form which altered the practical bearings of the theoretical view Locke had advocated. Thus in several ways his *Tracts* presented problems rather than solutions. Yet difficulty can be as rewarding, and more fertile than success. The *Two Tracts* provide the introduction to the works the world knows as characteristically Lockean.

III

Locke's aim of safeguarding civil society depended on the assumption that the magistrate was authorised to regulate things indifferent – understanding by that term, matters in which God had not issued regulations. Locke did not undertake to argue for the magistrate's authority in general (which was not at issue in the specific debate he addressed), but instead considered its limits. The principle he laid down to that end was that the magistrate could compel only outward performances. This would establish his fundamental aim.

By 'things indifferent' was intended matters about which God Himself had not declared views. In that sense 'indifferent' meant neither commanded nor forbidden by the greatest of superiors. God, of course, was not the sole superior. Terrestrial monarchs might see things indifferent as a field peculiarly suitable for *their* legislation. Matters about which God had legislated were not theirs to dispose, though they could enforce His dispositions with their own laws. This left indifferent matters to order as they chose: and because they were superiors they would require obedience. Hence we find a divine writing of 'a due matter. . .indifferent in it selfe: for in things simply good or euill, which are commanded or forbidden by God and Nature, No man hath power to crosse the will of God. And in these things mans power is declaratory and executory, not soueraigne of it selfe'; but, he continued 'In things indifferent there is a power to command for circumstances of time, place, order, and the like, and there is a necessity of obedience.' The authority of civil government in this case concerned those aspects of order God had not settled.

The principle itself depended on a view of the relation of intellect and will. We may recollect that in the psychology of the 'heart' it happened that God might work upon someone's understanding in order to determine his or her will to action. This notion presupposed the larger conception that the intellect was determined by the considerations placed before it, whether through the actions of God in particular cases or, more generally, through the evidence mediated through the senses and intelligence that He had provided. Whatever the way by which mankind was supplied with conceptions it was the case for Locke that 'God hath reserved the disposure' of 'the understanding and assent' to Himself and had 'not so much entrusted man with a liberty at pleasure to believe or reject'. Locke used this view at large in his subsequent writings on the human understanding and toleration, but (as is natural enough) it appeared first as an unargued assumption, deployed to argue a further conclusion.

The conclusion was that if God determined the intellect then, being beyond the range of human force, it was fruitless for the magistrate to try to regulate it: 'a magistrate would in vain assault that part of man which owes no homage to his authority'. But the conclusion was also a preface, for in those matters God had left to man it followed that 'it is far otherwise, which depending freely upon the choice of the doer will be entertained or neglected proportionally as the law shall annex rewards or punishments to them'.[38] Where a man commanded himself, the magistrate too could command effectively. Thus external actions, as divorced from states of assent, could be for the magistrate to control.

This suggestion served Locke's turn, though it said nothing about how the magistrate had been authorised so to act, because it was not a view which anyone was likely to dispute. If one took the ordinary view of fallen mankind's capacity for bad actions, or merely observed the fragility of order in this period, the need for the magistrate to regulate external performances was obvious: 'who knows not that the stubborn necks of the people do often call for yokes and those strong and heavy without which it would be impossible they should be kept in order?', Locke asked. Few would have disagreed, whatever their views about order within the church. William Perkins, at whose feet Samuel Crooke had sat at Cambridge and who was (according to John Cosin) the 'great Rabbi' of those sometimes ill-disposed to the Anglican hierarchy, had remarked that human laws could 'reach no further than the outward man, that is, to body and goods'. Edward Bagshawe the younger, whose specific views Locke wished to refute, agreed with him in the general view that the magistrate's true concern lay 'over the Body, to repress and correct those moral vices, to which our *outward* man is subject'. Hence all Locke needed to add to his principle was that the indifferent things of religion were outward performances and it followed that they were included in the magistrate's sphere just as much as were civil actions.[39]

These views, straightforward as they were, served a persuasive function when Locke wrote his *English Tract*, the earlier of the two, in 1660. Locke's personal opinions about church parties seem not to have survived, if they were expressed or even formulated, but he had moved on a smooth course of academic preferment at Christ Church whilst the Independent John Owen had been succeeded as Dean by the Presbyterian Edward Reynolds and he in his turn by the Anglican George Morley. Locke's family background suggested sympathy with Presbyterianism, at least as a response to Laudianism, and he may have had a personal respect for John Owen. The obvious way to ease his particular situation at Oxford was to foster church unity, for the restored Charles II, the supreme magistrate, was also head of the Church of England. The method which lay to hand was to voice his dislike of such ecumenical enemies as Quakers, Anabaptists and Fifth Monarchy men. After all, if Owen was a noted enemy of the Quakers, could not an appeal to the civil magistrate seem plausible?[40]

Locke's posture had relevance nationally as well as locally. It was assumed, not unreasonably after the Interregnum, that religious observance was a prop of civil order: as John Fell suggested 'Religion is the Cement of Government, without a publick profession of which, and the maintenance of Learning and Ministry, Atheisme and disorder must needs break in'. Of course this does not tell us the form of observance, but it was obvious from April 1660 onwards that the restored monarchy would be accompanied by a restored Church of England. Yet it was unclear precisely what form this church would assume. That there should be a unitary national church seemed natural to many. John Pearson, soon to be a bishop, thought 'that Union of all Parties, which, as at all times, so especially at this, is to be wished and embraced' and Bagshawe, professing himself 'a strict Assertor of the Doctrine of the Church of England', expressed a hearty wish 'that all Parties would agree to refer the whole Cause of Ceremonies to his Majesties single Decision'.[41] If such unity were accomplished on terms acceptable to Presbyterians (and perhaps even some Independents) it would have obvious advantages. It would settle differences which had pervaded the preceding decades of conflict, provide a common front marginalising the radical sects outside the Church of England, and, within the church, would balance the Laudians.

To put the matter broadly there were three ways of resolving the differences amongst religious parties. Everyone assumed that a national church of some kind would be upheld by the civil government and these solutions took their cue from that fact. The first method was simply for the state to support one existing party, and might include in that support for the use of sanctions against the others. The second was for two or more of the parties to agree to compromise on matters of worship and church government and thus accommodate each other. These two proposals were compatible with – but need not imply – applying civil sanctions against other parties. This the third method excluded. That was toleration, under which the state might patronise one party, but would not penalise the others. The situation was summarised by John Corbet. 'Religion is divided against it self,' he wrote

This dis-union is removed either by the Abolition of one Party, or by the Coalition of both into one. The former if supposed possible, cannot be accomplished but by violent and perilous ways and means. The latter is brought to pass by Accommodation or mutual yielding. Moreover there is a third way imaginable, Toleration indulged to the weaker side.[42]

These three courses characterise the ecclesiastical history of the Restoration. But alternatives are not pursued for their intellectual attractiveness alone.

The issue of 1660 lay in effect between the Anglicans and the Presbyterians. Corbet's formulation suggests as much by implying two sides. These, he thought, were 'two main ones. . .above the rest. . .they would take in, and carry along the whole stream and strength of the Nation'.[43] This was probably right, for in the situation of 1660 both parties had a strong voice in events. The Anglicans could presume that a restored monarchy would reinstate episcopacy. The Presbyterians had the major influence in parliament.

Nor did a project of unity seem implausible in 1660. By then there had been several conferences between Anglicans and Presbyterians, including the discussions between Baxter and Archbishop Ussher around the latter's *The Reduction of Episcopacy unto the form of synodical government received in the Ancient Church*, an essay whose title bespeaks its intention to reorganise the national church along lines acceptable to Presbyterians and those episcopalians who would part with some of the bishops' authority. When the Restoration looked likely such ideas had a definite appeal. Both parties agreed that there should be a national church. Neither had the strength to establish this on its own. The Presbyterian attempt to establish classes generally had failed, not least through the *de facto* toleration of a diversity of beliefs about church government under Cromwell. Anglicans could recognise that their brand of churchmanship was not overwhelmingly popular: as Herbert Thorndike remarked, without enforcement 'Unity in Religion will not prevail in the World.' Both looked to government for backing. This was unlikely to come from the army, which in 1659 appeared to be bent on toleration and, as it happened, republicanism. Royalists, on the other hand, looked equally askance at the army and certainly favoured a unitary church. Yet on their own they lacked the means to effect a restoration of the monarchy. Hence the political co-operation of the two, royalist and Presbyterian, in which the point of agreement was that there should be a single church for England.

But what kind of a church? By the 4 May 1660 when the Presbyterian party sent a delegation to Charles, it was apparent that whilst they could not be ignored in the Convention Parliament that body would not institute a purely classical church. If, therefore, the Presbyterians were to escape a powerful bench, it was necessary that they should be accommodated by the Anglicans in a national church where episcopacy would be moderated. Hence during April we find Baxter observing 'that the Unity of the Church should not be laid upon indifferent, small and doubtfull points' and that 'true Believers who differ in such things' should not separate from each other; read Corbet noting that many Presbyterians acknowledged that 'there is a vast difference between the ancient Episcopacy, and the height of *Prelacy* or *Hierarchy* of the latter times', the latter only being 'the true opposite of *Presbytery*'; and hear Reynolds preaching for 'all possible tenderness and indulgence towards the infirmities, especially the consciences of men of humble and sober, of quiet and peaceable Spirits'. In September Reynolds accepted a bishopric. More forcibly Ralph Farmer of Bristol, who had hard things to say about both bishops and presbyters asserted that '*Unity* and order is more *precious*, then to be *destroyed*'. From the Anglican party, Sancroft made soft noises about episcopal eirenicism and Pearson understood that 'His Majesty out of His most Princely care of the Church, and desire of Unity, intendeth to declare His gracious Pleasure in divers particular concessions for the satisfaction of all sober minds.' Accommodation was favoured by the king and Clarendon (though not, of course, by some of the bishops). Thus the union of a broad section of English Protestants looked practicable.[44]

A distinct but accompanying event secured Locke's primary aim by practically asserting the magistrate's authority over ecclesiastical causes. On 25 October was published His Majesty's Declaration Concerning Ecclesiastical Affairs. Its specifically political point lay in prescribing a 'synod of divines' to propose a 'proper remedy for all those differences and dissatisfactions which had or should arise in matters of religion' (which was to meet at some indefinite time). It promised that 'no bishop shall exercise any arbitrary power, or do or impose anything upon the clergy or the people but what is according to the known laws of the land'. In doing so it assumed what was necessary for the maintenance of civil order against the threat Locke had observed: that ecclesiastical authority, from the earliest times, was 'always subordinate and subject to the civil'.[45] Hence it was clear that the English government felt itself entitled to exert the force Locke required.

Yet there was a difficulty for accommodation in 1660 (or for 'comprehension' as it would soon be called). This lay not with the principle of the scheme, but with the matters involved. This had two aspects. One was the high value which some Anglicans put upon their distinctive practices. The other, which is of greater concern here because it confronted Locke, was the ambiguity of the Presbyterian position. The Presbyterians, like the Anglicans, acknowledged that there should be a national church, of which the monarch would be head, and that as such the monarch could impose his views in matters indifferent. Hence we find Corbet writing gracefully that 'His *Majesties* wisdom and authority will draw both Sides to submit to reason.'[46] But to desire *unity* and to agree to *uniformity* were not the same.

Whilst the Presbyterians acknowledged the royal right to impose, they denied that it should be used in a manner they disliked. About some things indifferent they held firm views: they objected to bowing at the name of Jesus, the wearing of surplices and the sign of the Cross in baptism. They thought that these were merely human inventions and not the work of God. As it happened these were just the practices that some Anglicans valued highly. If unity between the two parties was to be had, then uniformity of practice was not feasible. 'Uniformity in Religion is beautiful and amiable,' Corbet observed,

but we ought to consider not only what is desirable, but what is attainable. There have been, are, and always will be such points as the Apostle tearms *doubtful disputations*. When the severity of Laws and Canons inforce external uniformity in things of this nature, it exerciseth a tyranny over mens judgments, and holds them in a servile condition, that they are not free, but captivated to the Authority of men,

and this he would not countenance.[47] On the other hand, the Anglican party could take its stand on the Thirty-Nine Articles, the thirty-fourth of which prescribed that breaching the traditions and ceremonies of the church was a ground for rebuke: certainly they argued that there was no need of alteration.

Locke did not arbitrate between the parties' assertions about the status of these practices. His interest lay in a slightly different area. His concern was to vindicate the magistrate's authority to impose in things indifferent and to rebut the view that the magistrate could not employ it over a certain class of matters. In other words he was concerned with the question of principle. The adversary he confronted was one who acknowledged the royal superiority and yet had qualms about its application. Bagshawe shared Locke's general tenets, but dissented from them on particular grounds. Bagshawe agreed that external actions needed to be subject to the magistrate for the sake of peace. He assumed that Charles II was entitled to adjudicate quarrels over things indifferent in the English Church. Indeed he conceded that 'these Apples of *Ecclesiastical contention*' were in themselves 'very trifles'. His objection was simply that authority over ecclesiastical matters should not be *exerted* to impose practices in matters which had been left free in scripture: 'that none can Impose, what our Saviour in his Infinite Wisdom did not think Necessary, and therefore left Free'. Whilst Bagshawe accepted the principle, he reserved a class of matters from its operation.

The point had practical significance because some people did raise objections, as we have seen. The practices were indifferent in themselves and could be agreeable to those who had formed no aversion to them. But they were not in conscience acceptable to those who did object and, Bagshawe thought, it was 'utterly unlawful for any Christian Magistrate to impose the use of them'.[48] His objection thus had two aspects. One was the absence of scriptural authority for the content of some proposed impositions. This became significant in the light of conscience, whose dictates required respect. Before considering Locke's response we should turn to the matter of conscience in order to see why it had a special claim to tender treatment by the magistrate.

Conscience was the attribute of the soul which judged the rectitude of the agent's actions. God, as Perkins remarked, 'hath appointed our conscience to be our companion and guide, to shewe us what course we may take and what we may not'. As such it lay on the side of inner disposition rather than on an agent's external actions: and herein lay its significance for Bagshawe and Locke. If someone's conscience disapproved of their actions then their disposition obviously disagreed with their external performances: and, as we know, such performances were only sufficient for merit in God's eyes if they proceeded from an unconstrained heart. Bagshawe encapsulated the point by observing that 'god, as he loves a *cheerful Giver*, so likewise a *cheerful Worshipper*, accepting of no more, than we willingly perform'. By the same measure to act contrary to conscience's promptings was to sin. So it followed that if someone objected to impositions they could not conform to them safely: their very acts of worship would condemn them before God. Of course there remained external coercion: but the psychology of the heart suggested that this would work in vain against the understanding. So there remained Bagshawe's conclusion, that 'consciences, how erroneous soever, yet are to be tenderly and gently dealt with'.

Bagshawe's views on imposition demanded a reply of Locke. For they provided a case against the legitimacy of accommodation, unless on terms whose content excluded some practices which a powerful section of Anglicans were unlikely to forego. To achieve his end practically Locke had to remove the theoretical barrier provided by conscience. This barrier must have seemed all the more provoking for the admitted triviality of what was involved. Locke's *English Tract* tried to show the irrelevance of Bagshawe's supposed biblical warrant for freedom in things indifferent and to substitute texts grounding the magistrate's authority over them. To these arguments of principle he added the prudential view that without imposition 'I know not how a Quaker should be compelled by hat or leg to pay a due respect to the magistrate or an Anabaptist be forced to pay tithes.'[49] He had a further argument, which was needed to clinch his case and which, indeed, was significant for his later views.

Locke argued that it was impossible to distinguish clearly civil from ecclesiastical matters if one proceeded, as Bagshawe and the objects of Locke's distaste did, from a scriptural warrant. This view, of course, made plausible Locke's view that ecclesiastical matters were just as much under the civil magistrate as civil ones. 'There is no action so indifferent which a scrupulous conscience will not fetch in with some consequence from Scripture and make of spiritual concernment.' Locke gave examples that symbolised obedience to the civil order – 'a courteous saluting, a friendly compellation, a decency of habit according to the fashion of the place, and indeed subjection to the civil magistrate'. This spectrum may seem to range oddly from the trivial to the serious, but the principle was perceived to be the same. For instance Henry Stubbe the younger, like Locke and Bagshawe a Student of the House, argued that the ordinary forms of civility were 'anciently *condemned*', whilst Locke's friend John Parry complained that Stubbe's view 'is driven to so *wild* and Phantastick an *height*, as that *common civility* is lookt upon, as the mark of the *beast* . . . a seemly *reverence* to *Superiours* is without doubt a *worshipping* of *Antichrist*'. Locke himself pointed out that on this principle almost anything could be counted as being in divine worship. Hence it was hardly safe to indulge tender consciences, because of the use that might be made of them: 'though I can believe that our author would not make this large use of his liberty,' Locke wrote, ' . . . let him look some years back he will find that a liberty for tender consciences was the first inlet to all those confusions and unheard of and destructive opinions that overspread this nation.'[50] No doubt this emphasis was conscious, but it reproduced the conceptual point that when scripture was interpreted in an unusual way it might be difficult to distinguish and so defend the civil order adequately.

Indeed the difficulty helps to explain why Locke should write for the magistrate's power rather than for toleration. For he believed that religious parties could coexist peacefully, both with each other and with civil society. The difficulty lay elsewhere. In a letter, probably addressed to Stubbe in September 1659 he observed that it was possible for 'men of different professions' to 'quietly unite . . . under the same government and unanimously cary the same civill intrest and hand in hand march to the same end of peace and mutuall society though they take different way towards heaven'. The difficulty was simply that religion might come armed and that conscience could make almost any issue of directly religious significance: 'you know how easy it is under pretence of spirituall jurisdiction to hooke in all secular affairs since in a commonwealth wholy Christian it is noe small difficulty to see limits to each and to define exactly where on be gins and the other ends'. Locke's sympathy with conscience and his inability to indulge it owing the difficulty of delimitation appeared in the pages of his *English Tract*. There he admitted that 'I cannot deny but that the sincere and tender-hearted Christians should be gently dealt with and much might be indulged them,' and had to ask, 'but who shall be able to distinguish them, and if a toleration be allowed as their right who shall hinder others who shall be ready enough to lay hold on the same plea?'[51] In time Locke would suggest that civil society should be understood primarily through reason or a scripture that was coordinated with reason rather than scripture alone and so would be free to provide a clear distinction between civil and ecclesiastical. As yet that lay in the future. For the moment his solution was simply to insist upon the magistrate's authority over things indifferent, whether civil or ecclesiastical.

The solution, it must be said, was conceptually crude and by an historical irony would soon become practically discomforting. Its conceptual inadequacy lay in failing to reconcile conscience and the magistrate's authority. This could hardly be satisfactory in a frame of mind according to which Christian doctrine explained the order of civil society. If the demands of conscience and the magistrate conflicted one would become unavoidably involved in sin. If conscience were informed correctly then obviously it was a sin to follow another authority against God's. If it were ill-informed it would still be a sin to accept the magistrate's imposition, because God wished people to follow conscience. The point was accepted by those who wished to induce obedience to the magistrate. Sanderson, who thought things indifferent a most suitable subject for human legislation and who judged that men often professed scruples of conscience as a ground for disobedience, inferred that if those scruples were erroneous it would be a sin to disobey the magistrate. He noted, however, that it would be a greater sin to follow the magistrate against one's conscience, erroneous though its contents might be: 'one would sin more deeply if one obeyed without discarding that misconception'. Locke accepted the logic of the position, albeit somewhat weakly. 'God . . . abhors the sacrifice of the hypocritical compliant,' he observed, but commented merely that if the magistrate imposed against his subjects' conscience 'possibly he may increase their sin, whilst he endeavours to amend their lives'. Many years later he would gloss *Romans* xiv.23, the text which backed the claim of conscience, to mean that nothing was indifferent to a man unless his conscience said so.[52] Meanwhile the admission, though unavoidable, cannot have been particularly welcome.

Locke's position was all the weaker because in failing to reconcile Christianity and civil order it underlined the case for dissent. His aim was to uphold civil authority by showing that the civil magistrate could impose legitimately the use of things indifferent in religious worship. But obedience to the magistrate might imply a violation of what Locke recognised as 'the great business of Christian religion', namely a right disposition. Thus Christians with conscientious scruples were required to damn themselves for the sake of civil peace; understandably they might prefer to forego the latter. By 1667 Locke had come to treat this choice as politically destabilising. Bagshawe had already pointed out 'that dangerous *Dilemma*, either of breaking their Inward Peace and Comfort, by doing outwardly what they do not inwardly approve of: or else of running themselves upon the Rocks of Poverty and Prejudice, by disobeying what is commanded'. Locke's argument of 1660 could put the demands of conscience and civil life at odds.

No doubt in that year the problem of conscientious dissent seemed secondary to Locke when he urged unity amongst the central denominations. Firstly, the question of unity had not been settled, so that to argue was to offer persuasion rather than threats. Moreover, to some people's minds the prospect of applying civil sanctions 'in the present case. . .is so abhorrent to humane reason and Christian Charity, that we will not take it into consideration'. Secondly, if unity was attained the groups who were supposed to be socially obnoxious, like Quakers or Roman Catholics, would be marginalised. The sufferers (if there were sanctions), it might be hoped, would be chiefly those whose *fides* appeared less than *bona* and who were objectionable to civil society rather than merely offensive to the church. Then, of course, there was the primary aim of Locke's enterprise. His *Latin Tract*, written a little later and in a more systematic form, made his point clearly: that if conscience were allowed to nullify the magistrate's laws the civil order would be dissolved.[53] So, granted Locke's inability to separate civil from ecclesiastical adequately, the chief sufferer in his scheme would be conscience.

Locke's difficulty in reconciling conscience and the civil order was shared by others. Sanderson had recognised it. Bagshawe himself conceded in 1662 that if governments were to be guided by '*Prudential*

Motives' there would be nothing 'so contrary to *Reason of State*, as a *Toleration* of two or more Religions, or the least variation in the *Mode* and *Form* of *Publick Worship*'. The suggestion that conscience was really a mask for self-interest or sedition was to be exploited by Anglican opponents of comprehension and toleration alike, as by Samuel Parker.[54] In an obvious sense publicists faced a conceptual choice between conscience and order, which could be represented as mutually exclusive. Locke was able to resolve the claims of the two in 1667 to his own satisfaction, but meanwhile events were about to make the corresponding practical choice rather difficult for a number of people.

For the plan of accommodation was overtaken by events. On Christmas Eve, 1660 (less than two weeks after Locke had penned a letter which accompanied his *English Tract*) the Convention Parliament was dissolved. Opinion in the country seems to have been running against the Presbyterians and what we know as the Cavalier Parliament was returned. During 1661 the Commons and Convocation steadily pressed the king to maintain a strictly Anglican polity, whilst the Anglican clergy established an impressive grip on the ecclesiastical machine throughout the country. Charles went a certain distance with those loyal supporters whose prisoner he now was, but temporised and prorogued Parliament on 30 July. It was apparent, however, that accommodation was unlikely to work: the chief point in which the participants at the Savoy Conference (on the revision of the Prayer Book) had concurred was 'that we were all agreed on the ends for the Churches welfare, Unity and Peace, and for his Majesty's Happiness and Contentment; but after all our debates, were disagreed of the Means'. *The Book of Common Prayer* was restored on 17 March 1662 and the Act of Uniformity, prescribing ecclesiastical rites and ceremonies according to Anglican preferences, became effective on 24 August 1662. Nine hundred and seventy-one clergymen, of whom about half were Presbyterians, were ejected from their positions. Granted that they had conscientious scruples their secession could hardly be a surprise.[55] Dissent became a salient and, as it turned out, permanent fact.

It is not obviously the case that this development was pleasing to Locke. He had written in favour of a principle, at a time when it stood for unity rather than division. Certainly the scrupulous people whom his argument addressed were Presbyterian rather than Anglican; but he said nothing which implies belief in the importance of Anglican claims. Rather his arguments upheld the power of the civil magistrate.

Locke's *English Tract*, on the other hand, specified matters of

70

conscientious scruple that may seem to suggest an Anglican allegiance: in particular the use of the surplice. But this may not mean quite what it seems. Whatever the general case, it was certain from the start that surplices would reappear in royal foundations, collegiate chapels and cathedrals. Christ Church is all three of these: and in the House Bagshawe's position was therefore in *practical* terms aimed against the monarchy and the collegiate authorities. Equally Locke's tract in effect defended these. Besides, in the University generally the surplice was counted amongst 'signes of monarchy', so that there it was a mark of civil order.[56] Thus in the local context Locke's arguments need imply no more than an allegiance to peace and the monarchy rather than a specific adherence to triumphant Anglicanism. Certainly, whatever his feelings about the ecclesiastical settlement, to dissent would have been to belie the arguments he had advanced so recently.

IV

Those arguments, however, did not have the strength that makes for permanency. When Locke came to give formal statement to his primary aim in his *Latin Tract* his case had a touch of poignancy about it. He argued in terms of a hierarchy of laws, as he called them, rising from private vows through the fraternal law and human law to divine law. Divine law he divided in the ordinary way into positive and natural, which differed only in their clarity and mode of promulgation. Human laws were the work of the magistrate, to whom God was assumed to have delegated the regulation of civil society. The fraternal law required us to abstain from things which, though indifferent, might scandalise those who could not think of them as such. Under private law Locke categorised conscience. This organisation tells its own story. Yet Locke described the function of conscience as 'that fundamental judgement of the practical intellect concerning the validity of any ethical statement about what is to be done' and grounded in the fact that 'God placed the light of nature in our hearts and willed that there should always be present a sort of internal legislator, whose edicts it would not be permissible to transgress by a nail's breadth.' He inferred that nothing was indifferent unless we thought it so.[57] Where Bagshawe and Corbet admitted the civil magistrate's right to impose but denied that he should exercise it against conscientious scruples, Locke assumed the practice of the same right and was unable to overlook the problem of conscience. Both positions revealed the same problem. Thus conscience and the order of society were juxtaposed once more without an adequate reconciliation.

John Locke lacked not only a harmony between conscience and civil order but also a case in reason to ground his view of the latter. The order of society which Locke experienced was explained by a rational morality, rational in that it served certain ends. It was understood to be disclosed by scripture and reason alike, as we see when Locke placed at the head of his hierarchy of laws both divine positive law and natural law. But he knew that scripture, interpreted eccentrically, might be supposed to tell a different story. After all if the purported workings of the Holy Spirit could be believed might not what was understood ordinarily as the proper order of society be superseded? As Samuel Rutherford had put it, 'if conscience ought to be the ruling principle in all we doe in the acts of the second as well as the first Table of the Law . . . the sword hath no place at all over Christians'; and what could be said about the magistrate's authority could be said about anything else in society.[58] Whilst in a sense the most obvious remedy for this lay with that very sword, clearly a more considered response was needed. The validity of rational morality, which of course included the very idea of magisterial authority, ultimately required vindication. Scripture, as the object of dispute, hardly provided the means. Thus an examination of the conclusions and authority of reason was the complement to the defence of civil society.

The precarious nature of Locke's position is apparent in the paper against papal infallibility which he wrote about the same time as his *Latin Tract*. This answered the question 'Whether it is necessary that there should be provided in the Church an infallible interpreter of the Holy Scriptures?' with a firm 'No'.[59] The opposite belief was characteristic of Roman Catholicism, which identified the interpreter with the Pope. Locke shared his countrymen's distaste for distinctively Papal views. He disdained what Richard Field had called 'the monstrous conceit of Popish transubstantiation', taking time out to denounce it as nonsense. His precise objection in 1659 had been the common one, that Roman Catholics might be unreliable citizens because they were bound by a dual temporal loyalty, to the English government and to the Pope; and specifically that the latter would take first place since he could make them subscribe to whatever views he preferred, for as supposedly infallible it seemed that he could treat God's word according to his own ends. For instance he could release Roman Catholics from their oaths of loyalty to the government. Locke's distaste rested intellectually, in other words, on the same grounds he had for mistrusting the Quaker conscience. Roman Catholic and Quaker alike seemed to claim divine inspiration on terms which could be turned to their own advantage and to the detriment of the civil society to which they belonged. So the bulk of Locke's paper was devoted to arguing that there was no need for such an infallible interpreter and therefore none in fact.[60] Yet the direction of the text leads us to a difficulty for him.

We have seen that one whose conscience was at odds with the magistrate's impositions in religious observances was being asked to condemn himself before God for the sake of the civil order. This position appeared even more unsatisfactory when we are reminded that the civil magistrate's opinion of what was right and proper in church was quite as uncertain as the Pope's. For things indifferent in their nature concerned matters about which God had not disclosed His preferences. The magistrate and the conscientious worshipper were therefore equally ignorant of what God wanted. The claims of one were no better than the other, regarding them as aspirants to truth. From this point of view did the magistrate have any business to make anyone conform to his preferences? If not, it would be the case that he could have no business to impose in religious worship, whatever his authority over things indifferent outside church. In that case Locke's position on church and state, to say the least, would require adjustment. The question was perhaps an obvious one and it was natural that someone who had suffered for the cause of non-imposition should raise it.

Bagshawe, who had been ejected from his Studentship at Christ Church, shared Locke's distaste for transubstantiation and for the dependence of English Romanists on a foreign power, which could dispense them from 'their most sacred Engagements', and thought that the Pope was not infallible, but rather the Antichrist. But he also implied that rejecting interpretative infallibility made it improper for anyone to impose in things indifferent. This much might be anticipated from the similarity of the half-title of a work of his (*The Great Question about The Infallibility of the Pope and Church of Rome*) to that of *The Great Question concerning Things Indifferent in Religious Worship*. Anticipation would not be disappointed. If the Papacy was not infallible, he asked, how should the church deal with heresies? If they were plain in scripture, by excommunication. 'But, where the Scripture is either Dubious or Silent, there charitably to beare with dissenters. . .is the best way to winne them,' he observed, rather than 'to pretend to *Infallibility in determining*, or to practise *Tyranny in Imposing*,' because, lacking a warrant in scripture, these were 'onely the wayes of Ambitious and self-seeking men, found out not so much to promote Truth. . .as to Augment a party.'[61] There could be nothing in scripture more silent or dubious than things indifferent.

To meet this criticism Locke tried to distinguish the legitimacy of

73

imposition from any scriptural warrant it might claim. He repeated his *Tracts'* view that the civil magistrate could oblige the will but not the judgement of conscience, in other words that one was required to obey the magistrate without having to adopt any particular beliefs. He attempted to distinguish between definitive infallibility, which implied a right to command belief, and directive infallibility, which implied only an authority to regulate conduct. The latter, which the magistrate enjoyed, implied that the subject did have to obey 'the shepherds of the church' because 'obedience is the certain and indubitable duty of Christian people'. This restated Locke's position by claiming nothing for the magistrate's understanding but explicitly reasserting his title to be obeyed.

Yet this was rhetorically rather than substantively satifactory, for Locke's subsequent assertion that obedience was safe because a duty, though valid in itself, did not deal with the point at issue. He had not shown that the magistrate had any business to impress his preferences, which were necessarily as uninformed as anyone else's, on others' consciences when he could not claim to understand what God really wanted them to do. When Locke next dealt with conscience and civil order he observed explicitly that the magistrate as such 'hath nothing at all to doe with my private interest in another world', for 'having no more certain or more infallible knowledge of the way to attain it then I myselfe', 'he can give me no security that I shall not . . . miscarry'.[62] It was evident that the supposed magisterial power of imposition in the indifferent things of worship was conceptually unsatisfactory. How could Locke countenance this admission?

To admit the magistrate's ignorance implied a need for a different basis for the relation between the ecclesiastical and the civil. Locke lacked a reconciliation of conscience and order, and the question of infallibility made it apparent further that the terms he had chosen to defend civil society were unsatisfactory. A defence along lines other than the authority to impose was needed.

That defence would need to be conducted in some medium other than scripture. For Locke's paper also suggested that he could not use it satisfactorily for this end. For instance, he needed to show that obedience truly was a duty. To refer to St Paul, as would no doubt have been obvious, was simply to raise the matter of valid interpretation once more. Here Locke was at something of a loss. He could not determine the respective roles of reason and of the Holy Spirit in man's understanding of scripture. He feared alike that the Holy Spirit would be confused with mere personal delusion and that the Gospel might be neglected. 'What reason and what the illumination of the

Holy Spirit warrant is not easy and straightforward to determine,' he noted, 'to this extent, that we must beware of relying so much on our reason that we neglect our faith. . .and, on the other hand, we must carefully avoid enthusiasm lest we honour and worship our dreams whilst anticipating the inspiration of the Holy Spirit.'[63] Whilst this passage bespoke a desire to reconcile reason and scripture it hardly provided the means to do so. This defect was of some importance, for it left open the possibility of scriptural interpretations which disagreed with reason. The same lacuna, it was true, could be seen in Bagshawe, who thought '*Enlightned Reason*' was 'the best, if not the onely Interpeter of it'. But if the role of reason were not defined one could argue, with Stubbe, that as God had 'left the world no *infallible Judge* to expound the Scripture,' that the '*Spirit of God* in each Saint is the sole Authentique Expositor of Scripture'.[64] This implied a license for all that Locke disdained.

He required, in the first place, to show that reason's conclusions concerning civil society were authoritatively valid. That is to say he needed to show that they conformed to God's definitive intentions. For this the obvious medium was a discussion of natural law, which was conceived to comprise propositions disclosed by reason and which included a moral obligation to adhere to them. In the autumn of 1660 Locke had entered into an extensive exchange of views with Gabriel Towerson of All Souls on just this subject. In 1663–4 it fell to him as censor in moral philosophy at Christ Church to deliver the series of lectures which we know as *Essays on the Law of Nature*.[65] These exhibited the views Locke required, namely that reason could disclose definitively the purpose of civil society, delineate an appropriate code of ethics, establish magistracy and that God could give some of reason's conclusions an obligatory force.

Herein lay also the condition for relating the civil and the ecclesiastical adequately, specifically by dealing with conscience. Locke's establishment to his own satisfaction of what God willed for civil society also permitted him to solve the problem of determining what was and what was not properly a matter of conscience in respect of it. His paper on infallibility had suggested that scripture was 'the standard of faith and conduct'. In the absence of a proper light to interpret scripture the implications drawn from it for conduct could be inimical to what Locke understood by civil order. Locke's need of reason to ground that order was made clear in a question Stubbe had raised. He had suggested that Protestantism had made the Bible the sole object of faith and asked if it had not excluded 'all *extrinsecall Authority*' and left men to 'nothing but their own *phansies* to alleg, or false glosses?'.[66]

Natural law could bypass this difficulty in respect of civil society. If reason disclosed a definitive account of civil society, the *independent* authority of scripture and so eccentric interpretations of it would be superfluous. If an external interpretative authority was replaced with reason – which because a human faculty we might call an internal authority – there would be a proper measure of conduct for man to follow. Of course, this entails that reason must have some intellectual authority, a point Locke emphasised by dwelling upon its certainty. The adequacy of reason for discussing civil society suggested that conscience about civil matters would be guided authoritatively by natural law. Conscience figured in Locke's *Essays*, which did not treat of ecclesiastical matters, as informed by natural law. If civil order were established by natural law conscience could not be opposed to it.

The project of Locke's *Essays* in using reason to guide conduct in society pointed forward to a more extensive undertaking. Scripture was an important intellectual asset, disclosing man's duty in an uncomplicated way and revealing matters of salvation about which reason had known nothing. This very importance was what had made the sects' mistreatment of it so very shocking. It would hardly do merely to lay scripture to one side. So Locke would need to show how reason and scripture were compatible, of course doing so in a way that would prevent 'phansies' and 'false glosses' from having any claim to challenge a reasonable order. His writings on the human understanding indicated that reason could attain certainty, particularly in the matter of ethics, and that as such its authority was greater than the authority of revelation, because the conclusions reached through reason were certain where revelation would be at best probable. This upheld reason against the claims of eccentric scriptural interpretations. At the same time it gave revelation a legitimate place in a scheme of the understanding. Scripture could serve the social order and inform people in matters where reason had been silent. Clearly, if the two were both to be upheld and reason to be ultimately preferable in cases of dispute, these moves were needed. Locke adumbrated these views in 1663–4 by alluding to the difference between knowledge and faith.[67] For the moment Locke's thought had another implication.

It remained to reconcile conscience and the civil order. Locke had attained to a conception of the civil sphere, in which conscience could expect to be informed by reason (or scripture interpreted in reasonable terms) rather than prompted in a different sense by the Holy Spirit. It was in ecclesiastical matters alone that the latter could be supposed to work to another view. Thus Locke could distinguish two distinct spheres and be assured that any supposedly conscientious attacks on the civil order in the name of worship were spurious. Thus the boundary of the two was established. This permitted Locke to reconcile the claims of civil order and conscience. The inroads of the ecclesiastical on the civil could be seen for what they were and delivered legitimately to the magistrate. The ecclesiastical, in which the magistrate was as ill-informed as anyone else, need not concern him as such, once granted that its violent eccentricities could not legitimately control civil society: and conscience, confined to what could not harm civil society, could be left unconstrained. Thus Locke would be conceptually free to adopt the more relaxed posture characteristic of his later piece, 'An Essay concerning Toleration'. Because civil order was definitely established it could be reconciled with conscience.

Chapter 3

What distinguished the young Locke's treatment of natural law? The question may sound odd, but in fact is significant. It sounds unusual because Locke's name suggests at once a thinker of European stature, the author of *Two Treatises of Government* and *An Essay concerning Human Understanding*, and to ask about what distinguishes him seems curious indeed. But the question is important because in his early thirties Locke was an obscure figure whose vocation was as uncertain as his future fame was remote.[1] His *Essays on the Law of Nature* were one of the steps which marked his development. They do so because Locke formulated views in them which are fundamental to his later works. His conceptions of ideas and of God as the moral legislator are the most salient of these.

This intellectual growth, in its turn, provokes further enquiry. How one writer deploys a distinctive array of ideas, whilst another succeeds only in reiterating the commonplaces of others' work, is an extremely interesting matter. Also it is mysterious. At least much less work than one would expect has gone to show how conceptual originality occurs. This is easy to understand. The beginnings of thought are most often ambiguous and always tentative, so that to interpret them definitely impresses an interpretation in the manner in which heavy boots make patterns in a flowerbed. Locke's *Essays* belong to another category: they are academic lectures, set in the medium of a dead language and fixed with all the inflexibility of their genre, so that they present a public statement of a position rather than the ellipses of private reflection.

I

The doctrine of the lectures is straightforward in its main features. Locke's two cardinal points were, firstly, that God is the superior of the human race and as such entitled to give it directions (amongst which Locke included the law of nature) and that mankind was bound to obey Him, and secondly that God has fitted people to apprehend the content and obligation of that law by providing them with the data of sense and a mental apparatus to work on them, especially reason.

Locke had taken for granted God's authority: in his *English Tract* he had laid down that from God's 'authority all laws do fundamentally derive their obligation, as being either immediately enjoined by him, or framed by some authority derived from him'.[2] He now set out to prove his point by explaining that authority. The explanation, in effect, comprised two parts: God's superiority over mankind and the dependence of man on God that the particular character of God's superiority carried with it. Locke did not find these difficult, but his argument included an important assumption. Let us attend to both.

A superior, as we have noted, was one who excelled another in some important respect or respects. Usually these were understood to lie in those qualities that fitted the superior to direct the inferior, whether intellectual or otherwise. The inferior was held to be obliged to obey the superior. God's superiority over human beings was evidenced primarily by His greater degree of wisdom and power. As to power, Locke argued that man could not have produced himself, on the grounds that a being that created itself would give itself the power to exist indefinitely. This mankind did not have, and this pointed to another creator, whom Locke identified with God.[3] Creation meant the power of producing something out of nothing. God could do this because He was omnipotent, that is to say, able to do anything. That mankind had a degree of power rather less than this required little proof.[4]

God's superiority was exerted not only to create but to uphold mankind. Therefore mankind was *dependent* on God by reason of the latter's power. Locke's language was graphic: all things were subject 'to him by whom they were both made at first and are preserved continually', Locke wrote in one place and, in another, God 'can produce, preserve, and ruin us at His will'.[5] This notion of mankind's dependence, correlated to God's superiority and so His direction of mankind, is found late as well as early in Locke's works: writing probably in the 1690s he emphasised that 'The originall & foundation of all Law is dependency. A dependent intelligent being is under the power & direction & dominion of him on whom he depends and must be for the ends appointed by yt. superior being.' The emphasis on dependence was not fleeting: *An Essay concerning Human Understanding* compared 'an intelligent, but frail and weak Being, made by and depending on another, who is eternal, omnipotent, perfectly wise and good' and concluded 'that the Inferior, Finite, and Dependent, is under an Obligation to obey the Supreme and Infinite'. Dependence in point of power, of course, was not the sole reason for obeying God (for God was man's superior in wisdom also), but dependence in general was certainly fundamental. For in 1698 Locke may be found speculating privately on the logical possibilities of there being more than one Deity, but at the same time declaring unequivocally that with a multiplicity of Gods our obedience would be to the one God on whom we depended: *si tale ens existat, praeter Deum unicum a quo nos dependemus, illud ens minime nos spectare, quia ab eo non dependemus: Atque hoc nobis sufficere, ut Deum unum toto corde amemus et colamus.*[6] Dependence was thus central to God's superiority over mankind.

The specific form of direction which interested Locke was legislation. The notion that law is the direction of a superior is one familiar from jurisprudence.[7] Its intellectual home is the frame of mind discussed here – that is to say the notion of direction by one fitted to guide. This, of course, sets this notion of law in a light different from that in which it is often set: for if power is often mentioned by jurists, wisdom is not. At any rate, within this frame of mind, direction can take the form of law and, equally, law would be impossible without the presence of a superior. One of Locke's criteria for the presence of a law, accordingly, was the existence of a superior. In his own language, 'in order that someone may know that they are bound by a law, he ought to know that there is ... some superior power to which he is subject by right'.[8] It was human dependence on God that exemplified His superior power.

It was not the only example. Locke's God was not only powerful but also wise. Wisdom is not a term prominent in modern discourse, and it is as well to unpack the term. It refers essentially to the ability of the understanding to perceive and to judge. As James I noted 'To be wise, is vnderstood, able to discerne, able to iudge others.'[9] Locke's estimate that God's wisdom excelled man's reflected the common judgement that He was omniscient, that is to say, He knew everything. This attribute obviously fitted Him to direct mankind.

Locke interpreted God's wisdom to imply a significant feature in the world, namely divine purpose. He assumed that this meant God's actions embodied some end, for it was contrary to great wisdom to act for no end.[10] We shall see in a little while just what the ends were, but the general point of God's design should be registered first. For this assumption is central to the thought of Locke's day and to Locke's work, not only here but also subsequently. That God had constructed the human faculties with specific ends in mind characterises his view of the understanding. His political thought took this opinion and based upon it a view of human destiny and the content of morality. Indeed it is hard to conceive Locke's writings without it.[11]

God's wisdom and His goodness afforded further grounds for obeying Him, being aspects of human dependence on God. Wisdom was one of the two respects in which God excelled mankind, as we have noted, and so implied a reason for the latter to accept the former's directions. Of course wisdom and power by themselves need not imply that the superior wishes the inferior well, but Locke assumed that God was good to mankind.[12] The logic underlying the argument is that because God was able to provide benefits to mankind – whether creation, sustentation or benevolent and wise direction – that the latter was either unable or less able to provide for itself, therefore He was the superior and mankind the inferior. There is a further layer of logic which Locke used later in life, namely that benefits ought to be returned. Granted that God had conferred great benefits upon mankind, it followed that they 'should obey & revere love & thank the author of their being to whom they owe all that they are'. This point, of course, was not Locke's alone: we find John Flavel asserting that '*if God performs all things for you, see how obliged you are to perform all duties and services for God*'. Meanwhile, Locke assumed that contemplating God's power and wisdom would inspire people to revere God.[13] But he assumed also that God's power suggested that His directions were backed by sanctions.[14]

The *Essays*, as their manuscript title suggests, concerned the law of nature.[15] This indeed is the only form of God's legislation discussed at length. It was here that the accent fell when Locke treated the Deity's authority. Natural law, he wrote, 'can be described as that ordinance of the divine will which may be known by the light of nature'.[16] He emphasised that 'the light of nature' – that is to say, human faculties working without benefit of revelation – discovered rather than prescribed the law, since law implied the decree of a superior will.[17] But if God was the legislator, what of mankind's natural light?

Besides God as a superior and a moral legislator, the *Essays* contained the rudiments of a theory of ideas. The core of this was that sense perception furnished reason with ideas (or, as Locke sometimes said, images) and that equipped with these reason got to work.[18] Reason, according to Locke's usage, denoted a power of the human understanding. He attributed to the operation of reason on the data provided by sense and reflection the mind's ability to achieve anything, *omnium capax animus*.[19]

The model of the soul Locke had assumed in his *Tracts* was one in which the workings of the understanding were autonomous in relation to the will. God, we may recollect, had 'not so much as entrusted man with a liberty at pleasure to believe or reject'. This view connected the deliberations of the understanding with the evidence that God cared to present, whether by some extraordinary communication like revelation or by the everyday medium of ideas. What Locke had not provided hitherto was an explanation of how the understanding obtained ideas. If his account was to fit the demands of his model for mental activity unmediated by the action of the will, the understanding would not be able to refuse the ideas it received. Locke fulfilled this condition by suggesting that the understanding was unable to resist sense data and that all of its ideas were assembled out of sense perceptions. Sensation was irresistible because of the character of the organs with which God had equipped man: God, he thought, might have made people without eyes, but 'so long as they use their eyes and want to open them, and so long as the sun shines, it is a matter of necessity that they should know the alternations of day and night, perceive the differences between colours and see with their eyes the difference between a curved and a straight line'. This view remained constant, for in his *Essay concerning Human Understanding* he wrote that anyone might 'chuse whether he will turn his Eyes' to an object yet if he looked 'a Man with his Eyes open in the Light, cannot but see'. The understanding got to work on these ideas and composed new ones out of them, thus providing all the materials it could need.[20] From 1671 this account was stated formally in terms of a compositional theory of ideas, but Locke had already made the implication clear in 1667. The human agent could have no power over the conclusions of his understanding: 'that a man cannot command his owne understanding, or positively determine to-day what opinion he will be of to-morrow, is evident from experience and the nature of the understanding, which can noe more apprehend things, otherwise then they appear to it, then the eye see other colours in the rainebow then it doth'.[21] The understanding, then, worked in the first place with the evidence presented to it, and with the will only when a judgement had been formed.

This model accompanied a conception of reason as a discursive faculty. Reason, Locke thought, was that power of the understanding which permitted it to move from the known to the unknown, the known being understood as the data of sense experience. This function of connection fitted the view that ideas were all derived ultimately from sensation, at however great a remove, for the images sensation provided would have to be arranged and combined to yield further ideas. Locke identified as the business of reason to 'combine images drawn from sense, form others thence, derive new ones.'[22] This again was his constant view, for, whilst the account he gave in the *Essay* was more elaborate, reason's function there was to determine which ideas could be connected and perceive the connection between them.[23]

These two doctrines, a theory of ideas and of God as the moral legislator, have a prominent place in Locke's lectures. In the nature of lectures there are other doctrines besides them. The matter formed a continuous whole, unlike some series of lectures. The whole is a revision of the explanation of natural law in the light of contemporary difficulties. To this we should turn now.

II

The other doctrines of Locke's *Essays* – that the obligation of natural law is perpetual and universal, that the law itself is not based on self-interest, that sense and reason provide certainty whilst tradition and innatism do not, that a law implies a lawgiver – are obviously compatible with Locke's leading points but do not stand out on a first reading as integrally related to them as parts of a larger argument. But they are. It is the integrity of the design which is not immediately obvious.

The coherence of Locke's argument lies in offering a view of moral philosophy which differs radically from certain doctrines current in his day. Established views, whether those of Hooker or the innatists, of Grotius or Hobbes, were dispatched briskly. Doubtless this reflects the intellectual vigour of a young and probably obnoxious don,[24] but if so we should ask, with what end in mind? The end was twofold. Firstly, Locke wished to establish the intellectual authority of natural law – and so of the institutions he had seen under pressure, like morality, civil society and government. Secondly he did so in a manner that served the needs of another part of his mental life, one which (superficially at least) we should not expect to find connected with his moral philosophy. For either purpose it will be helpful to begin with Hobbes.

Hobbes had conceived ideas as the result of sensation.[25] His account of the formation of ideas did not make much use of reason, officially at least. His view of natural law was that in itself it was a body of precepts rather than a law properly so-called and that it counted as a law only when instituted by a government: 'the Lawes of Nature ... in the condition of meer Nature ... are not properly Lawes', he wrote, but when 'the commands of the Common-wealth' were 'actually Lawes'.[26] That these views differ markedly from Locke's is evident.

How did the difference arise? The answer will be found with a department of thought we might suppose quite unconnected with ethics and the theory of ideas. It lay with natural philosophy. The views of Locke's scientific circle in part resembled and in part differed from Hobbes' natural philosophy, but in both aspects it became desirable in the sixties to emphasise their distance from him.

The circle of natural philosophers at Oxford in the fifties and early sixties hoped to develop scientific knowledge on a new, non–Aristoteleian basis. Scientific discovery they understood to be a process beginning with sense data, collected by observation or by experiment, and continued by reasoning from these to formulate general propositions. They hoped these propositions would be certain, but did not always bring themselves to believe that they were: they did intend that they should have useful applications and to this end compiled catalogues of observation and experiment, or natural histories as we may call them. Hobbes was an inconvenience, both because his own scientific opinions differed from theirs and because they bore a sufficient resemblance to them to create unease when he became unpopular for quite different reasons. Hobbes held that certainty about nature could be obtained only at the most general level, that is to say about names and their implications. Experimental work could at best be probable. The difference in approach was illustrated by the dispute between Hobbes and Robert Boyle over the status of the results obtained from the latter's air-pump. If Hobbes was a grating adversary he was also an uncomfortable neighbour. Like the Oxford circle he was a mechanist, favoured experimentation, considered that philosophy should be useful and made sense-data central.[27] This made him an inconvenience when he acquired a distasteful reputation, albeit on quite different grounds.

The circle of criticism enveloping Hobbes from the later 1650s was wide. He was pre-eminent not least in making enemies and, to that extent, was an ecumenical figure. A mode of attack common with his critics was to question the coherence of his account of morality and latterly to fasten on to the marginal role of God in his thought. Sometimes this was a matter of detail, as Roger Coke's objection to one of Hobbes' assertions as 'destructive of all faith, and truth of Sacred History', and sometimes a more general disapproval, as William Lucy's lengthy critique. More especially Hobbes' assertion that natural law was not a law in the fullest sense until adopted by a terrestrial legislator was supposed to invert the proper order of things. 'God help us into what times are we fallen, when the immutable lawes of God and nature are made to depend upon the mutable lawes of mortal men, just as if one should go about to controll the Sun by the authority of the clock,' observed John Bramhall. Lucy emphasised what he took Hobbes to have omitted, that

every man is borne a Citizen of the World, and he must submit to that great Governour and *Law-maker* of the world, God, and that *Law* he hath made for him to doe; so that whether a man agree upon a *Law-maker*, or no, there is a *law-maker* and a *Law*, under which he is borne, and to which he ought to submit

that is to say, that people should answer in the first place to God, not to other people. This line of criticism might be extended to insinuate that for Hobbes there were no moral norms except the magistrate's command, or even that Hobbes met the best reception 'with such, as thought it *a piece of Wit* to pretend to *Atheism*'.[28] There was a sense that Hobbes had not treated God quite as centrally as he should have done.

In the England of the day this made it prudent to keep a distance from him, especially if Hobbes' views on other matters were at all akin to one's own. The task was grateful as well as necessary to Boyle. His method of distancing was shrewd enough. He insinuated that Hobbes' view of nature included no functional reference to God, 'that in the Physics themselves, his opinions, and even his ratiocinations, have no . . . great advantage over those, of some orthodox Christian Naturalist'.[29] Boyle, indeed, would make a speciality of insisting on God's centrality as a legislator for a correct understanding of nature.

For instance where some had understood omnipotence to indicate that God could do all things in nature, Boyle preferred to emphasise God as the immediate sustainer of everything. Where Donne had assured his listeners that 'often God admits into his owne Name, this addition of Universality, *Omne, All*, as though he would be knowne by that especially' and had added that 'he is Omnipotent . . . he *can* doe All' and Perkins had stated 'Gods omnipotencie, is that by which he is most *able* to perform euery worke', Boyle argued that physical nature and its laws reflected God's direction:

Sometimes, when it is said, that nature does this or that; [Boyle wrote] it is less proper to say, that it is done by nature, than, that it is done according to nature: so that nature is not to be looked on, as a distinct or separate agent, but as a rule, or *rather a system of rules, according to which those agents, and the bodies they work on, are, by the great Author of things, determined to act and suffer.*

Indeed Boyle suggested that it lay within God's power to alter the character of the nature He thus directed: 'indeed,' he remarked, 'if we consider God as the author of the universe, and the free establisher of the laws of motion, which depend perfectly upon his will, he may invalidate most, if not all the axioms and theorems of natural philosophy: these supposing the course of nature, and especially the established laws of motion, among the parts of the universal matter, as those upon

85

which all the phaenomena depend'. Thus all natural explanation, conducted in terms of the laws of physical nature, ultimately referred to God's omnipotence. Probably Locke held a similar view of physical nature.[30] No doubt rather than meaning to suggest that God was likely to seriously confuse or systematically supersede the present dispensation, Boyle intended to draw attention to his view of God's relation to physical nature. His writings, by drawing attention to physical laws of nature *eo ipso* dealt in the standing order of things.

This was only one general point. Boyle was equipped better to assault Hobbes' scientific practice than his philosophical assumptions. The latter too required attention. For the idea of natural law that was fundamental to the seventeenth-century mind was not physical but moral. For in Boyle's own words law was '*a notional rule of acting according to the declared will of a superior*'[31] a view which Locke would echo[32] and a view which was natural enough in a hierarchical society. So a full alternative to Hobbes would involve an account of moral philosophy.

This was the second matter mentioned earlier: an area of Locke's intellectual life superficially remote from moral philosophy called for an alternative to Hobbes' account of morals. But there was also a broader matter, of which Hobbes was a part but not the whole, namely the explanation of natural law. Both objectives required Locke to vindicate a theory of ideas commencing with particulars. For Hobbes' account of ideas did not include God and His purposes within the ambit of knowledge, and (as we shall see) the epistemological bases for natural law offered by others were equally unsatisfactory, though for different reasons.

In Locke's treatment of natural law we see a family of ideas being formed. That is to say a series of concepts were understood in a manner which groups them closely together and which as such distinguishes this arrangement from other groupings of ideas, even though some of the ideas may be shared. It would be easy to suggest that Locke's view turned out to be merely previous thought rearranged. But what is important are the innovative organisation of them.

Locke's manner was to take the resources which Hobbes had employed and to show that they could be turned to an entirely different effect and to use them, moreover, in a way which upstaged many doctrines apart from Hobbes'. To see just how we should refer ourselves first to Hobbes' views in more depth and then turn to Locke's intellectual situation.

III

Hobbes' philosophy spans an immense range, embracing concerns as superficially diverse as natural philosophy and sovereignty. Its range reflected an appetite for a universal scheme of knowledge, but its articulated form bespoke an objective. Hobbes' personal reaction to the English civil war, even in prospect, was to run away, but his intellectual response was to argue that the ruler's superiority should not be challenged.[33] The arguments that pointed to this conclusion deployed a view of the human understanding and necessitated a distinct treatment of natural law.

Hobbes aimed, firstly, to create a sovereign whom the citizen was not entitled to challenge. This was accomplished by a complete transfer of right by the latter to set up the former. The right transferred was the right to all things attributed by Hobbes to each agent and the reason for disposing of it was a desire to end the miseries Hobbes attributed to the state of nature (the condition of people without civil government). The construction of the right and the character of the natural state involved key suppositions. They depended respectively on Hobbes' treatment of morality and human nature.

Hobbes presented a conational view of human nature. That is to say, it was marked by its appetite for certain ends. In its most neutral form the appetite favoured what was pleasant and eschewed what threatened the agent.[34] But when Hobbes addressed politics he found it convenient to enlarge the appetites to embrace both wider advantages and more distant threats. This construction pointed towards conflict. The prospect of conflict implies danger, a danger moreover which had no measures of right sufficient to identify a juridically correct solution. For Hobbes posited a right to all things on the part of each human being and this legitimated a desire to possess anything. By the same token it failed to provide any standard to adjudicate disputes. Thus, in the absence of measures defining what pertained *exclusively* to each agent, disputes could be endless. An umpire entitled to resolve disputes and able to enforce a decision was clearly needed to terminate this condition.[35]

But though there was a necessity for a sovereign judge, so far no reasons for thinking him *absolute* have appeared. By absolute we may understand, in the first instance, free from any legitimate appeal or challenge from those under his adjudication. More generally absolutism denotes the doctrine that the ruler is in no sense responsible to the ruled because not merely superior to them, but also subject to no other terrestrial superior. Hobbes provided this through his right to all things and attributing it to everyone. If everyone transferred their right to the sovereign whom they created, then no one would have any rights in relation to him.[36]

It follows that the sovereign would be in no sense responsible to them or limited in his powers towards them (though it should be emphasised that absolutists supposed that rulers were answerable to God and bound to obey Him.[37]) Hence Hobbes' right to all things, like his assessment of the state of nature, was integral to his purpose.

This raises the further question of how the behaviour this countenances was permissible. For the agent's right to all things implies either the absence of law or the presence of a law constructed in a manner which did not constrain conduct. The latter was found in Hobbes' first law of nature. This permitted any conduct that struck the agent as tending to his survival. Of course there was the proviso that if possible the agent should endeavour peace, but the endeavour was rational only if it did not interfere with his survival.[38] Hobbes thus obtained both his ends. Conduct was permitted which engendered the expectation of violence and this condition encouraged the transfer of right creating the sovereign.

Hobbes complemented this doctrine of sovereignty with an account of obligation. The Hobbesian agent was obliged to whomever he or she had signified submission. The motive for doing this was the protection offered by the latter. So long as protection provided the obligation held good. There is an exception, but this accords with the purpose of creating the sovereign, namely self-protection. The result of this is that, terrestrially speaking, there is no obligation to *act* according to God's prescriptions: for God, it seemed, did not on the whole offer protection to people on earth. *That* was provided by the sovereign.[40]

The law of nature Hobbes conceived in a congruent manner. In its basic sense it involved no obligation. It was a theorem of reason. It was rational in that it was discovered by reason. It was rational also – and here Hobbes' emphasis lay – because it served the self-interest of the agent. We may add that congruently with this point, it was not to be acted upon where it might not conduce to that end, namely under conditions where the agent was not safe.[41]

When did it become law in full sense? Law in the full sense Hobbes defined as involving a command. The source of commands was the sovereign. For this there were two reasons, one positive and one negative. The positive reason we have seen already: the sovereign, not God provides protection. The point was underlined by Hobbes' discussion of the case where God, as sovereign of the Jews, provided various benefits to them.[42]

Secondly, and negatively, in Hobbes' eyes God was not part of our knowledge. Hobbes thought that the 'admirable order'[43] of the world encouraged a belief in God and, more firmly, announced that the study of causes led us to the first cause, which was God.[44] But these conceptions conveyed no knowledge of God's nature. Hobbes was emphatic that man's ascription of attributes to God were not descriptions. They were not descriptions because human information did not extend to formulating an idea of God.[45] Ideas were acquired originally by the mutual impact of external particles with organs of sense. On this basis other ideas could be formed. But all of these ideas related to finite things.[46] God, however, was nothing if not infinite and so beyond human conception. Indeed even His existence was not certain.[47]

The absence of a knowledge of God's attributes makes it impossible to characterise the world in terms of a knowledge of His purposes. Natural theology, which is the study of God's intentions through the mind's natural powers, assumes that those intentions can be inferred from God's attributes or have been translated into purposes which characterise the world. There is no suggestion in Hobbes that God organised the world according to a purpose or that the purpose was plain for people to read and follow: 'God has no Ends'.[48] This would have provided a guidance which would hardly have prescribed a right to all things. But such a knowledge is absent from Hobbes' thought.

Hobbes' organisation neither denied nor ignored Christian belief. It is compatible with *belief* in revelation, though it excludes knowledge of God and His attributes and so denies natural theology the status of knowledge: 'whether men will or not, they must be subject alwayes to the Divine Power'.[49] Indeed Hobbes paid tribute to the centrality of Christian doctrine in his time by interpreting it with the object of making it compatible with unquestioning obedience to the sovereign (not least by making the latter supreme pastor in his realm). Hobbes set out to ensure that obedience to God could not take precedence properly over obedience to the sovereign. He thought that this ground for disobedience had often been exploited:

The most frequent praetext of Sedition, and Civill Warre, in Christian Common-wealths hath a long time proceeded from a difficulty, not yet sufficiently resolved, of obeying at once, both God, and Man, then when their Commandements are one contrary to the other

he observed, adding that there was a difficulty in knowing 'in divers Cases, whether the command be from God' or merely from a designing interpreter.[50] The answer was to conceive that God's commands, rightly understood, could not differ from the sovereign's.

We may ask how this squares with a Christian belief in an afterlife. One of the considerations which put pressure behind the claims of God against government was the prospect that disobedience to God would entail posthumous punishment at His hands. This supposition was especially relevant to cases where conscience said one thing whilst the sovereign demanded a differing course of action. Hobbes avoided this by implying that the citizen is bound to obey God merely in the will rather than the deed too.[51] Thus it implies in practice the complete subordination of the church to the state.

Hobbes' object was to make the sovereign unchallengeable. In the course of arguing to this end he used a set of definitions artfully designed to form a coherent pattern, beginning with his right to all things and moving through his treatment of law to the sovereign. He offered a triumphant exemplification of his view that philosophy was the manipulation of definitions. Fundamental to the process is a view of the human mind in which knowledge derived from sense and concerned particulars so that God could not be known and could be separated sharply in significant ways from moral obligation and natural law.

Hobbes' triumphal march defied the conventional expectations of natural law, whilst exploiting its assumptions. It had been assumed that the law of nature provided a code of morals whose content was not dissimilar to Christian ethics (or at any rate ran parallel to them) and which was superior to the devices of man. We have seen as much in Samuel Crooke, but the examples could be multiplied.

Hobbes was able to transform natural law because its elements had not been synthesised properly. In particular it lacked a decisive, even an adequate treatment of obligation. Grotius, for example, admitted the need for a moral obligation to obey natural law, but omitted to provide one.[52] Also, the element of self-preservation had not been coordinated with duties to others, since Grotius (for example) had used it for his own purposes without including a systematic moral philosophy: this absence, in effect, provided Hobbes with an opportunity to use concern for self-preservation in a dramatic and unexpectedly subversive way.[53] The weakness of many responses to Hobbes testifies to his skill in stealing the clothes of the moralists whilst they were bathing. Hobbes was important not just for his striking explanations but also because he pointed to serious problems. The matter of moral obligation was especially important here. To suppose that this was absent in the first instance from the law of nature was vital to Hobbes' enterprise. Here he was helped, however unwittingly, by previous thinkers. The manner in which they wrote is worth noting, because it will help us to understand the character of Locke's doctrine.

Hobbes' project stands in an instructive contrast with Locke's. Like Hobbes, Locke began to account for ideas with sensation, but moved rapidly to a destination quite unlike his. Locke considered that God and His purposes could be known certainly, and that mankind knew also that they were obliged to obey God's directions.

Hobbes revealed the weakness of preceding explanations of natural law. These weaknesses, to Locke's mind, were not isolated. If he rejected Hobbes' inferences from sense experience and substituted another view he differed too from doctrines which suggested that morality could be known from consent or from innate ideas. The difficulty with these, apart from the fact that they disagreed with Locke's view of ideas, was that they provided neither an account of moral obligation nor a certain basis for morality.

Hooker had suggested a mode of apprehending natural law which did not use a theory of ideas in the Lockean sense. The view that the content of the law was disclosed through general agreement had a long lineage, being found in Aristotle.[54] Hooker suggested that there were two ways to apprehend goodness, one through its causes, the other through its signs and tokens. He passed by the former rapidly, remarking that it was 'the most sure and infallible way', but was difficult to execute and 'considering how the case doth stand with this present age full of tongue and weak of brain'. On the other hand 'the most certain token of evident goodness' was 'if the general persuasion of men do so account it'. He assumed that what was universal was natural and to be presumed to be God's work, so that 'the general and perpetual voice of men is as the sentence of God himself'.[55] Thus the question of whether God had acted legislatively was postponed to the general reception of the precept.

Grotius too emphasised consent, though in a slightly different way. Consent was a convenient device in his campaign to establish the law of nations. This was a law which quite definitely lacked a legislator, for there was no superior on earth above competing states and the law of nations considered matters on which the law of nature, even if God had promulgated it, was silent. Thus to distinguish the law of nations as a body of 'laws agreed on by common consent'[56] fitted Grotius' end, no reference to a superior being needed in this model to establish it. Certainly Grotius was aware that the findings of consent were not certain.[57] It could be argued plausibly that the universality of practice required for the 'voice of men' to qualify as 'the sentence of God himself' was lacking.[58] Locke, as we shall see, wished to assert God's role as legislator, for he was keen to distinguish human opinion from divine authority. For him it made sense to close the avenue of consent.

91

But before seeing exactly why, let us observe the model of law which befitted the consensual position.

We may distinguish in a broad way between two conceptions of law. These we may call 'internal' and 'external'. An external law would be one corresponding to the model we might have in mind in thinking of juridical law, namely a norm prescribed to an agent by another agent where the latter is accounted as the former's superior. It obliges because prescribed by a superior. The content of the law need not coincide by any means with the desires of the agent subject to it, though it may happen that a coincidence actually occurs in fact. The other model, which is of classical origin, places less emphasis on external prescription and is disclosed in conformity with the character common to the agents, both legislator and his inferior. The content prescribed corresponds as a matter of definition with the nature of both. It is something which is bound to be acceptable to the subject and as such it is considered primarily as a rule. Hooker, for instance, described a law as 'a rule directive unto goodness of operation'.[59] Under this hypothesis natural law becomes what is desired because of the way God has made us and obligation, insofar as it enters the discussion, comes to mean the need to follow the rule in order to achieve our end.

These points are clear in Ralegh's *History of the World*. According to Ralegh God Himself embodied an eternal law and 'by this eternall law all things are directed' for from it 'all laws are deriued'. The law of nature was 'that disposition, instinct, and formall qualitie, which God in his eternall prouidence hath giuen and imprinted in the nature of euery creature'. Its specific form in man was a law of reason. This meant both an inclination to what was good and a power of reason to disclose the good. Hence it corresponded to the nature of both God and man; and man was bound to follow it in that 'it imposeth a necessitie according to the nature of all things which it directeth'. We need scarcely add that if, as Hooker said, 'the laws of well-doing are the dictates of right reason' and people's natures are essentially identical it would follow that consent might disclose the law.[60] Hence we obtain a theory in which law means reason, specifically a correct conclusion reached by reason: right reason.

Locke was thus faced with a conception of law which was internal to man. This recommended right reason as the standard of law, which was related to what people in general found pleasant and might be found in consent. The trouble was that the events of the Interregnum had convinced Locke that reason might well not be right, in the sense that it would answer to self-interested passions and provoke dire consequences. 'Where is that Great Diana of the world Reason,' he had enquired in 1659 and now he asked whether his pupils would wonder why 'I have omitted to mention reason . . . because the law of nature is most often called right reason itself.' The answer was that human reason by itself (as we should say in the light of Locke's epistemological view, without sense perception) was unreliable. 'Where is that Great Diana of the world, Reason, every one thinkes he alone imbraces this Juno, whilst others graspe noething but clouds, we are all Quakers here and there is not a man but thinks he alone hath this light within and all besids stumble in the darke,' he had written, adding that 'every ones Recta ratio is but the traverses of his owne steps.' Now he stated that everyone attributed *recta ratio* to himself, *quamquisque se hominem putat sibi vindicat*. He added that 'right reason' was but a permission for a chaotic state where opinion pretended to be truth, 'it is this which the various sects of men fight about so bitterly'.[61] Going by an internal disposition had proved untrustworthy.

In effect, therefore, the preceding moralists, like Hobbes but for a different reason, were unsatisfactory to Locke. They had not taken account of modern requirements and difficulties. Whilst Hobbes had done so, it was in a manner that was disagreeable to Locke. His sense of certain matters resembled Locke's, but the trend of his solutions was unacceptable. For instance he abridged conscientious scruples about the civil order at the expense of all religious conscience. His view of God in relation to morals was under suspicion. What then was Locke to do?

Here we should remind ourselves of Locke's objectives. One of these, plainly, was to assert God's role as the moral legislator. The motives to this, however, lay not just in answering Hobbes, but also in providing an alternative explanation that authoritatively established moral order, unlike the vagaries of preceding moralists. In the light of this, another objective becomes clear. Locke's interest in the theory of ideas becomes intelligible, especially his desire to show how the human mind came by ideas about conduct. This allows us to understand his *Essays*' concern with the theory of ideas, whether in asserting sense and reason or (as we shall see) in criticising consent and innate ideas (the most respectable version of *interna lux*). Also, it becomes clear why the *Essays* gave an account of the obligation and basis of moral conduct: Locke's philosophical concerns with God and ideas had the effect of explaining the intellectual standing of the institutions he wished to uphold, but whose conceptual foundations required attention – civil society and civil government not least. Locke's task, then, was to develop a series of positions whose character would both yield an account of moral obligation and ideas, and rebut the alternatives he thought defective. On this basis the fundamental constituents of order would be intellectually secure.

Herein lies Locke's reason for asserting God's superiority in the specific form of insisting upon His legislative capacity. The general point that God was a superior, really *the* superior, was not in question. It is the manner of exercising His superiority that was of interest. Locke took up Hobbes' conceptions of right, law as command and knowledge derived from sense, and made them serve his turn in a rather different account of morals and God. He identified God's command as the element crucial to the law of nature. The view of law this implies – and the concept of right which accompanied it – agrees with Hobbes. But Locke meant to comprise more: he meant to relate God's will to the content of the law of nature. Locke desired to assert an integral relation between God and natural law. This implies that man can form, firstly, an idea of God and His attributes and, secondly, His exercise of them. The former is the more fundamental and we shall deal with it first.

Locke considered that he had an idea of God and His attributes because he used reason analogically. Like Hobbes he saw order in the world: but he differed in supposing that this told us something about the designer. For he pursued an analogy implicitly. The make of mankind and the world reflected an order, he thought; therefore we may infer the attributes of wisdom and power in the designer. As one can see this reasoning makes sense only on the assumption that the divine artificer could be conceived in a manner sufficiently analogous to a human for the adjectives which apply to a human being to fit Him. The point becomes clear enough in later writings of Locke, which argue that the only conception we can form of God's attributes is of some human attributes magnified.[62]

God's magnitude itself was important. For Locke required God to figure as mankind's superior and so as one entitled to control it. An argument of Descartes' was conveniently to hand to the effect that God was man's superior because He was his creator and sustainer.[63] This, of course, was something that Hobbes had omitted. To have mentioned these would have implied that people had reason to look up to God, both in the sense of being grateful to Him and in acknowledgement that He was their superior. In *Leviathan*, 'of the gratitude of mankind to their Creator, there is a deep silence'.[64] The silence matched Hobbes' desire to refer God's authority merely to His power, which fitted his views about sovereignty. For who has power can protect: where God did not protect there the sovereign could step into His office. As God, it seemed, did not protect people on earth, but the sovereign did, there could be no doubting who was the effective superior. It would have been quite otherwise if God had been recognised as creator and sustainer, functions that continued indefinitely (and which the sovereign, being merely human, could not perform).[65]

The magnitude of God and His uses of it were important because it grounded Locke's next step. It provided the means of supposing God's intention characterised the world. He created mankind with certain ends in mind and wrote them into the human character. From the make of people Locke inferred that God intended them to act.[66] Thus Locke felt able to make use of creation and purpose which Hobbes had entertained but not applied. ·

Hence Locke's fourth essay showed that sense perception, rightly handled, can provide the notion of God's superiority which we require to show His authority. We can add that concurrently the content of natural law would be shown from the same sources. But before we pursue that matter – and so the institutions that Locke wished to uphold – we should turn once more to his treatment of ideas.

IV

How did people come by ideas? Locke reviewed the resources of his age in his second lecture. These he identified as innatism, tradition and sense perception.[67] Hobbes had taken the latter. Locke agreed that sense experience furnished ideas of particulars and adopted a compositional model of ideas.[68] But the theory Locke outlined only briefly in his *Essays*. More deliberate was the use he made of reason in the formation of ideas. Reason was distinctly human in Aristotle's terms, a point helpful at Christ Church whose dean, John Fell, was a supporter of peripatetic views.[69] More generally, if sense and reason were the sources of certainty about morals, as Locke wished them to be,[70] it was necessary to dispose of both innatism and tradition. Locke needed to show that his choice was preferable to the alternatives.

Here the conception of certainty was important. Earlier thinkers had canvassed it freely and they had identified certainty as a desirable state of affairs. This reflected the phenomenon of scepticism. During the sixteenth century reflective minds had been struck by the diversity of practice embodied, albeit in different ways, by the split between Protestant and Catholic and by the disclosure of non-European moral habits, whether in Asia or the Americas. This diversity seemed to offer a *prima facie* suggestion that religious and moral institutions lacked that uniformity which would suggest that God had indicated His preferences for these matters unequivocally, or (more radically) that it was unclear that God (if He existed) was interested in these matters. This sceptical reaction bred in the next century a variety of responses, whose common denominator was an insistence upon the uniformity of the divine order, an insistence that was cast at a level intended to escape observed diversity.

One form was to suggest that beneath superficial differences there was a core of practice common to mankind. Sometimes this view referred to the make of human nature, shared by all and embodying the same needs and drives. This particular view helps to explain the prevalent interest in natural law. Sometimes it pointed to a variety of intellectual tenets about belief and conduct on which people were held to agree. Either way the notion that people really held certain matters in common was important, so that the notion of consent or agreement was central and the phrase 'common notions' prevalent. On occasion this view was underwritten by the theory of ideas that we know as innatism, which suggested that some ideas were common to mankind because they shared a common source, namely the human soul. Popularised by Herbert's *De Veritate* this view was developed by Descartes in a way that suggested that the soul had the conditions of certainty within it. For certainty was the obvious aspiration of a movement of thought bypassing scepticism.

Descartes' scheme turned upon the relation of the human intellect to God. More broadly, diversity of worship might be met by emphasising natural theology, so that truths about God's nature and intentions might be supposed known to the understanding without the mediation of revelation. In a sense natural theology underlies this whole movement of thought, for the view that there were fundamental features, whether intellectual or practical, common to mankind suggested that the human species reflected the purpose of a single designer, just as the sceptical reaction to a diversity of observed practice reflected the same view by supposing that valid institutions would be cast in a single mould. The being and intentions of God were thus fundamental, however construed.[71]

Locke's relation to this movement of thought was positive but critical. He was friendly to the project of establishing natural law and the existence of God, which complemented his scientific interests. But he was sceptical about claims to agreement in morals and about innatism too. To his mind they did not establish what was required of them. Additionally, he saw an important task that had been left undone.

The crucial task of obtaining a knowledge of morals and the existence of God with certainty had not been executed; or at least if the standard of certainty had been applied to ethics it was usually with an eye to their uncertainty. Grotius, for instance, had remarked that certainty in the fullest sense was not to be had in morals, whilst Hobbes had doubted mankind's ability to know rather than believe in God.[72] The way was open to seize certainty for the Lockean view of the understanding, which Locke took – or more precisely asserted that he had taken.[73] The next step was to consider the adequacy of other views.

Tradition was the easier target, for its doctrine assumed the vulnerable form that there was a universal consent to certain propositions. The events of the mid-century had made some Englishmen a little sceptical of this, just as the continued flow of anthropological data from the Indies and America augmented doubt on the continent too. Besides the advocates of tradition themselves indicated that its conclusions were uncertain.[74]

Innatism was a more imposing target. As a doctrine about knowledge generally, it had the backing of Descartes and Henry More. But More at this date had yet to develop an ethical doctrine (and, when he did, it would not dwell upon ideas in quite this sense). Descartes had said little on the subject.[75] Locke objected to innatism at this point principally because it did not provide a plausible case for positing a moral knowledge common to mankind.[76] Whilst something of the sort is required by the intellectual purpose that innatism served, this view is notable not least because it suited Locke's purpose to criticise it. That is to say, innatism was aligned with tradition in that they were represented alike as positing a universally shared understanding.

Thus notions of natural law being 'inscribed' on man's understanding and its being discoverable through consent, otherwise so different, were represented by Locke as identical in one respect, namely that if they held good then one would expect to find general agreement on moral values. The third essay, which was devoted to inscription, and the fifth alike rejected this view,[77] and in the latter the lurid locale of Soldania Bay, where men did not even acknowledge a god, made the ꞏꞏ ꞏꞏ of its many appearances in Locke's writings.[78]

The suspicion that agreement did not disclose natural law sprang from Locke's experience of the Interregnum. Hooker's 'as' had indicated that universal agreement of itself suggested only a presumption of divine authorship, for as he admitted it could result from a universal cause of error.[79] Locke thought the saying that 'the voice of the people is the voice of God' deeply deceptive, as we would expect from the man who had written in 1660 that most men were as beasts.[80] His scepticism fastened not only on the content but the diversity of morals: he insisted that the agreement required did not in fact exist.[81] So consent and inscription were both rejected.

Locke's replacement was reason accompanied by sense perception. People were not to look only on their desires and to do more than seek the means of their satisfaction. As we have seen he had to take into account the character of the world. That pointed to God and suggested that God's intentions for mankind had a higher authority than their own inclinations: God was mankind's superior. His superiority, we know, was supposed to issue in instructions to mankind. We shall see that these turned out to recommend what upheld society, rather than the chance promptings of human desire. It was true, of course, that God's will and the satisfaction of human desires could coincide – and in fact often did – but the coincidence was material rather than conceptual. Locke made his point clear in his eighth and final essay, which decided that the rightness of an action did not arise from its profitability; on the contrary God had arranged matters so that its utility was a by-product of its rightness.[82]

This argument turned ultimately on natural law being an external code, one prescribed by a superior according to a criterion which was not logically identical with the agent's nature. We may see this in looking at reason. Reason in any version of natural law was meant to disclose rules. If reason was equated with law, as it was in the internal model of natural law, then the rational satisfaction of desire was according to law. This would be true whatever the desires were. Whilst this might pass if an agreement in desires could be alleged, a diversity of morals suggested otherwise. Whilst Locke by no means neglected reason he wished to align it conceptually not to man's desire, but to God's will. Consent was not enough to establish a law. At the beginning of his first essay he contrasted a conception of natural law intelligible 'only' by the light of nature and one 'which is the decree of the will of God'. He added that it seemed incorrect to speak of the law as dictated by reason, since reason in fact only discovered what a superior had prescribed.[83] Both here and later Locke emphasised that what God was taken to prescribe as law and what reason discovered coincided in content, but of course what reason discovered was that God willed one course of actions rather than another and that it was supposed to be morally obligatory.[84]

V

Thus Locke asserted views of God as moral legislator and of the theory of ideas, views that respectively distanced him from Hobbes and provided an alternative to defective accounts of moral knowledge. But what was the content of that knowledge? Here again we find Locke developing alternatives to a variety of views. He asserted that moral obligation applied to everyone at all times, and that self-interest was not the basis of it. This continued his construction of an alternative to Hobbes, for Hobbes (of course) had made the interest of the individual pivotal to the content of morality. But apart from these formal matters, Locke considered too the content of natural law. It is worth considering the content first, for this will show how the vindication of order Locke was constructing made it helpful for him to bypass Hobbes.

Locke outlined briefly at the end of his fourth essay a series of precepts which were rational in relation to the desires which the human agent was assumed to have. The content assumed was not altogether novel, but that should alert us to the way in which it served Locke's end. For its rationality embraced the type of institution he wished to uphold.

Locke assumed that everyone was moved by a desire to preserve himself, that his needs would require him to coalesce with others to attain that end and that, besides, man had an inclination to the society of his fellows equal to his need for it. Whether considered in relation to the desire for self-preservation or to the desire for sociability it followed that the type of conduct which would maintain society was rational for man. It followed that it was also rational to adhere to any further precepts which were supposed to tend to that end. Thus people came by a series of measures adapted to sustain society.

Man was 'highly driven' by 'an internal instinct' for self-preservation, to the degree that Locke felt no need to insist upon it. To satisfy this desire the agent was 'driven by necessity and experience of life' to combine with others to form a society. This was complemented by 'a certain propensity of nature' for him to desire society as much as he required to preserve himself, which was evident in that he was endowed with a faculty that equipped him for society, namely speech, which would make a distinctively human society possible.[85]

On these terms it was as necessary to preserve society as to form it. Later in his *Essays* Locke specified good faith as the bond of society, *societatis vinculum*. This evidently denoted keeping to what was right in one's relations with others, whether in fulfilling promises or respecting others' property: in short acting according to rules, acting justly, for Locke also described justice as the 'bond of all society'.[86] It procured a list of benefits which dwelt on what the agent needed to preserve himself, as 'peace, harmony, friendship, safety, security, the possession of our goods'.[87] Locke, in other words, conceived the maintenance of society to lie in providing the agent with the benefits for which he had entered it. Since this suggested that the cooperation implied in society was ultimately rational, it followed that society and its preservation were throughout rational in terms of the agent's desires (as we shall see, Locke took care to emphasise the point in his eighth essay). The same sense of the significance of justice was to be maintained at length in *Treatises*, where it provides the ground of specifically political argument. Locke's political preferences for the moment were not directly engaged to the world of events, but to the foundations of society.

This type of view was anything but new when Locke enunciated them. It was adumbrated in the Aristotelian corpus, to go no further, where we are told that men combine 'because each is not sufficient for himself', as well as out of a desire for sociability, and that the community comes about from 'the bare needs of life' and continues 'for the sake of a good life'.[88] Through Cicero, whose *De Officiis* was a central textbook at Christ Church, was received the specific view that man was, like all animals, moved by a desire for self-preservation and had a corresponding affection for anything conducing to that end; but that he differed from the animals by pursuing the means to his end not through instinct but through reason. Cicero had added that the practice of justice maintained society.[89] These views were taken up in systematic form by Grotius, who suggested that every animal had an instinct for preservation and a correlated warmth towards whatever procured it. Cooperation was necessary, 'for the Author of Nature was pleased, that every Man in particular should be weak of himself, and in Want of many Things necessary for living Commodiously, to the End we might more eagerly affect Society'. To make society possible God had also equipped people with the gift of speech and with reason. For the understanding was supposed to disclose counsels which would uphold society, amongst which Grotius included respect for property and other forms of just action.[90] So Locke stood in a well-developed tradition concerning the content of rational conduct.

The content which Locke attributed to this thinking was rational not only in accurately correlating certain means and ends but also in that the means and ends were supposed to be disclosed by ideas and the exercise of reason on them. Human reflection on this 'internal drive' for self-preservation would inform him of the desire which moved the agent. Experience and contemplation of his needs, presumably in relation to the limited means of satisfaction available to each individual alone, pointed to cooperation with others to compass the ends which each desired for himself but could not attain without the help of others. Furthermore one could infer that since each agent entered society for his or her own ends an institution to assure them would be needed,

100

which was found in the enforcement of justice. So the practice of justice could be regarded as rational not only by satisfying man's desire but also because it could be inferred from the considerations disclosed to man by sense and reason.[91] Thus reason could be reckoned to disclose the precepts which sustained society.

Of course it was another matter to show that the same precepts were morally obligatory. It required no proof to say that they were obligatory as means to ends, as in Locke's observation that man was driven to society by need and disposition to the extent that he was bound to preserve himself.[92] But to show that rational precepts had a moral character on the model Locke had taken up it was necessary to show the obligatory force behind these precepts. After all, it is one thing to say a course of action is rational and another to say, additionally, that is is also obligatory.

It was for this reason that it was needful to assert an alternative to Hobbes' view of the extent of moral obligation. Hobbes took moral obligation to operate only under conditions of safety, because being obliged to obey A implied that A was providing effective protection. This in effect meant that obligation applied when measures were prescribed by the *sovereign*. As we have seen this view itself rested on the assumption that the fundamental – and sometimes the sole – concern of the agent was self-preservation. Thus Hobbes' view of self-preservation married with his view of obligation. His position, stated generally, was that obligation did not apply always and that the self-interest of the agent was morally paramount. Locke sought to deny both parts of Hobbes' view. He devoted the closing three *Essays* to developing a very different doctrine.

This view of Locke's implied that the agent was bound to follow God's law regardless of his or her terrestrial interests. Locke complemented it by arguing that as a matter of fact one's interests were served best by following it. The eighth of Locke's *Essays* argued self-preservation was not the fundamental law of nature.[93] By fundamental Locke meant here a standard of rightness for other measures, so that he did not imply the rejection of self-preservation as a duty or as a means of inferring other duties, merely its sufficiency as a criterion for assessing candidates for our moral conduct.[94] Locke's point was to stress that examination of our duty would lead us to what upheld society, even at some personal cost, as the eighth essay emphasised.[95] That cost, of course, might seem irrational, so Locke indicated that what upheld society was beneficial for everyone: it would procure the benefits each most desired.[96] Thus the convenient and the obligatory coincided, but not in the way attributed to Hobbes: rather the obligatory recommended conduct which was discovered on reflection to be beneficial.

The sixth and the seventh essays asserted the complementary view that obligations from God were permament and universal. Thus the content Locke required was seen to have a warrant that did not admit of exceptions. Of course there was the question of just *how* obligatory conduct was beneficial. Partly this was a matter of procuring terrestrial benefits: but Locke's case involved no elaborate calculations. Instead it adduced matters that could be reckoned to outweigh any terrestrial advantage, namely the rewards and punishments that God exerted in the afterlife, though Locke did not actually do anything in his *Essays* to prove their reality.[97] Once the existence of God and His legislative activity were treated as certain, it was an obvious recourse to treat the administration of the afterlife on the same basis.

A broader end than merely criticism of Hobbes was served by these views. Locke's argument about natural law implied a foundation for civil order which vindicated its authority against the threats to which he had alluded. This was not merely a matter of the thrust of his essays against uninstructed desire but also of the specific form of Locke's preference for a disclosure of precepts through reason and sense rather than consent. For consent and the whole attitude of *recta ratio* implied private judgement, which was also the principle which validated the judgement of conscience. By replacing private judgement with his alternative Locke restricted conscience to the conclusions he had outlined. These, as we have seen, were views which would support civil society. *Inter alia* Locke took himself to have established the authority of the magistrate in civil affairs. His *Essays* established the claims of civil order against those of conscience in respect of the matters they addressed. The title which religious groups had claimed to interfere in civil society was obviated.

The totality of people's judgement amounted to a general consent. Locke preferred the disclosures of sense and reason. In denying that consent disclosed natural law he observed that people did not know that something was good because they thought alike but rather that they might in fact agree because they knew something was good 'from natural sources'.[98] By natural sources Locke meant the conclusions of sense and reason, which we have seen were found in rational inferences from desire treated for moral purposes in the context of God's will. Since reason and sense thus led man to only one set of conclusions, natural law could be said to speak universally. Thus Locke substituted the precepts of law for each person's judgement of good. In his eighth essay he specifically denied that it was illegitimate for each person to judge for himself what would suit him.[99] The substitution of reason and sense for private judgement in considering morals showed that there was only one measure for human conduct.

It followed in particular that when conscience looked towards social actions as distinct from those towards God, which, in the common language, bore upon the Second rather than the First Table, it would not be informed except through people's proper capacities. These capacities, considered in the appropriate light, yielded only one set of conclusions and those of a kind which tended to support society. Conscience would attain knowledge (as distinguished from belief) concerning society only through Locke's brand of natural law. If God prescribed additional precepts, as He was of course free to do, they would be compatible with that law, since it harmonised with man's higher nature. Thus Locke would take it for granted that revelation would agree in content with the findings of reason. His project of establishing natural law thus tended to uphold the moral order. Thus, in the words of John Tillotson, if 'the *Law of Nature*' were '. . .every whit as much the *Law of God*, as the *Revelation* of his will in his *Word*;' then '. . .consequently, nothing contained in the *Word of God*, or in any Pretended *Revelation* from *Him*, can be interpreted to dissolve the obligation of Moral duties plainly required by the Law of Nature.' The practical implications were clear enough:

And if this one thing would be an effectual antidote against the pernicious Doctrines of the *Antinomians*, as of all other *Libertine-Enthusiasts* whatsoever. Nothing being more incredible, than that *Divine Revelation* should contradict the clear and unquestionable Dictates of *Natural Light*; nor any thing more vain, than to fancy that the *Grace of god* does release men from the *Laws of Nature*

so that the compatibility of the natural and the supernatural order would be assured.[100] Thus Locke's insistence that the law of nature was God's legislation, that it was established certainly tended to uphold the moral order.

Much more was implied in this position. One point of especial note is that reason and revelation should be congruent in their conclusions. This, of course, carried forward the doctrine which Samuel Crooke had addressed to his congregation. In that sense the use of reason in relation to revealed theology we find in so many divines of the Restoration was a continuation of an older position. What is significant is a change of emphasis: Locke's *Essays* did not suggest the older position that revelation clarified the conclusions of natural reason, but rather emphasised that natural reason was certain.[101]

There were further emphases on the congruence of any genuine claims about the supernatural with the natural order. Locke dwelt upon this point in respect of both the understanding and conduct. His subsequent writings on the understanding emphasised the congruence of reason and revelation and, more especially, argued that reason should judge the content of revelation. Likewise here he described the law of nature as *regula morum*. Claims of a similar tenor can be found in other writers of the period, and, whilst this need not reflect a specific influence in either direction, it does suggest a common sense of the social order.[102]

Locke's treatment of natural law served to establish his view of order in a specific way. When he mentioned conscience in the *Essays* it was either to emphasise its conjunction with natural law or to discount its merely uninformed reflections.[103] Any claims of conscience about civil society which conflicted with the ways of reason and sense could be discounted as ill-informed rather than divinely inspired. The authority of civil order was vindicated against the pretensions of religious groups straying out of their peculiar sphere into the concerns of civil society. The claim which the Locke of the *Tracts* had required to discount the sects, but had lacked, could now be made good. Thus his treatment of ideas yielded a view of God and His relation to natural law which pointed to a conclusion quite different from Hobbes'. Similar materials differently employed produced different conclusions.

The same was true of Locke's treatment of the character of obligation and what he termed the basis of natural law. Hobbes had suggested that natural law obliged only under conditions of safety – which meant where the sovereign made it his law – and that it was to be recommended insofar as it was rational for the purposes of the agent's terrestrial self-interest. Locke thought differently.

He insisted that the law of nature obliged continually, bearing upon all human agents and that perpetually.[104] Locke adduced not only the doctrine earlier announced, that men were bound to obey God, but also produced the further proposition that God had annexed rewards and punishments to natural law.[105] This view implied that the agent was bound to follow God's law regardless of his terrestrial interests. Locke complemented it by arguing that natural law was not based on self-interest[106] and that one's interests were served best by following it.

Just as reason indicated on these terms the moral fixity of the civil order so by a complementary process God's superiority could provide a basis for civil magistracy. Since God was superior to all things He created, it followed that He was the highest source of obligation. Locke

104

inferred that all the authority of lesser superiors was derived from Him.[107] It followed if one regarded a magistrate as the superior of his citizens that his laws were binding because God had delegated authority to him.[108] Of course, it remained to show that God had created magistracy, let alone which form of the institution was truly preferable, but as it was the foundation of the magistrate's authority rather than the authority itself that was in doubt, Locke had done enough for his own purposes.

Locke's *Essays on the Law of Nature* served to ground his conception of civil order in reason and sense, through advancing a particular conception of how the understanding was informed and placing it in the light of God's willing. Locke's subsequent views on the human understanding and his views about self-preservation and justice in *Two Treatises*, not to speak of his repeated allusions to God's superiority, indicate that he continued to base himself on these opinions later in life.[109] But a defence of society against the civil pretensions of conscience said nothing about the other piece of business standing over from 1660, namely accommodating conscience with civil order. Locke had yet to show how conscience in the properly religious matters of the First Table could be reconciled with magisterial authority over civil society.

Locke's *Essays on the Law of Nature* explained a rational morality. Their morality was rational in the sense that its precepts and presuppositions were disclosed by the reasoning faculty. It was also rational in a further sense, that the precepts were adapted to sustain civil society, just as the scriptural views of Samuel Crooke had been. The *Essays*, in other words, translated into the idiom of reason the type of conclusion Locke wished to reach. He outlined the content of what reason disclosed, showed how he meant to relate rational precepts to God's will and proceeded through a series of moves to show the definitive character of rational morality.[110]

The picture sketched in Locke's *Essays* suggests that the exercise of human reason on sense data would yield the conclusion that God was not merely the supreme legislator but also that His moral laws obliged. Locke had made use of Hobbes' conceptual resources to enforce a decidedly different conclusion about ethics. The deliveries of sense supported a reassuring view of the moral life and to Locke's mind did so more securely than tradition or innate ideas.

VI

Locke's early opposition to Hobbes may seem a surprising position. After all much of the secondary literature on *Two Treatises* either

105

devotes itself to showing or tacitly assumes that Locke was uninterested in Hobbes.[111] But the matter is evidently more complicated than that. Locke had declared himself about Hobbes much earlier. The form of the declaration was central to his future doctrines and ambitions, for he carried forward the conclusions of his *Essays* in both morals and epistemology.

We should not assume, of course, that Locke would develop his position on any question. His constitution was not robust and contemporary medicine was of doubtful use. If he survived, it was not obvious that he would pursue independent thought. A career in some form of practice, whether ecclesiastical, medical or diplomatic, might have been his next step. Neither should we suppose that the lines on which a thinker has worked must continue to be pursued, even if he remains a thinker: external events may point to other subjects. Events may also call forth possibilities that lie within an intellectual ambit but which otherwise might remain dormant. But if ethics and ideas were relevant, Locke would be likely to discuss them along lines not unlike these.

God continued to appear as a superior and giver of moral laws As such He was central to Lockean ethics. In 1667 He would be identified as 'the foundation of all morality'. The objections to Hobbes continued. Locke continued to regard the lack of coordination between self-preservation and other parts of morality as unsatisfactory, condemning the 'Hobbist' who, 'with his principle of self-preservation, whereof himself is to be judge, will not easily admit a great many plain duties of morality'.[112] A satisfactory relation between self-preservation and our duty to others would be achieved in *Two Treatises*. Locke came to think that a Hobbesian society would be held on civilised lines only by terrestrial pressures,[113] thus maintaining his sense that Hobbes and the morality of theism were some distance apart. Locke's mature view of ideas and certainty continued the lines of his *Essays*. Sense and reflection continued to be the sources of ideas to the Lockean mind, though the precise character of Locke's opinions was subject to change.[114] Locke's ambition would be to unite the two in a project of demonstrating the truths of morality. We shall see the success (or otherwise) of this project in the sequel. Thus Locke's response to Hobbes directed him towards a legislative view of ethics.

There were more immediate and particular consequences. Hobbes' edifice of knowledge and ethics had been crowned by a political doctrine. The Hobbesian sovereignty was immune from legitimate opposition and was entitled to command the religious conscience of the citizen. Whilst Locke's refusal to subscribe to Hobbes' ethics and epistemology does not imply a position about either state or church it certainly relieved him of any intellectual liability to agree with Hobbes' politics. Indeed it left open the avenues that Hobbes had tried sedulously to close.

Hobbes had argued that loyalty to God was in no sense prior to loyalty to government: he argued that the two were reconciled. His critics knew that to unpick the connections with which he had tied up political and religious dissent was to allow religion once again to be a cue for civil dissension. 'If divine law and humane law clash one with another,' observed Bramhall, 'without doubt it is evermore better to obey God than man.'[115] Specifically, in Locke's England two questions arose. One concerned the relationship between the conscience of the Christian believer and the magistrate in respect of things indifferent. Another was the conditions on which the magistrate held power. For though Locke's *Essays* maintained that civil government was an institution authorised by God, they did not explain precisely what form of authority was correct. If anything they implied that because people were bound to obey God an unreserved transfer of right to the magistrate was not necessarily the proper choice,[116] though that would be dependent on the character attributed to the latter. The avenue leading to *Two Treatises* and *Epistola de Tolerantia* was opened. Why did Locke pursue it?

Chapter 4

'An Essay concerning Toleration' presented a treatment of the problem of religious conscience and civil order different from Locke's *Tracts*. It did so in part because it implied a more securely founded account of natural law, as befitted the writer of *Essays on the Law of Nature*. But more pointedly it relied upon an implicit but ruthless treatment of the theory of the church. These together permitted Locke to settle the problem his *Tracts* had not touched on, to differentiate his arguments from his contemporaries' and so to set out a distinctive line of argument.

The problem with which Locke's *Tracts* had presented him remained unsolved. Two parts of the inherited framework of Christian thought had conflicted, namely the civil government's superiority over things indifferent and the uncoerced disposition implied in valid worship. In particular whilst Locke had aimed to establish the rights of civil government over Christian worship, he had not dealt with religious conscience adequately. He had argued that the civil government was entitled to regulate things indifferent within the ecclesiastical sphere. He had urged this on the grounds that no other arrangement could secure peace for civil society. But his position did not do justice to one case. A conscience which had a purely religious aspect and which differed sincerely in its view of things indifferent from the government, but did not in any way threaten civil peace would be subject nonetheless to the impositions of the civil magistrate. In other words, whilst not giving up the defence of civil society, intellectual clarity required Locke to manage it in a way that did not assault conscience of this kind.

This problem was pressing partly for intellectual and partly for practical reasons. The intellectual reason was that obedience to God and to man had not been satisfactorily ordered. To reconcile them was important, in that Locke had rejected the decisive solutions implicit in Hobbes and in Rome, but had not so far substituted a resolution of his own. It is to the intellectual grounds that we should turn first.

108

I

Locke's declared aim in 1667, to remove the grounds of dispute, focussed on 'the question of liberty of conscience, which has for some years bin so much bandied amongst us'. The two poles of disagreement over matters of indifference to which he alluded, 'absolute obedience' and 'universall liberty in matters of conscience', were well known to him. The former he himself had maintained and the latter was Bagshawe's position. As we have seen these positions had failed to do justice respectively to the claims of conscience and to civil order. Locke now observed that the error of the disputants had been to proceed 'without assigning what those things are which have a title to liberty, or shewing the boundaries of imposition and obedience'. He proposed 'to clear the way' for a better treatment.[1]

Locke resolved the intellectual problem by a pointed classification of principles, which afforded grounds for distinguishing what touched government from what did not. The scheme was threefold, but depended on one fundamental distinction. That distinction was between speculative and practical principles. This was a scholastic usage, denoting the difference between what affected conduct and what did not.[2] Practical principles Locke further divided into those actions about which God had disclosed no views and those where He had signified his views clearly. Thus there were three classes: speculative, practical but morally indifferent, and practical and morally relevant.

The principal division lay between speculative and practical principles: but this is not all. Not less important was how Locke identified the *contents* of each category, especially the first. For firstly came those actions which did not affect other people, whether by being speculations that gave 'noe bias to my conversation with men' and that did not influence 'my actions as I am a member of any society' or by being transactions only between the agent and God, and not other human beings. The contents of this category were alike in that none of them affected conduct in society and were all, in that sense, speculative only. Locke's other two categories concerned practice. The second category comprised opinions about conduct and the actions flowing from them that belonged to areas in themselves indifferent. Thirdly there were matters 'which are good or bad in themselves'.[3] These latter two categories did affect other people.

To these categories Locke juxtaposed a view of the civil government's purpose. He thought this consisted *only* in *civil* matters, in other words relations amongst people. It followed immediately that speculative matters were irrelevant to the magistrate's business. This turned out to be a point of the greatest relevance. In one direction it suggested that the business of government lay in sustaining civil society.[4] In another it suggested that the civil government had nothing to do with the matter of religious worship.

For Locke asserted, as we have seen, that religious worship fell into the class of speculation. His point about worship was simply that, as such, it had 'in its owne nature noe reference at all to my governor or to my neighbour', for 'bare speculations' could not 'by any meanes either disturb the state or inconvenience my neighbour'. This distinctness from the interests of civil society constituted a sphere which called for no action from the magistrate, whose function was to protect those interests. On the other hand Locke insisted that if religious figures 'out of pride or overweeningness' sought to 'force and compell others' to their persuasion then they became 'the worse subject' to the prince or the 'worse neighbour' to his subjects.[5] Thus if worship in itself implied nothing about conduct towards others it was not the magistrate's business.

Locke's distinction between actions in which liberty of conscience was legitimate and those in which it was not was made according to their relation to civil society. If an agent's action concerned the good of society it was to be subject to the magistrate. But if did not, whether because it passed between him and God alone or did not 'interfere with the advantages of the publique or serve any way to disturb the government' it was a matter for liberty of conscience.[6] In other words the line Locke drew lay between the matter of civil society and what did not affect that society's well-being.

Locke's criterion presupposed a clear sense of the good of society. One source of this was his *Essays*, as we may see by observing how he treated his third category. This, comprising matters 'which are good or bad in themselves',[7] did not claim much attention, for few claimed liberty of conscience here he thought: God had spoken and had already obliged the conscience. Thus Locke confidently dismissed claims of conscience in civil things indifferent, as befitted one who knew the authority concerning civil society could be had from God was a matter of rules which upheld both it and magistracy. He observed that to accommodate all that men 'pretend out of conscience' would undermine magistracy: but these scruples had no authority to oblige magisterial authority, because it was acknowledged 'on all hands' that the magistrate had jurisdiction over these matters. So 'the errours or scruples of any one's conscience' did 'not destroy the magistrate's power, nor alter the nature of the thing, which is still indifferent'.[8] Locke's clarity about the areas in which conscience had no legitimate claims reflected his sense that there it could claim no religious backing to the detriment of civil society.

In the same way Locke could identify the magistrate's function firmly. The magistrate's authority was identified in terms of what sustained each and every individual; he had a power 'to command or forbidd' opinions and actions insofar as they trenched on 'the preservation of the whole'. This suggests that the essay embodied a view about natural law. The magistrate's function was to preserve life. In other words Locke implied that magistracy substituted as the effective arm for the end of self-preservation recommended by natural law. So his essay takes its stand on propositions that Locke would count as certain because he assumed that they were demonstrable knowledge. Claims which would count merely as probability were not taken into account, as we shall see, and Locke accordingly focusses his account on the known.

The new doctrine, which suggested that the magistrate as such had no business to interfere with strictly ecclesiastical affairs, was permissible in terms of the defence of civil society Locke had made. For if conscience were informed in respect of society by natural law, which was a definitive measure of order, it followed that the claims of religious enthusiasm could not challenge legitimately the civil order. To state the matter in another way Locke had effectively distinguished the civil from the properly ecclesiastical by giving an account of the former in terms which a supposedly religious inspiration could not dispute. Since civil society was now securely grounded it would be feasible to reconcile the civil order with conscience, for it was no longer legitimately possible by Lockean standards 'under pretence of spirituall jurisdiction to hooke in all secular affairs'. The inroads of the ecclesiastical against the civil were placed in an unflattering light and appropriately to be delivered to magisterial direction. Since civil society could be defended on this ground from the religiously cloaked threat it would no longer be needful for the magistrate to claim an authority in ecclesiastical affairs, which Locke had recognised as intellectually untenable but had required as practically necessary.

The development of Locke's argument depends on the view that the civil magistrate existed only to deal with terrestrial interests. The argument is presented as one from means, but the content of the magistrate's work is plainly to uphold natural law. The latter suggested that people entered civil society in order to achieve their goal of self-preservation. The magistrate's function was to preserve each and every one under his control. Here his duty lay and nowhere else. It followed that ecclesiastical affairs *per se* were not his concern.

111

Of course it might be argued against this that religious practice often affected civil conduct. That point could hardly be ignored when theology was held to explain ethics, when religious inspiration was supposed to make people behave well, and where too religious prepossessions had been an element in civil conflict. But Locke carefully emphasised that the magistrate should encourage morality in order to uphold the state and should restrain religiously inspired disturbance. Indeed throughout his writings on toleration he refused to countenance civil disobedience on ecclesiastical grounds, even as a response to persecution. Such were the limits he drew.[9]

The limits, of course, divided the other way too. The magistrate as such had no brief to deal with religious affairs. The limitation of the magistrate's jurisdiction was complemented by the view that civil punishment could hardly serve the end intended. It was ill-adapted to produce conformity. If one were dealing with a case which reason and sense could determine, then the understanding was not subject to the agent's will in Locke's view and so could hardly be moved by force.[10] As to faith it was apparent that if God 'would have men forced to heaven' He would employ not external compulsion ('the outward violence of the magistrate on men's bodies') but the action of the Holy Spirit: for God could not be pleased by anything less than a conscientious obedience. Besides 'no consideration could be sufficient to force a man from, or to, that which he was fully perswaded was the way to infinite happiness or infinite misery'.[11] So civil sanctions would not be an effective means to reversing people's opinions.

Another view of the relations between intellect and will would have the opposite practical bearing. If one supposed that the will was somehow independent of the intellect, it followed in the psychology of the day that it would be moved by considerations of sense, just as beasts were moved by external stimuli. On this model the stimulus of coercion would be an effective means of moulding conduct. There is no reason why religious worship should not be moulded thus. One writer at least would suggest as much, Samuel Parker.[12] Thus views of the understanding reacted upon politics. Locke's position on the intellect and will is not less significant because he espoused it *before* favouring toleration.[13]

There remains a suggestion, which Locke did not foresee, but which was levelled some years later against his *Epistola de Tolerantia* by Jonas Proast. Proast suggested that whilst force could not effect a change of heart, a moderate application of it might encourage people to take seriously arguments which otherwise they would ignore.[14] The answer to that is simply that Locke had 'premised'[15] that the magistrate's

power could not extend legitimately to purely ecclesiastical opinions: however useful force might be it was illegitimate. He rested his case on the magistrate's limited field of jurisdiction.

II

Locke could be confident about what the civil magistrate was to do. He had a further reason for being confident about what the magistrate was *not* to do, a reason which is perhaps the most important point in his essay. The objectives of Lockean government were secular. For him the functions of civil government concerned only the relations amongst people in civil society. This followed from his use of the distinction between speculation and practice. Thus there is no question of the civil government having any business with worship as such.

It is important to understand the meaning of the word *secular*. It refers to matters which terminate in the terrestrial life, as distinguished from the eternal. We may see as much in Hooker's observation that 'Religion and the feare of God as well induceth secular prosperitie as euerlasting blisse in the world to come'. Locke himself used the word thus in 1659 when he contrasted 'spirituall jurisdiction' with 'all secular affairs', just as Maynwaring had treated the monarch as 'the sacred & supreme Head of *two Bodies*, the one *Spirituall*, the other *Secular*'. 'Secular' does not mean, as it is often taken to mean, the exclusion of theological or, more broadly, religious reference. Baxter combined the two, when he observed that 'The chief use of Kings and Magistrates is, to rule according to Gods Universal Laws, and to see them put into execution as far as the Ends of Government require in this World.'[16] Locke assumed with most of his contemporaries that God willed that there be government (though there was disagreement about precisely the *sort* of polity He intended), and he asserted that God was the moral legislator. To write the 'Essay concerning Toleration' assumed that religious worship was a central problem for the government. But Locke's solution to that problem presupposed that the business of government was with the conduct of the present life, and not with preparation for the next.

This position implies that Locke discounted some claims about the church. The silent manoeuvre behind his argument is – paradoxically – that he ignored the claims of faith to truth. Though the essay creates a space for religious conscience, it never enquires whether what conscience claims is true. It considers merely the temporal consequences of belief and leaves the believer to settle his or her account with God. This means that the claims of the churches to truth are left unconsidered.

All of this squares with Locke's earlier concerns. As in his *Tracts* he considered the question with reference to two of the three entities involved. The human agent, with his or her religious conscience and his civil interests, is considered. Indeed he or she takes priority (save over God), for the second of the three – the civil government – exists for the purpose of protecting him. Its need to do so is carefully considered and can take precedence over conscience. But because a different relation amongst the three is proposed there is an important consequence.

The essay accordingly eschews what we may call the Augustinian view of civil government as the servant of the true church. This suggested that the function of civil governments was to promote true belief, a view which found practical expression in enforcing adherence to one communion. This in effect was the presumption that made possible questions like the one Locke had addressed in 1660. For to argue that the magistrate had the role of regulating worship within a civil society implied that unity of worship was desirable. Unity itself was desirable because it reflected truth.

For the Augustinian view based itself on the assumption that the true church of Christ could be recognised. It would be marked out not only by true doctrine and the sacraments but also by church order. It would be a church in the singular, because God was supposed to work in a unitary way. Hence the church was united according to God's purpose into one body. As the church was clearly God's instrument it followed that the civil government should uphold His purpose. Since the church was in the business of diffusing truth the magistrate should assist it, by suppressing error, which in these terms included deviations not just from good conduct but also from church order. In short because the church was recognisably God's chosen vehicle it was the function of the civil government to aid it with the means at its disposal.[17]

When Locke decided that the magistrate did not enforce virtue because it was virtuous, but because it was useful to society, he added a gloss: 'however strange it may seeme'. It would have seemed strange to Anglican and non-episcopalian alike. For it had been assumed that the very point of magistrates was to uphold religion. 'Their office,' said Archbishop Whitgift, 'is to see God served, and honoured, and obeyed by their subjects' and according to one writing in defence of his royal mistress she was 'bound to direct all estates to live in the faith and obedience of Christian religion'. The Scottish Confession of Faith of

1560 argued that 'to kings, princes, rulers and magistrates we affirm that chiefly and most principally the conservation and purgation of religion appertains; so that not only they are appointed for civil policy, but also for maintenance of the true religion and for suppressing of idolatry and superstition'. John Knox observed with characteristic sweetness that it was the Devil who had 'persuaded princes, rulers and magistrates that the feeding of Christ's flock pertaineth nothing to their charge'. The position, in short was that rulers had under their charge both the spiritual and temporal concerns of their subjects. As Jewel put it 'a christian prince hath charge of both tables committed to him by God', so that monarchs had authority over their subjects in two aspects: they 'had care of their bodies and. . .also of their souls.'[18]

The assumption of this view was that if the ruler and the ruled were Christian then the state was also. 'I perceived no such distinction of the commonwealth and the Church that they should be counted, as it were two bodies, governed with divers laws and divers magistrates,' Whitgift observed, 'except the Church be linked with an heathenish and idolatrous commonwealth'. If the commonwealth was Christian it was substantially identical with the church: there was 'no difference between a christian commonwealth and the Church of Christ'. Obviously, under such conditions the magistrate could enforce his ecclesiastical opinions with the civil arm. But a distinction could be made, which Locke exploited. Hooker indicated how the case differed when the state was not Christian. Whilst Hooker regularly assumed a Christian monarchy, he insisted that the church was conceptually distinct from the state: it was when the church was found in a Christian state that they formed one society. To make the conceptual distinction implies that the state might be treated differently. Locke treated it as devoted only to man's temporal interests in order to place the punishment of ecclesiastical deviance beyond the magistrate's authority.[19]

Thus Locke was able not only to dismiss conscience in civil matters but also at once to indulge it in religious ones and to uphold civil society. This feat required that civil government be secular in its ends. Government was not Christian, in the sense of not existing for the purpose of defending Christian doctrine with its law and force. This, of course, was not to say that Christian doctrine did not support civil society, merely that civil society did not exist to support *it*. 'The lawmaker,' Locke thought, 'hath nothing to doe with morall vertues and vices, nor ought to enjoyn the duties of the second table.' Of course the practice of those duties was supposed to underwrite society and Locke therefore supported their enforcement to the extent that they were 'subservient to the good and preservation of mankind under government'. In other words 'the magistrate commands not the practice of vertues because they are vertuous and oblige the conscience, or are the duties of men to God. . .but because they are the advantages of man with man, and most of them cannot be loosened without shattering the whole frame'. Thus the civil and the ecclesiastical ceased to be aspects of the same entity. To look forward for a moment, the civil order of *Two Treatises* was devoted to upholding the terrestrial rights of the citizen; saving his or her soul and worship generally went unremarked there.[20]

Locke's account of the radical difference between the purposes of church and state was thus developed from suppositions which enabled him to discount the Christian character of the commonwealth. We may say that the results were more radical than Hobbes, in that the Hobbesian commonwealth may impress Christianity on the citizen. Locke would argue in his *Epistola de Tolerantia* that there was no such thing as a Christian commonwealth.[21] Thus the secular state appeared with the object of reconciling the commonwealth with Christian conscience.

It is worth emphasising once again that secular does not imply a divorce from theological reference, but this time with a slightly different point. That is to say, Locke's writing here has a theistic rather than a specifically Christian bent. In the essay Locke indicated his support for theism, for he specifically excluded the question of belief in God from merely speculative opinions as 'the foundation of all morality, and which influences the whole life and actions of men', but this hardly amounted to a specifically Christian religion, and the exception was made, as is apparent, for the good of society.[22] In other words whilst the problem Locke addressed arose from a Christian society, the terms of his solution were theistic rather than specifically Christian.

The point is of a wider relevance, for Locke's other works of this period involved theistic rather than strictly Christian arguments. *Essays on the Law of Nature*, by their character, argued in terms of a theological explanation that contained no peculiarly Christian terms. *Two Tracts* arose from a problem in Christian worship, a problem solved in 'An Essay concerning Toleration' partly by using natural law. If we may anticipate, Locke's early writings on the human understanding also made presumptions primarily about theism rather than Christianity and discussed faith in terms of the former. Christian doctrine became Locke's subject matter somewhat later.

This is not a point about the intellectual framework of Locke's society, but about his mode of working. Where Christian thought and practice had provoked problems, and where theology was assumed to be explanatory, the most helpful explanations would be those that were

116

based on theology but did not involve themselves in specifically Christian commitments. This emphasis tells us little about Locke's private beliefs: certainly, in the fullness of time, Christian doctrine would be important for him.

Locke's decision to treat civil society in theoretical abstraction from a Christian function grounded his argument because it allowed him to lay down the premise that the civil magistrate's authority existed 'for no other purpose' than to protect men 'in that society over which he is sett': and this evidently meant it being 'onely made to preserve men in this world'. When he had suggested in 1659 that it was easy 'to hooke in all secular affairs' to conscience, his reasoning had been that 'in a commonwealth wholy Christian it is noe small difficulty to set limits and to define exactly where one begins and the other ends'. Now he came to 'set limits' by suggesting that the commonwealth should be conceptually abstracted from Christianity. This abstraction permitted Locke to draw his distinctions, for it manifestly excluded matters outside secular concerns. Hence purely speculative opinions and religious worship obviously lay beyond the magistrate's legitimate concern. Equally matters of practice within society were his business, but here also the line Locke drew corresponded to the purpose attributed to the magistrate. His power extended only to 'command or forbidd', as laws, matters which 'tend to the peace, safety, or security of his people'. In short Locke's argument assumed that 'the magistrate as magistrate hath nothing to doe with the good of men's souls or their concernments in another life, but is ordained and entrusted with his power only for the quiet and comfortable liveing of men in society one with another'.[23] Civil society protected people for this life. Locke had solved a problem in which two parts of the Christian life were mismatched – the authority of the magistrate and the conscience of the believer. He solved it not least by conceiving the state as secular, in that its purpose was not to produce Christian belief but to pursue objectives which terminate only in the present life.

II

The practical attraction of the question for Locke sprang from the movement of events. Firstly it had turned out that there were important victims of the 1662 settlement. Secondly in 1667 Locke was able to entertain a wider range of views than hitherto, for he had broadened the basis of his support. He was no longer dependent for an interesting life on Christ Church when the service of Lord Shaftesbury opened a wider perspective. These provided a personal latitude. The passage of political events brought this practical latitude together with the intellectual considerations we have noted.

Several practical conditions bore upon Locke's views. That a more tolerant attitude was feasible for him was relevant because of the workings of the first Conventicle Act and opportune because it seemed possible that these might be ended. Ecclesiastical relaxation might secure the goal of Protestant unity at home, perhaps in the interests of a 'protestant' policy abroad. To this end a resolution of the disparity between conscience and civil order was needed, for the groups at variance in England were all Protestant amidst their differences. Locke had therefore to find terms on which the reformed communion could admit agreement. We have seen that he located these, paradoxically, in a clear distinction between the ends of the church and the state. So Locke came to articulate the position implied in the development of his views after 1660.

His position, though conceptually open, required support in the world of time and circumstance to be developed explicitly. The Christ Church which had deprived Bagshawe of his Studentship was probably not quite the place for this,[24] but from the Spring of 1667 Locke was freed from too close a dependence on the Dean and Chapter by the patronage of Shaftesbury. This was perhaps a case in which service was perfect freedom, for Shaftesbury had for some time been an advocate of toleration and the opinions Locke set out in 1667 can hardly have been unwelcome to him. But it is useless to speculate on the nature of their intellectual relationship given the void of evidence. This is no great hardship in this particular instance, for the arguments which Locke offered for his position in 1667 were unlikely to have been derived from Shaftesbury, as the latter used some of them in public only after, and not before, Locke's 'Essay' was written.[25]

The Conventicle Act of 1664 dominated the general situation in which Locke wrote. This measure had followed the Act of Uniformity and the Corporation Act when it had become clear that these were not sufficiently stringent for Archbishop Sheldon's purpose: they had removed dissenters from public authority rather than prevented the exercise of their ministry. This Act prescribed civil penalties for ecclesiastical dissent. As such it answered in one way to the state of affairs Locke noted when he suggested that 'the fantatiques, taken all together,' were 'numerous, and possibly more than the hearty friends of the state-religion'.[26] The majority in the Commons favouring such penalties were often narrow. In this context those who wished for another line towards dissent, whether of comprehension or toleration, could take heart. There were conferences between leading dissenters and churchmen in 1667 and 1668. The Conventicle Act expired when the parliamentary session of 1667 ended. It might seem worthwhile to write an essay advocating toleration on the narrow margins of the Commons' majority.[27]

For the dismissal of Clarendon, who had been the effective head of the administration, from his post of Lord Chancellor at end the end of August, 1667, seemed to open a new scene in politics. In the broadest sense Clarendon was the scapegoat for the series of disasters, natural and political, which had troubled the English government from 1665. Ignominious failure in the naval war against the Dutch complemented the Plague and the Great Fire of London. More especially his fall touched ecclesiastical politics. Though Clarendon had not been the most enthusiastic proponent of the penal code against dissent, he had become identified with it. Moreover, to settle the question of church and state might seem a fitting remedy for God's evident displeasure against England. At the same time the episcopate was not at the height of its popularity. In July 1667 a cousin of Pepys reported as 'a thing certain, that the Archbishop of Canterbury. . .doth keep a wench', whilst the bishop of Rochester was said to be 'given to boys'. By December Pepys observed that 'everybody is encouraged nowadays to speak and even print. . .as bad things' against the bishops 'as ever in the year 1640, which is a strange change'.[28] The time might seem ripe for another change.

The practical target of Locke's 'Essay' was the Anglican policy of imposing uniformity of worship on the other denominations on pain of civil sanctions. It identified the Anglican sufferers 'in the late times' as the present proponents of intolerance ('now soe forward to try it upon others')[29] and opposed their pressure for uniformity. Locke suggested that to go in that direction would unsettle civil peace, adducing the example of inability of moderate sanctions to contain 'puritans', arguing that intolerance failed to deal with 'the growth of puritans' before the civil war.[30]

But to what political end would this advocacy answer? The expression of a conviction, however firmly held or long meditated, occurs at a specific juncture and, as such, can answer to a particular aim. Locke's declared intention was 'to secure the safety and peace' of the realm. The threat to peace came partly from foreign inroads and partly from insurrection at home. Locke aimed to win dissent to the state 'both to secure it from disturbance at home and defende it against invasions from abroad'. The domestic troubles alluded to the rising of the Scottish Presbyterians, irked by the re-imposition of episcopalianism, which had culminated in the battle of Rullion Green on 28 November of the previous year. The fear of invasion would refer naturally enough to the incursions of the Dutch fleet into the Medway. But its general sense applied to the Dutch chiefly in retrospect. Peace was concluded with them in July, 1667. In 1667-8 the French invaded the United Provinces and so in prospect succeeded the Dutch as England's rival in the narrow seas. England was soon to join with the United Provinces in the Triple Alliance against France. Moreover Locke's strictures on the double loyalty of Roman Catholics would fit the view that France, rather than the United Provinces, was the more likely enemy, not least in view of the evident unpopularity of English Catholics in 1666.[31]

But though the piece criticised the imposition of uniformity, it did not attempt to undermine the existing institutional position of the Anglican body or any other denomination. It was written from within the former, for 'us' and 'our church'[32] referred clearly to the Church of England. Toleration was urged as a policy aimed at securing a common end: 'it is agreed on all hands that it is necessary the fantatique should be made usefull and assisting'.[33] There was nothing unfriendly in the essay to either unity without unformity or to the claims of the Church of England generally; but, at the same time, the essay did not reflect the church order of either Presbyterian or Independent. In fact it neither attacked nor advanced the claims of any Protestant denomination.

The essay was quite compatible with the Royal Supremacy. For though the trust of the civil magistrate was conceived in terms of civil society, there are no grounds for supposing that he may not have another capacity, standing on a different foundation. Its policy did not question the Supremacy. It considered the practical question before England as about safety, peace and welfare 'this one question in the whole matter'; and its phrase, 'whether toleration or imposition be the readiest way'[34] suggests a concern for the fortunes of the state rather than any church. On the basis of his principles Locke recommended a policy to authority and, indeed, one not unfriendly to non-Christian believers.[35] The very word *toleration*, after all, would be understood to relate in a political context to the magistrate's policy.[36]

Though Locke's view of the religious function of the state was clear, he developed *explicitly* no argument about the nature of the church in this essay. The status of his essay as a document about policy would have made an explanation of that point inappropriate. At a later juncture, when the author's practical posture was different, the view of the church implicit here would be made explicit. Principles are not the same as policies, and the needs of the latter may shade and colour the articulation or the development of the former.

To put the matter another way the principles of 1667 were compatible with a variety of practical policies other than the one Locke advanced at that date. Indeed in 1667 his intellectual trajectory suggested a focus of concern that differed from those of some other writers. We may say that Locke participated in the contemporary debate on toleration only to transcend it. For whilst the practical application of his views to the particulars of the day is clear, he pursued a different theoretical goal from the disputants in the controversy of 1667–8.[37] The most prominent of these argued in terms he had passed by, concerning the indulgence of conscience by a Christian state and the truth of ecclesiastical claims.

The state of the question was that penal legislation had helped to assert Anglican supremacy but had not disposed of the other denominations. The staple of the dispute was not church unity but church uniformity. There was agreement amongst Anglicans, Presbyterians and Independents about doctrinal articles and most marks of the church, but disagreement about church discipline and ceremonies. To this condition there were two possible responses, either that the penal legislation should be continued and perhaps strengthened or that because the differences were about the form of worship rather than its substance, it should be removed and arrangements made to accommodate and conciliate dissent. The latter school took the initiative in 1667.[38]

The tale of the 1667 attempt at comprehension and toleration is found on a flyleaf in the Bodleian Library. One of Thomas Barlow's collection of pamphlets[39] has a note to the effect that the Presbyterians heard in October, 1667 or a little earlier[40], that there would be a comprehension bill, that to prepare for it *A Proposition for ye safety and Happiness of ye King and Kingdome* would be published and that when the Commons met after Christmas there would be a toleration bill on the lines of the Declaration of Breda.[41]

In the event the comprehension bill was never presented, though it was meant for 10 October, 1667, for its parliamentary spokesman, Colonel John Birch, lost courage. There was a further plan. After the first proposal failed in this matter conferences between John Wilkins, a bishop friendly to comprehension, and a representative of Lord Keeper Bridgeman, on the government side, with Baxter and others from the Presbyterian party devised proposals to relax the rigidity of the Anglican liturgy into a form more acceptable to the Presbyterians. In particular Wilkins proposed that kneeling for the sacrament, the use of the cross in baptism and bowing at the name of Jesus in parochial churches should be 'left indifferent or. . .taken away'. A scheme for readmitting Presbyterian ministers to the Church of England without submitting to episcopal reordination (a sore point, as it implied the insufficiency of Presbyterian orders) came from the pen of Sir Matthew Hale.[42]

The proposals were accompanied by a flurry of pamphlet literature, which in effect was addressed to the parliament which would meet in November 1667. First amongst these was John Humfrey's *Proposition* which argued for comprehension of those who agreed doctrinally with Anglicanism and more widely for indulgence. It was by no means the last, but whatever their differences most of the pamphlets either make or assume certain common points.

The pamphlets embodied the view that church unity was desirable because the question of ecclesiastical truth was involved. Humfrey argued for the unity of 'the sober Protestant', urging comprehension ('Accommodation') for those 'that are sober in their principles, and Indulgence towards others who are so in their lives'. Tomkins, who answered him, assumed that 'our Antient Unity' was the goal and argued that force was applicable to prevent the spread of error.[43]

They assumed too that the state was Christian. This carried with it the consequence that ecclesiastical questions necessarily affected civil peace. So when Corbet asserted that England rested on Protestant worship, Perrinchief could argue that dissenters 'vex the *State* also, which being Christian, cannot be safe where the Church is in a Tempest'.[44] Whilst the proponents of uniformity argued that toleration or comprehension implied the disunity of faction and civil disorder – according to Perrinchief a standing army would be necessary to repress the tumults toleration would bring – the dissenters asserted on the contrary that the attempt to assert uniformity would cause ecclesiastical difficulties implying civil division.[45]

Both views assumed that worship was the business of a Christian state, but differed over the means to unity and civil peace. But their practical incompatibility at this level was paralleled by the assertion of different principles at another. The demand for uniformity assumed that in practice a little pressure would cause dissenters to reenter the Anglican fold. 'We do verily believe,' Tomkins asserted, 'That Uniformity if it were carefully maintained, and diligently looked after, would in a few years recall our Ancient Unity.' The other side naturally met this by arguing that peoples' views were not under their own control. As John Owen put it, 'Mens *apprehensions*. . .are not absolutely under *their own power*, or depend *on the liberty of their wills*.' To this the Anglican argument had no particular answer, but neither had the

122

dissenters to the reply that this ground for indulgence would accommodate Roman Catholics.[46]

The debate, then, was essentially irresolvable because of a critical difficulty which meant that the agreed goal of unity could not be translated into an ecumenical programme for uniformity. Everyone agreed about unity but for just that reason their attention focussed on uniformity, where agreement was unlikely. Anglicans equated, dissenters wished to distinguish the two. The assumption that a question of truth was involved made it difficult to come to terms. This was reflected in the common vagueness about how religious belief affected public order. The result was that the demands of uniformity and those of conscience could not be easily reconciled.[47] In short the problem which presented itself to Locke was left fundamentally untouched by the pamphleteering.

It was, however, possible to address the problem along other lines – by drawing limits, as Locke said. He had claimed that the inclusive claims of parties 'without assigning. . .or shewing boundaries'[48] were the cause of disputes. Locke was able to draw a limit, for the relation of religious belief and political conduct was obviously an example of the relations between belief and practice. As we have seen Locke argued that religious matters were not the magistrate's business unless they trenched on civil relations: and thus he found a limit. But to turn this argument into a resolution of the problem implied ignoring questions about truth and the nature of the church.

The situation of some other writers would have been easier had they adopted Locke's arguments. The view of Bagshawe and Corbet that the magistrate could impose in things indifferent but should not for the sake of their consciences would have been eased. Owen's views about toleration would have been placed on a firmer footing. But ease would have been purchased at a price. The Presbyterians' preference for uniformity (in a style they liked) would have been undermined and the Independents' view that church government should reside primarily in the hands of individual congregations might both have suffered.[49]

In general, Locke's position developed an argument which was distinct from his contemporaries' but which took account of their views, whether by incorporating or by answering them. Indeed neither these elements nor the practical concern for toleration were new.[50] It was Locke's *argument* which innovated in the situation of 1667.

Locke's essay thus participated in the debate only to transcend its terms. It does, however, bear a mark of its period in its loudly expressed distrust of Roman Catholics. This was necessary to free toleration from the canard of papal subversion. In a frame of mind

123

which valued unity as a component of order, disunity might suggest anarchy and weakness.[51] Locke laboured to avoid this supposition by suggesting that the state would benefit from toleration. But he had to do more: he had to show that the disunity of Protestants was not an opening for papal subversion.

It is worth contrasting Locke's theoretical posture and political opportunism towards a religious group, whom he took to be incompatible with civil society, with his view of groups who could be accommodated to it. Locke's ground for distrusting Roman Catholics, torn between the papacy and their king, was matched by a sense that they might be of little use for his project of peace. Their attributed infidelity to the government was used as a ground for non-toleration. Locke recommended severe penalties to diminish their numbers as not only legitimate but also, it so happened, unlikely to induce the public sympathy which he thought suffering in a religious cause would win in other instances. Added to which he thought that Rome won its converts not by proper persuasion but by adventitious means ('the art and industry of their clergy') and would suffer if these were removed. And, of course, the spectacle of anti-popery would bond the Protestants together and so to 'the king of England, as head of the protestants'. The case was different with dissenters. Locke supposed that soft treatment would conciliate them to the civil government, where harshness would be alienating. Hence he recommended toleration to the magistrate as 'a foundation whereon to establish the peace and quiet of his people'.[52]

IV

The 'Essay' presented a basic position, just as Locke's lectures on natural law had. Whether anything would be constructed upon it, still more what it might be, was obscure. For instance its indefinite view of policy was compatible with several courses of action. It set out principles of toleration, but Locke countenanced in passing a policy of comprehension too. It was unspecific about the source of whatever benefit was to be conferred, whether from the King or from his parliament. It was rather vague on what was comprised in the idea of a church, except negatively.

The 'Essay', however, suggests rather more definitely the lineaments of a theory of the state, because its argument was evidently incompatible with absolutism. An absolute ruler, as we have seen in looking at Hobbes, was one not responsible to his or her subjects, and one who enjoyed authority unrestricted in degree and subject matter. To restrict the magistrate's authority to certain purposes of civil reference and to exclude him *as such* from ecclesiastical affairs was obviously inconsistent with absolutism. Absolutism did not accord with Locke's idea that government was meant only for specific ends ('for no other purpose').[53] If this were not enough, Locke made his dissent from absolutism plain for those who cared to look. He thought the magistrate different from other men in small and accidental ways – he and 'his fellow-men, between whom and himselfe, in respect of the King of kings, there is but a small and accidentall difference'.[54] From here to his later view that 'absolute monarchs are but men' is a short step and (as we shall see in chapter 6) is one that undercuts the key assumptions of some absolutist views.[55] By 1667, of course, Locke had already distanced himself from one of the principal explanations of absolutism. To bind people firmly to God's direction made it difficult to think that they were free to bind themselves unconditionally to another superior. This would be admissible only if the purposes of God and magistrate coincided, a precarious condition. But to insulate Locke's views on toleration was not to encourage this connection.

Locke's view of toleration, then, implied a civil magistrate who was not absolute in the sense of having all matters, including ecclesiastical ones, under his authority. We should register the point that this is a limitation of *kind* only, and that there is no question of responsibility to the governed present at this stage of Locke's life. though a mention of Magna Carta may sound a different note[56]. But whilst there is no hint that civil government is in any way answerable to the citizen, clearly the burden of proof has changed. Where in 1660 the advocates of responsible government had been invited to produce their credentials, now in 1667 the theorists of absolutism were required to prove their case.

Locke's views as they stand here, though clear in their direction, were not fully worked out. His position about limited government was not explained at length just as no argument at all was offered for his view of the civil magistrate's function. Thus the internal foundations of his views had not been made good. The nature of the royal supremacy was not examined explicitly. The nature of the church remained to be considered, having been treated only by implication[57].

In particular it is questionable whether Locke had clearly worked out the juridical basis of his views about toleration. His understanding of the term 'right', as in 'right to toleration' seems to have conformed to a current model rather than to reflect special thought. The root meaning of the term in contemporary thought implied the possession of a means of acting – whether called power, faculty or aptitude.[58] To

125

act, of course, is to admit the possibility of encountering restriction, and the complement of this view was to suggest that a right subsisted where there was no prohibition, whether civil or divine, against action.[59] Locke continued this usage. He understood right as a power in the agent ('choice of the mind').[60] This was consistent with an area not touched by legislation, for Locke wrote of right as a 'perfect uncontrollable liberty' to act without 'any sin at all'.[61].

Arguably a more astringent view of right would be needed to make good Locke's purpose. For the magistrate's inability to abridge the right to free worship involved an unargued view of magisterial authority. Locke was here rather distant from the *Treatises'* view of right as an authority to execute God's purposes: but then the notion that it would be necessary to oppose God and the devices of government was not so important for Locke in 1667 as it would be in the future.

In the same way the implications of Locke's views were not explored. Apart from Locke's evident distance from absolutism very little can be discovered definitely about his views on political organisation. Certainly he made no attempt to explain his view of the magistrate's function or to show why absolutism was impossible. In short the conceptual validity of Locke's basic views had not been made clear, for the nature of civil magistracy and the church had not been explored.

This is hardly surprising given Locke's objectives. It was not necessary for his case to show just how magistracy was limited to certain ends or why absolutism was impossible. It is possible that the government of the day (of which Locke's patron was a member) might provide the article he wanted. In that situation theoretical clarity on these wider issues might have been uncomfortable. Over the next decade or so the situation would change, and Locke would deny not only an unrestricted scope to civil authority but also restrict the degree of power that authority could enjoy.

Thus Locke's position of 1667 on toleration involved, without explicitly arguing, a wider view of political theory. That its implications came to be developed clearly was not least due to the subsequent trajectory of English politics and of our author. His orientation, however, was clear enough. He had formulated an intellectually coherent position and had clarified his vision.

Chapter 5

Locke's *Essays* supposed that natural law and God's existence could be known, that is to say apprehended with certainty. These suppositions were matched by a view that the human understanding obtained knowledge through the exercise of reason on the data of sense. It is perhaps natural to suppose that these tenets proceed directly to *An Essay concerning Human Understanding*. In a sense this is obviously true, but in another not less significantly misleading.[1] Whilst Locke continued the type of view he had held in his *Essays*, and continued also to treat God as explanatory, his situation in 1671 helped him to develop his views in specific ways. The treatment of the understanding in Locke's *Essays* was an incident in a larger campaign and a distinct stimulus would be needed to develop it in its own right. Locke's earliest extended writings on the human understanding developed in a way that reflected his more general interests and developed too in the face of controversy. This controversy required that Locke should explain matters in a theologically respectable manner. He chose a manner that reflected his view of social life and had implications of special interest for his politics.

Locke's concern with political affairs had ensured that he should write about morality primarily in terms of natural law (though this implies no disbelief in authentic revelation). Natural law, as such, contained a sense of the need to worship God and, turning to terrestrial concerns, to attend to the preservation of the agent, and rules and institutional means conducive to that end. Its components, however, were likely to put people in mind of a more general project of human flourishing. For example, the notion not merely of living but of living well might suggest itself, as to one who remarked that 'the end for which men enter into society, is not barely to live. . .as other Animals: but to live happily; and a Life answerable to the dignity and excellency of their kind'.[2] Again, Christian ethics required people to look not just to their own preservation but to that of others. These, of course, are very general indications and it is right to ask about the forms they took in Locke's mind. These were three: ethics, political economy and natural science, especially medicine.

Fundamental to Locke's political economy was the assumption that the national wealth depended on population size or, more precisely, on the effective employment of the population. In 1667 he specified without troubling to argue that 'upon the number and industry of your people. . .depends the power and riches of the kingdome'.[3] This position was natural enough in an economy which, though characterised by commerce and manufacture, was not highly mechanised. The number of hands turned to an occupation was a basic determinant of its productivity. In this situation it was natural to understand power and riches in terms of 'numbers of men'.[4] Hence followed the preoccupation with population, so that we find that Locke later recommended easy terms of naturalisation by arguing that 'naturalization is the shortest and easiest way of increaseing your people'.[5] This concern with increasing the numbers of mankind would be central also to his *Treatises*, albeit with a different explanatory purpose in mind.

By the same token people had to be set to work. This meant in part exalting the usefulness of work and castigating idleness. Locke had associated idleness and poverty from his earliest jotting in his 1661 Commonplace Book. He would assume that 'Sobriety, Frugality, and Industry' brought 'daily Increase, to the growing Wealth of the Kingdom'.[6] He eventually brought industriousness under God's aegis, remarking that the need to work evidenced God's goodness, in that corporeal labour fortified the body.[7] This led easily to the conclusion that virtue and industriousness were correlated, 'virtue and industry being as constant companions on the one side as vice and idleness are on the other'.[8]

In part setting people to work involved the direction of labour to appropriate ends. The enduring difficulty was the secular decline of the woollen industries in the face of continental competition. Amongst the responses to these was the development of colonies. For if it had become difficult to export woollens to the continent, trade with England's own colonies might be substituted. Colonisation formed an obvious preoccupation, and it is hardly surprising that Shaftesbury's energies were directed towards Carolina and with them Locke's.[9] Besides the woollen trade there were more localised problems.

The paradoxical combination of unemployment and a shortage of labour in the sixties was one of especial concern. The problem was perceived to lie with a shortage of money. That is to say, Locke assumed that 'a certain proportion of money [was] necessary for driveing such a proportion of trade' and that this was lacking. Money was necessary for trade as the means to pay for the factors of production and for distribution.[10] It would not be available for this purpose, Locke

128

thought, if interest rates fell. Hence his concern with the rate of interest from the later sixties, the subject of his earliest extended reflections in political economy. A parallel concern lay with developing numbers and riches, which led him to emphasize trade.[11]

It followed from all this that those who did not produce or assist trade were, economically speaking, a burden. The point was important, for the margins on which the English economy worked were believed to be narrow. Locke noted in 1671 that most people had to labour diligently in their callings in order to survive[12] and later recognised that 'the poor Labourer and Handicraftsman. . .just lives from hand to mouth'.[13] Locke praised contributors to trade, writing that master mariners were 'to be cherished and esteem'd as the most industrious and most beneficial' of England's subjects, and identified those who did not contribute, listing with social impartiality 'such as are either idle and soe do not help, as Reteiners to Gentry and beggers or which is worse hinder trade as Retailers in some degree. Multitudes of Lawyers, but above all soldiers in pay'[14] and to this catalogue he would add 'the charge of the Government'.[15] This suggests a scepticism about the expense of armies and governments (though this was never a leading theme in Locke's explanatory writings).

Locke was suspicious, too, of gambling and luxury. The former, he thought, spent money without bringing it to bear on trade,[16] whilst the latter accompanied dubious practices and discountenanced useful activity, for 'the luxury of Courts and. . .inferior Grandees found out idle and useless imployments for themselves and others subservient to their pride and vanity, and soe brought honest labour in usefull and mechanical arts wholy into disgrace'. He recommended that governments 'suppresse the arts and instruments of Luxury and Vanity'.[17] Locke had an especial sense of those who had the capacity to labour but did not exert it: these he recommended be *compelled* to be useful.[18] Locke's practical attitude to the poor reflected the significance he attributed to work. His emphasis fell on the ethics of labour: if to work was to contribute, to be idle was to retard national prosperity. Hence Locke suggested that 'the true and proper relief of the poor' lay 'in finding work for them, and taking care they do not live like drones upon the labour of others'.[19] The necessity for work was present throughout Locke's economic analysis and (as we shall see) in a different way in his account of the human understanding.

It was not merely the increase but the maintenance of life which was necessary. 'Power consists in numbers of men,' Locke wrote, 'and ability to mainteine them.'[20] At one level this pointed to a concern with creating plenty. The trajectory of Locke's career focussed his mind upon the financial infrastructure, beginning (as we have seen) in the sixties and culminating with his involvement with trade, interest rates and recoinage during the nineties. At another level it knit with Locke's prior concern with natural philosophy and medicine.

Natural philosophy could be conceived in a congruent manner, namely the discovery and development of things useful to mankind in sustaining them or making their condition more comfortable. Medicine had been a subject of keen interest at Oxford during the fifties, pursued not least by Locke's schoolfellow Richard Lower.[21] Locke himself seems to have begun to be interested at Oxford, compiling lists of remedies and taking extensive notes from Thomas Willis' medical lectures. The subject had a personal interest, for Locke's immediate family all died during his early manhood: his mother in 1654, his father in 1661 and his brother Thomas in 1663, and Thomas' child probably soon after. His brother Peter had died in infancy: Locke noted that children often predeceased their parents.[22] In an age when disease was rife and its cure or prevention uncertain, the development of an effective medicine would look especially to the prolongation of life and the cure of disease. As one might conclude 'length of life with freedom from infirmity and pain as much as the constitution of our fraile composure is capable of is of soe great concernment to man kinde, that there can scarce be found any greater undertakeing then the profession to cure diseases'.[23]

These interests of Locke's in ethics, political economy and medicine, diverse as they are, might suggest a common supposition about God's intentions, namely that He desired the survival and increase of the human race. Their increase, evidently required by political economy, corresponded to God's observation of *Genesis* 2,18 that man should not be alone. Their survival, which after all necessary to their increase being continuous, was suggested by natural law. If we speak more generally (or vaguely) of the preservation of life, we find a constant theme in Locke. Medicine we need hardly mention, but his political economy presupposed the maintenance of mankind. The preservation of life became a general purpose: Locke recommended that if anyone dependent on the poor law 'die for want of due relief' then his or her parish be fined.[24]

The frame of reference which Locke was exploring in the 1660s placed an emphasis upon the preserving of life, on prosperity and practicality, and upon the need of human activity to fulfil these. The reader may ask about the relevance of these matters to his political thought. Their relevance is mediate but pervasive. It is mediate in that these concerns related immediately to something else, namely a view of the human understanding. That they were connected to *this* by way of a sort of politics is not unimportant. More significantly the view of the human understanding Locke evolved, with its emphasis on human superiority over nature, was a central requisite of his political theory. To understand this claim we should turn to that view of the mind and, firstly, to how it came to be developed. We shall find that Locke's preceding concerns led him, under a political pressure, to develop given views about the understanding and that he gave organised form to these in terms of the character and purpose of mankind.

I

In Locke's two early drafts on the human understanding (known to posterity by the banausic and unlovely titles of *Draft A* and *Draft B*), as in his *Essays*, all knowledge was derived ultimately from sensation or the mind's operations on it. 'I imagin that all knowledg is founded on and ultimately derives it self from sense, or something analogous to it & may be called sensation', he declared.[25] This applied also to the limitations of the mind. When Locke wrote *Draft B* he indicated that the point of his enterprise was to show what knowledge we could and *could not* have, in order that our attention should be focussed for best use.[26]

This focus resulted from a programme with two emphases, one positive and one negative. Locke's theory of ideas suggested the negative view that substance was not usefully knowable, indicated the more positive conclusion that a certain knowledge of morals and God was possible and pointed to a view of faith grounded on experience

Before we investigate Locke's treatment of theory of ideas, we must consider why he took up this agenda. After all, whilst there is an agenda about the theory of ideas and about morals implicit in the primary claims of *Essays on the Law of Nature* it was not as broad as this one; and if we abstract ourselves from our retrospective knowledge that John Locke wrote *An Essay concerning Human Understanding*, there is little reason to think that prior to 1671, when he composed his *Drafts*, he was preoccupied with pursuing the epistemological issues raised by his *Essays*. His interests lay in the areas just reviewed. In order to understand the shift of his attention we should turn to how Locke's motives were worked out in his initial account of the human understanding and then to how he provided an organising principle for his account.

II

There is something very curious about the agenda which Locke set himself in his writings on the human understanding. It embraced a range of subjects which might seem to have little intrinsic connection with each other – ethics, belief, words and physical nature (especially the rejection of substance as an explanatory principle). Their seeming diversity might appear to be confirmed by the modern philosopher's suspicion that really Locke treated concurrently a set of themes which modern thought would separate sharply.[27] Locke's interests were intimately connected. The connection consists in *jointly* answering the aspects of a challenge presented to Locke's preferred treatment of ideas and a related view of procedure in science and ethics, the way of discovery.

Let us consider Locke's views firstly in his earliest statement, *Draft A*. This found its subject matter in the theory of ideas, in nature (especially material substance), in relation (including ethics), in claims to universal knowledge and in probability. Its manner of treatment was to insist that the proper method of understanding them began with sensation and reflection. How are we to explain these features?

We may identify two general aspects, namely Locke's direction and his destination. In a very general way we might have guessed the subsequent direction of the writer of *Essays on the Law of Nature*. If he took up the subject, he would be concerned to continue along his line about sense and reflection (as he was about to call it) in the theory of ideas and to emphasise human claims to knowledge of God and ethics. His reliance on the knowable as against the merely probable in his 'Essay concerning Toleration' might encourage him to say something about faith as less than certain. But this tells us nothing about the rest of his interests, still less the combination of concerns that the drafts present.

Locke's direction was determined by being a friend to a procedure that we may christen the way of discovery at a time of religious difficulty and polemical challenge. Locke had espoused the way of discovery. That is to say, he assumed that knowledge was to be gained by considering particulars in the first instance. On this basis it would be possible to make statements of wider import. This applied both to ethics and to natural philosophy, though in differing ways.

Locke argued to the moral conclusions of his *Essays* from sense data via reason to God and from God to moral laws. In other words Locke implied that it was possible to move from the particular knowledge given by sense to general knowledge. We may say 'implied' because Locke did not explain in his *Essays* how we acquired knowledge of the obligations God prescribed, though the project was clearly implied.

The traditional mode of ethics, as practised by Sanderson for example, would have taken the existence of God and his law for

132

granted and then merely specified propositions about conduct and applied them to particular cases, using syllogistic reasoning. For instance, suppose we start with the proposition that theft is to be avoided. This proposition is not unreasonable (though it may require proof from those of a demanding disposition). At any rate this proposition would form a major premise; the action under consideration provided the minor premise; and from them a conclusion would be made clear.

> Omne furtum est fugiendum.
> Hoc quod mihi faciendum proponitur est furtum,
> *Ergo* est fugiendum.[28]

Whilst not every specimen was quite so banal, scholastic reasoning about ethics was directed rather at the elaboration of distinctions than at the establishment of fundamentals. Sanderson devoted much energy to treating conscience, obligation and oaths but he took the law of nature for granted. Less distinguished practitioners, such as Brerewood, devoted themselves to classifying virtues and digesting Aristotle's ethics.[29] Locke preferred to address ethical *explanation*. He began with sense data and reasoned from them, rather in the manner of a natural philosopher beginning with observable particulars. His procedure would grow more sophisticated, but his project remained the same. His commitment was therefore to a method of proceeding.

Locke's scientific interests lay with the observation of particulars.[30] The rejections of his *Essays* may be understood in parallel terms. The rejection of claims to *universal* knowledge resting upon unargued axioms was a common theme of Locke's negations in his *Essays*: tradition, innatism, and consent alike implied ambitions to general truth which the observation of individual cases did not bear out.[31] Innate ideas especially did not fit and contrasted with Locke's plan in his *Essay* to make inferences commencing from observable particulars.

Certainly this view of procedure, whether in science or in ethics was opposed to the assumptions of inherited thought. The tenets of scholastic natural philosophy in the seventeenth century may be divided under four headings. Firstly, it assumed that science moved from the universal to the particular (just as in ethics it moved from a fact of universal importance, God's existence, and from general rules to deal with particular cases). This, secondly, reflected the view that science consisted of necessary propositions, whose consequences were to be discovered. Thirdly there was the parallel point that the order of exposition, beginning with the universal and working to the particular, corresponded to the order in which discoveries were made. All this, fourthly, required the assumption that the general was apprehensible distinctly from the particular. This was founded upon the view that substance and, more especially, substance in general could be apprehended.

The first of these views, that science should move from universals to particulars, was asserted strongly by Aristotle himself.[32] He was echoed by Magirus and Burgersdyck amongst others.[33] This position was understood usually to imply dealing initially with genera and species.[34] Turning to the second view, we find Alstead, Magirus and Timpler accepting the Aristotelian view that science consisted of a certain knowledge of things present eternally through their causes.[35] The procedure that arose from this was to begin with a definition rather than an inductive process.[36] This helps to explain the assumption that universals and 'principles' were simple and that particular things were complex.[37] This suggested, thirdly, that the proper order of *procedure* was to seek the cause before looking for its effect. Hence Keckermann's statement that the order of knowing was 'from universals to particulars. . .from cause to effects'.[38] That it was possible to think this, fourthly, depended on assuming that genera and species were more clearly apprehensible than the individuals composing them.[39] This supposed not merely that substance but substantial form was apprehsible, a supposition reflected in the view that substantial form was the intrinsic source of the properties that distinguished substances of one species from another.[40]

This programme presented certain obvious openings to those who wished to begin with particulars rather than generalities. They could fasten on its predominantly speculative focus. Sennert, one of its exponents, suggested that it was superfluous to qualify the noun science with the adjective 'speculative'.[41] To criticise this enterprise as divorced from practice and utility was in fact a commonplace of the sixties. Whilst Locke did not forget this, he cast his criticism of scholastic science at a higher level.

Locke, obviously, would find the first and the third propositions unattractive. The fourth would be a target of his writings on the understanding. The second he did not decry as an ideal, but instead dwelt on the human inability to achieve it: *An Essay concerning Human Understanding* would suggest that a knowledge of nature, 'scientific' in the sense intended, had not been attained and in fact lay beyond the bounds of human faculties. Why did Locke's approach differ from his allies'? Partly, no doubt, it was a matter of intellectual capacity. But more generally, for Locke, who had applied the way of discovery to ethics as well as to natural philosophy, an attack on its methods in either would require defence, in morality as much as science. An attack came in the late sixties.

As people had feared religious excess in the fifties, in the sixties they talked of their anxiety about religion because of threats from atheism and infidelity. Thomas Sprat, writing in his *History of the Royal Society*, noted that Christian belief had less purchase on people's minds than hitherto. 'It is apparent to all,' he wrote, 'That the influence which *Christianity* once obtain'd on mens minds, is prodigiously decay'd.'[42] In this situation a challenge to the natural philosophy that concentrated on particulars might be cast naturally as a suggestion that it undermined religion. This much was clear from attack which some had mounted on Hobbes. The literature of the period is full of the challenge of epicureanism, by which was meant (if anything) a view of things centred on sensation and sensuality to the disregard of morality and God. We find so sober a pundit as John Owen complaining in the 1650s of a licencientiousness 'nearly epicurean' at Oxford. In 1671, the year when Locke wrote at length about the understanding, John North, preaching before Charles II, complained of atheists, described Epicurus as 'the grand Master of irreligion' and asserted that he 'roundly proclaims it our best and noblest design to gratifie our sence'.[43] A challenge duly came, stimulated by the ill-regulated enthusiasm of two friends to the new science. Here we may obtain a sense of Locke's destination.

III

Sprat intended his *History* of 1667 to vindicate the experimental work in natural philosophy undertaken by the Royal Society. So in many ways it did, offering copious evidence of its ingenuity, industry and practical orientation, and reporting the Society's achievements.[44] The difficulty was not with Sprat's evidence but with the framework of thought within which he placed it. This gave an easy opening to those suspicious of such work and perhaps did much to generate suspicion. In particular Sprat's claim that experimental philosophy was congruent with religion and morality was not so much serviceable as vulnerable.

Sprat defended experimental work as *compatible* with divinity and ethics. This was not a strong claim. The scientist's experiments, he said, were not opposed to religion. The world of sense was the scientist's proper preoccupation. Sprat suggested that experiment concerned what fell under the observation of the senses. He emphasised how discoveries tended to humanity's temporal happiness. He asserted that experimental work 'establishes' natural theology by evidencing God's power, wisdom and goodness, but asserted too that because the soul and God lay beyond the senses they were not the scientist's subject. Neither was morality. Sprat stated that the scientist as such was not concerned with morality, since the concepts involved in the latter (such as will or desire) were remote from sense. The experimental life was opposed to neither natural nor revealed religion, Sprat concluded: it did nothing against them.[45]

These claims were pacific, but not well-calculated for defence. Sprat had recognised a decline in Christian conviction. The form of his claims suggested that experimental science, though compatible with theism and with Christianity specifically, did nothing to uphold them. On the other hand, his account made it not unreasonable to think that experimental science directed human attention chiefly to sense, as John Worthington noted: Sprat, he observed, seemed obsessed by 'what gratifies externall sense, or what sense doth reach'.[46] This evident preoccupation with sense was not very sensible.

This was true for several reasons. Firstly, sense figured in contemporary thought as something likely to be distinct from reason and good conduct. For sense, as distinct from reason, was the attribute which characterised beasts rather than people.[47] People, equipped as they were with reason, might be supposed to be able to resist the promptings of sense, and (assuming the validity of ethical rationalism) distinguish good from evil. Beasts, locked into the world of the senses, could not aspire to intelligent or decent conduct. Thus, for instance, we find Thomas Sydenham remarking on how his mind gave him 'Dominion. . .over my Body in repressing the Sensual appetitions thereof, which are against my reason', Thomas Starkey hoping that 'none there is so rude and beastly, but, with care and diligence, by that. . .spark of reason given of God, they may subdue their affections and follow the life to which they be institute and ordained of God' and St German concluding that 'among all Gifts that God gave to Man, this Gift of Reason is the most noblest, for thereby Man precelleth all Beasts,. . .discerning Truth from Falshood and Evil from Good'. Hence mere sense and sensuality could be associated. Sprat himself could refer to 'the stupidity and slavery of Beasts'.[48] Secondly, even putting that aside, it remained to show that 'what sense doth reach' included theology and morals: if Sprat had insisted upon their compatibility with sense data, he had not shown how they could be explained in terms of a view of things preoccupied with sensation. Just what results would be produced was doubly doubtful.

It was dubious, firstly, because Sprat's account was unhappily close to Hobbes'. Hobbes too had descanted upon the usefulness of philosophy; he had identified it with the quest 'to search out the properties of bodies'; and on that basis announced that 'it excludes

Theology' and 'the doctrine of *God's worship'*.[49] This was not a happy juxtaposition, for Hobbes' tenet that all substances were material was taken by contemporaries to imply his disbelief in God, who was usually understood to be spiritual in nature. Doubtless this reading was malevolent, but it was nonetheless inconvenient for those whose energies focussed upon sensible particulars and upon matter. Secondly, assuming that this inconvenient company could be transcended, it remained to be shown just how it was to be done.

The question of just 'what senses doth reach' could not be brushed aside. For the preoccupation with matters accessible to sense characterised the experimental approach Sprat eulogised. 'The True Philosophy', he observed, 'must be first of all begun, on a scrupulous, and severe examination of particulars.'[50] This approach, implying observation and experiment, was congenial to figures like Boyle, Sydenham, Lower and Willis, who also took religion seriously. Not only was the question intellectually significant, it was also polemically relevant, not least because Sprat developed too a polemic against scholastic work which extended beyond natural philosophy.

Sprat began by arguing that the '*Schoole-Men'* had done little of practical value: their method was 'never able to do any great good towards the enlargement of knowledge'. He made it clear later on that scholastic exercises, bracing as they might be, had drawn attention away from useful works. This was not especially conciliatory and was remarkably unfortunate. For these disputations were supposed to fit the mind to defend religious truth against its adversaries. Sprat himself knew this: 'suppose. . .that they are most usefull in the controversies of our *Church'*, he wrote, 'to defend us against the Heresies and Schisms of our times'.[51] Suppose someone else thought *that*, what would they think of Sprat? It was natural enough for those worried about religion and for the adherents of the older science to express reservations about the intellectual posture of the new science.

Meric Casaubon's *Letter. . . to Peter du Moulin* put the question sharply. It did not gainsay the useful discoveries of the new science, but insinuated that they did nothing worthwhile for mankind's spiritual life. 'I ask,' wrote Casaubon, 'what is it that these account *useful*, and *useless?'*

For if nothing must be accounted *useful* (as some seem to determine) but what doth afford some use for the necessities or conveniences of this present life; I do not know but that a Brewer, or a Baker, or a skilful Horse-leech, or a Smith, or the like, may contest in point of true worth or desert with many, who for their learning. . .have been reputed generally, the great Lights and Ornaments of their age: though such, as never medled in their writings with experimental philosophy. They that beleeve that man doth consist of two chief parts, the body and a soul, whereof the soul [is] the more noble and more considerable part. . .natural reason will oblige them to beleeve, that a greater share of care and provision doth belong to that which is immortal, from the right ordering of which all true happiness, present or future, doth depend. . .Those men therefore, who have applied themselves by their writings to promote vertue and godliness. . .were generally thought to have deserved mankind, as well (if not better) as the most renowned inventours, or promoters of useful Arts or Trades.

That the latter's discoveries were useful only for the present life was complemented by the insinuation that such preoccupations immersed people in excessively terrestrial concerns. 'Whether those men who make it their work to reclaim men from that. . .*close adherence* of the mind to the body and senses. . .to the care and culture of their souls, ought in reason to be accounted *unprofitable* to the Common-wealth; or rather, of all Professions, the most *useful* and necessary,' wondered Casaubon. Before long he insinuated that Sprat meant to supersede Christianity with a neo-Hobbesian natural religion. More critically still he suggested that to concentrate on the evidence of sense might be to forget all religion, for those 'that are fixed upon matter and secundary causes and sensual objects. . .may in time. . .and by degrees forget that there be such things in the world as *Spirits*. . .and consequently discredit *supernatural operations*: and at last, that there is a God, and that their souls are immortal'.[52] Casaubon argued that the experimental life, if not incompatible with the spiritual, concentrated on the sensible and material, encouraging neither Christianity specifically nor theism generally.

It was only one step further to suggest that the experimental life was itself positively subversive of Christianity. Richard Baxter's *Reasons of the Christian Religion* was certainly understood to say that one of Boyle's views in natural philosophy undermined Christian faith, for it 'supplanted our future Estate'. This was not a comfortable assessment from 'ye popular discoursing of a popular man'.[53] The accusation of infidelity found a complement when South suggested that experiment meant sensation and a perversion of moral judgement. Whilst Sprat had been careful to suggest that natural philosophy did not touch upon ethics, he had hoped incautiously that natural philosophy would attract those that 'relish nothing but the *pleasures* of their *senses*'. South dealt with the matter joyously, speaking of

a set of fellows got together, and formed into a kind of diabolical society, for the finding out new experiments in vice. . .and scorning to keep themselves within the common, beaten, broad way to hell. . .are for searching out other

138

ways and latitudes, and obliging posterity with unheard of inventions and discoveries in sin; resolving herein to admit of no other measure of good and evil, but by the judgement of sensuality, as those who prepare matters to their hands, allow no other measure of the philosophy and truth of things, but the sole judgement of sense

a judgement, of course, that contemporaries would be disinclined to associate with moral good.[54] Yet this was not all, for to these problems about Christianity and morals were added a political difficulty.

Casaubon suggested that the experimental temper, by emphasising agreement rather than argument, tended to neglect the art of disputation. He was not alone in this fear. Thomas Barlow expressed the same view privately.[55] The matter was politically sensitive. As Stubbe pointed out the logical toughness encouraged by the practice of disputation was meant to protect Protestantism against the insinuating wiles of Catholicism.[56] A view with more general currency was that enmities and so disunity amongst the English engendered by natural philosophy would favour the papal cause. To understand how such divisions appeared to lay England open, we must remember that it was assumed that Rome ran a perpetual plot to subvert Protestantism. It was easy to apply this assumption to a specific case. Stubbe claimed that Campanella had recommended to the King of Spain that natural science should be encouraged amongst Protestants so that the best intelligences should be distracted from opposing Romish infiltrations.[57] Hence the new science was likely to diminish the strength in disputation that Protestant England needed to resist Popery.

More radically still, it was alleged that all theism was under threat. The new science undermined Aristotle, Stubbe suggested, whose *Ethics* were 'subservient to *Religion*'.[58] Moreover, the spectacle of public argument about science tended of itself to create scepticism about all truths. Baxter referred to the corruption of the young. More loosely the experimental life might be considered atheistic in that it made no use of theistic assumptions, as in Stubbe's accusation that '*intrinsecally* those *courses* dispose mens minds afterwards to *Atheism*, or an *Indifference* in *Religion*'.[59]

There was a large element of polemical inference in all this: that is to say, it was inferred that what the new science omitted to promote it must necessarily oppose or undermine. In Stubbe's case malicious fancies generated a papal and experimental plot. But there was nothing contained here that was too implausible for the contemporary imagination, which often thought in terms of polarities: what was not intimately allied with something was supposed to be against it.[60] Locke's own favoured order of presentation reflected this mental practice. He often prefaced his own views with a criticism of some other position, presented as their diametric opposite. In *Two Tracts* the criticism of Bagshawe in the *English Tract* preceded the *Latin Tract*; in *Essays on the Law of Nature* he developed his own views in the fourth essay, prefacing it with a critique of alternatives in the third; *An Essay concerning Human Understanding* dismissed innatism before proceeding to Locke's theory of ideas and *Two Treatises* devoted a great deal of space to the criticism of Filmer before developing Locke's own views. Besides, the tenor of the charges against natural philosophy was virtually traditional: as Sir William Alexander had remarked before the civil war, 'Young Naturalists oft Atheists old doe proue'.[61] Prudentially speaking there was a case to be answered.

The trajectory of Joseph Glanvill's views illustrates a corresponding defensiveness about the new science. Glanvill had begun by emphasising the extent of human ignorance (and so undercutting the claims to universal knowledge attributed to the reigning natural philosophy): he concluded that 'all will confess' 'the weakness of humane understanding'. This judgement was encapsulated in the unfortunately drastic statement that 'we cannot conceive any thing, which comes not within the verge of our senses'.[62] This statement, not especially prudent in itself, was coupled with allegations that the peripatetics were quarrelsome and a block on useful work.[63] This was in 1661. In 1668, when Glanvill wrote his *Plus Ultra*, he was more cautious, insisting that whilst true philosophy depended on sense yet the senses were 'of themselves. . .too narrow for the *vastness* of things, and too *short* for *deep Researches*' so that they required assistance.[64] The very interesting question of whence that assistance would come was not answered, a silence that was especially problematical in the face of charges of atheism against experimentalism (of which Glanvill was well aware).[65] This work had been intended as a defence of the Royal Society, but its chief effect was to unloose the deluge of Stubbe's polemic. Glanvill's tract of 1671, significantly entitled *Philosophia Pia*, emphasised that natural philosophy gave people a sense of God and that they needed to look beyond nature (affirming besides that atheists were merely pretenders to philosophy.)[66] Indeed Glanvill argued that natural philosophy focussed the mind upon religion and that philosophy helped to establish religion, praising Boyle and others for their efforts in proving the truth of Christianity.[67] This loud emphasis on theological respectability was matched by a retraction about sense. Glanvill dwelt upon the certainty about God provided through innate knowledge.[68] The trajectory is clear, if embarrassing enough.

The vulnerability of Sprat and Glanvill suggested that a more intelligent argument was needed. The need had not been fully met by 1671, though there was a hint of a fruitful line. Boyle had developed a strategy about nature itself, though in so doing he had said little of morality or theology.

Boyle, in effect, identified a problem. If it is necessary to label this, we may call it neo-Hobbesian or epicurean. Whatever we call it, its character identified all mechanical explanation with the atomists and materialists who claimed to have given an explanation of nature's events: an explanation which involved no reference to God but which was conducted merely through matter and motion. In other words, it was an explanation that emphasised the physical and omitted the spiritual. To distance oneself from such a position would obviously be prudent (not to say congenial after Boyle's brush with Hobbes over the air pump). Its prudence was clear even before Casaubon had commented upon 'those admirable Works of the Creation, which many now. . .taught by *Epicurus* and his mates, are apt to despise and vilifie, as being the works not of a wise *God*, but blinde *atoms*', and before Glanvil found copy in praising Boyle for using '*Philosophick Reason*' as the means by which 'he infinitely shames, and disproves the Follies of the *Epicurean Atheist*'.[69]

The obvious response to 'materialist' claims lay in insisting on two connected points: firstly, that our explanations of nature were not complete and, secondly, that one component in a valid explanation was God. The latter point was triply useful, for He was needed by the corpuscular hypothesis, but was ignored by the peripatetics as much as by epicureans. Boyle developed these themes concisely in his 'Essay . . .concerning Those that would Exclude the Deity from Intermeddling with Matter' of 1663. Boyle confessed ignorance of nature (for instance, of 'the true nature and adequate cause of gravity'), asserted that it would be difficult to understand 'without acknowledging an intelligent Author or Disposer of things', suggested that there was purposive design in nature which would be hard to explain by mere atomism and sneered at the 'Epicureans, who tell us they cannot frame a notion of an incorporeal substance or spirit' and announced that 'I ignore not[,] that not only Leucippus, Epicurus, and other *atomists* of old, but of late some persons for the most part adorers of *Aristotle's* writings, have pretended to be able to explicate the first *beginning of things*, and the world's *phenomena*, without taking in or acknowledging any divine Author of it'.[70] Boyle amplified these views in *Some Considerations*, which again attacked epicureans, atomists, peripatetics and materialists, who were said to have offered a complete explanation of nature without reference to God.[71] Subsequently Boyle would insist that nature depended upon God, for the laws of physical nature were expressions of His will.

The general form of Boyle's case suggested two further points. One was to indicate that the way of discovery, unlike peripatetic accounts, required direct reference to the deity. This we may refer to a mechanical style of explanation, since motion was explained there not by substance of a thing (as the peripatetics had said) but by impact – a feature which might be referred directly to God.[72] A helpful way of emphasising this point, faced with the inherited view that substance was the fundamental reality, was to insist that though substance was fundamental it was virtually unknowable. At the same time this ignorance pointed to the very limited knowledge we have of nature. The evisceration of substance as an explanatory category would be a helpful operation.

Locke's own views seem to have moved on a parallel trajectory in the later sixties. His *Essays* reveal him as a mechanist (and perhaps a corpusculiarian). There is no sign that he deviated from mechanism.[73] As he became a respectful member of Boyle's circle, he continued to regard the corpuscular hypothesis as the most probable explanation of the nature of atoms.[74] The *Drafts* were peppered with references which bespeak these allegiances.[75]

Mechanical explanation had failed to provide certainty or even many useful practical results. Locke's own practical interest in medicine provided him with a way of earning a living, whether by staying at Christ Church as a medical Student or by practice. But the success of his medical practice seems to have been due to native talent and practical experience rather than the deliveries of theory. His ability to deal with Shaftesbury's abcess was 'empiric', consisting in a steady hand with a knife and the commonsensical view that an abscess should be drained. Throughout Locke's medical career, he noted down remedies regardless of source. The successes of grander methods was not marked. At the theoretical level Thomas Willis' lectures on medicine, from which Locke took careful notes, failed to integrate observation and experiment with a conceptual framework, resorting for explanation either to conjecture or to the older assumptions of galenic medicine. Practical success was elusive. Both galenic and more modern remedies alike failed to save Locke's father. Less personal but no less obvious were the shortcomings of respiratory experiments on animals and the leaks in Boyle's air pump.[76]

In 1666 Locke met Shaftesbury and thereafter resided in his household in London as well as at Christ Church. The move was symbolic not merely for his future concerns but also for the treatment of at least one standing interest. Locke's view of our limited grasp of nature may have owed something to Thomas Sydenham. Sydenham's papers include assertions that earlier practitioners of medicine had been preoccupied with 'hidden causes' and 'principles'. Rather, he argued, the natural philosopher was ignorant of the working constitution of bodies: thus of the human body, 'he cannot possibly know' the 'organicall constitution' of the human body 'and that texture whereby it operates'.[77] Anatomy, rather, was concerned with sensible particulars rather than insensible ones.[78] The physician's concern lay with the 'outer husk of things' rather than the 'abyss of cause'.[79] Some of the writings in which these observations occur are in Locke's hand, so that it is not perfectly clear who was their author. But it is certain that in later life Locke reiterated this view of limited knowledge. It was evidently hard to know the character of life, he wrote,

Philosophers are at a loss about it after their most diligent enquiries; And Anatomists, after their whole Lives and Studies spent in Dissections, and diligent examining the Bodies of Men, confess their Ignorance in the Structure and Use of many parts of Mans Body, and in that Operation wherein Life consists in the whole.

Thus the earlier view of the limits of human knowledge evidently persisted.[80]

That there is a broad similarity between Boyle's position about natural philosophy and Locke's is clear. They concurred in giving a relatively low estimate of the adequacy of natural philosophy. But in order to understand Locke's direction exactly we need to go further. There was a gap to be filled in defence of natural philosophy, as we have seen. Since Locke had applied the way of discovery to ethics (and therewith to theology) also, the defence would have to be broad. In any case the insinuations of Casaubon and others applied as much to the ethical and theological adumbrations of natural philosophy as to its scientific credentials. There was needed a comprehensive vindication of Locke's interests from the charges levelled against sensation and the new science.

Unlike Sprat and Glanvill, Locke did not content himself with an apologia or a defence. Instead he purposed to remake the conceptual map in a way that gave his preferred views a central place. His prime need was to show how all the ideas anyone required, whether for morality or religion, could be made out from sense (to which he added reflection). He would need to show that the assumptions involved were not in fact divisive; that they rather tended to unravel perplexities; that on the other hand disputation was merely fruitless and traditional claims about procedure and about substance were misleading; and,

143

more pointedly, to establish that sense and reflection were the means to assert morality and a distinctly Protestant faith.

Locke's first draft undertakes these functions. It takes the controverted item *sense* and shows how it leads to morality and faith; that divisions are caused by quite another source; and indicates that a useful acquaintance with substance was hard of access.[81] We can see, therefore, why Locke should be interested in a very engaged way with the human understanding.

In this light James Tyrrell's well-known gloss on Locke's subject matter becomes clear, where otherwise it has been obscure. When Locke published *An Essay concerning Human Understanding* he included in 'The Epistle to the Reader' an account of how he began to write the book. This, he wrote, commenced when he and some friends '*discoursing on a Subject very remote from this*' found themselves perplexed, so that Locke decided that '*it was necessary to examine our own Abilities, and see, what Objects our Understandings were, or were not fitted to deal with*'. Tyrrell glossed the subject as morality and revealed religion. In the context of 1671, it is easy to see how a discussion of those subjects would lead Locke to treat the understanding and to do so in the manner that he did. To establish morality and revelation in terms of a theory of ideas was important in vindicating the intellectual respectability of the way of discovery.[82]

Locke's primary task was to show that in one direction the way of discovery would conduct us to knowledge: but in another, we would find ourselves largely ignorant. In the former his business was to demonstrate how sense, which was the mark of the way of discovery, would lead the discoverer beyond the presentiments of the terrestrial world. It would lead, specifically, to morality and to faith. By the way, since the senses were also the instruments of scientific discovery, it would be relevant to insist on the ignorance about substance in which they left us. This emphasis at once both vindicated the way of discovery from charges of presumptuous completeness and undercut peripatetic *scientia*.

Draft A proceeded directly to set out the foundations of these views. In the space of its first four sections, it had asserted that our ideas of substance were limited and that our ideas of relations (which included morality) were much greater. The key supposition for all these aspects was that 'all knowledg is founded on and ultimately derives its self from sense, or something analogous to it & may be cald sensation' which provided the mind, being 'conversant about particular objects', with 'simple Ideas or Images of things'.[83] This doctrine suggested that the understanding would be acquainted with the external features of things rather than anything more profound. Substance was presumed rather than properly known, for 'the senses by frequent conversation with certain objects finde that a certaine number of. . .simple Ideas goe constantly togeather which therefor the understanding takes to belong to one thing'.[84] It followed too that whilst this approach did not suggest a thorough knowledge of spirit, it implied an equally slight acquaintance with matter: 'the Idea of matter', Locke wrote, 'is as remote from our understanding & apprehensions as that of spirit',[85] so that the accusation that sense meant materialism was neatly turned.

So far the accent lay upon human ignorance. But if we move from substance to relations the picture was more optimistic. Relation denoted the 'compareing & considering' of things (loosely so called) with each other. This, Locke thought, gave rise to conceptions that were easier to denominate and describe than ones connected with substance.[86] He picked out one sort of relation especially, the idea 'which the minde hath which is of the rectitude of actions which is noething but the relation or conformity of the actions of men to some rule'. Whilst Locke supposed that delimiting ideas of 'the rectitude of actions' would not be easy, he did think that all the ideas involved in such a relation were accessible to the understanding.[87] This thought, of course, concerned ideas and did not imply knowledge. But from 1671 onwards Locke worked steadily at both.

The ideas involved in morality as he had understood it in his *Essays* included those of rule, obligation and God, to which Locke now added action. The idea of a rule was to hand, action would be conceptualised in terms of mixed modes from 1681, the idea of God was presented in *Draft A* itself. Obligation was considered in 1678.[88] Knowledge of these matters was a more subtle affair. Since God was assumed to be a substance (albeit a spiritual one) it might be supposed that His nature would be hard to apprehend: in these *Drafts* it was asserted that God might be known with greater certainty than even that of sense[89] and in his *Essay* Locke would argue that His being could be understood by inference from His works. A knowledge of mixed modes (which conceptualized actions) too was supposed possible by the terms of the view of knowledge Locke advanced. As we shall see, to know that God had in fact set obligations to mankind would prove more difficult. At any rate in both of these first *Drafts* Locke insisted that true morality lay in a knowledge of God's laws.[90] Some of these developments as yet lay in the future. But from 1671 the direction of Locke's concerns was evident.

His orientation suggested that relation, especially morality, as well as God, could be apprehended clearly and that substance could not.

145

That *Draft A* began with this combination of concerns betokened its high interest to Locke (not least because his presentation was headlong). *Draft B*, though organised more smoothly, maintained the same positions. Thus, speaking generally, human attention was directed to ethics and away from a complete science of nature as envisaged by the peripatetics.[91] More particularly a view of things which began with sense carried out on Locke's lines would look valid morally and theologically.[92]

The disposal of substance as a working item in explanation was complemented by two other blows at the peripatetics. These affected disputation and claims to universal knowledge. The content of the former consisted mostly in syllogistic reasoning. Locke himself seems to have found this tedious when an undergraduate and a young don. Predisposition and present need encouraged him to suggest that most of the disputes were about nothing. He referred this problem, appropriately enough, to the difficulties of identifying and naming natural substances properly. He deprecated the syllogism as a means of discovering the truth, for it might seem a rival to the way of discovery. In short the disputation to which the new science was said to be unfriendly appeared to be less a burnished weapon in dialectical conflict than a dubious item of impedimenta.[93]

Claims to universal knowledge had to be met with scepticism (if they could not be shown to derive from the particulars of sense from which Locke wished to begin). Hence, as he stated early in *Draft A*, 'we have noe knowledg of generall things' and the universals the mind manufactured were 'generall words'.[94] This claim was matched by Locke's vocal suspicion of the principles from which attributed claims to certainty often began. These, he thought, were usually untruths fostered by unavowable bias. By contrast, as we shall see, the truths derived from sense and reflection emerged in Locke's view as perspicuous and certain.

Why was certainty needed in knowledge? Locke had to work from sense and reflection: he wished to arrive at morality. Sense was often supposed to be deceptive, as by Hobbes, so that Locke would do well to show that, on the contrary, it was a means to certainty. Granted the need to vindicate the moral and theological credentials of the way of discovery, morals and, correspondingly, the existence of God were obvious candidates for the status of certain truths, not least in the face of fear about atheism and licentiousness.[95]

To produce a *demonstrative* knowledge of ethics had an especial attraction for Locke. In his *Essays* he had claimed that morality could be known with certainty. A demonstrative knowledge was understood

146

by contemporaries to be certain. Baxter, for instance, wrote of 'demonstrative evidence' from prophecy and tradition for Christ's mission. Others were less optimistic. It was understood by those who followed Grotius that mathematical knowledge was demonstrative, that ethics were a matter merely of 'moral certainty' and that reported matters of fact were the subject of credible testimony. A like view was attributed by South to Aristotle, who 'saies, *We are not to expect Demonstrations in Ethicks or Politicks*'. No doubt it was especially attractive to attribute certainty to ethics because preceding thinkers had claimed less and, for a like reason, to claim a certain knowledge of the existence of God. Moreover those who wrote of certainty often did so in a way that Locke found unattractive. Pufendorf's conception of demonstration was merely syllogistic, as was Hobbes'.[96]

The aspiration of treating ethics demonstratively suggested the complementary ambition of applying relation to a wide range of human conduct. Accordingly Locke conceived relation to embrace not only natural relations (as father and son), but also relations instituted by human invention. This breadth of subject matter contrasts interestingly with an earlier treatment. Sanderson had exemplified the idea of relation only with examples drawn from natural relations.[97].

To treat morality thus, left our knowledge of nature in a position of emphasised weakness. Where Bacon had taken over the peripatetic *ideal* of explanation through causes (including substance)[98], to be sceptical of substance's utility in speculation might help to vindicate the theological respectability of another approach. Substance was the obvious medium of explanation to provide universal knowledge: so, if you forego substance your knowledge would not be universal. We have seen why Boyle found it valuable to emphasise human ignorance. More aggressively the completeness of peripatetic and 'epicurean' views of nature could be represented as aspects of atheism. In general if an explanation were complete it left no role for God: we find Tillotson asserting that atheists could turn Aristotle's teachings to their own ends just as much as Epicurus', whilst Henry More had treated epicureanism and Aristotelianism in a similar way.[99] Like considerations applied to natural philosophy: completeness must be atheistic. Tillotson averred that a 'perfect knowledge of Nature is no where to be found but in the Author of it' and Samuel Parker asserted that natural philosophers could know only what came through 'Observations and Experiments' for 'it was never intended that meer Essences should be the objects of our Faculties'.[100] It was this point that Locke exploited, on the one hand by disparaging substantial explanation and, on the other, by emphasising that morals were truly God's law.[101]

147

In a congruent manner Locke asserted that his approach was eirenic. Its certainty debarred dispute. Its unravelling of linguistic and observational problems suggested that much past wrangling had really been pointless. This pacific posture, no doubt, masked real enmities. There was one respect, however, which was more obviously aggressive. Locke's account of revelation, conduced in terms of sense, had point, or rather two points.

Locke discussed revelation in his account of probability. He had indicated that some matters might be known with certainty, including morality and the existence of God. He added that others could be known with a less degree of assurance. These probable matters, Locke insisted, were alike in that the plausibility of statements about them depended upon their resemblance to experience, whether that of ourselves or of others. Thus, like knowledge, probability could be referred ultimately to sense and reflection:

Soe that as all our owne knowledg is noe thing but our owne Experience, The foundation of all our beleife is ultimately grounded in Experience too. Soe that at last the clearest best & most certain knowledg that man kinde can possibly have of things existing without him is but Experience, which is noe thing but the Exercise & observation of his senses about particular objects. & therefor Knowledg & Faith too at least resolve them selves into & terminate some where or other on Experience either our owne or other mens

and if so Locke had vindicated the intellectual respectability of sense, of beginning with particulars and so of the way of discovery.[102]

This experiential basis for probability allowed Locke to set faith in Protestant terms. Locke assumed without argument that revelation belonged to probability rather than certainty. He divided probable matters into two categories. In one stood matters capable of observation.[103] The other concerned 'matters out of the reach of our senses' but which had plausibility in terms of propositions established from. experience.[104] Either way 'all our reasoning bottoms & rests its self wholy upon experience & humane sensation'.[105] This, of course, implies the reliability of experience and the dubiousness of what lies beyond it. What lay beyond it to the Protestant mind was the Roman Catholic position that in the eucharist the bread and wine were actually turned into the body and blood of Christ. Locke was not slow to point the moral, writing of a Catholic 'prepard easily to swallow not only against all probability but even the clear evidence of his senses the doctrine of transubstantiation, & will believe that to be flesh which he sees to be bread'. In a like manner, by treating faith as probable Locke tended to undercut papal claims to infallibility.[106] The Protestant respectability of the way of discovery was evident.

Thus Locke's *Drafts* vindicated the way of discovery in terms of its moral and theological standing, as well as of its scientific implications. On these terms Locke and his like would be exempt from Baxter's canard about 'the *Atheistical Sensualists* of this age'.[107] How far Locke's mode of defence reflected his own religious sensibility, beyond an obvious adherence to natural theology, is unclear. It may be worth noting that where a previous writer had likened salvation to the relish of a pineapple, Locke used that fruit to illustrate a point about experience:[108] but the agenda he developed was important. For Locke gave a high place to establishing with certainty the sort of ethical explanation developed in his *Essays*. This approach would eventually encounter a problem, a problem which by that stage was integral to the bases of his mature political theory. In 1671, of course, *Two Treatises* lay in the future. But *Draft B* especially contained features that were important to its make up. To these we should turn now.

IV

Draft B, the more carefully ordered of the two, continued Locke's design more formally. It showed Locke, amongst other things, connecting his view of God's purposes with his theory of ideas. That is to say having decided the direction of his opinions about the human understanding in a context where God rated highly, he deployed a conception of God which vindicated that choice. That conception has important implications for his political thought.

Locke's *Essays* had affirmed that God had designed the human race for action. In *Draft B* Locke continued this line in a more specific way, God appearing as a designer who intended people to make use of their faculties. One of Locke's arguments against innate ideas was that God had equipped people with faculties which, if exerted, could discover all that they needed to apprehend. 'There is noe need of any such impressions of knowledg. . .', Locke wrote,

since he [God] hath furnishd man with such facultys that will serve him to all the ends requisite to such a being, & I doubt not to shew you that a man in the right use of his facultys may without any innate principles atteine a surer & more usefull knowledg, then he can by seekeing for or depending upon innate principles[109]

so that Locke relied upon his conception of God to suggest that sense and reflection, properly conducted, were adequate to humanity's purposes.

This reliance involves several matters. First amongst these is Locke's conception of God. The God of his *Essays* was characterised by wisdom, that is to say the ability to discern and judge. This was manifested not least in His acting with purpose.[110] Hence the way in which God had made things was a guarantee that they were adequate to the ends He intended. Conversely, it followed that what was superfluous to God's design need not be taken seriously. Thus we find Locke writing that 'I that am fully perswaded that the Infinitely great god made all things in perfect wisdome cannot satisfie my self why he should print upon the mindes of men some universall principles' *precisely because* He 'hath furnishd man with such facultys that will serve him to all the ends requisite to such a being' *without* any need for innate ideas. Locke's conception of God provided him with a license for assuming that what he located in man would be adequate.

Equally it was assumed that God would supply everything that was needed for the ends He prescribed. Locke could write, in a context of fulfilling a purpose of God's, that 'there must of necessity be a means'.[111] Hence it was incumbent upon the philosopher to show that the means he had identified were in fact adequate to the purpose attributed to God. This, of course, was not applicable only to God's design of man. Boyle, for instance, suggested that God ordered animal existence in a like way. He assumed that God intended animals to survive and to multiply. 'Since I must..refer many of the actions of irrational creatures', he wrote,

to a most wise Disposer of things, it can scarce seem strange to me that, in those particulars of which the Author intended, and it was requisite, that irrational creatures should operate so and so for their own preservation, or the propagation of their species, or the public good of the universe, their actions, being ordered by a reason transcending ours, should not only oftentimes resemble the actings of reason in us, but sometimes even surpass them

which was obviously testimony to the effectiveness of God's work as a designer, a testimony echoed by Sydenham.[112]

Secondly there is the manner in which God designed mankind. He had placed His emphasis upon the human intellect. Human beings were supposed traditionally to stand above animals, by more nearly resembling God. The resemblance was not least an intellectual one. William Ames catalogued the human resemblance to God in two ways, the inward and the outward. The inward consisted in the fitness of body and soul to adhere to God's will. For the latter he mentioned what equipped people to obey God's laws, that is to say 'those faculties by which it [the soul] was a free principle of its own actions, in understanding and will'. He went on to add 'also. . .gifts whereby man was made able to live well'.[113] This brings us to the outward way in which man resembled God.

God was superior to mankind, possessing perfections evidenced in His creating and sustaining of it. The same considerations applied to the world and its creatures, albeit in a slightly different way. God was the owner of these. Mankind resembled God in that both were understood to have dominion over nature, though mankind's (of course) was less than God's. Thus we find Ames writing that 'the externall perfection of man was his Dominion over other Creatures'. It is worth noting how the aspects of the image of God, in Ames' language the external and the internal, matched one another.

For the human superiority over animals consisted not least in intellect. We find Locke later in life contrasting 'the most excellent Part' of God's work 'our Understandings' with the condition of 'the Beast that perisheth'.[114] It was presumed that God would give the means to the end He had in mind. If mankind was to have dominion over animals, it followed that He would provide mankind with the means to control the animals. This was found in the human understanding. Thus Clarendon remarked that

When God vouchsafed to make man after his own Image and in his own Likeness, and took so much delight in him, as to give him the command and dominion over all the Inhabitants of the Earth, the Air, and the Sea, it cannot be imagin'd but that at the same time he endued him with Reason, and all other noble Faculties which were necessary for the administration of that Empire[115]

and so indicated how superior faculties produced control. Locke made the same point at the very beginning of *Draft B*, affirming that 'it is the Understanding that sets man above the rest of sensible beings & gives him all that dominion which he hath over them'.[116] Thus to explore the human understanding was to signal a sense of humanity's place in God's order.

Mankind's dominion extended not only over animals but over nature more generally, and was understood in terms of divine purpose. These points are revealed by the biblical warrant of the doctrine of human superiority. The view that mankind was superior to the animal kingdom in point of intellect was something that was taken to be apprehensible by the human mind. This view also had a scriptural parallel, whose particular form is of some importance, because it helps us to understand the extent of human dominion. In the words of *Genesis* 1, 26

God said, Let us make man in our image, after our likeness: and let them have dominion over the fish of the sea, and over the fowl of the air, and over the cattle, and over all the earth, and over every creeping thing that creepeth upon the earth

Thus the human understanding implied dominion over animals. The point could be and was extended to the earth itself. In the words of *Psalms* 115, xvi 'The heavens, *even* the heavens, *are* the LORD's: but the earth hath he given to the children of men.' Nature, in a wide sense, was subordinate to mankind.

Locke's own emphasis on human dominion over animals appears in the very first lines of *Draft B*. It signals a central interest, namely the direction of human attention. On the one hand, as we shall see, mankind was directed to tasks by God through the intellect: thus an exploration of the intellect would bear upon the matter of disclosing God's purposes. On the other the intellect implied humanity's dominion over nature. This motif was obvious enough for one with Locke's view of natural philosophy. For experimentalists had emphasised throughout the preceding decade or so that their work was useful because it brought mastery over nature.[117] As we shall see, Locke in effect combined a view of the human understanding with one of the proper direction of human attention: examination of the intellect would disclose that the purposes attributed to God required of mankind a concern with morality and control of nature. These are just those subjects that Locke's prior concerns would have suggested.

There are several implications in this understanding of humanity's position. The first is that God would direct people, as distinguished from animals, through the medium of their intellect rather than through instinct. The distinction would be appropriate: though both were subject to God, He required their obedience in different ways. Animals, who could not reason, conformed to laws inherent in their being; mankind had laws set before them for their reflective obedience.[118] Locke would declare the distinction clearly. When God had made man, the philosopher wrote, He 'directed him by his Senses and Reason, as he did the inferior Animals by their Sense, and Instinct, which he had placed in them to that purpose'.[119] The understanding would be God's medium of communication with mankind.

Secondly, 'mankind' here meant the species. The rationale of mankind's dominion over creation was the superiority of the human species over lower animals. To put the matter another way, the superiority existed not least by virtue of the human understanding, which was an attribute present in all normal members of the human race. This requirement of generality explains the otherwise curious fact that Locke should argue against innatism on the grounds that its hypothesised ideas were not apprehended by each and every member of the species.[120] In a like way sense and reflection were attributes of every member of the species not subject to accidental defect, for the former arose from the five senses and the latter from the contemplation of the the senses' operations.

The possession of the same understanding did not imply equality of intellectual achievement amongst mankind. To Locke's way of thinking, as we have seen, attainment supposed an exertion of mind. Thus 'the truest & best notions men had of god' were acquired 'by thought & meditation & a right use of mens facultys'. Not everyone made this effort, indeed 'the far greater number' did not. The latter's failure was one of practice rather than necessity, however, for it was the shortcoming of 'the lazy & inconsiderate part of men'.[121] In principle there was no reason why the truth should not be grasped by all. Whether Locke supposed that the principle turned into practice was another matter. We shall see that his political orientation produced a decision on this point. For the moment it is enough to note that the species was endowed with the means to do God's work.

It is worth adding here that Locke denied one very important claim suggesting that the knowledge of one man had exceeded all others. Traditionally Adam was supposed to have been gifted with insight into the nature of things which enabled him to give animals and natural objects names that expressed their real character. Locke did not accept this claim, remarking that by 'a specific name I know noe more of the specific nature or constitution of that sort of animalls then I did before.'[122] Presumably this was because it was inharmonious with his claims about ignorance of substance.[123] Certainly it implied that there had never been a human with better faculties than in the present.

Thirdly, there is the matter of the ends towards which God designed people to move. It was for Him to direct mankind in the use of dominion over the earth and its creatures. Since God was the proprietor of the earth (as Towerson put it, 'the Great Landlord of the World'), mankind was (so to speak) His tenant and as such subject to His directions. Hence human dominion ought not to be turned to any purpose, but to ones which furthered or were at least consistent with God's designs. As Ames observed, 'Dominion is a right to dispose perfectly of a matter so far as Lawes permit.[124]

God's purpose was made plain by *Genesis* at the same juncture that the *imago dei* was explained. He required the multiplication of the human race and it was to this end that He gave dominion to mankind not only over animals but over the earth itself:

God blessed them, and God said unto them, Be fruitful, and multiply, and replenish the earth, and subdue it: and have dominion over the fish of the sea, and over the fowl of the air, and over every living thing that moveth upon the earth

so that it was clear that mankind had the use of the earth and its creatures for specified purposes. The human superiority over the earth was intelligible in terms of the scale of creation. Mankind's standing implied dominion not only over animals but also over the world itself. For if mankind as rational stood above animals, which were governed by sense only, below the animals stood what was altogether inanimate. Thus, as Sydenham wrote, 'the rational faculties are so much more excellent and Superior then Brutal ones, as those are above Vegetables'. The point that there was a specification of use, indeed, was well understood. Ames had remarked of man's 'Dominion over other Creatures' that it was the means 'whereby he might use them freely to Gods Glory, and his own necessity' and inferred from the latter 'the tilling of the Earth, and getting of food out of the Plants of the Earth'.[125] Mankind's dominion, then, entitled people to turn the earth and its creatures to God's ends.

The notion of dominion was indeed an important one. It is easy to see that it fits easily into a frame of thought which dwelt upon superiority. One way in which an inferior might be dependent on a superior could be for the use of land or other material things, which happened to pertain to the superior and were his to dispense according to the conditions he chose to impose. There was a material as well as a conceptual coherence, for God, the greatest superior, was supposed to enjoy dominion over all the creatures of the earth and over the planet itself, all of which He had made. Dominion to mankind, then, would come from God to the degree that He chose. Locke made it clear, indeed, that God could adjust the degree of dominion He chose to provide.[126]

Dominion might denote also what was admittedly God's, but which inhered so closely to a given human agent that it excluded all other humans. That is to say, it could refer to matters over which only one human had direct control. High in this category were a person's attributes, as life and freedom of action, which might be supposed to be requisites of the agent's fulfilling God's purposes. Locke was proposing a teleology, a set of ends to which God directed mankind through His design and maintenance of their constitution. This may sound Aristotelian, but it is not. Aristotle, unlike Locke, had rarely ascribed purposive action to God, an ascription anyway inconsistent with the theology of his *Metaphysics*. Neither is Locke's teleology derived from the nature of matter, as it is with Aristotle. Locke's teleology resembles Aristotle's only in that the latter refers to design and so to purpose.[127]

What then were the ends to which Locke understood God to direct mankind? Our faculties were suited 'to the preservation of us to whome they are given or in whome they are & are accomodated to the uses of life'. This was a settled view, for it had appeared earlier in *Draft A*.[128] As preservation and 'the uses of life' were so central to Locke, we should explore them, but one point is worth noting first.

These ends both outlined and limited the proper exercise of the understanding. They outlined the objectives to which effort might be applied profitably. Locke assumed that our faculties were not only designed but designed by God to meet given ends. It followed that they would be adequate to achieve these, but likely to be inadequate to more extensive designs. 'For our facultys being suited not to the extent of beings & a perfect clear comprehensive knowledg of them, but to the preservation of us to whome they are given or in whome they are & are accomodated to the uses of life,' Locke observed, 'they serve to our purposes well enough if they will but give us certein notice of those things that either delight or hurt us, are convenient or inconvenient to us.'[129] This enlarged on a central assumption stated in *Draft A* too, that we can attain a knowledge sufficient for our purposes. The agent has what suffices 'as our condition needs'.[130] By the same token this specification implied that to pursue a fuller knowledge, 'a perfect clear comprehensive knowledg', was pointless. Having considered *Draft A* we have seen what Locke intended polemically by this. We see here, more generally, that by specifying given ends as within human endeavour he implied that others were beyond it.

The notion of preservation as God's purpose was a shrewd choice for several reasons. Firstly, no one would argue the opposite. Secondly, it adduced the concern of natural law writing with the survival of the agent. This would suggest itself obviously enough to Locke, and he placed the 'principle. . .of Self preservation'[131] next after God. Thirdly, it chimed generally with the general tenor of *Genesis*. After all, the increase of the species presumed that each individual should care for his or her own survival. Fourthly, it was a practical rather than a speculative end, and so aptly limited human attention. There was happiness and misery, 'beyond which we have noe concernment either of knowing or being'.[132] On these terms a knowledge without reference to practice was irrelevant.

Of course it was not self-preservation alone that was important. Locke's formula of 'the preservation of us' has a generality that extends beyond this. Whilst that same generality may preclude us from giving

155

its contents precisely, the tendency of Locke's views is evident. The 'uses of life' and things 'convenient or inconvenient to us' suggest a range of practical activities that would sustain or enhance life. More especially these phrases suggest various forms of dominion over nature, as licensed by God's requirement that humanity increase and subdue the earth and its creatures. It would not be unreasonable to think that this included the matters with which Locke and his associates had concerned themselves, the 'Experiments and Historical Observations. . .from which we may draw Advantages of Ease and Health, and thereby increase our stock of Conveniences for this Life'.[133] This would be clear even had he not delivered a panegyric on such pursuits whilst attacking the pretence of universal knowledge. For 'the schoolemen' to his mind

since aimeing at glory & esteeme for their great & universall knowledge. . .were noe wiser nor more usefull then their neigbours & brought but small advantages to humane life or the societys wherein they lived. . .for notwithstanding these learned disputers these all knowing Doctors it was to the unscholastique statesman that the governments of the world owed their peace & libertys, & from the illetrate & contemned mechanique. . .that they received the improvement of usefull arts

and indeed there is further evidence that Locke saw 'the improvement of usefull arts' as distinctly connected with the human understanding. We have seen how the understanding was connected with the human dominion over nature. Locke would assert that God's design that the species increase and subjugate nature 'contains in it the improvement too of Arts and Sciences, and the conveniences of Life'.[134] In short he conceived the understanding to answer to God's design for mankind, which in its turn authorised his preferred pursuits.

The concern for what preserves people or enhances the human condition derived from Locke's experience and pre-philosophical conceptions, as did his prepossession in favour of God. The frame of mind into which he was born, and his thinking about natural law, political economy and medicine would all have suggested a concern with human preservation, whilst the latter two would have put him in mind of 'the conveniences of Life'. But the thought that human faculties reflected a divine design for preserving their possessor was an innovation, serving the function of placing authority behind Locke's view of natural philosophy and the understanding.

The notices that the mind had about things outside it fell within the province of sensitive knowledge. Locke's scheme, as we know, aimed to include a wider knowledge extending to morality amongst other matters. Two points are worth making here. One is that the divine design apparent here was important because it meant that the understanding was provided with raw materials on terms which it could not reject. Locke's *Essays* had laid it down that the mind could reach great heights, but not without materials drawn from sense and reflection. *Draft B* echoed that point. It added that 'the minde is Fitted' to receive such impressions and suggested that in receiving them 'the understanding is mearly passive, & whether or noe it will have these beginnings & as it were materialls of knowledg is not in its owne power'.[135] Presumably this answered to God's intention about preservation, which would be a matter of reflex rather than deliberation for the agent. But these impressions were also the 'beginnings' of a more exalted knowledge.

To Locke's way of thinking, indeed, the human understanding was adapted by its nature to discoveries of the sort God required. Thus he could write of 'the facultys of the minde adapted to those discoverys which it is fit for man to make'. He was not alone in this supposition, Baxter writing of 'a certain aptitude to understand certain Truths' in 'the nature of Mans soul'.[136] But what was the sort of knowledge for which mankind was designed?

Locke suggested that 'the truth' of things 'realy existing without us' was 'the great concernment of our understandings'.[137] This description went far beyond sensitive knowledge, for Locke assumed the reality of God and the law of nature. He insisted, as one would expect, that sensation and reflection severally or together conveyed worthwhile ideas about relation, including morality, and the existence of God, and other matters. *Draft B* seems not to have been finished, but enough survives to show that the agenda of its predecessor was being expanded rather than denied.

In all this it was requisite to emphasise the distance between God and His creations. Though mankind stood above the animals, they stood a long way below God Himself, a point which required emphasis when His superiority was being exercised. This was true especially when it was needful to dwell on human ignorance of nature. We have seen already that Locke denied to Adam the height of knowledge others had assumed. More significantly, it was made clear that man could not create. Creation Locke referred to the case where 'the thing is wholy made new soe that noe part thereof did ever exist before, as when a new particle of mater doth begin to exist in rerum natura which had before noe being'.[138] Human power was limited to rearranging matter rather than producing it out of nothing. In a like way, simple ideas would be neither rejected, destroyed nor made by human beings. Locke, indeed, drew just this parallel. For

157

the dominion of man in this little world of his owne understanding being much what the same as it is in the great world of visible things, wherein his power however managd by art & skill reaches noe farther then to compound & divide the materialls that are made to his hand, but can doe noething towards the makeing the least particle of new matter, or destroying one attome of what is already in being. The same inability will every one finde in himself who shall goe about to fashion in his understanding any simple Idea not received in by his senses or the observation of his owne thoughts.[139]

The basic materials of more exalted ideas, which were also the means of human preservation, were the handiwork of God and not of humans. People could not create them and they evidenced God's design. Thus man was a dependent creature: God, not mankind, remained over all.[140]

But are not all these thoughts the parts of a vicious circle? Did not human faculties discover God and morality (at least in principle), and the reliability of those faculties depend on God's goodness?[141] The problem is a serious one, but perhaps it could be argued that within a given frame of reference, in this case the world, human knowledge had an operational validity. After all thinking properly was an attainment people required in order to *act* appropriately. As Locke put it, 'my cheife aim is to finde out those measures whereby a rationall creature put in that state which man is in in this world may & ought to governe his Opinions and actions depending there on'.[142]

More generally, these theological assumptions functioned not as blinds on what Locke would find, but rather figured as assumptions about how the understanding worked and how people should use their mental endowments. This is not unreasonable in terms of Locke's preceding views. If, as Locke supposed, God acted purposively and required man to preserve himself it made good sense that He should endow humanity with an understanding adapted to that end, and to whatever others that He might propose. Of course, the matter might look different to those with different theological opinions, especially if these were atheistic. But even the atheist would have to agree that Locke's views were rational in that he took them to be disclosed by the natural understanding (albeit with written confirmation from *Genesis*) and that they served the positions he wished to advance, namely the direction of human attention to certain matters.

In short Locke situated the view of the mind he wished to advance by arguing that the human understanding was designed by God to further preservation and the uses of the human condition. By the same token it furthered his view of ethical and scientific explanation. There is much in this that is relevant to Locke's political theory, not least his account of relations, though we should beware of supposing that the general concern for human preservation expressed in the drafts is *identical* with the *duty* to preserve others developed in *Two Treatises*. What is vital to Locke's politics is the supposition about the intellect contained in *Draft B*.

This matter is partly general and partly particular. The more general point is that *Draft B* indicated that the human species – or as Locke put it 'man'[143] – enjoyed a superiority over animals. We shall see that this placing of dominion in the whole species, as opposed to one man, was central to Locke's political argument. Though this assumption was current in Locke's day, we must not overlook its closeness to his intellectual heart. This point would be highly significant when Locke faced the elevation of Adam by Sir Robert Filmer to a dominion over both mankind and the earth: it implies a line of argument directly opposed to Filmer's. More particularly, Locke's view that the intellect was the characteristic part of humanity as a *whole*, capable in principle of reaching a knowledge of morality and God, would be integral to his account of political authority. But to understand why the human understanding should be important politically, we must direct our attention to some events in the decade after 1671.[144]

Chapter 6

In 1689 Locke would give to the world a view about the nature of the church and of its relations with the state in the English translation, made by another hand, of his *Epistola de Tolerantia*. That view conceived the church as a society voluntarily constituted by people, whose claims to be the embodied bearer of God's commission were unverifiable, but also as a body immune from the authority of the state so long as it did not disturb the public peace. The last point, of course, continued the principle of 1667. Constant too was Locke's view that the intellect governed the will but itself could be dictated to only by what it took for evidence. Locke, in short, augmented more than he altered in his preceding views.

How are we to understand this development? Locke's principle that peaceable conscience about religion be accommodated came to be set in a new intellectual situation. It is to the terms on which that principle could be realised that we should turn in order to apprehend Locke's reasons.

After 1672 Locke wrote under conditions which made it first less easy and then implausible to suppose that conscience as he conceived it, however peaceable, would be respected by the English state. The crucial reason for this was the posture of the Church of England, which was ready to assert its claims at the expense of others' beliefs, not least by using the agency of the state to impose civil penalties on dissent. Locke's final position reflects his response to these central facts. Events, of course, did not disclose the Anglican triumph all at once: Locke's views expanded in scope *pari passu* with developments in ecclesiastical politics.

Of course Locke's views, which embodied general principles and were expressed in appropriate language, cannot be reduced to their immediate situation. Though they were formulated to address a specific condition, they applied and developed propositions drawn from a larger intellectual ambit and expressed these in terms capable of being applied to many situations. As to the latter, it is pertinent to remember that though formulated with England in mind Locke's final view was addressed to the continent before being readdressed to England once more.[1] As to the former, much of what Locke said in 1689 may be taken to be *implied* in the principles stated in 1667. But more generally still (and perhaps more importantly) involved in Locke's treatment of the church in its relations with the state were suppositions of central importance for *Two Treatises of Government*. But let us turn to Locke and his situation.

Locke wrote 'An Essay concerning Toleration' from within the government of the day. His published works on political theory, concerning both church and government, bespeak a different point of view. His writings on toleration, both in their content and their intellectual bearings, help us to understand the nature of the change. Locke came to hold explicitly a view of the church which implied no integral relation with the state. He did so when it seemed that the Church of England was interfering successfully in the affairs of the state. It seemed to intrude not least by insinuating an unsatisfactory doctrine of the state. Thus Locke's views of church and state had an historical link. As we shall see they had a conceptual connection too.

We may understand this point most easily by recollecting that in 1667 Locke did not advance a theory of the church in its relations with the state, but rather a view of toleration,[2] but that in 1689 he did have a theory about this matter.

I

His views on toleration begin from a posture sympathetic to Charles II and his government because Locke conceived them as the instruments of his ends. His *Tracts* contain an appeal to the king. His 'Essay' may be addressed to the king and certainly is not antipathetic to the executive. Neither was Locke against governmental authority in general. His position of 1667 implies a view of the sovereign, since the civil magistrate's sole function was to preserve the subject in his civil concernments (which Locke in *Treatises* would identify with upholding the law of nature). This function stood in need of explanation – as did the sort of church Locke was implying.

For the moment, these explanations were not needed, for Locke was addressing the problem from within the civil government, and so a dissertation on its nature and relation to the church would have been superfluous and probably disconcerting. The 'Essay' of 1667 dwelt only on those general principles that explained why toleration was right and for whom it was right. To put the matter another way, the situation was one in which policy rather than the structure of church and state required adjustment. The king was presumed friendly and he probably hoped to relax or remove the penal laws against dissent. As it happened, the attempt was not successful, but this owed more to the maladroit execution of the design than to structural constraints. The same situation was reflected in a different style of writing when Charles and his advisors, including Shaftesbury, came up with the Declaration of Indulgence.

After the fall of Clarendon, Charles' principal ministers were men favourable to relaxing civil constraints on religious dissent. Buckingham and Shaftesbury favoured friendliness to Protestant dissent. Clifford and Arlington were secret Catholics and were thus not averse to such a policy if it could be framed in a manner favouring their co-religionists. That the king's private opinions veered in the same direction was known to virtually nobody, but he had a financial motive for a similar policy. His brother monarch, Louis XIV, was prepared to relieve his embarrassing finances in return for a quiescent foreign policy and domestic favour for Catholics, perhaps extending to a change in England's religion. It is unclear whether Charles took this last point at all seriously, but he did take the money. Indeed it was only prudent to do so: for parliament was likely to correlate its generosity to the monarchy with the monarchy's enthusiasm for Anglicanism. It was true that the Anglican enthusiasm of the Commons had been cooled, variously by the passing of many of its original members and by the obvious fact that the Conventicle Act had not persuaded dissent to capitulate to the Anglican body. But it was true still that the bishops in the House of Lords were resolute and influential, and that parliament had passed a new Conventicle Act in 1670. Thus it seemed that an improvement in the legal position of non-Anglicans would have to come from a source other than the Lords and Commons. Hence the Declaration of Indulgence of 1672 relied upon the twin notions that the king, as supreme governor of the Church of England, could act without the concurrence of Parliament and that, acting so, he was entitled to suspend the legislation against dissent.[3]

Locke's 'Essay' of 1667 had not disputed the royal Supremacy, but like much else, that institution was assumed rather than examined explicitly. Since it was now proposed that the king should exercise his Supremacy, it was helpful to understand its basis. There are amongst Shaftesbury's papers a document arguing that the king's ecclesiastical power derived from a source quite distinct from his authority as a civil magistrate.[4]

That this paper was intended to help a policy requires no comment. More interesting for our purpose is its relation to Locke's 'Essay'. The

162

paper is not merely compatible with it, but also admits of being related to it integrally if we make one assumption. They are compatible in that Locke's 'Essay' argued that the civil magistrate did not have authority over the church, other things being equal: this did not imply that the individual who held the office of civil magistrate might not have an authority over the church, assuming that this authority stood on a different basis to his civil power. The Royal Supremacy, interpreted in a certain way, provided just such an authority.

Indeed the authority was important in relation to church policy. It was not an authority extending over matters of doctrine, as writers as diverse as James I and Hobbes would have liked,[5] but it did cover matters like things indifferent in worship and toleration. In respect of these it gave the king latitude to behave precisely as he wished. He could tolerate (or, more precisely, indulge) as much or as little deviation from uniform practice within his church as he chose. In the case of 1672, where the king wished to indulge dissent, the latitude would be large; and, since matters of doctrine were not the subject of dispute, the king and his ministers would impart precisely the direction they wanted – and that too without any institutional changes in church or state. We may fairly call it erastianism without tears.

The objective of 1672 was to circumvent the recalcitrant Anglicanism of the bishops and their parliamentary friends. The avenue explored to this end was an exercise of royal power. No new theory of the church in its relation to the state was required to underwrite this policy, and no adjustment either in Locke's views on toleration. Though this course was theoretically economical, it had the weakness that its success depended entirely on the disposition of the monarch or at least on his ability to impress his will on others. If success were not obtainable in this way, what other route would there be to circumvent the militant Church of England? To put the matter at its simplest, the immediate problem was the exertion of force against dissent by the state at the behest of the bishops. If this could not be obviated by subordinating the church to the king it might be by insisting that religious dissent had no connection with the state and so, properly speaking, lay beyond civil sanctions.

II

Locke took up such a view after the Declaration. This had failed because the exercise of the royal supremacy not merely discountenanced Anglicanism and its friends, but also disquieted those suspicious of royal power in general. Where the former had been expected, the latter had not and when parliament assembled in February, 1673 Charles found himself the prisoner of an alignment between militant Anglicanism and the supporters of parliamentary government. Whilst the latter were not necessarily unfriendly to dissent, they were not prepared to help it by exalting the royal prerogative, a position that drew strength from the Commons' financial influence on the government.[6] The Declaration was withdrawn and the civil penalties against dissent were reimposed in a more virulent form

What remedy did Locke have? Locke recommendnd – if the suggestion is his – that Charles establish a vicar-general to reform the Church of England.[7] This came to nothing, as might have been anticipated. The avenue of dealing with the church through the royal supremacy seemed to be closed. Attention to the other route seemed sensible, at least for the moment.

The renewed legislation was inspired by the bishops and their friends. As such it could be represented as an effect of the church upon the state. This was certainly true in the sense that some of the personnel were in orders, but it was scarcely true in the prevalent state of the English constitution. For the episcopate were members of the House of Lords, and (to some eyes at least) the clergy were an estate of the realm. Locke did not direct his attention to these matters, but emphasised instead the impropriety of the church interfering with civil affairs. His piece 'Excommunicaan' of 1673–4 indicated that churches had no authority in the community save over their own members, that this authority extended merely to excluding deviants from the church and that it should involve no civil penalty. This position, which Locke carried forward to his *Epistola de Tolerantia*, imparted a new emphasis to the principle of 1667. He had argued for a division of the civil and the ecclesiastical, based on their differing functions and reflected in the principle that the state should concern itself with the church only if the latter threatened civil peace. He argued now that the church as such had no business to impinge upon civil affairs because its business lay elsewhere.[8] It might seem that the church and its lay sympathisers were a greater threat than the state as such to a congenial settlement of ecclesiastical affairs.

For instance this paper may relate to the attempt of February, 1674 to carry a bill through the Commons, removing all oaths and subscriptions, except that of Supremacy and Allegiance and to the articles of doctrine. Since the latter were not a subject of dispute this amounted to toleration of Protestant dissent, subject to security for civil obedience and to admission of the king's supremacy in ecclesiastical affairs. But Bishop Morley persuaded the 'great men' who were behind it to defer to a bill 'for composing differences in religion and inviting sober and peaceably minded Dissenters into the service of the Church', by repealing the 'assent and consent' clause of the Corporation Act and removing the renunciation of the covenant from the statute book. In other words he substituted a scheme of comprehension on an Anglican basis for one of toleration in terms close to Locke's. Both schemes came to nothing.[9]

Equally, we might look at the matter from another perspective. In order to understand the Anglican position it is necessary to grasp both the intellectual tenets that the Church of England espoused and that Church's situation. Both are relevant to Locke's concerns, the theoretical more especially. The Anglican mind registered the sense of unity, so important in the thought of the day, and raised it to a high power: it understood unity in a way unfavourable to those that stood outside its bounds.

The Anglican case rested on the view that the church was the vessel of God's grace. Of the church it was said that 'in her custody Christ hath left the treasure of his grace'.[10] Nowell's catechism even referred a 'fourth part' of the Creed, namely the Church.[11] Grace operated, in particular, to bond the members of the church into one under Christ's headship. A church was defined as 'a communion and a society of saints; that is, not only a society of all such as be, have been or shall be thy [God's] people, but also a society or partaking of Jesus Christ which is the "head" of the same'.[12] Christ was the 'head' because according to the thought of the day the head was understood to be that which gives the body life and because Christ was the conduit of divine authority to the Church. Under His influence Christians made a unity: in Cranmer's words, the faithful were 'turned into the body of Christ and are so joined unto Christ...that they do make but one mystical body of Christ'.[13] Hooker was even more graphic, remarking that believers were one with Christ 'by our actual incorporation into that society which hath Him for their Head, and doth make together with Him one body'.[14] The church and its members were one with Christ.

As such the church was a divinely constituted organisation. In the exotic language of Archbishop Sandys, Christ was planted as a true vine in the vineyard of the Church of England.[15] In the more prosaic style of Bishop Overall's convocation book He was described as the 'General' of the church, which was to be with Him for ever; He was also to be the Head ruling the church visibly by means of the bishops, priests and ministers He appointed.[16] Episcopacy, in its turn, represented Him and it could be said that the bishop was 'apt...to signifie a Principle of Unity, and to represent God and Christ under the Notion of a Head'.[17] Bishops, as well as Christ, evidenced God's

165

organisation. Indeed the *ecclesia Anglicana* was not only a true church, but in an important sense *the* true church. It embodied a direct lineage from God, unspotted more or less, and not besmirched in the way Rome had been.

Since the church was true, the office of the civil government was to uphold it.[18] The magistrate's authority, of course, covered things indifferent and included a power to impose civil penalties for dissent, as we have noted already.[19]

To separate from the church, since it was a divinely authorised church, was schism. To agree in matters of doctrine was not enough to constitute unity: separation from the body of the church on grounds that were inadequate was wilful and those who severed themselves from obedience to the church in matters of ceremony or church order, even though these things might be indifferent in themselves, were schismatics.[20] In Hooker's decided words, if people

break the bond of unity, whereby the body of the Church is coupled and knit in one, as they do which wilfully forsake all external communion with saints in holy exercises purely and orderly established in the Church, this is to separate themselves by schism.[21]

This followed from the church's role as the bearer of God's grace. Because schism was division from the organisation God had authorised, it was also division from God. The Anglican divine could dwell lovingly on the consequences of distancing oneself from the church. 'Whoever are *disunited* from the *Visible Communion* of the *Church* on *Earth*,' wrote Henry Dodwell,

and particularly from the *Visible Communion* of the *Bishop*, must consequently be *disunited* from. . .the *invisible* Communion of the Holy *Angels* and *Saints* in *Heaven*, and which is yet more from *Christ* and *God* himself, and from all the *Benefits* consequent to all these *Unities*

for these, he indicated, 'cannot be thought *communicable* to him who is *disunited* from the *origins* from whence they flow'.[22]

In sum the Anglican doctrine declared that the Church of England was a divinely warranted vessel of God's grace; that God's grace united its members into one with God; that the civil government should uphold the church, if need be by force; and that to leave the church was schismatic. These claims amounted to an assertion of ecclesiastical unity.

These claims for unity were set after 1660 in a context of ecclesiastical diversity. The collapse of episcopal order in the 1640s had allowed the growth of Presbytery and Independency, not to speak of the multiplication of sects over the next decade. For the first time in England since the reformation a multiplicity of Protestant bodies existed. It was clear from the later 1660s that this would be an enduring fact, for the goads applied by the Act of Uniformity and the Corporation and Conventicle Acts had not smoothed away Protestant dissent. To this fact several responses were possible. One was to comprehend some dissenters at least within the Anglican body by altering its terms of communion. Another was to tolerate dissent. These two could be combined (as in the notion of comprehending Presbyterians and tolerating Independents) or pursued separately (for comprehending some does not imply tolerating the rest). A third path was to persuade them to come into an unaltered Anglican church; a fourth to drive them into it or out of the kingdom. It was the last that was most congenial to Archbishop Sheldon.

Neither is it surprising that this was the course that a majority of Anglican divines seem to have favoured, for comprehension and toleration implied that something was adrift with the Anglican body. Comprehension implied that the matters to which Presbyterian objected were somehow unimportant, whilst the toleration of practices contrary to the Church of England's might seem to belie Anglican claims (though some advocates of toleration insisted that it was merely a favour, not an acknowledgement). Of course these points may well have meant more to the clergy than to the laity.

We should not assume, without examination, that the repressive policy would prevail. Locke had assumed quite another possibility in 1667, and he came to another view slowly and gradually. To put the matter of church and state with stark intellectual clarity it would be obvious enough that the conceptual antidote to Anglican claims was to complement Locke's principle of respecting peaceable conscience with an agnosticism about the marks of the church, a denial that tradition was important and an insistence that the church was not a supernatural entity constituted by God. Rather the church would be distinguished by its creeds and would itself be a body made by man, without any claims of truth to have its arrangements supported by the state. At length Locke would arrive at this position.

But it was not obvious that Anglicanism needed to be opposed so completely. The political conditions under which Locke developed a theory of the church – conditions under which it was clear that Anglican policy was intractable and the Anglican position politically impregnable – were not realised all at once. For some years after 1672 matters were not so clear.

Locke's position so far had not included any explicit theory of the church. He had specified that church and state had different objectives and that, broadly speaking, neither should impinge upon the other's purpose. But he had not explained definitely either that the church must be subordinate to the state or that the church must be conceived in a manner organisationally sundered from the state. The time for such a decision was not ripe politically. Though attempts to introduce toleration through state action had been frustrated so far, it was not obvious yet that they must be. For instance, the Declaration had been defeated by the combined efforts of episcopalians and parliamentarians. These bodies were joined by unity on that practical point rather than by any conceptual connection; without those who suspected royal power the bishops and their friends might not be so formidable; in 1675 someone friendly to Shaftesbury suggested that the bishops favoured divine right in the church and absolutism in the state.

A Letter from a Person of Quality, To His Friend in the Country argued that the bishops aimed to attribute to the Church of England to a basis in divine right and, by a sort of compliment, to extend the same basis to the monarchy. Any body established on divine authority, of course, was not subject to legitimate modification or challenge by man. Hence, *A Letter* insinuated, a malign monarch could not be challenged, whether through parliament or force by his subjects. The clergy, who were also attempting to establish a political party to back their claims, were thus interfering in the affairs of the state in a very sinister manner. No subversive intentions were attributed to Charles: but absolutism and Anglicanism were painted as the common enemy of England.[23]

As well as this ingenious theory of an hierocratic and absolutist plot, *A Letter* contained elements continuous or compatible with Locke's thought. Like Locke it argued that civil sanctions for religious dissent were improper, though it differed from him by doing so on pragmatic grounds. It suggested that the influence of ecclesiastics on the state was not for the best, arguing that the best kinds of church were those that were either firmly subordinate to the state or whose constitution implied their severance from political authority: this strikes resonances with Locke's use of the royal supremacy and his view that church and state had different goals. Most interestingly, in the same year that the *Letter* appeared, Locke noted that 'The great Clergy' were 'playnly inclining to goe back to theire Interest, w^{ch}: is highest exalted in that Religion', meaning Roman Catholicism, and declaring that 'They have found a Mistress call'd the pres^t pow^e that pay's them much better than truth can.' It is very unlikely that Locke did not know the contents of *A Letter*, but, whatever its origin, it expressed a doctrine of great importance for the future of his thought.[24]

A Letter noted the attributed claim that Anglican church order was *jure divino*.[25] The civil counterpart was the parallel ascription of absolute power to the English monarchy. By absolutism was understood the view that the ruler was in no way answerable to his subjects and therefore that these had no legitimate means of controlling his exercise of power: to which contemporary absolutism added, as we shall see, that rulers need not be bound by any terrestrial laws.[26] As in Locke's 'Essay' of 1667 the point was made that this did not accord with England's constitutional history. More particularly absolutism was said to threaten the liberties and properties of Englishmen; and to contradict the fact that England was a 'bounded' monarchy; by which was meant one where the subject was entitled to question and to repulse the inroads of the monarch, whether by parliamentary means of by force.[27]

Anyone who has read the *Treatises* with even the least attention can see that they transpose the features attributed to England by *A Letter* into a general key. They explain liberty and property and responsible government in a general way. But though there is a broad similarity between the stance of the *Letter* and the subject matter of Locke's *Treatises*, there are also differences. Most importantly, *A Letter* neither mentioned how political authority would be explained nor explained any of its views about liberty, property and 'bounded' government. Secondly, we need not read *A Letter* as an agenda for immediate action, but only as a conditional prospectus. In 1675 there was no reason to suppose that Shaftesbury would end his career in irreconcilable opposition to Charles, whom the piece treated with respect.[28]

Indeed the *Letter*'s desire to identify the Anglican body and its friends with absolutism, whilst indicating an enmity towards them, also bespeaks a desire to isolate them in parliament. There was as yet no reason to suppose that the state itself was intractable. After all the *Letter* attributed the woes of civil government to the church and not to the character of the monarchy or the monarch. Shaftesbury was in opposition, but did not wish to distance himself from office. Clifford rather than the king was made the scapegoat for malign innovation.[29] Absolutism was a convenient slogan to cultivate country opinion and so win support in parliamentary affairs. The popularity of absolutist language at court gave this a handle.

But it did come to be the case eventually that the claims of the Church of England and of political absolutism would need to be assailed and circumvented. To understand what was involved in this we need to attend to events, but to observe also that there was one set of assumptions about human faculties and political authority that was central to both.

169

III

Superiority, whether in church or state, involved a superiority of understanding. To the modern mind this may seem an unusual proposition, but it was so. We may recollect that the greatest superior of all was God, whose supereminence was embodied in his outstanding attributes of wisdom and power, specifically for Locke His omniscience and omnipotence. Other superiorities were modelled on the exemplar that God's authority presented.

We should focus especially on wisdom amongst the faculties, for superiority in this respect was an important title to direct others. Wisdom, perhaps, is a concept not familiar to the modern mind and it is best to clarify it. It may be classified generally as a property of the understanding. It denotes the ability to judge and discern. As James I noted 'To be wise, is vnderstood, able to discerne, able to iudge others'.[30] Hence we find a writer remarking that 'magistracie and offices of iustice bee not to be bestowed vppon the richest or most fauoured, but vppon the wisest and worthiest'.[31] Wisdom was above others a qualification to direct.

God, of course, was supposed to out-top all other agents in wisdom (as well as all other worthwhile attributes). It was natural that wisdom be treated as a quality distinguishing a properly ordered hierarchy. In other words, the model of God's superiority was generalised. God, of course, because omniscient could know everything without having to reason; in this respect all humans must be His inferiors: but the principle was the same. Hence, when we turn to other superiorities, for instance Halifax's account of the superiority of male over female, we find the same point being made. 'You must first lay it down for a foundation in general,' wrote the marquess, addressing his daughter

that there is inequality in the sexes, and that for the better economy of the world the men, who were to be lawgivers, had the larger share of reason bestowed upon them; by which means your sex is the better prepared for the compliance that is necessary for the better performance of those duties which seem to be most properly assigned to it.[32]

Thus authority ('the lawgivers') was linked with superior understanding ('the larger share of reason').

The authority that involved superior understanding was supposed to be exercised for the good of those directed. For God's wisdom was assumed to be matched by His goodness, so that it made sense that His wisdom should direct people benevolently. Hence it was supposed generally that rules and laws should be directed to the good of those receiving them. Locke remarked that '*Law* in its true Notion, is not so much the Limitation as *the direction of a*[n]. . .*Agent* to his proper Interest, and prescribes no farther than is for the general Good of those under that Law'; and Hobbes reflected the same assumptions when he observed that 'the use of Lawes is. . .to direct and keep them [agents] in such a motion, as not to hurt themselves. . .as Hedges are set, not to stop Travellers, but to keep them in the way'.[33] God's own legislation, natural law, directed people for their good, a point which Locke had laboured in his *Essays*.[34] Civil laws, it was assumed, should conduce to the good of the governed, so that Locke could state without argument that this was 'the standard and measure according to which' the civil magistrate 'ought to square and proportion his lawes'.[35] The same assumptions were used by some to suggest that measures which did not work for the good of the governed could not be counted as laws at all.

The origins of this doctrine and its implications for political order are not far to seek. To assume that an outstanding ability to understand means that those directed would be directed for their good conduces to the view that the wise should rule. The principle could apply in company with other outstanding qualities, such as the goodness we have seen attributed to God. The doctrine can be traced back to Plato and Aristotle and is well expressed by a contemporary of Locke's, who observed that 'virtue makes the distinction, which must be either simply compleat and perfect in it self',

so that he who is endued with it, is a God among men, or relatively, as far as concerns civil Society, and the ends for which it is constituted, that is, defence, and the obtaining of Justice. This requires a mind unbiassed by passion, full of goodness and wisdom, firm against all temptations to ill. . .tending to all manner of good, through a perfect knowledg and affection to it;

if so, he continued, 'Where such a man is found, he is by nature a King, and 'tis best for the Nation where he is that he govern.' Or, in the words of another writer, there were some 'that would prove Absolute Monarchy the best Government, as that which God himself governs the Universe by: because such Kings partake of his Wisdom and Goodness'. The first passage comes from Algernon Sidney, the second from *Two Treatises of Government*.[36] The correlate of this view, that those who utterly lack wisdom are fit to be subordinate without qualification to their betters, is also stated by Sidney: 'they are Slaves by nature', he wrote about those who 'have neither the understanding nor courage that is required for the constitution and management of a Government within themselves'. Locke himself understood the point,

171

remarking of some that 'their mean Souls fitted them for, Slavery'.[37] In short, superior understanding and other high attributes, such as goodness, marked their possessors as fit rulers; and their absence, in extreme cases, as properly slaves.

It was true especially that political rulers were conceived on the model of understanding. That is to say, they stood as terrestrial substitutes for God, in that they gave laws whose purpose was to further the design of His legislation and might be presumed to partake of wisdom and goodness (albeit to a lesser degree than the deity). Initially this model worked to the advantage of kings. James I emphasised the image of God in the monarch. 'Kings sit in the Throne of GOD,' he asserted 'and they themselves and called Gods.' For this reason 'all good Kings in their gouvernment, must imitate God and his Christ, in being iust and righteous'. Moreover, it was at once the monarch's duty to diffuse virtue to his people and his privilege to receive virtue from God, for

this glistering worldly glorie of Kings, is giuen them by God, to teach them to preasse so to glister and shine before their people. . .that their persons as bright lampes of godlinesse and vertue, may, going in and out before their people, giue light to all their steps. Remember also [James counselled his eldest son], that by the right knowledge, and feare of God (which is *the beginning of Wisedome*, as *Salomon* saith) ye shall know all the things necessarie for the discharge of your duetie. . .seeing in him, as in a mirrour, the course of all earthly things.[38]

On this reading the king, because the possessor of supereminent qualities, stood first in the political community.

The theory, however, need not work always to the exclusive advantage of monarchs. It asserted that outstanding attributes like wisdom formed a title to political authority. The logical form implicit in this would be that wisdom and authority should be correlated. To put the matter in a different language, in order to decide who should rule in a community it would be necessary to inquire about the *distribution* of wisdom within it. If one individual had a monopoly or a clear supremacy of understanding, like the Aristotelian natural monarch, then obviously he or she alone should rule: and if not, not.

To put the matter concretely, those who preferred monarchical rule would emphasise the superior understanding of kings and the inferior grasp of their subjects, even to the extent of denying the latter any rational capacity, and so relegating them to the status of animals. This had been the tactic of the young Locke when he asked,

Whence is most danger to be rationally feared, from ignorant or knowing heads? From an orderly council or a confused multitude? To whom are we most like to become a prey, to those whom the Scripture calls gods, or those whom knowing men have always found and therefore called beasts?

Ultimately this language tended to support absolutism, because 'those whom the Scripture calls gods', clearly, should be immune from responsibility to beasts. No doubt they were responsible to God for the beasts' welfare, but this was different from thinking they should answer to the beasts' judgement in the matter. On the other hand, empirical judgements leave room for disagreement – on some views of things, room for complete reversal. Certainly the older Locke declined to count absolute monarchs as gods, for to him '*Absolute Monarchs* are but Men.' It could be that claims like James' for divine support were not answered: for 'he that thinks *absolute Power purifies Mens Bloods*, and corrects the baseness of Humane Nature' would need little 'to be convinced of the contrary'. Instead oppressive rulers had become beasts (especially wolves, bears and tigers) whilst those who overthrew them displayed 'the sence of rational Creatures'.[39]

Reason, indeed, was the key to the matter. For it had a twofold function in the thought of the day. In the first place reason was supposed to distinguish good from evil, as we have seen Locke assume in his *Essays*. Secondly, it was supposed also to guide or control the passions, and thus to curb what one might call the sensual part of human nature into the courses of right conduct. Beasts stood in contrast with people, for they lacked reason and so could not control their sensual nature. How far reason controlled human beings was thus a measure of their fitness to guide themselves or others.

Absolutism supposed that rulers were somehow above the passions that diverted other people from the right. James I suggested that monarchy resembled 'Diuinitie, approacheth nearest to perfection' and Sir Thomas Elyot suggested that the queen bee 'is lefte to man by nature, as it seemeth, a perpetuall figure of a iuste gouernaunce or rule', because the bees 'hath amonge them one principall Bee for theyr gouernor', in whom 'is more knowledge than in the residue'. Locke himself emphasised the correlation of reason and fitness to rule: he suggested, writing of education, that the less children's reason was developed the more they should be subject to the unrestricted guidance of another: 'the less Reason they have of their own, the more are they to be under the Absolute Power and Restraint of those, in whose Hands they are'.[40] So absolutism and the possession of supereminent reason were correlated.

What Locke would not accept involved a small adjustment, but one

173

with serious implications. He did not believe that kings were any better supplied with reason than others, 'for Princes are but Men, made as others'.[41] What mattered here was how 'others' *were* made. Locke assumed that reason did not always triumph, that 'irregular Passion' might move action.[42] From this it follows straightaway that no one individual should be allowed to rule without restriction.

What distanced Locke from his original attribution of a superior understanding to 'those whom the Scripture calls gods'? Part of the answer, no doubt, is simply that he came to find absolutism uncongenial, for the conceptual adjustment required to discountenance that doctrine can hardly be called difficult. But there is a much more fundamental reason. The monarchical attribution could scarcely be said to have the support of an articulated view of the human understanding. The conception of the understanding that Locke had developed was one which looked askance at such a claim.

Between *Two Tracts* and *Two Treatises* Locke settled on his view of the human understanding. The central point about his views for our purpose is that they attributed intellectual superiority over lower creatures to mankind *as a whole*. At the outset of *Draft B* he had declared that 'it is the Understanding that sets man above the rest of sensible beings & gives him all that dominion which he hath over them'. This intellectual superiority placed mankind closer to God than to the beasts: in fact, in the language of *Genesis*, to which Locke alluded, it set people in the image of God:

And God said, Let us make man in our image, after our likeness: and let them have dominion over the fish of the sea and over the cattle, and over all the earth, and over every creeping thing that creepeth upon the earth.

If 'the Infinitely great god made all things in perfect wisdome', as Locke assumed, then His image was given to the whole human race and not to monarchs only.[43] Everyone, at least every normal member of the species, was provided with the same understanding.

This was not to assert that this set of faculties was present in just the same way in all human beings. Such a view excluded neither freaks of nature nor the possibility that some people had higher natural endowments of intelligence than others. Neither did it suppose ultimate equality of attainment, for that could be related to causes external to the understanding itself. But Locke did assert that people came from the hand of God with the same attributes, that they were 'born to all the same advantages of Nature and the use of the same faculties'. Nature in this sense signified God's intention, and as such was authoritative. If everyone was thus intended to 'the use of the same faculties'

174

it follows, granted that intellect was a title to rule, that each had the same political authority: none was superior in understanding and so none either in power. In Locke's own language there was 'nothing more evident,

than that Creatures of the same species and rank promiscuously born to all the same advantages of Nature, and the use of the same faculties, should also be equal one amongst another without Subordination or Subjection

Thus Locke maintained the assumption that superiority of intellect was a title to authority, but suggested that people were intellectually equal in principle. Hence by their natures people were in a condition 'wherein all Power and Jurisdiction is reciprocal, no one having more than another'.[44]

It may be asked whether the differences Locke admitted amongst intellectual attainments amounted to a contradiction of this position. After all, did he not decide eventually that there was 'great variety in men's understandings, and their natural constitutions put so wide a difference between some men in this respect that. . .their very natures seem to want a foundation to raise on it that which other men easily attain unto'? He did, but it was the *cause* of the difference that matters here. Locke assigned this less to nature than to subsequent acquirement: 'the difference so observable in men's understandings and parts', he wrote, 'does not arise so much from their natural faculties as acquired habits'. This being so, the difference matters less for our purpose. Of course, if the original endowments of some were inadequate, it would be otherwise. But Locke insisted heavily on the range of natural power. 'We are born with faculties and powers capable almost of anything,' he wrote, 'such at least as would carry us further than can be easily imagined.'[45] The differences Locke admitted did not touch his purpose. This is important, for even after his time opinion did not always concur. When Burke wrote that virtue and wisdom were titles to govern, when the younger Mill recommended special representation for the intelligent and cultivated and when Bagehot lamented 'the supremacy of ignorance over instruction and of numbers over knowledge', they had a different conclusion in mind.

If we say 'inadequate' it may be asked fairly, 'inadequate to what?' The answer is, adequate to self-direction. For there was another side to the intellectual superiority of governors, namely the assumption that their inferiors were ill-equipped to guide themselves and so needed direction from others. Locke's doctrine that people were 'born to. . .the use of the same faculties' implies that no human agent by nature is superior to another. Who then directs each agent, but himself or

175

herself? To underwrite this doctrine plausibly, of course, it was necessary to produce an account of the agent showing how this could be so. The answer that was congenial to Locke, since he assumed that the understanding determined the will, was that the agent's understanding was equal to directing his or her actions. Hence we read that 'the agent determines himself to this or that voluntary action upon some precedent knowledge. . .in the understanding'. In other words Locke had to posit an ability to form knowledge and to act upon it before he could suppose that his agent required no direction by others. Locke's writings on the human understanding had supplied the former. The latter was added in his *Treatises*, where we are told that 'God having given Man an Understanding to direct his Actions, has allowed him a freedom of Will'.[46] Endowed with an appropriate understanding and the ability to act freely as it directed, an agent was thus independent of the need to be guided by a superior:[47] indeed he or she had no one entitled to be called superior. Hence Locke could state that the 'State all Men are naturally in. . .is. . .a *State of perfect Freedom* to order their Actions. . .as they think fit. . .without asking leave, or depending upon the Will of any other Man.'[48] Freedom from direction by a superior implied an intellect and a will adequate to self-direction.

It should not be supposed that Locke meant to undermine God's superiority or to question superiorities in society that did not impinge upon political authority. He qualified the assertions of his agents' freedom from superiors and equality of faculties by referring to God's laws and reserved the possibility that God might 'by. . .manifest Declaration of his Will set one above another, and confer on him by an evident and clear appointment an undoubted Right to Dominion'.[49] Indeed without the precedent of God's supereminent attributes Locke's explanation of authority would have ceased to make sense. Again, he did not intend to undermine the idea of social hierarchy.[50] His point related to political order rather than other kinds.

It is reasonable to ask how far Locke's attitude to political superiority flowed from a distaste for absolutism. Some effect there must have been, for even if all the intellectual components necessary had been present in his mind already, it required a motive to devise and settle his argument. Certainly the components were present by 1671 and in fact a disposition to treat them in a certain manner was hinted at as early as 1667. Locke had suggested then that though magistrates might be set above citizens, yet between them 'in respect of the King of kings, there is but a small and accidentall difference'. In his *Treatises* monarchs would be 'in comparison of the great God, but as a Drop of the Bucket': the tone has become harsher, the note was the same.[51] One point is especially worthy of note, for it could not be referred to conceptual considerations (unlike his view of the human understanding), is Locke's choice of juncture at which to consider intellect and authority. Had he taken his stand when the monarch and the ploughman were well advanced in life, instead of when they came into the world, 'born to all the same advantages of Nature', his verdict about intellectual superiority might have been different.

It is probably fair to hypothesise that Locke's political involvement caused him to articulate sharply what was implicit earlier. Between 'An Essay concerning Toleration' and *Two Treatises* Locke had penned his *Drafts*, which dwelt *inter alia* on God's requirement that people exercise their minds. To be intellectually lazy was to ignore this requirement. It was also to make oneself rather docile. One of Locke's objections to innatism was that it tended 'to take off' people 'from the use of their owne reasons & judgements & put them upon beleiving & takeing upon trust without farther examination'. 'In which posture of blinde credulity,' Locke concluded, 'they might be easily governd by & made usefull to some sort of men who had the skill & office to principle & guid them.'[52] To guide oneself was quite opposed to this temper.

There was another point implicit in the choice of juncture. In effect, though tacitly, it excluded reference to the operation of God's grace on rulers, marking them out above others to do His work. This was a recognised gambit. For if the people at large were 'beasts', it might be that a special effect was needed to endow monarchs to govern well. God, John Novell declared, 'gives to his Special Minister the Supreme Magistrate, special grace, wisdom, counsel, courage, justice, love to his people, and a tender care of their Welfare'.[53] By determining where authority lay at the earliest possible point, Locke excluded such grace from the reckoning as to who should rule.

The point has its relevance. For the same Lockean claims about the understanding that tended to undermine the superiority of absolute monarchs tended also to weaken the claims of the Church of England. Absolutism and Anglicanism did not by any means stand on the same conceptual foundations. There was, however, a similarity of assumption. The authority of the Church of England, like that of monarchs, rested on a claim to know better, to be endowed with a superior title to understanding. The Anglican case was that God had established the Church of England under the headship of Christ, and that from Christ flowed gracious benefits. Those not under the its aegis lacked these. Because the church had clear evidence that it was God's chosen vessel those who opted out committed a grievous intellectual error and *eo ipso* were not capable of guiding themselves. Thus, like the monarchy, the

Church of England in effect presented itself as superior to non-episcopal believers by reason of the understanding of order that it claimed to have received from God.

The monarchical claim depended on wisdom. The Anglican title differed in that it turned on a claim to apprehend the truth. It was therefore vulnerable to counter-claims and, more radically, to assertions that the truth was not firmly within human grasp. This might take the form of suggesting that the relevant claims were not certain or, more pointedly, that their truth was unknowable. Or, again, it might be suggested that insofar as judgement was possible each individual was as well equipped as the next to make it, *ceteris paribus*.

The matter may be brought into focus by drawing a contrast. The Anglican position would call for an exercise of mind as much as any other: the question was one of destination. If Anglican claims were correct, people would do best to concur with them rather than to exercise their faculties towards any independently conceived destination. But if each agent were responsible for his or her own direction each must judge individually. Hence we not only find Locke reiterating that God gave no warrant for forcing people into churches against their judgement (1678), but emphasising also the absence of intellectual authority in matters of salvation. That is to say, no such authority had been provided ('god has noe where given such power to any man or society'), and so nobody could claim to have grasped the truth of the matter: 'man in all states being liable to error as well governors as those under them. . .it would be unreasonable to be put under the absolute direction of those who may erre'. Because of this nescience, no one could be expected to surrender his responsibility to another ('nor can man possibly be supposd to give it an other over him absolutely').[54] That the governors of church and state were not decisively in possession of the truth made it irrational to rely upon them.

Equally voluntary action was important. Coercion would be ineffective because, as in 1667, it affected the body and not the understanding, which determined action. The ineffectiveness of coercion in inducing conformity was parallelled by a strange case in which non-imposition induced submission to uniformity.[55]

These reflections, of course, were not favourable to Anglican claims. They undercut the claim to understand God's intent for church order and implied that the Church of England had no claim to force others to conformity. Thus the civil and the ecclesiastical parallel each other. On the one hand, there were claims that superiors, whether in church or state, knew better than their inferiors. On the other hand, there was an assertion of parity: that for the purposes of political authority each agent was as well fitted to govern as the next, and that for ecclesiastical purposes all were unsure of the truth.

Again, if the truth was accessible at all, each human agent could be as well endowed as the next with the means to get it. This, indeed, would be Locke's position. 'GOD has furnished Men with Faculties sufficient to direct them in the Way they should take, if they will but seriously employ them that Way,' he wrote in *An Essay*.[56] In effect this involves a further view. If Locke wished to maintain that everyone could direct themselves towards Heaven he had to suppose that the terms and conditions involved were easy for everyone to understand. This married easily enough with the Protestant view of the Bible, but it required additionally that Christian doctrine, so far as vital for salvation, was straightforwardly intelligible, that each individual was sufficiently endowed to find their way to Heaven, especially that the Bible could be grasped by the human understanding. This, of course, would be the position of Locke's *The Reasonableness of Christianity*.

However, all this is to anticipate. It is to anticipate in the sense that though Locke's jottings of the mid seventies made these presumptions and suggested certain lines of development, they did little to explain the former and nothing to extrapolate the latter. It is anticipation more pointedly because some time elapsed between the mid seventies and Locke's developing alternatives to absolutism and Anglicanism. It is to the conditions under which this happened that we should turn now.

IV

It was not entirely obvious in the later seventies that Anglicanism, for all its principles, was bound to oppose comprehension or toleration *entirely*. Political circumstances might make friendliness to dissent prudent. The success of the episcopate in imposing a traditional Anglican church order and in maintaining its dominance depended on support from the laity. This had been forthcoming in the sixties not least because of Anglican success in identifying religious dissent with political subversion. But this appeal began to look a little implausible as the chief figures of the generation of the civil war passed from the scene and younger men came forward to people public life. Neither could English dissenters, whom a decade or more had shown to lack the strength and the will to overthrow the government that penalised their worship, compete with the spectre of Roman Catholicism.

The theoretical dangers of Catholicism in political life gradually took hold of the country's practical imagination in the seventies. It took its footing from the evident fact that the heir presumptive to the throne

179

was a Roman Catholic. The many evidences of Charles' virility did not include a legitimate child; whilst his surviving brother and heir, James, Duke of York had turned to Rome. The exact date of James' conversion was unknown, but keen observers inferred it by 1672[57] and it was public property in 1673. Of course Charles was the elder of the brothers by merely three years, but his illness of 1679 made a Catholic succession seem close.

The terror of a Catholic future took hold fully with the advent of the Popish Plot, a conspiracy by Jesuits and others to murder Charles – probably an imaginary event and certainly not one which made any practical distance.[58] Thus the nonconformists were displaced as a threat in the popular imagination by the Roman Catholics. Displaced is perhaps too weak a word, for though both dissenters and Catholics were in fact numerically marginal the catholic danger seemed far more terrible.[59]

The Popish Plot was Shaftesbury's opportunity. The Plot summoned up a spectacle of absolutism, the subversion of liberty and property, foreign influence and Catholic domination. It was thus capable of alarming those (at least those who believed in its reality) who cared for constitutional government, who cherished the rights of Englishmen, who hated foreigners and feared Roman Catholicism. In the England of 1679, in other words, it was an ecumenical cause. Shaftesbury did his best to encourage credence in it, and used the support he attracted to further appropriate causes.[60]

It would be wrong to suppose that the Whigs, as Shaftesbury and those who associated with him at this point are known to posterity, were homogeneous in principles or policy.[61] The common denominators, insofar as they can be recognised, lay in relieving dissent at the expense of the Church of England and in ensuring, by whatever means, that the English monarchy would not become a vehicl for the absolutism that a Catholic king might import. This latter end might be achieved by using parliament to limit the power of the monarchy or to impose special limitations upon a Catholic king or to exclude altogether a Catholic from the throne in favour of a protestant candidate. Shaftesbury favoured exclusion, and the crisis of the years following 1679 has become known as the Exclusion crisis. But whilst the direction of Shaftesbury's actions is clear enough, *precisely* what he intended has never been established with certainty, not least because his movement was deflected.

The Popish Plot made the court defensive, but did not defeat it. Initially there was no turning the anti-Popish tide. The rational policy was to be sufficiently concessive – or to seem to be so – in order to establish credentials free from papistical and absolutist taint. Amongst these were an apparent receptiveness to limitations on the monarchy, whether by a diminution of its power or by constraints on a Catholic king. Charles, however, did not countenance exclusion: his brother, though a political nuisance, was his brother and lineal successor. Charles would not vary the succession. When the hysteria about the Plot began to subside in 1681 and when he had summoned parliament to meet in Oxford, outside the turbid atmosphere of a capital dominated by the Whigs, Charles struck. Parliament was dissolved, whiggery and dissent represented as the real enemies of liberty and property and as the friends of disorder. Public opinion, insofar as it can be gauged, remained indifferent or hostile as the blackening of the Whigs was succeeded by their persecution. The Rye House Plot of 1683 (which, if there was such a plot, aimed to assassinate Charles and James) seems to have projected no appeal to the country, whilst the rebellions of Monmouth and Argyll in 1685 (aiming to upset the newly succeeded James) obtained little popular support.[62] But our concern is presently not with the state but the church.

In 1679–80 the obvious response to the papal threat was the unity of Protestant denominations against the common enemy. Schemes for this end were floated.[63] Whether conceived as comprehension or toleration, they placed unity above uniformity. They enjoyed some approval from dissenters, Whigs, moderates and even the royal party, which was keen to establish its non-Popish credentials. They even seemed to acquire the support of the Anglican hierarchy.[64]

That support, however, was evanescent, for it sprang from an exigency that passed with the reassertion of Charles' authority.[65] It was evident in any case that the church was prepared to give little ground. Edward Stillingfleet's *The Unreasonableness of Separation* showed clearly that the hierarchy would offer nothing that would compromise the validity of their assertions. It countenanced comprehension only in a marginal way and contemplated toleration under license. It treated both as concessions of policy rather than admissions of principle. Concerning those 'Dissenting Protestants, who agree with us in all the Doctrinal Articles of our Church; and only scruple the use of a few Ceremonies, and some late Impositions' Stillingfleet suggested that '*it would be a part of Christian Wisdom and Condescension in the Governors of our* Church, *to remove those Bars from a freedom in joyning in full Communion with us*', though he did not think that such dissenters had good grounds for their scruples.[66] The '*many. . .zealous Protestants*' whose objection to Anglican liturgy and church government was more thorough, he hoped, might be granted an indulgence on subscription to the thirty-four doctrinal Articles and the Test Act, as well as payment of fines to the Established Church (which they were not to criticise). They would not be allowed '*to breed up* Scholars, *or to teach Gentlemens Sons* University-Learning', as this would propagate their views, and must submit to episcopal supervision.[67] In other words he suggested that right lay with the Church of England.

This is evident in how Stillingfleet treated dissenting clergymen. He would not admit that anyone who subscribed to the doctrinal Articles only was to be counted as an Anglican clergyman. His case was that this contradicted the existing terms of the church and this he would not countenance. '*We do heartily and sincerely desire* Union *with our Brethren,*' he wrote,

If it may be had on just and reasonable Terms; but they must not think, that we will give up the Cause of the Church *for it.*[68]

The 'Cause of the Church' was evidently at the heart of Stillingfleet's views. What precisely did it comprise?

If we consider Stillingfleet's tract as a piece of policy it was ambiguous. If events had taken a turn for the worse from the Anglican viewpoint it could be represented as an opening move. For there was some room for expansion in its views (just as Stillingfleet became a bishop after the Toleration Act of 1689). If, on the other hand, no concessions were necessary its principles embodied the grounds on which the Anglican church stood.

These grounds, of course, were essentially that it claimed truth. The Church of England understood itself to be a true church. It had besides more distinctive claims. An extensive repertoire of scholarship was deployed to prove the unsullied derivation of its essential practices from the early church. Its claims to independence from Rome were defended through intensive argument, as by Stillingfleet himself. As a true church it claimed connection with God. By this was understood not that the entire structure of the church was *jure divino* but that it provided a conduit from God to convey the benefits of His benevolence to man. In other words because Anglican claims were true, adherence to the Church of England was warranted.

Anglican assertion implied no hostility to foreign churches. The Church of England claimed a national standing. Stillingfleet argued that the fall of the Roman Empire had liberated the churches of its provinces to form autonomous bodies. 'By *Whole Churches*,' he meant 'the *Churches* of such *Nations*, which upon the decay of the *Roman Empire*, resumed their just Right of Government to themselves, and upon their owning Christianity, incorporated into one Christian

182

Society, under the same common ties and Rules of Order and Government.'[69] Foreign churches within their own realm enjoyed in principle a parity with Anglicanism in England. But two sorts of deviation were less acceptable.

The claims of the papacy were incompatible with the standing of Anglicanism. The Church of Rome asserted a headship of all churches, based on its claim to have continuously maintained the transmission of authority from Christ and His apostles. As such it could claim too that its doctrine came from God and was therefore incontestable. Most characteristically this took the form of asserting the Pope's infallibility. Naturally the Anglican church resisted all of these claims, not just by denying that anyone was infallible but by arguing a purer preservation of the Christian tradition. To Rome's assertion that the Anglican body was schismatic, it replied that an episcopal succession was adequate to the true church.

The claims of dissent were offensive in a different way. Where Rome undermined the legitimacy of Anglicanism, dissent queried its claims to truth. For conscientious objection to the institutions of any church implies that they are false or at least insufficiently proven. Hence the very large volume of literature in which the divines of the Restoration church set out to persuade the dissenters to the Anglican view.[70] Hence too the assertion that dissenting scruples should be discounted, as either malign or trivial.[71] Both of these responses to dissent reflected the same assumption: that the true church was identifiable and accordingly that to satisfy conscience was a matter of demonstrating the fact. Evident truth turned casuistry into argument rather than persuasion and, if the arguments were held to be decisive, a conscience which was not convinced by them was defective in some way, whether intellectually or morally. If Stillingfleet was prepared to be concessive he yielded only the inessential and that without any intellectual compromise.

Stillingfleet had a reputation as a liberal divine. Indeed he emphasised his tenderness towards nonconformity. If his writings are sharp it was merely in finding formulae for submission to Anglicanism which gave very little ground to the dissenters. Others were less tender. The assertion of truth demanded the support of the civil arm. Parker had called vocally for it in the past and did so again.[72] Stillingfleet was a subtle enemy to toleration as understood by Locke.

The document which Locke and James Tyrrell, his former pupil and friend, wrote in response to Stillingfleet's writings adopted the mode of argument which Stillingfleet himself had employed against dissenters. The *Defence of Nonconformity* replied to each assertion in his *ad*

183

hominem argument by rejection in detail. But within this commentary positive views can be discerned, which show how Locke's views implied conclusions very different from the Anglican divines'.

In part the manuscript dwelt upon the Catholic danger, arguing especially that a Church of England under royal control would become a vehicle for 'a Popish Prince' to impress his views upon the nation.[73] At one level this was merely a response to the standard Anglican gambit that the separation of Anglicanism from dissent weakened the common Protestant front.[74] At another it suggested one good reason why the use of the royal supremacy Locke had countenanced in 1672 had become inappropriate. Accordingly the *Defence* conceived churches not as bodies subordinate to the state, even in respect of things indifferent in worship, but as entities distinct from it, and from each other, membership of which was voluntary and whose sanctions could not include civil punishment.[75] Congruently, it bypassed the notion of a true church as understood by Anglicans suggesting that authority was inapplicable to the ecclesiastical, so that each must choose for himself.[76] Likewise it suggested that it was 'being perswaded in conscience' that they were right rather than the actual possession of 'the truth of the doctrine & worship' that had given Anglicans 'a reason to reforme & set up in now separate churches'[77] and, indeed, was sceptical about 'those, who would perswade the world, yᵗ any one forme of Church Government is Jure Divino'.[78] In short the evidently immovable posture of Anglicanism suggested that it was needful to focus upon the alternative to a state church.

A Defence was never published. It seems probable that it was overtaken by events. Toleration and comprehension alike had been lost even before the Oxford parliament was dissolved.[79] But there was a more profound point. It was more obvious than ever (if possible) that Anglicanism was unfriendly to the style of religious settlement that Locke desired and that Anglicanism was politically immoveable. That implied an unfriendliness to both a church detached from politics and to a state church in the sense intended by *A Letter from a Person of Quality*. Neither of the alternatives envisaged in Shaftesbury's circle in the seventies looked practically plausible. Moreover, in the course of defeating the exclusion movement, the king had allied himself with the bishops and their lay supporters. The implication was that for the foreseeable future the English state had nothing to offer for toleration or comprehension. Certainly, it must have seemed so to Locke when he left England for Holland in 1683.

V

Though the practical situation in England was unfavourable, the continent and the higher ground of theory remained open. Accordingly the work we know as *A Letter concerning Toleration* is more properly *Epistola de Tolerantia* and develops a theory of the church and its relation to the state. The lineaments of such a theory, in part at least, may be seen beneath the surface of Locke's pieces on toleration from 1667, but so far had not been articulated into an explanatory account. By the same token the effects that Locke's view of the church adumbrated for his other concerns had not become clear. It is to Locke's theory that we should turn now.

Locke's domicile on the continent was part of the process that elicited a general theoretical statement from him. His *Epistola* was written with a new audience in mind. Where Locke's English writings were concerned primarily with the question of indifference, here a broader statement was appropriate. To write in Latin was to write for an audience spanning Europe and whose mutual divergences were more marked than those amongst English Protestants.

The materials from which Locke constructed the bases of his argument, of course, had been generated in his earlier reflections, whether or not they had been developed explicitly or not. His view of the purpose of civil government, his principle that religious conscience should be unmolested as long as it was peaceable and his sense of clerical claims to embody a true church were present already. Their theoretical shape and the explicitness with which they were articulated, however, reflected a more general focus of attention.

Mutual forbearance amongst Christians, so the tenor of Locke's case went, was appropriate. For the churches stood in a common condition of ignorance about which of them was the true one. A church, as conceived by Locke, was not the embodiment of an authority handed down from God but instead an organisation created by human beings. Hence the notion of the civil government having a duty to uphold God's truth by supporting an individual church became irrelevant. Claims to divine authority for any specific scheme of worship, by the same token, were beside the point.

That Locke was advancing a theory of the church and its relations was apparent from the outset of the *Epistola*. He announced his subject as reciprocal tolerance between Christians, *de mutua inter Christianos tolerantia*.[80] This was a different agenda from that of 1667, which had concerned 'liberty of conscience'. The subject matter of the latter had been the attitude which the civil magistrate should adopt towards those who conscientiously eschewed a given church or, to put the case in different terms, a matter of the deviations permitted from a church with some claim to centrality. Now, however, he discussed Christians in relation to each other.

His central point was that a church was a body constituted by human action. This had been implicit in his remarks of 1679 that there was a 'power of every society or profession of religion to establish within them selves confessions of faith & rules of decency & order'.[81] Now Locke defined a church as 'a free society of people joining together of their own initiative in order that they might worship God in the manner that they believe pleasing to the deity for the salvation of their souls'.[82] There was no hint that such a society was constituted by anything except a coalition of human wills. As Locke added a little later 'a church grows out of members by their own initiative'.[83]

This doctrine rested upon several presumptions, the most important of which concerned human capacities. Locke did not suppose that people were born into churches, but rather that they adhered voluntarily to the body in which they believed true religion was found.[84] This presumed that people had understanding enough to judge for themselves and had a will to carry through their decisions. It would be on these terms, as we noted above, that they would be able to direct themselves.

That such a decision should be legitimate as well as feasible supposed the absence of human superiors set over the agent in his or her religious capacity. In other words, Locke was making suppositions about the divine warrant of the church and about the civil government.

To Locke's mind the identity of the church related to Christ. Christ's work was conceived in a mode that was personal rather than institutional. His mission lay with the Gospel, with the preaching of peace and with the exemplary figure He presented to mankind. This message of peace, decency and holiness indicated to Locke's mind that the function of the church was to encourage faith in God's word and good deeds.[85] These two matters, faith and works, are the constituents of goodness in the full sense as Locke's century understood it, the sense required for salvation. In short, he conceived the mission of the Christian church to lie with the preparing the individual for his or her future life. There was no hint that its business was broader, though Christ's mission was placed in polar constrast with cruelty and immorality.[86]

The notion of a true church, that is to say a body authorised by God and providing a conduit of His grace not available to those outside it, was bypassed by the disclaimer that this was not the proper place to discuss it. Despite this modest observation, Locke felt able to make the points that suited his purpose. That is to say, he enquired whether Christian churches should not understand themselves purely in reference to the scriptures, suggested that the apostolic succession was superfluous for a true church and argued that the dissensions of its bearers gave a free hand to the individual believer.[87] At any rate, if Locke did deal with the matter of ecclesiastical truth with his left hand, so to speak, the tenor of his own views was apparent.

By eliminating the question of the true church in effect, Locke deprived the church of jurisdiction over believers at large. As we have seen, superiority involved a claim to know better and, more precisely, to embody the ecclesiastical truth. To omit the question of the true church was thus to deprive the ecclesiastic of his superiority over other Christians. Hence we find Locke asserting that churches stand to each other in the same relations as private individuals to one another: that is to say, 'one has no rights over another'.[88] The same conclusion was reached by a different route when Locke denied that there was any judge of orthodoxy on earth.[89] No church, to his mind, could claim a superior warrant from God.

By the same token, the magistrate could have no special function in upholding the truth about the church. Locke identified the magistrate's task in terms of civil life and as such separated it from a distinctly Christian responsibility. Locke denied vigorously that a political superior as such had a privileged understanding of ecclesiastical affairs. Neither did the magistrate's office confer any special grasp of ecclesiastical truth. He was as ignorant as others, because 'neither the office of state nor the right to legislate discloses to the magistrate the way that leads to Heaven more certainly than his study as a private individual'.[90] Locke asserted more pointedly that though princes were superiors in power, their natural endowments were no more than other people's. Insight into civil government, he argued, implied no certain knowledge of anything else, including the true religion.[91] Church and state stood on an equal footing of understanding, or rather nescience.

These views legitimated the possibility that churches were constituted by human action and that membership of them too was voluntary. That a church should be constituted by man rather than established by God supposed not merely that people had the understanding and will necessary to the task but also that God had not preempted them: for if princes were equal to others by nature, God remained everyone's superior. Likewise, for people to be entitled to opt for churches according to their own decision supposed that God had not signified which church had His special approval.

187

Generally speaking, Locke's view of the church presupposes a view of divine activity. The Lockean God would be distinguished by treating people at the outset in a fundamentally identical manner and by making the organisation of their lives a matter for their own responsibility. That it is to say, firstly, that people came from the hand of God with the same faculties. These faculties fitted them to direct their own lives, subject of course to God's legislation. That legislation, as we know, combined precepts concerning the worship of God with others about conduct towards others. If the duties of the First Table required an institutional setting, the devising of it was left to man rather than being imposed by God, so far as people could tell. The same would be true of the institutions required to facilitate the practice of the Second Table, namely civil government. To put the matter another way, God did not exercise Himself to produce specific arrangements in church or state. Congruently, Locke asserted that dominion was not founded in grace.[92]

His view of the church may be said to suggest, though not to imply, something about grace more generally. The view that the church was divinely authorised made it an obvious vehicle for God to convey grace. Whilst Locke's agnosticism about the true church did not exclude such an operation, it made it rather difficult to say anything about it. This was true especially after he responded to one of his critics, Jonas Proast, by suggesting that it was hard to distinguish the marks of the church (except that a true church would be tolerant).[93] If Locke himself came to discuss Christian doctrine, he would have to treat grace primarily in other terms – instead of discussing the sacraments administered by the churches, for instance, he would have to concentrate on matters such as revelation and covenant.

The implications of God's dealings in politics will be pursued in the next chapter. One important implication for Christianity itself was that its character would be understood in a credal rather than in a traditionary way. We have seen that Locke by-passed the view that the identity of the church was handed down from God through Christ and His apostles. A traditionary lineage, indeed, would carry little theological weight if it were supposed that ecclesiastical institutions were man made. Locke understood the church's message in terms of the work of Christ, and especially in terms of what made for salvation. This, of course, comprised works and appropriate beliefs. These beliefs, no doubt, could be formulated as a creed. We may add that the content of the creed would focus neatly enough on Christ's work. So indeed it turned out, though this is to anticipate.

Certainly Locke would include amongst desirable tenets a belief in

God. For though Locke favoured tolerance amongst Christians, he preferred them (and the civil government) to turn against atheists. Locke's *Epistola* continued the principles he had stated in 1667 about magisterial toleration. The business of the magistrate as such lay with the protection of civil interests so that beliefs, whether speculative or practical, were of concern to him only if they trenched upon civil life. Religious groups with pretensions that disturbed a peaceable existence continued to be suspect (though Roman Catholics were not distinguished by name). Atheists were not to be tolerated, because their belief (or lack of it) was understood to be a danger to civil society. Why was this?

Locke assumed that the understanding determined the action of the will. This was not an uncommon position and, in fact, it was one he had articulated before composing his *Drafts* of 1671. Nonetheless it was an important part of his case for tolerating religious dissent. Because the will (which moved action) was itself moved by belief, it was useless for the civil government to coerce the will: this would not change anyone's conscientious beliefs about religious ceremonies. And force could do nothing to change the mind. But the same view that helped Locke to favour toleration for religious dissent turned him against atheism.[2]

The view that the understanding determined the will and so action implied that intellectual tenets would direct action, if the agent acted at all. The character of the tenets would inform the sort of actions he or she undertook. It happened to be the case that Locke believed that God explained good and evil; as he insisted in 1667 the being of God was the basis of morality. Thus believing in God would be a condition of behaving morally.

It follows from this reasoning that an atheist would not conform to morality. That is to say, because the atheist did not believe in God he or she could not believe in morality; and since the understanding governed the will the atheist would not seek to act morally. Thus because thought governed action, the theoretical denial of God implied there was nothing moral: in Locke's words, the taking away of God, even in thought, dissolves all things.[94]

In particular it dissolved society. Locke in his *Essays* had assumed that the practice of justice was the bond of society. This assumed that a community, whose existence conferred benefits on its members, could be had only on a basis of fair dealing. It was natural in a theistic climate to suppose not only that God explained morality but also, more generally, that to attest one's fair dealing by an appeal to Heaven was to offer a guarantee. Hence Locke assumed that 'Faith and Truth, especially in all Occasions of attesting it upon the solemn Appeal to Heaven by an Oath, is the great Bond of Society'. Granted too that the civil government should uphold society it followed that it should encourage such veracity, 'this it becomes the Wisdom of Magistrates carefully to support, and render as sacred and awful in the Minds of the People as they can.'[95] The atheist seemed to threaten all this.

It follows, too, that this line of thought must exclude atheists from religious toleration. That is to say, atheism was a position about religion that had practical implications; as such, in the Lockean scheme, it fell within the magistrate's oversight, and the magistrate would see that atheism was inconsistent with morality and that because morality (or parts of it) supported society, atheism undermined society. So the magistrate would have to proceed against it. Thus where Locke was friendly to the conscientious believer he was unfriendly in the extreme to the conscientious unbeliever.

There is one line of criticism against this of which Locke is unlikely to have been unaware, which in fact was published before he wrote his *Epistola*. This was Pierre Bayle's *Letter on the Comet* of 1682, which the author expanded the next year as *Miscellaneous Reflections on the Comet*. The work, written as its title suggested on the occasion of the great comet of December, 1680 seen over Western Europe, argued against the supposition that celestial events reflected divine displeasure at impiety and sin, suggesting instead a mechanistic explanation of natural phenomena. This was accompanied by the suggestion that God would not use such a method of recalling people to obedience, because most people (Bayle thought) happened to worship Him in an idolatrous manner: hence to cause them to become more fervent in their devotions would augment idolatry. The anti-Catholic polemic implicit in this and the mechanism would have pleased Locke, no doubt. The inference Bayle drew was less attractive. His implication is that God would rather not be worshipped at all than worshipped idolatrously: so an atheist would be more acceptable to Him than an erroneous believer.

Bayle's view was not more palatable because it suggested that theistic belief was not necessary to sustain moral practice. In the course of exploring atheism, Bayle suggested that a society of atheists was a practical possibility. That is to say, although atheists lacked theistic beliefs to inspire good conduct, they would nonetheless behave well.[96] They would understand that moral conduct sustained society, without which they would all suffer. Alternatively, if atheists were unmoved by this consideration, the sanctions of the civil magistrate and a regard for their own reputation would stimulate them to behave well. Whatever the mechanism of causation, it was apparent that if Bayle were right people could behave well without looking to God and that He was not needed to explain a viable ethical code.

Bayle himself was not entirely comfortable with some consequences of his own opinions. The effectiveness of terrestrial pressures in producing conduct to which the agent did not give a sincere assent might encourage religious persecution.[97]

Locke's response was indirect. Bayle had challenged the view that theistic belief was the cause of good conduct. Locke did not deny that some Christians behaved badly. His own views about those who persecuted in the name of Christianity and his conclusion that the practice of morality upheld society precluded that, as did his sense that some people at least were moved by the codes of conduct embodied in the law of their land or by the operative opinion in their own country. His response, in effect, was that it would be possible to contrive the external pressure imposed on the agent by his love of repute in such a manner that it would implant in him or her a love of the conduct God prescribed: in other words people could be motivated to act morally, from the love of God, through one of the agencies Bayle supposed would make people behave rightly without such theistic conviction. Again, there remained the project of demonstrating morality from a theistic basis which, because it was intended to be certain, would cut out the insinuation that a genuine ethical code could dispense with God. But for these we should turn to Locke's writings on education and the human understanding.

More immediately, his writings on toleration presumed a position in political theory. Locke's view that civil government existed only for the purposes of civil interests presupposed a distinct view.[98] We are all familiar with the view that the rights for whose protection government was instituted according to Locke were life, liberty and property. The protection of religion, whether as worship or as truth, were not included, though contemporaries as diverse as John Owen, Hobbes and Jonas Proast supposed that the promotion of Christian religion was an objective of civil government.[99] Religion appeared in this light only once in *Two Treatises*, and that in passing. But unless Locke explained civil government on terms that did not include religion, his argument about ecclesiastical matters would lack logical insulation. *Two Treatises of Government* is the complement of the *Epistola de Tolerantia*.

Chapter 7

Locke's theory of the church involved a parallel treatment of civil government, explaining that the latter's authority concerned the matters of this life rather than the next. The phrase 'civil government' is embodied in the proper title of what we call habitually the *Second Treatise of Government*, and it is a much apter designation. For Locke's explanations there refer exclusively to a secular organisation. Of course this concentration upon the civil, which was remarkable in the seventeenth century, does not exclude theological explanations. Indeed these are vital to Locke's argument about civil government, both because they provided him with a set of purposes to explain his preferred view of that institution and because those purposes, being God's, could be taken as authoritative. Locke explained the secular state in theological terms. The need for an explanation of political authority may be referred partly to the political situation of Locke's day, as we shall see, and partly to his pre-existing posture on such matters as toleration. But before we turn to Locke's situation, it will be as well to outline the general characteristics of his book.

Two Treatises of Government is an explanatory work. It argued that absolutist explanations did not make sense and that the true explanation of political power was quite different. Its discourse was directed principally to these ends. Locke applied the word 'demonstration' in his text and often criticised Sir Robert Filmer for preferring assertion to explanation. He criticised the quality of Filmer's work, terming it 'glib Nonsense' and describing Filmer's reasoning as 'nothing but a Rope of Sand'. But though Locke expressed disdain for its cogency, he treated it as an explanation. Filmer's argument was '*his* Hypothesis' and its refutation provides 'premises' for Locke's conclusions, whose first book aims to refute Filmer's *False Principles* and whose second to reveal *The True Original, Extent, and End of Civil-Government*.[1]

The object of Locke's distaste was absolutism. Absolutism is a concept foreign to the modern fashion. We are all used to the idea of constitutional government, in which the governors are responsible to the governed because from the latter derives authority and that authority is given on specified terms. Absolutism is the doctrine that the ruler is not responsible to his subjects because his power derives to him in a different manner. Two sorts of derivation figured prominently. One assumed that authority came directly from God. The other took authority to derive from the people in a way that freed rulers from responsibility to them. In the latter way, as well as in the former, power came from God, this time indirectly, for He was supposed to have left it to the people's discretion how they organised government. Thus it assumed that theology was explanatory, attributing certain specific intentions to God in order to assemble ideas for a given destination. If, however, one alters this family of ideas, by rearrangement as much as by substitution, a very different political destination may be reached. The intellectual need to deal with absolutism is evident in Locke's own thought. Neither his view of toleration nor his view of the church as an organisation constituted by voluntary membership sat easily with an absolute authority, assuming the latter to be of unrestricted scope, or with the view of the human condition which countenanced absolutism and compulsory churches. By the same measure it did not consort well inferentially with his view of the human understanding. Neither did it fit the practical circumstances of the day, in which the Anglican church seemed to hymn the merits of absolutism in England.[2]

Absolutism, besides, did not harmonise with the political prepossessions of the circle in which Locke moved. As early as 1675 Shaftesbury had signalled his distaste of it to his peers.[3] He insinuated that absolute governments were not entitled to unlimited obedience.[4] *A Letter from a Person of Quality* had made a similar point, distinguishing 'bounded' from 'absolute' governments. A 'bounded' government was one 'limited by humane laws', denoting a contrast with absolute governments whose rulers were bound only by God's laws. The relevance of the distinction became clear when *A Letter* asked 'how can there be a distinction. . .between Absolute, and bounded Monarchys, if *Monarchs* have only the fear of *God* and no fear of humane Resistance to restrain them'. England, *A Letter* added, had a bounded government and, we must infer, one in which monarchs should be subject to 'fear of humane Resistance'.[5]

Explanation is far from being the sole constituent of political discourse. Practical ends can be connected or annexed to theoretical writings. There has been some question about Locke's hypothesised involvement in political affairs and about the possible practical use of his writings.[6] But we should not be diverted from considering their explanatory character. The work sets out to show how 'political power' is specific in its goals and limited in its authority, the latter being revocable. The practical activities Locke may have projected and the possible uses of his volume are conceptually distinct from this and from each other.

To give give birth to political thought answering to such a destination is to synthesise greatly. It is to combine ideas, perhaps modifying many of these, perhaps inventing some more and certainly combining them in a distinct way. Thus a family of ideas is laid out. These ideas may concern not only matters of hypothesised fact but also explanatory constructs, whether suppositions in moral theory, philosophy or theology. It is to combine ideas, in particular, in a manner which explains certain features of political life *distinctively*. Often this manner of explanation will produce conclusions designedly inconsistent with other specimens.

Locke's *Two Treatises* display these features. Together they lay out a theory which embraces many items in social and political life – whether liberty, property, education, the family or civil government – and explain, through such means as God, His revealed and natural laws, mankind's dominion over nature, natural rights and the idea of relation, that government is to have an authority which is conditional and revocable. Thus Locke reached conclusions inconsistent with absolutism of whatever sort.

To show how Locke constituted his argument, it is necessary to consider in turn his treatment of explanatory matters and the understanding of social and political life he effected through them. But before proceeding to this we need to understand Locke's agenda a little more fully by examining the character of absolutism.

I

Absolutism, in its most basic sense, suggested that those who ruled were not answerable to any terrestrial superior. In the English usage of the day 'absolute' denoted primarily complete and perfect: a ruler subject to no human superior was clearly that. If a ruler were without a superior, it followed that he was not responsible to anyone on earth. Thus we find Charles I remarking that 'Princes are not bound to give accompt of their actions.'[7] By the same token no one was entitled to oppose themselves to the prince's will or to question his authority. This formulation, however, tells us little about the extent of that authority or its relationship to God.

Whilst this style of ruling was supposed to be compatible with God's directions, whether because consistent with them or, more strikingly, specified in them, it was not the case that rulers stood above God. On the contrary it was His superiority over them that situated their superiority over other people. If Charles I announced that 'Princes are not bound to give accompt of their actions', he added, 'but to God alone'. By the same token rulers answered to His directions, whether revealed or natural. It is worth emphasising especially their subordination to the terms of divine laws. As Bodin put it,

All the princes of the earth are subject to them, and they must bow their heads in fear and reverence before His divine majesty. The absolute power of princes and sovereign lords does not extend to the laws of God and of nature[8]

for just as rulers stood above subjects so was God the superior who stood above them all.

This indicates that in one case rulers were answerable to laws they themselves did not make. Traditionally people had conceived another case. It was often supposed that rulers were at once absolute and at the same time bound to respect the customary, traditional or fundamental laws of the kingdom which neither they nor their predecessors had legislated. Bodin embodied this understanding of the matter. He emphasised that absolute authority implied 'conditions of appointment' specifying 'only such as are inherent in the laws of God and of nature', and indicating that rulers need not be bound by the undertakings of their predecessors.[9] Only the ruler was entitled to legislate, and rulers did not need the consent of subjects in law-making. But simultaneously Bodin indicated that 'the constitutive laws of the realm. . .cannot be infringed by the prince'.[10] Hooker alluded at once to royal superiority and to such rules when he remarked that 'though no manner of person or cause be unsubject to the king's power, yet so is the power of the king over all and in all limited, that unto all his proceedings the law itself is a rule'.[11] In the concise formula of John Rawlinson 'A King. . .though he be free from *coaction* to keepe the law, yet must he voluntarily submit his will to the *direction* of the law' or, in the fuller statement of Charles Merbury, the king 'is subiect vnto lawes both ciuill, and common, to customes, priuileges. . .and all kinde of promises'.[12] The point was repeated by Baxter, who suggested both that the king was 'under those contracts which are called *Fundamental* or *Constitutive Laws*, made by common consent to secure the subjects rights' and also that 'the *Soveraign Power* is *unlimited* and *absolute*, as to any limitation of any *superiour humane Power*'.[13] To be absolute, that is subject to no superior, to be the sole legislator, was not to be free from fundamental law.

How does such a notion make sense? It is intelligible in terms of two points, one about the theory of dominion and one about property. If we conceive dominion in a context of feudal ideas we discover that a multiple superiority is possible. That is to say, agent B has superiority over object C, but A has superiority over B and thus over object C also. Thus we find Richard Fitzralph observing that there could be several rights of dominion over a single thing that belonged to one alone: a baron had dominion over one barony, his lord the earl over the same barony and the king over it too.[14] It follows from this that the dominion of a king is of the same kind, though higher in degree, as that of a baron. Thus, in the language of Fortescue, just as a piece of land which is given to me is called my right (*jus*), so the power given to the king is properly called the king's right[15] or, as a Prussian put it as late as the nineteenth century, 'the king is a large estate owner and landowner; the noble estate owner is a small king'.[16] Thus the royal authority figured as a right which was of the same type as a subject's right over property and, moreover, a right not logically inconsistent with the latter.

This hierarchical structure suggests that a superior would have the use of his inferior's possessions and, indeed, Fitzralph suggests that there were conditions under which this was so.[17] But it would be possible to qualify this arrangement by conceiving a political organisation in which royal superiority was not unrestricted. Fortescue, for instance, mentioned three sorts of lordship, *dominium regale, dominium politicum* and *dominium despoticum*.[18] Let us attend to the former two, putting aside *dominium despoticum* for the moment. Fortescue suggested that a *dominium regale* was one in which a monarch 'mey rule his peple bi suche lawes as he makyth hym self'. This legislative power covered their property; 'And therfore he mey sett vppon thaim tayles and other imposicions, such as he wol hym self, with owt thair assent.' Fortescue contrasted this with *dominium regale et politicum* in which a king 'may not rule his peple by other lawes than such as thai assenten vnto' so that their property was beyond his sphere, 'he mey sett vpon thaim non imposicions with owt thair owne assent'.[19] Clearly, under this arrangement there were some matters beyond a monarch's control, but we may ask why. There is no hint in Fortescue of the monarch's subordination to other people, despite the occasional commentator: Fortescue's monarch was absolute, in the sense of having no superior on earth. But as we see the monarch did not have authority of unlimited extent. The reason for this was given in another place, the *De Laudibus Legum Anglie*. Fortescue argued that the laws constituting a kingdom were structural to it, that 'the law, under which the people is incorporated, may be compared to the nerves or sinews of the body natural'. Hence the monarch could not interfere with such laws:

And as the bones and members of the body preserve their functions, and discharge their several offices by the nerves; so do the members of the community preserve their rights by the law. And as the head of the body natural is unable to change its nerves or to deny to the several parts their proper energy, their due nourishment of blood; neither can a king, who is head of the body politic, change the laws thereof, nor take from the people what is theirs by right against their will. . .For he is appointed to protect his subjects in their lives, properties and laws; for this very end and purpose he has the delegation of power from the people; and he has no just claim to any other power but this[20]

and so a monarch might be absolute but not entitled to alter the laws structuring his or her kingdom, just as we have seen in Bodin.

The notion that such laws were fundamental to the being of the kingdom suggested a special status for them. It suggested that they were laws of nature, at least in the sense of laws governing the nature of a certain body. Fortescue, for instance, included amongst the sinews of the state the laws of nature and Merbury wrote of the king's subjection to laws and customs 'So farre forth as they are agreable vnto the lawe of God.'[21] The person and property of the subject would obviously figure as items under natural law. For these constitutive laws included not least financial matters. Fortescue juxtaposed the power to make laws with the power to raise taxes. Amongst the laws a monarch could not alter Bodin mentioned especially those regulating the king's estate. Bodin, too, indicated that the subject's property was beyond monarchical control, so that because 'the prince has no power to exceed the laws of nature which God Himself. . .has decreed, he cannot take his subjects' property' without good cause. Thus, in the formula of Seneca that was quoted from time to time, *ad reges enim potestas omnium pertinet: ad singulos, proprietates.*[22] On this reading there were certain matters beyond absolute monarchs' authority to alter because they were comprised in the laws of God.

This was an obvious restriction on the extent of authority a ruler could enjoy. Under its terms a ruler might be absolute, that is to say answerable to no authority on earth, but at the same time not entitled to breach certain rules. As Locke himself observed '*absolute Power. . .is not Arbitrary* by being absolute'.[23] Some may think this a rather untidy theory, juxtaposing as it does an authority subject to no terrestrial superior and a limitation on the authority's subject matter. Some writers would suggest that this limitation should cease, emphasising *regale dominium* rather than *dominium regale et politicum*.[24] Thus absolutism would extend its meaning, embracing not only an authority subject to no terrestrial superior but also one subject to no limitations of extent.

Absolutists, of course, could not pretend that rulers escaped subjection to God. But they could and did argue that they were bound by no terrestrial laws. James I insisted that he was not bound by the laws of the land. For though 'a good king will frame all his actions to be according to the Law; yet is hee not bound thereto but of his good will'.[25] Filmer emphasised 'the superiority of princes above laws' and, when he excerpted Bodin, omitted all passages qualifying the extent of rulers' authority.[26] Thus in relation to man-made laws, though not divine ones, rulers were arbitrary: they were entitled to act according to their own will. Locke recognised thus much by referring, frequently enough, to absolute authority as arbitrary. Whatever the use *he* made of the term, it does not of itself imply irregularity, either through abrogating existing laws or through impulsive action: it was assumed that rulers would act for the good of their subjects, since their reasonable nature equipped them to govern well[27] and, after all, they had an interest in doing so.[28] Thus, though unrestricted, rulers were not supposed to be tyrants. Bodin distinguished tyrannical monarchy, describing it as a condition in which natural law was ignored and subjects treated as slaves.[29] Locke himself distinguished between despotism and tyranny, at least in that he dealt with the latter as a distinct subject.[30]

Rather monarchs would be despotic, understanding that word in its technical sense. Despotism, Fortescue's *dominium despoticum*, does not imply oppression, which was what people understood by tyranny. A despot was one who had at his or her disposal the lives and goods of those they ruled. As Bodin put it 'a despot can be a just and virtuous prince, and an equitable governor of his people, but he is the master of their persons and their goods'.[31] The point was understood by contemporaries and in dealing with absolutism Locke referred to it sometimes as despotism.[32] Despotism may not sound an agreeable word and it is not less illuminating to take a leaf from Aristotle's *Politics*. Aristotle described[33] a form of kingly rule in which the monarch had the disposal of all, likening it to a household. Perhaps the aptest term for this family of ideas would be 'oeconomical' rule. Here certainly we may situate patriarchal language, that deliberate assimilation of rulers to heads of households or, more precisely, to fathers and especially to the father of all, Adam, from whom kings might thus derive authority. Its significance is apparent in the denials it encountered, as Matthew Kellison's assertion that Adam 'had the power called Oeconomica, yet had he no power of governing a Citie or Common wealth' or Selden's distinction between 'Oeconomique rule' and 'the common state'.[34] But whether we refer to despotism or

'Oeconomica' the ruler had at his disposal the subject's person and goods.

In this model all terrestrial laws must originate from rulers, for otherwise an independent source of regulation could continue. The most obvious form for this claim to assume was that all laws took the form of commands from a superior, as we find in Filmer and Hobbes[35] alike. It found its complement in the further view that there was only one source of law within a community, that is to say in the idea of sovereignty. But whilst Bodin had emphasised sovereignty, he had not insisted that its claims embraced all matters, including the property of subjects.[36] These moves suggested that all fundamental laws either proceeded from monarchical authority or were not properly laws at all. The former manoeuvre was executed through the resources of historical scholarship. James I insisted that the 'Fundamentall Lawes' of Scotland denoted only rules for the descent of the crown and so was 'that which is called IVS REGIS'.[37] Others took up Bodin's point that despotic rule was acquired by conquest, suggesting that monarchs had authority as the heirs of conquerors.[38] Alternatively, it might be argued that people had handed over their rights, including rights over themselves and their properties, to rulers without reservation. Bodin had suggested this,[39] though he had qualified it by references to natural law and the laws constituting kingdoms. Whatever the mode of argument – and several variations could be played on these themes[40] – their destination was the same.

Absolutists insisted in particular that the monarch's will was the sole source of the subject's possessions. James I exploited the theory of dominion for this end, remarking that 'the King is *Dominus omnium bonorum*, and *Dominus directus totius Dominij*, the whole subjects being his vassals, and from him holding all their lands as their ouer-lord, who according to good seruices done vnto him, chaungeth their holdings from tacke to few, from ward to blanch, erecteth new Baronies, and vniteth olde, without aduice or authoritie of either Parliament or any other subalterin iudicall seate'.[41] The law of nature, so far as it referred to property, was omitted from this discourse, Filmer for one making little structural use of it.[42]

Absolutism thus came to embrace four items. One was the notion that monarchs were not answerable to anyone but God. This was a notion with a long lineage. Another was the view that their authority was subject to no limitation by terrestrial rules – that it was not merely absolute but arbitrary. This involved, thirdly, the notion that all law must proceed from a legislator. Coupled with these was the view that rulership was despotic or 'oeconomical', that is to say that the person and property of the subject was at the monarch's disposal. The matter had a practical relevance. We have seen that one of the leading items attributed to natural law or to fundamental law was the property of the subject. The government of England was never rich and frequently exigent, a condition to which the Lords and Commons were not uniformly sympathetic. Absolutism explained why parliamentary consent to levies upon the subject's property was unnecessary, by suggesting either that the source of law was the king's own will alone (not parliament's) or that since all property was his anyway he could dispose of it as he chose.[43] Absolutism was convenient for a financially perplexed monarchy: perhaps otherwise it would have obtained little vogue in England.

A wide variety of responses to these positions was possible. We have seen already the notion that inherited custom embodied some of the content of natural law.[44] Another suggestion was that if England had been conquered this somehow did not signify, either because the Norman Conquest had not abrogated inherited laws or because if abrogated these had been rapidly restored.[45] A third was to argue, more dramatically, that political authority was located in a way quite different to the one the absolutists proposed. The most popular variant was mixed monarchy. This suggested that the monarch was not the sole constituent of the legislative, but rather was a member of a trinity with the Lords and Commons.[46] This had the merit of respecting the monarch's claim to be superior whilst rebutting his claim to rule alone and without the consent of his subjects. It also maintained the notion that there were fundamental laws, for by definition a monarch could not *authorize* such an arrangement. Like arguments about conquest and fundamental law generally this claim turned upon historical scholarship.[47]

Contemporary absolutism, with its claims to unrestricted scope, and the response to it alike suggested three modes of argument. About the first they agreed. Both accepted the supremacy of natural law and regarded other conclusions as acceptable to the degree that they consisted with it. Secondly, there was the theory of law in general. Absolutists used arguments about law as command and about the location of legislative authority. Their opponents disputed the latter. This brings us to the third matter, for the applicability of conclusions from the second dispute turned on suppositions about history, where (as one would expect) different stories were told. These three sorts of argument, at any rate, were common to political discourse. We find them used, in varying proportions, by most thinkers who aspired to a general treatment of political matters. Tyrrell and Sidney differ from Hobbes and Filmer in many respects, but not in this one.[48]

So far we have discussed absolute authority and its extent. What of the practical checks on rulership? These would be found in the distribution of power in the community, as in any political society, but that distribution consisted partly of the constitutional apparatus. Contemporary absolutism implied that there was no constitutional standing by virtue of which subjects were entitled to restrain or, more radically, remove rulers. The earlier view that lower magistrates might restrain their superiors presupposed a ground of authority independent of the ruler they opposed. Mixed monarchy suggested that authority did not lie with one agency alone. But it was possible to undercut absolutism more radically. Absolutist writers often suggested that rulers' authority resulted from a transfer of rights from people at large.[49] An obvious response to that was to suggest that if there was a transfer it was of a more limited character. If it were supposed that people by nature possessed an authority requisite for government, it would be argued that they would part with only that portion of it necessary to yield an effective magistracy rather than surrender themselves utterly to a ruler.

Filmer presented a dramatic challenge to that supposition. To suppose that people could constitute political authority, whether limited or absolute, supposed that originally they were without a political superior. The 'oeconomical' model was compatible with this, if we consider it as a destination. But if instead it *explained* political authority it presupposed that there was always a superior. Filmer claimed that the authority of a father over his offspring and over his household generally implied at the same time political authority. It followed that people always had a superior and, as Filmer understood fatherly power to be absolute, an absolute superior at that.[50]

What line, then, would a writer take who wished to oppose contemporary absolutism and to provide terms on which monarchs could be checked legitimately? Like everyone else our writer would make use of natural law. But though the contents of natural law were agreed generally, its applications varied widely. Of course, he or she would seek to devise an apparatus which explained political authority in a way that was both inconsistent with absolutism and offered grounds for rebutting the activities of rulers, should these be unacceptable. But how are we to explain the particular line which Locke took?

II

It is worth beginning negatively. It has often been remarked that Locke did not use arguments drawn from fundamental law.[51] At one level this is less surprising that might be supposed. For if fundamental law was referred ultimately to natural law, as it was, it follows that to discuss the former was primary and that discussions of constitutional history were secondary. Indeed in Tyrrell's *Patriacha non Monarcha* the discussion of the English constitution largely *followed* the exposition of natural law.[52] At another level, this subordination may make Locke's omission the more remarkable. Whilst we cannot be categorical – for it is perfectly conceivable that he discussed the matter in the absent part of his *First Treatise* – there was a general reason which reduced its importance for Locke. That was his view of law. In the early sixties he had taken over Hobbes' view of law as the legislation of a superior. Though he had done so with a rather un-Hobbesian view of ethics in mind, the definition had general relevance. It was a definition inconsistent with custom, traditionary codes and so on being counted *as law*. It was true that the content of these might coincide in some cases with natural law, but that merely laid the emphasis more firmly on the latter for theoretical purposes.[53]

This is not to say that constitutional history was unimportant to Locke. Hobbes constructed *Leviathan* without this sort of historical reference, but nonetheless argued in *Behemoth* and *A Dialogue* respectively that its criticisms of mixed monarchy were illustrated by the course of English history and that English law properly understood reflected his view of sovereignty. Though Locke did not write books of this kind, he did recommend works of constitutional history as part of a gentleman's education.[54] The point is simply that his view of law directed his theoretical attention elsewhere.

Where did it lie? Locke's *Second Treatise*, as we shall show, offered an explanation of political authority that was incompatible with absolutism and which explained also that the terms on which rulers held political authority implied that they could be challenged legitimately. In doing so it constructed an account of mankind's destiny which provided a theological and ethical basis for discounting the most powerful arguments for absolutism. It was natural for Locke to present an account contrasting with those of Bodin, Grotius, Hobbes and Pufendorf. That he preferred an alternatve account to a detailed refutation accorded with his practice elsewhere: as we have seen his writings on the human understanding offer a conceptual programme meant to upstage peripatetics and others rather than attacking them point by point. In any case it was surely sensible to oppose himself to the most powerful arguments for other views.[55]

But equally it was Locke's habit to offer a critique of another view before embarking upon his own exposition, as he had prefaced a refutation of Bagshawe in the *English Tract* to the development of his own in the *Latin Tract* and had used innatism as a critical preface to his own theory of ideas from 1671. As everyone knows the exposition of the *Second Treatise* was preceded by the attack on Filmer in the *First*. But why? Filmer's patriarchal hypothesis ruled out the supposition that people were ever free of a political superior and so excluded the possibility that political authority derived, in whatever way, from them. Other absolutists had taken a different view. Not only did Locke wish to address these in his *Second Treatise*, he also wished to show that popular freedom, properly assessed, would produce the sort of political authority he desired. Filmer was thus doubly objectionable. Objectionable, perhaps, all the more because until the publication of his principal manuscript in 1680 the patriarchal character of Filmer's position was not fully obvious. Those of his tracts published earlier, whilst deploying the patriarchal hypothesis on occasion, neither developed it nor made it their subject.[56] Thus, Filmer's challenge to the premises Locke required was a powerful innovation. Because it was a challenge to the premises that Locke required, it had to be dispatched before his own exposition proceeded.

How was that exposition conducted, generally speaking? Locke's strategy was to trump the absolutist account of superiority by adducing a superior yet higher than theirs and by attributing to Him certain intentions. Locke identified God as the greatest superior of all and made Him operative in explaining political matters, whether the nature of a political agent, the terms on which he or she can acquire property or the bases of governmental authority. The general attitude this implies was integral to Locke's *Essays*, in which God had been represented as the greatest of superiors. Locke, of course, had connected the Deity's superiority primarily with morals. But the notion of superiority was capable of a wider locus, whether the human species' dominion over nature or the superiority of one human over another or of a human being over property. To interpret God's superiority in a given way was, of course, open to anyone. But Locke's preceding thought pointed firmly to this possibility: for, as we shall see, motifs from Locke's past became components in his political explanations. For if God's superiority was a common datum, it was the use that Locke made of it that was significant.

But what was to be explained? Locke's task was not simply to explain that absolutism was unacceptable and to establish 'bounded' government. Quite distinct from these questions about polity were the objectives for whose sake civil government existed. To argue against absolutism and for a limited style of government implied that these items needed to be accommodated within the frame of the latter. Better still these items should be explained in terms at once congruent with those establishing 'bounded' government and inconsistent with absolutism. Chief amongst these were the substantive values of liberty and property. The formulation of 'bounded' government suggested that inroads on these were not to be suffered quietly. They needed to be displayed safely in the setting of limited government, for they were values dear to the political nation.

The duke of Buckingham reminded the House of Lords that 'there is a thing called *Property*. . .that the People of *England* are fondest of' and from quite a different perspective John Nalson agreed that there was nothing 'of which they are more Jealous, than. . .the *Property* of their Estates'. Others celebrated it equally. Edward Chamberlayne claimed for the English 'an absolute power' to 'dispose of all they have how they please'. A little later a justice in King's Bench reminded a felon that her 'offence hath been in a nation where property is better preserved than in any other government in the world' and Ambrose Philips rhapsodised 'O Property! O Goddess, English-born!'[57]. Property was an item which political thought in England could not discount.

Neither could it ignore liberty. Civil liberty was bound to figure highly in a society structured by hierarchy. After all, a superior was distinguished as such by his capacity for directing his inferiors. The latter could not dissent reasonably from this, if they could not direct themselves, and in this sense did not have freedom within the sphere of his judgement. So it was important to distinguish what lay beyond a superior's jurisdiction, liberty in this sense 'being only an exemption from the dominion of another' in Sidney's words. In law this took the form of financial immunities from governmental levy, not least those accorded to communities. In the less technical thought of the day liberty was closely connected with property, for property established the status of being free from servitude. Liberty and property came to be connected, as in Filmer's complaint that 'liberty and property' were 'the two grand favourites of the subject'.[58]

It was necessary for the advocates of 'bounded' government, especially, to explain property and civil liberty in terms which accommodated them to their view of polity. *A Letter from a Person of Quality* had insinuated that they should be protected but had not *explained* how that was to be done. Explanation was necessary for both general and particular reasons. Generally absolutism or thought compatible with it occupied the central place in European thought. Absolutism, we have been told often, looked *à la mode* in the seventeenth century.[59] Certainly some of the most powerful specimens of political thought developed absolutist explanations of government. Filmer and Hobbes were not alone.[60] Hobbes, besides, was a host in himself: for whatever may be said about the ostracism of his person from polite intellectual company after 1660, his ideas could not be ignored so easily. Others, whose arguments were not aimed at proving absolutism often admitted it, Grotius for instance. An intellectual alternative was required.

This was true too for reasons that were particular, but which required general explanations. It may be unduly categorical to connect *Two Treatises of Government* exclusively to any particular juncture in the history of English politics. Certainly its propositions are cast in a universal form, and its author believed its principles to be of general importance. We see that its subject matter reflects general concerns in contemporary thought and politics when we recollect that Shaftesbury observed that 'Monarchy, if of Divine Right, cannot be bounded or limited by humane laws' in 1675 and that Sherlock declared that 'an absolute Monarch is under the Government of no Law, but his own will' in 1684.[61] This is not to say that the book was irrelevant to more particular matters or that general propositions cannot have specific applications.[62] Indeed the explanatory framework of *Two Treatises*, the dismissal of absolutism and its supersession by a different view of polity, was relevant to one of the central problems of the Exclusion crisis.

Though exclusion was itself a narrow issue of particular reference, its institutional setting admitted questions of general importance. To exclude the Duke of York was to alter the succession through parliamentary legislation. Exclusion thus opened the question of parliament's authority, especially whether this extended thus far. At one level the answer turned upon matters of fact concerning parliamentary title and precedent, but it was possible to deliver a trump to parliamentary claims. Those who wished to deny that parliament's authority extended to the succession would hope to rest their view upon an authority that was unequivocally higher, namely God's ordinances. So if we find a writer declaring that 'it were a most dangerous thing to have an opinion prevail, that the King in concurrence with his Parliament should not have power to change the direct order of succession', we find another insisting that by natural law (and the law of nations) 'the Crown ought to descend according to Priority of Birth, and Proximity of Blood'. Of course this involved a step back: succession presumed monarchy so that to conduct the argument to its destination a divine warrant for the latter had to be alleged: all monarchy, we learn, 'does owe its immediat Foundation and Constitution to God Almighty'. Now one does not think ordinarily of natural law in this manner, for the term strictly denotes a series of rational precepts about conduct. But, by a kind of loose courtesy, the usage extended to what reason suggested – as for instance that fathers ruled children and that somehow kings stood in the room of fathers. Thus one might conclude that by natural law there was monarchy and an unalterable succession:

By the Law of Nature the Father hath the Rule over his Children; and the King over his Subjects. . .The Descent makes the King, Allegiance is due to the King by the Law of Nature; the Law of Nature cannot be abrogated by Human Power; *ergo*, The right then of Blood cannot be excluded by Parliament, which is a Human Power

so that Exclusion was *ultra vires* for parliament precisely because monarchy and its forms were directly instituted by God.

It was possible to extend this argument to embrace fundamental law. The fundamental or constitutive laws of a country, we may recollect, were supposed to embody the relevant contents of natural law. If, therefore, the succession were settled by the law of nature, it followed that the succession might be also a fundamental law. Some were not slow to draw this inference: 'the Succession of the Crown to the next Heir of the Blood Royal, is a fundamental and primary Constitution of this Realm; and, indeed the *Basis* and Foundation of all our Laws.' So fundamental law might be understood to embody the same terms as *jure divino* monarchy.

The tendency of these arguments was to make monarchy absolute. For their terms, which were calculated to prevent exclusion, implied that monarchy was set up by God Himself. As such it could not be subject to human preference, which implied that it could not owe its authority to popular consent. Of course, this does not indicate that what God established was precisely an absolute monarchy and, strictly speaking, to argue for monarchy *jure divino* is not identical with absolutism. But, as any reader of Filmer knows, the two can be linked.

From exclusion arose the question of absolutism, for a monarchy warranted by God was beyond legitimate human control. More generally, the exclusion crisis implied a demand for explanation. If monarchy was established by God and, according to some, settled upon Adam in particular, it was necessary to offer evidence for such views. If one took the opposite line, that monarchy or government in general was a human institution, and so liable to alteration, that 'every form of Government is of our Creation and not Gods. . .And was never intended unalterable, or at least inflexible, but was intended and made under reservations', that too needed to be established.

Explanation had a practical importance. No doubt it was difficult to argue that the government established in England enjoyed a power independent of its subjects *in fact*, when it was true that the monarch was 'under a necessity to fly to his People in Parliament for supplies upon the least extraordinary accident, or Emergency of State'. But Exclusion *raised* the issue of whether or not the monarchy should be *explained* as absolute. This bore upon the practical point of who should be the next king. It had wider implications for practice, as (of course) an absolute monarch would be entitled to levy upon his subjects without their consent. To put the matter at its most general, theory was part of what government might become in fact. Thinking retrospectively, we know that the Revolution of 1688 and the Act of Settlement in effect resolved the matter in favour of a man made and indeed a parliamentary explanation for monarchy. Of course that is not how contemporaries could see it. The two most sustained explanatory accounts, Sidney's *Discourses on Government* and Locke's *Two Treatises*, proceeded from the losing side in the Exclusion crisis. At any rate, the explanation of political authority was a central item in political practice.

If explanation was central, what were its modes? One very obvious response from those disinclined to admit Whig claims, as we have seen, was to allege that political authority was beyond any human authority, because God settled the course of succession. Hence 'proximity of Blood does give a Title unchangeable by any Humane Laws'. Two sorts of argument were offered for this judgement, each of which corresponds to the concerns of one of the *Two Treatises*. One involved 'a Divine Patriarchal Right, which Kings as Natural Fathers of their People have derived down to them from *Adam*'. The other was favoured by those

who being desirous to bestow upon the Crown a compliment of the like nature, which they were at the same time obtaining from it, have declared in general, That Monarchy is of Divine Right, That Princes succeed by the Laws of God, That their Title is not subject to any earthly cognizance, nor owing to any consent of the people

and thus 'a Jurisdiction which is of Divine Right, is not alterable by the will or power of man.'[63] The former of these arguments was represented classically by Filmer and became the subject of Locke's *First Treatise*. His *Second Treatise*, of course, arrived at a conclusion inverting the second argument. Thus *Two Treatises* attended to two arguments which would have precluded exclusion.[64] Hence *Two Treatises*, whose architecture indicates a concern with general principles, was relevant to a particular issue precisely because that issue presupposed a view upon the larger question of absolutism.

One may ask, of course, why Locke did simply not treat *jure divino* argument to the piecemeal attack to which he subjected Filmer. A full and specific answer would be very long, but it is worth offering a general remark and indicating one or two points, points united by a need to offer an alternative scheme of explanation.

Generally speaking, it was necessary for Locke to offer a deliberate account of natural law. Natural law was a term used by anti-exclusionists to mean merely a dictate of reason. At one level the necessary response to this was simply to show the irrationality of patriarchal claims: it is a measure of the importance of this task (rather than its intrinsic difficulty) that Locke devoted so much time to it. At another something more sophisticated was needful, to show that natural law implied quite a different destination. As we shall see, Locke's treatment of the law of nature was calculated not only to show how people could produce a congenial kind of civil government, but also that an absolute one was not available to them legitimately.

The first specific point concerned the legitimacy of forcibly opposing civil governments. Since the magistrate was *ex officio* a superior, the notion of disobeying him, let alone actively opposing his rule, was difficult. It was especially difficult because some divines had constructed a doctrine of non-resistance on the basis of St Paul. The apostle had stated that 'they, that resist, shall receive to themselves Damnation'. Seth Ward's *Against Resistance of Lawful Powers* declared that 'Saint *Paul's Theory* concerning *Government* is an authentick *Christian* Theory' and asked that 'if *harsh Administration* of *Power* will exempt men from *Obedience*; at that Time, when *Claudius*, or *Nero* was Romane Emperour, why should the *Holy Ghost* move *Saint Paul* to write to the *Romans, They, that resist, shall receive to themselves Damnation?*' Since Ward conceived Charles II '*as an Angel of God*' it is unlikely that he thought contemporary opposition more acceptable.[65] On this reading of St Paul it followed, if the state was regarded as a Christian organisation, that resistance was unacceptable and Shaftesbury's hope of constraining governments by 'fear of humane resistance' was illegitimate. The apostle's injunction was plain, so that, in Sprat's words, 'it is most true Divinity. . .that not the most vehement persuasions, or dissuasions of Conscience, not the greatest pretences to new Light, or Divine Inspirations can justify any member of a Christian State, or Church, nor any whole Church, to violate the establish'd Laws of their Country by resisting'.[66] This obviously posed a problem for those who wished to admit a different conclusion.

The solution was obviously to explain that matters were different.

The starting point was to insist that if rulers were superiors their authority rested on quite a different basis, one which did not entail Christian sanctions against those who opposed. Locke, of course, explained the authority of civil government in terms very different from those of divine right, terms, moreover, which showed that opposition to errant rulers could not be classed as resistance.[67] This was possible not least because his argument, though involving *theistic* explanations, was not specifically *Christian*. There is no sign in the *Second Treatise* that the authority of civil government was to be understood in terms of the New Testament, nor that one of its objectives was to inculcate Christian doctrine and worship. Rather, its object was to protect the citizen in the enjoyment of terrestrial goods. This complemented Locke's account of toleration, which turned on the assumption that the state was not a Christian organisation. In short Locke did not assume, as Ward and Sprat did, that the state was Christian: his explanation he cast in different terms.[68]

To implicate unseating a government in one's account of politics was to unsettle people. This much is apparent from contemporary assumptions of the *raison d'être* of civil authority, as it is from Locke's own view of why that authority was necessary.[69] As such it might seem to threaten liberty and property, both of which should be *protected* by civil government. Additionally, as we have noted, some explained property through governmental action.[70] The question of whether it was possible to uphold liberty and property whilst admitting 'bounded' government, or whether these were in fact better located in absolutist theory, was therefore of some importance.

On the one hand, the obvious resource was to suggest that absolutism would allow arbitrary inroads against the liberty and property of the subject. On the other, it might be alleged that these would be less safe with Shaftesbury or his ilk. Where Shaftesbury pointed to the Duke of York's rule in Scotland to show people 'having their lives, liberties and, estates subjected to the arbitrary will and pleasure of those that govern', *Heraclitus Ridens* suggested that he and his followers 'would have no body Arbitrary but themselves'. This accusation lay not merely against persons, but also against their views: as Nalson put it, 'they who make all the noise about it, are the most Arbitrary principled persons in the world'. It was therefore necessary not merely to ask with Shaftesbury 'what is present power, or riches, and a great estate, wherein I have no firm fixed property?' and to observe that 'it is the constitution of the Government. . .that secures. . .every man. . .in what he hath' but more especially to show how liberty and property were to be protected and *explained*[71]. That is to say, it would be necessary to explain property in terms different to those consistent with absolutism and to develop a view of government that would uphold liberty and property, regardless even of the wishes of Lord Shaftesbury. For these reasons explanation rather than refutation was the order of the day.

In fact the explanatory agenda would have to be set more widely still. Filmer's argument embraced a wide range of social relations, involving fathers, mothers, children, servants and slaves.[72] The explanations would need not only to explain a given style of government and to accommodate certain values within it, but also to discount absolutism. The seventeenth century thought in terms of polar opposites: to refute one view was to validate its opposite.[73] Besides, it was not merely a matter of developing a case but of depriving the other side of theirs. Thus we find both negative and positive arguments in *Two Treatises*, both arguments against absolutism and ones for limited government.

We find argument also in two modes. Of course the argument has one primary subject, namely political authority, but to this there were not one but two origins. All power was of God, but derived from Him either directly or indirectly. The former source worked when God conveyed power by His command to some individual or group. This in effect meant conveyance through scripture, or through the para-scriptural explanations of patriarchy or divine right. The latter source suggested that power was mediated through a longer route, as for instance popular consent. This would be discovered most characteristically through reason.

Locke had therefore to deal in the media of both scripture and reason and needed to both dispatch absolutism and establish another style of civil government. This sounds a complicated agenda, but the structure of Locke's argument is straightforward enough. The first of his *Two Treatises* dealt primarily in arguments about scripture and his second in reason, though Locke deployed both media in each. He criticised absolutism and developed his alternative *pari passu*. For in his attack on Filmer throughout the first book Locke laid down several premises from which his own argument about civil government in the second proceeded, whilst that argument itself offered an alternative to the devices of absolutism by explaining another sort of government. The two books of *Two Treatises of Government* form a continuous treatment of Locke's theme.

III

The argument as a whole assumes superiorities, as we should expect from the nature of Locke's England. The common presumption of

210

hierarchy, however, leaves it unspecified just how government would be founded. Here there were competing theories, of course. But, as we know, there was one trump. The greatest superior was God and the explanation of other important superiorities proceeded from Him. The question was not about the ultimate origin of authority, but about the way it derived to terrestrial superiors, whoever they might be.

The point is plain in St Paul's famous text 'all power is of God'. Whilst this settles the ultimate source of power,[74] it does not explain how God mediated His authority to others, as is apparent from the differing constructions that Filmer and Sidney placed on the passage: Filmer thought it referred only to kings, whilst Sidney applied it also to other forms of rule.[75] The passage, for instance, did not explain whether authority came directly of God, or indirectly. The former meant that God settled authority specifically – as when He defines its terms or gave it to a specific individual or located it in a given line of descent. The latter means that He prescribed only that there be political authority, and left open the specification of where it should reside. The differences amongst political theories of Locke's day were located not least in questions of specification.

His *Two Treatises* are complementary, for each considers one of two routes. The first book considered one of the explanations that power is directly of God. This was the one developed in Locke's day by churchmen like Ussher and Sanderson, and found most extendedly in Filmer.[76] Locke set out to destroy Filmer's explanation of absolutism. Locke's second book provided an account of power in the other model.

They are not merely complementary in subject matter, but also in their manner of treating it. For Locke's *First Treatise* provided a description of God's purposes which provides a large part of the basis of the *Second Treatise*. The *First* is usually conceived as a refutation of one explanation of absolutism, and a rather tedious one at that.[77] This judgement of tedium perhaps obscures the fact that the manner in which Locke executed his attack on Filmer's view of political superiority involved also the rebuttal of Filmer's view of God's purposes: and therefore brought a relocation of His intentions and, conformably, a new explanation of superiority.

The two destinations of absolutism and responsible government corresponded respectively to attributions to God's authorship of differing sorts of terrestrial superiority. Absolutism, as explained in the terms adopted by Filmer and those who asserted that power was directly of God, required God to set one person above another in explicit terms. An indirect derivation of power to civil government implied that God had not set up any such superiority of one agent over others: thus each agent had as much authority as the next. Since each had equal authority, it followed, for this purpose at least, that no one had a superior. Lacking a superior they must be free of direction by another (except, of course, God and His directions). They could set up a superior, of course, and the general assumption that government was necessary required this. As Gilbert Burnet remarked, 'it is certain, that the *Law of Nature* has put no difference nor subordination among Men. . .so that with Relation to the Law of Nature, all Men are born free'.[78] On this understanding, government would be created in whatever way 'Men' thought suitable.

It need hardly be emphasised that this is a point of the highest importance, for on the judgement of human discretion turns the question of governmental form and revocability. A government set up by God Himself could not be changed by man in any respect. A humanly determined institution, however, might be subject to the changes people chose, including complete alteration. Hence there is deliberate point to Locke's relaxed classification *Of the Forms of a Commonwealth*, emphasising the different sorts of polity for which people could opt.

Locke's method of dealing with superiorities, whether negatively or positively, was demonstrative in the sense that he set out to show the terms in which political superiority was created by tracing out connections amongst ideas. This method befitted his general concern with philosophy and his explanatory mode of writing. By demonstration Locke intended 'noe thing else but shewing men how they shall see right'.[79] In his first book Locke was concerned to break the connection Filmer had set up, whilst in his second he aimed to establish connections of his own.

Filmer dealt essentially in one superiority, on the basis of which he attempted to establish a wide range of connections. In his view God had conferred on Adam a universal superiority over the earth and mankind. God's medium of expression was preserved in scripture and His conferral was direct. The contents of the grant comprised a superiority over the world as a whole: an authority, subject to no superior but God, over all Adam's descendants and unlimited in extent, as well as a parallel lordship over the whole earth and its creatures. This authority, Filmer argued, passed by descent to subsequent monarchs so that they enjoyed an absolute authority over person and property.[80]

Locke was not much amused by these connections. He required for the purposes of his own argument about government that people by nature be free from any superior (excepting God).[81] Filmer asserted

212

that everyone had a superior, and that the superior had an authority that was complete in every way. Locke's first book was devoted to unpicking Filmer's connections. Sometimes his method was to suggest that these were insecurely grounded in scripture. At other times he argued that Filmer had not connected his ideas properly. These arguments are in their nature *ad hominem*. They are fairly exhaustive, though those who have not been exhausted before reaching section eighty know that Locke went beyond the text that found its way into print to discuss grant, usurpation and election as titles to government[82]. But in the course of breaking Filmer's connections Locke suggested some of his own. There were two points of especial importance. Both turned on suppositions about the connection between authority and intellect. We may recollect that intellectual superiority suggested fitness to direct others less well endowed.

Firstly, the absence of a direct allocation of authority to one individual, allows us to suppose that the same faculties presume the same moral standing for all, since God had made those faculties and their make reflected His intentions. That is to say, the similarity of people one to another afforded no grounds for setting one human above another: and so (as we observed earlier) they should have the same status. As Locke put it, 'Creatures of the same species and rank promiscuously born to all the same advantages of Nature and the use of the same faculties, should be equal one amongst another without Subordination. . .unless the Lord and Master of them all, should by any manifest Declaration of his Will set one above another.'[83] To this equality is correlated freedom from direction by others, for Locke assumed that the faculties possessed were adequate to self-direction, and so direction by another was intellectually superfluous: thus, in Locke's own words, people were in '*a State of perfect Freedom* to order their Actions. . .as they think fit. . .without asking leave, or depending upon the Will of any other Man'.[84] Self-direction was the product of adequate and equal faculties, subject (of course) to God's superiority. He, after all, was omnisciently wise.[85] This identity of status amongst people 'born to all the same advantages', as we shall see in a moment, was important in explaining the duty of preservation, which in its turn was integral to Locke's view of political organisation. But central to many more matters is our second point.

Locke provided an explanation of a superiority common to the whole human race, a superiority over the world and its creatures, whether as dominion or as right, and suggested duties addressed to all. All these are cast in terms of the very point to which Locke alluded in

213

his statement of equality, namely that the human intellect was a salient aspect of the image of God in man.

These are found in what Locke termed 'the great design of God'.[86] This design, as its name suggests, signified God's purpose for the human race. The direction was straightforward: people were required 'to promote the great Design of God, *Increase* and *Multiply*'. This language alluded to the narrative of God's setting the human race over lower animals recorded in the first chapter of *Genesis*. Indeed Locke adduced just this to emphasise the purpose. The specification in full runs as follows:

And God Blessed them, and God said unto them, be Fruitful and Multiply and Replenish the Earth and subdue it, and have Dominion over the Fish of the Sea, and over the Fowl of the Air, and over every living thing that moveth upon the Earth, I Gen.28

and it is unambiguous. The God of Locke commanded the human race to propagate themselves, subdue the earth and have dominion over creatures. This was the 'great and primary Blessing of God Almighty'.[87]

Though the great design was cast as a command, it implied a right. To be specific, it explains how mankind collectively had a right to dominion and indeed property over the earth and over its creatures. Locke, of course, was keen, for the purposes of his polemic against Filmer, to distinguish the concepts of dominion and property. But he was clear that the benediction of *Genesis* ix, 1–3 to Noah and his sons gave to the human race 'the utmost Property Man is capable of, which is to have a right to destroy any thing by using it'.[88] Thus mankind collectively had a right to property in the earth and its creatures.

How was the presence of a right made clear? We might say, simply, through revelation, but though true this would not be complete. The allusion to *dominion* should make the point clear. Dominion over animals, we may recollect, derived to mankind from their intellectual superiority. The common assumption of the day that animals did not reason or even think or, if they did, that their thought was so conspicuously beneath human cogitation that they were still manifest inferiors. Thus people were their superiors or, as Locke put it, had '*Dominion*, or Superiority' over them. As he had remarked in *Draft B*, 'it is the Understanding that sets man above the rest of sensible beings & gives him all that dominion he hath over them'.[89] For mankind resembled God, in that people had superior understandings, 'for wherein soever else the *Image of God* consisted, the intellectual Nature was certainly a part of it'.[90] The possession of the *imago dei* implied superiority.

Superiority or dominion, of course, are general terms and do not disclose precisely how people were entitled to act in relation to animals, or, for that matter towards inanimate nature. Here we should attend to the terms of the grant which God made to mankind in His 'great and primary Blessing'.

God made the grant for the sake of a purpose, of course. Locke had long ago decided that He did nothing without a purpose.[91] The phrase common to both *Genesis* texts Locke mentioned (1,28 and 9,1) specified the same purpose for mankind's performance, namely: be fruitful, and multiply, and replenish the earth. This general formula may be mediated into a number of particular forms. One of these is worth especial attention. The intention implicit in the grant required people to preserve themselves. Locke, indeed, indicated that there was a duty of self-preservation,[92] a duty which was matched by a desire for survival and whose content pointed towards the perpetuation of God's design.[93] We may infer that the great design gave people a right to the means of self-preservation; for example, to destroy an animal in order to eat it. Locke inferred as much himself, remarking that God would be unlikely to give property to Adam alone because

it is more reasonable to think, that God who bid Mankind increase and multiply, should rather himself give them all a Right, to make use of the Food and Rayment, and other Conveniences of Life, the Materials whereof he had so plentifully provided for them.[94]

In short the great design suggested that God had given the earth to all mankind, having in mind that the human race should survive and increase. A duty to preserve oneself was implicit in this. More generally, as we shall see, an interest in the propagation of the species is implied, but of that more later.[95] The grant, then, was a means to God's purpose, to which was correlated a duty to preserve oneself.

Here we see Locke deploying conceptions gathered from the thought of the day, not least his own preceding reflections. Self-preservation was a concern of writing about natural law, including his own *Essays*. The notion of human dominion over animals had appeared in his writings about the human understanding. These assumed also that God had equipped people with apprehensions fitting them to survive. We may add, if we care, that the great design's prescription for the increase of mankind captured Locke's assumption, seen in his early writings on political economy, that large populations were best. Indeed it was not merely the growth of mankind, but its 'perfection' for which he argued, including in the great design the development of the arts and sciences – 'the improvement too of Arts and Sciences, and the conveniences of Life'.[96] More pointedly, we may say that Locke had taken these motifs and formed from them a determinate pattern. That pattern, as we shall see, was central to his political theory.

We should attend to the generic form behind these formulations: that God had signified an intention for mankind. The design presents a teleology – an end or ends marked out by God for man to follow. The general intention is not itself a duty, though it gives rise to what Locke termed duties. Mankind could be expected to follow it without introducing moral obligation because God had constructed human nature in a manner conducive to that course. The 'great Design' is an example of the sort of intentionality Locke had quietly attributed to God in constructing his account of the human understanding in his *Essays* and *Drafts*. The general principle that there was such a divine plan does not imply the *content* of the example that Locke adduced in his *Treatises*, of course. But there is a continuity of thought between his early writings on the understanding and his political doctrine. For Locke assumed in the former that God had equipped mankind with apprehensions adapted to survival and to allow people to dominate the earth and its animals: in the latter the 'great Design' embodied these suppositions. For it was human 'Senses and Reason', as well as desires, that set people on the path God had indicated.[97] Thus Locke's view of the human understanding informed the bases of his politics. We should now turn to the superstructure.

IV

These points were significant for Locke's larger intention. They provided some of the major bases for his argument about political power in his second book and concurrently about society too. The *Essay concerning... Civil-Government*, like the first book, is concerned with superiorities in society. Locke took care to distinguish these from each other. His prime concern was the superiority of the civil government over the citizen. This was differentiated carefully from the superiorities of lord over slave (or, as Locke calls it, absolute power), parent over child and master over servant. This project sprang from Locke's intention of interpreting political power to imply constitutional government. Those of an absolutist persuasion had understood it in terms resembling those from which Locke set out to disassociate it. The power to contract away irrevocably one's rights implied simultaneously the power to surrender one's self to slavery. Filmer had assimilated political power to power in the household, whether of father, husband or master. Locke needed to show that these identifications were illegitimate.

216

To this end of distinguishing amongst sorts of power. Locke was concerned not just with demonstration but also with relations. For unlike Sanderson, for example, Locke included amongst relations not merely natural connections but also instituted relationships. Hence he could include in his discourse not merely matters of the family but also a wider range of social and political relations. For Locke wished to distinguish the relation between magistrate and subject from that between father and child or between master and slave, amongst others: in his own words:

I think it may not be amiss, to set down what I take to be Political Power. That the Power of a *Magistrate* over a Subject, may be distinguished from that of a *Father* over his Children, a *Master* over his Servant, a *Husband* over his Wife, and a *Lord* over his Slave. All which distinct Powers happening sometimes together in the same Man, if he be considered under these different Relations, it may help us to distinguish these Powers one from another, and shew the difference betwixt a Ruler of a Common-wealth, a Father of a Family, and a Captain of a Galley.[98]

To these we might add the control which an owner enjoys over property, for Locke treated this in a manner congruent with his view of political authority. Locke's objective was to distinguish what Filmer had combined. Filmer's argument, in effect, made Adam father, king and lord: in his own words 'a son, a subject and a servant or a slave, were one and the same thing at first'.[99] Thus the *Essay concerning. . . Civil-Government* presented an alternative to Filmer's conflation of these different relations. It did so, of course, in the interests of explaining a non-absolute form of polity.

This argument required that people by nature have no superior. This meant a political superior. Locke was not disposed to deny the superiorities inherent in the society of his day, of parents over children or the owner over his property, for instance.[100] But Filmer himself had identified freedom by nature from a political superior as the central assumption that his explanation of absolutism needed to surmount.[101] Locke was as good as Filmer's word.

Locke's method of explaining the difference amongst different relations was to outline their source – in his vocabulary, their original. The original, in fact, was one, in that they were all referred to God's intentions. These are best understood by referring to the 'great Design'. All the relations important to Locke's argument are explained, wholly or partly, in terms of the great design, except for the relations of master and slave. It is this common explanation which united the terms of Locke's *Essay concerning. . . Civil-Government*. Viewed as a list of contents, the principal items of the *Essay* might appear somewhat miscellaneous. Duties of self-preservation and preservation, slavery, property, parenthood, the household and political society, to name no others, follow each other in a succession which does not seem entirely orderly at first blush. But there is a connection between these items. The laws of self-preservation and preservation explain the terms on which government is instituted, just as slavery illustrates how God's purposes limited these terms. Property, parenthood and the household all appeared in contemporary eyes as bases of political power so that it was incumbent on Locke to show how these, whilst explicable in terms of God's intentions, were actually quite distinct from political power.

The great design had a major role in all of these arguments. The duty of self-preservation was correlated to the design. We shall see that the law of preservation follows from it, once set in conjunction with freedom, equality and the golden rule. God's superiority, prescribing self-preservation, ruled out slavery and suggested that men must remain free. Property in general, we know from the *First Treatise*, derives to mankind from the great design. We shall see that property could be made private through an aspect of freedom; and that privatisation was required by the terms of the design. Parental power Locke explained through the function of fitting children to be free and the design will explain the binding character of the function. After all this, it is natural to reflect that rights traditionally associated with Locke's name, all relate to the design. Government, of course, existed to protect them. In short, Locke's account of political power is related to the view of human purpose which he called the great design of God.

V

If we start with government we soon find ourselves drawn back to the great design. Locke argued that civil government was empowered by two rights – rights belonging to the individual and whose exercise he or she delegated to ensure that they would be applied efficiently. These were the rights to execute the law of nature and to preserve oneself. These rights themselves derive from two duties, to preserve others and to preserve oneself.[102]

We are familiar with the duty to preserve oneself from the explanation Locke gave in book one, but what of duty to preserve others? He had mentioned this, but had not explained it. The idea of a duty to preserve others is quite intelligible in itself. Its explanation is another matter. It does not figure in scripture, but could be inferred from it according to the principles of interpretation practised in Locke's day: we find it, indeed, in Samuel Crooke's writings. Locke did not allude to that (indeed his sense of scripture would scarce allow it). Instead he indicated that because we have a duty to preserve ourselves, we have a duty to preserve others: that 'Every one as he is *bound to preserve himself*. . .so by the like reason. . .ought he, as much as he can, *to preserve the rest of Mankind*.'[103] How can we explain it?

Locke, as often in his *Treatises*, may seem to write elliptically in explaining the law of preservation. But he had no need to be more than allusive because he employed an idea well known to his contemporaries. The law of preservation he explained by combining the human desire for self-preservation with the golden rule. The golden rule was a central item in the thought of the day. The agent's duty, therefore, could be summarised in the form: love God, and thy neighbour as thyself. This thought figured in a variety of Christian sources, from St Matthew to Hooker (to go no further). So habitual was its use that there was evidently little need to set it out in explicit language. But its role becomes clear as we pursue the reasoning in chapter two of his *Essay concerning. . .Civil-Government*.[104]

Locke reminded the reader that men were in a state of freedom and equality and went on to say that Hooker had made 'this *equality* of Men by Nature' 'the Foundation of that Obligation to mutual Love amongst Men, on which he Builds the Duties they owe one another'.[105] To what was Locke alluding? Here we should turn to the passage from Hooker which he subjoined and which accordingly bears quotation in full:

The like natural inducement, hath brought Men to know that it is no less their Duty, to Love others than themselves, for seeing those things which are equal, must needs all have one measure; If I cannot but wish to receive good, even as much at every Man's hands, as any Man can wish unto his own Soul, how should I look to have any part of my desire herein satisfied, unless my self be careful to satisfie the like desire, which is undoubtedly in other Men, being of one and the same nature? to have any thing offered them repugnant to this desire, must needs in all respects grieve them as much as me, so that if I do harm, I must look to suffer, there being no reason that others should shew greater measure of love to me, than they have by me, shewed unto them; my desire therefore to be lov'd of my equals in nature, as much as possible may be, imposeth upon me a natural Duty of bearing to themward, fully the like affection; From which the relation of equality between our selves and them, that are as our selves, what several Rules and Canons, natural reason hath drawn for direction of Life, no Man is ignorant.

The passage involves three components. It involves our duty to love our neighbour, an inducement to perform that duty which lies in one's own desires and the relation of equality. It also suggests that rules may be inferred from this complex of notions. The golden rule we have met already, so let us review the other components, beginning with equality.

Hooker argued that each man should expect no more from his neighbour than he himself performed, for they were equal by nature and so in that respect there was no ground for differentiating between them. He also wrote of taking care to satisfy what one supposed one's neighbour to desire. This follows on the basis of equality. Let us put these considerations more formally.

The conjunction of the golden rule with desire we may describe first in very general terms. It implies the procedure of putting oneself, mentally, in another's place. There one considers how one would like to be treated if really in his or her shoes. One formulates one's conclusion as a rule and one should treat others according to it if one wishes to deserve like conduct from them towards oneself. As Atterbury suggested, 'put thyself into such or such a Man's Condition, and Consider, what Treatment, what Favours, in that case, thou might'st fairly and justly expect from Others; and be Thou sure to deal with Him according to those thy just and regular Expectations'.[106] The procedure could be stated formally in these terms: it cannot be right for A to treat B in a manner in which it would be wrong for B to treat A, merely on the ground that they are two different individuals, and without there being any difference between the nature or circumstances of the two which can be stated as a proper ground for any difference of treatment. But there are two further points which need to be made before we can see the golden rule in action with desire.

The first concerns the equality on which Hooker and Locke were so keen. Equality by nature follows obviously enough from the possession of the same natural attributes, at least in the absence of any superiority superadded by God. But this equality has an important role in Locke's argument. The formal statement of our rule includes a *ceteris paribus* clause, referring to the absence of any proper grounds for distinguishing between persons for the purposes of morality, namely grounds in their natures or circumstances. We can hardly proceed further without filling out this clause, for if it were possible to adduce salient differences between persons the same conduct would not be appropriate in regard to both.

Locke took the bold course: he declared that there was no possible ground for differentiation between people's natures, so that they should be regarded as equal. Equality was also a condition of showing that in their circumstances too there was no ground for making a difference. Being equal there was no natural criterion for distinction, so that no one except God could produce grounds for subordinating one man to another. Filmer's case for the absolute power of monarchs consisted in supposing God had introduced a salient distinction between them and other men: Locke's whole case against Filmer was to show that He had not. His disposal of Filmer meant that for Locke those who were not dependent on another human being and so in 'a *State of perfect Freedom* to order their Actions. . .without asking leave, or depending upon the Will of any other Man'. Thus people's nature and circumstances alike ensured that there should be only one code of conduct towards all, for they were 'all equal and independent'.[107]

What of the desires people entertained? This brings us to the second point, which is that it is necessary for some content of desire to be applied to the golden rule in order to yield a determinate rule of conduct. The golden rule in itself provides no positive guidance to the content of what people are to do or not do. It merely requires us to treat others in a way we would not disapprove of, if it were applied to ourselves. As such the rule merely throws the *onus probandi* onto the person who applies to others a treatment of which he or she would complain if applied to himself or herself. This lack of guidance can be alleviated only if we apply to the golden rule some material content, such as desire.

What *natural inducement* did Locke choose, what *desire, which is undoubtedly in other Men, being of one and the same nature?* The answer is the 'strong desire of Self-preservation' which we have seen correlated to the great design, 'The desire, strong desire of Preserving his Life and Being. . .Planted in him, as a Principle of Action by God himself.'[108] This desire, joined with the golden rule, brings us to duties towards others.

Thus in the case Locke discussed immediately after the Hooker passage, the golden rule and the desire of self-preservation yield a duty to refrain from harming others. The rule prescribes that it cannot be right for *A* to treat *B* in a manner in which it would be wrong for *B* to treat *A* without there being a difference in their nature and circumstances. According to Locke people are equal in their natures and independent in their circumstances. Man wishes to preserve himself and would wish rationally for nothing to obstruct that end; which we may call harm. On the showing of the rule he should do nothing to harm others, in order to deserve the same restraint from them. So the golden rule suggests that if we wish to deserve no harm from others then it would be rational not to harm them; or, as Locke put it, 'the *State of Nature* has a Law of Nature to govern it. . .And Reason, which is that Law, teaches all Mankind. . .that being all equal and independent, no one ought to harm another in his Life, Health, Liberty and Possessions'.[109] So the desire to preserve oneself and the golden rule together prescribe that people should do each other no harm; or, as

221

Locke remarked later, 'Love permits us to doe noe harm to our neighbour.'[110]

Locke turned next to what people should do more positively. Here he adduced God's superiority once more. People, he explained, were bound to the ends God prescribed. That is to say, they were obliged morally to perform the duties he prescribed. They were 'all the Servants of one Sovereign Master, sent into the World by his order and about his business'. In his *Essays* Locke had argued that God was mankind's superior (He possessed superior perfections of power and wisdom) and therefore entitled to prescribe obligatory rules to people. Hence people were obliged to follow God's purposes rather than their own or each others': they were 'made to last during his, not one anothers Pleasure'.[111] But what was the content of their duty? Here we meet again the desire of self-preservation. For this desire, joined with the golden rule, brings us to the law of preservation.

Consider self-preservation. *A* has a concern to preserve himself. How does *A* also become subject to a duty to preserve others? According to our reasoning the way we would have ourselves treated is the way we should treat others, *ceteris paribus*: in Atterbury's words, 'the principle of *Self-love* in us', the golden rule 'makes the Ground and Rule of all that Love we owe to others'.[112] Hence the golden rule allows us to observe that self-preservation is explanatory of the preservation of all. Consider the application of the golden rule to *A*'s attitude to *B*, assuming, as we may in Locke's scheme, that *A* strongly desires to preserve himself. *A* perceives that he would like *B* to assist him, if need be, in attaining *A*'s own desire of self-preservation. So *A* comes to see that if he is to deserve such assistance from *B*, he would have to be disposed to assist *B*, in case of need. So *A* has a duty to assist *B*. Since people are equal by nature and independent in circumstances, we may generalise with the permission of the *ceteris paribus* clause, and say that *A*'s duty lies equally in respect of *C*. . .*Z* and that by the same measure *B*. . .*Z* have a duty to preserve *A*. Each agent thus has a duty to preserve himself and to preserve all others, the two being intimately related. For one's desire to succeed in the former particular is part of the explanation of the duty to preserve all.

Preserving other people, specifically the rest of mankind, thus became a duty. It was one of the items which Locke meant by God's business. The superiority ascribed to God in his *Essays* had been accompanied by a catalogue of duties rather concisely described. Here Locke's purposes required that he should emphasise God's prescriptions rather more strongly. That is to say, Locke's argument that people were bound always to give their first obedience to God rather narrowed the window of opportunity for absolutism founded upon a surrender of right. For as Filmer himself noted 'what they have not, they cannot give'.[113] But to close that window completely it was necessary to add that God wished people to act in a manner *incompatible* with absolutism. Here we should turn to self-preservation once more.

The significance of God's regard for human self-preservation was that it prevented absolutism on the terms preferred by modern thinkers. To trace power directly from God was one route to the absolutist destination. But the same result could be had by an unreserved transfer of right from free men, as Grotius had suggested and Hobbes exploited. Grotius suggested that he wished to

> reject their Opinion, who will have the Supreme Power to be always, and without Exception, in the People; so that they may restrain or punish their Kings, as often as they abuse their Power...I shall refute it with these Arguments. It is lawful for any Man to engage himself as a Slave to whom he pleases; as appears both by the *Hebrew* and *Roman* Laws. Why should it not therefore be as lawful for a People that are at their own Disposal, to deliver up themselves to any one or more Persons, and transfer the Right of governing them upon him or them, without recovering any Share of that Right to themselves? Neither should you say this is not to be presumed: For the Question here is not, what may be presumed in a Doubt, but what may be lawfully done?...A people may choose what Form of Government they please: Neither is the Right which the Sovereign has over his Subjects to be measured by this or that Form, of which divers Men have divers Opinions, but by the Extent of the Will of those who conferred it upon him.[114]

Hobbes was more categorical, suggesting that the exigencies of the state of nature induced people necessarily to set up an absolute sovereign.[115] Their arguments presupposed that 'the Will of those who conferred' political authority was unrestricted, to the degree that people could make themselves slaves. On these terms an authority absolute in the fullest sense was possible.[116]

Locke precluded this by asserting that people were answerable to God and that God required of them conduct incompatible with an unreserved transfer of freedom. God required man to preserve himself and self-preservation was ensured by freedom from absolute power. According to Locke the only reason why anyone would attempt to gain absolute power over another was to threaten his life.[117] To subordinate oneself to a superior without reservation was therefore out of the question:

> *Freedom* from Absolute, Arbitrary Power, is so necessary to, and closely joyned with a Man's Preservation, that he cannot part with it...For a Man, not having the Power of his own Life, *cannot*, by Compact, or his own Consent,

enslave himself to any one, nor put himself under the Absolute, Arbitrary Power of another, to take away his Life, when he pleases. No body can give more Power than he has himself; and he that cannot take away his own Life, cannot give another power over it.[118]

So people could not countenance submission to absolutism in this mode because they were answerable to God and because the content of God's purposes required them to retain their natural freedom. Freedom, that is to say, could not be utterly alienated. We shall see that it could be transferred in order to execute other purposes, but that only on conditions which admitted recall. Thus the operations Locke attributed to God restricted the range of possible civil governments.

VI

Locke had not only to explain political power but also to explain those values his society prized. Once the ability to direct oneself and so the basis of civil freedom had been established, property was the most important of these. Hence the second of *Two Treatises* passes from freedom (in chapters 2–4) to property (in chapter 5). This ordering had a logic beyond psychological linkage. For having established political authority in terms of God's design, including intellect and freedom, it was incumbent upon Locke to explain property in a like manner.

Locke placed the retention of freedom significantly, for freedom would be his instrument of explaining how property could be private. To explain it thus was important, for the prevalent style of explanation founded private property on terms that favoured absolutism. To substitute a version that grounded private property in freedom rather than subjection would be a major coup.

What was the task before Locke? The great design of God gave property in the earth and its creatures to mankind collectively. The question, then, was how to move from that to private property. Locke explained this in terms of freedom, for he argued that it was an attribute of a free man that his labour was his own. It was free labour, under the auspices of the great design once more, that produced appropriation and was present in the accumulation of more sophisticated forms of property.

A dictionary of the seventeenth century distinguished an individual's property by its independence from others' control, defining it as 'the highest right that a man hath or can have to any thing, which is no way depending vpon any other mans courtesie'.[119] The writer followed the usage we employ today by applying this definition only to material possessions. Locke is well known for construing the term in a broader

224

way. He embraced not only property as land and goods but also the property each man had in his person. This dual usage is important because it situated 'property' in his wider political explanation.

Locke needed to treat private property in a certain way in order to sustain his own political theory. His *Second Treatise* undertook to explain political authority in a way which distinguished it from paternal and from absolute or despotic power. The basis of political power was present in people by virtue of their intellect and (consequently) their natural freedom and the absence of any superior set over them by God directly.[120] Locke's objective was to explain political authority in terms incompatible with despotism or, more soberly, 'oeconomical' absolutism. Of course the plausibility of his doctrine to contemporary readers would depend not just on his reasoning about political authority itself but also on showing that property could be explained adequately within the terms Locke proposed. His wider argument would not be acceptable if it did not base their cherished property soundly.

The need to explain property was strong on theoretical grounds too. Neither the law of the land nor current political theory explained it in terms incompatible with absolutism. If anything they cohered with it. English law before 1660 embodied the feudal explanation that all landed possession derived from the king, which obviously ruled out property in land 'in no way depending vpon any mans courtesie'[121] and indeed explained it as the ruler's creation. What he had created he might revoke, so that property on these terms bespoke his power rather than disclosing any limit to it.

Political theory likewise explained property in terms which made it easy to refer it to government. The most powerful explanation was Grotius'. He assumed that mankind originally held property in common and subsequently agreed to partition it amongst themselves, thus producing private property. Pufendorf added the refinement of classifying the original ownership by the whole community in two ways, as negative (which was common because not marked out by any action) and positive (which was common to a given group but not to outsiders), but he did not modify the fundamental theory.[122] Whilst this view of itself implies nothing about government, the two combined easily in the suggestion that only government could produce an enforceable and therefore stable partition. Hobbes asserted that 'there can be no Propriety, no Dominion, no *Mine* and *Thine* distinct' without government.[123] Hence private property turned out to be the creation of governmental power. Thus the sovereign alone would be the source of property: 'the constitution of *Mine*, and *Thine*, and *His*; that is to say. . .*Propriety*. . .belongeth. . .to the Soveraign Power'.[124] These explanations of property therefore fell easily into a larger pattern of absolute authority.

The pattern would suggest itself naturally to the seventeenth-century mind. For although property and political authority were distinguishable they were not completely distinct. Both could figure as examples of the *dominium*. Conceived as authority, *dominium* suggested an exclusive title to direct based upon superiority. God, as mankind's superior, held it in *dominium*. The magistrate bore a similar relation to the citizen and the parent to the child. In the same way the citizen's exclusive control over his or her possessions – 'which is no way depending vpon any other mans courtesie' – counted as *dominium*. Edward Gee explained '*Moral power*. . .that which we call *property* or *dominion*' in terms which embraced both property and political authority. Edward Stillingfleet wrote of 'Dominion and Propriety'. In the seventeenth century when the English franchise and other aspects of political status depended upon the possession of property it was natural to associate political authority with property.[125] As illustrations of the same idea they might be expected to fall into the same conceptual pattern.

The opponent of absolutism would do well to produce another pattern, embracing both political authority and property. This was true especially because the Grotian explanation of the latter had wide currency in Locke's England. Stillingfleet remarked that 'in a state of Community it was the right of every man to impropriate upon a just equality, supposing a preceding compact and mutual agreement'. This assumption cohered with the view that the title to property could in fact be defined by government. Samuel Parker in 1669 assumed incidentally that justice in 'its particular Cases depend[s] upon Humane Laws, that determine the bounds of *Meum* and *Tuum*'. A little later an MP could remark disturbingly that 'when you abjure a government, you abjure your lands'.[126]

Neither had a plausible alternative been provided. Locke himself, before writing his *Treatises*, thought that 'Men. . .must either enjoy all things in common or by compact determin their rights.'[127] Sidney (whose *Discourses* remained unpublished in any case) accounted for private property in England and Europe with terms which did not escape decisively from the Grotian explanation.[128]

That the most persuasive criticism of Grotius came from a source radically hostile to natural freedom did not help. Filmer had pointed out an acute difficulty in producing a division of common property because he disliked the implications of the natural freedom it implied.[129] Such a division, he argued, would require a consent of all mankind. Hobbes' view that the state of nature could hardly sustain a viable

226

agreement about property was equally unhelpful to anyone who wished to explain property without relying on government. Their arguments in effect required a new explanation of private property from one who wished both to uphold natural freedom and to explain property in terms free of governmental attachments. Locke noted the difficulty[130] and proceeded to solve it. The *Second Treatise* set out an explanation of property which was founded on natural freedom and was *incompatible* with absolutism. Locke reasoned from the assumption that man was by nature free of a political superior: people retained their natural freedom, for they were not free to alienate it as Grotius had envisaged. That left open the way to set property in terms of freedom. How was this accomplished?

If a man were free it followed that 'every Man has a *Property* in his own *Person*'.[131] If a human being enjoyed freedom from another's control it followed that they had authority over themselves. As we have seen the seventeenth century called this exclusive control *dominium*. Sometimes too it was called property or *suum*. This control referred to the qualities inhering in a person and was thought to comprise his life, limbs, liberty and so on. Grotius described it as life, liberty, limbs, honour and reputation. Those who opposed absolutism emphasised that material possessions belonged with these, so that property in the ordinary sense was classified as *suum* rather than explained through government. Hence within the framework of *dominium* property in the sense of control over oneself came to include property in goods and estates. The Lockean trinity of life, liberty and property is only one example of this.[132]

It was one thing to move property (in the concrete sense) on the conceptual map and another to explain it in terms that would securely locate it there.[133] Writers before Locke had not attempted this. He did so by suggesting that a deployment of the agent's *dominium*, his property in the wider sense, produced property in the narrower one. When Locke emphasised the property each had in his person, he added that the '*Labour* of his Body, and the *Work* of his Hands. . .are properly his'.[134] That labour Locke used as the means to property. It was easy to describe this as appropriation, since it implied taking something to oneself.[135] The activity had been mentioned by Grotius and Pufendorf, but only marginally.[136] Locke made appropriation the instrument of acquiring property.

But why should this use of the agent's property, his 'labour', produce property in the ordinary sense? It is a mystery why applying one's labour to something, even consuming it, makes the thing taken one's own.[137] After all we call one variety of this activity theft. The solution is that the world already belonged to someone, who required mankind to use it for an end which necessitated labour.

Locke had argued for God's superiority in his *Essays* and assumed it in his *Treatises*: and indeed His ownership of the world was a datum common to all writers on the subject of property. They assumed, additionally, that He had given the world to man: Filmer argued to one man, Adam, and Grotius and the rest to all mankind. His donation was supposed, by Grotius and Filmer amongst others, as by Locke, to take the form declared in *Genesis*: *be Fruitful and Multiply and Replenish the Earth and subdue it*. Locke, of course, had used this passage to found his God's great design, and here we see its special bearing on property. That lies in a point which is itself quite small, but which has important implications. Most writers treated this instruction of God's merely as a permission – Filmer described it officially as a blessing or benediction and Grotius as a right – which entitled people to live on the earth but did not demand anything of them. Locke by contrast treated it as a direction from God to man. This interpretation was crucial for his argument about property.[138]

The command was conveyed through both revelation and reason. The former, on Locke's interpretation, disclosed that God had set up 'the Dominion of the whole Species of Mankind, over the inferior Species of Creatures' and that this was entailed by His command. 'God who bid Mankind increase and multiply' intended to 'give them all a Right to make use of the Food and Rayment, and other Conveniencies of Life, the Materials whereof he had so plentifully provided for them'. The latter was made as an inference from the nature of man and the world to the effect that God meant man to use the earth to preserve himself:

God. . .spoke to him, (that is) directed him by his Senses and Reason. . .to the use of those things, which were serviceable for his Subsistence, and given him as means of his *Preservation*.[139]

So God not only gave the world to man but also gave it for a purpose. That purpose, the preservation and increase of the human race, was integral to Locke's account of property.

In the first place it required appropriation as the means of God's design and therefore legitimated that activity. Locke was quick to insist that this required appropriation. 'God, who hath given the World to Men in common, hath also given them reason to make use of it to the best advantage of Life, and convenience', he remarked and reason pretty soon concluded that 'there must of necessity be a means *to appropriate*' things before they could be used by anyone. The means of appropriation was labour. Hence the man who laboured in order to sustain life acquired property because He did by doing as God willed with God's creation. 'The Law Man was under,' in Locke's words, 'was rather for *appropriating*.'[140]

It may be said that the labour, like the creation itself, was God's own property. This is true, but it suited Locke for just that reason. He emphasised man's dependence on God and thus expressed a single sequence of thought. God had been used as a bar against absolutism, for man, as answerable to Him, could not transfer control over himself to another human. God's authority was now seen to direct man to acquire property in a manner which involved freedom and which did *not* involve government. In effect Locke substituted dependence on God for dependence on man. Whereas in Hobbes (let us say) government created a title to a property good against other people but not against the ruler, in Locke God created a title good against other people and prior to government. That it was not good against Himself was important only because He prescribed the very purpose which explained property.

The character of God's 'great Design' had a wider importance for Locke's account of property. That it prescribed the increase of mankind suited his need to accommodate the types of property valued in the England of his day. This did not require him to deal with property in the sea, which had exercised Selden and Grotius. Locke's audience most characteristically were concerned with property in land and commercial wealth.

Whilst appropriation of itself suggested consumption or seizure, it could also be the instrument of service to the end attributed to God. His command to subdue the earth could be glossed to legitimate property in land. 'God and his Reason commanded him to subdue the Earth', we read, '*i.e.* improve it for the benefit of Life' which was achieved through appropriating land and farming it. The increase of mankind could be sustained, it seemed, by fencing in ground and more pointedly by improving land.[141] Locke insisted eventually that at least 90 per cent 'of the *Products* of the Earth useful to the Life of Man' were 'the *effects of labour*'.[142]

The institution of money would encourage improvement still more, for it removed the limit to rational labour and acquisition set by the perishable character of natural products: people could exchange their produce for money.[143] Thus both land and money turned out to be terms in God's design, for they both implied an increase in the resources available to sustain the human race.

Locke wrote near the end of his life that 'Propriety, I have no where found more clearly explain'd than in a Book intituled *Two Treatises of Government*.'[144] The outstanding immodesty of the assertion bespeaks the importance of a plausible explanation of property for his purposes. It accommodated the principal varieties of property in a way which relied upon man's natural freedom; it avoided the difficulties which Filmer and Hobbes had seen in the Grotian account; and it was incompatible with absolutism. So property and political power fell into the same pattern of explanation for Locke.

So the 'great Design', because it involved freedom, made possible on the explanation of private property in terms congruent with Locke's view of political power. But if freedom had gone to explain property, what did it say about the family?

VII

Locke's explanations would need to separate the paternal from the political in order to show that the relation of father (or rather parents) and child did not involve the authority that Filmer had attributed to fathers. This would have to be done in a manner that was not subversive of the family. For household order was at the heart of Locke's England. The power of the head worked to coordinate its members activities to serve order rationally. This form of authority was supposed to be as vital not only to England but to any society. For that reason it was indispensable for Locke that he should explain it adequately in terms that securely established some authority in the household. Here too the great design served Locke's turn. That is to say, where he had used the 'great Design' to explain private property its terms could be turned to explain paternal power in a way that divorced it from political power. Fatherly rule would turn out to be paternal compliance with God's design, and as such at once authorised and limited by God's intentions.

Paternal power, Locke explained, was the means to do a duty. That duty is to bring up children to be able to obey reason. How was this duty explained? Our knowledge of book one reminds us that a natural instinct drove people to become parents in order to sustain numbers or, in Locke's words, 'God in his infinite Wisdom has put strong desires of Copulation into the Constitution of Men, thereby to continue the race of Mankind.'[145] To ensure that parents nurtured their offspring He also implanted in them a very powerful instinct to protect their young: He 'makes the Individuals act so strongly to this end, that they sometimes. . .seem to forget that general Rule which Nature teaches all things of self Preservation, and the Preservation of their Young, as the strongest Principle in them over rules the Constitu-

230

tion of their particular Natures'.[146] The duty of preservation constituted a juridical complement to these instincts. Parental care, Locke decided, should extend beyond preservation alone to education, for God's design required parents to raise their children to a given condition.[147] What was that condition? It is perhaps unsurprising that it was the ability to use reason.

This goal is intelligible enough in terms of the distribution of rational conduct Locke's view of political power required. We have seen that some contemporary writers attributed the power to think and act rationally to monarchs and denied it to people in general. Locke was concerned to be able to suppose that people were rational. We have seen the intellect at the basis of political authority, and seen the exercise of reason both implied in the derivation of the duty to preserve others and exercised explicitly in the acquisition of private property in land. Soon we shall see it is integral to Locke's account of government. The plausibility of Locke's political theory required him to show that rational conduct was feasible, at least in principle. Hence education became central to his political concerns.

By this token it was necessary to explain how people became rational. For it was obviously true, as Locke himself observed, that at birth people tended not to act rationally. He explained that the power of reason was present from the outset, but suggested that it came to fruition through the educational process: hence children had need of education. Locke was not slow to argue that there was incumbent on parents a duty 'to take care of their Off-spring, during the imperfect state of Childhood' and to assert that this extended 'to inform the Mind, and govern the Actions of their yet ignorant Nonage, till Reason shall take its place'.[148] Hence parenthood and education were central to God's, or Locke's, design.

The centrality of education to the design of the Lockean God provided parents with a role, which otherwise they would have lacked. The demotion of fathers from their Filmerian eminence might have seemed disturbing had superiority and purpose not been attributed to them or, at least, to parents. But the superiority of parents was necessary for the sake of their children for so long as the latter lacked the power of reason: 'the *Power. . .that Parents* have over their Children, arises from that Duty which is incumbent on them'. By the same token this authority extended no further than the task in hand.[149] Thus Locke explained parental power, but in terms which point to his view of political power yet which show how different were the authority of parent and ruler.[150]

VIII

Locke had indicated that political authority resided in the first place with each agent. He had explained property in a way which showed that it was prior to civil government and unrelated to the underpinning of it. He had argued that parenthood, likewise, implied a superiority that fitted people to govern themselves rather than constituting civil government itself. Instead he referred both property and parenthood to his view of God's intentions in the great design. But one great task remained: to treat government itself in the same terms.

For Locke's task was at once to explain civil government and to limit it. To explain government was necessary because otherwise the obvious safeguard of liberty and property would be absent. For despite the suspicion of rulers built into the structure of *Two Treatises* both of its books assume the need for government. The explanation would have to be managed in terms of freedom too, in order to show how Locke's argument, which had begun without political superiors, conducted his reader to a secure government. That government had to be limited, in order to fulfil the aim of establishing 'bounded' government. One task, then, was to show how a polity could exist on his terms and the other was to show its limitations.

To show that government could exist legitimately was straightforward enough. The rights of each and everyone to preserve themselves and to execute the law of nature, which we have seen flow from Locke's general views, explained government easily enough. Locke supposed that in order to secure the objectives corresponding to these rights, people would consent to creation of a political society, that is to say a society whose superiors were entitled to pursue just those objectives.[151] To suppose these rights inhered to each individual presupposed that everyone by nature was free of a political superior. So government was founded on terms compatible with freedom.

The working assumptions behind each agent's consent to such an arrangement were that the agents were free and rational. It was no accident that Locke's account moved from property and parenthood to discuss the cases of women and servants. In part, no doubt, this reflected the facts these cases, belonging as they did to the household, might seem to lend themselves to treatment in terms of patriarchy. But more particularly the alternative explanation of their place that Locke offered was a preface to his political society. For wives and servants obliged themselves to a superior by free acts that presupposed their possession of reason, both by consenting freely and at that to strictly defined terms.[152] These cases provided Locke with a type of rational conduct which he carried forward to his discussion of government.

In this model Locke assumed that each agent consents to the formation of a political society in his or her own person. That is to say, although it not transparently clear from Locke's account just who 'the people' are (for precision on this point was not required by his purpose of advancing responsible government), yet it is evident that each agent acts primarily on behalf of himself. For it to be otherwise would undercut Locke's view that agents were equipped intellectually to guide themselves. As ever, his treatment of mind informed his view of politics. All this, of course, presumed that God had set no one over them. Not everyone subscribed to the natural freedom of man, of course. One opinion of another hue contrasted significantly with Locke's. Just as some attributed superior intelligence to Adam, some conceived him as politically superior

Filmer had assumed that God had made Adam the political representative of mankind. As every school boy knows (if he is sufficiently erudite) Filmer argued that kings enjoyed a power derived from Adam, a power political in its reference and absolute in its extent. In order to make good this case, Filmer had to show *how* Adam's political power devolved to subsequent monarchs. This was partly a matter of adducing descent, though Filmer was rather chary of producing specific family trees. But it was also a matter of representation. 'What was given unto Adam,' Filmer assumed, 'was given in his person to his posterity.'[153]

How can we make sense of this proposition, 'given in his person to his posterity', so surprising as it sounds? The task would not be easy from the text alone, for Filmer was at no pains to explain it. But that untroubled reticence suggests that he was using a common assumption. Filmer *was* deploying an idea familiar to his readers. This notion of representation is one from a certain sort of Christian theology.

It figures in one account of the Fall of Man. In this account Adam was the representative of mankind. When Adam sinned by eating the forbidden fruit he was erring not only on his own account but also on behalf of everyone else. In that sense he was the representative of mankind.

How did the doctrine arise? Here, as in so many places, it is best to begin with St Augustine. Augustine put a peculiar construction on scripture. At *Romans* V.12 Paul stated that sin exists, ἐφ ᾧ πάντες ἥμαρτον Version puts it, 'for that all have sinned'. Augustine understood the phrase ('because all have sinned') to refer to Adam and to mean *in quo omnes peccaverunt* ('in whom all have sinned'). This reflects an insecure grasp of the Greek language; but if an error it is historically important, for it was general amongst the Reformers.[154]

How can one make sense of the doctrine? How had all sinned with Adam? Augustine himself had no particularly clear answer to the conundrum[155] and declared frankly that nothing was more difficult to understand that the consequences of Adam's Fall.[156] But you can always rely on Calvin to be outstandingly resourceful. He declared that mankind was derived from Adam, as he put it, not only 'seminally' but also 'federally'.[157] This 'federally' may seem *obscurum per obscurius*. Yet what it means is fairly straightforward. 'Federally' affords an explanation of how Adam was mankind's representative at the Fall. Clearly it was not enough to suggest that Adam was representative merely because he was the first man or a parent of mankind (to which Calvin's 'seminally' alluded delicately). Something besides is needed, which might make use of Adam's priority. 'There is a further step,' remarked Gilbert Burnet – and who more alive to transitional manoeuvres than a Scotsman who had become an English bishop? – 'made by all the disciples of St Austin, who believe that a covenant was made with all mankind in Adam, as their first parent: that he was a person constituted by God to represent them all'[158]. Burnet's testimony is borne out by William Perkins, who had stated without argument that 'Adam was not . . . a private man, but represented all mankind.'[159] What covenant was made? It was suggested that Adam was party to an agreement in which obedience to a law of conduct would be rewarded with felicity and deviation from it punished with misery. If we assume – as evidently it was assumed – that mankind needs representation whilst Adam was the only person in the world, God would not have far to look for a type of mankind. So, as Edward Reynolds wrote, 'we were in him parties of that covena[n]t, had interest in the mercy, & were liable to the curse which belonged to the breach of that covenant'.[160] Adam figured as not just mankind's ancestor but also as its representative.

Of course his natural role of ancestor was important. For the function for which the device of representation was needed, involved descent too. Augustine had wished to explain how the sin of Adam was visited on his descendants. This account of representation fitted part of that bill. It showed how mankind would be liable for whatever punishment Adam incurred in breaking God's law: people would be liable for what their representative did. If, as Gabriel Towerson put it, a law were 'given to *Adam*, not only in his personal capacity, but as he was the Representative of Mankind', then, 'this Law must be consequently supposed to have been obligatory to us, as well as to him to whom it was immediately given'.[161] But it remained to show how punishment was transmitted. The answer was that because Adam was the ancestor of all mankind, whatever punishment marked him would be passed on to them quite unavoidably. To put the matter shortly, the entire human race would be liable for punishment and it was certain that everyone in fact was punished. 'Wee all are sharers,' Reynolds concluded, 'because *Adams* person was the Fountaine of ours, and *Adams* Will the Representative of ours.'[162] Because of Adam's capacity his sin could be imputed justly to mankind as a whole.[163]

On what assumption does the whole theory turn? It involves thinking that the human race was inextricably one with Adam. As we might say, in the eyes of God they made but one person with Adam; as a seventeenth-century writer in fact put it 'we are some ways, one person with him, either by Nature, or Law, or both, and God did so account of us'. We can hardly do better than summarise the theory in the words of George Lawson:

By Nature, for he was the Root, and all men the Branches. By Law, for . . . God did account *Adam*, and all Mankind as one. And so far as God judged him one, and made *Adam* the Head and Representative of all: so far in *Adam* all men might be bound to obedience or penalty . . . And if God had not considered *Adam*, and all his posterity as one person, By one man sin could not have entered into the World . . . so as to pass upon all men.

Mankind was represented in Adam and the punishment of his transgression fell upon all, for they were 'one person with him'.[164]

It is in this light that Filmer's statement is explicable. He had written that 'what was given unto Adam, was given in his person to his posterity'. This makes sense if one understands mankind as 'one person' with Adam. He represented his posterity: so whatever referred to him referred just as much to them: as another writer observed 'Whatsoeuer he receiued of God, he receiued for himselfe and for them all'.[165] The theory besides helps us to understand Filmer's reasoning. With the representative theory Adam receives and transmits punishment for sin. With Filmer he obtains and transmits political power. The logic is the same: what Adam obtains he receives as a representative figure and transmits as a natural ancestor. Filmer's political theory assumes the type of reasoning employed in the Augustinian view of the Fall of Man.

The motif of Adam's representation appears in the *First Treatise*. To be specific, it figures in at least two contexts. The first is in the discussion of Eve's subordination to Adam. The second is when Locke discussed the Filmer's explanation of how Adam's regal power descended to his descendants.[166] In whatever context the supposition was vital to Filmer. The mere fact of descent from Adam was inadequate to his purpose. If one were dealing with a kingdom which

235

had standing laws of succession, one could locate an adequate title to the throne simply by finding the line of descent specified by legislation. But this could not apply to descent from Adam, certainly not in the first instance, for there were no positive laws in being. The function of explaining that regal power was inheritable was fulfilled by our motif: what was given to Adam was given to his posterity in his person.

Locke had little difficulty in dealing with *this* use of the motif. In the second of his two discussions he simply pointed out that Adam's posterity comprised the whole human race. Let him speak for himself, in his inimitable, knowing style:

Here again our *A.* informs us, that the *Divine Ordinance* hath limited the descent of *Adam's* Monarchical Power. To whom? *To* Adam's *Line and Posterity*, say our *A.* A notable *Limitation*, a *Limitation* to all Mankind.[167]

But if this particular employment of the motif itself could be dispatched with ease, the motif itself was more significant. We should turn to Locke's first context.

The motif was significant, because if conceded to Filmer, a large part of Locke's case in both *Treatises* went with it. The principles on which Locke constructed both his attack on Filmer's theory and his alternative to it involve the exclusion of Adam's representative quality.

In the first and most important place Locke's method of interpreting scripture was incompatible with Filmer's use of Adam's person. Filmer's case depended at many points on scriptural interpretation. Locke responded by showing that his adversary's citations did not agree with the literal sense of the text. In other words he treated a literal interpretation as the standard of canon.

For example, let us turn to one of Filmer's key assertions and to Locke's treatment of it. If Adam's transmission was going to be valuable for Filmer, he had to posit a grant to the father of mankind from God. Specifically, Filmer supposed that God gave Adam an exclusive dominion over 'all creatures', 'being commanded to multiply, and people the earth, and to subdue it'.[168] Locke observed that the literal sense of the texts adduced would not support Filmer's contentions: there was no grant to Adam *alone*, and the grant made was not actually political

Tis nothing but the giving to Man, the whole Species of Man. . .the Dominion over the other Creatures. This lies so obvious in the plain words, that any one but our *A.* would have thought it necessary to have shewn, how these words that seem'd to say the quite contrary, gave *Adam Monarchical Absolute Power* over other Men, or the *Sole Property* in all the Creatures.[169]

When Filmer claimed that the donation is addressed to Adam alone, Locke suggested that scripture spoke in the plural.

Locke's choice of a literal interpretation against Filmer's looser one was dictated by polemical convenience. But it involved a choice between scriptural methods. One might take the line that scripture presented a repertory of types or patterns for interpreting future cases, as John Pearson in *The Patriarchal Funeral* (which likens Joseph the son of Jacob to Christ) or John Dryden in *To His Sacred Majesty, a Panegyrick on His Coronation* (which likens Charles II returning to England to Noah landing on Mount Ararat).[170] Locke himself used typology to the end of his life, describing Adam as 'the figure and type of Christ who was to come'.[171] This, however, was not the chief emphasis of his *Treatises*. There he preferred a more literal interpretation. John Worthington's verdict that 'we are not to value' the work of interpreters 'if they speak what is plainly cross to the unforced and easy meaning of the text' parallels John Locke's view that our prepossessions 'cannot Authorize us to understand Scripture contrary to the direct and plain meaning of the Words'.[172]

It was in this frame of reference that Locke raised the matter of representation. In chapter five of his *First Treatise* he argued the case that *Genesis* 3,16 referred not, as Filmer had argued, to sovereignty, but merely to conjugal authority. In particular he considered the condemnation of Adam to labour: this he said was not a time 'when *Adam* could expect any Favours, any grant of Priviledges, from his offended Maker'. But what if the text were taken more generally? 'It will perhaps be answered again,' wrote Locke ' . . . that these words are not spoken Personally to *Adam*, but in him, as their Representative, to all Mankind'.[173] What was the Lockean response?

Locke could not admit that God was addressing 'all Mankind'. It would have upset his attack on Filmer's view of Adam's political authority. Locke asserted in chapter four of his first book that *Genesis* 1,28 was addressed to mankind in general and not Adam alone. His case depended on taking the text literally – to refer the text's 'them' to the plural number and not to a singular. Locke, in consistency, could not admit that the singular address of the passage in hand, its 'thou', was meant for mankind in general. We may infer, what Locke's treatment of scripture in his subsequent works evidences, that for him the Bible would have to be interpreted literally.

The wider implication of this rejection was that Locke could not easily admit Adam's representative capacity at all. For *Genesis* 3 was the text by which that role was traditionally warranted. For instance, Henry Ainsworth's popular *Annotations upon the first Book of Moses, called Genesis* commented at this place that 'neither was it his owne sinne onely, but the common sinne of us all his posterity'.[174] This note is silent in Locke's *Treatises*. The theory, it is true, is considered, but at that merely hypothetically and in relation to woman only, not the human race as a whole: if indeed, Locke queried, any command were properly present at all.

Certainly the view implied, that a representative is appointed by God immediately, is dissonant with the doctrine of the *Second Treatise*. For the people that are free and equal must be supposed, in one sense or another, to choose their representatives for themselves: having, as Locke says, 'reserved to themselves the Choice of their *Representatives*'.[175] So the view of representation implied in Filmer and the Augustinians was incompatible with Locke's politics.

Of course one could say that political representation is an idea distinct from what is involved in the Fall of Man: and so it is. Yet they involve the same *sort* of reasoning: and the seventeenth century did not overlook the analogy. It applied the theological idea to political representation. We find Thomas Tuke declaring that '*Adam* was no priuate person, but represented all mankinde,' and reasoning that

therefore we stood and fell with him. For hee was the root, and we are his branches: he was the spring, and we are the streams: he was the head, and wee are as the members. As the King, his Nobles, Knights and Burgesses represent the whole realme in the Parliament: even so did *Adam* represent the person of his whole posteritie.[176]

So that to allow Adam's representative position in theological discourse involved the corresponding admission in political theory.

It is important to register just how significant this sort of Adamic reasoning was. In itself it exemplified the point that God could set a superior, whether father or ruler, over mankind: but it suggested also that people could be represented (and be liable for their representative's actions) without their *own* consent. This had a wide currency in the thought of the day. It was held valid, for instance, that one who committed treason forfeited his possessions not merely on his own account but also on behalf of his heirs. Samuel Parker interpreted the law of treason thus. 'If any Person be convicted of Treason against the Crown, he is thereupon attainted,' he wrote, 'and not only his Estate escheats to the King as Supream Lord, but his Blood too is corrupted, so that his Posterity are not capable of Inheritance.' On what assumption did Parker base this account? 'And thus,' he continued, 'that Entaill of Priviledges, which God of his free goodnesse had settled upon *Adam* and his Heirs forever, upon Condition of their Obedience . . . was by the disobedience of *Adam* cut off from himself and his Posterity.' In a like way, it was assumed that the children born to those who had become slaves, whether through their own intent or otherwise were themselves slaves. It was the Adamic model that suggested that the descendants of slaves must have servile status. 'As poison is carried from the fountain to the cisterne,' wrote Edward Reynolds, 'as the children of traytors have their blood tainted with their Fathers treason, and the children of bondslaves are under their parents condition,' so 'We were *all one in Adam. and with him.*[177] If indeed agents were supposed to consent, as in Bodin, their consent might be an acknowledgement of a superior constituted by God rather than one constituted as such by their acts. Again, even if such consent or contract by free agents was hypothesised, so that representation might be founded upon choice at some original point, political power might move rapidly from this basis. Hobbesian people consent to set up a sovereign, but there is no hint that their sovereign was juridically dependent on them subsequently or that their descendants and successors had any voice in authorising the commonwealth.[178] Thus the assumption present in the Adamic model informed the notion that absolutism could be erected by contract.

The political implications drawn from the Augustinian view, indeed, disagreed with Locke's politics. Locke's political position was at odds with the motif to which Filmer had alluded. The view of the Bible which his treatment of Filmer deployed, the premises of his *Second Treatise* did not agree with Adam's representative quality and the political inferences which could be drawn from it. Filmer's assumption of a certain kind of Christianity did not accord with Locke's politics. We find him proposing alternative conclusions about the consequences for children of their parents' actions. His chapter on conquest in the *Second Treatise* argued, amongst other things, that even the conqueror with a just cause had at his mercy only the person of the vanquished. The latter's goods and his posterity could not be touched legitimately, for 'the Father ... can forfeit but his own Life, but involves not his Children in his guilt or destruction'.[179] In a like way he denied that the children of slaves were themselves born to a servile life.[180] More fundamentally his view of consent was inconsistent with the notion that one agent could transact on behalf of another.

There were negative and positive aspects to this. To state the negative point generally Locke eschewed forms of political power that arose from a natural process. Adam's attributed power was the exemplar of this. We need not dwell on Locke's denial that Adam had political power over mankind, since Locke himself dwelt on it at length. He denied too *jus in generos*, the notion that fathers enjoyed authority over their children by reason of begetting them.[181] For that doctrine had a significant application: it implied that the acts of a father could oblige

239

his descendants. As Stillingfleet remarked 'in Contracts and Covenants made for Government, men look not only at themselves, but at the benefit of Posterity . . . [each] must be supposed to oblige his Posterity in his Covenant to perform Obedience; which every man hath power to do, because children are at their parents disposal'.[182] This ability to transact on behalf of others, even if for 'the benefit of Posterity' could lend itself to uses Locke could not countenance. He could hardly have been more explicit than to deny that if 'Fathers or Progenitors passed away their natural Liberty' they also 'thereby bound up themselves and their Posterity to a perpetual subjection to the Government' for whilst

'Tis true, that whatever Engagements or Promises any one has made for himself, he is under the Obligation of them, but *cannot* by any *Compact* whatsoever, bind *his Children* or Posterity. For this Son, when a Man, being altogether as free as the Father, any *act of the Father can no more give away the liberty of the Son*, than it can of any body else[183]

so that for Locke, political authority could not arise from the processes of nature, though it might be referred to humanity's natural endowments.

More positively he conceived how those natural endowments, reason and will, could be used to establish political power on terms that suited him. Firstly, setting up a government was a rational act. Civil government was a device designed to secure the ends embodied in God's design. It was supposed to secure them better than individual agents considered separately could secure them; for people could do do collectively what they could not accomplish individually.[184] Locke argued, in effect, that the creation of civil government was an exercise of rationality.

The very act of *setting up* a civil government implied adding something to nature. In this sense government for Locke was artifice. As such it appeared at an intelligible stage in the text. For having begun the second book of *Two Treatises* with natural matters, such as the endowments of mankind and their duties under natural law, Locke had moved to matters that required action, such as the acquisition of property and the exercise of parenthood. These activities, of course, accorded with God's prescriptions. But they involved people acting to better the nature they had received, whether by improving the earth or educating a child. Making a government, too, meant bettering the state of nature and was a deliberate act of artifice. But to what, precisely, did people consent? Locke's answer was cast, unsurprisingly, in terms of reason and freedom.

IX

Political authority was a rational construction: it was both set up for a purpose and existed by virtue of acts that implied reason in the agent. Each agent transacted for himself[185], not for others,[186] and was thus responsible for political arrangements, just as he was responsible for his own worship. Self-direction in this case implied the exercise of reason, which (as we have seen) was facilitated by education.

The end for which civil government existed in Locke's view, it need hardly be said, was the protection of property, understanding by 'property' life, liberty and estate.[187] This broad definition of property served at least two functions for Locke. Firstly, the matters specified were explained in terms of his 'great Design'. Liberty, understanding by that freedom from the arbitrary control of another, Locke presented as a condition of survival.[188] Estate was in its simplest forms acquired in terms of the great design and in its more sophisticated forms authorised by it. The generality of the formulation 'life' accords with the design. 'Life' is certainly general and seems oddly so, till we remember that the activities to which it relates are as various as the preservation of the self and of others and the raising of children.[189] Liberty and property, of course, were values important to contemporary society. Locke's scheme explained them as something rather more important, namely values important to God. Secondly, and by the same token, it emphasised the place of civil government. The objective of the latter was to protect these values, which is obvious enough: but Locke's scheme explained civil government in terms that *subordinated* it to these values. It was a means to secure them and, were it not, consent to it would be irrational.

In a similar way the emphasis on property in the broad sense prevented the notion of protection of the person from becoming too central to the argument. This is not to say that this was unimportant for Locke – far from it – but rather that his doctrine is constructed in a manner which complements the protection of life with other functions. The contrast is fairly obvious. Hobbes had argued that the protection of the person by the government was implicated with the obligation of the citizen to obey. On these terms government could enjoy an authority over the remaining areas of civil life that was subject to neither rule nor restriction, as indeed was the case in Hobbes' view.[190] Locke's government, by contrast, has a broader range of purposes to consider. In a like vein, citizenship and protection were not as such correlated, for receiving protection was not sufficient to make an individual into a citizen: 'this no more *makes a Man a Member of that Society* . . . than it would make a Man a Subject to another in whose Family he found it convenient to abide.[191] Thus Locke's view of the purposes of government is inconsistent with Hobbes' argument.

This, of course, corresponds to Locke's famous distinction between tacit and express consent. Tacit consent referred to those who enjoyed the benefits of government and thereby, Locke thought, were obliged to obey the rules it prescribed: these people, by their actions, implied submission to the government,[192] But they did not *state* that they wished to be citizens under that government, which act alone *made* people so.[193] This, of course, emphasises that it is only an act of one's own that implies subjection to a government. Since protection was afforded to those who were not citizens, it indicates also that citizenship and protection were not formally correlated.

The supposition that people, presumed to be rational, gave their consent to a government for certain purposes implies that those purposes provide a *raison d'être* for that government. On this understanding government could not be arbitrary, as contemporary absolutism might be supposed to imply, but had a purpose to guide it. The purpose, of course, was the preservation of property in the broad sense. The absence of government advertised the need for terrestrial laws, their impartial administration and their enforcement in the face of the human propensity for mischief: thus people were driven to 'take Sanctuary under the establish'd Laws of Government, and therein seek *the preservation of their Property*'.[194] Thus the making of terrestrial laws and the execution of them became the primary tasks of civil government. Locke was perfectly clear that it existed for just these purposes: as it was 'only with an intention in every one the better to preserve himself, his Liberty and Property' that government arose, its function was 'to secure every ones Property by providing against those three defects . . . that made the State of Nature so unsafe and uneasie'.[195]

It was a purpose, too, which the civil government was bound to respect in the terms of its existence; it was, in Locke's language, 'obliged to secure every ones Property'.[196] That is to say, its business was to uphold property in this broad sense and not to make inroads against it. This is illustrated clearly in Locke's treatment of the legislative and the executive. These two bodies corresponded in function to the making and the enforcement of terrestrial laws.[197] Locke was quite clear that the law of nature (which required the preservation of human beings) and the intention with which government was created precluded a legislative that was arbitrary, either in violating natural law or in governing without stated rules or in making levies on possessions

242

without consent.[198] The executive was bound to congruent purposes, always by being subordinate to the legislative and that to the degree of not being part of the legislative in 'well-framed Governments'.[199] Thus no part of government could be called 'arbitrary'.

Locke's treatment of the legislative helps to explain a mode of civil government requisite for Whig purposes. Those purposes, whether for exclusion or for the limitation of monarchical powers, emphasised the importance of parliament in law-making because they turned upon its legislative authority. Since the proposed legislation was supposed to prevent papist tyranny and so protect everything worth having, it followed that parliaments were essential to the constitution. This, indeed, was the position that Somers set forth with considerable emphasis, arguing '*That Parliaments constitute and are layd in the Essence of the Government*', reasoning that

a Parliament is that to the Common-Wealth which The Soul is to the Body, which is only able to apprehend and understand the Symptoms of all Diseases which threaten the Body politick.

That a Parliament is the Bulwark of our Liberty, the boundary which keeps us from the Innundation of Tyrannical Power, Arbitrary and unbounded Will-Government

and emphasising

That Parliaments do make Laws and abrogate old-Laws, Reform Grievances in the Common-Wealth, settle the Succession, grant subsidies; And in summe, may be called the great Phisitian of the Kingdom

but not completing his message. For though the tenor of all this was that parliament was competent to change the succession (*inter alia*) and was entitled to do so as the protector of the country, Somers did not explain why parliament had such high authority. The Lockean explanation identified the body that legislated for society as authorised in terms of people's natural rights (and so ultimately God's purposes) for the sake of the common good. This, obviously enough, established the legislative as the supreme authority within the state: and so Whig requirements, it seemed, were fulfilled by the purposes of the Deity.

The anti-absolutist implications of the purposes for which Locke supposed civil government existed are clear enough. They may be amplified, if we care to take the exercise. Locke's specification of the distinction of powers within a government serves the same turn. Having distinguished political authority thus, Locke examined its character. Polity, according to him, had three aspects – besides the legislative, there were the executive and federative. The distinction, as stated in his text, was amongst functions. One agency was to legislate, another to execute the laws and so on, and another still to conduct foreign relations. These were not necessarily distinctions amongst personnel, for in government one agent might have more than one function. It was the distinction of those functions that mattered, for it was integral to the responsible character of government. That is to say, Locke wished to subordinate the executive and federative to the legislative and to show that the latter depended on the governed.[200] These dependencies inverted the order of absolutist explanation. Above all sat the ruler, who might (or might not) have a legislative assembly: but that assembly was not supreme and depended on the ruler for its being and powers, which might be severely limited.[201] His authority thus involved no responsibility to the governed. In other words Locke revised government in the interests of his view of political authority.[202] The design of his polity, however, was not entirely aggressive.

It had a strong defensive aspect. This was not simply a matter of illustrating a reassuring respectability by dwelling upon how a Lockean government upheld property and order generally. For if the legislative and executive could not be arbitrary, this stipulation told as much against the accusation that Locke's political friends wished to 'have no body Arbitrary but themselves' as against the modern theory of absolutism. Again, where a Tory ballad apostrophised Sir John Moore

> May Moore ne're cease to stand up for the Crown
> 'Gainst the Presumtuous Rabble of the Town

and many sources suggested that the Whigs were anti-monarchical, Locke indicated his indifference to forms of government and emphasised the importance of prerogative.[203] The point was important, for as well as alleging that liberty and property were under threat from the Whigs, monarchical sources emphasised that republicanism meant arbitrary rule. Charles II enquired in 1681, 'who cannot but remember, That Religion, Liberty and Property were all lost and gone, when the Monarchy was shaken off, and could never be reviv'd till that was restored.' The point would have sounded plausible, for if eventually the political nation might grow sceptical of James II's declaration that 'I will never Invade any Mans Property . . . I shall still Go as far as any Man in Preserving it in all it's [sic] Just Rights and Liberties' this as yet lay in the future. Again, Locke distinguished legislative, executive and federative powers as means to different purposes. This was an important insistence because adversaries of Shaftesbury and his ilk had insisted that government based on popular consent would be ineffective to the proper ends of government. It would confound powers of executive and federative power with the legislative. A Tory parody of a

Whig petition asked Charles to 'grant the Right of Calling and Dissolving Parliaments, Entring into Associations, Leagues and Covenants, The Power of the Militia: War and Peace: Life and Death: the Authority of Enacting, Suspending and Repealing Laws, to be in your Leige People, the Commons of England'.[204] Locke decisively avoided this confusion, and thus illustrated the reassuring nature of the explanations he wished to maintain.

X

Locke's concern, once he had outlined a government which could not be arbitrary, was to cast the positions he rejected as the disturbers of the peace. The last five chapters of his book perform this function. In a sense they do so just by displaying a train of undesirable conditions – despotism, tyranny, usurpation and the destruction of civil government – as a preface to the citizen's right to oppose forcibly ill-natured rulers, so delivering the reader to the destination which Locke's circle had signified in 1675. More pointedly they provide an explanation of how such action was not to be understood as resistance but as repelling an aggressor.

The key term in Locke's explanation was despotism. This term denotes the condition in which the person and possessions of the subject were at the ruler's disposal. It corresponded to the substance of the modern view of absolutism as an arbitrary or 'oeconomical' condition. Locke, naturally, emphasised that '*Despotical Power* is an Absolute, Arbitrary Power one Man has over another'[205] and made it clear that neither paternal authority nor political authority were anything like it in his view. This is an unsurprising conclusion, and to spend a chapter reaching it may seem otiose.[206]

In fact it is important to Locke's argument. Despotic authority accrued to a conqueror, according to Bodin, and this view was alive in Locke's own time,[207] though not universally shared: Hobbes and Hale alike rejected it.[208] It was significant for Locke, partly because he wished to refute it as incompatible with his view of political authority, partly because he wished to insist that the descendants of the conquered had no responsibility for their ancestors' acts[209] and partly for another reason. That was to suggest that a conqueror as such had no right to rule, but was an aggressor. Usurpation was represented in a similar light.[210]

Both conquest and usurpation introduced the notion of rule extending beyond right. As Locke described conquest it did so by definition. In describing usurpation he added, quite gratuitously, that 'if the

Usurper extend his Power beyond, what of Right belonged to the lawful Princes. .'tis *Tyranny* added to Usurpation'.[211] Tyranny was a concept that no one favoured and the introduction of it fitted Locke's purpose. Tyranny he defined as *'the exercise of Power beyond Right'*.[212] Before turning to the political implications of tyranny, we must look at how Locke understood 'right'.

Locke specified the purpose for which government existed was to sustain rights. How does this relate to the matters discussed so far? Right in Lockean can be understood in relation to superiority. In its root sense the latter involved an ability to direct. To say that A had authority over B would imply that A was able to direct B more successfully that B could have managed for himself. This would be partly a matter of intellect and partly of other faculties. Hence, for example, God's authority over people derived from His superior ability to direct and to reward or punish them. This superiority, Locke thought, gave Him a right to deal with mankind as He chose.[213]

On this model, right would be an attribute of a bearer of superiority. It would be attributable in respect of a superiority, meaning by that both that it accrued to a superior and referred to the aspect in which he or she excelled the inferior. Since God was superior to all forms of existence, His right held good over all aspects of creation. But we need not assume that the right enjoyed by a mere human agent over another would be so complete.

In particular we might note that God's super-eminent superiority gave Him a right over everything. It followed that His inferiors enjoyed a right only in terms of the aspect and extent granted by Him. We have seen already that mankind enjoyed a right to the earth and its creatures because God decided it was so. God indeed enlarged the original extent of that grant (to extend to destroying animals for consumption).[214] It is worth adding the more striking illustration that people enjoyed life only as God chose.[215] On this basis, then, rights would be grants made by God.

This affects how we understand the concept of right. Most importantly, the attribution of right to an agent would relate to God's purposes. After all, God would not deal out rights without purpose. Rights would be attributed to those capable of doing His work and, by the same measure, discontinued if the capability were misused. Thus, for example, all human agents have the same faculties, faculties which were supposed to be adequate for self-direction. Hence each agent was entitled to direct himself or herself. This implies a right to be free from the direction of others, 'the Right of my Freedom'.[216] Again, each agent had a superiority over their persons, described by Locke as their right (and sometimes their property). The language suggests an exclusive possession, beyond the proper control of other human agents: now so much was common in contemporary writing, but Locke indicated that this self-direction was subject to direction by God. We find that Locke's statement of the agent's independence was subject to natural law. By the same measure we find that those who contravened God's purposes decisively lost their rights, most dramatically by forfeiting their lives.[217].

Secondly, there may be an extension of usage, an extension relating to purpose. It happens several times in Locke's thought that rights are attributed to people by reason of the fact that they correspond to the means necessary to do God's work. Amongst these we can list the right to use the earth and its creatures as a means of self-preservation (without which the duty to preserve oneself would be impossible), and the right to punish aggressors (glossed immediately after its appearance as the right to execute the law of nature; without supposing this, as Locke pointed out, natural law could not be enforced terrestrially).[218]

Thirdly, what contradicted God's purposes could not be classified as right. Whilst right involved an ability to do something, the requirement that right should be related to natural law precluded ability to do *alone* being sufficient to constitute right. For example, theft implied an ability to appropriate, but this was not a right because it lacked an authorisation from God.[219]

This brings us to a further sense which right denoted, namely agreement with measures prescribing proper conduct. This was present generally in the seventeenth century, as in Hobbes' view that right existed where the laws were silent.[220] With Locke there is the special assumption that rights would not merely accord with law but would relate to the purpose for which the latter was made. This was true, for example, of the rights protected by government. These, of course, were the famous trio of life, liberty and property that we encountered earlier.[221]

Because the creation of a polity was an exercise in rationality, the same purposes for which it was created bounded its activity. This meant, firstly, that just as the agent had only a limited range of actions open to him or her legitimately, so too the government was restricted. The authority of polity came from the power an agent enjoyed over herself under the terms of the great design. That was limited and so polity at the utmost would enjoy no more. Locke put the matter with a clarity edging on pleonasm. 'No Body can transfer to another more power than he has in himself;' he wrote,

247

and no Body has an absolute Arbitrary Power over himself or over any other, to destroy his own Life, or take away the Life or Property of another. A Man, as has been proved, cannot subject himself to the Arbitrary Power of another; and having in the State of Nature no Arbitrary Power over the Life, Liberty, or Possession of another, but only so much as the Law of Nature gave him for the preservation of himself, and the rest of Mankind; this is all he doth, or can give up to the Common-wealth.[222]

Where with Marvell, 'The same arts that did gain/ A power, must it maintain', with Locke the same purpose which did a power create bounded it.

Restricted as the government was to these purposes, we might think this a 'minimal' state, if we were so disposed. The disposition is a valuable one only to the extent that it helps to lay bare an intention – after all 'minimum' and its cognates denote comparison and any historically informed comparison should attend to the very limited resources available to any government in the early modern period. But Locke's limitation expressed a purpose. The set of values that government protected would have excited little comment in his way, save perhaps for the exclusion of religion from the list.[223] The manner in which government was restricted to upholding those was the significant matter.

For '*Power beyond Right*' in this case would involve conduct prejudicing the purposes for whose sake government existed, namely those encapsulated in the broader sense of property, and that by virtue of exceeding the extent of the proper authority of government. If we contrast Locke's position with James I's, the difference made to the ruler's right comes into relief. James and Locke alike understood that a tyrant would be concerned for his own private advantage, not that of his subjects.[224] But where James suggested by contrast with a tyrant that 'the righteous and iust King doeth . . . acknowledge himself to bee ordeined for the procuring of the wealth and prosperitie of his people', Locke had a rather fuller picture of tyranny as the use of governmental power 'to impoverish, harass, or subdue' the governed, 'to the Arbitrary and Irregular Commands' of their rulers.[225] In other words tyranny was government carried on for purposes negating those for whose sake it existed.

On this basis it was easy to see that tyranny, implying arbitrary rule, would threaten everyone's property: as Locke put it 'their Laws, and with them their Estates, Liberties, and Lives are in danger'[226] and that such a threat would dispose people to reject 'Arbitrary and Irregular Commands'. It implies, more importantly, that to do so would not be illegitimate. For in the terms Locke had argued, arbitrary rule implied the ending of political authority.

Political authority was an instrument created for a specific end and therefore ceased to be valid when it no longer served that end. Locke specified a variety of conditions under which this event could occur: the unifying factor was that government as he understood it, based on right, was replaced by arbitrary rule.[227] Thus Locke's consideration of despotism, conquest and tyranny led him to a destination in which arbitrary rule implied an end to government.

If government were dissolved, it followed obviously enough that two rights were returned to people. Since people set up a government in order to have terrestrial laws tending to their good and to have such laws enforced, they were reckoned to tender to the government their rights to self-preservation and to punish aggressors, though strictly for the purposes specified.[228] If the government were dissolved, people resumed those rights.

It followed that forcible opposition to such rule was not to be classed as resistance: arbitrary rulers were not governors. Resistance is a relative term, like so many in the *Second Treatise*. As Seth Ward had put it, '*Resistance* is a *Relative Act*, and it implies some *Person*, or *Thing*, to be resisted'.[229] The crucial question concerned the status of the person or thing to be resisted. Ward had preached against resisting lawful powers. Locke's argument implied that arbitrary rulers were not legitimate powers: it follows that opposing them was not to *resist* authority. It was instead merely opposing force with force or rather, since the ruler was making inroads against the citizens' rights, it was opposition to improper force: '*Force* is to be *opposed* to nothing, but to unjust and unlawful *Force*.'[230] In Locke's terms, indeed, it was such rulers who were rebels: 'those, whoever they be, who by force break through, and by force justifie their violation of them, are truly and properly *Rebels*'.[231] To oppose such inroads, then, was not to resist authority but to defend property, a proposition which harmonises with the conservative prepossessions of Locke's day.[232]

On these conditions to oppose rulers was not to resist powers ordained of God, but to oppose those who (to adapt Gladstone) proposed to erect the negation of God's intentions into a system of rulership – and to oppose them equipped with the right to punish aggressors, derived from God's law. As the arbitrary rule was not authority in Locke's eyes, so an absolute ruler could not be a superior. To oppose such a figure was not to resist a superior but to repel an aggressor: 'to resist Force with Force . . . ' Locke wrote, '*levels the Parties*, cancels all former relation of Reverence, Respect and *Superiority*'. Indeed the superiority now lay elsewhere. For then the odds that remains is, That he, who opposes the unjust Aggressor, has this *Superiority* over him, that he has a Right, when he prevails, to punish the Offender, both for the Breach of the Peace, and all the Evils that followed upon it[233]

so that it turned out that the agent breaching God's ordinance by 'resistance' was the ruler (strictly, former ruler) and not the governed. Locke was not a resistance theorist in a meaningful sense. We can refer his position to two sources. One we have just seen. Complementing his treatment of natural rights and government, this was conducted in terms of natural reason and texts from the Old Testament. The other, if it can be called a source, is the non-Christian character of the Lockean commonwealth. Locke treated civil government without reference to Christianity. Denis Grenville, Locke's erstwhile correspondent, would write that 'Rebellion ... is ... esteem'd by the Church of England ... the worst as it was the first of sins.'[234] Locke, by omitting Christianity as a means of explaining the state was able to put to one side Anglican claims about the need to submit to all rulers rather more elegantly that some Anglican writers were to do after the Glorious Revolution. Rather than being a theorist of resistance he was a thinker whose constructions intended to turn the terms of theological currency to the task of uprooting and replacing absolutism.

XI

Locke's political theory took elements from his preceding thought and treated them in a manner that combined them with the devices and the needs of current thought in order to explain his preferred style of civil government. Two items were especially significant in his project. These were his view of God as mankind's legislative superior, drawn from his moral theory, and his assessment of human faculties, based upon his writings on the human understanding, but not developed there in this direction. He used these devices, in company with his view of relations, to attribute a divinely warranted purpose to mankind, which comprised an understanding of morality and of human life inconsistent with absolutism and favouring a different sort of polity.

There are a great many other elements in *Two Treatises*. What is significant about the constituents of the book is less their origin than the total ensemble Locke produced from them. Many of the ideas he used were the generally shared currency of the day, as indeed befits his requirement of placing the commonly shared constituents of theology and ethics behind his political arguments. The golden rule, for one, may be found in the works of virtually any theologian or moralist of

250

the period, running from Hooker to Atterbury and beyond. Of course they did not all make the same use of it, as its appearance in the work of both Hobbes and Locke indicates.

Here we meet the matter of conceptual families. A number of ideas may be grouped and formed into a single argument by a thinker in a manner which bends them towards some particular conclusion. Many of the same elements may appear in quite a different argument. Partly this is a matter of just which ideas are included. Hobbes and Locke, for instance, share not only the golden rule but also a view of the nature of law, a concern with self-preservation and similar views about the theory of ideas: but Locke made a crucial use of Grotius' notion of a right to punish aggressors, which Hobbes did not. Partly it matters just what the character of an idea admits – whilst Hobbes and Locke both referred some ideas to sense experience, Locke made use of ideas of reflection, where Hobbes did not, and was able to conceive God as within human knowledge. At any rate an overlapping set of constituents may produce two quite different conclusions. For ideas are sufficiently plastic to be organised in a manner that will answer to a number of different conclusions about some matter in particular.

Our account suggests that Locke was a more powerful and single-minded theorist than the figure found in our textbooks. This may be a surprise, but should not be. For it should hardly be anticipated that the author of *An Essay concerning Human Understanding* should be less acute in dealing with politics. However, this is not to say that his writings are without difficulties, elisions and omissions.

There is an important omission from *Two Treatises*. There is no attempt to show the presence of a moral obligation to the rational precepts Locke proferred. His recipe for natural law required rational precepts, God as superior and His exercise of superiority to make those precepts obligatory. Rational precepts are apparent in *Two Treatises*, as in mankind's use of the world to preserve itself. God's superiority is alluded to, and (indeed) functioned importantly in Locke's argument. But no evidence of His moral legislation was adduced, though it was evidently assumed, as Locke's unpremeditated use of 'bound' suggests.[235] This was not a major omission in its place, for this was a matter unlikely to be raised in the political conflict of the day. But the credentials of Locke's argument, so far as rational precepts were supposed to be obligatory, remained to be made out. The task of proving that they were was carried forward to *An Essay concerning Human Understanding*.

Chapter 8

Locke had organised *Two Treatises* according to the divine design for mankind to which *Draft B* had alluded. God's design required the preservation and increase of the human species. This doctrine had helped to explain the opinions about political organisation that Locke preferred. It had appeared also in the morality he had encountered from his youth and more diffusely in the course of his mature but pre-philosophical interests in natural law and political economy. It accorded with his view of the experimental life. These grounds of predisposition and consistency made it natural that his matured views about the human understanding should fall into a congruent pattern.

It becomes clear in reading *An Essay* that Locke conceived the human intellect not least as an instrument in God's designs. *Draft B* had suggested as much by stating that intellect set mankind above the beasts, for this alluded to God's ordering of being. *An Essay*, which repeated that point,[1] reflected a more specific view. The human intellect was fitted to God's purpose of preserving mankind, whether in the basic sense of leading people to good in the natural and moral worlds or directing their attention profitably in natural and moral philosophy or regulating their faith.

Central to this project was rational conduct. Reason directed the mind in its undertakings. For instance, convenience in material life would be attained by the direction of the faculties to their proper ends in natural philosophy and medicine, whilst a rational morality sustained society. The way to the next life required reason to demonstrate the existence of God and the proper measures of faith. But it was not just reason which was important, but the exercise of it too.

Locke had understood 'reason' to mean a faculty and its exercise, rather than a given set of conclusions, from the first. Its denomination as a faculty continued in *An Essay*, where Locke described it as 'that Faculty, whereby Man is supposed to be distinguished from Beasts, and wherein it is evident he much surpasses them'. He emphasised especially the functions of the faculty. Both of these were active. The first was to enlarge our knowledge, which to Locke meant discovering and ordering ideas. The other was to regulate assent, which of course emphasises the role of the understanding in guiding the will. Locke, indeed, maintained the warm assessment of the power of reason first stated in his *Essays*, but he now emphasised also the importance of reason in regulating probability.[2] In whatever role, Locke's emphasis lay upon reason's action.

The notion of *activity* was fundamental to Locke's treatment of the human understanding. He had announced in his *Essays* that God intended mankind to be active. Doubtless there was a temperamental bias towards the necessity of effort, instilled by the austere circumstances of contemporary life, inculcated by a morality which served to master them and embodied in the assumptions of political economy. There was also a translation of this into a specific form, just as in Locke's *Treatises* his sense that God had given the world to 'the industrious and rational' is mediated into his view of property. Here it took the form of insisting that the deliberate exercise of the intellect was necessary to discover truths about God, morality and nature: it was not by innate ideas, for instance, but 'barely by the Use of their natural Faculties' that people 'may attain to all the Knowledge they have'.[3] This assumption unites many arguments in *An Essay*, especially those indicating that the mind constructed complex ideas, the rejection of innatism, the proof of God's existence and the account of faith. Locke assumed that God had endowed mankind with the ability to reach the knowledge they needed. To explain their evident failure to do so and to maintain the assumption of divine benevolence at the same time required the fault to lie squarely at mankind's door. It had to be a failure, too, which was not bound to happen in principle for that would have implied a defect in the divine design.

These considerations had been present in *Draft B*, where Locke had suggested that it was the lazy and inconsiderate who failed to discover the truth.[4] This suggestion was now made more forcibly, for Locke linked together knowledge and activity when he observed that his intellectual method meant to stem scepticism and idleness.[5] This renewed the views of his *Drafts* and fitted the need of mental independence and so mental activity to Locke's political position. His view that people had sufficient intelligence to choose their own mode of worship and set up their own government assumed the adequacy of the human intellect to the tasks God proposed, even if only in principle. The positions Locke had eschewed – those supposing that people in general were no better endowed with reason than beasts – involved the contrary assumption. Reason in this sense underwrote toleration and limited

253

government. That is to say, it did so if it were exercised: for the view of the understanding Locke had developed in his early *Drafts* suggested that the discovery of significant truths implied mental activity.

In other words, *An Essay* embodied a natural theology that assumed that God had designed the human agent and designed it for certain ends. The sufficiency of human faculties to certain purposes was taken for granted because God required those purposes. By the same measure human aspirations to knowledge which was not required in executing God's purposes could be discounted. Locke had yet to draw the theological implications of this programme, but would do so within the decade.[6] More central to developing these assumptions was showing how relevant knowledge (in ethics, for instance) could be obtained whilst irrelevant ambitions (as in substance) could not. There was much for Locke to do. He had yet to give a demonstration of the law of nature, so central to his designs.

The programme of activity may remind us of *Draft B*, but it was strengthened in an important way by Locke's treatment of pleasure and pain. As before he mentioned with deliberate point ideas in whose reception the mind had no part to play. For the human intellect was 'fitted to receive . . . Impressions' through either the senses or reflection.[7] The nature of the fitness is adumbrated by a difference between ideas drawn from the senses and those acquired by reflexion. Through the external senses the former were *given* whereas the latter had to be worked up.[8]

Locke, as before, insisted that the business of the senses was to take notice of what helped and hindered life. Here *An Essay* embodied a technical advance over Locke's earliest drafts. The latter had assumed that happiness was the objective of human endeavour, an assumption common enough in Locke's day.[9] After 1671 he developed a view of psychology which connected human nature and God's designs. His psychology dwelt on pleasure and pain, identifying these as 'two roots out of which all passions spring'. He assumed that the construction of human nature answered to God's purposes, but initially was unspecific about the content of the latter: 'God has so framed the constitutions of our minds and bodies that several things are apt to produce in both of them pleasure and pain, delight and trouble, by ways that we know not, but for ends suitable to His goodness and wisdom.'[10] By the time Locke composed *Draft C* he had decided that God's arrangement answered to two general ends. In the first place he linked pleasure and pain with his sense that mankind was meant to be active. It now turned out that God had designed matters so that pleasure and pain spurred mankind to act. 'The infinitly wise author of our being haveing given us the power over severall parts of our bodys to move or keepe them at rest as we think fit and soe also by the motion of some parts to move the whole . . . He having also given us a power to our mindes in severall instances to choose amongst its Ideas which it will thinke on and to pursue the enquiry of this or that subject . . . ', wrote Locke,

to excite us to those actions of Thinkeing and motion that we are capeable of he has been pleased to joyn to severall thoughts and severall sensations a perception of *delight* which if it were wholy seperated from all our outward sensations and in word thoughts we should have noe reason to prefer one thought or action to another, negligence to attention or motion to rest, and soe we should neither stir our bodies nor imploy our mindes but let our thoughts (if I may soe call it) run a drift without any direction or designe and suffer the Ideas of our mindes like unregarded shadows to make their appearances there as it hapened without attending to them, in which state men however furnished with the facultys of understanding and will would be a very idle unactive Creature and passe his time away in a lazy lethargique dreame. And therefore it hath pleased our wise creator to annext to severall objects and the Ideas we receive from them as also to severall of our thoughts a concomitant pleasure and that in severall objects to severall degrees that these facultys he had indowd us with might not remaine wholy Idle and unimployed in us.

Thus the constitution of human nature was seen to answer to God's general intention that people should be active.[11] Pleasure and pain also served a more specific design, namely explaining how the senses gave warning of what helped and what harmed human life. For

the wisdom and goodnesse of our maker who designing the preservation of our being annexed pain to the application of many things to our bodys to warne us of the harme they will doe, and as advices to withdraw from them. But he not designeing our preservation barely but the preservation of every part and organ in its perfection hath in many cases annexed pain to those very Ideas which delight us . . . which is wisely and favourably soe orderd by nature that when any object does by the vehemence of its operation disorder the instruments of sensation . . . to withdraw before the organ be quite put out of order and soe be unfited for its proper function for the future.[12]

Thus the intention attributed to God in 1671 had found a conceptual vehicle by 1685.

More generally pleasure and pain served a number of functions for Locke. In the first place it provided an idiom for the assumption that happiness attracted the human agent. Secondly, it could be used to remove the possibility that something other than happiness attracted the agent. Thus Locke's psychology complemented his scepticism about accounts of morality in terms of 'right reason'. His notes of 1676 suggested that moral goodness was attractive to the agent to the extent that it was perceived to bring pleasure, rather than being compellingly attractive simply by virtue of being morally good.[13] Of course this necessitated an explanation of just how his psychology could be connected with moral goodness. The resources lay to hand in Locke's view that morality was properly conceived as law and that law implied rewards and punishments. Moral good and evil, he decided, were relative to these features.[14] This makes sense in terms of the assumption that Locke had deployed in his *Essays* and declared in his *Drafts* that morality properly so-called resided with God's legislation.[15]

God had annexed to His laws a feature which marked them for this purpose. Some ideas had delight and others its opposite annexed to them, so that mankind could apprehend what respectively aided and harmed it. These ideas of pleasure and pain served also to direct action. Pleasure was annexed to make man prefer some thoughts and actions and so to work towards them, whilst pain had the same power to stimulate him to work.[16]

Locke's account of psychology continued his aim of setting mankind to work at God's purposes. For the absence of pleasure stirred man to industry and action, as we have seen. Moral psychology in particular was tailored to Locke's specifications. Locke's God evidently meant to organise pleasure so that it would be found with actions which He wished man to undertake. What God willed man to do must be good and what He wished man to avoid must be evil. Hence it was easy for Locke to argue that good and evil were relative to pleasure and pain respectively. Of course it was possible that man might fall into error by following a pleasure more apparent than real or, we may add, lesser rather than greater[17] but that was another matter.

The Lockean account of the relations between intellect and will falls into the same pattern. His aim required that ideas of pleasure and pain should determine the agent to act. In its turn this required the view that the mind conceived an idea which in turn moved the will, the will being the power to act.

Thus we see in Locke's reading of freedom of action as doing or not doing according to the mind's dictates.[18] Locke was able to conclude on this basis that freedom pertains not to the will, but to the agent.[19] The point he wished to make was that the will was bound to follow the intellect. This may not be what everyone understands by freedom, but it is what Locke's purpose required: if to break loose from reason was to be free then 'madmen and fooles are the only free men'.[20] Granted the role of reason in Locke's ethics and politics it could hardly be otherwise.

The implications of this psychology are evident when we turn to Locke's account of uneasiness. He described uneasiness as a condition of 'pain of the body' and 'disquiet of the mind'.[21] Desire he understood as 'a state of uneasiness'.[22] It is easy to see the implication that action would follow from an idea of uneasiness which would guide man towards pleasure: and so to God's purposes. The Lockean God in fact organised human uneasiness to make people preserve themselves. Indeed He directed them to continue the species, thus making good the promise of Locke's political writings:

thus we see our All-wise Maker, suitable to our constitution and frame, and knowing what it is that determines the *Will*, has put into Man the *uneasiness* of hunger and thirst, and other natural desires, that return at their Seasons, to move and determine their *Wills*, for the preservation of themselves, and the continuation of their Species.[23]

Philosophical innovation thus explained points Locke had taken as read and deployed earlier.

It is well known that Locke has two accounts of how ideas determine the will. The first and earlier one, given in the first edition of *An Essay*, suggested that the will would pursue the greater of two goods set before it.[24] This accorded with Locke's general views. But it failed to take account of a case central to a counter argument suggesting that the connection between intellect and will was quite different. This is encapsulated in the phrase *video meliorem, deteriorem sequor*. The case in which the intellect identifies the greater good and the will follows quite another course is too commonly experienced to discount easily.[25] By 1694 Locke had become dissatisfied with his first account.

His revised position suggested that present uneasiness moves the will, so that a more distant prospect of pleasure might be overlooked.[26] Hence it was not necessarily the greatest good but the nearest which determined action.[27] This revision was important in explaining moral error. The notion of error accorded with Locke's larger views of morality. For whilst he acknowledged that different things might please different people he maintained two views besides. One, which we have seen, is that pleasure and pain were annexed to some ideas by God in a way which related to the preservation of the species. The other was that God had located a preponderance of pleasure in Heaven and a corresponding pain in Hell. Hence a good which overbalanced others was annexed to God's moral organisation.[28] The greatest pleasure, accordingly, would be found with one scheme of conduct and any other scheme presented a lesser good. But it was notoriously the case that many eschewed God's scheme. Locke's revision in psychology explained this mistake (for such it was on his assumptions), in that God's dispensation of justice was more distant from the agent than other, immediate and seductive pleasures.

257

The revision placed yet more weight on the intellect. Since Locke plainly supposed that the rational destination was eternal bliss, the intellect must have the task of directing people there rather than to an exclusively terrestrial reward. This implied overriding the intellect's own preference for close goods. Locke accomplished this by his doctrine that the agent could suspend choice until the intellect had appraised the relative merits of different courses.[29]

God evidently intended man's preservation in the world, by annexing pleasure to what sustained and pain to what harmed man. He had taken steps too which made the right course easy to follow, in that the relevant ideas were visited on man with no effort on his own part. But to exploit God's benevolence in a thoroughgoing way, man had to exercise his intellect. This was as true as much of natural as moral philosophy.

I

Locke outlined three categories of complex ideas, namely substances, modes and relations. This was a traditional classification. Substance and relations we have met already. Modes, which were mentioned in the early *Drafts* only in passing, were dependencies on substance. For example, an action performed by an agent presupposes the substance by virtue of which the agent exists. But though Locke had not made much of modes in 1671 he would have an important function for them in *An Essay*. These, then, are his principal classifications.[30]

Our concerns direct us to substances primarily in connection with natural philosophy (though God, of course, was a spiritual substance) and to modes and relations with moral philosophy. As we might anticipate, Locke worked in two different ways. Where he wished to emphasise the scope of human knowledge, God was said to have given man all that was needed. On the other hand, where Locke preferred to curtail it, the little that he claimed to know was said to correspond to the lowly function for which God destined such knowledge. Substance exemplifies the pessimistic interpretation and ethical knowledge the optimistic one.

Locke assumed the existence of substance, but emphasised our limited acquaintance with it. He described it in terms of a supposed but unknown substratum which supported those properties of things and agents. Thus we had an idea, albeit a rather obscure one, of what it did, but no idea of what it was. His pessimistic ambitions for natural philosophy and his desire to relegate more optimistic views of it demanded a downgrading of substance in explanation. Here the idea of God's benevolence was helpful. This is plain in his account of how we get the idea of substance, which shows how little it comprises. For God has given us what we need for the convenience of life and indeed no more.[31] The pendant to this limitation was found when Locke explained that more ambitious estimates of our knowledge of substance were derived from imagination only.[32]

Locke underlined the point by insisting on our ability to conceive relations and exemplified this by discussing cause and effect. Discussing the latter emphasised our ignorance of substance. For example, Locke argued that the relation was clearer than things related where these were substances.[33]

One of the most helpful tactics for a philosopher in a critical mood is to erect criteria of judgement which the views he dislikes cannot meet. Locke proposed four tests for ideas: that they be clear, real, adequate and true.[34] Simple ideas were real, true and adequate to God's purposes.[35] Complex ideas of substance, however, were meant to be real and fail the test and indeed were false.[36] We can understand, then, that complex ideas of substance were not of much use.

A similar conclusion was enforced in the discussion of what knowledge they could yield. Locke emphasised again that mankind was concerned to know only what affected human life, writing of 'our Happiness, or Misery, beyond which, we have no concernment to know, or to be'.[37] This principle was located by discussing two types of knowledge, namely relations and actual real existence agreeing with ideas. These two types afforded three degrees of knowledge – the intuitive, the demonstrative and the sensitive.

Sensitive knowledge concerned particular objects. Locke was quick to suggest in discussing our knowledge of the external world that it would always be largely sensitive. This matches the assertion that our knowledge of substances will extend very little beyond our experience.[38] The point, if not already apparent, becomes evident in Locke's discussion of the reality of knowledge.[39] The attempt to make general propositions about substance was doomed.[40]

Locke complemented this lengthy series of negations by asserting a rather less ambitious programme for natural philosophy. It was not a knowledge, properly so - called, of nature that God required of man, but merely the discovery of what was convenient or the reverse for human life. For instance when Locke discussed our knowledge of other things he indicated that our knowledge was of particular things. Our faculties had evidently been constructed *only* to inform us of what is convenient and inconvenient.[41]

An Essay thus directed the attention of the natural philosopher to securing advantages for human life. It is hardly surprising that Locke should treat natural philosophy as concerned with procuring conveniences and that this was identified with what was feasible. Locke concluded 'that the weakness of our Faculties in this State of *Mediocrity*, which we are in in this World . . . makes me suspect, that natural Philosophy is not capable of being made a Science' and that it was through 'Experiments and Historical Observations', he hoped, that 'we may draw Advantages of Ease and Health, and thereby increase our stock of Conveniences for this Life: but beyond this,' he added, 'I fear our Talents reach not, nor are our Faculties, as I guess, able to advance'.[42]

So, granted that God had given man faculties sufficient for the ends He had in mind, we see that Locke's delineation of our faculties tells us a great deal about their purpose. Since our faculties were sufficient to obtain conveniences it followed that man's proper work lay there: in useful research rather than in any large ambitions.[43]

II

If we cannot have science in the terms Locke proposed, can we have a certain knowledge of morality? Locke considered that the state of human faculties suggested that we should look to morality, 'that *Morality* is *the proper Science, and Business of Mankind in general*'.[44] After all happiness and misery were the subjects of interest God had put before us. Whilst this does not of itself imply that morality can be known *certainly*, any more than it implies a knowledge of nature, Locke projected a demonstrative knowledge of morality.

Locke's requirements had been specified in his *Essays on the Law of Nature*. Of course law or, more specifically, natural law is not the only form in which morality can be understood, but the political character of Locke's concerns had confirmed that he would write about it primarily in these terms. His requirements for morality, then, comprised a law and the possibility that it be apprehensible by human faculties.

Law in the full sense denoted five points. Firstly, it implied a superior, that is to say one who excelled another in some salient respect to a degree that it was for the inferior's good to recognise his superior. Secondly, there was moral obligation. Locke, like other writers of the day, assumed that the expressed will of a superior morally bound the inferior. If this notion were to be effective, there were presumed also our third and fourth points. That is to say, thirdly, if there is an obligation there must be present considerations that the inferior is being required to respect: Locke thought of these primarily as rules. Fourthly, the superior must make those considerations, whether rules or otherwise, obligatory: that is to say he or she must signify that they are willed as laws. Lastly, the agent must be aware of all these points or at least be able to know them. Locke included amongst such knowledge the knowledge of reward and punishment, since he had long considered that these were components of an effective law.

Nature denoted (inter alia), firstly, that all this was apprehensible by mankind through its natural faculties; secondly, that the subject matter consisted of ends natural to mankind; and, thirdly, that those ends included the satisfying of some desires found in human nature. The latter two we have seen in *Two Treatises*, where desires of self-preservation, procreation and security lead to the formation of society and government. Rules relating to these ends were disclosed through exercise of sense and reason.

Let us turn to see what would be comprised in fulfilling Locke's agenda. Firstly, there was the matter of the superior. The superior in this case would be God, as He alone had dominion over mankind and, more generally, over the whole world: in Stillingfleet's words, 'Who by being sole Creator and Governour of the World, hath alone absolute and independent Dominion and Authority over the souls of men.'[45] The presence of the inferior we may take for granted, but it was necessary to prove God's existence. Locke considered that he had done this satisfactorily.[46] Secondly, there was the ability of the inferior to recognise a superior and His laws. That is to know that God exists, that He is capable of being a lawgiver, that there are rules and that they are obligatory.[47] Thirdly, this presupposes an actual provision of laws, i.e., that the superior actually signifies that certain rules were obligatory. All this would have to be accessible to mankind's natural faculties.[48]

It is obvious that both superiority and acts of legislation and promulgation were required. Locke specified this in his *Essays on the Law of Nature*. It was not his view alone. Stillingfleet too suggested that 'mans obligation to any thing as a duty, doth suppose on the part of him from whose authority he derives his obligation, both *legislation* and *promulgation*', i.e., 'a *Legislative Power* commanding it' and 'a *sufficient promulgation* of the Law made' whilst Baxter remarked that 'subjection, being a general obligation to obedience, would signifie nothing, if there were no particular duties to be the matter of that obedience'. The same point was put if anything more forcibly by Locke's acquaintance Gabriel Towerson, who argued that it is not enough to make a law obligatory to us, that it hath God for its Author and Promulger, unless it do also appear to have been intended for our direction and obedience; therefore before we proceed to infer our own obligation by it, we must enquire how it comes to do so, and what appearance there is of Gods intending it for our direction and obedience[49]

for whilst superiority implied that the inferior was bound to obey his superior, it was necessary for the superior to specify what actions he meant to be obligatory.

What had Locke achieved in this connection? His earliest drafts had been devoted mostly to considering human abilities, especially investigating sense and reflection, and exploring demonstration, where he was not minimising our knowledge of substance and undertaking connected tasks. Though both presumed that God was mankind's superior and that He provided laws of nature, neither did much to prove the point. These omissions were doubtless evident to Locke, for he devoted much of his attention from the middle seventies to making them good.

He considered that he had knowledge of the existence of a superior in God. His existence was assumed throughout Locke's works. Locke offered arguments in the fourth of his *Essays*. He recurred to this topic in the 1670s, whilst *An Essay* said that God's existence could be known with intuitive certainty. Locke was still sufficiently interested in the question during the 1690s to make some notes on a Cartesian proof of God's existence.[50]

Locke was keen to insist that God was the *moral* superior. Locke's own society contained superiors, including magistrates and parents, but God alone was reckoned capable of moral laws. For His superiority over man consisted not only in an infinitely greater power and wisdom but also in His goodness.

Mankind's means of forming ideas and developing knowledge about ethics were a major preoccupation in *An Essay*.[51] Locke's most important advance over 1671 lay in conceptualising actions through ideas of mixed modes. These appeared first in some journal notes.[52] He took it that modes were given combinations of simple ideas (of course excluding from this the obscure idea of substance). He divided ideas of modes into two sorts. Simple modes were combinations of simple ideas of the same kind: for instance the idea of a dozen was composed of twelve units of the same kind. Mixed modes were combinations made up of ideas of several kinds. For instance the idea of a lie would be composed of simple ideas including articulate sounds, the connection of these sounds to ideas, whose marks the sounds would be; the combination of marks in spoken sentences in a way differing from the arrangement of

262

ideas in the mind of the speaker; and the speaker's consciousness that he or she misused the marks deliberately. A modern commentator helpfully describes ideas of mixed modes as 'action concepts'.[53] This is true not just in the sense that they conceptualise acts but also in that they were examples of the mind doing work. Mixed modes were complex ideas and as such the product of humanity's active power. That is to say simple ideas were united to form a new idea.[54]

Locke expressed a hope that we could reach a knowledge of our duty, remarking that we are 'funished with Faculties (dull and weak as they are) . . . to lead us to the Knowledge of the Creator, and the Knowledge of our Duty'.[55] How far do mixed modes take us in that direction? They give us both the idea of a rule and an account of the content of rules. The idea of a rule insofar as it consists in a generalised description of action may be framed in terms of mixed modes, though there is no hint of the moral or obligatory status of the rule. Again, supposing we assigned some definite content to our rule, we could compare actions with it.[56] Of course we should enter the rider that ideas of mixed modes would be in the indicative rather than the imperative mood. Since they are descriptive it is hard to see how it could be otherwise, and none of Locke's examples of mixed modes concern normative rules.[57]

The viability of mixed modes was evident, in that they pass the criteria for ideas which Locke had specified.[58] Clearness could be attained easily. Locke suggested that confusion in complex ideas was best avoided by ennumerating the simple ideas they contained. He supposed this was easy for mixed modes. The question of their reality did not arise, for they were not supposed to conform to the real. This suggested that their adequacy would have to be conceived in other terms. Since there was no question of their conforming to any real archetype, the adequacy of an idea of mixed modes would have to be judged against its own original.[59] In a similar way their truth had an internal reference: since they were complex ideas, falsity was possible if the simple ideas comprising them were not assembled properly.

These, of course, were difficulties in formulating ideas of mixed modes, not with our ability to know these ideas once formulated properly. Locke conceived that we can know mixed modes, because complex ideas of this type were their own archetypes. The point was made clear and, if necessary, clearer still by the pendant discussion of complex ideas of substance.[60]

This deals with actions. Another development we find in pages of *An Essay* is the matter of defining terms involved in ethical discourse. Locke's objective was to provide self-evident propositions. His examples included '*Where there is no Property, there is no Injustice*', his reasoning being that the definition of the terms made the proposition true by virtue of their meaning.[61] This was certainly an accession to Locke's intellectual armoury, though one which would underlie an argument rather than provide its whole content. However, it does not obviously fulfil Locke's wider programme. To define words, even to define them certainly, is not to disclose what is obligatory

Locke offered a conceptualisation of actions which satisfied the criteria he himself had specified for ideas and which he conceived could provide certain knowledge. He had satisfied himself also that he had an intuitive certainty of God's existence. How far did this go towards satisfying his ambitions about morality?

Locke claimed that our knowledge of morals is demonstrative. By demonstration he meant that reason could be used to show the connection between ideas.[62] It is apparent that Locke meant to demonstrate not merely general points but also moral rules.[63] The key matter, then, is to provide all the ideas necessary to suppose we know an obligatory morality. We have seen that in Lockean terms this comprises a knowledge of God's existence, an acknowledgement of His superiority, a conceptualisation of rules and an apprehension of their content and an awareness that God has signified that the rules are obligatory. All this Locke had provided to his own satisfaction – except the last.

III

It is perhaps needful at this point to insert a few words underlining precisely what was at stake. There is little doubt that Locke omitted to provide a full account of the law of nature in the sense he had outlined and this, at least, may be taken as a datum of scholarship. It is less clear, however, just why this omission arose. In order to determine the nature of Locke's difficulty, we need to begin by making two distinctions. Firstly, it is important to distinguish the notion of a mixed mode from that of morality and, secondly, to make a distinction between two sorts of moral condition.

The class of mixed modes, if it conceptualises action, has *as such* no reference to good and evil. That an action can be understood in these terms tells us nothing of its moral character. To refer to actions in the way that mixed modes do is to colligate simple ideas. Locke did not suggest that simple ideas, which are the deliveries of sense or of the mind's reflection on its own activity, tell us anything about the moral or the obligatory character of the action or actions the mind considered. It would be true, no doubt, that the mind could conceive ideas of mixed modes such as gratitude or fidelity or obligation itself, but this conception does not of *itself* identify the practice of the idea as good, let alone obligatory. Not all good actions are obligatory (as we shall see in a moment), and in any case the mere conception of an idea does not of itself identify the practice conceived as good.

This raises the question of how one knows which practices are virtuous. Locke, writing in 1681, proposed the criterion of doing good. His note *Virtus* observed, as one might expect, that the obligation to virtue 'is ye will of god, discovered by naturall reason, & thus has ye force of a law'. More pointedly, he stated that the content ('matter') of virtue 'is nothing else, but doeing of good'. Good, we have seen, he related to pleasure and the highest degree of pleasure, we know, can be called happiness. The part of the content Locke had in mind we could infer from his *Essays* or the *Two Treatises*, where he identified several forms of conduct as productive of good. Assuming with other theorists of natural law that the objective in view was the satisfaction of specified human desires, it was easy enough for Locke to suggest that reason would identify what leads to that end. Ethical rationalism, understanding by that term the tenet that reason discloses good, makes sense obviously enough in this frame of reference. But having said so much, we need to identify why it was the satisfaction of one set of desires, rather than another, that was important. One route at this point is to take the consequentialist path, and to suggest that the real object is to consider the aggregate of human happiness. Another, supposing with the natural law school that the satisfaction of some desires, as opposed to others, is important for upholding society, is to distinguish legitimate from illegitimate desires, and that suggests this we attend to the notion of law.[64]

Ultimately there is another reason that leads us back to the notion of law. For Locke assumed that the greatest happiness lay in obeying God's laws, for annexed to these (as he took it) were rewards and punishments of infinite weight. Were it otherwise his criterion of good action would become consequentialist. That is to say, he would look at the consequences of actions to determine which produced the most terrestrial happiness. Now whilst the laws of nature were supposed to produce happiness, they were not consequentialist, for, firstly, their criterion was God's purpose (that God might design them by looking at happiness was another point) and, secondly, they took into account happiness as a whole and not merely the terrestrial variety. Consequentialist *reasoning*, moreover, might undercut Locke's position about the rights of conscience – a point of which he was well aware.[65] Locke understood ethics primarily in terms of divine law.

This brings us to the second point, which is that obligation and virtue are not conceptually identical. An action may be virtuous without being obligatory or obligatory without being virtuous. Even if we assume that we are dealing only with virtuous actions (which we may define for this purpose, concurring with Locke, as those specified by rule)[66] and assume too that virtuous actions are to be obligatory the two concepts are not identical. Locke himself distinguished them when he wrote that 'vertue as in its obligation it is ye will of God, discovered by naturall reason, & thus has ye force of a law, so in ye matter of it, it is nothing else, but doeing of good'. For the purpose in hand, if Locke had discovered what was good by natural reason he needed also to show what was obligatory.

Locke had marked out his agenda in his *Essays on the Law of Nature* and it is there that the crucial point (or its absence) can be observed most easily. For there is a component omitted from amongst those which Locke needed to include to make his point fully. He had provided a superior entitled to legislate and provided also a declaration of his will: but he had not shown that the rational precepts he had selected were also to be taken as an expression of God's legislative will. God might express His will without it being meant for a moral law. To put the matter simply Locke had shown that certain precepts were rational, but had said nothing to show that God had prescribed them as morally obligatory.

The omission is apparent at the opening of Locke's sixth essay. He had established two requisites for a law in the fourth essay, namely that (i) there is a superior, i.e., someone entitled to give laws, and (ii) he declares his will as a lawmaker. To have the latter it is necessary to show that a rule had been meant as a law and so had moral obligation annexed to it. This Locke had omitted to do. He wrote that to understand the obligation of a law we must know that someone should have the right to prescribe it and added that when that person gave his commands he only made use of his right. Locke's conclusion was significant; for in asserting the superior's right to legislate and mankind's subjection to the legislator, Locke wrote that 'in so far as we are subject to another so far are we *liable* to an obligation,' but gave no grounds for saying that God had in fact signified what He had prescribed as being obligatory. Again, he had laid down 'that no one *can* oblige or bind us unless he has right and power over us'.[67] The lacuna was plain a little later when Locke pointed to a right to legislate and a right to impose an obligation without mentioning the condition that there be an act declaring prescriptions to be meant as moral laws.[68] The omission was present most pointedly, however, in the fourth essay itself where, as we saw, certain rational precepts were presented as according with God's will for mankind: but no explanation was given of how these precepts could be recognised as not merely willed by God but willed specifically as of moral obligation. Such an explanation would be needed to distinguish moral obligation from what was willed in other senses. The alternative would be that Locke intended everything willed by God to be morally obligatory, which is indeed what his definitions suggest.[69]

This alternative, which is attractive because it rescues Locke from his omission, is only a way of encountering a difficulty at another remove. Locke distinguished two senses of the idea of obligation, 'terminative' and 'effective'. Effective obligation resided in the 'prime cause of all obligation', namely 'the will of a superior'. This corresponded to Locke's first requisite for moral obligation, the presence of a superior and an expression of his will. The second requisite, a knowledge that the superior had declared his will as law, corresponded to the 'terminative' sense of obligation. An obligation had a terminative, or as we would say determinate, character, when it had been specified to *what* performances we are obliged: 'we are not obliged to anything', Locke noted, 'except what the legislator has made known in some way and promulgated that he wishes it'.[70] But the passage specified no criteria by which it could be judged that the legislator disclosed that he willed a precept to be a law, a rule which he was making morally obligatory, and not a mere expression of intention or will without that specific character. Clearly, we may add, there are such expressions. The Lockean God, for instance, willed the increase of the human race. Whilst this direction can be shown to have a content compatible with a number of precepts which Locke did take to be obligatory (such as preserving others and oneself), its conceptual form is not the same. A direction, whilst an indication of divine will, can hardly be understood as requiring an act as a matter of obligation. If it did, to make an *ad hominem* point, Locke the bachelor was singularly lax in omitting his part in this instance (so far as we know). In other words there was outlined no way to distinguish what was meant legislatively. This being so it was unclear that *any* of God's intentions were disclosed as morally obliging. Locke had shown that we can apprehend rational precepts and that on his assumptions God was entitled to will moral obligations: he had not shown that He had actually done so.

What did Locke do to make good this omission? Let us consider the matter demonstratively, in the sense of looking at the ideas Locke would need to connect. To conceive morality in terms of law presupposes a superior whose character gave him or her a right to prescribe, which in Locke's mind would be God. This much Locke provided to his own satisfaction. Equally he conceived a variety of rational precepts. But to demonstrate morality in this mode presupposed also a declaration of will about what was obligatory.

An Essay is remarkable for the absence of a chapter on this subject. Locke did, as a matter of fact, begin an essay on the subject. He entitled it 'Of Ethick in General'. The *general* conforms with his promise to demonstrate 'the certainty of general propositions in morality' as distinguished from 'the particular existence of anything'.[71] The essay as a whole was intended for a chapter of *An Essay*, though Locke was undecided about where it would appear.[72] Whatever its intended place it is eloquent by omission on the subject of our knowledge of moral obligation. It emphasised that the true measure of morality lay in 'the commands of the great God of heaven and earth, and such as according to which he would retribute to men after this life'[73] and contrasted this view with other notions which lacked this divine authenticity.[74] So, like Locke's *Essays* and his early drafts it contrasted 'God and the law of nature'[75] with other ethical codes. Yet when Locke came to the crux of producing an account of what matters God had made obligatory, it pulled up short. Locke observed that

to establish morality . . . upon its proper basis & such foundations as may carry an obligation with them, we must first prove a law wh always supposes a law-maker: one y^t has a superiority & right to ordain, and also a power to reward & punish according to the tenor of the law established by him. This Sovereign Law maker, who has set rules and bounds to the actions of men, is god their Maker, whose existence we have already proved.

This much we might anticipate. Locke continued:

The next thing then to show is, that there are certain dictates, wh it is his will all men should conforme their actions to, and that this will of his is sufficiently promulgated & made known to all man kinde

and here the paper broke off.[76] Locke had yet to demonstrate which were the 'certain dictates' God had prescribed to mankind. The published text of *An Essay* offered nothing in this line.

If there is an omission in this area, neither was the matter of rewards and punishments worked out. Locke's view of obligation required these as features of a genuine law. As he says in *An Essay*, God 'sees Men in the dark,' and 'has in his Hand Rewards and Punishments, and Power enough to call to account the Proudest Offender'. In the more sober language of a contemporary, 'Lawes are Rules of Duty, with Rewards annext to the obedyent and punishment to the Stubborne'.[77] Locke had in mind not least the law of nature. The character of this law required that its rewards and punishments be known to man's natural faculties. This task was obviously difficult, since God's administration of justice was assigned by Locke, as by others, to the afterlife. Locke thus had to argue that reward and punishment could be known by inference. But where he had been content to argue for God's existence and attributes on that basis, he was less definite about His treatment of the dead. In the seventies Locke suggested an argument which involved no more than a presumption. He proposed a variant of Pascal's wager.[78] *An Essay* did not produce any arguments pretending to certainty.[79]

The difficulty was not surmounted by Locke's contemporaries, though they frequently made stronger claims for their conclusions, Samuel Parker, for example claiming to have proved the reality of posthumous sanctions. Behind this lay a sense that the survival of the soul after bodily death and the consequent possibility of reward and punishment in the afterlife were necessary to complete the destiny God had projected for man. As Sydenham put it, 'that there should be found in mankind a certain appetition or reaching out after a future happiness, and that there should be no such thing to answer to it . . . is to me very improbable'.[80] In the end these assertions assumed that what was required to complete God's schemes would be forthcoming. This is a fair inference from His omnipotence, but of course no certain evidence that in fact He had exercised it in the requisite manner.

Though it was hard to establish the certainty of posthumous justice it was necessary to make out Locke's claim to know the obligation of natural law. We can evidence this much from his other writings. His view that God would decide claims which lay beyond the view of any earthly court[81] depended on it. For this judgement would concern desert. 'God alone, I say, is the judge in this case,' Locke wrote, 'who at the last judgement will repay each according to his merits.[82] Indeed the account of personal identity that Locke added to *An Essay*'s was cast in terms relevant to this concern.[83] This, of course, underlines the necessity of proving the afterlife.

Since Locke had neither shown that some rational precepts were obligatory nor proved the reality of an afterlife with certainty, he cannot be said to have fulfilled his agenda of providing a knowledge of what was morally obligatory. We may ask, why?

To the incurious reader the matter may seem to be one of omission due to personal defect. The omission was certainly personal, for Locke had set himself an agenda and had not fulfilled it. At this level one might think of likening Locke to John Austin, who failed to write the volumes on jurisprudence that everyone expected of him. But Locke's omission, like Austin's reflected a more serious intellectual problem.[84] To see Locke's difficulty in its proper perspective, let us examine the lacuna in *An Essay*.

The lacuna may be noted in several ways. Firstly, let us recollect Locke's model. Locke required a superior, whose will obliges morally, whose rules were apprehensible by reason (and which were also rational in another sense), and whose rules could be distinguished as obligatory. Obligation is one matter, goodness another. Where would goodness lie, if anywhere, in Locke's model? Of course this is a different question from Locke's, but the answer does something to illuminate his problem.

His model assumes you are bound to obey a superior. You are bound to Him, to do as He requires. Why? There are several possible reasons. We are used to the idea of contract. This doesn't apply to God in His capacity as creator and sustainer, since His power and wisdom sets Him over us whether we will or no. As Baxter put it, '*consent* to Gods Laws was required indeed, as *naturally necessary* to ... obedience, but not as necessary to the *Being* or *obligation* of the Law [of God]'. Putting aside the prior question of whether this law was *known*, our attention focusses upon the key point: mankind are supposed to be dependent upon God. Because dependent beings had received benefits from Him, they should make a return in the form of grateful worship[85] and more generally through obedience to His will. But this explains merely why we are bound to obey *Him*.

Mankind, then, was bound to obey God. In this model, goodness does not lie with the notion of law. The very definition of law presumes nothing of the sort – *regula agendi subdito a superiore potestatem habente imposita*[86] – and Locke himself insisted, in respect of terrestrial rulers, that laws were not always good. More generally, it is hard to see how law could distinguish good and evil. If we suppose a law obedience to which is a matter of moral indifference, then obviously *that* law discloses nothing about good and evil. But if we suppose a law that it would be good to obey, but evil to disobey we would also be supposing that good and evil are antecedent to the law, so that obeying the law meets our idea of good and disobeying it conforms to our view of evil.[87]

Did Locke show that God Himself was good? He certainly referred to God's goodness quite frequently, sometimes in contexts where his sincerity is not open to doubt,[88] but offered no proof of it. His chapter *Of our Knowledge of the Existence of a GOD* indicates Him to be eternal, omnipotent and omniscient,[89] but offers no arguments for His goodness. Neither had *Essays on the Law of Nature* discussed the matter. Locke seems not to have treated God's goodness at length in terms of reason.

This is certainly an important omission, and it is worthwhile to scrutinise it a little. Locke had made it clear that goodness, in respect of an agent, referred to its pleasure and evil to its pain. Thus things 'are Good or Evil, only in reference to Pleasure or Pain'[90] or (more loosely) 'Good and Evil ... are nothing but Pleasure or Pain, or that which occasions, or procures Pleasure or Pain to us'.[91] If goodness is understood in these terms, what of moral goodness in particular? Locke, seized as he was of the significance of dependence, assumed that 'it would be in vain for one intelligent Being, to set a Rule to the Actions of another, if he had it not in his Power, to reward the compliance with, and punish deviation from his Rule, by some Good and Evil, that is not the natural product and consequence of the Action it self'.[92] Accordingly moral good and evil are a distinct class amongst the sources of pleasure and pain. '*Morally Good and Evil* ... is only the Conformity or Disagreement of our voluntary Actions to some Law, whereby Good or Evil is drawn on us, from the Will and Power of the Law-maker; which Good and Evil, Pleasure or Pain, attending our observance, or breach of the Law, by the Decree of the Law-maker, is that we call *Reward* and *Punishment*.'[93] So good is relative to pleasure and moral good is a special source of pleasure.

Locke's treatment of good has two important consequences, one for the characterisation of God and another for the meaning of 'good' itself. The first is, in a sense, the more serious. If good is intelligible to people in terms of pleasure, how does it make sense to attribute 'goodness' to an agent? Presumably it would relate to his or her disposition or ability to give pleasure. This is problematic enough if one pauses to consider the range of human activities which bring pleasure, but which it is hard to conceive easily as good. Locke, perhaps, had a point of that sort in mind by distinguishing moral good (though that distinction introduces in its turn the difficulty that no one without power to reward or punish could be a source of moral goodness): but here lay a difficulty in characterising the Deity. God's goodness encountered a serious problem. If God is 'good' because a source of pleasure, then He must be 'evil' too: for Locke's God brings pain upon those who breach His laws.

This is not a happy conclusion, but it is (at least) not circular. A circularity results if we assume that God's goodness is in some sense 'moral'. For 'moral good' and 'moral evil'in Locke's hands relate to the pleasure and pain annexed to a rule by a legislator. Hence to say that God was morally good would be to tell us that He wills what He wills. Thus we come to the position of Hutcheson, that 'to call the Laws of the Supreme DEITY good, or holy, or just, if all Goodness, Holiness and Justice be constituted by Laws . . . must be an insignificant Tautology, amounting to no more than this "That GOD wills what he wills"'.[94] The conclusion is not more happy for having been attributed by Locke to someone else.[95]

The consequence for the meaning of 'good' runs on similar lines. The connection between pleasure and good is clear enough, but where does it leave the idea of moral legislation proceeding from God? If all we can be said to know about God's character as a legislator is that He wills what He wills we have not been told very much. Hence, perhaps, the rather unforthcoming response Locke made to Thomas Burnet after the latter had enquired about the basis of God's legislation. Locke would say no more than that

Whoever sincerely acknowledges any law to be the law of God, cannot fail to acknowledge also, that it hath all the reason and ground that a just and wise law can or ought to have[96]

which was to leave Burnet's question unanswered. Locke stated nothing about whether the rule or its divine author could be accounted good.[97]

There may be a way out of this difficulty within the framework of Locke's thought, though it was not one that he explored. Whilst there are evident difficulties in applying 'good' to God, He could be described as benevolent. That is to say, it could be argued that God willed to do good. Locke could refer to God as one 'from whom we receive all our Good, who loves, and gives us all Things'. True, this might seem not to touch the fact that God punished delinquents and so inflicted pain on them: but it could be argued that God's benevolence was contingent on the agent's obedience: as Locke said, He 'does all manner of Good to those that love and obey him'.[98] At any rate divine benevolence, if not goodness, was within Locke's grasp.

Thus, if measures might be recognised as conducive to good there were nonetheless difficulties with the notion of good in Locke's thought, not least in attributing goodness to God or to law in general. The significance of this point for our present enquiry is that the mere fact that directions came from God would be insufficient by itself to bring them within the purlieu of morality. That is to say, we have seen that goodness is not a property of law as such and that Locke did not obviously provide grounds for thinking God was good. Where, then, is the *moral* element in obligations proceeding from Him? This may be thought to compound the problem of identifying which rational courses He had made obligatory. Rather it explains that the exercise of pinning down precepts that obliged in a special sense involved an insoluble difficulty.

For the model of hierarchy embodied the notion of a superior being one able to direct an inferior for the latter's benefit. The direction made sense because the superior, in some respect or respects, excelled the inferior significantly. The superior thus provided something which the inferior could not have produced independently and, in return for this, the inferior was supposed to be bound to obey the superior. Contemporaries assumed, once this relationship was recognised, that the inferior was bound to obey the superior in all relevant particulars (except those which proceeded from an authority yet higher). The obligation therefore lay not in any *specific* instruction given by the superior but in being bound to obey *him*. Hence when we turn to the case of moral obligation, that is to say to distinguish which members of the class of rational precepts God intends to oblige, there is nothing within the resources of the model to help us. We know that we are bound to obey God, but the model tells us nothing about the respects in which this is so.

Indeed when we turn to the way in which the word obligation was used in Locke's day, we perceive an elision. That is to say, that A provided B with a benefit was understood to require a return from B to A. It is perhaps unexceptionable enough to suppose that a service requires a return, but this is not the same as suggesting that we are *obliged* to return it: for to do so is to suggest that what is good is *ipso facto* obligatory. But this is just what contemporaries did suppose. We find Tillotson equating benefit with obligation when he observed that 'we find it true which *Seneca* says, *Nihil citius senescat quam gratia, Nothing sooner grows old and out of date than obligation*', and Aubrey writing that Selden, being thwarted, received a 'disobligation'.[99] In this usage it becomes easy to overlook the question of just what God has signified as obligatory to mankind.

Thus the state of the case becomes intelligible. It was easy enough to argue that there were rational precepts and that God was mankind's superior. It was unclear which precepts He had determined to make obligatory because the obligation from humanity to obey inhered to Him rather than any specific command of His. Hence there is an absence of a criterion to distinguish precepts which were merely rational (and good) from those which are rational and morally oblige, for it cannot be supposed that everything which is rational is obligatory. Of course we might argue that God wishes us to do good: but since it was established neither that God Himself was good nor that good was obligatory this supposition gets us no nearer solving the problem.

Not every proposition formed through use of natural faculties can sensibly be supposed to express an obligation: as Jeremy Taylor remarked 'every natural proposition is not a law'.[100] The result of taking it as such would be either that we simply have to discount those rational courses that are not obligatory or we have to insist that everything which is rational is also obligatory. Roger Coke, objecting to Hobbes' definition of natural law as the dictate of reason, put the point memorably:

If the law of Nature be the Dictate of Right reason, [he wrote], then does the Law of Nature exclude every thing else from being the Dictate of Right reason, or this cannot be the definition of it: I would know of Mr *Hobbs*, whether all Arts and Sciences, and Prudent actions, be the Laws of Nature, or not. If they be the Law of nature, then is every Inscientifical and Imprudent man, an unjust man[101]

which is not a very sensible conclusion. Whatever the niceties of definition, Locke himself wished to pick out areas not subject to the demands of moral obligation. His correspondence with Denis Grenville on leisure suggested as much. Again, the presence of things indifferent in worship assumed that there were concerns about which God had nothing to say. If we are to think that God had not prescribed in respect of some matters, it follows that there are areas of life in which we can pursue rational conduct without supposing that such conduct relates to moral obligation. The distinction was recognised at the time, in a slightly different context. It appears when distinguishing what is supposed to oblige from what is merely true. Stillingfleet remarked that 'some of the School-men say, that although the Law of Nature be immutable, as to its precepts and prohibitions, yet not as to its demonstrations ... as, *Do as you would be done to*, binds always indispensably; but, *that in a state of nature all things are common to all*, This is true, but it binds not men to the necessary observance of it. These which they call Demonstrations are only such things as are agreeable to nature, but not particularly commanded by any indispensable precept of it.'[102] This remark omits to show how the 'precepts and prohibitions' themselves oblige, of course. The problem seems not to have been evident to Stillingfleet.

It is improbable that Locke was unaware that he had a problem, though there is little evidence to show positively how he conceived it. Firstly, his interest in demonstration implied tracing out the connections between ideas that would draw his attention to the matter. Just as 'Of Ethick in General' broke off when it turned to show that God had made known His dictates about conduct, so the jottings which Locke made about ethics in the early 1690s did nothing to advance the question.[103]

The promptings of friends likewise drew attention to Locke's omission. When *An Essay* was first published Tyrrell read it with 'great satisfaction' and discussed it 'with some thinkeing men at Oxford'. The Oxonians, however, read the text in an unfriendly way. They seized on one of the passages in which Locke had emphasised the several divergent standards by which people, as a matter of fact, regulated their conduct, congruently with his aim of denying the government of conscience by an innately known natural law.[104] They apparently took him to mean that such diversity indicated his own disbelief in any authoritative ethics, that 'there is no moral good or evil: vertue, or vice but in respect of those persons, that practice it or thinke it so.' They read the absence of an explicit account of natural law from *An Essay* as evidence that Locke eschewed that moral norm. The particular form of their accusation was that Locke was a Hobbist.

Hobbes had argued that the laws of nature did not oblige people to action except under conditions of safety. Further, he considered that under a government these laws might oblige only the sovereign to action. Whilst there were natural laws on this reading in effect they did not always oblige most people to act, perhaps oblige them to act, if at all, infrequently. This view, as we have seen, was suspect to Locke and to others. Indeed the polemical malevolence of the day had no difficulty in imputing to Hobbes the position that there was *no* natural law and that people could espouse whatever ethical views suited them. Locke himself had entertained this view, if not of Hobbes then of Hobbists, whom he grouped with those who gave themselves up to their appetites.[105] It was hardly surprising that Locke's prepossessions made him receive the charge of Hobbism with distaste and disquiet:[106] his omitting to provide a knowledge of natural law lent a pointed if mischievous and misleading plausibility to the charge.

Locke did not do very much to make good his case in his ensuing correspondence with Tyrrell. His reply to Tyrrell's letter has not survived, but Tyrrell's response to it has. It pointed out that Locke had formulated his apparent references to natural law in *An Essay* so vaguely ('The *Divine Law*')[107] that it could be taken for an appeal to revelation. To Tyrrell's accompanying request for a demonstration of natural law and to William Molyneux's reiterated demands for a demonstrated ethics Locke returned scant answer or none,[108] but these requests must have reminded Locke of his promise to demonstrate ethics. After all, he had set the terms of his task explicitly and friends were keen for him to undertake it

For others, who had not worked in this manner, it was possible to overlook the question. In the first place, most thinkers devoted themselves more to using than to arguing for natural law. For instance, Grotius registered the point that the obligation of natural law was important, scarcely attempted to prove it and moved on serenely to write about other matters. He was not alone. Stillingfleet, for instance, had insisted upon an act of legislation and on promulgation of the law once it was made. Without promulgation, he observed, there would be no proper conviction of delinquents, as 'unless there be a sufficient promulgation and declaration of the will of the Lawgiver, mans ignorance is exscusable in reference to them'. But this was in reference to positive laws. He had edged away from the task of showing how natural law was promulgated, implying that promulgation was scarcely necessary, because 'in reference to the dictates of the natural Law, . . . though man be at a loss for them, yet his own contracted pravity being the cause of his blindness, leaves him without excuse'.[109] In this light – if that is the word – the question of legislative status need not be raised. The rather keener mind of Hobbes did not produce a consistent judgement on this point. In one place he asserted that 'every man that hath attained to the use of Reason, is *supposed* to know' the law of nature.[110] In another, despite his sense that reason was not univocal, he insisted that the 'Lawes of Nature . . . need not any publishing nor Proclamation; as being contained in this one Sentence, approved by all the world, *Do not that to another, which thou thinkest unreasonable to be done by another to thy selfe.*'[111] We may be forgiven for thinking that it was the destination rather than how to obtain it that people apprehended. Ultimately it was simply assumed that God would not have left mankind without direction. As Baxter put it, 'I think that the interest of mankinde will not suffer him to be so erroneous to deny . . . a Law of Nature made by the God of Nature.' This was not the isolated judgement of a cleric: the worldly Halifax suggested that God would not leave mankind without a law.[112]

Locke was not able to overlook the problem in this way. Neither could he find a way out by developing a sentimentalist account of moral knowledge, such as the one Henry More had published, Cudworth had used in private and Thomas Burnet would assert against Locke himself.[113] Locke's commitments forbade this. These included not merely his public adherence to ethical rationalism but also something more substantial. The validity of his political theory turned on people being dependent creatures, subject inescapably to the will of a superior, a will whose content and obligation alike were disclosed through reason. To have recourse to sentimentalism would discard this structure of thought, for it necessitated only that people were created beings rather than implying a more extensive dependence.[114]

We may ask how so acute a thinker as Locke found himself in this awkward situation. Intellectual honesty and thoroughness, certainly, and the ambition to take over Hobbes' account of law and set it in a very different relationship to God were certainly part of the matter. Besides this a certain looseness in his usage of the word 'law' may have muted the problem at some early stage of ambitious and unreflective optimism, or even obscured the problem altogether. The second of Locke's tracts on government grouped divine and human laws together as laws with private resolutions and vows.[115] Even late in life, albeit in a composition he did not live to revise, Locke could treat the 'light of nature' as equivalent to 'law'.[116] No doubt it was easy, in a framework which assumed God and His goodness, to think that good as such had obligatory force: we find so keen a thinker as John Wallis write of 'Good, which *must* be done' and Tillotson could elide a standard into a law, beginning by stating that 'A *Rule* . . . is a Metaphorical Word. . .A *Moral Rule* is the Measure, according to which we judge, whether a thing be *good* or *evil;*' and concluding that 'this kind of Rule is that which is commonly called a *Law*'.[117] Certainly Locke's own vague formulation about natural law, 'reason which is that law',[118] was not likely to expose the intellectual difficulty, certainly not to anyone of a superficial cast of mind. But Locke did come to recognise the problem and was indeed criticised by Lowde on just this point: reputation, Lowde argued, not a law because a law implies an obligation.[119]

It is easy to see how this looseness of usage could occur. Locke wrote in terms of God's superiority and lived in a society conceived in terms of inferiors and superiors, a society in which many people issued directions. The question of the moral status of their instructions would be masked by the practice of an habitual obedience: civil government and the church were exceptions with Locke only because they became controversial. It would be ironic but intelligible if an unexamined custom were a cause of his difficulty.

Locke required to prove an obligation to natural law and show it with certainty. He had dealt with several of the components involved – the existence of God, His assumed superiority over mankind, the discovery of rational precepts – but he had not shown where the moral obligation lay. He could not take refuge in darkness, for his programme was quite clear. But his problem was very serious, perhaps insoluble. Another resource, however, presented itself along lines Locke laid down in *An Essay* itself. This did not solve the difficulty, but provided an opportunity to alleviate it in a manner.

IV

Locke dealt not only in certainty but also in probability. *Draft A* had suggested that probability should be conceived in terms of experience. The account in *An Essay* did not belie this position, but treated it as an assumption in an account which Locke developed in a different way. He treated probability as an example of the mind conducting itself in terms of reason, even where reason could not provide knowledge.

His object was to show that we are still bound to conduct ourselves in accordance with reason in cases where certainty cannot be obtained. That is to say, we should follow the connection of our ideas as far as it will take us and, if we must go further, to accept nothing which disagrees with what reason has disclosed.

Locke continued the intellectualist position he had taken about knowledge and the will. The mind was unable to resist ideas of sense and any ideas involving uneasiness determined the will. Generally speaking the will could not determine the position the mind would assume in the face of any evidence at all. This stipulation was important, for Locke supposed that many of life's concerns involved probability rather than certainty. The scheme, once created, moved to the optimistic view that the ordinary ground of probable belief left little room for doubt[120] and to the assertion that if it did the mind would determine the will's assent.

Locke's God had evidently designed matters so. Certainly probability was needed for God's purposes and Locke supposed that He would reward adherence to it. Moreover Locke supposed that the mind gravitated naturally to probability,[121] which again suggests the hand of the creator.

This intellectual policy had a particular application to revelation. Locke was keen, as we should expect from his past, to show that reason and revelation agreed in their conclusions. But this was necessary not only to underwrite his views about morals and his procedure in *Two Treatises*, which made pivotal use of *Genesis* as well as arguing from reason, but also to complete his scheme for God's direction of man. For belief in the truth of revelation was obviously a condition of attaining a better life.

The crucial question for Locke was not God's veracity – which he took for granted here – but the grounds for supposing that putative revelations actually came from God.[122] Locke was true to the priority of reason which all his work embodied. He assumed that faith should be regulated by reason.[123] By the same measure the content of revelation was acceptable to the degree that it did not contradict reason.[124] This dealt with cases which the findings of reason and the dictates of revelation had in common, as we have seen in the great design where God had made specific declarations which ran parallel to rational thinking about man and the world.

The cases in which revelation gave information about which reason could say nothing required inclusion. For the revelation Locke had in mind primarily was biblical and much of the Bible consists in statements about past events. Reason could not inspect these, but merely scrutinise the evidence for their plausibility. Locke's test of this lay in conformity to the findings of reason.[125] His point was underlined in the chapter on enthusiasm which he added to the fourth edition of *An Essay*.[126] The same view was presented along the way in Locke's ready contrast between reason and probability on the one hand and on the other error.

Matters of probability as well as knowledge conformed to Locke's treatment of reason. Thus his reading of God's purpose suggested its essential continuity of method. In matters of natural philosophy and moral philosophy mankind's business was to act by the measures God made disclosed. The same was true of probability.

Continuity in method was paralleled by continuity in content. For reason was supposed to be not merely the means of conducting philosophical work but also of disclosing the content of ethics. On this basis it would not be out of the way for Locke to propose a substitute (not a solution) for his deficiency in ethical knowledge by suggesting that Christ came to promulgate the law of nature, which we find in his *Reasonableness of Christianity*. It was a substitute, rather than an adequate resolution, because the law of nature, in the fullest sense, had to be known to all mankind. Whilst the Christian revelation had a content which was parallel to the precepts of natural law, yet, as a matter of fact, it had not been diffused to all mankind and, even if it had, obliged only those who accepted Christ. We find a small but significant revision in the second edition of Locke's *Essay*. In 1690 he had announced boldly that 'GOD has given a Law to *Mankind*, I think, there is nobody so brutish as to deny'. In 1694 'The *Divine Law*' was now understood as 'that Law which God has set to the actions of Men, whether promulgated to them by the light of nature, or the voice of Revelation', which was to say 'that God has given a Rule whereby *Men* should govern themselves, I think there is nobody so brutish as to deny'. Thus Locke disembarrassed himself of the suggestion that the law was known to all, to mankind, rather than to men indefinitely specified.[127] But this is to anticipate a little, for it is one matter to see a deficiency or have it made plain by a reader and another to be moved to repair it.

Chapter 9

Education may seem at first sight distant from Locke's other concerns. His interests in ethics, politics and the human understanding are related to each other. As we shall, see his account of Christianity too is related to this complex of ideas. Where then does education stand? In one sense Locke's treatise *Some Thoughts concerning Education* is an occasional piece, generated to oblige friends and published because the results seemed timely. But in another it is integral to the corpus of Locke's work, for it undertakes the practical formation of the view of man deployed in his theoretical writings.

Theological explanation was central to Locke's enterprises in ethics and government and was only less important in his views about the church. He conducted the former in terms of the intentions and attributes of God and in the latter worked in terms meant to be compatible with these. His writings on the human understanding, which assume a divine teleology, he devoted in part to showing the truth of his claims about God and ethics, though with imperfect success. But to all this we can oppose a question. Do these considerations have any practical relevance? That is to say: could there be an account of ethics which did not refer to God but which functioned to guide conduct effectively? The answer was important, for if man's subordination to God were superfluous then Locke's case against Hobbesian ethics and absolutist theory became at best irrelevant and at worst untrue. Besides, much of the fabric of his intellectual life would become an elegant but marginal folly.

This was just the challenge Pierre Bayle had posed. He had argued that theism was inessential to good conduct by pointing out that theists were known to behave badly and atheists could behave well. More generally, Bayle's supposition that people were effectively moved by terrestrial pressures rather than divine regulation would limit the relevance of Locke's theoretical writings. Besides, Bayle's case had the merit of observational truth. It was not reassuring that it also struck resonances in Locke's own mind. He had emphasised how badly pretenders to authority from God could behave in his early *Tracts*, and had made similar points in his *Treatises* and *Epistola de Tolerantia* too. He had taken for granted that it was the law of the land rather than the laws of God which restrained wrong-doers. He had noted how people regulated their conduct by laws which were not God's. He himself has even been criticised, however erroneously, for identifying such behaviour as right.[1] In the second edition of his *Essay* he would explain how people came to eschew God's laws for other norms. But he set out to obviate Bayle's case first.

I

Bayle's case had several aspects but fundamentally it exploited an ancient understanding of human nature, one founded on people's longing for approbation. That people are moved by a desire for the approval of others is an observation so inescapable that it is hardly surprising that it should appear in many varieties of thought.[2] Bayle's particular use was to suggest that far from being motivated by God's laws, people were moved by terrestrial considerations, amongst which, we may observe, contemporaries included the desire to look well in the lights of prevailing opinion. In other words, because certain types of conduct were approved by society people would tend to practise them. Hence it followed that belief in God need not be an index of practical rectitude. Bayle rubbed in his point by alluding to examples of Christian wickedness and pagan virtue, suggesting besides that atheists could understand as well as anyone that virtue not only sustained reputation, but also upheld the social fabric from which everyone benefited. The point could be generalised: terrestrial consideration moved people and amongst these considerations figured approbation.[3]

Like Hobbes, Bayle exploited constituents from the common currency of thought to obtain an uncommon conclusion. For instance Locke had argued from 1667 that atheists should not be tolerated because their beliefs undermined the practice of virtue.[4] It scarcely needs saying that his view was diametrically opposed to Bayle's.[5] But Locke also thought that virtue upheld society and that this truth was perfectly clear. So far he would find himself in unwilling agreement with Bayle. Further, he held a congruent view of approbation and its effects

The desire for the approval of others resolves itself in one mode into following the dominant mode of conduct. Under this description we can locate Locke's view of the law of honour – an adherence to the norms prevailing with those people whose opinion the agent valued. This was not a fleeting opinion.[6] Neither was Locke alone in his judgement of its effects. His French contemporaries had built a system of conduct around this measure, calling it *honnête*, and their moralists frequently descanted upon its shortcomings. We read in the memoirs of Cardinal Retz how the desire of appearing well governed his ecclesiastical conduct. If we had not this direct evidence we could have guessed as much from Corneille's heroes or the aphorisms of Rochfoucault. Descartes himself had recommended a provisional morality in lieu of a code of ethics proven certainly; the content of this morality corresponded to the common code of the place where the agent happened to live.[7] Locke in France had seen as much in the conduct of the natives.[8]

The doctrine of approbation in general was far more ancient, being found in Augustine, and had a future before it in places as unexpected as de Tocqueville's and the younger Mill's concern with the effects of democracy, besides James Mill's view of the law of nations. Tocqueville and James Mill suggested that modern societies tended to produce a uniformity of opinion. This was difficult to resist because of the pull of approbation (and all the more so because the majority would not be friendly to different habits of thought and conduct).

On the whole the doctrine had suffered a worse press than even that. Augustine had used the appetite for approval in explaining how mankind behaved well not from any internal disposition of love towards God or good but because they were moved by external considerations, whether a fear of punishment or a relish for esteem. It was just this which the French moralists had emphasised. It was this point, in effect, that Bayle used. In his view human conduct was not governed by reverence for God but by the pull of terrestrial considerations: so God was irrelevant to good conduct. Therefore an atheist as much as a theist could behave well.

The arguments about approbation were well-known to Locke, for he had translated some essays relevant to the subject. Pierre Nicole's essays on the weakness of man and on the way of preserving peace embodied the views that people were governed by opinion. The former suggested that they valued the approbation of others, not least because it reflected their own high opinion of themselves. But it suggested too that the standard of judgement they often applied, namely worldly greatness, had a bearing that was only terrestrial. It decided that to measure oneself by the opinion of others was therefore a sign of weakness. The latter essay pointed a related moral. Its first part treated civility as a duty, arguing that to treat others with consideration and good manners was incumbent on the agent because these gave pleasure to others. Hence to practice civility was also a means of living at peace with others. The second part of this essay, however, stated that most civility was ethically worthless. It was neither motivated by a good disposition nor directed towards worthwhile actions. Rather it was mostly moved by and directed towards a concern for esteem. In short, Nicole suggested that approbation guided people and did so in a way that reflected neither a good disposition nor right actions.[9]

We may assume that Locke broadly endorsed this position when he translated these essays in the seventies. He selected the essays and modified their content where he wanted.[10] His stated reasons for translating them were not very explicit, but the essays may have embodied Locke's sense of how people behaved. If so they imply a measure of distaste for the world in which he found himself.

Locke turned both the distaste and the explanation to his advantage in composing *Some Thoughts concerning Education*. This treatise indicated how to turn approbativeness to the cause of virtue. The *Thoughts* took the agent's desire for approval and used it for a different end: that of *creating* virtue within the agent. By adapting approbation to the formation of a good disposition Locke reasserted the integral relation between theism and good conduct. It was not merely that approbation could be used to build up a disposition to the good within the agent. More pointedly that disposition coincided not with any sort of conduct which happened to be prevalent but with theistic morality, which it was the business of parents to inculcate.[11] Thus through education Locke showed how theism could be a motive to good actions.

The form of Nicole's writing offered two cues to this move. Firstly, Locke's *Thoughts* were directed to the education of gentlemen's sons in the first instance. This object was suggested partly by Locke's original concern for Edward Clarke's offspring and partly because he thought that '*if those of that Rank are by their Education once set right, they will quickly bring all the rest into Order.*' If, as William Gouge had suggested, 'necessary it is that good order be first set in families: for as they were before other polities, so they are somewhat the more necessary: and good members of a family are like to make good members of church and government', it followed that the education of the gentry was especially important[12]. Nicole had suggested a need for this guidance from above, remarking that 'all the poor, and almost all those that live of their hands, all children, and the greatest part of ordinary women' did not govern themselves rationally but 'are comprehended in the herd'.[13] Secondly, a hint of how desirable it would be to turn approbativeness to the good was contained in Nicole's question, 'how free would he live, who valued not the love or hatred of men: But neither desiring the one nor fearing the other, did yet upon another principle all those things which might deserve their affection?'.[14] Locke aimed to form people who would be free, which to his mind meant governed by reason. He aimed also to make them morally deserving. He set out to make them so by treating approbation in a striking and unexpected way.

These concerns, of course, are not the whole of Locke's book. *Some Thoughts* is indeed a book about education in a wide sense. It follows Aristotle's order of treatment, dealing firstly with the body, then with the character and finally with the academic education of the child; and like Aristotle it is concerned with yielding an individual fitted to cope with life rather than to expound a theory of pedagogy.[15] It continues Locke's view that parents should bring up their children to the use of reason. It adds an explicit treatment of the dominion of reason over inclination to the catalogue of Locke's superiorities. But it differs in content from Locke's own writings on education before Bayle and from most contemporary works.

This latter point may be made very simply by drawing attention to a particular difference amidst general similarities. Gilbert Burnet composed a long memorandum on education in 1668. It contains many details that resemble those of Locke's *Thoughts*, although it was not published during the philosopher's lifetime. It dwells on the force of emulation, the effectiveness of praise and blame, the success of sweetness in dealing with children, as well as recommending that beating should be used only as a last resort (but then severely) and suggesting too that Latin be taught by dialogue and that current 'logics' were repositories of pedantry.[16] But it did not argue that praise and blame could be the means of forming a good disposition.

The same is true of the literature on education current in Locke's day. This fell into three broad categories. There was, firstly, works about the method and substance of teaching. Prominent examples were Milton's *Tractate on Education* and Ascham's *The Scholemaster*. Secondly there were works on the raising of gentlemen, which dwelt upon civility and other matters of good form. Amongst these were Obadiah Walker's wide-ranging *Of Education*, as well as two books by Henry Peacham and Jean Gailhard, both entitled *The Compleat Gentleman*. The third division emphasised virtues like civility, respect and love, matters treated not least by Montaigne. As will be readily seen the three overlapped in several respects. Whilst it would be surprising had Locke not drawn some matter from these, the significant point is that the treatment of the formation of character present in *Some Thoughts* is absent from them.

Locke's piece 'Of Study' was concerned with intellectual matters, especially the habits of the contemplative life and the proper direction of intellectual attention.[17] It overlapped with *Some Thoughts* chiefly in dwelling on the nurture of the body as a condition of mental activity. Again *Some Thoughts* is an explanatory work. Before the mid 1680s Locke's interest in education did not extend to this. He had identified virtue, religion and civility amongst the ends of education early in his career, but offered no specific recipe for how to inculcate them.

Virtue was the object of Lockean education: he insisted that 'Vertue then, direct Vertue, . . . is the hard and valuable part to be aimed at in Education.'[18] Virtue he understood here as the victory of reason over desires incompatible with it.[19] Clearly to show that reason could govern at least some people effectively was important for Locke's claims about ethics, politics and the human understanding. But where did reason direct?

II

According to Locke nature came from the hand of God in a way which made external stimuli likely to prevail upon it. In the manner of *An Essay*, nature was presented as liable to pleasure and pain.[20] It was likely to act on these. This provided a footing on which the outside agencies would affect man's nature.

For just this reason Locke thought that violence should be eschewed in dealing with children. The punishment of the rod was likely to impress an immediate dislike of its intended object – whether learning, civility or morality. This point was scarcely new, being found in Ascham (if not earlier).[21] But it was a preface to a point important for Locke's argument.

He considered that immediate impressions could be overcome to yield a virtuous habit. He had in mind an opposition between desire and reason.[22] Of course this did not amount to an irreconcileable dichotomy in his view, for Locke was keen to combine pleasure and pain with reason in ethics. But he did suppose that in many cases to follow virtue meant ignoring the immediate promptings of pleasure and pain. There is no need to think of examples, for Locke himself provided some.[23] This obviously implies that if someone is to be virtuous they must learn to ignore such promptings. Locke thought this quite feasible. How did he suppose it could happen?

It was achieved through a parental regime which esteemed virtue and shamed vice.[24] For Locke took it as true that the pleasures of esteem and the pains of shame were sharper than the other stimuli which a child might meet. In other words he supposed that the force of the child's desire for approval would override other desires and so induce virtuous conduct. This point, simple as it is, turns external stimuli towards virtue.

The force of the example is quite evident in this account, as it is in Locke's other writings. For in his *Treatises* he had taken the line that the use of reason was not present fully in youth, but had to be developed. This, of course, was part of his view about human destiny: not much was to be had without work. But it meant that though the child was to be reared to the use of reason it had to be led thither by another route. Hence the approval of others was all the more important. Locke, believed, specifically, that manifested behaviour was important. In other words example rather than explicit precept was important in the first place.

This is apparent in his detailed treatment of the parental regime. Locke suggested that parents guide their children into the ways that reason had marked out by example rather than merely by precept: parents should always behave virtuously before them, always praise virtue and condemn vice, and always confine their approbation to the project of habituating the child to morality. This parental regime was to be continued by different means with the tutor and the governor.

This inculcation was to be done gratefully, so that it stuck with its objects. The lessons of virtue were to be introduced in the manner most pleasurable to the child, and so most likely to be absorbed and remembered with pleasure. Likewise once parents had established their sway of approval over their offspring, they should strive to win the infants' affection, reinforcing further their influence.

The other side of the coin was that external stimuli of the opposite tendency were to be managed carefully. At the earliest age children had to be kept out of wrong company, lest the habits of thought and conduct their parents were inculcating so earnestly should be countered by other examples.[25] Obviously this isolation could not continue always. The youngster's exposure to the way of the world should be exercised in a way that ensured he remained resistant to its bad features. Locke tempered virtue with civility. Indeed he counted civility as a virtue (at least according to Lady Masham).[26] For this high place there were two reasons. One was that Locke wished to make the compatibility of a virtuous disposition and civility clear.[27] The traditional line, whether in the hands of Augustine or of Bayle, tended to separate conduct formed by external pressure from a good disposition. This ran against the tenor of Locke's view, as he intended. His project was thus happily rounded by suggesting that the two were compatible. The other reason was that Locke was attentive to the requirements of worldly contentment, amongst which he rated civility highly. It was not to be cast adrift.

III

The materials from which Locke worked were not entirely new. So much is in the nature of thought, which often proceeds as much by rearranging ideas as by innovating with entirely original reflection. But what is more significant is the twist imparted to certain of them.

For instance Locke's insistence on the comparative malleability of youth was not new. The importance of dealing decisively with children when young, because their dispositions were set early in life, was a common datum. It appeared in Crooke and Peacham before it appeared in Locke[28]. Neither was the correlate, that education was suited to mould people to the good, a novelty. Milton had suggested this and Baxter went as far as to say that education was a medium for the working of grace[29].

More generally the large literature on education that preceded Locke, although it was coordinated to purposes different from his own, contained many points that Locke took over. It assumed that one of the prime objectives of education was to inculcate a knowledge of God.[30] This was complemented by a love of Him and of mankind.[31] It was asserted that this basic teaching was the duty or trust of a child's parents.[32] In teaching it was thought that kindness was better than the rod.[33] The rod, however, should be applied as a last sanction.[34] Furthermore, it was understood that the opinion, not least that of its parents, was important to a child.[35] On the same understanding, the child should be shielded from bad company.[36] The same sense of the importance of opinion tended to make the educational theorists treat fashion in a pejorative manner but caused them to regard opinion itself as significant.[37]

These judgements concur in regarding virtue as important and approbativeness as operative. But they do not suggest the latter as a method of inculcating the former. There was at most a hint in Burnet's memorandum.[38] This cue, however, was not worked out in Burnet's text.

Locke's striking innovation was to find an explanation of how this could be. Works on education were stronger on precept than on explanation. Locke was adapting what he has learnt from Nicole to provide a means to virtue. During a stay in France Locke had selected and translated three of Nicole's moral essays. Of these the last is the one important for our purpose. It drew a contrast between external conduct and disposition, suggesting along lines now familiar to us that the former need not issue from the latter. In fact it was externally governed and, however, virtuous it might be in itself implied no decency within.[39]

Locke found the means to his end in Nicole, odd though it may sound. Nicole had emphasised how conduct was formed by approbation. He had dwelt especially on how the repeating of an example tended to form the disposition within.[40] In effect Locke proposed to contrive the environment of the child so that it became a means of inculcating virtue rather than merely imposing good form on a disposition that was untouched by goodness.

Locke's personal emphasis on this theme of character, if not sufficiently apparent already, is found in the order of composition. His essential points about the role of approval, the ingrafting of virtue and civility, are found in his drafts of 1684.[41] But his account of the mechanics of child-rearing were added to his corpus of material in the later 1680s in response to further queries from the Clarkes, whilst his observations on the academic curriculum and social accomplishments of the child and adolescent were mostly the fruit of reflection during the 1690s, possibly prompted by earnest parental enquiries.[42]

IV

Locke's argument rather suggests that the conventions of the world and virtue were compatible to a degree. If the child's environment inculcated virtue and if civility was compatible with virtue it could not be otherwise. What the degree was Locke did not specify precisely, but it is evident that the published version of *Some Thoughts*, as distinct from his letters and drafts, was directed to what he supposed was a public need. *Some Thoughts* was keen to locate virtue in a proper regard for property and labour and to discountenance prodigality.[43] This accords with Locke's distress with the moral climate of the 1690s and his sense that industriousness was the key to national prosperity (though physical labour was not the main preoccupation he intended for the gentry).[44] But the chief significance of *Some Thoughts* in Locke's oeuvre lies elsewhere.

Locke had executed a manoeuvre which characterises the great thinker. He had taken a concept strongly associated with one mode of thought and made it integral to quite another. The human liking for approbation served often to show how man's disposition did not answer to God's will: Locke showed that it was precisely the means of building a disposition of obedience in man. He may speak for himself in conclusion:

288

The great Business of all is *Vertue* and *Wisdom* . . . Teach him to get a Mastery over his Inclinations, and *submit his Appetite to Reason*. This being obtained, and by constant practice settled into Habit, the hardest part of the Task is over. To bring a young Man to this, I know nothing which so much contributes, as the love of Praise and Commendation, which should therefore be instilled into him by all Arts imaginable. Make his Mind as sensible of Credit and Shame as may be: And when you have done that, you have put a Principle into him, which . . . will be the proper Stock, whereon afterwards to graft the true Principles of Morality and Religion[45]

so that approbation and virtue would be connected intimately. But if *Some Thoughts* emphasised virtuous practice, what further progress did Locke make in apprehending 'the true Principles of Morality and Religion'?

Chapter 10

We have seen Locke hitherto deploying theological devices, sometimes to indicate the respectability of his opinions and most often to provide explanations of the kind he wanted. When we turn to his version of Christian doctrine the scene is different. It bears the impress of his preceding writings. *The Reasonableness of Christianity* shows how Locke's opinions are important to the central constituents in his revealed theology.

This is true in two senses. We would expect Locke to devise a revealed theology that conformed to his procedural requirements, so that in a formal sense his views about revelation would agree with *An Essay*. The latter's categories, especially its view of faith and reason, are not forgotten in *Reasonableness*, as its very title indicates. But there is a second feature which is not less important: that the content of *Reasonableness* is informed by his preceding opinions about human capacity and destiny.

Locke had developed the view that the human agent was responsible for his or her own opinions and actions. On the basis of a properly directed use of sense and reason he could estimate the probabilities of evidence. In principle, at least, his character could be formed to follow reason and virtue unerringly. Man's responsibility extended not merely to conducting himself, but also to judging civil government and to choosing his own ecclesiastical path to salvation. All this was the outcome of the natural powers of humanity.

These views had positive implications for Christian doctrine. Every estimate of human nature affects how the answers to questions of justification are to be conceived and these in their turn bear a relation to the nature of the church and the Godhead. For theology is no more isolated from other bodies of doctrine than they are from each other. This is true for the general reason that the propositions used overlap in content. It is evidenced in theology by the variations Christian doctrine has recorded over the centuries.

It is true in particular of theories like Locke's which frequently attribute intentions to God and which are supposed in all cases to have a content agreeing with His will. We have seen that Locke conceived God as a superior and, for the purposes of his moral and political theories, as a legislator. The political theory of *Two Treatises* presupposes not only this but also that God has organised human destinies in a highly deliberate way, directing the race to multiply, subdue the earth and preserve each other. Locke's writings on the human understanding assume more generally that God had expressed His benevolent concern for this preservation in His design of human faculties. Theology, that is to say a doctrine of God's attributes and intentions, was an instrument in all these designs of Locke's.

Yet if this means that Locke's thought in many of its most characteristic features relies on theology, it turns out to be true also that theology depends on it. For revealed theology can be conceived in a manner which matches a broader body of thought. This is at one level merely a matter of consistency, that last infirmity of notable thinkers (and especially those who wish to coordinate faith and reason). More importantly it reflects continuity of substantive thought, for to Locke morals, politics, the human understanding and theology would scarcely seem disconnected. Hence if Locke discussed Christian doctrine he would develop positions he had attained previously.

This applies in two senses. The more obvious is that Lockean Christianity would neither contradict nor retract his previous thought. For instance, his views on faith and reason would not be denied. Locke emphasised the 'design and fore-sight' as well as the 'Divine Wisdom' of Jesus' work, and indicated that "'Tis no diminishing to Revelation, that Reason gives its Suffrage too' in some matters.[1] It would have been unthinkable for him to do otherwise, for this would be to deny the larger view of which that was a part, namely of mankind's ability to exercise the human faculties adequately for both intellectual and practical purposes. Some positions would be transposed into a theological key. For instance Locke's view that Adam was not representative in politics would be matched by a theological judgement. Again the doctrines Locke had developed or implied about the church would find their place, a credal Christianity concentrating on Christ's work amongst them.

The less obvious sense was that revealed theology could soften (though not remove) some of Locke's difficulties. For if Lockean man was self-reliant under God, that independence might be a shade optimistic. Locke's political position had involved a high place for the agent's ability to practice self-government under reason. Since Locke's central claim concerned the abilities with which people came into the world rather than their mature attainments, the structure of his political theory would not be weakened by shortcomings of practice: but the applicability of the theory would be. This was important to Locke, for he was a political practitioner of a sort. More especially he maintained that the revolution of 1688 had embodied his principles, for whatever the genesis of *Two Treatises* we must not forget that the work was published in order to '*establish the Throne of our Great Restorer, Our present King* William ... *And to justifie to the World, the People of* England'.[2] Unfortunately observation suggested that the practice of reason was honoured more in the breach than the observance.

Firstly the possibilities of reason were scarcely realised in every individual. Locke was troubled by them shortly after publishing his *Treatises*, observing in 1690 that a countryman would be hard pressed to master even the Bible fully[3]. His concern continued and in 1693 we find him noting privately the 'horid ignorance and brutality' of 'the bulke' of 'man kinde' and reflecting publicly that '*the early corruption of Youth, is now become so general a Complaint'*.[4] Locke hoped to put this right by educating the offspring of the gentry and nobility on the right model: and they, after all, led the political nation. But he sensed a political weakness in the intellectual dependence of their inferiors. 'The populace well instructed in their duty and removd from the implicit faith their ignorance submits them in to others would not be soe easie to be blown into tumults and popular commotions by the breath and artifice of designeing or discontented Grandees', he thought.[5] Locke's political commitments had involved him in claims about reason which some people at least had failed to meet. Accordingly the practice of reason was one of Locke's major interests in his final years, not merely in his educational works but also in the manual he meant to append to *An Essay, Of the Conduct of the Understanding*.[6]

There was, secondly, a shortfall in the reach of the theory. Had 'the populace' and their superiors been equal to Locke's reasoning they would have found that it stopped short of showing the moral obligation he had promised. Locke's *Essay* produced arguments for the existence of God and presented Him as a superior to mankind in point of wisdom and power. The *Treatises* had displayed a variety of precepts, rational in different ways. But Locke had not fulfilled the programme of his *Essays on the Law of Nature*: he had not shown which rational precepts carried a moral obligation. Such an obligation played an important political role for Locke, and its absence was an intellectual inconvenience. Thirdly, the position was the same with reason's discovery of natural law's sanctions, for this remained a promise rather than a performance. Revelation could not *solve* these problems, of course, for its deliveries had a status different from that of knowledge in Locke's mind, but it could provide information which made their solution less important by providing a substitute useful for practical purposes.

The plasticity of thought is such that quite another relationship is imaginable. Loyalties in revealed theology could have found a congruent conception of man, just as Augustine's view of grace seems to have generated a congruent view of human nature. But the order in which life had presented matters to Locke had helped him to develop a view of man before he turned to revealed theology.

We may note especially that there is not much material devoted to justification in Locke's writings before the 1690s. There were certainly matters of import for revealed theology. For instance, Locke's doctrine of the church suggested that saving Christianity in his view would be credal rather than traditionary in scope and that the creed would concentrate on Christ. But the many adumbrations in Locke's previous thought cannot of themselves tell us precisely what his revealed theology would be. No doubt we can infer something from an assertion of man's natural powers, from a rejection of Adam's representative role, from an emphasis on creeds rather than churches and from Locke's difficulties with rational morality. But inference needs to be informed about how theology works. For revealed theology *explains* the answers to various questions – questions about justification and related concerns. Substantive views like Locke's are some of the materials embodied in such an explanation rather than its sum. In any case it has still to be asked why Locke should make the transition from deploying theological gambits to explain revealed theology.

I

An impetus to reflection came from the criticisms with which Jonas Proast greeted Locke's *Letter for Toleration*, or more precisely from Proast's rejoinder to Locke's response. Proast's first statement, *The Argument of the Letter concerning Toleration*, objected less to toleration but to Locke's arguments for it. Proast laid his finger on Locke's assertion that force was inappropriate to convince the mind. Proast agreed that it was not a means of inducing sincere belief, but asserted that it might be a necessary precondition. For mankind had shortcomings which discouraged a proper consideration of the issues. 'Lusts and Passions' distracted the judgement, people supposed unthinkingly that they had reason on their side and 'either through Carelesness or Negligence' overlooked important arguments. Force applied by the magistrate was useful because it stimulated thought and focussed attention. In other words Proast assumed that superiors – amongst whom he listed 'Parents, Masters of Families, Tutors, &c' – knew better than those in their charge and were entitled to apply force to encourage them to agree.[7]

Locke's reply, *A Second Letter concerning Toleration*, took the opposite line and upheld his previous view that in principle people could and certainly should judge for themselves. Assuming this, it argued that because Christianity was true it would triumph by the force of its own reasonableness and therefore required no coercive assistance. 'A religion that is of God wants not the assistance of human authority to make it prevail,' Locke thought.[8] In short he supposed that the understanding could be expected to operate effectively in governing conduct. Thus Proast and Locke deployed opposed views of how religion took hold of human nature and drew opposite conclusions about the use of force.

Proast's rejoinder, *A Third Letter concerning Toleration*, made explicit the bases of his argument. Force was needed because the human will was recalcitrant to the truth. Proast insisted that Christianity needed either miracles or civil power to impress itself on people because of 'the Corruption of Humane Nature'. That corruption was evidently thoroughgoing. Idolatry triumphed 'meerly by the advantage which it had in the Corruption and Pravity of Humane Nature'. The 'depraved Nature of Man' thus meant that 'the Christian Religion' was 'contrary. . .to Flesh and Blood'. Hence Christianity had needed force to support it from the beginning and needed it still in the present day.[9]

Proast had mounted a serious challenge which, if valid, undermined many of Locke's views. It hit at his view of error as the product of an intellectual confusion personal to the individual rather than a defect engrained in the species. On this view of Locke's, the truth would become clear if only people troubled to exercise their minds correctly. Along with it went Locke's view of toleration, which assumed the worshipper's capacity to be responsible for his or her own salvation; and Locke's views of the church and of civil government went also, founded as they were on the exercise of reason. His account of education showed how these claims of principle could be realised in practice. *An Essay* indicated the terms on which the natural understanding would be exercised best. Proast's observations were not more pleasing because they fastened on Locke's admission that as a matter of present fact most people were incapable of judging for themselves.

Proast's language suggests, but does not state directly, that he alluded to original sin and believed its effects were thoroughgoing. His lavish language of 'Corruption and Pravity' about 'the depraved Nature of

Man' and his emphasis that Christianity was 'contrary. . .to Flesh and Blood' suggested a malady deep seated. Original sin was a convenient explanation of this.

What is original sin? Original sin usually has a reference wider than the first man. It can be taken to mean the sin Adam committed at the original point in human history. But more frequently it refers to the involvement of mankind, without exception, in the consequences of Adam's action.

How is the latter doctrine intelligible? It can make sense as part of the story of the Fall of Adam, told in a certain way. Mankind would be diminished in some way by his defection. The matter can be illustrated in several ways. The Fall might involve the loss of some amenity, like Eden, or of some feature intrinsic to man. For instance, there might be some loss of moral perception or self-control, or, again, mankind might lose the immortality which they had possessed by nature. At any rate, whatever the specific character and extent of the loss, loss there was supposed to be.

This notion is distinct from Adam's representative quality. That suggests that through Adam's representative character mankind as a whole was *guilty* of his sin. For mankind's liability to original sin can be explained merely through descent from Adam without supposing that there was any juridical liability to suffer a penalty. Adam, for instance, might be supposed to be punished by being deprived of certain powers to perceive or do good. This deficit would be passed on in an entirely natural manner to the children he fathered after his loss and so to all mankind. In other words it is not necessary to espouse imputation in order to explain original sin.

It is important to recognise two aspects to original sin, one fixed, the other variable. The former is that original sin must be universal in its operation. It would affect all of Adam's descendants, which would be the whole of mankind. The variable point was the *degree* and *kind* of loss to which people would be liable. Suppose we were considering moral loss. The human race might be thought to suffer from a total obliteration of their powers for good or perhaps merely a more limited kind of damage. The degree and kind were variable, for no warranted explanation could be given on the basis of *Genesis* for what mankind's affliction was, save ejection from Eden and certain other physical inconveniences. Indeed, it is hardly out of the question that some of the consequences of Adam's sin could be escaped by natural means if one supposed that the Fall involved only a mild degree of damage.

At any rate, because original sin lacked a biblical specification a variety of opinions about its extent were expressed. If the account of

Genesis is silent, so too is the Judaic literature of apocalypse and, for that matter, the Rabbis too. The spokesmen for the Eastern Church on the whole and Jerome in the West did not believe in an hereditary propensity towards sin. The Western Church and Gregory of Nyassa in the East attributed a limited weakness to Adam's descendants.[10] Stronger lines were possible.

One could take a high line, as Augustine and Calvin did, which suggested that every human power was turned to evil. The view finds a full-blooded expression in the work of William Whately, who informed the world in 1619 that

A man in the state of corrupt nature, is nothing else but a filthy dunghill of all abominable vices: hee is a stinking rotten carrion, become altogether vnprofitable and good for nothing: his heart is the diuels store-house, an heape of odious lusts; his tongue is a fountaine of cursing and bitternesse, and rotten communication; his hand is a mischieuous instrument of filthinesse, deceit, and violence; his eyes great thorowfares of lust, pride, and vanity; his feet are swift engins, mouing strongly to reuenge, wantonesse and lucre; his life a long chaine of sinfull actions, euery later linke being more wicked than the former: yea it is but (as it were) one continued web of wickednesse, spun out, and made vp, by the hands of the diuell and the flesh, an euill spinner, and a worse weauer.[11]

This particular view lies at an unambiguous point on a spectrum.

A diversity of opinions was current in seventeenth century England. Gilbert Burnet's *Exposition of the Thirty-Nine Articles of the Church of England*, published almost at the end of the century, mentioned several views. One was that mankind suffered nothing at Adam's Fall. Another, 'in opposition to this', suggested that Adam forfeited the tree of life and so his descendants were born mortal. A third maintained that 'there is a corruption spread through the whole race of mankind, which is born with every man'. This view, the Augustinian interpretation, suggested that corruption was thoroughgoing. Or one might suppose that there was a damage to man's nature, but that it was of a less grievous degree. Specifically, that there was a 'great disposition' in man 'to appetite and passion', so that 'pains' were needed to attain 'an ordinary meaure of virtue': in other words, virtue would not be easy for post-lapsarian beings, yet effort might bring them to it.[12]

Locke, in his early writings, did not maintain a definite view of the juridical standing of original sin or the character of its consequences. In the face of this baffling diversity of explanation – and, really, only a tithe of the views possible have been presented – it was natural enough for the layman not to commit himself very definitely. For instance, in the *English Tract*, we have a graphic statement about human conduct but no distinct explanation of it. 'We cannot doubt,' he declared, 'there can be anything so good or innocent which the frail nature or improved corruption of man may not make use of to harm himself or his neighbour,' and added that 'Ever since man first threw himself into the pollution of sin, he sullies whatever he takes into his hand, and he that at first could make the best and perfectest nature degenerate cannot fail now to make other things so too.'[13] The point is clear enough: man is entirely capable of sin. But we are left at a loss for an explanation. Locke's second sentence suggests the view that the Fall had utterly destroyed man's capacity for good: but, read again, it is seen to assert a temporal rather than a causal sequence. The first sentence, with its reference to 'frail nature' bespeaks a milder view. As, indeed, does the reference to 'improved corruption', for you cannot improve a corruption which is complete and ineffaceable, even if you mean the word 'improve' in an ironic way.

Locke's *Essays on the Law of Nature* tells a similar story. Whilst there was less sense of a complete corruption of human faculties, it is hard to see any particular explanation for the characteristics man actually has. There was an insistence that everyone acknowledges that good and evil are distinguishable by nature, that the law of nature was knowable by man's natural faculties and indeed that a knowledge of it could be kept only from those who preferred to cast off nature. This assertiveness, however, was coupled with a silence about original sin as an explanation of moral or immoral conduct. Locke's sole mention of it is to remark on its irrelevance to his purpose: it would not affect what one was describing[14]. Evidently Locke had no particular desire to declare himself about original sin at this point.

Two Treatises are more definite. They were not only incompatible with imputation but also with any extreme view of man's moral debility on account of the Fall. Certainly man is viewed as a creature liable, indeed likely to commit sins. Yet the propensity to do wrong is not explained through original sin. For instance, let us turn to concupiscence.

Concupiscence is interesting because central to the Augustinian assessment of post-lapsarian humanity. Augustine understood it as an incontinent desire, significant because in its sexual manifestation it explained at once the propagation of the species and the sinful nature of its continuance. This generous treatment was founded on the notion that children begotten by parents in a state of concupiscence would partake of it themselves. Adam and Eve were in that state when they fell, since at '*enmitie*' to God and so, as universal parents, transmitted it to the world: Samuel Crooke, we may recollect, described mankind's corruption as 'an hereditary disease'.[15] As such, because of the Fall sin was unavoidable for everyone.

Locke had a view of quite a different temper. For instance, a sexual instinct was the deliberate handiwork of the Deity, for 'God in his infinite Wisdom has put strong desires of Copulation into the Constitution of Men'.[16] This in itself indicates merely that Locke did not share Augustine's assessment of the *extent* of mankind's punishment for the Fall. If we read further in the *Treatises* we shall find that human concupiscence could hardly be attributable to the Fall of Adam at all. For Locke mentioned concupiscence in the eighth chapter of his *Second Treatise*. He discussed its prevalence in terms which suggested that there was a time when it had not been manifest, an age 'before vain Ambition, and *amor sceleratus habendi*, evil Concupiscence, had corrupted Mens minds'. The time is plainly post-lapsarian, for Locke suggests that there was government. And as well as being post-lapsarian, it was a '*Golden Age*'.[17] But if concupiscence came upon the scene some time after the Fall, indeed after a golden age, it must be true that not all people were inescapably liable to it. Some people, those living after the Fall but before vain Ambition did its work, were presumably exempt from its operation. Indeed if we follow the phrase *amor sceleratus habendi* to its source, we find Ovid's *Metamorphoses* describing quite a late stage in the development of society.[18]

Would it be right to think that Locke considered that the Fall did not affect nature at all? The *Treatises* are inexplicit. What we have just seen is compatible with an interpretation of the Fall which does not allude to concupiscence. But, if damage there was to human nature, it was evidently limited so far that it did not preclude good conduct. It is virtually needless to remark that the God of *Two Treatises* had 'given Man an Understanding to direct his Actions, has allowed him a freedom of Will, and liberty of Acting, as properly belonging thereunto, within the bounds of that Law he is under'.[19] In other words, whatever difficulties mankind laboured under, they were sufficiently limited for people to be able to conduct themselves rationally: which was quite enough for Locke's ends. It was also enough for them to be good in disposition as well as in act: for Locke had stated in his *Essays* that natural law included the requirement of a good disposition and clearly it was now possible to prefer right actions.

Of course Lockean people can and do deviate into sin. The whole point of constructing a polity was to guard against those men who were no greater respecters of justice, which, bluntly, was most of them; and we need hardly mention the Lockean menagerie, populated by wolves, which absolute monarchy would admit. Yet the text suggests that these specimens were deviating from norms they could well have met, 'whereby a Man so far becomes degenerate, and declares himself to quit the Principles of Human Nature, and to be a noxious Creature'.[20] This is not the sort of language one employs about people who are bound or even inclined towards evil by a force beyond their control. If these errors were in some significant sense unforced, what does this tell us about Locke's view of human nature?

Locke's educational works suggest that he felt able to discuss human nature without reference to the Fall. His confidence is apparent in the very mention of Adam in the *Directions concerning Education* which he wrote for Edward Clarke. 'Few of Adams children,' he observed, 'are so happy as not to be borne with some byas in their natural temper'.[21] These biasses, were soon attributed not to the Fall but to nature, as the corresponding passage in *Some Thoughts concerning Education* makes clear. There we read that 'the Byass will always hang on that side, that Nature first placed it'.[22] Anyhow Locke's view that 'Seeds of Vice ... must be carefully weeded out'[23] is hardly suggestive of the depth of evil which a *pronounced* degree of moral debility from the Fall implies: and if 'few of Adams children' had escaped bias then *some* must have done so, which is incompatible with the universality original sin must have. This was at some distance from Launcelot Andrewes' 'general corruption' that Adam had 'brought into the whole race of Mankind'.[24] Should we add that Locke mentioned the Fall in order to illustrate the compelling attraction of fruit?[25]

It seems hard to deny that if human capacities were impaired by the Fall it was to a degree hardly worth mentioning for Locke's purposes. Of course, it would be possible to admit any sort of damage which did not impinge upon his intentions. For instance, if we recollect Burnet's view that virtue was acquired by effort and turn next to Locke's educational writings, we see that their views agree in this respect. Yet Locke did not explain the need for effort as a product of the Fall.

Whether or no Proast alluded to original sin in this mode, a view centred on Adam was unlikely to attract Locke, for his *Treatises* were incompatible with the political use of the Adamic motif. It made sense for him to consider the doctrine at its root.

There were two alternatives before Locke. One was to restructure the body of his thought in order to meet Proast's views. Perhaps this did not attract him. The other was to show that Proast's views about human nature were untrue or, if true as a current description, not necessarily true in principle. To make good this line it was necessary to *preclude* a debility in human reason and will which could not be erased. In terms of the intellectual currency of the day, this meant treating original sin in a way which would not allow it to include the corruption of human faculties.

Original sin thus became a matter of general importance to Locke. It might involve suggesting that everyone was personally responsible for Adam's sin. As such it suggested a view of responsibility that jarred on the position, developed in the course of Locke's political writings, that each adult agent was responsible for guiding himself or herself only.

This pattern could hardly be admitted comfortably by Locke, even had he been able to forget the inconvenient motif of Adam's representative role. For like Bayle and 'Hobbism' it could be taken to imply that people were incapable of guiding themselves to follow God's laws of their own disposition. Bayle and 'Hobbism' presumed the priority of external, terrestrial pressures in determining conduct. Original sin opened the door for a like determination: intellectual or moral debility implied an agent whose powers of self-guidance were weak, possibly useless. All of these could be conceived to involve an inability to act well unless constrained by external, immediate pressures like approbation or coercion.[26]

The arguments Locke added to the second edition of *An Essay*, published in 1694 marked a sharp difference from these positions. The additions, as is well-known, concerned personal identity and freedom.

Locke revised his doctrine of the will in terms which both explained personal sin in a way which did not require the effects of original sin to be adduced and which indicated how each agent was capable of withstanding immediate pressures to regulate his or her conduct by God's law. It would obviously assist the viewpoints Locke disliked if the agent were moved by the most immediately powerful inducement to pleasure. Locke eradicated this possibility from 'Of Power' in the second edition. The effect of his revision was that the agent has 'a Power to suspend his determination' and therefore need not be causally determined to yield to the nearest carrot and stick of pleasure and pain. Rather Locke spoke of the power of suspending the will as a means of conforming to God's will, namely doing one's duty. For,

This as seems to me is the great privilege of finite intellectual Beings . . . that they can *suspend* their desires, and stop them from determining their *wills* to any action, till they have duly and fairly *examin'd* the good and evil of it, . . . This we are able to do; and when we have done it, we have done our duty,

that is to say, arrived at the conformity to good properly so-called, found in picking the way to the greatest felicity, 'a careful and constant pursuit of true and solid happiness'.[27] Thus Locke took himself to have provided people with a freedom to consider the ultimate pleasures and pains and so to be free to choose the laws of God rather than those of terrestrial coercion or reward.

By the same measure this model of freedom understood moral error to arise not from the will but from the understanding. There was no hint that mistakes could occur because the will acted in ways the understanding knew to be wrong. This was impossible, for it was made clear that the will was not an independent power as we have seen: hence Locke's famous statement that it was the man who was free, not the will. Error occurred when the understanding preferred a present pleasure to the prospect of a more distant one, despite the latter's promising a greater degree of felicity. This, of course, explains why some people might be moved by immediate stimuli. But it explained their propensity as *error*. At the same time it suggested that if the agent thus moved had taken more care, he or she could have done better. In other words, the agent would be capable in this model of adhering to God's law.[28]

The operative term is *capable*. Locke's assessment of human nature suggested that people were capable of both good and evil. We have seen how good was possible, and how evil resulted from attractive misunderstandings. That both good and evil were possible was important for Locke's moral and ethical position. This required that some people should guide themselves by reason, whilst others, the menagerie from whom political order protected the rest, did not. Hence a view of the matter by which people necessarily all acted well or ill did not suit Locke's requirements. In particular any extreme view of the impact of original sin upon intellect and will would be inconvenient for him.

A moral agent had not only to be capable of obeying God's rules but also to bear some actual relation to them. The chapter on identity and diversity that Locke added to his second edition explained that the identity of a moral agent consisted precisely in his or her conscious relation to rules, especially divine rules. Thus, once more, the agent was understood in terms that transcended merely terrestrial concerns, this time in respect of his or her very identity. It was true too that personal identity so conceived excluded Adam's representative role.

Locke conceived personal identity in terms that excluded mankind's complicity with Adam's sin and which instead intimately connected the very idea of a person with God's law. Personal identity Locke referred to consciousness. This precluded the imputation of Adam's sin to mankind. The representative theory, in George Lawson's words, reasoned that God regarded '*Adam*, and all his posterity as one person'. For Locke 'person' stood for 'a thinking intelligent Being, that . . . can consider it self as it self'. The latter operation was accomplished by the consciousness Locke found inseparable from thinking: 'for since consciousness always accompanies thinking, and 'tis that, that makes every one to be, what he calls *self*; and thereby distinguishes himself from all other thinking things, in this alone consists *personal Identity*'. Plainly this is inconsistent with Adam and his posterity being one person: a posterity as yet unborn could hardly be conscious of anything at the Fall. As Locke himself remarked of the self 'whatever past Actions it cannot reconcile or appropriate to that present *self*, by consciousness, it can be no more concerned in, than if they had never been done'.[29] It is hard to see how this could be reconciled with an imputationist view of the Fall.

This view of personal identity was also instrumental in helping Locke to show that the moral agent could be defined in relation to God's rules. As such it implies several points, of which the most important is that as such the agent would be subject to God's sanctions. Without this the authoritative character of God's rules would vanish. The necessity of sanctions bearing on him implied further that the account of the moral agent must include an afterlife. Obviously, therefore, the agent could not be defined in terms of his corporeal body, or, as Locke put it, as a man. Likewise, the agent should be aware of his actions as pertaining to himself (otherwise there could be no moral responsibility). Where was Locke to find this? Certainly not in the soul, for the soul implied substance, something which Locke could not bring into an explanation self-consistently. Instead Locke referred himself to the resources of conscience.

Conscience, as understood traditionally, presumed (i) a knowledge of moral rules present innately (or at least without mental effort) to the conscience, (ii) an awareness or consciousness that certain actions were one's own and (iii) on the basis of (i) and (ii) that one's actions could be judged right or wrong. But this is not to say that conscience was not useful in Locke's exigency to give an account of the moral agent, once he had ruled out both body and soul. For it had been claimed by a thinker well-known to Locke that conscience was a faculty distinct to people. Of angels, said Sanderson, we know little; beasts have no conscience; so it was a distinguishing feature of humanity to have a conscience: '*est ergo Homo proprium Conscientiae Subjectum, ut et Rationis: isque omnis non exclusis aut Ethnicis, aut Impiis, aut ipsis etiam Infantibus*'.[30] So if conscience distinguished humanity, so did the components of conscience taken collectively. One need hardly add that a thinker of sufficient ruthlessness might take one of those components alone and use it to define the moral agent.

This Locke did. He chose to pick out his criterion of personal identity from amongst the parts of the inherited account of conscience. As (i) would not do so (iii) was impossible. Hence (ii), a person's consciousness of their actions was distinguished as the criterion of their identity. Consciousness, of course, continued to be understood as of one's moral conduct. A person was described as 'a conscious thinking thing. . .which is sensible, or conscious of Pleasure or Pain, capable of Happiness or Misery'. One should add that the alteration was of emphasis, not of content, for Sanderson amongst others had emphasised that conscience concerned *Actus particulares Proprii*, and in the first edition Locke himself had located personal identity in consciousness without comment. But thus, at any rate, the agent could be understood in terms of moral rules and especially of God's laws. Hence the famous description of 'person' as 'a Forensick Term appropriating Actions and their Merit; and so belongs only to intelligent Agents capable of a Law, and Happiness and Misery'.[31] Locke's modification was to emphasise consciousness rather than conscience.

Consistency obliged Locke to write about Christianity in a way which agreed with his other doctrines. Those doctrines disregarded Adam's being mankind's representative and accordingly *The Reasonableness of Christianity* took Adam's representative capacity as a target. If *Reasonableness* did not build on imputation, what had it to say about original sin? The major losses incurred by mankind at the Fall were said to be immortality and the Garden of Eden. This was original sin only in the narrow sense that it directs us to a sin committed in the original position of mankind. Adam suffered the loss of immortality and Eden as a punishment for his action. The rest of mankind suffered them as a consequence of their descent from him. The consequence displayed original sin in terms of a loss of immortality and Eden rather than a propensity towards evil on mankind's part.

How are we to understand the logic of Locke's position? Let us consider it as a series of answers to questions. The questions are found in a short piece in his papers entitled *Peccatum originale*, which dates from 1692.[32] The paper is subtitled 'Queres concerning yᵉ Imputation of Adam's Sin to his Posterity'. At the most general level the 'queres' divide into two and these correspond to two disjunctive alternatives: either God 'reputes' mankind to have committed 'yᵗ Sin in Adam' or He 'only subjects them for yᵉ Sake of yᵗ Sin comitted by him alone yᵉ same Evills wᶜʰ he incurred by comitting it'.

The former alternative, which assumes Adam was representative, was subjected to questions about 'how they can be said really to participate wᵗʰ Adam in yᵗ Sin who did not concurr to it by any act of theirs, nor were in being when 'twas comitted?'. If we answer the question affirmatively in the terms set, we are clearly in the world of Burns' 'Holy Willie':

> I, wha deserve most just damnation,
>   For broken laws,
> Sax thousand years 'fore my creation,
>   Thro' Adam's cause

so let us pass on to the second set of queries. Answering these goes some way to showing how the relevant parts of *Reasonableness* assumed their shape. These queries enquire about three matters: (a) the evils which Adam incurred, (b) to which of these his posterity was subject and (c) whether suffering these made it better to be or not to be. But before answering them, let us turn to Locke's treatment of Adam's representative role.

Reasonableness proceeded by rejecting, as one of two undesirable extremes, the view that Adam was mankind's representative. Adam, Locke wrote, 'Millions had never heard of, and no one had authorised to transact for him, or be his Representative.' This criticism follows naturally from Locke's view that representation involves the agent's own consent. It was a criticism which could hardly have been stronger: the Augustinian view as a whole Locke described as having 'shook the Foundations of all Religion'.[33] Such critical intensity imposes the task of providing an alternative, just as it suggests a keenness to perform it.

What would an alternative involve? There would be two requirements of a doctrine which should at once satisfy Locke's view of representation and be properly Christian. These requirements had to be satisfied together. On the one hand, if Adam alone sinned then only he could be punished; on the other, was there any work for Christ to do in redeeming man? Locke was quite clear, as his view of responsibility required, that credit or discredit related only to personal action: so '*God will render to every one . . . According to his deeds*' and, conformably, 'none are truly *punished*, but for their own deeds'.[34] His treatment of Adam demanded as much. In a like way, to emphasise *personal* responsibility made it difficult to think that one man could suffer for another's sins. So the question arose, why did mankind, guilty of no original sin, require Christ? In observing how Locke answered the question, we should attend to the three questions to which he was alive.

What was Adam's punishment? Locke supposed the immortality Adam had enjoyed depended on maintaining a state of perfect obedience to the laws of conduct God had set him. By sinning he therefore lost immortality. He was also turned out of Paradise and subject to the inconveniences of work. This, then, was his punishment.

How far were his descendants involved in his Fall? It was not strictly a matter of punishment, but of suffering. There was no alteration by way of punishment in respect of mankind's moral task. Locke supposed that the same standards applied to his descendants; 'if any of the posterity of *Adam* were just,' he wrote, 'they shall not lose the Reward of it, Eternal Life and Bliss'.[35] Again, though the loss of Eden was a punishment for Adam it was merely suffering for his descendants. For Locke reasoned that no one was *entitled* to enjoy felicity: so 'they could not claim it as their Right, nor does he [God] injure them when he takes it from them'.[36] So there was suffering rather than punishment for the human race.

The suffering was in fact carefully specified to give a role to Christ. Whilst it was true that anyone who was perfectly righteous was entitled to immortality, it so happened that the standard of righteousness was set too high for anyone to meet out of their own resources. So, down to the coming of Christ, 'no one of *Adam's* issue had kept' the law of works.[37] It followed that they were liable to the same fate as Adam, namely a loss of immortality. One might suppose that this ran against the tenor of Locke's third 'quere', but he had an answer. It would certainly have been true that 'a state of extreme irremediable Torment is worse than no Being at all', but 'that such a temporary Life, as we now have, with all its Frailties and ordinary Miseries, is better than no Being, is evident, by the high value we put upon it our selves'.[38] Thus Locke established a version of the Fall congruent with the views about responsibility developed in the course of his political speculations.

Locke needed to include other elements, not least of which was a role for Christ. He did so by developing a view of Christianity in terms of natural man's willing dependence on the supernatural message provided by Christ.

II

If it were necessary to state the fundamental logic of Christian doctrine it could be done in three sentences. The proper destination of the human agent lies not with his or her present existence but with eternal life. However, his or her own conduct is not sufficiently just to deserve this according to the standard God sets. But for the sake of Christ the Deity accepts people, at least some people, into Heaven. From these propositions follow many others at a greater or a less remove.

These further propositions are numerous and very diverse. They differ not least because the original propositions can be filled out with different contents. These propositions can be referred to matters whose

305

status is factual and as such admit of wide variations. For, firstly, some of the hypothesised facts are not open to inspection – as, for instance, God's relations with Christ. Others might be observable by some people, but to most are available only by report – such as miracles. Some are observable always, like the facts of human nature, but admit of differing explanations. The facts about man's moral debility are especially important.

This is because they condition the account of Christ's work. The function of Christ in saving man depends on *why* man is unable to save himself. The explanation of *that* in its turn depends upon how the Fall is taken to affect man. In short how a theologian treats the Fall is correlated with his or her account of Christ's work.

In Locke's view the Fall of man affected not the faculties but the immortality of human beings. Adam and Eve had been immortal because they had access to the Tree of Life. Their ejection from the Garden of Eden separated them from the Tree and so reduced them to mortality. There is no sign in Locke's text that the Fall implied any other damage to human nature. This did not imply that he thought that people actually behaved well – 'the greater part', he thought, were 'no strict Observers of Equity and Justice'[39] – but that the cause of their misdemeanours lay elsewhere. Sometimes he attributed their sins to their situation in society, sometimes to the influence of others, sometimes to the bias of nature. So Christ's work would be described in terms of restoring immortality

This, of course, implies a logical insulation against a certain kind of representation and one possible set of consequences. Locke's view of representation thus preserves the assumptions it embodies. It protects the operation of a reason and will adequate to their intellectual and moral tasks. Thereby it implies responsibility for self. This correlation of consent and personal adequacy is interesting, not least because it contrasts with Hobbes' view. Hobbes did not suppose that people were able to conduct themselves adequately. Neither did he suppose that representatives, whether political or theological, need always be acknowledged by consent. Political superiority subsisted on terms which included an initial consent, but under conditions that scarcely required much exercise of the understanding; and theological representation did not involve that much.[40] By the same token, as we shall see, Christ's leadership had to be acknowledged by deliberate individual consent. So revealed theology, philosophical anthropology and political theory made a continuous pattern, though not the same pattern for each thinker, of course.

Christ's work was measured by man's abilities or, to speak more precisely, inabilities. Lockean man could do much, but he could not do everything. For instance he could not accumulate enough merit to earn salvation. As befitted his estimate of man's abilities Locke supposed that God had set a law of works to him. But he coupled this with the insistence that this law demanded more than flesh could manage. It was, he wrote, 'such a Law as the Purity of God's Nature required'. If this seems evasive, the point became clear in another place, where Locke observed that 'perfect Obedience was the Righteousness of the Law of Works; and then the Reward would be of Debt, and not of Grace': if people could earn salvation they would not be dependent on God in a crucial particular – as Locke's own manuscript note ran, 'They stood upon their own legs'[41] – just the particular where Locke required their legs to fail.

This may seem rather odd. It is contrary to the tenor of Locke's account of intellect, will and law and his insistence in *Reasonableness* itself that God expected errors.[42] But Locke had a specific purpose in mind. Our sketch of Christian doctrine suggests that Christ's work was to do on man's behalf what he could not do for himself. If people could earn salvation there would be no need of Christ. So Locke suggested that the law of works was more difficult than it looked. To this end he treated the law of works as 'that law which requires Perfect Obedience, without any remission or abatement'.[43] Thus in the face of people's continuing capacities it was a strict legalism which made room for Christ. Besides, there was a reason for this estimate of the law's difficulty. This supposition conveniently provided Christ's opportunity.

It might seem that an emphasis on mankind's moral capacities obviates Christian redemption, but this would be a superficial conclusion. Locke insisted on the need of 'the Redemption by Jesus Christ'[44] but this emphasis on distributive justice told against a belief in original corruption rather than belief in Christ.

Thus Locke reconciled his estimate of mankind with his sense of Jesus. That is to say, Locke's view of personal responsibility implied faculties which, in principle, were capable of following good by choice rather than by constraint. On the other hand, Locke required Christ to have a redemptive role, which does not reconcile (at first appearance) with the human capacity for virtue. Locke's suggestion was that though mankind were capable of virtue as a matter of fact they did not attain it fully, by the standards God had set.

The precise character of Christ's function was related to what mankind could do. This was true of both content and procedure. The content of His work was to make an offer to man that obviated his moral failure and supplied him with information he needed but otherwise lacked. Procedurally this function accorded with Locke's canons of truth because there was appropriate evidence that Christ was divinely authorised.

The fundamental part of Christ's work was to offer a covenant to mankind, abridging human defects and offering eternal life in return for acknowledgement of Christ as the Messiah, that is to say, the lawgiver sent by God. All Christian thinkers refer to a New Covenant – that is to say an offer made by God to man, in terms of which his failure to keep God's commandments adequately is forgiven and, hence, he can be received into Heaven – but the form of it varies.[45] Let us turn to Locke's version of it.

The specific content of the divine instruction Christ provided, apart from the offer of redemption, was twofold. The history of Locke's opinions makes neither a surprise. One was the obligation of natural law and the other was the afterlife and its rewards and punishments.

Allowing to Locke both the existence of God and rational precepts, it remained for him to show that these precepts in fact had obligatory force. We have seen that there were acute difficulties in the way of Locke's project, whose common feature was an absence of proof that God was good and that, if He were, He willed this obligation. Probably their solution was impossible within the terms Locke had set. This is not to say that Locke eschewed reason – we have seen that he did not – but that he was not perfectly successful in using it. *Reasonableness* confessed as much. 'It should seem', Locke wrote, 'by the little that has hitherto been done in it; That it is too hard a task for unassisted Reason, to establish Morality in all its parts upon its true Foundation'. Locke dwelt not least on the absence of proof of moral obligation. He assumed that there was a law of nature: 'But who is there that ever did, or undertook to give it us all entire, as a Law; No more, nor no less, than what was contained in, and had the obligation of that Law?'[46]

It was Christ's role to relieve the difficulty. It was true, of course, that revelation counted not as knowledge but as the object of belief for Locke: but revelation supplied information that reason had not discounted. This was acceptable because, after all, the objective was to discover God's will. If reason could not achieve this in the required way, then another route was needed. As Locke put it

wise Men ... could never make a Morality, whereof the World could be convinced, could never rise to the force of a law, that mankind could with certainty depend on. Whatsoever should thus be universally useful, as a standard to which Men should conform their Manners, must have its Authority either from Reason or Revelation ... He that any one will pretend to set up in

308

this kind, and have his Rules pass for authentique directions; must show, that either he builds his Doctrine upon Principles of Reason, self-evident in themselves; and deduces all the parts of it from thence, by clear and evident demonstration: Or must show his Commission from Heaven; That he comes with Authority from God, to deliver his Will and Commands to the World.[47]

The net result of Locke's intellectual failure was that 'Authority from God' rather than 'Doctrine upon Principles of Reason'[48] provided the source of information about obligation. Thus to conceive Christ as a lawgiver was central to Locke's concern of vindicating legislative ethics. Hence we have his view, which otherwise must seem so extraordinary, that Christ came to establish the law of nature.

The reality of an afterlife was an important component of obligation, since in Locke's view sanctions were necessary for a rule to become a law. Christ indicated that there was an afterlife, a point that had been unclear before His time. It is especially noteworthy that the reality of posthumous rewards and punishments vindicated Locke's view that morality was rationally preferable (even to an egoist) because of the great benefits the moral legislator possessed.

It was the obligation rather than the content of natural law which was lacking. Though Locke insisted that its contents were not apprehended entirely before Christ, he noted that a good part had. This view was consistent with Locke's regard for some pagan moralists (and indeed with his own success in producing rational precepts). What had been utterly lacking was any moral obligation. Locke insisted that 'such a body of Ethicks, proved to be the Law of Nature, from Principles of Reason, and reaching all the Duties of Life; I think no body will say the World had before our Saviour's time'.[49] Those who had not received the Gospel lacked obligation to natural law rather than information about its contents. As Locke said, people 'were under no obligation: The opinion of this or that Philosopher was of no Authority.'

How does the Gospel repair the law of nature? After all the New Testament does not correspond in content to much of *Two Treatises*, even if we go beyond the synoptists to John and the Epistles. But it does contain one very important precept, from which others could be inferred, namely the golden rule. Contemporaries inferred from it not only the contents of the second table but also those of the law of nature. Locke presumably shared their view, for he declared that 'our Saviour's great rule, that "we should love our neighbour as ourselves", is such a fundamental truth for the regulating human society, that I think, by that alone; one might without difficulty determine all the cases and doubts in social morality'.[50]

So belief stood in the room of knowledge. On occasion Locke wrote a little generously of the matter, suggesting that the New Testament afforded 'knowledge of true Morality'. Of course it did not, for (as Locke himself insisted against Stillingfleet) revelation provided grounds of probability rather than certainty.[51] There was also the matter of its audience. Knowledge was available to all in principle, but revelation only to those to whom the word had been delivered. As a matter of history the latter was not the whole of mankind in fact. Some had lived before Jesus, whilst not all of those who lived after Him had received His word. Does this involve a want of divine benevolence in disclosing natural law? Locke suggested that the Gospel was *addressed* to the whole of mankind, which indicates a uniform benevolence of intent, if not performance. But the difficulty is less than it seems, at least in respect of morals.

The discrepancy between the general address of the Gospel and the actual audience by whom it was received in fact signified more for the purposes of salvation. Those who had not received Christ could not be saved, presumably. However, this was a difficulty for the future, in that though present in Christian doctrine it was not a subject of controversy when Locke wrote. The deists would change that.

Salvation brings us to the human acknowledgement of Jesus. This took the form of accepting him as a ruler. The Lockean Jesus 'declared to all Mankind, that whoever would . . . take him . . . to be their King and Ruler, should be saved' This may seem curious, but conforms to the pattern of Locke's ideas. His treatment of the Fall, as we have seen, implied that mankind's natural powers of reason and will were unimpaired. Choice was therefore possible. A deliberate acceptance of Christ could be signified. That is to say, if His authority was to be accepted by the individual some sign of consent was necessary. For just as Adam would have required consent to make him mankind's representative, so the individual needed to signify his subordination to Christ. Hence

those who would have the Priviledge, Advantage, and Deliverance of his Kingdom, should enter themselves into it; And by Baptism being made Denizens, and solemnly incorporated into that Kingdom, live as became Subjects, obedient to the Laws of it.

The evident similarity between theological and political authority requires no comment. But the form of the act does. It took the form of acknowledging His right to legislate because the Lockean Jesus worked principally in this way. It was not just that He came to promulgate the law of nature. His message to mankind was a new covenant. The first covenant contained the law of works. The new covenant lifted man from his failure to meet that law. It did not abridge his duty to behave morally, but suggested that those who tried to do so earnestly would be saved if they acknowledged Jesus' authority and believed in Him. In other words adherence to Him would be reckoned to abridge the deficiency of human conduct. This act of faith, like political consent, was a voluntary act. The covenant of faith was said to be 'offered'. Christians were said to 'take' Christ, 'for their ruler'. Locke said that believing in Him made people 'denizens of his kingdom', revealing the voluntary character of their obedience, 'for a man must be a subject before he is bound to obey'. In short, Christians were 'voluntary subjects' and Christ their 'politique head'.[52]

This was not a question of creating an authority but of submitting to it. Jesus' authority came from God. Unlike the authority of a terrestrial ruler it was not constituted by human consent but derived from God's superiority. On the other hand the individual did need to acknowledge his acceptance of Jesus' rule. For that marked his agreement to the terms of the new covenant: and that underlay the applicability of its conditions.

This emphasis on Christ's legislative role and the conditions of the new covenant make Lockean Christianity seem a little academic. In a sense it is, but not in a besetting way. Locke indicated that the simplicity of Christ's message suited the limited acquirements of 'the vulgar, and mass of Mankind'.[53] The same was true of the simplicity of the new covenant's terms. Though Locke was constituting his revealed theology in a manner that continued his preceding views it was also the case that he wrote with an eye to religious need. We shall find that this was true in an unexpected way, relating to the character of belief. We will find that Locke thought that not only credence in God but also adherence to Him was required: and that adherence was ultimately to the unknown.

The acceptance of Jesus was a matter of belief, which brings us to the question of evidence. There had to be adequate evidence that Jesus was a lawgiver sent by God for belief to be warranted. This was provided in two ways, coherence with God's previous policy and examples of His power. The first was found in the consistency of Jesus' mission with the Old Testament. He fulfilled its prophecies of the second coming. Indeed He took great care to do so, avoiding conflicts that might have curtailed His mission. In like manner the content of His message did not abrogate but complemented the moral prescriptions of the Old Testament. Again, He performed miracles to authenticate His claims to God's backing. This also corresponded to

Locke's view that the predictions of miracles, contained in the Old Testament, should be fulfilled.[54] So reason found its continuation by other means in probability.

So did the human response, in that it is an act of belief in the evidence presented to the agent. For most people that evidence has the status of report. Those who witnessed Christ's work could claim knowledge founded on their experience. But those of a later day could base their assent merely on their appraisal of the scripture reporting the experiences of the Evangelists. This was not inappropriate because Locke was concerned less with what convinced Jesus' contemporaries than with the objective grounds of belief.[55]

The individual based assent on personal consideration of the evidence, not on reliance on a church. For in Locke's reading of probability the claims of tradition were less strong than those of a direct report. We may suggest that the two be considered together. If they agreed their convergence strengthens the plausibility of the alleged result (assuming that they do not derive from the same source). But Locke's heart did not embrace a fondness for ecclesiastical traditions, in England at least. His coolness suffused priestly claims in general with a layer of ice.[56]

There was a more fundamental reason for this distance. The whole transaction about salvation was between the individual and God. It was the individual's belief and actions which counted according to Locke's new covenant. Earlier Locke had decided that each agent was responsible for his or her own worship. Locke had decided by 1679 that he could not hand this over to anyone else. Since his formula had widened from worship to salvation in that place, the application to *Reasonableness* is obvious. Here each human being was responsible for his whole destiny: 'as I remember every one's sin is charged upon himself only', Locke wrote. There is no hint that one might covenant or act on behalf of others, as Moses did on behalf of the Israelites (which Locke did not mention) or as some thought Adam had done for mankind as a whole.[57]

Lockean Christianity builds upon the natural endowments of mankind rather than superseding them. True, as any scheme of redemption does, it repaired the results of human weakness. It does so by providing a further avenue for humanity's own efforts. Whilst its moral endeavours evidently fell short of the law of works, the ability to exercise belief was evidently pleasing in God's sight. For in company with continued moral effort belief satisfied the new covenant.[58]

The new covenant, however, was an act of grace on God's part. Without it no one could be saved, but in the nature of things no one could be said to have earned it. To provide it was a matter of graciousness rather than debt. In fact it was the principal form of grace in Lockean Christianity. Locke alluded to grace in other connections but did not explain them. Neither did they play an explanatory role in his view of Christian doctrine. This silence accorded with his emphasis on the agent's own activity, whether in moral effort or in the act of belief. Grace most smoothly takes a form congruent with the economy of salvation. If action is central to this then grace must fall naturally into a form which flatters action. It is noteworthy that Locke suggested that the merits of Jesus were imputed to a human only after his or her own efforts.[59]

If Jesus performed a service to man, man also performed one for God. For Locke thought man's belief should take a form which indicated his confidence in God's goodness. The attribute of goodness had not come out quite fully in *An Essay*. For the Lockean God inflicted pain on some people, and pain was the correlate of evil. Neither had Locke shown that his God had the attribute, though he had dwelt on His power and wisdom in explanatory contexts. But Locke had another resource in God's promises. Whilst 'the works of Nature shew his Wisdom and Power:' Locke wrote, 'But 'tis his peculiar Care of Mankind; most eminently discovered in his Promises to them, that shews his Bounty and Goodness.'[60] In other words the new covenant was evidence of God's goodness. But this was not all.

Christ's role in establishing natural law was also evidence of God's goodness. For God was supposed to reveal to people what they needed to understand in order to conduct themselves. The absence of a definitive law, in Locke's judgement, would have opened the door to moral relativism. By precluding this God had acted with goodness. But this meant that the evidence of His goodness turned on revelation.

Correspondingly Locke's God placed an extremely high value on human trust in His goodness. For the new covenant was the occasion for a striking affirmation about God on man's part. It was the human reliance on God, Locke argued, that pleased Him. The appropriate belief in God was not merely an intellectual assent but a trusting dependence. Partly no doubt this thoroughgoing reliance is simply what we should expect if God functioned as mankind's superior. This took a remarkable form – a belief in God's goodness.[61]

This trust in God helps us to understand the great role of the act of belief in Locke's explanation of salvation. He instanced Abraham, whom God justified not for believing any propositional creed but for simply trusting Him: 'the Faith which God counted to *Abraham* for Righteousness,' Locke decided, 'was nothing but a firm belief of what God declared to him, and a steadfast relying on him for the accomplishment of what he had promised'.[62] This evident need for emphatic credence in God makes sense in terms of showing more directly that God was good.

The precise meaning of 'good' is worth noting here. God's conduct did not afford proof that goodness was one of His attributes as omniscience and omnipotence were taken to be. For these were supposed to be known by inference from God's works in nature, whereas this was evidenced by particular actions. However, the same acts evidenced that God was benevolent, for He manifested a concern for the happiness of His creatures. These actions, of course, were apprehended not through reason but revelation and so afforded grounds for belief rather than certainty.

These considerations explain the centrality of Jesus' role as the Messiah. The need to vindicate God's goodness and the requirement for man's active assent to the covenant both required this. The former was found in the fulfilment of the divine promise of a redeemer. The latter required consent to a new dispensation, which was to be found within the resources of theology most obviously in the Messiah – one who would lead man. Since both components were essential to Locke's account of Christianity it is evident that Jesus' role as Messiah had to be central.[63]

The human reliance on God, in fact, was more profound than even this would suggest, as we may see by reverting for a moment to Locke's treatment of good and evil. People knew things as good or evil strictly by their connection with pleasure or pain. As Locke stated in *An Essay*

what has an aptness to produce Pleasure in us, is that we call *good*, and what is apt to produce Pain in us, we call *Evil*, for no other reason, but for its aptness to produce Pleasure and Pain in us, wherein consists our *Happiness* and *Misery*.

In Locke's frame of reference this implied that God had ordered matters in this way: but it did not disclose whether their goodness is prior to God's willing or a result of it. This, indeed, is the conundrum about morality implied but not explored in *An Essay*.[64] But there is one further implication to it that requires to be examined.

Locke located the evidence of God's *goodness* in His promises to mankind. But, what evidence did Locke have that these promises were valid? What, in other words, if God was a deceiver, who had made untrue promises? The guarantee against this would be that God was good or benevolent. No doubt one could argue that the content of revelation was continuous with what was known to reason and therefore reliable, just as reason was. *But* what reason disclosed was merely that God existed and that there were precepts rational in terrestrial terms. It did not evidence His goodness or benevolence. These were inferences from revelation. But it is precisely the truth of revelation that is under scrutiny. In this light to say that revelation continues reason offers a presumption that revelation may be true: it affords no evidence that it is *in fact*.

The problem of a deceiving God is no doubt a theoretical difficulty rather than a practical probability. It was not, however, a difficulty that Locke could meet. Locke's evidence of God's goodness was His promises, but the evidence that His promises were true was revelation. The difficulty may be illustrated through the logic of Locke's earlier judgement that the scriptures were 'an eternal foundation of truth as immediately coming from the fountain of it':[65] this judgement becomes circuitous if the evidence that the fountain gives truth is the truth it gives. When Thomas Burnet enquired after the standard by which Locke supposed God worked, he received an answer that was circular:

Whoever sincerely acknowledges any law to be the law of God, cannot fail to acknowledge also, that it hath all the reason and ground that a just and wise law can or ought to have

and thus Locke left unanswered the question of what that ground was.[66] The annexation of divine rewards and punishments to rules, as Burnet observed, could only be apprehended from revelation:[67] but revelation was under question.

Of course, there was the assumption that God would not break His promises because that would imply self-contradiction. It was a common assumption that God could not contradict Himself (e.g., will *A* and *not-A* simultaneously). Promises were counted relevant to the notion of self-contradiction. On this line, God could not break His promises. Locke subscribed to this view, declaring emphatically that '*Grants, Promises* and *Oaths* are Bonds that *hold the Almighty.*' By the same token biblical prophecies were binding. Hence we find Locke taking care to emphasise Christ's insistent concern to fulfil the Old Testament prophecies of a Messiah. Thus the coherence of the parts of the divine message lent credence to it.[68] Yet this was not enough.

Suppose that God had two different plans. It might be the case that the two agreed in their ultimate tenor, but suppose rather that they did not. The resources of theology in fact included not only God's revealed will but also His secret will. The *voluntas dei signi*, commonly called his signified or revealed will – signified or revealed in scripture, that is to say – was contrasted with the *voluntas dei beneplaciti*, the direct or eternal will of God. The latter need not be revealed to people or understood by them if it were.[69] Though it may be comforting to assert that the latter would coincide with the former, was there any guarantee of this?[70] Presumably not, unless it was understood that God had guaranteed the ultimate validity of his revealed order. But the value of the guarantee depended on His veracity. This is just what Locke had not proved. On this reading it could be true that His promises and His non-self-contradiction belonged alike to a regime that was God's plaything rather than His purpose: that told mankind nothing of the true character of His order. Burnet did not hesitate to emphasise the point,

for tho' you have a Revelation, if there be no immovable Rules of Good and Evil, Just and Unjust; nor any fixt Rule of Right betwixt God and his Creatures, you can never be assur'd of Performance, whatsoever is promis'd or threatned. There may be a Reveal'd and a Secret Will, for any thing you know: And we may follow one, and the other be finally executed, according to a Secret Intention;

'which', he continued, 'will lay a Ground for an incurable Scepticism'.[71] But perhaps we can treat the matter in another light.

It may be more appropriate to treat God's goodness as an assumption rather than something to be proved. Locke, in effect, had failed in undertaking the latter. But this does not preclude treating divine goodness as a postulate of a body of thought. Locke's work, viewed in its historical development, had done just that. Of course this makes human dependence on God much more radical than Locke had suggested.

Whilst Locke continued the view of faith and reason in *An Essay* he had explored revelation in depth. He had emphasised revealed theology not just in a manner that agreed with his preceding views but by advancing a content continuous with his previous commitments. That content, however, ultimately involved a dependence on God far more fundamental than might have been supposed at the outset.

But we should remember, after this fideistic discovery, that *The Reasonableness of Christianity* was a treatment of revealed theology designed to show its conformity to and continuity with the conclusions of reason and, more intimately, to resolve some intellectual difficulties in which Locke had found himself. It did not pretend to be exhaustive and did not give a complete and systematic treatment of Christianity. Indeed it did not conform to what some of Locke's contemporaries understood by Christian doctrine. For instance his treatment of original sin and the consequent adjustments of soteriology received criticism, unsurprisingly, from a devoted Calvinist.[72] But there is no room in a study of Locke's politics and its immediate setting to pursue the more distant connections of his doctrine, though there are many of these. It is more pertinent to emphasise a point of general significance: that what a writer understands by Christian doctrine may bear the impress of his or her own broader intellectual prepossessions, and this is as true of Locke as anyone else.

Conclusion

We have considered Locke's political thought and its relations with his other concerns. The task has led us to traverse many of his writings, beginning with his earliest reflections on things indifferent in the 1660s and finishing with his account of Christianity in the 1690s. Though this does not pretend to constitute an exhaustive account of his thought, it does not lend itself to brief summary. If Locke's writings were so straightforward that they could be peptonised easily, he would scarcely be a rewarding subject of study, and probably of limited historical importance. Some elements of significance, however, do bear mention.

These concern the general character of Locke's vision, and more especially the meaning of some of its elements. To understand this, it is perhaps best to look at a theological doctrine which is the antitype of Locke's. In considering how Locke came to compose his vision and develop a technique, we have encountered an older view of things. This has appeared piecemeal, just where reference to it assisted in understanding the growth of Locke's views. It is time to consider it connectedly.

The Augustinian model of mankind and its destiny involved a collective view of responsibility. It assumed that Adam bore responsibility for all people, so that the punishment appropriate to his delinquency would fall upon everyone. The penalty for Adam's sin happened to involve a diminution of the human faculties of intellect and will to a degree that they became inadequate to both distinguishing duty entirely and performing it fully.

This theological doctrine, because it presented a specific view of human nature, had the widest implications. Its general significance was that authority, whether political or ecclesiastical, was essentially something imposed upon people. Post-lapsarian mankind was incapable of doing what was right spontaneously. Any right actions that people performed, flowed not from a good disposition, but from external pressures like coercion, fashion or public opinion. Political direction, for instance, however just its terms, would command obedience through its sanctions. It was obvious, on this view, that people would not turn

319

to God of their own will, and therefore could not expect to be saved on the basis of their own performance. How then could they find salvation?

This problem was resolved by conceiving God's grace to operate not least by providing the means of saving people without spontaneous action of their own. High amongst these was a church constituted not by human endeavour but by the direct action of God Himself. Such a church, because it was God's, obviously was unitary. The same divine warrant suggested that the state should support it and, as some people might be so far from God that they might rebel against His order, the state's support might very well take the form of protecting the church against heresy or of coercing the recalcitrant to worship. Certainly it was the business of the state to uphold Christian doctrine and institutions.

This codirection of church and state implied divine direction. Priests were only human and if they did well it was due to God's grace working upon them directly. The same applied to civil rulers. This doctrine might be extended to suggest that God directly empowered civil government of some specific sort. That sort might turn out to be absolutism. The latter doctrine implies that the ruler was not answerable to the governed. This accords well with the notions that can be added easily to the Augustinian view: for instance, if people in general were not equipped to do well, to the degree that they were incapable of self-direction, whilst God had endowed their ruler with capacities adequate to guide them all. Thus a divinely established church might be complemented with a state warranted in the same way.

The centrality of Adam marks a correspondence in this model. Authority exists without popular basis and does its work without popular direction. Adam was given the authority to transact on behalf of mankind by God alone. Adam's sin and its consequences were abridged by divine action without a cue from any human and without any contribution of human merit. Christ was mankind's representative without human consent and His action, rather than mankind's, undid Adam's sin. The civil ruler was established by God rather than by man and acted for his subject's sake rather than at their behest, even to the degree of being responsible for their salvation.

This is a general model. Many variations are possible within it, not least because some of the connections within it depend upon assessments of fact rather than upon purely conceptual considerations (as, for instance, the seriousness of Adam's punishment and, consequently, the degree of it). It corresponds exactly to the views of no one thinker. But its tendency is apparent in a great deal of thought, in which a central role for Adam, a serious diminution of the human powers for good, and a divinely warranted form of organisation in church and state are connected to a view of authority which, in various forms, is imposed upon people rather than arising from them.

The reader will recognise this as quite contrary to the family of ideas that Locke formed. Since that family arose in part as a response to specific problems, its constitution was gradual. His recognition that the consciences of religious dissidents were not necessarily perverse, present in his writings from the beginning and integral to his view of toleration from 1667 found a complement in ignoring claims about the divine credentials of churches and consequently their claim to political support. Under the pressure of political circumstance, this was embodied in the larger claim that churches were organisations constituted by people and, more extendedly, in a theory of civil government which presented the state as secular in its objectives and powers. This ran against the tenor of inherited views of organisation. The society into which Locke was born had assumed in many ways that one agent had an authority over and, correlatively, a responsibility for others. Heads of households were responsible for guiding their members, just as monarchs bore responsibility for guiding their subjects and, in a more exalted capacity, Adam transacted on behalf of the whole human race. This notion of one agent having responsibility for others gradually came to be removed from Locke's work and to be replaced there by the notion that each agent was responsible for himself or herself in some respects at least. Where originally he assumed that the civil magistrate had a responsibility to regulate his subjects' worship, he decided that this matter lay between the individual worshipper and God only. In a way that was connected, Locke came to think that each agent was responsible not merely for conducting his or her own worship but also for decisions relating to civil government, to the conduct of the mind and to the larger question of Christian salvation.

This, then, was Locke's family of ideas. Involved here is a definite view of personal responsibility. Locke's mature theories presupposed that in principle the human understanding and will were adequate to the agent's self-direction and bypassed claims which suggested that God had endowed some people with special authority in church and state: rather, Locke thought, such authority derived from each person because each (at the the outset) had the same intellectual endowments as the next. His view of church and state thus makes presumptions about a view of the human understanding which referred differences in the understanding to effort more than to endowment. Locke's view of salvation complemented his revision of ecclesiastical and political authority by suggesting that divine assistance, in the form of Christ's help, was something rationally offered to human beings as a personal choice rather than impressed upon them.

This view of responsibility, as one might expect, embodies the tendency of thinkers to reproduce in one place an intellectual motif devised in another. This tendency is not confined to Locke alone, as one may see by comparing the views of some of his contemporaries about the logic of original sin with their views about political matters, or, for that matter, by looking at the work of many other thinkers. The specific shape of Locke's pattern of ideas reflects also his response to the circumstances of the day. But putting the matter in terms of its conceptual basis it reflects Locke's view of the human understanding. He conceived that the intellect, conducted with application and care, was capable of knowing truths about morality and God with certainty and of apprehending other matters, such as faith, with a reasoned attitude. Since these were the most salient concerns in the thought of the day and, not least, the bases of contemporary reflection about political and ecclesiastical order, Locke was in effect suggesting that each human being was capable of effective thinking about such matters. This capacity, even if only a matter of principle, was of central significance for some other departments of thought. For contemporaries assumed that it was reason that enabled a human being to guide himself or herself in matters of conduct. Locke assumed additionally that reason disclosed truths about God and should regulate faith. In short the human understanding, as he conceived it, was the instrument that equipped people to guide their own destinies in matters of government and worship. His view of the mind is fundamental to some of his other positions.

For the model of thinking which assumed the responsibility of one agent for another assumed too that the former was fitted to direct where the latter was not. The superior understanding of monarchs, churchmen and fathers suggested that they should guide the destinies of their less gifted inferiors. Locke's conclusions, which were mediated as much by his sense of political need as by the philosophical character of his writings about the human understanding, suggested otherwise.

They thus implied a revision of the allocation of authority in society. This was a matter both of conclusions about authority and of the means by which authority was constituted. In respect of the former, the conclusion that the means of salvation were sufficiently clear to be understood by the simplest of people and were not obviously mediated by ecclesiastical organisations tended to undermine the claims of churchmen to authority over the laity. Again, Locke's sense that monarchs were no better endowed intellectually or morally than their subjects tended to undermine claims that monarchical authority should be unrestricted. These reflections suggested also a revision of the mechanisms by which authority was constituted. Those who so conspicuously knew better than others how affairs should be regulated might be supposed to have an authority independent of the latter. But if people stood on a footing of intellectual equality, even in principle, the matter was rather different. If authority was necessary – and Locke assumed that political authority at least was needful – then it arose from the rational reflection of people rather than being something that needed to be imposed upon them from above. In the particular form Locke himself developed, civil government arose legitimately from popular consent rather than being imposed by God.

This view of autonomy is restricted in Locke's vision to certain aspects of political theory, namely those which excited his enmity in preceding explanation and which, accordingly, he wished to replace. That Locke's position arose not least from what he was *against* indicates, procedurally speaking, the importance of treating him historically. It indicates, substantively, that it was not his object to set up the autonomy of mankind as a comprehensive doctrine. Central elements of his vision, of course, require the subordination of mankind to God, and that subordination was important for Locke's political argument. But within the latter there is a question to which Locke returned no answer and which has very radical implications.

There were large exceptions to Locke's revision of authority. For instance, the notion that parents were set above children without the latter's consent remained in place in his thought. But since its significance was as the means of fitting children to direct themselves through the exercise of reason, we can hardly say that this was an anomalous exception.

In a similar way, Locke did not subject the authority of God to revision. God's place as the superior of mankind assumed His possession of attributes that were so far in excess of any human endowment that there could be no question of His fitness to direct people in general or, indeed, to enforce His view of how they should behave. The intentions Locke attributed to Him, it is true, differ somewhat from those that other thinkers laid at His celestial door, but that is a different matter and one which the nature of theological explanation admits.[1] Indeed it was a matter quite vital to the constitution of Locke's thought. The Lockean view of mankind's intellectual endowments rests on the assumption that the possession of reason distinguished mankind from animal and vegetable life. This assumption, like the terms of Locke's 'great Design' and the golden rule, were the common coin of contemporary religious thought, just as the view that reason should guide conduct was a common assumption of moral thought. But coupled with Locke's view of the power of reason to disclose morality and with his political prepossessions, they generated a body of thought about the church and political organisation that produced Locke's allocation of responsibility and authority in society. In this sense theology is an indispensable element in the constitution of Locke's thought.

These developments did not imply a revision of the social structure in Locke's mind. Partly this reflects his sense that whatever the capacities in principle that the human understanding might have the actual attainments of the mass of the population were rather limited. Partly also it reflects Locke's social disposition. Certainly it is difficult to conceive Locke as radical about social hierarchy or about the question of which strata of society were fitted in fact to administer the government of the day or to have seats in parliament. But supposing a different distribution of intellectual attainment in the community might imply supposing also that social hierarchy should be subject to revision or at least be required to explain itself.

Locke's political argument required him to emphasise the human understanding as a source of superiority. Whilst he emphasised that mankind excelled animals intellectually, he argued that people came from the hand of nature with the same faculties and, therefore, without subordination one to another. As we have noted, he did not explore the consequences for the social order that might be inferred from this position. How age, wealth and human power were located in his mind is unclear. What is apparent, on the other hand, is that they cannot be fitted readily into his scheme of explanation. The understanding, power and (hopefully) the good will of God indicated the most important of superiors: but in Locke's political theory authority derived in terms of intellect chiefly. We have seen how this defined the authority of civil government and qualified ecclesiastical claims, limiting both. The completeness of this explanation leaves no space for the appurtenances of social position (or, for that matter, mere power) as claims to authority.[2] In relation to the order of his day, or of early modern Europe generally, the implications that could be drawn from his thought were decidedly radical.

It is wrong to begin by extracting 'implications' from the thought of those who, quite evidently, did not draw them or anything like them and to finish by calling the results 'X's position'. Intellectual positions are taken deliberately. That is to say, to formulate a view is not a matter simply of extracting the properties of ideas, except possibly in the more austere branches of logic and in mathematics. The nature of ideas, especially those of general significance, is not such that they lend themselves necessarily to only one interpretation or one relation to another idea. They are sufficiently capacious or, if one likes, sufficiently ambiguous to be conceived in different ways and in different relations. This applies *a fortiori* if we consider a cluster of ideas rather than only one or two. To take up an intellectual position is thus an act which admits of choice as well as reflection or which bears the impress of a thinker's preceding view of things rather than arising from a neutrally reflective survey of all the possibilities. Indeed this is one of the reasons why there is a history of thought and why it demands the attention of posterity: the families of ideas that thinkers give to the world are contingent examples of how thinking gets done rather than simply a logical development whose course is to be taken for granted.

Having said this much, we may see that the conclusions of a powerful thinker are important to his or her successors: they present a family of ideas in a form that may be important to posterity, but which the latter otherwise might not have devised for itself. The combination of ideas Locke connected with the agent's responsibility for self – constitutional government, toleration, a simple creed, a rejection of the centrality of Adam and all that went with it – were linked to an interpretation of the human understanding. In this important sense Locke's political posture and much else makes use of his view of the human understanding. Whilst the thinkers of the next century did not concur, by any means, with the all the arguments of *An Essay concerning Human Understanding*, it is easy to see how its bearings were central to the temper of a great deal of the century's intellectual attitudes. *An Essay*, by dwelling upon the individual's equipment to direct himself or herself, facilitates an attitude to political and ecclesiastical institutions that must be reflective and may be critical. If one juxtaposes Locke's cluster of ideas with the practices of the *ancien regime* in Europe it is not difficult to see that change in the latter might be supposed desirable.

Much could be written on this subject, and more on the question of how Locke was adapted and absorbed by the Enlightenment and by thinkers down to the present day: but, in an obvious and significant way, that would not be a study of Locke but of the reasons that made him important to posterity. Neither is this the place for an extended examination of these. But if individuals are important in the history of thought because they present families of ideas which, by reason of their contingent formation, might otherwise not have appeared, it is true too that that the features of a given thinker will illuminate the distinctive difficulties in wider movements of opinion.

Amidst this large story it is perhaps worth picking out one item, the idea of self-direction, which has significance for our understanding of Locke himself. This idea depends, of course, on the human agent's intellectual capacity, especially his or her reason. To bring reason to the fore in this way exposed two problems of enduring difficulty, one concerning the actual distribution of intellect amongst people and the other concerning the conclusions which the demands of morality make upon reason.

The former, put very simply, is that everyone is supposed to be rational in thought and deed, but isn't. Or, to put the matter more soberly, a theory which supposes that individuals do not need to be directed in fundamental ways, postulates a view of their rational capacities and their attainments. Whilst Locke maintained the adequacy of the understanding to its purposes, he came to think that the actual attainments of the majority of mankind were decidely limited. The implications of this painful contrast are numerous, but one in particular is worth mentioning. Presuming that some members of the community have higher attainments than others, whose attainments are inadequate. then in terms of Locke's view of authority it becomes the business of the former to guide and instruct the latter. This has implications beyond the conduct of education and of summarising Christian doctrine for the sake of simple folk: it may involve guidance about ethical and political matters too. Whilst we should beware of reading a specific social or institutional form into this general point, it does suggest the guidance of some members of society by others. Herein we come to a tense place: because such guidance is not the most obvious sequel to declaring that everyone belongs to the same rank.

The other problem relates to a question of morals. The morality of the West places an accent upon altruistic conduct. The form varies in Judaism, Christianity, Kantianism and Utilitarianism, but the point is apparent in all of them and in other ethical doctrines besides. But this assessment of morality is not matched by the dominant view of human psychology, which conceives people as essentially egocentric. Between the demands of altruistic morality and the pull of egocentric psychology there is an obvious tension, which in many instances passes into a decided enmity. Moralists have tried to resolve the tension by suggesting in one way or another that to behave altruistically is rational for the egocentric agent: that is to say, that reason can show that altrustic conduct in fact satisfies or overrides egocentric desire. One of the most persistent attempts to prove that reason does this comes in the form of a moral obligation upon the agent to behave well. Locke adduced both the idea of a superior whose will legitimately overrode the desires of human agents and also the notion that this superior had annexed sanctions to His will in a way that made altruistic conduct into the interest of the most radically egocentric agent. The difficulty lay in rationally identifying just what was involved here, a difficulty which Locke did not succeed in solving properly.

Those of his successors with a concern for moral obligation, but without his theological framework, did not do appreciably better. Both Kant and Bentham assumed that human beings were ethically autonomous, the former more clearly than the latter. Neither explained very clearly why people were bound to follow the moral prescriptions that they recommended, a point as apparent from the labyrinthine obscurities of the *Groundwork to the Metaphysics of Morals* as from the silences of the *Introduction to the Principles of Morals and Legislation* and the *Deontology*. Whether the younger Mill's explanation that moral obligation for utilitarianism was to be referred to progress is more convincing is an open question, though his account is certainly transparent. What is clear is that Kantian deontology and utilitarianism continue to have a central place in moral and political thinking. What is absent is a compelling account of why anyone is obliged to act upon them.[4]

At any rate two central difficulties appear in Locke's thought. They are theoretical difficulties, which is to say that they do not necessarily obstruct practice, but at the same time suggest that practice may be imperfect. To put the matter another way, a great deal of contemporary thinking attempts to close the lacunae which Locke, evidently against his will, placed on the conceptual agenda. Much reflection on the character of representative government, on ethics and on the philosophy of the social sciences dwells upon these problems, in ways different to Locke's but not always with conspicuously more success.

If Locke thus encapsulates a modern difficulty, how far does he fit modern categories of thought? The central value in contemporary social and political thought is freedom. Locke did certainly not conceive that the freedom of mankind in relation to God was either desirable or possible. Since God was the source of moral obligation it is hardly possible to conceive Locke as concerned with freedom in this respect.

This is true the more so because Locke had a view of the purpose of life more broadly conceived. The Lockean God, expressing Himself in *Genesis*, indicated a clear purpose which He required mankind to pursue – to multiply and to subdue the earth. This purpose, in Locke's view at least, comprised also the establishment and growth of private property, the development of the arts and sciences, and education in the use of reason, as well as what he called 'the continuation of the

Species in the highest perfection'. It is true, obviously enough, that these activities are unlikely to exhaust the possibilities in anyone's life: but it is true also that there is no room here for practices that would detract from that purpose. The 'great Design' suggested a range of lifestyles that Locke thought acceptable, and, concurrently, suggested ones that he rejected. He listed 'Adultery, Incest and Sodomy' as 'Sins, which. . .have their Principal Aggravation from this, that they cross the main intention of Nature, which willeth the increase of Mankind, and the continuation of the Species in the highest perfection, and the distinction of Families, with the Security of the Marriage Bed, as necessary thereunto'.[5] Presumably also contraception, on this reasoning, would be suspect.[6] Turning from the content to the presuppositions of Locke's argument, his view that God created mankind in His image and set people decisively above animal creation, if not absolutely inconsistent with natural selection, certainly expresses a pre-Darwinian conception of nature. Since Locke plainly conceived society generally in a highly hierarchical way, it is difficult to think that his vision of life was free in the sense of being structured according to the preferences of individual taste. In a sense this detail is superogatory, for it implicitly juxtaposes Locke, living in the seventeenth-century, with contemporary attitudes and practice. But it is not the less valuable for that reason. Locke is often supposed to be an ancestor of contemporary thought, which has a rather different conception of how people should live their lives.

A similar finding arises if we turn to Locke's mature politics. It is true that the Lockean commonwealth arises as a result of individual wills and that Locke had a relaxed attitude to forms of civil government, provided that they were not absolute and conformed to certain general requirements. But it is true also, and not less important, that the purposes for which that commonwealth exists were prescribed and bounded by the Lockean God, just as He explained the character of Lockean morality.

It is when God is removed from explanation – probably the greatest conceptual breach in the history of modern thought – that matters take a different turn. The significance of Hume's philosophy lay in subverting every assumption about a divine direction of mankind that Locke had assumed, and therewith his central explanatory assumptions. Hume's treatment of cause and effect precluded the notion that we could know a divine design in the make of things, a project carried over into his treatment of the passions. In this respect Hume's general intentions resembled Hobbes': but unlike Hobbes he drew radical inferences for explanation in morals and politics. Hume explained ethical distinctions in a way that made no use of God as a legislator and which referred them instead to the make of human nature and to social usefulness. He referred the human artifice of government not to human necessity and to God's intentions but to necessity and utility. Hume's thought is thus radically anti-teleological, a posture complemented by his picture of English history as a process in which the political and social values that his contemporaries prized arose from the intentions of neither God nor man but from caprice and contingency.

The implication of this view is that mankind is not obviously responsible to God. How such a view came to achieve prominence is as much a matter to do with historical changes like the destruction of the ancien regime, the industrial revolution, urbanisation and the character of mass education as it is to do with the work of any thinker or thinkers. It is again, worth reflecting just how many of the world's population would subscribe to theological explanations, albeit not necessarily ones that have Christian resonances. But Hume embodied a range of conceptions that have achieved a pervasive place in western thought and which, by effectively extruding the Deity, suggest that mankind is to be directed not by God but by itself.

This is, in other words, a change in the sorts of reasons for action that can be offered. In the absence of a direction beyond human devices, the question of how to act becomes a matter of preference: reason, in Hume's famous phrase, is the slave of the passions. One might be disposed to suggest, on the other hand, that Locke's own account of reason admits of a like conclusion. After all, to treat reason as a faculty or to think of its exercise as connecting ideas does nothing to prevent it from being a tool of desire. The difference of direction lies elsewhere. Locke treated God as a fact of existence, whose reality makes all the difference to where human conduct *ought* to be directed. Whilst recognising that reason can be the slave of the passions, he did not share Hume's sense that it *ought* to be.

This is not merely a matter of saying that there are some elements in his writings that are recognisably modern and others that are not. It is something rather more important than that. It is more salient to Locke's own concerns and more relevant to wider problems that Locke's writings indicate difficulties. They raise questions about the importance of reason to moral and political thought, whether of moral obligation or political responsibility, and crucially of the character of autonomy, problems which they do nothing to answer and which are with us still. For in many ways the terms in which contemporary thought is set derives from the seventeenth and eighteenth centuries. That the derivation is as much by rejection of some early modern views as by by acceptance of others does not affect this fact. Reflection on contemporary difficulties may suggest either that we should revise our intellectual expectations or that we should seek a new scheme of thought.

Notes

INTRODUCTION

1 Leo Strauss (1953); C.B.Macpherson (1962).

2 Strauss discounted the evidence of Locke's *Essays on the Law of Nature* (which were published after his own book was issued), in his essay on 'Locke's Doctrine of Natural Law' in his (1959), pp.197–220. Macpherson, it should be said, handled a wider range of texts.

3 Amongst critiques of Macpherson and Strauss, see John W.Yolton (1958), pp.477–98, Peter Laslett, (1964), pp.150–4, Alan Ryan, (1965), pp.219–30.

4 John Dunn (1969), cf. (1985), pt.i, (1990) ch.1; Geraint Parry (1978), Francesco Fagiani (1983), esp. chs.3 and 4, Patrick Riley (1982), ch.3, Alan Ryan (1984), ch.1. See also Raymond Polin (1960) and Charles Taylor (1989), ch.14.

5 Cf. especially, in different ways, Julian Franklin (1978), James Tully (1980), Mark Goldie (1983), Richard Ashcraft (1986, 1987).

6 This is not to say that there have been no general works: for two significant examples, see John Dunn (1984) and John W.Yolton (1985).

7 For an anthology of recent work on Locke's *Epistola*, see John Horton and Susan Mendus (eds.) (1991), with bibliography, and for a treatment of Locke's political theory that includes his views on toleration, see James Tully (1991) in Burns (ed.) (1991). Philip Abrams' edition of John Locke *Two Tracts on Government* (Cambridge, 1967), however, has a more inclusive approach.

8 James Gibson (1917).

9 It should not be forgotten that Gibson wrote long before the recovery of Locke's *Essays on the Law of Nature* and his drafts for *An Essay concerning Human Understanding*: for the degree to which the publication of *Draft B* affected Gibson's perspective, see (1933), pp.29–51.

10 R.I.Aaron (1971) where morals and politics are placed in pt.iii of the book.

11 John W.Yolton (1970), G.A.J.Rogers (1981) in Brandt (ed.) (1981), pp.146–62 and Michael Ayers (1991), esp vol. II.

12 The principal exception is P.H.Nidditch and G.A.J.Rogers (eds.), *John Locke: Drafts for the Essay concerning Human Understanding, and other Philosophical Writings*, vol. I (Oxford, 1990); for Locke's philosophy and his educational views, cf. John W. and Jean S. Yolton (eds.), *John Locke: Some Thoughts concerning Education* (Oxford, 1989).

13 For mixed modes and *Two Treatises*, see Tully (1980), ch.4 and Ruth W. Grant (1987), ch.1.

14 Especially Abrams' edition of *Two Tracts* (see n.7 *above*), Wolfgang Von Leyden's edition of *Essays on the Law of Nature* (Oxford, 1954), and Patrick Kelly (ed.), *Locke on Money* (2 vols., Oxford, 1991), and A.W.-Wainwright (ed) *A Paraphrase and Notes on the Epistles of St.Paul* (2 vols, Oxford, 1987)

15 See esp. E.S.de Beer (ed.), *The Correspondence of John Locke* (8 vols., Oxford, 1976–89, with an index volume by other hands to follow). Forthcoming work include Henry Schankula's edition of Locke's journal and John Biddle-Higgins' of *The Reasonableness of Christianity*.

16 Conveniently possible through Roland Hall and Roger Woolhouse (1983), which covers 1900–80, with annual updates in the *Locke Newsletter*. For a sample of the journal literature, see Richard Ashcraft (ed.) (1991).

17 *Pace* Peter Laslett's treatment in s.4 of the introduction to his edition of *Two Treatises of Government* (second edn, Cambridge, 1967).

18 The *logical* relationship between the first and second books of *Two Treatises* is, of course, distinct from the question of which Locke wrote first.

19 See the collections of his writings, (1969, 1976, 1979, 1991).

20 For their influence in England at a later period, cf. R.W.Church (1891), p.3 on the rural incumbent: 'When communication was so difficult and infrequent, he filled a place in the country life of England that no one else could fill. He was often the patriarch of his parish, its ruler, its doctor, its lawyer, its magistrate, as well as its teacher, before whom vice trembled and rebellion dared not show itself.' But see too C.J.Sommerville (1992).

21 *The Reasonableness of Christianity*, pp.272f.

22 This is a study of Locke's mind, not of his sources and for that reason does not attempt to show that he drew this or that idea from someone else. There are general and particular reasons for this. The general reason is that the state of our understanding of the thought of Restoration England, and of seventeenth-century British thought generally, takes place often in categories that have a limited explanatory use and are sometimes suspect in themselves: for an astringent treatment of one of these, see John Spurr (1988a). In any case a treatment of Locke done purely in terms of schools of thought (or, as the misleading phrase often is, in terms of context) is likely to yield chiefly the negative result that Locke belonged to no one school. The particular reason is that a treatment of sources is unlikely to do justice to Locke's purposes. In any case, we have been told very frequently that there are few new ideas in Locke's political theory: if so we should attend to the way in which he used them to argue for his political purpose. Besides, Locke's 'borrowings' may turn out not to be such on further examination: compare Franklin (1978) with Conal Condren (1990).

CHAPTER 1

1 Assembly of Divines (London, 1647), pp.34ff; J.H.Blunt (ed.) (1893), p.467f; for Crooke see s.3 of this chapter; Gabriel Towerson, *An Explication of the Decalogue* in (1676), fifth commandment.

2 Humphrey Sydenham (1637), pp.135; Sir John Fortescue (1869), pt.ii, ch.lix.

3   See below ch.3, p.78-81 for Locke's treatment of God's superiority in terms of wisdom and power; Henry King (1621), pp.25, 27.

4   For the terms in which Locke's revision of political superiority was cast see chs.6-7, esp. pp.170-9, 212-14.

5   Sir John Cheke (1807-8), vol.III, p.993; James I, *The Trew Law of Free Monarchies* in James I (1918), p.55; *Speach in the Starre-Chamber* (20 June, 1616), James I (1918), p.341, see also James I *Basilikon Doron* in (1918), p.39; for the church, see below, pp.163,363n.5.

6   For a patriarchal use, see Sir Robert Filmer, *Patriarcha*, ch.1.10 in Filmer (1991), p.12.

7   Locke's reassessment of political superiority is set out at length in chs.6-7 below. Locke revised neither God's supreme place in the hierarchy nor the social order, except insofar as is politically relevant. More radical revisions might be possible in principle: cf. 'Conclusion', pp.323-5 below.

8   James I, *Basilikon Doron*, p.23. See also p.36.

9   All biographical data in this chapter, unless otherwise stated, is from Maurice Cranston (1957), ch.1.

10 *Two Treatises of Government*, II.v.43, p.316.

11 *Ibid.*

12 *Ibid.*, II.v.40, p.314.

13 *Ibid.*, II.v.42, p.315; *ibid.* II.v., p.314; *An Essay concerning Human Understanding*, II.xxxii.17, p.390.

14 *Two Treatises*, II.v.42, p.315.

15 *Essays on the Law of Nature*, no.8, fol. 112(210), *Nobiscum non nascitur vestitus*. In 1679 Locke listed first amongst the evidence showing that man was superior to animals that he alone wore clothes. See his 1661 Commonplace Book, p.52, *Homo*, 79.

16 Thirsk (ed.) (1985), pt.i, p.375.

17 *Ibid.*, pt.i, pp.375, 370.

18 *Ibid.*, p.360.

19 T.G.Barnes (1961a), p.2n.1, cf. A.J.Howard and T.L.Stoate (eds.) (1975). David Underdown (1985), appendix i.

20 K.G.Ponting (1957), pp.26, 112.

21 Eric Kerridge (1985), p.25 and p.263n.6; for population, a report of 1623 cited in Joan Thirsk (ed.) (1967), p.80.

22 The former estimate is from Gregory King and was accepted by Robert Trow-Smith (1957), p.233. The latter is recorded in R.H.Tawney and Eileen Power (eds.) (1924), vol.I, p.180. For a brief synopsis of Somerset farming, see David Underdown (1973), pp.13ff and at greater length Thirsk (ed.) (1967), ch.1.6 and (1985), pt.i, ch.11.

23 D.W.Jones (1972), pp.567-87 and for the channelling of west country wool through Blackwater Hall, Julia de Lacy Mann (1971), pp.64-8.

24 W.G.Ward (1953), p.9.

25 For the industrial importance of wool, see P.J.Bowden (1962), *passim* and D.C.Coleman (London, 1975), pp.25-32; for the significance of the west country, Bowden (1962), p.45; for its wool, Bowden (1962), p.33; for broadcloth G.D.Ramsay (1943), p.1.

26 Bowden (1962), p.33.

27 These details are drawn from Mann (1971), ch.10, but the point about E.Somerset wool comes from p.10. See also Kerridge (1985), ch.1.

28 Mann (1971), app.iii, tables e and f; Kerridge (1985), p.240. The first figure may be an underestimate, cf. Mann, p.34.

29 Ponting (1957), p.74; cf. Kerridge (1985), p.169 on the spinning wheel.

30 D.C.Coleman, 'Textile Growth' in N.B.Harte and K.G.Ponting (eds.) (1971), pp.1–20 at p.7.

31 The labour-intensive character of the process is evoked in a poem from 1641 about the wool trade of Shepton Mallet: 'At first, the Parter, that doth neatly cull / The finer from the coarser sort of wool. / The Dyer then in order next doth stand, / With sweating brow, and a laborious hand. / With oil they then asperge it, which, being done, / The careful hand of Mixers round it run. / The Stockcarder his arms doth hard employ, / (Remembering Friday is our market day:) / Then the Knee-carder doth (without control) / Quickly convert it to a lesser roll. / Which done, the Spinster doth in hand it take, / And of two hundred rolls one thread doth make. / The weaver next doth warp and weave the chain, / . . . and cries, come boys, with quills. / Being filled, the Brayer doth it mundify, / From oil and dirt that in the same doth lie. / The Burder then (yea, thousands in this place), / The thick-set weed with nimble hand doth chase. /. . ./ The Fuller then close by his stock doth stand, / And will not once shake Morpheus by the hand. / The Rower next his arms lifts up on high, / And near him sings the Shearman merrily. / The Drawer last, that many faults doth hide, / (Whom Merchant nor the Weaver can abide), / Yet he is one in most cloths stops more holes/ Then there be stairs to the top of St Paul's.' From Watts, *The Young Man's Looking Glasse*, pp.42–4 in *Victoria County History: Somerset*, vol. II, pp.411f; Locke *Two Treatises*, II.v.42, p.315.

32 'An Essay concerning Toleration', p.103, cf. *Two Treatises*, II.v.42, p.315f and 'For a Generally Naturalization' (1693), *Locke on Money*, vol. II, pp.487–92.

33 Bowden (1962), p.46, cf. *Victoria County History Wiltshire*, vol. IV, pp.148–55; for the severity of the depression Mann (1971), p.102.

34 Bowden (1956), pp.56–7, cf. Mann (1971), pp.xivf. Though vital to the trade this was not so helpful to the growers (see the complaint of 1684 quoted in Bowden (1962), p.216).

35 Ramsay (1943), p.103, cf. pp.112, 114–16 and M.Priestley (1951), pp.46–7; Kerridge (1985), pp.38–9 for its diffusion. Its success was due to its superior texture, Ramsay (1943), p.106.

36 Noted in Barry Supple (1959), p.149. Mann observes that there is no evidence for its use earlier in any other county (1971), p.xvii, cf. Kerridge (1985), p.35.

37 For conditions in general, cf. Ramsay (1943), chs.3,7, Supple (1959), chs.2–3, 5–7; for the sources of wool, Bowden (1962) pp.58ff, 61f, cf.pp.208 and 89n.4, Kerridge (1985), p.35. The area south of Bristol obtained wool from Gloucester, see T.S.Willan (1938), pp.168–75; for foreign artisans, cf. Kerridge (1985), pp.145f. It is worth nothing that Spanish wool lost only 12 percent in scouring, where English lost 28 percent (Mann (1971), p.285).

38 Thirsk (ed.) (1985) pt.i, pp.387f. For the oak woodlands of N.Somerset, Underdown (1985), p.7 citing other literature.

39 Thirsk (ed.), pt.i, p.382. For Peter Locke as a tanner, Ms.Locke b.5, fol.12 (dating from 1668).

40 Ms.Locke, c.25, fol.6 (John Locke senior's will, dated 7 February, 1660, endorsed on the back 'J. *Locke* 15 Dec *60*'). How 'convenient' this item really was, is not clear; the will shows that the furnace was on loan to one William Heale.

41 Ms.Locke, f.12, p.5. This entry dates from 1665.

42 Shaftesbury to Locke, 20 March, 1680, *Correspondence*, no.532 (vol. II, p.161). There may be some antiepiscopal point here, cf. Locke's Presbyterian antecedents in ch.2, s.1 below.

43 *Two Treatises*, II.v.42, p.315. The phrase 'the ordinary provisions of life' comes from this passage.

44 Thirsk (ed.) (1985), pt.i, p.364.

45 Barnes (1961a), ch.5; *Two Treatises*, II.v.42, p.315; II.v.37, p.312.

46 Kerridge (1985), p.203.

47 Cf. D.C.Coleman (1960), *passim* and (1975), pp.23–34; for the west country (1975), p.27.

48 Kerridge (1985), p.195; the last figure is from Thirsk (ed.) (1967), p.425.

49 Kerridge (1985), p.230; and p.206 for evidence that foreigners worked more cheaply.

50 Herbert, 'The Church Porch', line 91 from *The Temple* in Herbert (1974); Herbert (1986), ch.32, p.230. In Locke's 1661 Commonplace Book, p.16 the heading *Paupertas* is accompanied by the quotation 'Sloth' from *Proverbs*, 6.6; on p.22 *Divitia* is accompanied by 'Diligence' from *Proverbs*, 10.4.

51 Samuel Crooke, 'A Short Prayer for the Morning' in (1614b), D_4, p.58.

52 For examples see Underdown (1985), pp.36f; cf Beier (1986).

53 Cranston (1957) p.474.

54 Paul Slack (1974), pp.360–79 at pp.374–5, cf. John Patten (1973), pp.23–4, 30.

55 Slack (1974), pp.364–6; for further details about the west country, cf. Slack (1972) in P.Clark and P.Slack (eds.) (1972), pp.164–203.

56 See the evidence in Underdown (1985), pp.47, 49. G.R.Quaife, however, in his (1979), pp.84–7 finds no connection between revels and illegitimacy: but see also R.L.Greaves (1981), pp.214, 466–7. Much illegitimacy appears to have resulted from broken marriage contracts amongst servants. See P.Laslett, K.Oosterveen and R.M.Smith (eds.) (1980), chs. 1–3, 5–6.

57 The list is in T.G.Barnes (1959), p.109 n.1 and add one for 1612 (Underdown (1985), p.49 n.21). The description of 'feasting, dancing and strenuous exercises' is Barnes' (p.107).

58 E.H.Bates [Harbin] (ed.) (1907–19), vol. III, p.285. For other examples as late as this cf. pp.302, 324.

59 For 'obedience' and 'duty' see Richard Cust and Peter Lake (1981), p.45; for the cloth-making district, cf. Underdown (1985), p.84 and note 49; for a more general linkage of depression to crime see J.S.Cockburn (1977) in Cockburn(ed.) (1977), pp.49–71; for general concern, Keith Wrightson (1981) in Yeo and Yeo (eds.) (1981), ch.1.

60 Underdown (1985), pp.15–17.

61 For an account noting regional differences, see Keith Wrightson (1982), pp.125–45; for the figures on mobility see P.Spufford (1973–4) and P.Clark (1974) and Slack (1974); for some examples see Julian Cornwall (1967), pp.146, 150; Keith Wrightson and David Levine (1979), p.76; Peter Clark (1972) in Clark and Slack(eds.) (1972), p.127.

62 Underdown (1985), pp.100–3; and for the local variant in Somerset and Wiltshire, the skimmington, see Martin Ingram (1981), pp.251–64; for evidence of magisterial concurrence, Anthony Fletcher (1986), pp.71ff.

63 Samuel Crooke (1614a), s.8, p.28; Locke *Some Thoughts concerning Education*, s.56, pp.115f, cf. *Directions concerning Education*, s.50, p.61 and Ms.Locke, f.3, p.201 (15 July, 1678) and pp.381–2 (12 December, 1678).

64 *Some Thoughts concerning Education*, s.33, p.103.

65 *Ibid.* s.38, pp.107f; s.45, p.111.

66 Cf. *ibid.*, s.39, p.144 'The *younger* they are, the less, I think, are their unruly and disorderly Appetites to be complied with; and the less Reason they have of their own, the more are they to be under the Absolute Power and Restraint of those, in whose Hands they are'; and compare the passage at s.40, p.109 with that in Cranston (1957), p.12; and see *Proverbs*, 13.24 cited in Locke's 1661 Commonplace Book, p.44.

67 *Two Treatises*, II. vi., esp. s.58, p.324.

68 *Venditio*, 1695 (1661 Commonplace Book, p.268): 'Upon demand what is the measure that ought to regulate the price for wch any one sells soe as to keep it with in the bounds of equity & justice, I suppose it in short is this. The market price at the place where he sels. Whosoever keeps to yt in what ever he sels I think is free from cheat, extorsion or oppression or any guilt in whatever he sels, supposeing noe fallacy in his wares.'

69 according to Anon (ed.) (1966), p.38 in 1633–4 charitable bequests of £4–11–6 and 10s-1d were made, some of which seems to have been spent on Irish vagrants; £4–10–0 was spent on bread and wine for a year (p.31). For Locke's bequest Cranston (1957), p.474; he also left money for the poor of High Laver, Essex (near Oates, where he was living); for further details of Locke's charitable activities see Ms. Locke, c.25, fols.67–9 (High Laver 1702–3) and c.26, fol.38 (Pensford, 1665), noting his insistence on the industriousness of the poor. The 1661 Commonplace Book at p.38 has beside *Liberalitas* a quotation from *Proverbs*, 11.25, 'The liberall soule shall be made fat.' For Locke's view of the proper extent of charity see the present writer's (1994). It is worth noting that masters in textiles were obliged to support their sick workers, see Kerridge (1985), p.205.

70 Crooke (1614b), s.27; *Epistola de Tolerantia*, p.134.

71 John Aubrey (1862), p.266. Aubrey was writing of Wiltshire, but the contrast of the 'Cheese' and the 'Chalk' is elaborated more generally by Underdown (1985), esp. ch.4 (cf. p.72 and the map on p.87); for some limitations on the application of this thesis see Martin Ingram (1987), pp.101–3 and Collinson (1988) p.153f.

72 'Daily orator' W.G. (1662), p.45; 'vulgar auditories' William Thomas *et al.* (1653), p.5 and cf. Patrick Collinson (1982), p.97; popularity Thomas *et al.* (1653), p.67.

73 Crooke (1614b), epigraph; he also recommended instruction at home to supplement preaching, cf. (1614a) and (1614b), both A$_2$. *Some Thoughts concerning Education*, s. 2, 1, pp.83–4. At the top of many of the pages in the 1661 Commonplace Book (from pp.6 to 52) Locke noted aphorisms from the Book of Proverbs.

74 For preserving, cf. *Life*, p.36; for popularity *ibid.*, p.53.

75 (1614a), s.24, p.89; for the Two Tables generally, cf. J.S.McGee (1976).

76 (1614a), s.24, p.90.

77 *Ibid.* s.30, pp.110, 112; (1614b), s.30, p.31. It is not clear that either a duty not to kill or a duty to preserve need forbid doing harm, provided the harm neither killed nor impaired preservation. But for this understanding of the directive cf. the material in John Dunn (1969), p.88n.3.

78 5th: (1614b), s.29 p.30; cf. (1614a), s.29, p.107.
   8th: (1614b), s.32; cf. (1614a), s.32, p.117.
   10th: (1614b), s.34, p.36; cf. (1614a), s.34, p.124.
   7th: (1614b), s.31, pp.31f; cf. (1614a), s.31, p.115.
   9th: (1614b), s.33, p.33; cf. (1614a), s.33, p.121.

79 Crooke (1658) pt. i, ch.5, p.30.

80 Assembly of Divines (1643) Crooke (1613) in (1615), B$_3$; John Winthrop quoted in E.S.Morgan (1958), p.38; Thomas Hooker (1656), p.63; Thomas Shepard (1972), pp.41f.

81 *Two Treatises*, II.ii.11, p.292, *pace* Laslett *ad loc*.

82 Crooke (1614a), s.23 p.87, cf. s.6 p.20.

83 Crooke (1658), p.30.

84 E.g., Robert Filmer (1991), p.210; or, again, we might distinguish between the law of nature as what was not only discoverable but also performable by man's natural capacities without special assistance, as with John Winthrop (1963), pp.196f.

85 Crooke (1614a), s.3, p.3, (1614b), s.3, p.11; Sir Thomas Browne (1955); Nathanael Cole (1618), p.69. See also John Donne, (1953–62), vol. VI, pp.297f and Richard Sibbes (1639), p.19. Examples could be multiplied.

86 Benjamin Whichcote (1930), no.321, p.39; Ralph Cudworth (1678), p.886. Of course this does not preclude that we should honour God: cf. the continuation of the passage in Browne, n.85 above.

87 See for examples Arnold Williams (1948), pp.73–4 and the literature cited there. Locke, *An Essay concerning Human Understanding*, I.i.1, p.43. Crooke (1614a), s.6, pp.18f. Cf. Milton, *Paradise Lost* (in Milton (1952–5), bk. VIII, 1.440 'Expressing well the spirit within thee true/ My image, not imparted to the Brute.'

88 Milton, VIII, 445, 450–1; Locke, *Two Treatises*, II.vii.77, p.336; Donne (1953–62), vol. II, 279, cf. e.g., vol. V, 113, vol. VI, 81, vol. VIII, 155. Petty (1927), vol. II, p.49 and cf. (1928), p.154.

89 Crooke (1614a), s.6, pp.18ff; Richard Sibbes (1638), vol. II, 255; Cudworth (1647), p.19.

90 Milton (1642) in Milton (1931–8), III, p.260; *I Corinthians*, 13.5; John Preston (1639), pt. i, p.58.

91 Francis Quarles (1640), F$_2$; Richard Sibbes (1639), p.17.

92 Arthur Lake (1629), vol. I, pp.18f; John Preston (1639), pp.8f; Cudworth (1647), p.19.

93 Jeremy Taylor (1656) in Taylor (1847–54), vol. VII, p.563.

94 *Two Treatises*, I.iv.23, p.174, quoting Genesis, 1,28. The phrase 'great and primary Blessing' comes from *Two Treatises*, I.iv.33, p.182.

95 Crooke (1614a), Preface, s.4; s.1, p.1. See also (1613), B₃.

96 Edmund Spenser (1596), II.ix.2, p.1.

97 George Herbert, 'Faith', line 32; St Jerome, cited in Robert Sanderson (1627), p.116; Crooke (1658), pt.ii, ch.3, p.602.

98 Crooke (1614b), s.17, p.18, cf. (1614a), s.17, p.60.

99 For original sin (1614a), s.7, pp.23f; for the definition of sin, s.8, p.24; for 'actuall sinne', s.8, p.26; for concupiscence, s.8, p.25; for enmitie (1614b), s.8, p.8, cf. *Guide*, s.8, p.24; for hereditary disease (1658), pt. ii, ch.2, p.586, cf. ch.5, p.619.

100 (1614a), s.8, p.28.

101 (1614b), s.12, p.12, cf. (1614a), s.12, p.45.

102 (1614b), s.19, p.20, cf. (1614a), s.19, p.67; for Crooke as a daily orator cf. W.G. (1662), p.45; for his lectures W.G. (1662), pp.39f; Anon (ed.) (1966), p.31.

103 *Essays on the Law of Nature*, no.5, fols.74f (172); no.4 fol.61 (156/8).

104 For justice as necessary to society, no.8, fol.115 (212); no.8 fol. 118 (214) *ut omnia uno verbo complector, faelicitas, 'Morality'* (Ms Locke, c.28, fols.139–40 at 139).

105 *Essays*, no.4, fols.60f (156).

106 *Essays*, no.4, fol.61 (158). For *Two Treatises*, see generally Ian Harris (1994).

107 *Essays*, no.7, fol.95 (194) and cf. *An Essay concerning Human Understanding* I.iv.7, p.87; *Essays on the Law of Nature*, no.2, fol.27 (128), cf. *An Essay concerning Human Understanding*, I.iii.5, p.68.

108 *Essays on the Law of Nature*, no.1, fol.16 (114); no.5, fols.66f (164); no.4, fol.47 (146), see also. fol.56 (154) and cf. no.5, fol.78 (174).

109 *The Reasonableness of Christianity*, pp.14, 24f, 193.

110 See Ingram (1987), ch.4 and pt. ii *passim*. This study concerns Wiltshire, Sussex and Ely, but for related views see R.A.Marchant (1972), pp.1–11, 243 *et passim* and Ralph Houlbrooke (1979), p.271; and for the diocese of Bath and Wells in particular Margaret Stieg (1982), p.223. For Nicholas Locke, see F.A.Wood (1903) p.166

111 *Two Treatises*, 'The Preface', p.156; for some remarks on the reception of the clerical message in a broad if not precise way, see Ingram (1987), pp.93–8.

112 Crooke (1614b), s.19, p.20.

113 'An Essay concerning Toleration', p.91.

114 *An Essay concerning Human Understanding* I.iii.6, p.69.

115 'honest and civilised', Sir Richard Cocks, 1694, cited by Fletcher (1986), p.169; *A Second Letter concerning Toleration Works*, vol. II, p.356, cf. *English Tract*, p.3 (138), *Latin Tract*, p.6 (194/223).

116 Milton, *Paradise Lost*, IX, 11. 1121–6; for the magistrate as head cf. James I's utterances collected by C.H.McIlwain in James I (1918), p.xxxv.

117 *Latin Tract*, p.11 (200) *mortales inter se quasi in unum corpus coalescant*;
    Hobbes, (1983) V.9 p.89; Hobbes (1651), ch.17; cf. Bodin (1576), III.7;
    Two Treatises
    II.viii.95, p.349; for the corporal metaphor, see also, II.xii.145, 151,
    pp.383, 386.
118 Richard Hooker (1977–82), I.x.1; *Latin Tract*, p.11 (201), *in omni republica
    debet esse aliqua suprema potestas sine qua res publica esse non potest.*
119 Cf., n.105, n.107 above.
120 Cranston (1957), p.10 says merely that he was clerk to the JPs. But he
    appears not to have been one of the two official clerks to the JPs in the
    county, not being numbered with those listed in T.G.Barnes (1961b),
    pp.7–10. On the other hand, the contents of his memoranda book for
    1630–55 (British Library, Add.Mss.28273) correspond closely to the preoc-
    cupations recorded for the clerks of the individual justices, *ibid.*, p.11.
    J.S.Cockburn (ed.) (1971), no. 162 records under 18 December 1654 that
    'Mr John Locke of Penseford' was to 'grant replevins' at the county court.
121 J.H.Gleason (1969), esp. ch.7. Memoranda Book: bastardy, pp.4–5, cf. 6–
    7; drink pp.1, 13–15, cf. 137; poor 9–10, cf. 8; trade 2; hospitals 46–51, 60;
    for the Mendips Bates [Harbin] (1907–19), vol. I, p.xlv; for alehouses in
    general Peter Clark (1983), chs. 3–7; for Cannington Hundred,
    J.S.Cockburn (ed.) (1976), p.252.
122 For instance the memoranda book records at p.35 an assize order for 1630
    for a bridge to be repaired. Since on 30 July, 1632 Richardson CJ noted
    that Robert Tucker, titheing man of Ham, had refused to collect a rate to
    repair bridges at Pensford and elsewhere (Cockburn (ed.) (1971), no.254,
    cf. T.G.Barnes (ed.) (1959), no.52) magistrates evidently had to face a
    degree of recalcitrance.
123 See Barnes (ed.) (1959); paupers, nos.5, 14, 16, 21–3, 32, 41, 46, 51, 70,
    75, 80–1, 88–90, 97, 104, 140, 144, 167, 169, 171–4, 186, 188; bastardy,
    nos. 56, 99, 105, 112, 116, 121, 124, 132, 150, 170, 172, 185–6, 188;
    vagrants nos. 23, 42, 70, 108, 144, 184, 186–8; bridges and highways
    nos.1, 19, 36, 44, 50, 52, 65–6, 115, 122, 130; alehouses nos.12, 39, 54, 94,
    181, 186, 188. Note the overlap in categories, esp. nos.170, 172, 186 and
    188.

CHAPTER 2

1 See this chapter, pp.60–77 for Locke's treatment of things indifferent.
  The ensuing account of Stuart politics is meant only as a general sketch of
  tendencies. It pretends to neither originality nor detail.
2 For the significance of 1688, cf. David Ogg (1955b), Clayton Roberts
  (1966), Jennifer Carter (1969) and Henry Horwitz (1969), both in Geoffrey
  Holmes (ed.) (1969), and the essays in Beddard (ed.) (1991).
3 On the financial structure of the state, see Joel Hurstfield (1958), Robert
  Ashton (1960), G.E.Aylmer (1974), Conrad Russell (1973) in Russell (ed)
  (1973), ch.3, J.P.Cooper (1972) C.D.Chandaman (1975) and Russell (1990)
  ch.7.
4 On the variable success of foreign policy, see in general J.R.Jones (1966)

and J.L.Price (1979), and for detailed studies, Keith Feiling (1930), Charles Wilson (1957), K.H.D.Haley (1953) and (1986).

5 See below, ch.7 for a brief analysis of the theoretical position. The classic analysis of first half of the century remains M.A.Judson (1949). For a very clear recent account, see J.P.Sommerville (1986).

6 But see T.Lyon (1937) and W.K.Jordan (1932–40).

7 Below pp.47–59.

8 Kenneth Fincham (1990); Nicholas Tyacke (1987).

9 The most recent and most balanced survey is Ann Hughes (1991).

10 See ch.1, s.4 with s.1 of the present chapter and ch.4

11 John Aubrey (1949), pp.50–1; John Locke *Further Considerations Concerning Raising the Value of Money* in *Locke on Money* vol. II, p.461.

12 Edward Gee (1658), preface s.2 A$_4$.

13 Gee (1658), preface s.2 A$_4$.

14 *English Tract*, p.23(160); [William Sancroft] (1652), D$_5$.

15 *English Tract*, p.1(119).

16 Barnes (1959), esp. pp.110–19; the last quotation is from Underdown (1985), p.67.

17 Stieg (1982), pp.287–309, esp. pp.292f for Peirs' interference at Pensford.

18 Memoranda Book, p.136.

19 *Ibid.*; for N.Somerset lectures of 1630s, *Somerset and Dorset Notes and Queries*, 24(1943–6), p.136; for Peirs' attention to them, Stieg (1982), p.291; for classes, cf. F.A.Wood (1903) p.206; for the conventicle of 1605, Stieg (1982), p.247.

20 Stieg (1982), pp.96f, 115f (and p.148 for the profits laymen had been accustomed to make from the church). It is worth noting that about 25 per cent of Jacobean incumbents 'inherited' their benefice from their father, Collinson (1982), p.115. Presbyterian and other anti-Anglican sentiment might marry with a desire for financial gain from the church. For the west country activities of Cornelius Burges, for example, see David Underdown (1963) pp.18–48, cf. Gauden (1660).

21 For the elder Locke's notes on levies, Memoranda Book, pp.16–27, 36–45, 58–9, 61 and for ship money, pp.89–101. Barnes (1961a), pp.204, 213 and n.5; Underdown (1973), p.17; Barnes (ed.) (1959), no.184, pp.60–1, cf. p.234.

22 For the suffering of the county Ian Roy (1978), esp.pp.128, 141, cf. Underdown (1973), pp.81, 87, 90f, 95, 12f, 128, 135ff, 156; for murder Cockburn (ed.) (1971), nos. 15, 24, 31, 41–3, 45, 49, 53, 55, 57, 60, 66, 75, 95, 137, 142, 152; for bridges nos. 14, 52, 56, 58–9, 63, 93, 97–9, 101, 104–7, 131, 136, 151; for sexual morals, see the evidence in Underdown (1985), p.285; for billeting, Underdown (1973), p.114 and for its burdens, (1985), pp.150–2; for 'ransoms', Memoranda Book, p.119; for poor relief Cockburn (ed.) (1971), no.82.

23 Underdown (1973), pp.81, 86, 133, 135ff.

24 Underdown (1973), p.46; for the clubmen (1985), pp.148ff; and note (Underdown (1973), p.159) the vocal resistance of Richard Mogg to an attempted sequestration, 'I care not a fart from the highest to the lowest of them all, nor for any man in England. 'Tis my house and my goods.'

25 Calvin (1559), I.vii.4; Samuel Petto (1654), pp.71, 26; John Owen (1674),

ii.16. For the possibility that Locke respected Owen, cf. Richard Ashcraft (1986), pp.77n.7.
26 Owen (1850–5), vol. VIII, p.165; Richard Sibbes (1853–62), vol. IV, p.225; for the conjunction of the Spirit and the Word, G.F.Nuttall (1946), Ch.1, s.1–2; Thomas Burton (1828), vol. I, p.69, cf. pp.76, 86.
27 Quaife (1979), p.64; Gertrude Huehns (1951), p.66 (and see ch.6, esp p.98 for the anarchic implications of antinomianism); for a concise account of radical religion in the Interregnum, see J.F.McGregor and B.Reay (eds.) (1984), esp. chs.2, 5–6; for the Somerset ranters, Underdown (1985), p.249.
28 Fox (1952), p.34; Fox (1656), p.12; George Bishop [really Fox] (1657), p.20; Fox (1952), p.260; for outward testimony and natural reason, Robert Barclay (1678), proposition ii; Fox (1952), p.21, cf. pp.110, 369, etc.; for social reorganisation, T.L.Underwood, 'Early Quaker Eschatology' (1970) in Peter Toon (ed.) (1970), p.98; for conscience, Barry Reay (1985), p.34, cf. Fox (1952), p.30.
29 For 'thee' Richard Bauman (1983), ch.4; the quotation is from Fox (1952), p.416; Cockburn (ed.) (1971), pp.46ff; Fuller, cited in Reay (1985), p.58; oaths, Underdown (1985), p.251; for 'magistracy and ministry', Edward Butler (MP for Poole) in Burton (1828), vol. I, p.137.
The view of Reay (1985) and Christopher Hill (1972), that Quaker opinions were chiefly negative, should be qualified by noting that their negations proceeded from their view of the Spirit.
30 For numbers compare W.C.Braithwaite (1979), p.512 with M.R.Watts (1978), p.270 and Reay (1985), p.27; for Oxford see Wood (1891–1900) s.a. 1654 (vol i p.190) and for Bristol, see Ralph Farmer (1656), esp p.45, as well as Blair Worden (1984), pp.199–233 at p.225 and Nuttall (1946), p.131. William Grigge (1658), pp.3f, cf. Ralph Farmer (1654), p.2. For an answer to Grigge see Anon (1658). *Correspondence of John Locke*, no.30, 15 November 1656, Locke to his father (vol. I, p.43) and for another account of Nayler under questioning, see Grigge (1658), esp. pp.6–9. De Beer notes that Grigge was probably a connection of Locke's.
31 'Philanthropoy' (Ms.Locke, c.27 fol.30ᶜ); 'sceane of mirth', *Correspondence of John Locke*, no.59 (vol. I, p.83); for nonsense and self-interest, see *Correspondence*, no.30 (vol. I, p.44): 'after a little pause they [the Quakers] went over the same round, without answering any questions which by the standers by were proposd, and those which by the committee were urgd. I observd they either not answerd or did it with a great deale of suttlety besides the cover and cunning of the language which others and I beleeve they them selves scarce understand'; Fox *et al.* (1654) pp.10f; *English Tract*, preface, p.3 (121). It is worth noting that Fox distanced himself from Naylor, see Fox (1657) pp.3f.
32 *An Essay concerning Human Understanding*, IV.xviii, 2, 5, pp.689, 691f; IV.xix.3, 7, 14, pp.698f, 704; IV.xvii.24, pp.687f.
Quakerism became markedly more conformist after the Restoration, see Christopher Hill (1984), ch.5.v. In particular Barclay's (1678) argued that the immediate action of the Spirit would not in practice supersede reason or the ordinary understanding of scripture. It is interesting to note that after 1678 Locke, who owned a copy of Barclay's book, dropped 'Quaker' and substituted

the generic 'Enthusiast'. Cf. *Draft A*, s.42, p.71 with the corresponding passage of *An Essay concerning Human Understanding*, IV.xx.10, p.713.

33 Bernard Capp (1972), esp. p.68 and Austin Woolrych (1982) pp.31–2, 52, cf. pp.112–13, 148, 209–17; *English Tract*, preface, p.2(120).

34 Reay (1985), p.88, cf. Woolrych (1982), pp.58–9; Grigge (1658), p.34; for Jupiter's log, Reay (1985), p.91.

35 Underdown (1985), pp.247, 244; I.M.Green (1979), p.530; 'utter dislike', Reay (1985), p.97; it is worth noting that part of Grigge's object in exhibiting Naylor (two years after his entry into Bristol) was probably to undermine toleration, see Grigge (1658), p.50 and cf. Anon (1658), pp.3ff; for joint action against Quakers, Underdown (1973), p.188; for Booth's rising, J.F.Maclear (1950), pp.240–70. For the disquiet of a Presbyterian about the sects, albeit one who died in 1658, see Paul Seaver (1985) with J.S.Morrill's review in *History*, 72 (1987), p.343. For the view that the decline of ecclesiastical discipline had encouraged vice, see Richard Allestree (1660), p.31.

36 For liberty and property, Underdown (1973), pp.193–94; for Quakers, Reay (1985), pp.84–8, 95; [Ralph Farmer] (1660), p.6 and cf. Richard Baxter (1660b), p.45 complaining that people allow the Quakers revile the clergy; 'a Pilot', *The Correspondence of John Locke* 8 November, 1659, no.82 (vol. I, p.125); for Lucy Hutchison (1968) p.317; Josselin (1976), pp.457f; [John Fell] (1659), p.15; 'joy and satisfaction', *English Tract*, p.2 (119), cf. *Latin Tract*, p.1 (186). On the other hand T.C. (1660) set out to show *how deeply the Nation resents the thought of Capitulating, now, with his Majestie*
We should add that the instrumental light in which the monarchy was viewed would dissolve the transition between Abrams' 'conservative' Ashcraft's 'radical' Locke, if indeed there is a transition. In 1660 Locke looked to the monarchy to secure peace: later he decided that at least under one king it was unlikely to serve that end. In other words since at neither point in time did he owe allegiance to any given set of political structures for themselves, there is no transition to be explained. What changed was his perception of the monarchy's fitness to his own, distinct end.

37 Samuel Rutherford (1726), pp.6–7.

38 John Buckeridge (1606), pp.6–7; *English Tract*, p.2 (127f).

39 *Ibid.*, p.16 (149), cf. p.27 (166) and for the view of sin underwriting it, p.19 (155); for Perkins (1596) in Thomas F.Merrill (ed.) (1966), pp.31–2; for Crooke, W.G. (1662), p.26; for Cosin's view of Perkins, see G.Ornsby (ed.) (1869–72) vol. I, p.54; for Bagshawe, see (1660), p.16, cf. p.12 and see also (1661), p.7 against '*Drunkenesse*, and other Disorders, which the Apostle *cals Works of the Flesh.*' For religious things indifferent as outward perform-ances, *English Tract*, p.2 (126); for their being subject to the civil magistrate as much as civil things indifferent, p.8 (136), cf. p.19 (153).

40 For the date of the *English Tract*, Abrams in *Locke: Two Tracts*, p.11 (probably before 11 December, 1660); for Locke's career, Cranston (1957), chs. 3 and 5; for his family background and views on Quakers, above ch.2, s.1; for Owen as an enemy of Quakerism, see Henry Stubbe jr. (1659a), p.81.

41 [John Fell] (1659), p.6; John Pearson (1660a), p.2; Bagshawe (1660), preface.

42 John Corbet (1660a), p.16.

43 Corbet (1660a), p.16 cf. Corbet (1660b), p.1.

44 For Ussher, see *The Reduction*, printed in R.B.Knox (1964), pp.26–35; for the failure of the classical movement, see G.R.Abernathy (1965), pp.6–16, cf. R.S.Bosher (1951), pp.28–9, 44–5; for the army, Abernathy (1965), pp.25–34; For Thorndike, Herbert Thorndike (1662), 'To All Christian Readers', A_2; for the Convention, Godfrey Davies (1952), pp.211–35, H.W.Mukerjee (1934), pp.398–403, 417–21, J.R.Jones, (1963), pp.159–77; for Baxter see Richard Baxter (1660a), pp.323f, for Corbet (1660a), p.19, for Reynolds, (London, 1660), p.34 and for Farmer, [Farmer] (1660), p.26; for Sancroft, see William Sancroft (1660), p.37 on the bishops' concern for peace; for the king and Clarendon, Abernathy (1965), p.75, cf. I.M.Green (1978), pp.1–2 and for some obstacles to their policy, cf. R.B.Knox (1967), pp.128–31. It is worth noting that Grigge (1658), p.56 preferred a reduced episcopacy to the abolition of bishops.

45 *Journals of the House of Lords*, 11, pp.179–82.

46 See ch.6 below, for Anglican views; Corbet (1660a), p.111. Roger Thomas (1962) dates the notion of comprehension a little later, but 'Accommodation' was being used in 1660 and Corbet (1660b), p.11 referred to 'an inviolable Union between these Comprehensive Parties'.

47 Corbet (1660b), pp.60f. For Anglican and Presbyterian views on the question of alteration, compare Cornelius Burges *et al.* (1660); John Pearson (1660a); Henry Savage (1660); Cornelius Burges (1660); John Pearson (1660b); for the thirty-four articles, John Pearson (1660a), p.9.

48 Bagshawe (1660), preface and p.2, cf. pp.3f.

49 Perkins (1596) in Merrill (1966), p.41; Bagshawe (1660), p.3, cf. p.12; Bagshawe (1660), p.12; for Presbyterian objections to imposition on similar lines, cf. Cornelius Burges *et al.* (1660), esp pp.33ff; for Locke's treatment of Bagshawe's inferences, see *English Tract*, pp.5–18 (131–53); for Locke's view that the magistrate's authority was founded in scripture, cf. *English Tract*, p.18 (153), *Latin Tract*, p.8 (197/226) and cf. Robert Sanderson (1660), V.xxii–xxiv, pp.150–4; see also *English Tract*, p.32 (171), *Latin Tract*, p.12 (203/33) for the view that the scriptures have little to say about forms of civil government; for tithes, *English Tract*, p.9 (138).

50 *English Tract*, p.10 (140), cf. esp p.21 (157); p.10 (139); for Stubbe, (1659a), s.52, pp.163–5; for Parry (1660), p.3; *Latin Tract*, p.2 (187/213); *English Tract*, p.23 (160).

51 *Correspondence of John Locke*, no. 75 to (?) Henry Stubbe jr (?) September, 1659 (vol. I, pp.110f); *English Tract*, p.23 (160), cf. p.21 (157) and *Latin Tract*, p.2 (187).

52 Sanderson (1660), V.xxiii, pp.152f, cf. VI.xv and xxii, pp.184f, 192f: the quotation is from VI.xvi, p.186, *gravius tamen peccaturum, si errore illo nondum deposito obediret*; see also Richard Allestree (1684) Sermon, V. p.72 and cf. Roger Williams quoted by Abrams (ed.) *Two Tracts*, p.43; *English Tract*, p.14 (145); *Paraphrase and Notes*, II, p.595 and, for earlier admissions of the same point, 'An Essay concerning Toleration', p.86, *Toleratio* (Ms. Locke, d.1, fol.125) and *Epistola de Tolerantia*, pp.106, 108.

53 *English Tract*, p.26 (164), cf. 'An Essay concerning Toleration', p.84;

Bagshawe (1660), p.12; Corbet (1660a), p.73, cf. p.16; *Latin Tract*, pp.8f (197/226f); for the date of *Latin Tract*, see Abrams, *Two Tracts*, p.16.

54 Bagshawe (1662a), preface; Samuel Parker (1670), esp. the preface.

55 For anti-Presbyterianism, Abernathy (1965), p.78, cf. Bosher (1951), pp.140–1, 204–6, 212–13, 256–7; for the resumption of ecclesiastical control, Green (1978), chs.3–6; for the Savoy, Richard Baxter (1696), pt. ii, p.357; for the ejected, A.G.Matthews (1934), pp.xii–xiv; for an example of their scruples of conscience, cf. Pepys' Dr Bates (entry of 17 August, 1662 in Pepys (1970–83)), 'it is not my opinion, faction, or humour that keeps me from complying with what is required of us, but something which after much prayer, discourse and study yet remains unsatisfied and commands me. Wherefore, if it is my unhappinesse not to receive such an illuminacion as should direct me to do otherwise, I know no reason why men should not pardon me in this world, and am confident that God will pardon me in the next.' At length see Edmund Calamy *et al.* (1663).

56 For *English Tract* on the surplice, p.9 (138), cf. 2 (127); for various aspects of Christ Church and the uses to which they could be turned, cf. Anon (1661), p.15 on cathedral chapters: 'neither *Scripture, Antiquity* nor *Covenant*, forbid or exclude such *Societies* or their *Endowments* . . . Yea in the late times, when some of *those in power* stiffly pleaded the *Covenant for extirpation* of them, to justifie *Sacriledge*, the *Dean and Prebends of Christs Church* in *Oxford*, would not be perswaded to believe themselves concerned in that *Article*, because they stood barely in a *Collegiate Capacity.*'

Anthony Wood (1891–1900), s.a. 1660 noted that 'the first matter. . .that the restored persons looked after was . . . to restore all signes of monarchy in the Universitie, the Common Prayer, surplice and certaine customes'; the significance of this point was evident to the Presbyterians 'whos number was considerable, seeing their disciples dayly fall off, endeavoured to make these matters ridiculous either in their common discourses, libells, or some idle pamphlets that they caused to be dispersed'. For the general significance of sartorial matters in Oxonian church politics, see Wood s.a.1659 on Presbyterians and Independents 'laughing at a man in a cassock or canonicall coat' and on John Owen, who as Vice-Chancellor 'had alwaies his hair powdred, cambric band with larg costly band-strings, velvet jacket, his breeches set round at knee with ribbons pointed, Spanish leather boots with Cambrig tops. And all this was in opposition to a prelaticall cut.' (vol i pp.357f, 300)

57 For Locke's classification, *Latin Tract*, pp.6–8(193–6/222–5); for conscience, p.7 (196/225). Locke's treatment of the fraternal law was an ingenious way of restating a rather more important principle, or rather instancing an example of it, as may be seen by tracing the law back to the principle. The fraternal law was an other-regarding rule. How could one explain it? There is a danger of a man being led against his conscience and thence into sin. One would not like the same to happen to oneself, as it would if one were in his place. In his place one would be dependent on others not to lead one astray. One would like them to act towards one's hypothetical self as one acts towards them. The general principle which subsumes this is therefore 'do unto others as you would have them do unto

you'. We need hardly remind the reader that this is a summation of the Second Table. Locke's subordination of ethics to the magistrate's will is remarkable (and see also 'An Essay concerning Toleration', p.90).

58 Samuel Rutherford (1648), p.262.

59 [A]n necesse sit dari in Ecclesia infallibilem Sacro Sanctae Scripturae interpretem? negatur, long known amongst the Shaftesbury Papers in the P.R.O., and printed fully for the first time with a translation and useful introduction by J.C.Biddle [-Higgins] as 'John Locke's Essay on Infallibility', *Journal of Church and State* 19(1977), pp.301–28. I have amended the translation in places.

60 Richard Field (1847–52), vol. IV, p.304; for transubstantiation see *Draft A*, s.42, p.71, journal 26–8 June, 1676, Ms.Locke, f.1, pp.421–6 (printed in *Essays on the Law of Nature*, p.277), *An Essay concerning Human Understanding*, IV.xx.10, p.713; for the papacy see 'An Essay concerning Toleration', esp. p.96; for the English distaste, see for an introduction to a large literature, John Miller (1973); 'Essay on Infallibility', pp.316–22.

61 Bagshawe (1662b), B_1 and B_3; for his attack on the grounds of infallibility, pp.3–34; for Antichrist, C_1; for the half-title, p.1; for imposing, p.33, cf. B_3 'they ought not to impose upon the Judgment of others, there being nothing more unreasonable than this, that they should *Lord it over the Faith, or Conscientious Perswasion* of other men, who are not certain but that they may Erre and be deceived themselves'.

62 'An Essay concerning Toleration', p.84, cf. p.87 see also *Toleratio*, fol.125 and *Epistola de Tolerantia*, p.94.

63 'Essay on Infallibility', p.326 '*quid . . . praestat ratio, quid spiritus sancti illuminatio non adeo facile et pronum est statuere, maxime autem cavendum est, ne, rationi nostrae nimium confisi, fidem negligamus, et posthabitis evangelii mysteriis pro religione philosophiam amplectamur, ex altera vero parte enthusiasmus caute vitandus, ne dum spiritus sancti afflatum expectamus nostra miremur et veneremus somnia*'.

64 Bagshawe (1662b), B_3; Stubbe (1659b), p.39.

65 For Locke's exchange of views with Towerson, see *Correspondence of John Locke*, nos.104, 106, 108, esp no.106 (?) c.3 November, 1660 Towerson to Locke (vol. I, pp.158f). The date 1664 is given for the final version of *Essays on the Law of Nature* in no.8, fol.119 (214) for 1663 see the editor's remarks pp.11f.

66 Stubbe (1659b), s.xi, pp.92f.

67 *Essays on the Law of Nature*, no.5, fol.79 (176).

CHAPTER 3

1 For Locke's attitude to a clerical career and to other sorts of practical work, see Cranston (1957), chs.6–8.

2 *English Tract*, opening leaf (124), cf. *Essays on the Law of Nature*, no.6, fol.84 (182).

3 *Essays*, no.4, fol.54–5 (153).

4 For creation as production *ex-nihilo*, cf. Hugo Grotius (1616), VI.xi, p.341; Nathaniel Culverwell (1654), p.89, 'Creation being the production

of something out of the barren womb of nothing'; Robert South (1665), p.19 on omnipotence as 'a Power able to fetch up . . . the World, out of the abyss of Vanity and Nothing, and able to throw it back into the same Original Nothing again'; James Ussher (1677), p.75 on creation as the execution of God's decree 'whereby of nothing he made all things very good' and p.76 that 'nothing in Heaven and Earth can give a Being unto a Creature but God'.

5 *Essays*, no.6, fol.85 (184); no.4, fols.55–6 (152), cf. no.4, 58(156/8) alluding to *Romans*, 9, 21–3 on which Locke commented (*Paraphrase and Notes on the Epistles of St Paul* vol. II, p.567) that 'the nations of the world. . .are by a better right in the hands and disposal of god than the clay in the power of the potter may without any question of his justice be made great and glorious, or be pulled down and brought into contempt as he pleases'. Cf. James Ussher (1677), p.82, 'The absolute Authority that God hath over Man; as the Potter hath over his Pots, and much more, Rom 9.21.'

6 'Ethica B', Ms.Locke, c.28, fol.141; *An Essay concerning Human Understanding*, IV.xiii.3, p.651; Locke to Philip van Limborch, *Correspondence of John Locke*, no.2410, 22 March, 1698 (Vol. VI, 355).

7 Most characteristically, of course, in Blackstone, Bentham and Austin.

8 *Essays*, no.4, fol.52 (150).

9 James I, *A Speach in the Starre-Chamber* (20 June, 1616) (1918), p.326.

10 *Essays*, no.4, fol.59 (156).

11 See esp ch.5 and 7 *below*.

12 E.g. *Essays*, no.4, fol.60 (156) *tanto tamque beneficio authore*; for Locke's difficulties with proving God's goodness and for his problems with moral obligation, see ch.8 *below*.

13 For the logic see esp. *Essays*, no.6, fol.84–5 (182); 'Lex naa', Ms.Locke, f.3, pp.201–2, 15 July, 1678; John Flavel (1678), p.182; *Essays*, no.4, fol.61 (156), cf. Ms.Locke, f.1, p.321 (shorthand entry transcribed in *Essays*, p.261) on worship of God, 'whereby we acknowledge His power and sovereignty and our dependence and thankfulness'.

14 *Essays*, no.6, fol.85 (182–4). By this point it should be clear that dependence, whether in respect of God's power of His wisdom, is central to His superiority over mankind. Thus mankind would be dependent on God not only for creation but also for many other purposes. James Tully (1980), a most interesting volume, draws attention helpfully to the idea of creation, but emphasises chiefly one part of Locke's complex of ideas by emphasising God's right through the act of creation (see esp. p.36 (which mentions continued dependence, but no use is made of this)). Certainly creation was important to Locke, but not creation merely in this sense, as the production of mankind and the world. Thus:

(a) Creation in this sense was only part of Locke's usage. He wrote (*Essays*, no.6 fol.85 (184) cf. fol.84 (182) of God, by whom people were made at first are perpetually conserved. Later he referred to God as 'the infinite Author and Preserver of things', *An Essay concerning Human Understanding*, II.i.10, p.108. Cf. also the entry from Ms.Locke, f.1, p.321 in n.13 *above*.

The point is evident from John Colman's odd decision to refer to 'the right of creation' and then to discuss dependence more generally: see (1983), pp.45–6. The usage of a right of creation seems to be limited to one passage within the *Essays* (for instance, *First Treatise*, I.vi.52, p.196 produces a biblical quotation that places our dependence on God in the present tense).

(b) Indeed it was only part of the usage of Locke's day, which dwelt on a much wider range of dependence. Contemporaries dwelt on both creation and subsequent sustenance. For instance John Novell (1662), p.6 referred to God as 'the only just possessor . . . of all Dominion, Government and Rule over the Nations of the world, as their Sole Creator and Upholder' and Gabriel Towerson (1685), pt.ii: *Containing An Explication of the Decalogue*, Discourse One *Of the Law of Nature*, p.2 described God as 'Creator and Sustainer of the world'. Stephen Nye wrote of 'a Creating and Preserving Power', (1696), pt.i, s.6, p.39, whilst John Tillotson observed of God that 'we are all his Creatures, and the Work of his hands, that *it is He that hath made us, and not we our selves*: That He continuously preserves us, and gives us all good things that we enjoy', Sermon 51 in Tillotson (1704), p.609. Most graphically, William Ames (1642), bk. i, ch.9.17, p.41 observed that 'Gods conservation is necessary for the Creature because the Creature doth every way depend upon the Creator, not only as touching its *Fieri* .i. being to be made, but also touching its *Esse, existere, permanere & operari* .i. Being, Existence, Continuance, and operation: so that every Creature should returne into that nothing whereof it was made, if God should not uphold it, and the very cessation of Divine conservation, would without any other operation presently reduce every Creature into nothing.' Grotius (1625), *Prolegomena*, s.11, adds dependence for posthumous rewards.

(c) Contemporaries understood God's right over mankind, therefore, as relating not just to the act of creation but to continuous conservation. Thus, for instance, George Lawson wrote that 'By Creation he began, by Conservation he continued to be actually the Proprietary of all things: for he made them of nothing, and gave them being and existence, so that they wholy always depend upon him and are absolutely his. Therefore he hath power to order them to those ends he created them', (1660), I.i., p.1, and again in (1657), p.150 that 'God. . .createth and preserveth them, so that their being is more his than theirs' cf. (1659), I.viii.16, p.46; Richard Baxter observed that 'GOD is *jure Creationis & Conservationis*, the most absolute Owner or Proprietor of Man and the whole Creation', (1667), pt. i, ch.6, s.4, p.34.

(d) Creation alone does not provide a logical foundation for the wider purposes of God in respect of human life as conceived in Locke's day, for these included the supernatural. It is hard to see how a right deriving from creation alone can give authority to God's *super*natural activities. These may relate to another world and, as they plainly do in the case of the afterlife. A right based on dependence on His continuing support can cover such matters, for that would be required *always* by human beings. For instance, God's supernatural acts included giving revelations. More generally, the afterlife was certainly central to contemporary speculation – for instance, the notion that God could reward the good and punish the wicked in the hereafter. Whilst some writers hoped that these sanctions could be discovered by natural reason, they could scarcely count them as part of the natural world. Locke, of course, eventually came to the conclusion that apprehension of these, and much else, depended upon revelation. See ch.10 below.

15 Locke's lectures on natural law have been re-edited as *Questions concerning the Law of Nature* by Robert Horwitz, Jenny Strauss Clay and Diskin Clay (Ithaca, 1990), but as this revision does not alter the argument of the present volume, Von Leyden's edition will be used here.

16 *Essays*, no.1, fol.11 (110).

17 *Essays*, no.1, fol.12 (110/12).

18 *Essays*, no.4, fols.47–9 (146).

19 *Essays*, no.4, fol.48 (146).

20 *Essays*, no.7, fol.101 (200); *An Essay concerning Human Understanding*, IV.xiii.1, p.650; *Essays*, no.4, fol.48 (146).

21 'An Essay concerning Toleration', p.83.

22 *Essays on the Law of Nature*, no.4, fol.50 (148); fol.48 (146).

23 *An Essay concerning Human Understanding*, IV.xvii.2, p.668.

24 Anthony Wood (1891–1900), s.a.1663 (vol. I, p.472) on Locke at Peter Stahl's chemistry class.

25 Hobbes (1839–45a), ch.25.1.

26 Hobbes (1651), II.xxvi, p.138.

27 For science at Oxford, see the documents collected in R.T.Gunther *et al.* (1923–67); for the experimentalists at Wadham, see Barbara J.Shapiro (1969); for a valuable account of one area, see Robert G. Frank, Jr (1980); on Hobbes, cf. (1839–45a), ch.1.8 for the exclusion of natural history, and generally 25.1; for the air pump, R.E.W.Maddison (1969), pp.92–5, 227–33; for the dispute, Simon Schaffer and Steven Shapin (1985); for Hobbes on the use of science (1839–45a), 1.6–7. For Hobbes as an ecumenical enemy, cf. S.I.Mintz (1962) and Noel Malcolm (1988) in Alan Ryan and G.A.J.Rogers (eds.) (1988); cf. Tuck (1992) in Hunter and Wootton (eds.) (1992).

28 Roger Coke (1660), p.26; William Lucy (1663), chs.12–18. John Bramhall (1677), p.881; John Wallis (1662), pp.11, 6; Lucy (1663), xxi.3, p.155. For criticisms of Hobbes' ethics, to the effect that he maintained that there was no morality in a proper sense, see Robert Sharrock (1660), ch.2, n.5, and John Tillotson, Sermon 3, Tillotson (1704), p.47, attributing to Hobbes the view, 'That Virtue and Vice are arbitrary things founded only in the imaginations of men and in the constitutions and customs of the World, but not in the nature of things themselves.'

29 Robert Boyle (1661) in Boyle (1772), vol. I, p.187.

30 John Donne (1953–62), VII 247 (last emphasis added); William Perkins (1591), A$_7$; Boyle (1686) in Boyle (1744), vol. IV, p.400; (1673) in Boyle (1744), vol. III, p.516; Locke *Some Thoughts concerning Education*, s.192, p.246 'it is evident, that by mere Matter and Motion, none of the great Phaenomena of Nature can be resolved, to instance but in that common one of Gravity, which I think impossible to be explained by any natural Operation of Matter, or any other Law of Motion, but the positive Will of

a Superiour Being, so ordering it. And therefore since the Deluge cannot be well explained without admitting something out of the ordinary course of Nature, I propose it to be considered whether God's altering the Center of gravity in the Earth for a time (a thing as intelligible as gravity it self, which, perhaps a little variation of Causes unknown to us would produce) will not more easily account for *Noah's* Flood, than any *Hypothesis* yet made use of to solve it.' For William Molyneux's construction of this passage, see Molyneux to Locke, *Correspondence of John Locke*, no.2131, 26 September, 1696 (vol. V, 702).

31 Boyle (1686), s.2 in Boyle (1772), vol. V, p.170.
32 *Two Treatises*, II.vi. 57, p.323.
33 Save that if the sovereign threatens the citizen's life, the latter may disobey his commands in the interests of self-preservation (1651), II.xxi, p.112.
34 (1839–45a), ch.25.12–13.
35 See esp. (1651), I.vi, xiii–xvi, II.xvii.
36 Or them: Hobbes supposed that the sovereign could be an assembly as well as an individual, (1651), II.xxvi, p.137. Hobbes' view of representation is integral here, see, e.g., II.xxviii, p.163.
37 (1651), II.xxx, esp. p.175, III.xliii, *passim* and II.xxi, p.109 for David and Uriah.
38 (1651), I.xiv, esp. p.64.
39 I.e., the logic implied is of an exchange of benefits, namely protection for obedience. See further ch.8, p.273 below.
40 It is in his^c eternall Kingdome' that the Hobbesian God provides 'Protection and Life everlasting' (1651), III.xlii, p.285.
41 Esp. (1651), I.xv, p.79.
42 (1651), III.40, II.xxvi, p.137. Note that Hobbes conceived God's actions towards people in this life in terms of the natural consequences of actions (1651), II.xxxi, pp.193f.
43 (1651), I.xi, p.51.
44 (1651), I.xii, p.53.
45 (1651), II.xxxi, pp.190f, I.xi, p.51.
46 (1651), I.i, p.1, I.ii, pp.5f, I.xii, p.53.
47 Cf. generally (1651), I.xi.
48 (1651), II.xxxi, p.190; on the sovereignty of the Jews, cf. III.xlii, p.285, cited n.40 above.
49 (1651), II.xxxi, p.186.
50 (1651), III.xlii, pp.295ff; xliii, p.321.
51 (1651), III.xliii, p.322; for Samuel Crooke, see ch.1, pp.28–43 above.
52 Grotius (1625), I.i.ix.1.
53 Roger Coke (1660), preface on how Hobbes 'does lay down his Principles, and persue his method much more clearly then *Grotius* does' and how '*Grotius* his Principles are so perplexed, and equivocal, that it is not possible for any Man to understand any thing clearly from him'.
54 Aristotle, *Nichomachean Ethics*, VII.14; or so Hooker said.
55 Hooker (1977–82), I.viii.3.
56 Grotius (1625), *prolegomena*, s.18.
57 (1625), I.i.12.

58 Samuel Pufendorf (1672), II.iii.7–8.

59 Hooker (1977–82), I.viii.4.

60 Ralegh (1614), II.iv, s.5, 6, 5, pp.189, 192, 195, 188; for the book's popularity, see Patrides' introduction, p.15n.1, 35f; Hooker (1977–82), I.vii.4.

61 *Essays*, no.2, fol.24 (124); *Correspondence of John Locke*, no. Locke to ? Tom Westrowe (vol. I, p.123); *Essays*, no.1, fol.10 (110).

62 *Essays*, no.4, fols. 53ff (150/2); *An Essay concerning Human Understanding*, IV.x, esp.5, p.5, p.620.

63 Descartes (1641), no.3.

64 Bramhall, (1677), p.871, cf. p.872.

65 (1651), II.xxxi, p.187 'The Right of Nature, whereby God reigneth over men, and punisheth those that break his Lawes, is to be derived, not from his Creating them, as if he required obedience, as of Gratitude for his benefits; but from his *Irresistible Power*. I have formerly shewn, how the Soveraign Right ariseth from Pact: To shew how the same Right may arise from Nature, requires no more, but to shew in what case it is never taken away. seeing all men by Nature had Right to All things, they had Right every one to reigne over all the rest. But because this Right could not be obtained by force, it concerned the safety of every one, laying by that Right, to set up men (with Soveraign Authority) by common consent, to rule and defend them: whereas if there had been any man of Power Irresistible; there had been no reason, why he should not by that Power have ruled, and defended both himselfe, and them, according to his own discretion. To those therefore whose Power is irresistible, the dominion of all men adhaereth naturally by their excellence of power; and consequently it is from that Power, that the Kingdome over men, and the Right of afflicting men at his pleasure, belongeth Naturally to God Almighty; not as Creator, and Gracious; but as Omnipotent.'

66 *Essays*, no.4, fols. 59–60 (156). Hobbes had objected to such a use of creation in the *Third Objections* (see Descartes et al (1647) to Descartes' (1641)): its reassertion was thus an obvious counter-move against him.

67 *Essays* no.2.

68 Locke's view of ideas here had been referred to Gassendi, see F.S. and E.Michael (1989), but the point for our enquiry is Locke requires the mind to do work: for this theme at more length, see ch.5 below.

69 For Fell and education at ChristChurch, see E.G.W.Bill (1988), pp.268–308. John Owen had been friendly to experimental natural philosophy and passingly contemptuous of scholastic efforts, see his (1971), no.2, p.15 (from 1654).

70 Cf. ch.5 below.

71 On the question of scepticism, see generally R.H.Popkin (1979) and for its impact on one British thinker, see Richard Tuck (1989), pts.i–ii and further literature cited therein. For Herbert, see Edward Herbert (1937); for Grotius' reaction to scepticism, see Tuck (1987) in Pagden (1987), pp.99–119 and for some practical effects of scepticism on policy, see Tuck (1988).

72 Grotius (1625), I.i.xii.1–2 for the view that morals considered *a posteriori* are not certain, but nearly so; cf. Grotius (1616), I.i, pp.8f for the

connected concession that he was not interested in the views of nations whose reason had been eclipsed by savagery or wildness.

73 *Essays*, no.4, fol.54 (152) for the certainty of God's existence and of His design of the world; no.5, fols.79–80 (176) for the point that consensus, if it subsisted, would provide opinion, not knowledge (*fides enim est sed non cognitio*).

74 for the Interregnum, see Aubrey (1949) in ch.2 above, p.47; W.G.Batz (1974), pp.663–70 usefully collects data on Locke's anthropological reading.

75 For More, see his (1668); for Descartes' reticence, see G.Rodis-Lewis (1957).

76 *Essays*, no.3, *passim*. Locke doubted in the first place whether this project had met with any success, *ibid.*, fol.38 (136).

77 See apart from *Essays*, no.3, no.5, fol.66–7 (164/6).

78 *Essays*, no.5, fols.68–78 (166–76) for Locke's doubts about whether there was any such agreement. Note too that he picked on the practice of self-preservation, Grotius' candidate for an agreed datum, in *Draft B*, s.6, p.111; and see *An Essay concerning Human Understanding*, I.iii.9, p.70–2 for an especially lurid catalogue of moral variations.

79 Hooker (1977–82), I.viii.3.

80 *Essays on the Law of Nature*, no.5, fol.62 (160); *English Tract*, p.22 (158).

81 cf. ns.77 and 78 above.

82 *Essays*, no.8, fol.119 (214).

83 *Essays*, no.1, fol.11 (110).

84 See esp. *Essays*, nos. 6 and 7.

85 *Essays*, no.4, fol.61 (156/8) '*ad vitae conjunctionem cum aliis nominibus conciliandam et conservandam non solum vitae usu et necessitate impelli, sed ad societatem ineundam propensione quadam naturae incitari eamque tuendam sermonis beneficio et linguae commercio instrui, quantum vero ad se ipsum conservandum obligetur. Cum ad eam officii partem interno instinctu nimium quam impellatur, nemoque repertus sit qui se negligit, se ipsum abdicet, et in hanc rem omnes forte magis attenti sint quam oportet, non opus est ut hic moneam*'.

86 *Essays*, no.8, fol.117 (214). For *amicitia* in this context as sociability or cooperation, cf.Cicero, *De Officiis*, I.xvii.

87 *Eudemian Ethics*, VII.10; *Politics* I.ii.

88 *De Finibus Bonorum ac Malorum*, III.v; *De Officiis*, I.iv.

89 *De Officiis*, I.xliv, cf. on *justum*, I.vi. For *De Officiis* at Christ Church, cf. Bill (1988), pp.276ff.

90 Grotius (1625), I.ii.1; *Prolegomena*, s.17, 7, 8.

91 see *Essays*, no.5, fol.70 (168) where the practice of justice is rational in relation to this end (*omnis societatis vinculo*) and apprehensible by reason (*lege naturae*).

92 *Essays*, no.4, fol.61 (156). That obligation in this passage should be read in this sense is clear from *Two Treatises*, II.vii.77, p.336, 'God . . . put him under strong Obligations of Necessity, convenience and Inclination to drive him into *Society*.'

93 *Essays*, no.8.

94 *Essays*, no.8, fol.107 (204). This should be distinguished from the

historiographical debate as to which of the laws of nature is fundamental for Locke, meaning which is the one from which in his view the rest may be derived. For this see Ian Harris (1994).

95 *Essays*, no.8, fol.109 (206).

96 *Essays*, no.8, fol.107 (204).

97 *Essays*, no.6, fol.85 (182). In no.5, fol.76 (172/4) Locke observed that God's existence and the soul's immortality must be presumed if natural law were to subsist.

98 *Essays*, no.5, fol.80 (176).

99 *Essays*, no.8, fol.108 (206).

100 John Wilkins (1675), preface by Tillotson, A₄. Cf. Locke *Essays*, no.7, fols.99–100 (198) for the argument that natural law relates so closely to human nature that they stand and fall together and therefore, fol.101 (200), no human can abrogate the law of nature.

101 For Crooke, ch.1 *above*; for reason in the restoration, cf. John Spurr (1988b).

102 For *regula morum*, *Essays*, no.1, fol.9 (108); for Locke on faith and reason, see chs.5 and 9 *below*.

103 *Essays*, no.1, fol.17 (116), cf. fol.10 (108), no.6, fol.85 (184), fol.90 (188); no.5, fols.67f (166): but see no.4, fol.51 (154).

104 See generally *Essays*, nos.5 and 6.

105 Cf variously, *Essays* no.6 fol.85 (182), no 1 fol.20 (118) cf n.97 *above*.

106 *Essays*, no.8.

107 *Essays*, no.6, fol.87 (186).

108 *Essays*, no.6, fol.89 (188).

109 *Two Treatises*, II.ii.6, p.289; *An Essay concerning Human Understanding*, IV.iii.18, p.549; IV.xiii.3, p.651.

110 A project which became fashionable a little later in response to the range of problems Locke had identified. See, for example, Richard Cumberland (1672) and Samuel Parker (1681b). The latter (p.iii) attributed to Hobbes the view attacked by Locke, 'That there are no Principles of Good and Evil but onely every Man's Self-interest.' In a different idiom, Henry More's (1668) had similar aims.

111 See esp. Peter Laslett's seminal introduction to his edition of *Two Treatises*, pp.67–91, followed tacitly by many others. This interpretation clearly reacted against Leo Strauss' view of Locke as a closet Hobbist, see his (1953), ch.5(B).

112 'Of Study' (1677) in Axtell (ed.) *Educational Writings of John Locke* (Cambridge, 1968), pp.416f.

113 *An Essay concerning Human Understanding*, I.iii.5, p.68.

114 For Locke's awareness of difficulties in his doctrine of sense experience, cf. the changes between *Draft A*, s.1, *Draft B*, ss.17–18 and *An Essay concerning human Understanding*, II.i.1–3.

115 Bramhall (1677) p.889.

116 But cf *Essays* no.6 fol.85 (184).

CHAPTER 4

1 'An Essay concerning Toleration', p.81 (hereafter 'An Essay'). For a general treatment of the composition of this document, see C.A.Viano (1961), pp.285–311. It may be worth noting that the general view that toleration be allowed to religious worship, subject to protecting civil society, seems to have been current in Locke's circle: see Boyle (1649) in Boyle (1772) vol. IV, p.384; 'the liberty of serving God, by such ways, as are not repugnant to the light, or laws of nature, or the welfare of civil societies, is the common right of mankind, and cannot be denied man, without injustice'. For a general survey of the development of Locke's views on toleration, see Molyneux (1957) and for an important study of their ecclesiastical setting, see Spurr (1991), cf. (1985).

2 see, e.g., Bartholomew Keckermann *Praecognitorum Philosopicorum*, I.ii, in Keckermann (1614), vol. I, cols.16–18.

3 'An Essay', pp.83, 86, 90.

4 see pp.115–17 and chs.6-7 *below*.

5 'An Essay', pp.84f, 83, 85. see also Mackenzie's remarkable (1663) esp pp.10f, 19f (first pagination)

6 'An Essay', pp.94f.

7 'An Essay', pp.83, 86, 90.

8 'An Essay', pp.89, 87.

9 'An Essay', p.89; *Epistola de Tolerantia*, pp.126–30; pp.128, 130 hint at forcible repulsion of the magistrate, but do not authorise it on grounds of religious conscience: the argument is conducted in terms of *civil* interests and their invasion.

10 'An Essay', p.83; pp.88,98. The position admits of some obvious qualifications. See (e.g.) *An Essay* IV.xiii.1-2 pp.650-1, and especially IV.xx.15 p.716.

11 'An Essay', p.84.

12 Samuel Parker (1670), and for the opposite view, see Anon (1668b), p.7 asking whether the civil magistrate should not deal with men 'like rational Creatures, not to persecute them with force and corporal Punishments, and so deal with them like Beasts?'. For the latter view, cf. Locke, 'An Essay', p.98.

13 It does not seem, then, that Locke's view of the relations of intellect and will was *inspired* by the debate Ashcraft supposes (1986), ch.2; and see John Spurr (1988b), pp.563–85 at p.567ns.17–18. In any case Locke did not discuss the matter at length in his two earliest *Drafts* on the human understanding.

14 [Jonas Proast] (1690a), *passim*; Jeremy Waldron (1988b), esp. p.67. This line of thought is examined in Goldie (1991), in Grell *et al.* (1991).

15 'An Essay', p.82.

16 Hooker (1977-82) V.lxxvi.5; Maynwaring (1627) no.1 p.5; Baxter (1680) ch.3 s.15 p.37. '*civill*' is a secular body.

17 This matter is part of a larger frame of mind, for which see 'Conclusion', pp.319–21 below.

18 John Whitgift (1851-3), vol. III, p.592; Anon (1958), p.46; Knox(1949), vol. II, p.271; Knox's *Petition* in Knox (1846–64), vol. IV, p.485; John

Jewel (1845–50) vol. II, p.97, vol. IV, p.1126; for the monarch as keeper of both Tables, see too James I, *Basilikon Doron*, (1918), p.39.

19 Whitgift (1851–3), vols. I, pp.21–2; Vol. III, pp.313 and 360; Hooker (1977–82), VIII.iii.6; VIII.iv.7; VIII.i.2.

20 An Essay, p.91; cf. Two Treatises II.xviii.210 p.423.

21 'An Essay', pp.90, 91; *Epistola de Tolerantia*, p.116 *sub Evangelio nulla prorsus est respublica Christiana*.

22 'An Essay', p.86, and note on p.83 a number of Christian tenets are included amongst purely speculative beliefs.

23 'An Essay', pp.81, 88, 91.

24 Roger L'Estrange alleged that Bagshawe had voided his Studentship by accepting a benefice incompatible with it; see (1662), p.9, whilst Bagshawe (1662a), preface stated that he had been deprived of 'a Freehold I had at *Ch*.Church' For Bagshawe's adventures, see White Kennett (1728), pp.43–4, 603, 681, 703, 741, 784–6, 854, 937. L'Estrange's and Kennett's attention suggests that Bagshawe was not a negligible figure on the national stage, which helps to explain Locke's earlier attention to him.

25 Shaftesbury was styled Lord Ashley when Locke met him, but for the sake of clarity he will be called by his best-known title throughout. For speculations of the relationship, cf. Cranston (1957), chs.9–12, 14–16; for Shaftesbury using Locke's views, cf. K.H.D.Haley (1968), p.288. It has been suggested that the document in question was actually by Locke: see Haley, (1968) pp.391–3 for a discussion.

26 'An Essay', p.100.

27 R.A.Beddard (1979), p.168; C.G.Robertson (1947), p.66.

28 See Pepys (1970–83), vol. VIII, pp.585, 596, .364. For Archbishop Sheldon's lady friends, see Andrew Marvell (1963), in G. de F. Lord *et al.* (eds.) (1963–75), vol. I, p.133. For further evidence of episcopal unpopularity, cf the reprinting of William Prynne (1668), as well as the tracts against bishops, such as (1667b) (which mentions Bishop Peirs, p.9) and (1667c), esp. p.4. For the setting of 1667, see Seaward (1989), and, more generally, Hutton (1983).

29 'An Essay', p.98.

30 'An Essay', p.101. For Presbyterianism in Locke's family background, see ch.2 *above*.

31 'An Essay', pp.95,97; David Ogg (1955a), vol. II, p.412; Haley (1968), pp.268f; 'An Essay', esp pp.95f. For Locke's reasons for distrusting Roman Catholics, see the present writer's (1994), s.2. 'An Essay', p.97.

33 'An Essay', p.97. The multitude of mishaps that befell England in 1666–7 – the Plague, the Great Fire of London, difficulties with Scotland, poor trade, monetary crisis and the Dutch wars – induced a sense of general crisis which the advocates of ecclesiastical relaxation exploited, see [John Humfrey] (1667), p.7; [John Corbet] (1667a), p.26 and Anon (1668b), p.3.

34 'An Essay', p.95.

35 See 'An Essay', p.86 for Locke's reference to the Jews

36 Cf. 'An Essay', p.84, where toleration is of something under the magistrate's authority or, again, p.91.

37 Note that Locke's rhetorical strategy was to emphasise that he stood apart from existing positions on the question, 'An Essay', pp.81f, or was building upon agreed points, 'An Essay', pp.87, 97.

38 See [Robert Perrinchief] (1668b), p.38 (*recte*, p.46); [John Owen] (1667a), p.12, that it was 'only things relating unto *Outward Order and Worship*, wherein our *dissent* from the present *Establishment of Religion*, doth consist', cf.p.15; [Humfrey] (1667), p.19 and Anon (1668c), p.8 for the common recognition of this point. See also Wolseley (1668)

39 See the collection of pamphlets, Bodleian Library B.14.15 Linc p.4. For a version see too the notes in Thorndike (1851–6), vol. V, pp.301–8.

40 B.14.15 Linc, p.18, beginning of August 1667.

41 *ibid.*, pp.9ff.

42 For the Bridgeman/Wilkins proposals, see Roger Thomas (1962), pp.191–253 in G.F.Nuttall and Owen Chadwick (eds.) (1962), pp.198–203. This essay offers a valuable narrative of this and related transactions during the reign of Charles II, to which the present writer is indebted at various points.

43 [Humfrey] (1667), p.8 suggests 'Accommodation' for those 'that are sober in their principles, and Indulgence towards others who are so in their lives: So far I mean as over it will stand with the Rules, both of Civil and Religious Prudence, and the good order of the Land'; and argues that an Act of Parliament was wanted (pp.11, 62); [Thomas Tomkins] (1667), p.6.

44 [Corbet] (1667a), p.22, cf. A$_2$.; [Robert Perrinchief] (1668a), s.6, p.10.

45 [Perrinchief] (1668b), p.50, cf. [Tomkins] (1667), p.36, 'we do verily believe, That Uniformity if it were carefully maintained, and diligently looked after, would in a few years recall our Antient Unity'; [Humfrey] (1667), p.38. cf. Thorndike (1667), (1667-8) for the Anglican case:

46 [Tomkins] (1667), p.6; [John Owen] (1667), p.17. See too [Humfrey] (1667), p.33, 'To meddle with their persons is but to torment the body, not heal their conceptions', cf. p.77, 'Force may make men hypocrites, not Converts to a Faith which is enjoyned', and Corbet (1667a), p.24. Catholics: [Tomkins] (1667), p.21, [Perrinchief] (1668a), p.25, [John Pearson] (1668), p.8.

47 Cf. 'An Essay', Cf.p.81.

48 'An Essay', p.81.

49 For Bagshawe and Corbet, see ch.2, p.60–66 above. For the Independents, cf. Douglas Nobbs (1935), pp.41–59. In general, it should not be forgotten that Locke's treating toleration in terms of speculative and practical principles, rather than the truth (or otherwise) of ecclesiastical claims, was distant from the positions of Anglican and Dissenter alike.

50 See, e.g., the transcription of a Cromwellian edict, Ms.Locke, c.27, fol.11. 'The Government of the Commonwealth as it was publickly declared at Westminster 16 december 1653. Published by his Highness the Ld Protectors special Commandment.' P.43, Article 37. 'That such as profess *faith in God, by Jesus Christ*, the differing in Judgment from the Doctrines, Worship or Discipline publickly held forth, shall not be restrained from, but shal be protected in the profession of the faith, & exercise of their Religion, so as they abuse nott his liberty to the civil injury of others, & to the actual disturbance of the publick peace on their part. Provided this liberty be not

extended to Popery or Prelacy, nor to such as, under the profession of Christ hold forth, & practise licentiousness.'
For a contemporary pamphlet going much further, Anon (1667a).

51 For Locke's view of Roman Catholicism, cf. pp.72-3 *above*.
52 'An Essay concerning Toleration', pp.95, 96, 97–101.
53 'An Essay', p.81.
54 'An Essay', p.89.
55 *Two Treatises of Government*, II.ii.13, p.294. See ch.6, pp.170-9 *below* for a consideration of the significance of passages like these.
56 'An Essay', p.82.
57 For these, see chs.6-7 *Below*
58 cf. Grotius (1625), I.i.iv.
59 E.g., Hobbes (1651), I.xiv, p.64; Jeremy Taylor (1660), II.i, pp.167–8; Pufendorf (1660), I.xiv.3, p.194.
60 'An Essay', p.84.
61 'An Essay', pp.83, 85.

CHAPTER 5

1 Even apart from Locke's continual development of his doctrines.
2 [Sexby] (1657), p.278.
3 'An Essay concerning Toleration', p.103.
4 'Trade' (1674), *Locke on Money*, vol. II, p.485.
5 'For a Generall Naturalization' (1693), *Locke on Money*, vol. II, p.487.
6 'Paupertas' (1661 Commonplace Book, p.16); *Some Considerations of the Consequences of the Lowering of Interest and Raising the Value of Money* (1692, 1696), *Locke on Money*, vol. I, p.270.
7 'Labor' (1693; in 1661 Commonplace Book, p.310), *Locke on Money*, vol. II, p.493.
8 'Representations', H.R.Fox Bourne (1876), vol. II, p.378. For Locke on the poor generally, see A.L.Beier (1988), pp.28–41.
9 For Shafesbury's commercial policy, see Haley (1968), ch.6. After his final political defeat, Shaftesbury would suggest to the king, as one possible course, that he retire to overseas, see Bodleian Library, Ms. Clarendon State Papers 88 (1681-8), fol.5 (28 October 1681), arguing that he would thus escape 'perjur'd Rogues' in England and 'shall extend his Matie's Dominions there; & his Customes here'.
10 Land and labour are counted by Locke: but, very interestingly, capital as such is not mentioned. See 'Some of the Consequences that are like to follow upon lessening of Interest to 4 per cent' (1668, etc.), *Locke on Money*, vol. I, e.g., pp.172–3, 179, *passim*.
11 'Trade', *Locke on Money*, vol. II, p.485.
12 *Draft B* s.10, p.116.
13 *Some Considerations, Locke on Money*, vol. I, p.275.
14 'Trade', *Locke on Money*, vol. II, p.485; on the non-productive, see 'Some of the Consequences', vol. I, pp.176f, and (for a further list) *Some Considerations, Locke on Money*, vol. I, p.240, 'Scholars of all sorts, Women, Gamesters, and great Mens menial Servants'.

15 *Further Considerations Concerning the Raising the Value of Money* (1695, 1696), *Locke on Money*, vol. II, p.453.

16 'Some of the Consequences', *Locke on Money*, vol. I, p.177.

17 'Labor', *Locke on Money*, vol. II, pp.493, 495. This suggests a certain blindness about consumer goods, which, as Thirsk notes, was shared by contemporaries. See Joan Thirsk (1978), pp.14–5, 164–9.

18 Whether by applying the existing poor laws or by hard labour or being forced to work for low wages, 'Representations' in Fox Bourne (1876), vol. II, pp.379–81

19 Fox Bourne (1876), vol. II, p.383.

20 'Trade', *Locke on Money*, vol. II, p.485.

21 Cranston (1957), pp.39ff.

22 *Draft B*, s.28, p.138.

23 Sydenham 'De Arte Medica or Ars Medica, 1669' in Kenneth Dewhurst (1966), p.79.

24 'Representations', Fox Bourne (1876), vol. II, p.390.

25 *Draft A*, s.1, p.1.

26 *Draft B*, s.1, p.101: see also *Draft A*, s.3, p.11.

27 W.H.Walsh (1947), p.3 (from whom the example is drawn unfairly).

28 Sanderson (1660), I. xi, p.11.

29 For example, Edward Brerewood (1641) is devoted to the classification of virtues and vices, and to reasoning about them, whilst Bartholomew Keckermann (1607) outlines the virtues rather than explaining why they are virtues.

30 Locke's medical journals are printed conveniently (if not always with perfect accuracy) in Kenneth Dewhurst (1963). For some specimens of Locke's mature notetaking, see, for example, pp.121–7. 130–3, 139–41.

31 *Essays on the Law of Nature*, nos.3, 5.

32 Aristotle, *Physics*, I. i (184a24), cf. *Physics*, I. vii (189b1).

33 Johannes Magirus (1642), I. 2. A, p.11, Franco Burgersdyck (1625), disp. i, s.10, p.12.

34 But see Francis Toletus (1579), I. i. 3–4, p.10.

35 see John Alsted (1649), vol. I, pt. ii, bk xiii: 1.i.1, p.97; Magirus (1642), I. i.A, p.2; Clemens Timpler (1605–7), I. i.2.

36 Cf. the literature cited in n.34 for natural philosophy and in n.29 for ethics.

37 Eustachius of St Paul (1649), Physics, proemial questions, qu.3, p.113.

38 Bartholomew Keckermann, *Systema Logicae*, pt. iii, posterior, ch.1 in (1614), vol. I, col.826.

39 Mark Wendelin (1648), I. ii.6, p.15.

40 see Keckermann, *Systema Physica*, I. 3, (1614), vol. 1, cols.1366–3507, Daniel Sennert (1664), I. 3, pp.42f.

41 Sennert (1664), I. ii, p.15, Keckermann, *Praecognitionorum Philosophorum*, I. 3, (1614), vol. I, col.250. For a view of the scholastic writers' *receptiveness* to change, see Feingold (1984), pp.11–4.

42 Thomas Sprat (1667), p.376.

43 Owen (1971), no.1 (1652), p.5; John North (1671), pp.3, 17. For Epicurus in english dress, see Charleton (1656).

44 Sprat (1667), pp.130, 149, 370–403; 158–320.

45 Sprat (1667), pp.82f (cf. 111), 325, 347–56: Sprat's view is especially clear on pp.82f.

46 John Worthington to Henry More, 5 February, 1668 in Worthington (1847–86), vol. II.ii, p.265.

47 See ch.1 above.

48 Sydenham 'Theologia Rationalis', Dewhurst (1966), pp.149f; Thomas Starkey (1948), p.153; Christopher St. German (1751), p.42; Sprat (1667), p.428.

49 Hobbes (1839–45b), 1.6, 1.8.

50 Sprat (1667), p.31.

51 Sprat (1667), pp.15f, 326f, 21.

52 Meric Casaubon (1669), pp.6f, 7, 17f, 30. For Casaubon generally, see Michael Spiller (1980).

53 Henry Oldenberg to Boyle, 24 December, 1667, no.735 in Oldenberg (1965–), vol. iv, p.80.

54 Sprat (1667), p.344; South (1842), vol. I, pp.287–8.

55 Thomas Barlow (1693), pp.157–9.

56 Henry Stubbe jr (1670a), dedication.

57 Cf. Campanella (1653), pp.64–5, 236–7 with Stubbe (1670c), esp. p.12.

58 Stubbe (1670c), p.13.

59 Baxter (1667), 'A Conclusion, defending the Soul's Immortality', p.498; Stubbe (1670b), p.17.

60 Christine Larner (1981), pp.161–2; Stuart Clark (1980), pp.98–127.

61 Alexander, dedicatory poem to John Abernathy (1630), A_7.

62 Joseph Glanvill (1661), ch.7, pp.62f (cf. p.13, ch.3, p.23).

63 (1661), ch.17, ch.15, pp.139f.

64 Glanvill (1668), ch.7, pp.52f.

65 (1668), conclusion, p.141.

66 Glanvill (1671), ch.1, s.4, pp.15, 16; ch.2, s.2, pp.23f.

67 (1671), ch.4, s.1, p.44; ch.5, s.4.

68 (1671), pp.161f, 172, 203.

69 Casuabon (1669), p.23; Glanvill (1671), ch.5, s.4, pp.78f.

70 Boyle (1663), pp.156, cf. 171, 157, 170, 172, 154 (a bracketed comma inserted for ease of reading). See esp pp.156f 'There are divers effects in nature, of which, though the immediate cause may be plausibly assigned, yet if we further enquire into the causes of those causes, and desist not from ascending in the scale of causes till we are arrived at the top of it, we shall perhaps find the more catholic and primary causes of things to be either certain primitive, general, and fixed laws of nature (or rules of action and passions among the parcels of the universal matter); or else the shape, size, motion, and other primary affections of the smallest parts of matter, and of their first coalitions or clusters, especially those endowed with seminal faculties or properties; or (to dispatch) the admirable conspiring of the several parts of the universe to the production of particular effects – of all which it will be difficult to give a satisfactory account without acknowledging an intelligent Author or Disposer of things.' On Stubbe see also Oldenberg to John Evelyn, 8 July, 1670, Oldenberg

(1965-), no.1482 (vol. VII, p.58). See also Peter Nelson to Oldenberg, 15 December, 1670 enquiring 'whether Dr Spratt or any body else be engaged in defence of the R.Society and its' history against the vapouring cavills of the Hectoring Stubbs'. For the feeling that a response was needed, see Michael Hunter (1988), pp.63–6. For the general setting of the Royal Society, see Michael Hunter (1981), and for a report of contemporary suspicion, see Harold J.Cook (1986), p.179.

71 Boyle, (1663-71).

72 Cf. Boyle's re-iterated point, 'An Essay', p.165 that motion was not intrinsic to matter.

73 It has been suggested by Howard Duncan (1985), pp.11–22 that Locke was not a wholehearted mechanist. Three passages were produced from *An Essay concerning Human Understanding* to support this contention. It is unfortunate that none of them do so. One (*An Essay*, II.viii.25) is confessed to support mechanism in Locke (Duncan, p.15); the second concerns the point that the clearest idea we can have of active power is from spirit (*An Essay*, II.xxi.4), which has nothing to do with any alternative to mechanism; the third (*An Essay*, II.xxiii.28, p.311) shows Locke asserting that we are entirely in the dark about certain phenomena. In the last passage Duncan omits to quote lines 21–3, in which Locke disowned precisely the position Duncan wishes him to hold.

74 Nicholas Jolley (1984), p.59.

75 Whilst there are many mechanical and corpuscular references in the *Drafts*, their argument does not depend on them, though there is an analogy between Locke's view of sensation and Boyle's corpuscular hypothesis, cf. Michael Ayers (1981) pp.209–25. The fullest account of Locke's intellectual relationship with Boyle is in Peter Alexander (1985) and of his professional contacts in M.A.Stewart (1981), pp.19–44.

76 For Locke's treatment of Shaftesbury, see Haley (1968), pp.203–5; for Willis, see Willis (1980a), pp.45, 69, 80, 92ff, 98 for his inability to choose between galenic and mechanical explanations, for his very brief and metaphorical explanations of cases, see pp.43f and for his vague empiricism see pp.53, 128, 164. For some fanciful reasoning, see Willis (1980b), pp.67f, 122, 128; for a confident theory being translated into practice with a 'perhaps' see pp.85f; for metaphorical explanations, p.117; for trial and error in remedies p.133n.7; for Locke's father, see Cranston (1957), pp.68–70; for the dog, Frank (1980), esp pp.183–8; for the air pump Shapin and Schaffer (1985), p.77. Sydenham 'De Arte Medica' and 'Anatomie' (1966), pp.80, 85.

78 'Anatomie' (1966), p.87 'Tis no doubt we see gall and urin comeing from the liver and kidneys, and know these to be the effects of those parts, but are not hereby one jott nearer the cause nor manner of their operation . . . it is cleare that after all our porings and mangling the parts of animals we know noething but the grosse parts, see not the tools and contrivances by which nature works, and are as far off from the discovery we aime at as ever.'

79 Sydenham, quoted by Dewhurst (1966), p.64.

80 *Two Treatises*, I.vi.52, p.196.

81 *Draft A*, s.34, pp.63f; on substances, cf.s.25, pp.39ff.

359

82 *An Essay concerning Human Understanding*, 'The Epistle', p.7; Tyrrell's copy, British Library, C.122, f.14: 'this was in winter 1673 as I remember being myself one of those that then met there where the Discourses began about the Principles of Morality and reveald Religion'; Lady Masham in Masham (1955–6) at pp.35f lists Tyrrell and David Thomas amongst the friends. Curiously, Tyrrell there gave 1670 or 1672 as the date and it is possible that Locke originally dated *Draft A* to 1672 – see *Draft A*, p.1, note c in *Drafts for the Essay concerning Human Understanding and other philosophical writings*, ed. P.H.Nidditch and G.A.J.Rogers (Oxford, 1990).

83 *Draft A*, s.1, p.1; 'sensation' would soon be re-named as reflection', see s.4, p.12.

84 *Draft A*, s.1, p.1; note, s.2, pp.8f, how Locke's assertion that sense and reflection are the only sources of ideas reverses the peripatetic order: from the observation of particulars one moves to genera and species, which, Locke insisted, were mental constructs.

85 *Draft A*, s.1, p.2, cf.s.2, p.7.

86 *Draft A*, s.3, pp.11f.

87 *Draft A*, s.4, pp.12f, esp p.12 'sense or sensation' to 'simple Ideas'.

88 For the reflections that look forward to mixed modes, see Ms.Locke, f.5, fols.77f (26 June, 1681) (Aaron and Gibb, pp.116ff), see too Ms.Locke, f.3, fol.263 (25 August, 1678) (Aaron and Gibb, p.112); for obligation, lex naa, Ms.Locke, f.3, pp.201–2, 15 July, 1678

89 *Draft A*, s.39, cf. s.12.

90 *Draft A*, s.26, p.41; *Draft B*, s.160, p.269.

91 How was this acceptable? After all it suggests a very uneven degree of knowledge over various fields. but contemporary canons permitted this. Aristotle had suggested that different degrees of precision were appropriate to different activities, *Nichomachean Ethics*, 1,3. This suggestion obtained generally currency: see, e.g., Hugo Grotius (1616), p.95n; John Wilkins (1675), I.3, p.23.

92 The great coup here was to adduce ideas of reflection (or, as Locke called it, *Draft B*, s.41, internal sense). Suppose we confine ourselves to ideas drawn from sense – these are unlikely to disclose an idea of God. but reflection on the operation of our own minds might lead in just that direction, cf. *Draft A*, s.2, p.10. Note, in reference to this, that neither Hobbes nor Hume discussed ideas of reflection, whilst we may say with only slight exaggeration that Reid did little else.
Locke's procedure was doubly elegant. For the denial of a useful acquaintance with substance suggested that reasoning needed to begin not with universal propositions but with the deliveries of sense. The peripatetics could not deny the importance of sense in the face of Aristotle's own authority, however often they had ignored this point in practice.

93 *Draft B*, s.60–3, 67–73, pp.162–7, 170–9; for the syllogism, cf. *An Essay concerning Human Understanding*, IV.xvii.

94 *Draft A*, s.2, p.9.

95 *Draft A*, s.39; *Draft B*, s.94, p.214 and, at length, *An Essay concerning Human Understanding*, IV.x.

96 Baxter (1667), pt.ii, ch.6, p.289; Grotius (1625), I.i.xii.1–12; South (1660),

no.1, p.13; Hobbes (1969a), p.56; Pufendorf (1672), I.ii.2; Hobbes (1839–45b), VI.xvi, cf. VI.xi.

97 *Draft A*, s.19–23, pp.34–7, cf. *Draft B*, s.145–55, pp.260–6; Robert Sanderson (1618), I.xii, pp.40–2.

98 Francis Bacon, *Novum Organum*, pt ii, aph.2–3 (1857–74), vol. i p.157); *De Augmentis Scientiarum* III.iv (1857–74), vol. i esp. pp.360, 550.

99 John Tillotson, Sermon 1 in (1704), pp.7f, 14ff, 17; Henry More (1655).

100 Tillotson, Sermon 1 in (1704), p.1; Samuel Parker (1666), p.64.

101 To draw attention away from substance is also to push to the fore God's work as creator and sustainer. Substance suggests the idea of self-sustenation: only God fell *properly* into that class and the term was extended by courtesy to other entities. Hence it was appropriate for Locke to continue the presumption of his *Essays*, that God was the moral legislator. I do not mean that Locke would have denied this otherwise, merely that it made good sense to *emphasise* it in the *Drafts*.

102 *Draft A*, s.33, pp.62f.

103 *Draft A*, ss.33–7, pp.63–5.

104 *Draft A*, s.38, pp.65f.

105 *Draft A*, s.39, p.66.

106 *Draft A*, s.42, p.71 for transubstantiation and papal infallibility.

107 Baxter (1672), epistle dedicatory.

108 Francis Rous, *Works* (1657), pp.622f, cited by G.F.Nuttall (1946), p.139. *Draft A*, s.1, p.7, *Draft B*, s.66, p.170 and see too *Essays on the Law of Nature*, p.269.

109 *Draft B*, s.12, p.119.

110 Cf., in a different context, *An Essay concerning Human Understanding*, IV.xvi.13, pp.667 for God compassing ends.

111 *Two Treatises*, II.v.26, p.304; 'An Essay concerning Toleration', p.84; Halifax, (1699) in Halifax (1969), p.51.

112 Boyle (1663), p.161; Sydenham 'Theologia Rationalis', (1966), p.145.

113 William Ames (1642), I.viii.66, p.38.

114 *An Essay concerning Human Understanding*, IV.xviii.5, p.692f.

115 Clarendon (1676), p.27.

116 *Draft B*, s.1, p.101.

117 Cf. Charles Webster (1975), ch.5.

118 Cf. Boyle (1663), p.159 'how mere and consequently brute bodies can act according to laws, and for determinate ends, without any knowledge either of the one or of the other. Let them, therefore, till they have made out their hypothesis more intelligibly, either cease to ascribe to irrational creatures such actions as in men are apparently the productions of reason and choice, and sometimes even of industry and virtue; or else let them with us acknowledge that such actions of creatures in themselves irrational, are performed under the superintendence and guidance of a wise and intelligent Author of things.'

119 *Two Treatises*, I.ix.86, p.223.

120 *Draft B*, s. 4ff, esp s.4.

121 *Draft B* s.5, p.108.

122 *Draft B* s.76, p.184, cf. s.62 but see s.89. This is despite the fact that this

point was specified in *Genesis*. Locke, like everyone else, took items from scripture that informed his purpose. This, of coure, makes his allusion to the dominion of mankind all the more remarkable.

123 For Boyle's rejection of the Adamic language and for an important treatment of Locke's handling of it in *An Essay concerning Human Understanding*, see Hans Aarsleff(1964)repr. in Aarsleff (1982), ch.1; and see *Draft B*, s.60–3 pp.162–67 on the ideas of substance that we do have.

124 Ames(1642), II.xx.4, p.325.

125 *Genesis*, 1,26; Sydenham (1966), p.146; Ames (1642), I.viii.74–5, p.38

126 Cf. *Two Treatises*, I.iv.39, p.185.

127 Aristotle and God: Aristotle, *De Caelo* 271^{a}33 and *De Generatione et Corruptione*, 336^{b}32; matter, Aristotle, *Posterior Analytics*, 94^{b}27–31; design, Aristotle, *De Partibus Animalium*, 639^{b}16–21.

128 *Draft B*, s.39, p.147; *Draft A*, s.10, p.21.

129 *Draft B*, s.39, p.147; the comparable pasage, *An Essay concerning Human Understanding*, IV.xi.8, pp.634f, restricted itself more closely to preservation.

130 *Draft B*, s.10, p.21. Locke affirmed this in discussing predication of things outside the mind, but it has a more general application.

131 *Draft B*, s.6, p.111.

132 *Draft B*, s.39, p.147, cf. *Draft A*, s.10, p.21.

133 *An Essay concerning Human Understanding*, IV.xii.10, p.645.

134 *Draft B*, s.88, pp.194f; *Two Treatises*, I. iv.33, pp.182f.

135 *Draft B*, s.21, pp.132f.

136 *Draft B*, s.13, p.121; Baxter(1667), pt.i, ch.10, s.4, p.70.

137 *Draft B*, s.11, p.119.

138 *Draft B*, s.134, p.254, cf. ch.3; n.4 above p.345.

139 *Draft B*, s.20, p.131.

140 This knits well with Locke's limitation of the sources of ideas to sense and reflection: he insisted that the ideas we have depend upon their deliverances and that with these we cannot meddle. This view fits too with the effective limitation of mankind to certain concernments, to a useful rather than a universal knowledge of things.

141 Cf. Michael Ayers (1991), vol. I, p.123. See further on God's goodness, chs.8 + 10 *Below*.

142 *Draft B*, s.3, p.103.

143 *Draft B*, s.3, p.101.

144 There are several matters not addressed in Locke's second draft which had been considered in his first (as faith). There were others to which Locke had yet to attend – e.g., *actually* proving God's existence and attributes rather than merely insisting that he could, would and indeed needed to do so – or which he had not yet placed on the intellectual agenda – e.g., the conceptualisation of moral actions: and there was one case which neither Locke nor others had readily conceived – the problem of moral obligation. These will be considered when we address *An Essay concerning Human Understanding*. For the moment it is enough to say that we have the beginnings of an answer to the question of why Locke wrote about the human understanding. He needed to vindicate the way of discovery. In this task, God was supposed to have ends

towards which He was keen for us to work. Thus Locke situated his view of things in a scheme that contemporaries could regard as respectable.

CHAPTER 6

1 That *Epistola de Tolerantia* was written in Latin evidences that it was intended for a continental audience. On Locke's position generally, cf. Dunn (1991) in Grell, *et al.* (eds.) (1991).

2 See ch.4 p.109-17 *above*.

3 For the Declaration generally, see Frank Bate (1908).

4 Public Record Office, P.R.O. 30/24/6B/430. See also, e.g., [John Humfrey] (1672), p.23 'The King is head over his people as a Nation, and that in Ecclesiasticalls, as well as Civils.'

5 James I, *Speach in the Starre-Chamber* (20 June, 1616) (1918), p.327 'It is the Kings office to protect and settle the trew interpretation of the Law of God within his Dominions', cf. p.341 on his subjects 'they for whose soules I must answere to GOD'; Hobbes (1651), III.xlii, esp p.284, cf. p.296.

6 See Dering (1940): for interest in the growth of Popery, see pp.70, 87, 94, 146f, 148–9 (and see too William Lloyd, 1673); for supply and the Declaration, see p.111 (7 February, 1673); for the debate on the Declaration, pp.114–18 (10th February, 1673); for parliamentary willingness to relieve dissenters, see pp.122–6, 133f, 145f (19 February to 19 March, 1673) and esp debate of 14 February, 1673, p.119, 'it was moved to add that we would pass a vote that a bill should be brought in for giving ease to dissenters in matters of religion, which they said would very much please his Majesty, to let him see that we did not dislike the matter of his declaration but the manner, and did not doubt the prudence but only the legality of it.' See also Shaftesbury in the House of Lords, as reported in Anon (1675), p.4 '*the power of the King's Supremacy, which was of another nature then that he had in Civills*'.

7 Public Record Office, P.R.O. 30/24/6B/429.

8 'Excommunicaan', Ms.Locke, c.27, fol 27a (endorsed on the back, '7¾', i.e., January to March 1674).

9 Baxter (1696), III, s.256–7. For the position of dissent throughout this period, cf. Tyacke (1991) in Grell *et al.* (eds.) (1991).

10 Thomas Cooper (1850) p.174; cf. Edmund Bunny (1595), p.16.

11 Alexander Nowell (1570), p.171.

12 J.Bradford (1848–53), p.146, cf. Edmund Bunny (1576), p.22.

13 Thomas Cranmer (1844), p.42, cf. (1846), p.224.

14 Hooker (1977–82), V.vi.7; on the Holy Spirit, V.vi.11 and 13.

15 Edwin Sandys (1841), p.59.

16 John Overall (1606), II.vi, pp.124f, xi, pp.197, 203. Most bishops hold office *by divine appointment* and a few by *divine permission*; the day was yet to come when Bishop Hensley Henson would observe that many do so by divine inadvertence.

17 Henry Dodwell (1683), ch.13, s.10, p.388.

18 Hooker (1977–82), VIII.iv.5–6, 9, cf. VIII.ii.3.

19 See chs.2, 4 above.

20 Whitgift (1851–3), vol. I, p.95, vol. II, p.240.
21 Hooker, *Sermon V* s.2 in (1888), vol. III; note the qualification in the adverbs, of course. For schism after 1660, see John Spurr (1990), pp.408–24.
22 Dodwell (1683) ch.13, s.9, p.387.
23 Anon (1675), pp.1ff.
24 Anon (1675), cf. p.6 (civil sanctions); pp.1f, 5f, 24f (clerical influence); p.24 (erastian or separate); for Locke, see 'Philanthropoy or the Christian Philosopher's', Ms.Locke, c.27 30ᶜ.
25 Anon (1675), p.24.
26 See ch.7, pp.194–201 below.
27 Anon (1675), pp.16, 18, 27.
28 Anon (1675), pp.29.
29 Anon (1675), pp.7f (*recte* 3) 5f.
30 James I, 'A Speech in Starre Chamber', James I (1918), p.326.
31 Edward Forset (1606), pp.91f, cf. p.86.
32 George Savile, marquess of Halifax, (1688) in Halifax (1969), p.277.
33 Locke, *Two Treatises*, II.vi.57; Hobbes, (1651), II.xxx p.182.
34 See *Essays on the Law of Nature*, esp. no.8.
35 'An Essay concerning Toleration', p.81.
36 Sidney, (1698) III.xxiii p.359 paraphrasing Aristotle *Politics*, III.17; *Two Treatises*, II.xiv.166, p.396 – see II.v.42, p.316 for an interesting variant. Sir William Temple (in Gilbert Burnet (1897–1900), ch.14, vol. II, p.352 n.2) suggested that Sidney had himself in mind for such a role.
37 Sidney (1698), III.iv, p.269, *Two Treatises*, II.xix.239, p.444.
38 James I, 'A Speech in Starre Chamber' and Basilikon *Doron*, both in (1918), pp.326, 12.
39 *English Tract*, p.22 (158); *Two Treatises*, II.ii.13, p.294, cf. *Epistola de Tolerantia*, p.94; *Two Treatises*, II.vii.92, p.345; xix.230, p.436.
40 James I, 'The Trew Law of Free Monarchies', (1918), p.54; Sir Thomas Elyot (1907), I.ii, p.9; *Some Thoughts concerning Education* s.39, p.108. See also Glanvill(1667).
41 *Two Treatises*, II.xiv.165, p.395.
42 *Two Treatises*, II.xviii.199, p.417.
43 *Draft B*, s.1, p.101; *Genesis*, 1,26; *Draft B* s.12, p.119.
44 *Two Treatises*, II.ii.4, p.287 and I.vi.67, p.208: 'Man has a *Natural Freedom*. . .since all that share in the same common Nature, Faculties and Powers are in Nature equal, and ought to partake in the same common Rights and Priviledges, till the manifest appointment of God, who is *Lord over all, Blessed for ever*, can be produced to shew any particular Persons Supremacy, or a Mans own consent subjects him to a Superior.'
45 *Of the Conduct of the Understanding*, ed.F.W.Garforth (New York, 1966), s.2, pp.33f; habits, *ibid.*, s.4, p.43; ingrained, s.4, pp.41f.
46 Understanding, *Conduct*, s.1, p.31; freedom of will, *Two Treatises*, II.vi.58, p.324.
47 Cf. *An Essay concerning Human Understanding* IV.xvii.4, p.673, 11.27–30.
48 *Two Treatises*, II.ii.4, p.287.
49 *Ibid.*
50 *Two Treatises*, II.vi.54, p.322.

51 'An Essay', p.89; *Two Treatises*, II.xvi.195, p.414.

52 *Draft B*, s.13, pp.122f.

53 John Novell (1662), p.6.

54 *Toleratio* (Ms.Locke, d.1, fol.125).

55 Ms.Locke, d.1, p.5.
'Conformitas. Severall protestants not of the Church of England resident at Constantinople had leave of S[r] J. Finch the English Ambassador there to have a roome in his house to meet to pray in they being most of the French church. But at last it was thought fit that if they would continue that privledg they should come & receive the sacramt in his chappel administerd there by his chaplain according to the discipline of the Church of England. Of w[ch] they haveing notice they accordingly came. But presented themselves to receive it according to the severall fashions of their churches or perswasions of their owne mindes some siting & some standing though the Ambassador & all the usuall congregation of the English there had received it kneeling. However the chaplain thought he could not refuse it any one that came solemly & seriously to receive it for any posture he presented himself in & therefor administered the breed to them all. w[ch] significant declaration that kneeling was noe essential part of receiving the Ds supper & noe necessary part of worship had soe powerfull an effect upon them that when he came afterwards to give them the cup, they of their owne accord received it, every one kneeling. This was if it were at litle more practised would perhaps be found not only the most Christian but the most effectuall way to bring men to Conformity Mr Covell.'

56 *An Essay concerning Human Understanding*, IV.xx.3, p.708.

57 Shaftesbury knew by 1672, see Thomas Stringer in W.D.Christie (1871), vol.II, p.xxiii and cf.Colbert to Louis XIV, 7 June, 1672, vol.II, p.xiv, on the 'almost certain proofs' of York's conversion and the disquiet it caused; Reresby noted (in an entry for 1670, but presumably written later), that the duke was converted to Roman Catholicism by his sister, the duchess of Orleans, and in his entry for 12 December, 1672 noted York's refusal to conform to the Test Act (which really belongs under 15 June, 1673): Reresby (1936), pp.80,87.

58 See generally J.P.Kenyon (1972).

59 For the history of anti-catholicism in the seventeenth century, see Robin Clifton (1973), ch.3, (1984), pp.129–61; John Miller (1973); K.H.D.Haley (1975), pp.102–19 and M.G.Finlayson (1983).

60 For the exclusion crisis, see generally K.G.Feiling (1924) and J.R.Jones (1961); Haley (1968), pp.463–741; Haley (1985), ch.4; Ashcraft (1986), ch.4–6, with C.B.A.Behrens (1941), pp.42–71; Tim Harris (1987), chs.5–7 and Jonathan Scott (1991), *passim*. Leopold Von Ranke (1875) is a forgotten classic: see esp. Bk.XVI (vol.iv, pp.1–206).

61 Jones (1961) provides a clear guide to the varieties of whiggery; the interpretation of Scott (1991) runs cross Jones'.

62 For Rye House, see D.J.Milne (1951), pp.91–108; for the campaign against the whigs, see Haley (1968), chs.28–9, Tim Harris (1987), ch.6 and B.J.Rahn (1972), in P.J.Korshin (ed.) (1972), pp.77–98. For Monmouth, see C.C.Trench (1969) and Robin Clifton (1985), with the striking interpretation of Scott (1991), p.274

63 Henry Horwitz (1964), pp.201–17.
64 See Thomas (1962), pp.224–5.
65 Thomas (1962), p.226.
66 Stillingfleet (1681), preface, pp.lxxi–lxxxii.
67 Stillingfleet (1681) preface, pp.lxxxv–lxxxviii.
68 (1681), preface, p.lxxxix.
69 Stillingfleet (1680), p.9.
70 See Symon Patrick's instalments of 'friendly debate' with dissenters and such collections as Anon (ed.) (1694).
71 Samuel Parker (1670).
72 Parker (1681a).
73 Ms.Locke, c.34, p.14.
74 E.g Tyrrell's reply to *Mischief*, Ms.Locke, c.34, p.14. The charge was levelled against Locke's *Epistola* as late as 1689 by Thomas Long (1689). Long had written a defence and continuation of Stillingfleet's (1681).
75 Ms.Locke, c.34, p.20 (distinction from state), pp.75, 118f (things indifferent); pp.16–19, 145 (voluntary); p.13 (no civil sanctions).
76 Ms.Locke, c.34, p.3, cf. pp.48f on the right an agent has to take care of his or her own soul.
77 Ms.Locke, c.34, p.40.
78 Ms.Locke, c.34, p.71.
79 The Anglican interest in unity and indulgence evaporated immediately on the loss of the exclusion bill in the House of Lords, 15 November, 1680. See Edmund Calamy (1724), pp.72–3.
80 *Epistola de Tolerantia*, p.58. For the difference between this and toleration as Locke had discussed it in 1667, see the point made in Ms.Locke, c.34, p.7 for 'Toleration, wch is a businesse of the state, not of the Church, & so not properly belonging to the subject before him [Stillingfleet], for a Church properly as a Church meddles onely with its owne body but neither gives nor denyes toleration to those without. . .the Question of Toleration is whether the Magistrate shall tolerate different Churches'.
81 *Toleratio* (Ms.Locke, d.1, fols.125–6).
82 *Epistola de Tolerantia*, p.70.
83 *Ibid.*, p.72.
84 *Ibid.*, pp.70, 72 '*Dico esse. . .invenisse*'.
85 *Ibid.*, p.64, cf. p.116.
86 *Epistola de Tolerantia*, pp.74, 76.
87 *Ibid.*, pp.72, 74, 76 note that the examples on p.98 illustrating magisterial variations in religion are all English.
88 *Ibid.*, p.80.
89 *Ibid.*, pp.80, 82, cf. 84.
90 *Ibid.*, p.92.
91 *Ibid.*, pp.92, 94, cf. 96.
92 *Ibid.*, p.130,132.
93 [Jonas Proast] (1690b) and Locke *A Second Letter for Toleration*, cf. Peter Nicholson (1991), pp.163–87 for Locke's responses to Proast.
94 But the point remained the same as in 1667.
95 *Some Considerations, Locke on Money*, Vol. I, p.213 – see the whole passage.

96 Pierre Bayle (1682), esp. pp.391ff for the speculations about atheism. More generally see Bayle (1686) in Bayle (1727), vol. II, pp.355–561 and (1683), Bayle (1727), vol. III, pp.1–161, and accompanying texts ((1727), vol. III pp.162–417). For Bayle himself see Elisabeth Labrousse (1983) and more recently John Kilcullen (1988) and David Berman (1988), pp.271ff. For Bayle's *Lettre* in Locke's notebook, see Ms.Locke, f.8, p.38/294 (16 October, 1685).

97 Which harmonised with the view that religious dissent was less the outcome of conscience that perversity, which could be corrected.

98 Note, *Two Treatises*, II.xviii.210, p.423, that when religious worship makes it solitary appearance in the text that the religion favoured by the government is scarcely the right one.

99 John Owen, *Of Toleration*, Owen (1850–5), vol. VIII, pp.188f, cf. *Sermon, 9, Christ's Kingdom and the Magistrate's Right* (1652), (1850–5), vol. VIII, p.375; Hobbes (1651), III, esp. xxxix, p.248, xlii, pp.295ff; [Proast] (1690a), pp.18f.

CHAPTER 7

1 *Two Treatises*, preface; I.1.1; II.1.1; title page; pp.155, 159, 285, 153.

2 Locke mentioned ecclesiastical support for absolutism at *Two Treatises*, II.xix.239, pp.442–4, cf. preface, p.156. See also [James Tyrrell] (1681), preface A₂. For a specimen of clerical patriarchalism, see James Ussher (1661), with Robert Sanderson's preface. For a fuller list of clerical absolutists, including Sibthorp and Maynwaring, see Anon (1675). For an example of the clerical use of Filmer, see Nathaniel Alsop (1682), esp. pp.9f.

3 Shaftesbury, speech in the House of Lords in W.D.Christie (1871), vol. II, p.xcii, cf. p.c 'the most dangerous destructive doctrine'.

4 Shaftesbury's speech on 20 October, 1675 in Shaftesbury (1675), p.10: 'If ever there should happen in future ages (which God forbid) a King governing by an Army, without his Parliament, 'tis a Government I own not, am not obliged to, nor was born under.'

5 Anon (1675), pp.1, 16.

6 For differing versions of Locke's practical activities, see the important statements in Peter Laslett's introduction to his edition of *Two Treatises*, sections 2–3 and in Richard Ashcraft's (1986). (See also Ashcraft's (1987), appendix, pp.286–97 for a summary of the author's views on the dating of *Two Treatises*.) Laslett offered some response to Ashcraft in the so-called 'student edition' (Cambridge, 1988) of his edition (in fact a slightly updated and shortened reprint). Ashcraft's fascinating volume has attracted a good deal of comment, much of which is used by David Wootton (1992), pp.79–98. See especially Jeffrey Friedman (1988), pp.64–101. Ashcraft defended and restated his position in (1992), pp.99–115.

7 Charles I (1628), p.9.

8 Bodin (1576), I.8, p.29.

9 Bodin (1576), p.20.

10 Bodin (1576), pp.32, 31 (translation amended).

11 Hooker (1977–82), VIII.ii.13.

12 Rawlinson (1619), p.7; Merbery (1581), p.44.

13 Richard Baxter (1680), ch.3, s.34, p.58; s.18, p.38 and see s.19, p.38 also.

14 This and the next citation from Fitzralph are taken from *De Pauperie Salvatoris*, I.ii in Wycliffe (1890), pp.279–80.

15 Fortescue (1869), I.xxvii, p.218.

16 Cited by Robert M. Berdahl (1988), p.84.

17 Fitzralph also suggested that inferiors had no right to refuse imposts for reasonable purposes.

18 Fortescue 'Declaracion upon certayn Wrytinges' (1869), p.533.

19 Fortescue (1885), p.109.

20 Fortescue (1949), ch.13, pp.31, 33 (amended).

21 Fortescue (1949), ch.13; Merbury (1581), p.44.

22 Bodin (1576), I.8, pp.31, 35; Seneca *De Beneficiis* 7.4.2; the Senecan phrase was quoted (e.g.) by Bodin (1576), I.8 (not in Tooley).

23 *Two Treatises*, II.xi.139, p.379, in slightly different context.

24 This is distinct from the question of which kingdoms belong to which category. Fortescue placed England in the latter and France in the former, see (1885), ch.3, pp.113, ch.4, pp.116–17, whereas Bodin placed both in his category of royal monarchies, which meant that both the constitutive laws, like the subject matter of natural law generally, were beyond the monarch's authority to alter.

25 James I, *Trew Law of Free Monarchies*, (1918), p.63.

26 Filmer, *Patriarcha*, 3.1 in Filmer (1991), p.35; *The Necessity of The Absolute Power of all Kings* (1648) in Filmer (1991), pp.173–83.

27 See ch.6 above pp.170–73 and cf. Thomas Floyd (1600), p.31 'the iudgement and sentence of a king [should] be incorrupt and irreprehensible in all points'.

28 Filmer, *Patriarcha*, 1.1 in Filmer (1991), p.5; James I, speech of 1603 (1918), p.278.

29 Bodin (1576), II.ii, p.57.

30 *Two Treatises*, II.xviii, esp. s.199, p.417 on the use of power 'for his own private separate Advantage'. See also, amongst many references, Aristotle, *Politics*, III.vii, Aquinas (1932), 1.1, Fortescue (1885), ch.4, p.117 and (1869), I.xxviii.

31 Bodin (1576), II.iii, p.59. To Bodin's eyes despotism was acquired under special conditions, see pp.245–6 below.

32 *Two Treatises*, II.xv.172, p.400.

33 Aristotle, *Politics*, III.14.

34 Matthew Kellison (1621), p.44; John Selden (1614), p.2, cf. Hooker (1977–82), I.x.4, VIII.ii.5. The 'oeconomical' model does not determine the role of patriarchy in explaining political authority: Filmer's use was much more complete than James I's or Bodin's in that respect. Bodin, again, made use of authority in the household, but did not suppose that it implied an unrestricted extent of monarchical authority.

35 Filmer, *Patriarcha*, 3.9 in Filmer (1991), p.45; Hobbes (1651), II.xxvi, p.137.

36 We have been told often that Bodin's reservation of property was

inconsitent with his view of sovereignty, – see, e.g., Richard Bonney (1991), p.313 – but this omits the simple point that Bodin placed certain matters outside the scope of sovereignty.

37 James I, speech of 1607, (1918), p.300.

38 Bodin (1576), II.ii pp.56f, for some examples see p.245–6,377n.207 below.

39 Bodin (1576), I.8, pp.27f.

40 With the greatest virtuosity by Hobbes, of course.

41 James I, *Trew Law*, (1918), p.62.

42 Note the absence of natural law from Filmer's explanation of political authority.

43 For absolutism and monarchical entitlement to levy taxes without consent, cf. p.377n.202 below.

44 Sir John Davis (1628), 'preface dedicatory', 'Therefore as the *lawe of nature*, which the Schoolmen call *Ius Commune*, and which is also *Ius non scriptum*, being written onely in the heart of man, is better then all the written lawes in the world to make men honest and happy in this life, if they would observe the rules thereof: So the *customary law* of England, which we doe likewise call *Ius commune*, as coming neerest to the lawe of *Nature*, which is the root and touchstone of all good lawes, and which is also *Ius non scriptum*, and written onely in the memory of man . . . doth far excell our *written* lawes, namely our Statutes or Acts of Parliament.'

45 Coke (1658), ii, preface, p.x; viii, preface, p.iv.

46 For views on mixed monarchy, see classically Sir Thomas Smith (1982) and cf. Hooker (1977–82), VIII.1–3,6,9, Charles Herle (1642) and (1643). For commentary cf. C.C.Weston and J.R.Greenberg (1981).

47 J.G.A.Pocock's remarkable (1987) should be compared on this point with Ashcraft (1986), p.189 n.26.

48 Filmer, of course, made the least use of natural law, as the territory of the writers he wished to supersede, though he did acknowledge it. Ashcraft's claim (1986), p.187, that Filmer 'stressed at some length the natural law basis of his argument', reads rather oddly. His general point that Filmer's writings suggested that the questions at issue would need to be addressed at the plane of natural law is, however, important (cf. Locke *Two Treatises*, I.xi.126, p.251), but Filmer's writings were not alone in this – see n.63 below.

49 See *below*, pp.223 and, more generally, the important treatment in Richard Tuck (1979), esp. chs.2 and 3.

50 Filmer presented his basic position most forcibly in *Patriarcha*, ch.1.

51 J.G.A.Pocock (1987), conclusion; David Resnick (1984); M.P.Thompson (1987).

52 [James Tyrrell] (1681) devoted his energies to the criticism of Filmer and the assertion of an opposing point of view; his discussion of the English constitution appears in this context, see, e.g. p.4.

53 See *Essays on the Law of Nature*, no.1 and, generally, ch.3 *above* for Locke on the force of custom and agreement. It is true more generally that Locke was sceptical of the value of some established practices, especially intellectual ones, current in his own day – see chs.5,8 + 9 *below*. For one further reason why reference to custom or fundamental

law was not suitable for Locke's purposes, see Burnet in n.63 below.

54 See Hobbes (1969b) and (1971). For Locke, see *Some Thoughts concerning Education*, s.186–7 pp.239–40 and app.iii 'Mr Locke's Extempore Advice', pp.321–3. But for Locke's casualness on this subject, see *An Essay* II.xxvi.3 p.326.

55 For Bodin and others, see this chapter pp.194–201, 224–30, 241–50. Concerning Locke's allocation of attention, it is worth bearing in mind that by offering an *alternative* explanation of political authority to the absolutists, the question of whether or not he was addressing Hobbes becomes otiose. Obviously the project was much broader than that, and Hobbes was being transcended along with several others.

56 For the chief references, see Filmer, *The Anarchy of a Limited or Mixed Monarchy* (1648) in Filmer (1991), p.138, *Observations concerning the Originall of Government* (1652) in Filmer (1991), pp.202, 210, 217, *Observations upon Aristotles Politiques* (1652) in Filmer (1991), p.237. For Locke's knowledge of Filmer before *Patriarcha*, cf. Ms. Locke, f.28, p.118 (dated '79') and f.14, p.5, where he is referred to as 'Sr Thomas Filmore', and p.16. Curiously, many years *after* Filmer's authorship of the relevant tracts had become known, Macaulay referred to Sir Thomas Filmer (see Macaulay (1974–81), vol. IV, p.47). Perhaps Locke and Macaulay supposed 'Thomas' a name appropriate for one who doubted their premises.

57 George Villiers, second duke of Buckingham (1675), p.13; [John Nalson] (1681), p.1; Edward Chamberlayne (1669), ch.19, p.447; Mr Justice Powell in T.B.Howell (ed.) (1809–14), vol. XIV, pp.632ff (a case of 1702); Ambrose Philips cited in G.M.Trevelyan (1932), p.84n.

58 Sidney (1698), III.33, p.406; Filmer *Observations upon Artistotles Politiques* in Filmer (1991), p.276; for property and status, see David Ogg (1955b), ch.3.

59 For a collection of diverse modern views about absolutism, see John Miller (ed.) (1990) and for the history of the idea, Burns (1986).

60 see, e.g., J.P.Sommerville (1986), chs.1–4.

61 Shaftesbury (1675), p.20 (also in Christie (1871), vol. II, p.xciii); William Sherlock (1684), ch.6, p.208.

62 For a variety of clear or probable references to contemporary events see, e.g., preface p.155, ix.131, xiii.157, xiv.161, xviii.205, 210, xix 212–19.

63 'it were' [John Somers] (1681a), p.15; 'the Crown ought' and 'God Almighty', [Robert Brady] (1681), pp.25f; 'Human Power', Anon [E.F.] (1679), p.4; 'our Laws', *ibid.*, p.8. See also Gilbert Burnet (1897–1900), ch.10 (vol. II, p.216) 'some argued against the exclusion that it was unlawful in itself, and against the unalterable law of succession, (which came to be the common phrase.) Monarchy was said to be by divine right: so the law could not alter what God had settled.' Burnet mentioned, amongst other points, that 'All lawyers had great regard to fundamental laws; and it was a maxim among our lawyers that even an act of parliament against Magna Charta was null of itself.' This latter point helps to explain why Locke thought that reference to constitutional history was unsuitable for his *Treatises*; 'every form of Government', Anon (1680), p.9; 'under a

necessity', Anon (1682b), p.3; 'when a man' [Somers] (1681a), p.15. For a direct response to Somers, see [Brady] (1681).

64 This is not to say anything so crude as that *Two Treatises* was merely an 'exclusion tract', rather that its explanatory concerns to discount absolutism and to provide an alternative were *relevant* to exclusion. It does mean, however, that the views that it was not a very competent exclusion tract (Dunn (1969), pp.53) or that elements of revolution are uppermost in the text (Ashcraft (1986), esp.chs.7–8, cf., e.g., (1987), p.285n.69) require revision. More importantly, it indicates how Locke's concerns *embody* points relevant to the problem of exclusion.

Somers (1681a) also indicated two further sorts of argument aiming to establish monarchy beyond human control. One concerned conquest, to which Locke attended (see p.245-6 below). The other was fundamental law, for which see p.205-6 above and n.63.

65 St Paul, *Romans*, 13,2; Seth Ward (1661), pp.6f, 30, cf. 18, ep.ded.

66 Thomas Sprat (1682), p.21. See also Sherlock (1684), ch.4, p.101 and ch.5, p.141 (on Paul and Peter respectively).

67 See p.249–50 below.

68 For toleration see chs. 3 and 6 above. It is not being argued that Locke's position is *inconsistent* with Christian doctrine. The common interpretation of St.Paul rested upon the assumption that what was resisted was lawful, whilst (as we shall see) Locke argued that dealing with *unlawful* power was *not* to be conceived as resistance to government. *Two Treatises* does make extensive use of Old Testament devices. For the logic of Christian belief, see Gilbert Burnet (1688), s.9, p.3 'It is indeed clear from the *New Testament*, that the *Christian Religion* as such, gives us no grounds to defend or propagate it by force. It is a Doctrine of the Cross, and of Faith, and Patience under it: and if by the order of Divine Providence, and of any constitution of Government, under which we are born, we are brought under sufferings, for our professing of it, we may indeed retire and fly out of any such Country, if we can; but if that is denied us, we must then according to this Religion, submit to those sufferings under which we may be brought, considering that God will be glorified by us in so doing, and that he will both support us under our sufferings, and gloriously reward us for them.'

69 See ch.1, s.3 *above* for the manner in which civil magistracy upheld society.

70 See p.225-6 *below*.

71 Shaftesbury, speech in the House of Lords, 25 March, 1679 in Christie (1871), vol.II, p.ci; [Roger L'Estrange] (1681–2), no.11 (12 April 1681); [John Nalson] (1681), p.1; Shaftesbury speech in the Lords, Christie (1871), vol.II, p.lxxxix.

72 Filmer, esp. *Patriacha*, I.3–4 in Filmer (1991), pp.6–19.

73 Cf. ch.5, p.139f above.

74 In the vocabulary of the seventeenth century 'power' connoted the Latin *potestas*, which embraced both authority and the ability to enforce one's will. Hence Locke's project of explaining political authority used the word 'power' with an emphasis on the normative.

75 Filmer, *Patriarcha*, 3.3 in Filmer (1991), p.39, cf. *Observations on Aristotles Politiques* in Filmer (1991), pp.238–40; Sidney (1698), III.x, pp.292f.

76 for Ussher and Sanderson, see Ussher (1661).

77 John Dunn (1969), p.ixn.3; that this is a general opinion seems to be testified by the relatively brief treatment in Geraint Parry (1978), ch.4 and by Laslett's sparse commentary on the text. But see also M.P.Zuckert (1979), pp.58–74, Charles D.Tarlton (1978), pp.43–73.

78 Burnet (1688), s.1, p.1.

79 *Two Treatises*, II.x.132, p.372; *Draft B*, s.44, p.179.

80 Found fully, of course, in *Patriarcha*, cf. p.203 and n.56 above. For patriarchalism generally, see Daly (1979) and Schochet (1975).

81 *Two Treatises*, II.ii.4, p.287.

82 *Two Treatises*, I.viii.80, p.220, a passage that, curiously, Dr Laslett and the other commentators have overlooked in trying to discover the contents of the lost ending of the *First* Treatise.

83 *Two Treatises*, II.ii.4, p.287.

84 *ibid.*

85 See ch.6, pp.172–8 above for a fuller account of the significance of this passage.

86 *Two Treatises*, I.iv.21, p.174.

87 *Two Treatises*, I.iv.33, p.182.

88 *Two Treatises*, I.iv.39, p.185; for all this, see ch.5, pp.150–9 *above*.

89 *Draft B*, s.1, p.101. Sensible: accessible through sense experience, of course; a contrast is being drawn implicitly between the sensible and other spirits supposed to be beyond detection by human faculties, at least usually.

90 *Two Treatises*, I.iv.30, p.180.

91 See ch.3, p.95 above.

92 *Two Treatises*, I.ix.86, p.223 'For the desire, strong desire of Preserving his Life and Being having been Planted in him, as a Principle of Action by God himself, Reason, *which was the Voice of God in him*, could not but teach him and assure him, that pursuing that natural Inclination he had to preserve his Being, he followed the Will of his Maker.'

93 *Ibid.*, pp.222f 'God having made Man, and planted in him. . .a strong desire of Self-preservation, and furnished the World with things fit for Food and Rayment and other Necessaries of Life, Subservient to his design, that Man should live and abide some time upon the Face of the Earth, and not that so curious and wonderful a piece of Workmanship by its own Negligence, or want of Necessaries, should perish again, presently after a few moments continuance'.

94 *Two Treatises*, I.iv.41, p.187.

95 *Two Treatises*, II.vi, see below pp.230–1.

96 See *Draft B*, s.39, p.147; 'An Essay concerning Toleration', pp.102f; 'Trade' in *Locke on Money*, vol. II, p.485; *Two Treatises*, I.iv.33, pp.182f, 59, p.201, cf.I.iv.33, p.183, 41, p.188 on depopulation under absolute monarchies.

97 *Two Treatises*, I.ix.86, p.223.

98 *Two Treatises*, II.i.2, p.286; on relations, see ch.5, pp.147 above.

99 Filmer, *Observations on Aristotles Politiques* in Filmer (1991), p.237.

100 See notably *Two Treatises*, II.vi.54, p.322.

101 Filmer, *Patriarcha*, I.i in Filmer (1991), pp.2–5.

102 In logical sequence, *Two Treatises*, II.ii.8–11, pp.290–2; vii.87–8, pp.341–3. For a similar logic, see Burnet (1688), s.2, p.1 'It is no less certain, that as the light of nature has planted in all men a natural principle of the love of Life, and of a desire to preserve it; so the common principles of all religion agree in this, that God having set us in this World, we are bound to preserve that being, which he has given us, by all just and lawful ways. Now this duty of self-preservation, is exerted in instances of two sorts; the one are, in the resisting of Violent Aggressors; the other are the taking of just revenges of those, who have invaded us so secretly, that we could not prevent them, and so Violently that we could not resist them: in which cases the principle of self-preservation warrants us, both to recover what is our own, with just damages, and also to put such unjust persons out of a Capacity of doing the like Injuries any more, either to our selves, or to any others.'

103 *Two Treatises*, II.ii.6, p.289.

104 For a fuller account of this derivation, see the present writer's (1994), s.2.

105 *Two Treatises*, II.ii.5, p.288.

106 Francis Atterbury (1704), p.3.

107 *Two Treatises*, II.ii.4, p.287; ii.6, p.289.

108 *Two Treatises*, I.ix.86, p.223.

109 *Two Treatises*, II.ii.6, p.289.

110 *Paraphrase and Notes on the Epistles of St. Paul*, vol. ii, p.590 on *Romans*, xiii, 10.

111 *Two Treatises*, II.ii.6, p.289.

112 Atterbury, *A Sermon*, p.10.

113 Filmer, *The Free-Holders Grand Inquest* in Filmer (1991), p.129.

114 Grotius (1625), I.iii.8.1–2 (anonymous translation of London, 1738), p.64.

115 Hobbes (1651), I.xiii–xvi, II.xvii.

116 The general form of the argument comes from Bodin, but without his reservations, see pp.199 above.

117 *Two Treatises*, II.iii.17, p.297.

118 *Two Treatises*, II.iv.23, p.302. The point about slavery was noted by Parry (1978), pp.69–70. See also p.247-8 below for the effects of this.

119 John Cowell (1607), s.n. *Property*.

120 *Two Treatises*, II.1–2, 4, 7 and I, *passim*.

121 Cowell (1607), s.n. *Property* 'and this none in our kingdome can be said to have in any lands, or tenements, but onely the King in the right of the Crowne. Because all the lands through the realme, are in the nature of fee, and doe hould mediately or immediately of the Crowne.'

122 Grotius (1625), II.2.ii, esp. 1, 5; Samuel Pufendorf (1672), IV.v.2, 4. For Grotius and Pufendorf, see Karl Olivecrona (1974), pp.211–30.

123 Hobbes (1651), I.xiii, p.63, cf. II.xxiv, p.127.

124 Hobbes (1651), II.xxiv, p.127.

125 Gee(1658), I.ii.2, p.15 '*Moral power*, is that which we call *property* or *dominion*; it consisteth in a right title or interest, to order dispose or

govern. This Moral Power, as seated in Man, may be taken either more extensively, so the object of it may be inanimate, or brute beasts. . .or more strictly, as it respecteth Man only; and this Power thus related we peculiarly call Authority'; Stillingfleet (1662), I.vii.1, pp.132f. For political authority compare Filmer, *Observations upon Aristotles Politiques* in Filmer(1991), p.252 'the first grounds or principles of government (which necessarily depend upon the original of property' with George Lawson (1660), I.i, p.1 'Propriety is the ground of Power, and Power of Government.'

126 Stillingfleet (1658), I.1.2, p.9, cf. I.vii.1, pp.132f 'Dominion and Propriety was introduced by free consent of men.' Cf. Cumberland (1672), ch.7, s. 8–9, pp.321–4 of Cumberland (1727); Samuel Parker (1670), ch.2, p.79 and cf. more vaguely (London, 1681a), pt. i, s.6, p.40; Sir H.Goodricke in Grey (1769), vol. x, 80.

127 Locke, 'Morality', Ms Locke, c.28, fols.139–40. Patrick Kelly (1988) suggests 1677–8 as a dating for this.

128 'I may grant that Mannors, &c. were enjoyed by tenure from Kings; but this will no way prejudice the cause I defend, nor signify more, than that . . . to avoid quarrels that might arise, if every man took upon him to seize what he could, a certain method of making the distribution was necessarily to be fixed; and it was fit, that every man should have something in his own hands to justify his Title to what he possessed. . .This must be testified by some body, and no man could be so fit, or of so much credit as he who was chief among them', Sidney(1698), III.xxix, pp.393f.

129 'Certainly it was a rare felicity that all the men in the world at one instant of time should agree together in one mind to change the natural community of all things into private dominion. For without such an unanimous consent it was not possible for community to be altered' which Filmer disdained because 'If our first parents, or some other of our forefathers did voluntarily bring in property of goods and subjection to governors, and it were in their power either to bring them in or not, or having brought them in to alter their minds and restore them to their first condition of community and liberty, what reason can there be alleged that men that now live should not have the same power?' Filmer, *Observations concerning the Originall of Government* in Filmer(1991), p.234. Sanderson's preface to Ussher(1661), d-d₂ objected to popular consent more generally by enquiring who convened people for this purpose.

130 *Two Treatises*, II.v.25, pp.303f.

131 *Two Treatises*, II.v.27, p.305.

132 For an objection to slavery, without Locke's argument against it, see [Henry Parker] (1644), pp.36f; for property as a quality inhering in a person, see Thomas Fuller (1642), V.xiii, p.409; for Grotius on *suum*, see *De Jure Belli*, I.2.i.5 and II.17.2,1. There is a discussion of *dominium* as property in the narrow sense in Tully(1980), ch.4 and in the wider sense in Tuck(1979), esp. chs.4, 6 and 8.

133 For instance Hobbes had included material possesions in his catalogue of 'propriety', but had been able to suggest that along with other examples of

suum they were explained by the sovereign's acts, see (1651), II.xxx, p.179.

134 *Two Treatises*, II.v.27, pp.305f.

135 For the usage of 'propriety' see, e.g., Pepys' 'heard exceeding good argument against Mr. Harrington's assertion that over-balance of propriety was the foundation of government', (1970–83), vol. I, p.17.

136 Pufendorf only discussed appropriation after partition (see(1672), IV.iv.12) and Grotius used the verb *arripere* to describe prior appropriation, which scarcely suggests a legitimate title to property (see(1625), II.2.ii.1).

137 For some gamineseque queries, see Robert Nozick (1974), pp.174–82. For a more sophisticated approach, see Cohen (1985)

138 Filmer *Observations concerning the Originall of Government* in Filmer(1991), p.217; Grotius(1625), II.2.ii.1.

139 *Two Treatises*, I.iv.28, pp.179f, cf. s.40–1 186-8, and ix.86 p.233.

140 *Two Treatises*, II.v.26, pp.304f; v.35, p.310.

141 *Two Treatises*, II.v.37, p.312 'he who appropriates land to himself by his labour, does not lessen but increase the common stock of mankind'.

142 See *seriatim Two Treatises*, II.v.28–9 (consumption), 30 (seizure), 32 (improvement), 40 (labour), pp.306–14.

143 *Two Treatises*, II.v.48, 50, pp.319–20.

144 Locke to the Rev.Richard King, 25 August, 1703, *Correspondence of John Locke*, vol.VIII, p.58. Here, if anywhere, is the place to juxtapose Jeremy Waldron's important argument that labour does not establish a title to property in the term Locke sets out (Waldron(1988a)ch.6) with Alan Ryan's query that theology appears less than one might suppose in Locke's chapter on property (Ryan(1984)p.24). The point is that Locke's terms *include* a reference to labour, but labour is significant as licensed by and as a means to fulfilling God's ordinance; the latter is structural to chapter five, but deployed rather than set out there.

145 *Two Treatises*, I.vi.54, p.197.

146 *Two Treatises*, I.vi.56, p.199, cf. II.vi.63, p.327.

147 *Two Treatises*, II.vi.56, p.323.

148 *Two Treatises*, II.vi.58, p.324.

149 *Ibid.* II.vi.64, p.328.

150 *Two Treatises*, II.xv.170, p.399.

151 See generally *Two Treatises*, II.vii-ix.

152 *Two Treatises*, II.vii.78–88, pp.336–43.

153 Filmer, *The Anarchy of a Mixed or Limited Monarchy* in Filmer(1991), p.138.

154 Augustine, *De peccatorum meritis et remissione*, I.ii (Migne(1843–66), vol.xl, 116; H.Heppe(1950), pp.347f.

155 *De Civitate Dei*, XIII.14 (Migne(1843–66), vol.xli, .386) says that all are justly damned as his progeny.

156 Augustine, *De Moribus Ecclesiae Catholicae*, I. 40 (Migne(1843–66), vol.xxxii .1328).

157 Calvin(1559), II.i.4–6,8; v.19; cf I.xv.4 and see esp. II.5 for Calvin consciously improving on Augustine's explanation.

158 Gilbert Burnet(1699), sub. art.ix, p.128.

159 William Perkins, (1970), p.191.

160 Edward Reynolds(1631), p.134.

161 Gabriel Towerson (1685), *An Explication of the Decalogue*, p.8.

162 Reynolds(1631), p.135.

163 For this reason the terms 'representative' and 'imputationist' will be used interchangeably in this context.

164 George Lawson (1659), I.xv.5, p.74.

165 Thomas Tuke(1609), pp.56f.

166 *Two Treatises of Government*, I.xi.111 pp.239f; I.v.45–7 pp.190–2.

167 *Two Treatises*, I.xi.111 p.239.

168 Filmer, *Observations upon Aristotles Politiques*, preface in Filmer(1991), p.236.

169 Locke, *Two Treatises*, I.iv.40, pp.186f.

170 John Pearson(1658), John Dryden (1661), esp. lines 1–10.

171 *Paraphrase and Notes on the Epistles of Saint Paul*, ii, p.525, note on *Romans*, V.14.

172 Worthington(1847–86), vol. II.i, p.47; Locke, *Two Treatises*, I.iv.36, p.183; on obscure writers, see also *An Essay concerning Human Understanding*, III.ix.10, p.481.

173 *Two Treatises*, I.iv.45, p.191.

174 Ainsworth(1639), p.15.

175 *Two Treatises* II.xix.222, p.431.

176 Tuke(1609), pp.56f.

177 Samuel Parker (1667), pp.137f; Edward Reynolds(1631), p.31. Contrast, Locke, *Two Treatises*, II.xvi.182–3; pp.407–9.

178 Bodin(1576), I.x, p.40; compare Hobbes (1651), I.xvi with I.xviii and II.xxx.

179 *Two Treatises* II.xvi.182, p.407.

180 *Two Treatises* II.xvi.189, p.411.

181 *Two Treatises* I.vi.50–1, pp.194–6. For the doctrine, see, e.g., Grotius (1625), II.v and, for another critique, Hobbes (1651), II.xx, p.102.

182 Stillingfleet (1658), p.34.

183 *Two Treatises*, II.viii.116, p.364, cf.vi.73, p.333.

184 *Two Treatises*, II.ix, esp. 131, p.371.

185 *Two Treatises* II.xv.169–74, pp.398–402.

186 It is unclear from Locke's account precisely who would be in a position to consent explicitly, save officeholders and property owners.

187 E.g., *Two Treatises*, II.xi.134, p.373.

188 *Two Treatises*, II.iii.17, p.297.

189 To these we should add charity, for which see Ian Harris (1994), s.2.

190 Hobbes (1651), I.xvii, p.87; this is not to say that the sovereign does not have functions – in Hobbes' word 'offices', but he is bound to obey God rather than obliged to the citizen to perform his office. See II.xxx.

191 *Two Treatises*, II.viii.122, p.367.

192 *Two Treatises*, II.viii.119, p.366. This assumes, of course, that the proper return for a benefit is another (cf. s.121, p.367) and presumes, fundamentally, a rule to the effect that benefits ought to be returned – see ch.8, p.273 *below*.

193 *Two Treatises*, II.viii.119, pp.365f.

194 *Two Treatises*, II.ix.127, p.370.

195 *Two Treatises*, II.ix.131, p.371.

196 *Two Treatises*, II.ix.131, p.371.

197 *Two Treatises*, II.ix.127, p.370.

198 *Two Treatises*, II.xi.135–8, pp.375–9. Of course it was also helpful to establish property in terms congruent with those that established 'bounded' government, in order to show that the latter implied no weakening of the former.

199 *Two Treatises*, II.xiii.156, esp p.389; xiv, 159 p.392.

200 [John Somers] (1681b), pp.2–3; *Two Treatises*, II.ix; *Two Treatises*, II.xiii, esp. 149, pp.384f.

201 see, e.g., Filmer, *The Free-holders Grand Inquest passim* in Filmer (1991).

202 Polemical convenience, as on other occasions, was served by this explanatory sequence. By Locke's principles, taxation without consent was not admissible. This obviously contradicts the absolutist argument that rulers are entitled to their subjects' possessions, as does Locke's explanation of private property in terms not of governmental action but rather of God's intentions. But taxation by consent was important if the House of Commons' ability to influence the government was exercised by withholding supply. Examples could be multiplied.

203 For 'no body Arbitrary but themselves', see above p.209; for Moore, Anon (1681b) in N.Thompson (ed.) (1685), p.79; for Locke on forms of government see *Two Treatises*, II.x, esp. 132, p.372. Cf.II.xiv, *passim*, esp. s.165, p.395.

204 For Charles II, see (1681), p.10; for James II, see (1685), p.4; [Roger L'Estrange] (1681–4), no.27.

205 *Two Treatises*, II.xv.172, p.400.

206 See Laslett's strictures on II.xv.169, p.398n.

207 For Bodin, see above p.199. For contemporary interest, see J.M.Wallace (1968) on the engagement controversy, Fell (1659), p.5 for the Restoration ('the *Royalists* pretension of having the K[ing]. an absolute Conqueror, as it would destroy the interest of all parties that have appeared against him or his Father, would infringe the Liberties of the *English* Subjects in general'); [Somers] (1681a), p.16 ('There is a third sort of men, who tell us this Realm, being entirely subdued by the Conqueror, and by him left to descend to his Heirs, none of those Heirs who derive a Title under him, can deprive those who are to succeed of any Right'); for the view that monarchy can be acquired either by consent or by conquest see, [Settle] (1681), p.21; and for the exclusion crisis generally Tarlton (1981), pp.49–68.

208 For Hobbes, see (1651), II.xx, p.104 and esp. 'A Review, and Conclusion', pp.719–21; for Hale (1971), pp.49–52.

209 *Two Treatises*, II.xvi, esp. s.175, 182.

210 *Two Treatises*, II.xvi.196, p.414; xvii, s.198, pp.415f.

211 *Two Treatises*, II.xvii.197, p.415.

212 *Two Treatises*, II.xviii.199, p.416.

213 *Essays on the Law of Nature*, no.4.

214 *Two Treatises*, I.iv.39, pp.185f.

215 *The Reasonableness of Christianity* (London, 1695), p.8 for the fact that

human life was understood to be God's: 'if God afford them a Temporary, Mortal Life, 'tis his Gift, they owe it to his Bounty, they could not claim it as their Right, nor does he injure them when he takes it from them'. Cf. *Essays*, no.4, fol.56 (p.154).

216 *Two Treatises*, II.iii.17, p.297.

217 *Two Treatises*, II.ii.11, p.292.

218 *Two Treatises*, I.ix.86, p.223; II.ii.7, pp.289f; the supposition of the latter right obviated Hobbes' view that God's law was not enforced *as such* on earth, but only as a terrestrial sovereign's command): but the Lockean God gave people a legitimate title to enforce His commands. The 'some Men' to whom Locke's doctrine 'will seem . . . very strange' (II.ii.9, p.290) presumably refers to Hobbes; cf. (1651) II.xxviii, p.161. See also for Hobbes and Locke Wolfgang Von Leyden (1981) in Reinhard Brandt (ed.) (1981). Generally, see Simmons (1992), ch.3.

219 Cf. *Two Treatises*, II.iii.18. p.298f.

220 E.g., Hobbes (1651), I.xiv, p.64; Jeremy Taylor (1660), II.i (1660), pp.167–8; Pufendorf (1660), I.xiv.3, p.194 and the young Locke, *Essays on the Law of Nature*, no.1, f.11 (p.110).

221 See above p.241.

222 *Two Treatises*, II.xi.135, p.375.

223 Cf. ch.4 and ch.6, p.191 *above*.

224 James I, speech of 1603 (1918), p.278; Locke, *Two Treatises*, II.xviii.199, pp.416f.

225 James I, speech of 1603 (1918), p.278; *Two Treatises*, II.xvii.201, p.418.

226 *Two Treatises*, II.xviii.209, pp.422f.

227 See *Two Treatises*, II.xix.211 on conquest; 214 on arbitrary rule; 215–16 on arbitrary power against the legislatve; 220 on tyranny and esp. 222 on arbitrary power and slavery.

228 See esp. *Two Treatises*, II.ix.131, p.371.

229 Seth Ward (1661), p.8.

230 *Two Treatises*, II.xviii.204, p.420.

231 *Two Treatises*, II.xix.226, p.433.

232 see V.F.Snow (1962), pp.175–87. This is not to say that Locke's conclusion was attractive to all his contemporaries, but merely that his project stood on a ground that it was desirable to capture.

233 *Two Treatises*, II.xiv.226, p.440.

234 Denis Grenville (1861), p.31; since Locke is not a resistance theorist in this fundamental sense, it seems rather doubtful that one can set one's bearings by *Two Treatises* as the culmination of resistance theories as Quentin Skinner did in (1978), vol. II, pp.347–8, cf. 239. For a related point, see J.H.Burns (1983), 369–74.

235 *Two Treatises*, II.ii.6, p.289.

CHAPTER 8

1 *An Essay concerning Human Understanding*, I.i.1. p.43.

2 *Essays on the Law of Nature*, no.4, fol.50 (148); *An Essay*, IV.xvii.1, cf.4;

IV.xvii.2, p.669, cf. IV.vii.2, p.591, IV.xx.1, p.706 and IV.xvii.15, 18,
IV.xvii.2, p.669, cf. IV.vii.2, p.591, IV.xx.1, p.706 and IV.xvii.15, 18,
pp.683, 685; IV.xvii.9, p.681, cf *Essays*, no.4, fol.48 (146).

3 *An Essay*, I.ii.1, p.48.

4 See ch.5, p.153 *above*.

5 See *An Essay*, I.ii.6, p.46 sub-heading '*Knowledge of our Capacity a cure of Scepticism and Idleness.*

6 See ch.10, *below*.

7 *An Essay*, II.i.24, p.118.

8 *An Essay*, II.viii.4, p.133; II.i.25, p.118; II.i.8, p.107, cf. II.i.22, p.117.

9 For the common view that happiness was the end of human activity, cf Locke's own note cited p.388 n.28.

10 Ms.Locke, f.1, p.326, 16 July, 1676, shorthand entry deciphered by Von Leyden, *Essays*, p.265, cf. *Essays*, no.4, fols.56 and 59 for wisdom and goodness.

11 *Draft C*, II.vi.4, cf. *An Essay*, II.vii.3, p.129.

12 *Draft C*, II.vi.5, cf. *An Essay*, II.vii.4, pp.130f.

13 For distrust of 'right reason', see ch.3, p.93 *above*; Ms.Locke, f.1, pp.336f, deciphered in *Essays*, p.268. In the latter place Locke distinguished three varieties of good: *utile, honestum* and *jucundum*. These three denoted respectively what was good because useful, what was good in itself and what was good because pleasurable. An obvious source of the distinction was Cicero, *De Finibus Bonoroum ac Malorum*, esp. II.iv, xv, xxiv, IV.xviii. Locke had already rejected the idea that good was attractive because good in his *Essays on the Law of Nature*, no.1, fols.10–11 (108/10).

14 For morality as law and for rewards and punishments, see ch.3, pp.80-83, 101-2 *above*; for moral good and evil, see pp.255-6, 270-1 *below*.

15 *Draft A*, s.26, pp.41f, *Draft B*, s.160, pp.269f.

16 It is worth noting in passing that when Locke came to discuss qualities (II.viii, see s.8 for a definition of quality) he continued this purpose. The point of *pain* was to guide us from what harms us towards that 'which is necessary to the preservation of life', for God had not designed 'our preservation barely, but the preservation of every part and organ in its perfection' (s.4 p.130 cf II.i.10 p.108 and II.x.3 p.150).

17 *An Essay*, II.xx.2, 14, pp.229,231f.

18 *Ibid.* II.xxi.5, p.236.

19 *Ibid.* s.10, 14, cf.21–9, pp.238, 240, 244–9 in the same way.

20 *Draft C*, II.xxv.31, p.251, cf. *An Essay*, II.xxi.50, p.265.

21 *An Essay*, II.xxi.31, p.251.

22 *An Essay*, II.xxi.32, p.251.

23 *An Essay*, II.xxi.34, p.252.

24 *An Essay*, II.xxi.35, for Locke's retractation.

25 The quotation is from Ovid, *Metamorphoses* vii.20–1. For an example, compare the idea of compromise, in which two people agree to do that whih they both know is wrong.

26 *An Essay*, II.xxi.36–7, pp.254–5.

27 *An Essay*, II.xxi.43–4, pp.259–61.

28 Which fails to deal with the determined masochist. For a recognition that

people were attracted to different pleasures, cf. *An Essay*, II.xxi.54–5, pp.268–70. For the causes of error and for right choice, cf. s.56–70, pp.270–82.

29 *An Essay*, II.xxi.47, cf. s.8,15, p.237, 241: for a fuller treatment of the revision, see ch.10, pp.300–02 *below*.

30 *An Essay*, II.xii.3. p.164.

31 *An Essay*, II.xxiii.12–13, pp.302-304.

32 *An Essay*, II.xxiii-xxiv.

33 *An Essay*, II.xxv–xxvi.

34 *An Essay*, II.xxix-xxxii.

35 *An Essay*, II.xxxii.14; xxi.2.

36 *An Essay*, II.xxxi.6, cf. II.xxxii.5, 18.

37 *An Essay*, IV.ii.14, p.537.

38 *An Essay*, IV.iii.14 p.545f.

39 *An Essay*, IV.iv.12. p.568f.

40 *An Essay*, IV.vi.13.

41 *An Essay*, IV.xi, esp. ss.5, 8.

42 *An Essay*, IV.xii.10, p.645.

43 *An Essay*, IV.xii.11–12, pp.646–7.

44 *An Essay*, IV.xii.11, p.646.

45 Stillingfleet (1662), I.i.3, p.11.

46 see *An Essay*, IV.x.

47 Cf. *An Essay*, I.iii.12, p.74 'what Duty is, cannot be understood without a Law; nor a Law be known, or supposed without a Law-maker, or without Reward and Punishment'.

48 Cf. Clarendon (1676), p.36 'That is only properly call'd the Law of Nature, that is dictated to the whole species.'

49 Stillingfleet (1662), I.i.3, p.11; Baxter (1667), pt i, ch.10, s.2, p.70; Towerson (1685) *pt ii . . . An Explication of the Decalogue*, disc. iii. p.12.

50 Proofs of God, *Essays on the Law of Nature*, no.4; Ms.Locke f.1, fols.367–70, 29 July 1676 (Aaron and Gibb pp.81–2); *An Essay*, IV.x; Descartes, Ms.Locke c.28, fols.119ff. For the effects of logomachies in France about God's existence, see Kors (1990).

51 Despite a long and distinguished tradition in Locke scholarship concentrating on such matters as substance and knowledge: see above 'Introduction' p.3.

52 Ms.Locke, f.3, fol.263 (25 July 1678), f.5, fols.77ff (26 July 1681) (Aaron and Gibb, pp.116f), cf. Ms.Locke f.3, fol.18 (22 January 1678) (Aaron and Gibb, p.104).

53 John Yolton (1970), chs.7-8.

54 *An Essay*, II.xxii.2,5.

55 *An Essay*, II.xxiii.12, p.302.

56 *An Essay*, II.xxviii.14–15, pp.357-9.

57 It is true that II.xxviii.14, p.358 says 'If I have the Will of a supreme, invisible Lawmaker for my Rule: then, as I supposed the Action commanded, or forbidden by God, I call it Good or Evil, Sin or Duty'; but the passage does nothing to explain *how* 'I have the Will'. Again whilst the concept of obligation could be analysed in terms of mixed modes, (*An*

Essay IV.xxii.1 p.283) this is quite another matter to proving the presence of an obligation.

58 *An Essay* II.xxix-xxxii.

59 *An Essay* II.xxx.4, xxxi.3 cf. 14, xxxii.17 but mixed modes were not without potential inadequacies, see, e.g. II.xxx.4 on inconsistent composition.

60 *An Essay* IV.iv.5, 6-7, 12

61 *An Essay* IV.iii.18, p.549f.

62 *An Essay* IV.ii-iii; IV.iii.18, esp pp.548f.

63 *An Essay* I.iii.1 p. 66 'these moral Rules are capable of Demonstration'.

64 For Locke's problem, cf.Dunn (1969), ch.14, Riley (1982), ch.3; *An Essay* IV.xxii.1 p.283; *Virtus* (1681), 1661 Commonplace Book, p.10. For Locke's location of the content of good, cf.Simmons (1992) ch.1.5.

65 *A Second Letter for Toleration* (*Works*, twelfth edition (10 vols. London, 1823, vol.5, pp.69, 131, 133) reveals the force of Locke's anti-consequentialism. This precludes the arguments advanced by Proast against Locke's view of toleration (for which see ch.10 below pp.293-5), against which, indeed, it was advanced.

66 *Draft B* s.100 p.223 cf 'An Essay', p.95.

67 *Essays on the Law of Nature* no. 6 fols. 83f (p.180/2) '*ut vero cognoscamus unde oriatur illud juris vinculum, sciendum est neminem nos ad quodvis agendum obligare vel astringere posse nisi qui in nos jus et potestatem habet; et dum imperat quid fieri velit, quid non, jure tantum. utitur suo: adeo ut vinculum sit ab illo dominio et imperio quod superior quivis in nos actionesque nostras obtinet, et in quantum alteri subjicimur in tantum obligationi obnoxii sumus.*'

68 *Essays* no. 6 fol.87 (p.186). The point can be seen at fol.89 (188), where it is said that it is the will of the supreme Deity that provides the basis of moral obigation, *fundamentum enim obligationis.*

69 cf *Essays* no.4 fols.52f (150) '*Primo . . . ut se lege teneri quisquam cognosat, scire prius oportet esse legislatorem superiorem scilicet aliquam potestam cui jure subjicitur. Secundo scire etiam oportet esse aliquam superioris illius potestatis voluntatem circa res a nobis agendas, hoc est legislatorem illium, quicunque is demum fuerit, velle hoc agere illud vero omittere, et exigere a noblis ut vitae nostrae mores suae voluntati sint conformes*'

70 *Essays* no. 6 fols.86f (p.184/6).

71 *Second Reply to Stillingfleet*, Works I, p.103, cf, *Postscript to Reply* p. 576.

72 Locke's uncertainty about where to put 'Of Ethick in General' is revealed by the numerous suggestions, amendments and crossings-out at the head of the pages. Ms.Locke c.28 fols.146, 147, etc.

73 'Of Ethick in General' s.4. fols.147-8

74 *ibid* s. 4-6, 9.

75 *ibid.* s.11, fol.151 'without showing how he hath declard his will & law I must only at present suppose this rule till a fit place to speak of these viz. God & the Law of nature and only at present mention what is immediately to ye purpose in hand . . . That this rule of our actions set us by our lawmaker is conversant about & ultimately terminates in those simple ideas before mentioned.'

76 *ibid*, s. 12. fol. 152 It is of marked interest that one of the best treatments of Locke on natural law, G.A.J. Rogers (1981) pp.146-62 collects no evidence that Locke discovered that there was an obligation to the law of nature.
The ms. of *Draft B* ends at precisely the same point. Whilst it is conceivable that a continuing passage from B is lost, it is unlikely that any further argument on this subject has perished. On this point there is not only the evidence of 'Of Ethick in General' but also the fact that the corresponding passage in *Draft A* ends and moves off the subject without further development.

77 *An Essay* I.iii. 6 p. 69; Petty (1928), p. 277.

78 Ms. Locke f.2 fols.49-50 (29 June 1676) (Aaron and Gibb p. 87), cf. *An Essay* II.xxi.70 pp.281f.

79 Whilst there are no arguments in *An Essay* proving posthumous sanctions, their reality is assumed, see I.iii.6 p.69 II.xxviii.8 p. 352.

80 E.g. Samuel Parker (1681b) I.xvi pp.84-8; Sydenham 'Theologia Rationalis' (1966) p. 154.

81 *Two Treatises* II.xiv.168, xix.241 pp.397f, 445; *Epistola de Tolerantia*, p.128.

82 *An Essay*, II. xxvii.22, 26 pp. 344, 347.

83 See ch.10, p.301–3 below.

84 For Austin, see the present writer in *Cambridge Law Journal* 48 (1989), pp.340–2.

85 *Essays on the Law of Nature* no.4; 'lex naa', Ms.Locke, f.3, pp.201–2(15 July, 1678); Ms.Locke, f.1, p.321 (15 July 1676), deciphered in *Essay*, p.261; Baxter (1673) IV. 3.19, p.12.

86 Sanderson, (1660), V. iii p.129.

87 The latter part of this paragraph is drawn from Adam Smith (1976), VII. iii.ii.4, pp.318f, itself based on Ralph Cudworth (1678), I. ii.3–4.

88 *An Essay concerning Human Understanding*, II. xxviii.8, p.352.

89 *An Essay*, IV. x.3–5, pp.620–1.

90 *An Essay*, II. xx.2, p.229.

91 *An Essay*, II. xxviii.5, p.351 cf. II. xxi.42.

92 *An Essay*, II. xxviii.6, pp.351f.

93 *An Essay*, II. xxviii.5, p.351.

94 Francis Hutcheson(1897) VII.v in L.A.Selby-Bigge (ed.) (1897), vol. I, p.158.

95 *An Essay concerning Human Understanding*, I.iii.18, p.78 'let us consider this Proposition as to its meaning. . .*viz*. *Virtue is the best Worship of God*; i.e. is most acceptable to him;. . .If *Virtue* be taken for Actions conformable to God's Will, or to the Rule prescribed by God, which is the true and only measure of Vertue, when Vertue is used to signifie what is in its own nature right and good; then this Proposition, *That Vertue is the best Worship of God*, will be most true and certain, but of very little use in humane Life: since it will amount to no more but this, *viz*. *That God is pleased with the doing of what he Commands*; which a Man may certainly know to be true, without knowing what it is, that God doth command'. cf. *Draft B*, s.6, p.111f.

96 *An Answer to Remarks*. . . appended to *Reply to*. . .*the Bishop of Worcester*,

Works, vol.i, p.576. This was despite the hectoring observations on p.575 about Burnet's anonymity: 'I cannot much blame him in another respect, for concealing his name: for, I think, any one who appears among Christians, may be well ashamed of his name, when he raises such a doubt as this, viz. whether a infinitely powerful and wise being be veracious or no'. Burnet riposted, aptly enough (1697b), pp.2f 'as to the Crime of concealing my Name. . .I think, of all Men I know, Mr. *Lock* had the least Reason to make that Criminal, He who hath writ so many Books without putting his Name to them, and some in confutation of the Principles of other Men'.

97 It my be worth adducing Richard Price's view (1948), p.43, '*Mr. Locke . . . represents rectitude as* signifying conformity of actions to some rules or laws. . .From whence it follows, that it is an absurdity to apply *rectitude* to rules and laws themselves' or 'to suppose the *divine* will to be directed by it. But, it is undoubted, that this great man would have detested these consequences; and indeed, it is sufficiently evident, that he was strangely embarrassed in his notions on this, as well as some other subjects.'

98 *Some Thoughts concerning Education*, s.136, p.195. There is, however, the further difficulty that God's infliction of punishment in the afterlife, as usually understood, was not obviously for the good of the sinner: but this difficulty could be obviated by conceiving posthumous punishment as a means of expiation or reformation. Locke did not reach this position, but towards the end of his life made notes which suggested that punishment might not be eternal and so, implicitly, indicated that it might be proportionate to sins.

99 There is the additional point that the comprehensive range of God's benefits to mankind would afford no clue as to what particulars were especially worthy of presenting to Him in acknowledgement, though worship might be a suitable one in general terms, cf. *Essays*, no.4; for Tillotson, see 'Sermon 54' in (1704), p.641 and for Selden, Aubrey (1949), p.435, 'He intended to have given his owne Library to the University of Oxford, but received disobligation from them, for that they would not lend him some MSS.' Of course, it might be supposed that society depended upon a continual exchange of benefits, in which case the obligation would become one of the necessity; it may be that the usage captures this point.

100 Taylor (1660), II.i, s.54, p.183.

101 Coke (1660), preface.

102 Stillingfleet (1662), I.i.9, p.9.

103 For the identification of *Ethica*, *Ethica* B etc. as notes for the project of demonstration, see Aaron (1971), p.256n.

104 *An Essay concerning Human Understanding*, II.xxviii. 7–13, pp.352–7.

105 'Of Study', p.417 'An Hobbist with his principle of self-preservation, whereof himself is to be judge, will not easily admit a great many plain duties of morality.' Other self-deceivers, as they were conceived by Locke, unsurprisingly included Roman Catholics and enthusiasts.

106 Cf. Dunn (1969), ch.7.

107 *An Essay concerning Human Understanding*, II.xxviii.7, p.352. *Correspondence* no.1301 (30 June, 1690).

108 Molyneux's letters (all in *Correspondence of John Locke*, vol.IV) are nos. 1530 (27 August, 1692), 1579 (22 December, 1692), 1661 (16 September, 1693). Locke's sole surviving reply is no.1538 (20 September, 1692). His response to Tyrrell is striking: 'Will nothing then passe with you in Religion or Morality but what you can demonstrate? If you are of sonice a stomach I am afraid If I should Examine how much of your religion or Morality you could demonstrate how much you would have left, not but that I thinke that demonstration in those matters may be carried a great deale farther then it is But there are perhaps many millions of propositions in Mathematiques which are demonstrable which neither you nor I can demonstrate and which perhaps no man has yet demonstrated or will do before the end of the world.' *Correspondence* no.1309, 4 August, 1690 (vol.IV, pp.111f). See also nos. 1301, 1307, 1312 and 1394.

109 Grotius (1625), I.i.ix.1; Stillingfleet (1662), I.i.3, p.12.

110 Hobbes, *Leviathan*, II.xxvii (my emphasis).

111 *Ibid*, II.xxvi, cf. I.v for right reason.

112 Baxter (1667), pt. i, ch.8, s.4, p.44; Halifax, see (1699) in (1969) p.51.

113 see Henry More (1668); Thomas Burnet (1697a), p.5 and Cudworth's 'As the first spring of vital action is not from the speculative understanding, so neither is dry and inspid ratiocination the only measure and rule of good and evil...It is not sapless speculative knowledge that is the proper rule or judge of good and evil but vital touches, tastes and savours' (British Library Mss.Add.4982, 8–9, quoted by J.A.Passmore (1951), p.66).

114 A point which the third earl of Shaftesbury and Hutcheson exploited in disconnecting ethics from God's capacity as a legislator.

115 *Latin Tract*, pp.6–8 (193–7).

116 *Paraphrase and Notes upon the Epistles of St.Paul*, vol.II, p.499.

117 [John Wallis] (1643), ch.12, p.82; Tillotson (1666), I.i.3, p.4.

118 *Two Treatises*, II.ii.6, p.289.

119 James Lowde (1694), preface; (1699), p.11, cf.40. For Locke's usage, cf. *An Essay*, I.xxviii.13, 15, pp.357, 359.

120 *An Essay concerning Human Understanding*, IV.xvi, esp.6–8.

121 *An Essay*, IV.xiii.2, IV.xx.12, p.715.

122 *An Essay*, IV.xix.14, cf. xviii.5, p.692.

123 *An Essay*, IV.xix.14.

124 *An Essay*, IV.xviii.5.

125 *An Essay*, IV.xviii.6.

126 *An Essay*, IV.xix, added in the fourth edition; for the sort of phenomenon which this addressed, cf, ch.1, pp.53–7. *above*.

127 *An Essay*, II.xxviii.8, p.352 (the emphases on mankind and men are added).

CHAPTER 9

1 See James Lowde (1694), preface and (1699), p.11, cf. p.4.

2 For a broad treatment, see A.O. Lovejoy (1961).

3 See above ch.6, pp.189–91 *above*.

4 'An Essay concerning Toleration', p.86.

5 But Bayle was not personally hostile to Locke and Locke recommended Bayle's dictionary, albeit with no special enthusiasm: see 'Mr Locke's Extempore Advice', p.326.

6 'lex triplex', Ms. Locke, f.3, p.201; 'Thus I thinke', Ms. Locke, c.28, fol.143.

7 For all this, see Alban Krailshamer (1962).

8 Cf. Nicole's argument to the effect that just as the monastic life made the road to Heaven easier so the life of a royal court facilitated the path to Hell (1670), pp.190–220. See also Nicole (1828), no.2, s. 4, p.28.

9 See Nicole (1828), nos.2 and 3.

10 See Thomas Hancock's preface to Nicole (1828), pp.ix–xii and notes on no.2, pp.66–8. For the translation, cf., e.g., Ms. Locke, f.1, fol.367 (29 July 1676), f.3 (2 July 1678) (in John Lough (ed.) *John Locke's Travels in France, 1675–79* (Cambridge, 1953), p.202 and for an idea drawn from it congruent with it, see Ms. Locke, f.2, fol. 49 (8 February 1677) (Aaron and Gibb, p.87).

11 *Some Thoughts concerning Education*, s.138, p.197. For a general treatment of some thoughts, see Nathan Tarcov (1984) and more especially the editors' introduction to J.W. and J.S. Yolton (eds.) *Some Thoughts concerning Education*.

12 Nicole, (1828), no.2, s.52, p.80; for Gouge, see William Gouge (1622), Epistle. The education of the leaders of society seems to have given especial concern about this time. Cf-Viscount Lonsdale (1808), p.viii–ix: 'He had frequent occasions of regretting how very defective this nation was in the education of gentlemen. He remarked that there was sufficient provision for those who devoted themselves to the study of divinity, physic, and the study of the civil law at the Universities; but that the education of gentlemen was a thing so foreign to the notions, birth and studies of those men and the discipline with regard to them so loose, that for a very long time it hath very manifestly been the ruin of all those young persons, who are easily susceptible of bad impressions; while the naturally good and virtuous are instructed in nothing but a little useless sophistry, an awkward garb and habit which requires a long time to unlearn, and which nothing less than two or three years' travel is able to remove.' See, on national degeneracy [Stephen Penton] (1694), pp.1–2

13 Nicole (1828), no.2, s. 45, p.71.

14 (1828), no. 3 pt. ii, s. 43, p.214.

15 Aristotle, *Politics*, VII.15 (1334b), cf. Plato, *Republic*, III. 410.

16 Gilbert Burnet (1761), pp.19, 21, 22f (emulation), 19f (praise and blame), 48ff (kindness), 19ff (few and severe beatings), 43f (Latin by dialogue), 63 (logics)

17 'Of Study', printed in Axtell (ed.) *Educational Writings* esp. pp. 406–12, 415–22.

18 *Some Thoughts concerning Education*, s. 70, p.132.

19 *Ibid.*, ss. 33, 38, pp.103, 107f.

20 *Ibid.*, s. 48, p.112, cf. s. 45, p.111.

21 Roger Ascham, *The Scholemaster* (1570), bk I in Ascham (1904), p.183, cf. preface, p.176.

22 See *Some Thoughts concerning Education* s. 33, p. 103.

23 *ibid.*, 45, p.111

24 *Ibid.*, ss. 61–2, p.119.

25 *Ibid.*, s. 68, pp.126f.

26 See Lady Masham's report that Locke regarded civility as 'not only the great ornament of life, and that that gave lustre and gloss to all our actions, but looked upon it as a Christian duty that deserved to be more inculcated as such than it generally was', quoted in Fox Bourne (1876), vol. ii, p.533 and see Nicole (1828), no.3, pt.i, s. 88–90, pp.169–73 for a possible explanation of this.

27 *Some Thoughts concerning Education*, esp. s. 142–3, p.199–201, cf. s.70, p.131.

28 Henry Peacham, *The Complete Gentleman* (1622) ed. (with *The Truth of Our Times* (1638) and *The Art of Living in London*) by V.B.Heltzel (Ithaca, 1962), ch.3, p.32.

29 John Milton, *Of Education*, Milton (1974), pp.182f; Baxter (1696), I.i. p.7.

30 Milton (1974), pp.182f, cf. Peacham, *Complete Gentleman*, ch.5 (1962), p.52.

31 Milton (1974), p.181, cf. Ascham, *Scholemaster*, bk I in (1904), p.188, Peacham, *The Truth of Our Times* (1638), (1962), p.222 on religion as the basis of virtue.

32 Obadiah Walker (1673) pt. i, ch.2, p.13.

33 Walker (1673), pt. i, chs.2, 4, pp.24, 38; John Aubrey (1972), p.52. Cf. [Stephen Penton] (1688), pp.74f.

34 Ascham, *Scholemaster*, preface, (1904), p.176, cf. Walker (1673), pt. i, ch.5, pp.39f.

35 Peacham, *Complete Gentleman*, ch.5, (1962), p.34; Ascham, *Scholemaster*, bk I, (1904) p.183, cf. bk I, (1904), pp.187, 188, 201.

36 Peacham, *Complete Gentleman*, ch.5, (1962), p.50, cf. *The Truth of Our Times* (1962), pp.203ff, 218, 224; Ascham, *Scholemaster*, bk I (1904), p.211; Walker (1673), pt. ii, ch.3, p.239.

37 Peacham, *The Truth of Our Times*, (1962), p.197; Walker (1673), pt. i, ch.2, pp.14f.

38 Burnet (1761), p.33, indicating that children should be taught 'a high esteeme of vertuous persones and actions, and as great a contempt of vicious ones'.
   The suggestion that in society virtue would win honour can be found earlier, e.g. [Richard Lingard] (1670), p.5 that moral conduct 'always secures a firm Reputation, let the World be never so Wicked. No man ever gains a Reverence for his *Vice*, but *virtue* commands it'; but see [William Ramesey] (1672), pt. ii, s.3, 2, p.77 for a different accent 'As Honour is obtained by revealing thy Virtue without disadvantage, so Praise is but the reflection of thy Virtue, which represents it self in so many various shapes, as we may justly expect it but a Juggle, and Deceit.'

39 Nicole (1828), e.g., no. 2, s.28, p.50; no. 3, pt. i, s.5, p.102, ss.26–38, pp.121–7, no. 3, pt.ii, ss.14–22, pp.187–94, s.62–3, pp.228–9.

40 Nicole (1828), e.g., no. 3, pt.ii, ss.18–23, pp.190–4.

41 Naturally the care of the body came first in *Some Thoughts concerning Education*, following the Aristotelian order of treatment. Whereas a good

deal of this material was prompted by questions from Edward Clarke and his wife, Locke's arguments about character formation appears no earlier than his draft of 1684. It is possible, of course, that some earlier correspondence is lost, but the evidence at present stands thus. (An exception of some biographical relevance is that the account of toilet training, *Some Thoughts concerning Education*, ss.23–8, derived from Locke's own experience: see *Directions concerning Education*, ed. F.G.Kenyon (London, 1933), s.28, p.47.

42 See M.G.Mason's important essay on the order of Locke's composition (1961) pp.244–90.

43 *Some Thoughts concerning Education*, s.70, 94, 126, pp.131, 156, 188.

44 *Labor* (1693), *Locke on Money*, vol. II, 493–5, encapsulates all these points. It also recommends physical labour as a recreation for the sedentary and genteel. For this, see too *Some Thoughts concerning Education*, s.209–10, pp.260–1.

45 *Some Thoughts concerning Education*, s.200, p.255.

CHAPTER 10

1 *Reasonableness of Christianity*, pp.152, 158, 278. 'Reasonableness' was not a new idea for Locke in 1695, see *A Second Letter for Toleration* (*Works*, edn 12, vol. 5), p.63, and see too the works of Samuel Crooke (ch.1, above pp.29–30) and for Restoration England the references collected in Spurr (1988b). For general treatments of Locke's views in revealed theology, see W.M.Spellman (1988), and M.S.Johnson (1977).

2 *Two Treatises*, 'preface', p.155. This point seems to have got rather lost in the various attempts to re-date the composition of the text. After all, Locke did intend the volume to refer to the events of 1688–9; besides which the explanatory nature of much of his writing in them suggest an applicability to more than one situation.

3 *A Second Letter for Toleration* (*Works* edn 12, vol. 5), p.102.

4 *Labor*, *Locke on Money* vol II p. 494. *Some Thoughts concerning Education*, preface, p.79.

5 *Labor*, *Locke on Money*, vol. II, p.495. For the literacy of labourers, see also Nicole (1828), no.2, s.44, p.70.

6 For the intention that *Of the Conduct of the Understanding* should be added to *An Essay*, see Locke to William Molyneux, 10 April 1697, *Correspondence*, vol. VI, p.87.

7 [Jonas Proast] (1690a), pp.4–6, 7f, 16.

8 *A Second Letter for Toleration*.

9 [Jonas Proast] (1690b), pp.6, 7, 6.

10 C.A.Patrides (1966), p.98.

11 William Whately (1618), pp.7–8.

12 Glbert Burnet (1699), pp.122, 123, 128.

13 *English Tract*, p.19 (155).

14 *Essays on the Law of Nature*, no.1, fol.16, p.114; no.2, title, p.122; no.6, fol.89, p.188, cf. no.4, p.154 and no.7, p.200; no.3, p.138.

15 Samuel Crooke (1614b), s.8, p.8 (1658), pt. ii, c.2, p.586.

16 *Two Treatises*, I.vi.54, p.197.

17 *Ibid.*, II.viii.111, p.360.

18 Ovid, *Metamorphoses*, I. 11. 89-150 at 1.131.

19 Locke, *Two Treatises*, II.vi.58, p.324.

20 *Ibid*, II.ii.10, p.291.

21 *Directions concerning Education*, s.70, p.74.

22 *Some Thoughts concerning Education*, s.102, p.163.

23 *Ibid.*, s.100, p.162, cf. *Directions*, s.36, p.50 for parents corrupting nature. The idea that tendencies to sin derived not from Adam but from parental conduct was aired publicly by a friend of Locke's after *Directions* was composed but before *Some Thoughts* were published. See Philip Van Limborch (1686), III.iii.iv, p.182 on the propensity to sin *cum si ab Adamo esset, in omnibus hominibus debet esse aequalis: jam autem admodum est inaequalis.*

24 Launcelot Andrewes, *A Preparation to Prayer*, p.5, in his (1642).

25 *Directions*, s.18, p.42.

26 For Bayle and 'Hobbism', cf. ch.6 and ch.8, pp.189–91, pp.275 above.

27 *An Essay concerning Human Understanding*, II.xxi.52, p.267 (and see the whole section); II.xxi.51 p. 266.

28 *Ibid.*, II.xxi.59, p.273, 61–2, pp.274–5, 71, pp.282–4. Locke evidently supposed that people moved towards pleasure and away from pain; but this does not mean that they were *automatically* prone to what was definitively right, of course. See his note on p.9 of Thomas Burnet's (1697b), 'Men have a natural tendency to what delights & what pains them. This universal observation has established past doubt. That the soul has such a tendency to what is morally good & from what is morally evil has not fallen under my observation.'

29 George Lawson (1659), I.xv.5, p.74; Locke, *An Essay*, II.xxvii.9, p.335, 26 p. 346. It is significant that this succeeds the chapter on relations, all of whose examples are of moral relations, and is succeeded by 'Of Other Relations' (xxviii), whose half-title is 'Moral Relations'.

30 Sanderson (1660), I.xx, pp.21f.

31 *An Essay*, II.xxvii.26 p.346. Note also Locke's journal entry of 5 June, 1683 (Ms.Locke f.7 p. 107), 'Identity of persons lies not in haveing the same numerical body made up of the same particles nor if the minde consists of corporeal spirits in their being the same but in the memory & knowledg of ones past self & actions continued or under the consciousnesse of being ye same person whereby every man owns himself.' See, more graphically, Locke's annotation on p. 265 of John Sergeant *Solid Philosophy Asserted* (London, 1697), 'A man has the individuality of a man before he has knowledg but is not a person before he has knowledg.'
This emphasis, as well as the requirement that consciousness relate to a law for forensic purposes help to explain the firmness of Locke's emphasis that 'Conscience is the iudg not ye law' and that 'It is not conscience yt makes the distinction of good and evil conscience only judging of any action by yt wch it takes to be yt rule of good & evil acquits or condemns it' (marginal notes on pp. 11, 5 of Burnet (1697b)).

32 The questions will be found on pp.294–5 of the *Commonplace Book* of 1661.

33 *The Reasonableness of Christianity* (London, 1695), p.1 cited from Locke's

own copy, now in the Houghton Library of Harvard University. See also Locke on *Romans*, V.12ff in *Paraphrase and Notes*, vol. II, pp.523ff for his treatment of Adam's fall.

34 *Reasonableness*, p.9 (order of quotations reversed).
35 *Ibid*; p.11.
36 *Ibid*; p.8.
37 *Ibid*; p.14.
38 *Ibid*; pp.8f.
39 *Two Treatises*, II.ix.123, p.368.
40 Hobbes, *Leviathan*, I.xiii, xiv, p.68, xvii, p.85 but see III.xxxiii, pp.195f on the intellect and I.xvi, II.xxx and III.xlii, esp. p. 267 on representation. In general, despite Jean Hampton's admirable (1986), Hobbes' argument does not depend upon *reasoning* or calculation by the individual.
41 *Reasonableness*, p.14, 213.
42 *ibid.*, p.213 cf. pp.247, 252, 290, 301.
43 *ibid.*, p.16.
44 *Ibid.*, p.6.
45 See, for a distinguished treatment, Charles Gore (1922).
46 *Reasonableness*, pp.265, 272.
47 *Ibid*, p.271.
48 *Reasonableness*, p.271.
49 *Ibid*, p.270.
50 Locke *Conduct*, s.43, pp.122f. In *Reasonableness*, p.224, the Lockean Christ 'closes all his particular Injunctions with this general golden rule, Matt.vii.12, "All things whatsoever ye would that men should do to you, do you even so unto them, for this is the law and the prophets."' A little later (p.226) Locke included the golden rule in his comment on Luke, xvii, 18, writing in the margin of the Harvard copy, 'Eternal Life'.
51 Against Stillingfleet's view that revelation was certain, see Locke's (first) *Reply to the Lord Bishop of Worcester* (*Works*, twelfth ed, vol. IV), p.275. Cf. Burnet (1697b), pp.18f. But in Locke's own more casual moments he could refer to acquaintance with the Bible as knowledge of revelation. See Locke to [Richard King], 27 September 1703, *Correspondence*, no.3339 (vol.I, pp.69f).
52 *Reasonableness*, pp.210, 193 ('offered'); for 'take', 'denizens', 'for a man' and 'voluntary subjects', see *A Second Vindication of the Reasonableness of Christianity*, *Works*, vol.III, pp.152, 150, 153, cf. p.153 for the 'performance' of belief; for 'politique head', Ms.Locke, c.27, fol.278^r. The process of consenting to rule seems not dissimilar to someone becoming a citizen in *Two Treatises*, II.viii.121, p.367.
53 See pp.291–2 above for the general situation and, for the specific point, *Reasonableness*, p.265; cf.*Reasonableness*, p.260 for the situation before Christ.
54 *Reasonableness*, p.55.
55 Cf. *An Essay concerning Human Understanding*, IV.xvi.13, p.667.
56 Cf. *An Essay*, IV.xvi.10, pp.663f and see *Reasonableness*, p.257 for priestly obscurantism blotting out the true faith before the coming of Christ. For Locke's mature views on priests, see *Sacerdos* (1698), 1661 Commonplace

Book, p.93 and note the remarkable observation in *Reasonableness*, p.214 that 'I do not remember that he [Jesus] any where assumes to himself the Title of a Priest, or mentions any thing relating to his Priesthood.'

57 *Reasonableness*, p.6, cf., for Abraham Hobbes, (1651), III.35, pp.216ff, e.g. but for a different view in respect of Moses, Hobbes (1651), III.xl, p.249.

58 *Reasonableness*, p.199.

59 *Reasonableness*, p.233 'A sincere Obedience, how can any one doubt to be, or scruple to call, a Condition of the New Covenant, as well as faith'. In the margin Locke added 'Obedience a Condition'. Cf. *Reasonableness*, pp.232f 'This Righteousness. . .a compleat Obedience and freedom of Sin, are still sincerely to be endeavoured after.' For a rather indefinite account of auxiliary grace of another kind, see *Reasonableness*, p.289.

60 *Reasonableness*, p.245 'The works of Nature shew his Wisdom and Power: But 'tis his Peculiar Care of Mankind; most eminently discovered in his Promises to them, that shews his Bounty and Goodness; And consequently engages their Hearts in Love and Affection to him. This oblation of an Heart, fixed with dependence and affection on him, is the most acceptable Tribute we can pay him'.

61 *Reasonableness*, pp.244f 'This faith in the promises of God; This relying and acquiescing in his Word and Faithfulness; The Almighty takes well at our hands, as a great mark of homage, paid by us poor frail Creatures, to his Goodness and Truth, as well as to his Power and Wisdom; and accepts it as an acknowledgement of his peculiar Providence, and Benignity to us.'

62 *Reasonableness*, p.24, cf. p.23 'this Faith, for which God justified *Abraham*, what was it? It was the believing God, when he engaged his Promise in the Covenant he made with him.' See also p.245.

63 For Christ as Messiah, see *Reasonableness*, e.g., pp.180, 199. Locke's position (p.199), that 'Faith and Repentance; *i.e.*, believing Jesus to be the *Messiah*, and a good Life; are the indispensible conditions of the New Covenant' is not identical with Hobbes' (1651), III. xliii, p. 322) that 'all that is NECESSARY to *Salvation*, is contained in two Vertues, *Faith in Christ*, and *Obedience to Laws*' because of Hobbes' distinctive view that 'all the Precepts of the Bible. . .is there onely Law, where the Civill Soveraign hath made it so; and in other places but Counsell'.

64 Cf. *An Essay concerning Human Understanding*, e.g., II. xxi. 42, and see ch. 8, pp.271–2 above.

65 'Of Study', *Educational Writings*, p.409.

66 *An Answer to Remarks*. . . appended to *Reply to the Bishop of Worcester*, W i, p.576. Cf. above ch.8, pp.271–2.

67 Thomas Burnet (1697b), p.24.

68 For the view that contradictions could not proceed from God, see Ms. Locke, f.2, fol.121, 19 February, 1682 (Aaron and Gibb, p.119). For divine promise, see *Two Treatises*, II. xvi. 195, p.414 and I.ii.6, p.162 'Promises and Oaths, which tye the infinite Deity'. Locke, of course, showed a long-standing interest in the work of Nicholas Toinard, who meant to show the internal harmony of the Bible.

69 For the secret and revealed wills of God, cf. Ames (1642), p.100, Walter Charleton (1652), pp.352–4, John Wallis (1791), no.10, p.356 and Tillotson

Sermon 13 (1704), p.145; cf. Robert Sharrock (1673), p.185. For Locke's awareness of the point, see *Essays*, no.4, fol.60 (156), though it was lost on Von Leyden.

70 See, e.g., Ussher (1702), p.40; John Wallis (1791), no.10, p.356.

71 Thomas Burnet (1697b), p.24. None of the foregoing aspects of the interchange between the two are mentioned in S.A.Grave's otherwise excellent (1981).

72 John Edwards' position is revealed most clearly in his (1699), esp. pp.5–7.
   It should be remembered that *Reasonableness* sets out to deal with a limited range of themes and not to give a complete view of Christianity.

CONCLUSION

1 See 12–13 *above*.

2 Ch.6, pp.173–7 *above*.

3 Thus Locke's thought has implications far more radical than the interpretation of Locke as a seventeenth century radical supposes; for the latter, cf. 'Introduction' p.2 *above*.

4 The point seems to have been understood by Selden: see Selden (1927), p.70 'whence then comes the restraint? from a higher power, nothing else cann bind, I cannott bind my selfe (for I may untye my selfe againe) nor an equall cannott bind me (wee may untie One another) It must be a Superior. even God Almightie, If two of us make a bargaine, why should either of us stand to it, what need you care what you say, or what need I care what I say, certainly because there is something above me, tells me, ffides est servanda, and if wee after alter our minds & make a new bargaine, there's fides servanda there to[o].'

5 *Two Treatises*, I. vi. 59, p.201.

6 but cf. *Ibid*, I. v. 47, p.191. There again, the command to increase and multiply was promulgated at a time when the best estimate put the world's population at two.

Bibliography

Citations in this volume have been made according to the author-date (or 'Harvard') system, for reasons of space. Two exceptions to this are: (i) Locke's own works, which are cited by a short-title system in order to make it immediately clear to the reader just what work is being cited, and (ii) a small number of classical works, which lack a real publication date (and whose use in this work, would not be any different if they were cited from a critical edition). The latter are also cited by a short-title system.

Many seventeenth-century books have titles that furnish material enough for a modern preface: reasons of space require that they be curtailed. The full titles are given here only when they communicate something it may be helpful for the reader to know.

PRIMARY WORKS

(I) WORKS BY LOCKE AND SOME MANUSCRIPTS AMONGST HIS PAPERS (in approximately chronological order)

English Tract and
Latin Tract, both in
Two Tracts of Government, ed. Philip Abrams (Cambridge, 1967).
'*An necesse sit dari in Ecclesia infallibilem Sacro Sanctae Scripturae interpretem? negatur*' (Public Record Office), ed. J.C.Biddle [-Higgins] as 'John Locke's Essay on Infallibility', *Journal of Church and State*, 19(1977), 301–28
Essays on the Law of Nature, ed. Wolfgang Von Leyden (Oxford, 1954, etc.)
Questions on the Law of Nature, ed. R. Horwitz, J.S. Clay and D. Clay (Ithaca, 1990)

An Essay concerning Toleration, 1667' in C.A. Viano (ed.), *Scritti Editi e Inediti sulla Toleranza* (Turin, 1961)
'Some of the consequences that are like to follow upon lessening of interest to 4 per cent' (Ms. Locke e.8) in P.H. Kelly (ed.) *Locke on Money* (2 vols., Oxford, 1991), I pp.165–202
Draft A and
Draft B [of *An Essay concerning Human Understanding*], both in *Drafts for the Essay concerning Human Understanding, and other philosophical writings*, vol. I (Oxford, 1990), ed. P.H. Nidditch and G.A.J.Rogers)
Notes on ecclesiastical affairs, Public Record Office P.R.O.30/24/6B/429 and 430

'Excommunicaan', Ms. Locke, c.27, fol. 27[a]

'Trade' (Ms. Locke, c.30, ff.18–19, 1674) in Kelly (ed.) *Locke on Money*, vol. II, pp.485–6

'Of Study' (1677), in J.L. Axtell (ed.) *John Locke: Educational Writings* (Cambridge, 1968) pp. 405–22

'Morality' (Ms. Locke, c.28, fols. 139–40), in T. Sargentich, 'Locke and Ethical Theory', *Locke Newsletter*, 5(1974)

'*Homo*' (1679), in 1661 Commonplace Book, p.52

Virtus (1661 Commonplace Book, pp.10–11:1681)

Toleratio (Ms. Locke, d.1, f.125: 1679)

'The Defence of Nonconformity' (Ms. Locke, c.34)

Two Treatises of Government, ed. Peter Laslett (second ed, Cambridge, 1967: corrected reprint, 1970)

Directions concerning Education, ed F.G. Kenyon (London, 1933)

Epistola de Tolerantia, ed. Raymond Kilibansky (Oxford, 1968)

Draft C of *An Essay* (?1685), Pierpont Morgan Library, New York

An Essay concerning Human Understanding, ed. P.H. Nidditch (Oxford, 1975, corrected reprint 1979)

Some Considerations of the Consequences of the Lowering of Interest, and Raising the Value of Money (1692, 1696) in Kelly (ed.) *Locke on Money*, vol. I pp. 207–342

Some Thoughts concerning Education ed. J.W. and J.S. Yolton (Oxford, 1989)

Labor (1693: 1661 Commonplace Book, pp.310–11) in Kelly (ed.), *Locke on Money*, vol. II, pp.493–5

'For a Generall Naturalization: 1693' (Houghton Library) in Kelly (ed.), *Locke on Money*, vol. II, pp.487–92

The Reasonableness of Christianity, as delivered in the Scriptures (London, 1695)

Venditio (1695: 1661 Commonplace Book, p.268) in Kelly (ed.), *Locke on Money*, pp.496–500

Further Considerations Concerning Raising the Value of Money (1696) in Kelly (ed.) *Locke on Money*, vol. II pp. 401–81

Of the Conduct of the Understanding, ed. F.W. Garforth (New York, 1966).

'*Sacerdos*' (1698), 1661 Commonplace Book p.93

Paraphrase and Notes of the Epistles of St. Paul ed. A.W. Wainwright (2 vols., Oxford, 1987)

There are a number of items that relate to the whole period of Locke's intellectual activity:

The 1661 Commonplace Book, used by Locke at intervals from 1661 to the late 1690s: I have received no authorised information concerning the location and ownership of this volume at the time of writing.

The Works of John Locke, the eighth edition (4 vols., London, 1777; probably edited by Edmund Law)

The Works of John Locke, the twelfth edition (10 vols., London, 1823)

The Correspondence of John Locke, ed. E.S.de Beer (8 vols., Oxford, 1976–89)

A number of printed volumes contain exercpts from Locke's journals and papers. R.I.Aaron and J.Gibb (eds.), *An Early Draft of Locke's Essay* (Oxford, 1936), which contains philosophical passages from his journals (cited as Aaron and Gibb), as does Von Leyden (ed.), *Essays on the Law of Nature*. Other parts of his journal are printed in John Lough (ed.), *Locke's travels in France, 1675–79* (Cambridge, 1953). Transcripts of some theological papers are contained in Wainwright (ed.), *Paraphrases and Notes on the Epistles of St Paul*. Many of Locke's medical papers are printed in Kenneth Dewhurst, *John Locke, Physician and Philosopher* (London, 1963) and his notes of Thomas Willis' lectures appear in Kenneth Dewhurst (ed.), *Thomas Willis' Oxford Lectures* (London, 1980).

See also Pierre Nicole, *Discourses*, translated by John Locke (London, 1828).

(II) MANUSCRIPT COLLECTIONS CONSULTED FOR MATERIALS BY LOCKE OR RELATING TO HIM

Beinecke Library, Yale University
Locke's marginal annotations on Thomas Burnet, *Remarks on an Essay concerning the Humane Understanding* (London, 1697) and *Third Remarks on an Essay concerning Human Understanding* (London, 1699) – K8 L79 Zz 697 Pa and Pb

Bodleian Library
Ms. Locke, b.4, 5; c.1, 2, 25, 26, 27, 28 30, 31, 33, 34, 39, 42, 43; d.1, 10; e.9, 10, 17; f.1, 2, 3, 4, 5, 6, 7, 8, 9, 10, 11, 12, 13, 14, 15, 27, 28, 29

British Library
Add.Mss. 15, 642

Houghton Library, Harvard University
Locke's copy of the first edition of *The Reasonableness of Christianity*, with marginal classifications, index and passages to be added to the second edition (*Ec65 L7934 695ra) and the ms. of 'For a generall naturalization' (f.Ms Eng. 818)

Newberry Library, Chicago
Copy of a first edition of *An Essay concerning Human Understanding*, with marking said to be Locke's

Pierpont Morgan Library, New York
manuscripts of Locke's translation of Nicole and of *Draft C*, and of Locke's notes in his copy of Nierop *Niew gein Verteerde Koopmans . . . almanach*

Public Record Office
PRO 30/24/6B/429 and 430

St John's College, Cambridge
Locke's marginal annotations on John Sergeant *Solid Philosophy Asserted* (London, 1699)

Somerset Record Office, Taunton
DD/SF 3064 pt. and DD/SF 3079

(III) OTHER MANUSCRIPTS

Locke, John (the elder) memoranda book, 1630–55, British Library, Add.Mss. 28273

Will (15 December, 1660), Ms.Locke, c.25, f.6

Lord Shaftesbury's petition, Bodleian Library Ms.Clarendon State Papers, 88 (1681–8), fol.5 (28 October 1681)

    Tyrrell's annotations to his copy of *An Essay concerning Human Understanding*, British Library (C.122, f.14); his corrections to a copy of *Patriarcha non Monarcha*, Bodleian Library 8xRawl 432.

    Thomas Barlow's annotations to his collection of pamphlets on toleration, etc., 1667–8, B.14.15, Linc., Bodleian Library

    Ms. Douce 357, Tanner 43 and Carte 77 in the Bodleian Library

(IV) PRINTED WORKS

Abernathy, John (1630), *A Christian and Heavenly Treatise Containing Physicke for the Soule* (third edn., London)

Ainsworth, Henry (1639), *Annotations upon the First Five Books of Moses* (London)

Allestree, Richard (1684), *Forty Sermons, Whereof Twenty are now first publish'd, the greatest part preach'd before The King and on solemn occasions* (London)

[Allestree, Richard], (1659), *The Practice of Christian Graces: or, The Whole Duty of Man* (London)

Alsop, Nathaniel (1682), *A Sermon Preached at the Assizes at Leicester* (London)

Alsted, John (1649), *Scientiarum omnium encyclopaedia* (2 vols., Lyons)

Ames, William (1642), *The Marrow of Sacred Divinity*, tr. anon (London)

Andrewes, Launcelot (1642), *A Preparation to Prayer* in Andrewes *The Morall Law Expounded* (London)

Anon (1641), *A learned and necessary Argument to prove that each Subject hath a Propriety in his Goods* (London)

    (1644), *England's Monarch or a conviction and refutation by the common law of those false principles. . .of Albericus* (London)

    (1658), *Rabshaketh's Outrage Reproved: Or a Whip for William Grigge*

    (1661), *Terms of Accommodation, Between those of the Episcopal, and their Brethren of the Presbyterian Perswasions* (London)

    (1667a), *Bentivolyo* (London)

    (1667b), *The Cobbler of Gloucester*

    (1667c), *Omnia Comesta a Belo*

(1667d), *The Late Apology In behalf of the Papists Re-printed and answered, In behalf of the Royallists* (London)

(1668a), *Dolus an Virtus? An Answer to A Seditious Discourse Concerning the Religion of England: And The Settlement of Reformed Christianity in its due habitude* (London, really November, 1667)

(1668b), *A Few Sober Queries, upon the late Proclamation, For enforcing the Laws against Conventicles* (London)

(1668c), *A Modest and Peaceable Letter Concerning Comprehension* (London)

(1670a), *Some Seasonable and serious queries Upon the late Act against Conventicles* (London)

(1670b), *A Letter to Mr Henry Stubs concerning His Censure upon certain passages contained in the History of the Royal Society* (London)

(1675), *A Letter from a Person of Quality to his Friend in the Country* (n.p.)

(1679), [E.B.], *A Letter from a Gentleman of Quality in the Country, to his Friend. . .being an Argument Relating to the Point of Succession to the Crown* (n.p.)

(1680), *The Great and Weighty Considerations, Relating to the Duke of York, or, Successor of the Crown* (London)

(1681a) [C.B.], *An Address to the Honourable City of London* (London)

(1681b), *The Humble Wishes of a Loyal Subject* in N.Thompson (ed.), *A Collection of Eighty-Six Loyal Poems*

(1682a), *A new Discourse about the Fire of London, and the Probability of Self-Murther* (London)

(1682b), *Plain Dealing is a Jewel, and Honesty the Best Policy* (London)

(1958), *Queen Elizabeth's Defence of her Proceedings*, ed. W.E.Collins (London)

(ed.) (1694), *A Collection of Cases and other Discourses, Lately written to recover Dissenters to the Communion of the Church of England By Some Divines of the City of London* (London)

(ed.) (1966), *Wrington Village Records. Studies in the History of a Somerset Village* (Bristol)

Aquinas, Thomas (1932), *De Regimine Principum*, ed. G.B.Phelan (Toronto)

Aristotle, *Eudemian Ethics*

Nichomachean Ethics

Physics

Politics

De Caelo

De Generatione et Corruptione

Posterior Analytics

De Partibus Animalium: all in

Aristotle (1984), *The Works of Aristotle*, ed. and trans. Jonathan Barnes (2 vols., Oxford)

Ascham, Anthony (1649), *A Discourse: wherein is examined, what is particularly lawfull during the Confusions and Revolutions of Government* (London)

Ascham, Roger (1904), *The English Works of Roger Ascham*, ed. W.A.Wright (Cambridge), including Ascham, *The Scholemaster* (1570)

Assembly of Divines (1643), *The Westminster Confession* (London)

(1647), *The humble advice of the Assembly of Divines* (London)

Atterbury, Francis (1704), *A Sermon Preach'd before Her Majesty* (London)

Aubrey, John (1862), *Topographical Collections*, ed. J.E.Jackson (Devizes)

(1949), *Brief Lives*, ed. O.L.Dick (Harmondsworth, 1972).

(1972), *On Education*, ed. J.E.Stephens (London)

Bacon, Francis (1972), *Essays*, ed. M.Hawkins (London)

(1957–74), *Works*, ed. J.Spedding, R.L.Ellis and Heath, D.D. (7 vols., including:

Novum Organum

De Augmentis Scientariam

Bagshawe, Edward (the younger) (1660), *The Great Question Concerning Things Indifferent in Religious Worship* (Oxford)

(1661), *The Second Part of the Great Question* (Oxford)

(1662a), *The Necessity and Use of Heresies, or the Third Part of the Great Question* (London)

(1662b), *A Brief Enquiry into the Grounds and Reasons Whereupon the Infallibility of the Pope and the Church of Rome is said to be Founded* (London)

Barclay, Robert (1678), *Apology for ye true Christian Divinity as held forth by the Quakers* (London)

Barlow, Thomas (1693), *The Genuine Remains of. . .Dr Thomas Barlow* (London)

Barnes, T.G. (ed.) (1959), *Somerset Assize Orders, 1629–40* (SRS)

Bates, E.H. [Harbin] (ed.) (1907–19), *Quarter Session Records for the County of Somerset [1603–1660]* (SRS, 4 vols.)

Baxter, Richard (1660a), *Catholick Unity: or the only way to bring in all to be of one Religion* (London)

(1660b), *Right Rejoycing or the Nature & Order of Rational Warrantable Joy* (London)

(1667), *The Reasons of the Christian Religion* (London)

(1672), *More Reasons of the Christian Religion* (London)

(1673), *The Christian Directory* (London)

(1680), *The Second Part of the Nonconformists Plea for Peace* (London)

(1696), *Reliquiae Baxterianae* (London)

Bayle, Pierre (1682), *Lettre à M.L.A.D.C sur la Comète* (Amsterdam)

(1683), *Pensees diverses a l'occasion d'une Comète* in Bayle, (1727), vol. III, pp.1–161.

(1686), *Commentaire Philosophique sur ces paroles de J.C. contraignez les d'entrer* in Bayle, (1727), vol. II, pp.355–561.

(1727), *Oeuvres Diverses* (3 vols. in 4, The Hague)

Blunt, J.H. (ed.) (1893), *The Annotated Book of Common Prayer* (London)

Bodin, Jean (1576), *Les Six Livres de la Republique*, trans and selection M.J.Tooley as *Six Books of the Commonwealth* (Oxford)

Boyle, Hon. Robert (c.1649), *The Martyrdom of Theodora and of Didymus* in Boyle, *The Works of. . .* (vol. V, 1772)

(1661), *An Examination of Mr T.Hobbes His Dialogus* in Boyle, *The Works of . . .* (vol. I, 1772)

(1663), 'An Essay, Containing a Requisite Digression, concerning Those that would Exclude the Deity from Intermeddling with Matter' in Stewart (ed.), *Selected Philosophical Papers*

(1663–71) *Some Considerations touching the usefulnesse on Experimental Naturall Philosophy*

(1674), *Of the Reconcileableness of Reason and Religion* in Boyle, *The Works* (vol. III, 1744)

(1686), *A Free Enquiry into the vulgarly received Notion of Nature*, in Boyle, *The Works* (vol. IV, 1744 and vol. IV, 1772)

(1744), *The Works of. . .Robert Boyle*, ed. T.Birch (5 vols., London)

(1772), *The Works of. . .Robert Boyle* (second edn, 6 vols., London)

(1979), *Selected Philosophical Papers of Robert Boyle*, ed. M.A.Stewart (Manchester)

Bradford, J. (1848–53), *Sermons* in *Writings*, ed. A.Townsend (2 vols., Cambridge)

[Brady, Robert] (1681), *The Great Point of Sucession Discussed* (London)

Bramhall, John (1677), *The Catching of Leviathan* in Bramhall, *The Works of the Most Reverend Father in God, John Bramhall* (4 vols. in 1, Dublin) vol. III

Brerewood, Edward (1641), *Tractatus Ethici: Sive Commentarii in aliquot Aristotelis Libros ad Nichomachum De Moribus* (Oxford)

Browne, Sir Thomas (1955), *Religio Medici*, ed. J.J. Denomain (Cambridge)

Buckeridge John (1606), *A Sermon Preached at Hampton Court before the Kings Maiestie* (London)

Villiers, George second duke of Buckingham (1675), *Two Speeches. . .II The D. of Buckingham's Speech in the House of Lords the 16th November, 1675* (Amsterdam [really London])

Cornelius Burges (1660), *A Postscript to Dr Pearson* (London)

Burges, Cornelius *et al.* (1660), *Reasons shewing the Necessity of Reformation of the Publick Doctrine, Worship, Rites and Ceremonies, Church Government and Discipline of the Church of England* (London)

Bunny, Edmund (1595), *Truth and Falsehood* (London)

(1576), *The Whole Summe of Christian Religion* (London)

Burgersdyck, Franco (1625), *Collegium Physicum, Disputationibus* (second edn, Leyden)

Burnet, Gilbert (1688), *An Enquiry into the Measures of Submission to the Supream Authority: And of the Grounds upon which it may be Lawful or necessary for Subjects, to defend their Religion, Lives and Liberties* (London)

(1699), *An Exposition of the XXXIX Articles of the Church of England* (1699, edn. Oxford, 1845)

(1761), *Thoughts on Education* (London)

(1897–1900), *A History of My Own Time: part one: The Reign of Charles II*, ed. Osmund Airy (2 vols., Oxford)

[Burnet, Thomas] (1697a), *Remarks upon an Essay concerning Humane Understanding* (London)

(1697b), *Second Remarks upon an Essay concerning Humane Understanding* (London)

Burton, Thomas (1828), *Diary of Thomas Burton*, ed.J.T.Rutt (4 vols., London)

T.C. (1660), *Vox & Votum Populi Anglicani* (London)

Calamy, Edmund *et al.* (1663), *Farewel Sermons Preached by Mr Calamy, Dr Manton...* (London)

Calamy, Edmund (1724), *Memoirs of the Life of.. John Howe* (London)

Calvin, Jean (1559), *Institutes of the Christian Religion,* tr. F.L.Battles (London)

Campanella, T. (1653), *De Monarchia Hispanae* (Amsterdam)

Casaubon, Meric (1669), *A Letter of Meric Casaubon...to Peter du Moulin...Concerning Natural experimental Philosophie, and some books lately set out about it* (Cambridge)

Chamberlayne, Edward (1669), *Angliae Notitia* (third edn., London)

Charles I (1628), *His Maiesties declaration to all his loving subiects, of the causes which moved him to dissolve the last Parliament* (London)

Charles II (1681), *His Majesties Declaration To all His Loving Subjects, Touching The Causes & Reasons That Moved Him to Dissolve The Two Last Parliaments* (London)

Charleton, Walter (1652), *The Darknes of Atheism Dispelled by the Light of Nature* (London)

(1656), *Epicurus's Morals: Collected, And faithfully Englished,* ed. Frederic Manning (London, 1926)

Cheke, Sir John (1807–8), *The hurte of sedition how greeous it is to a commonwealth,* in Raphael Holinshed, *Chronicles of England, Scotland and Ireland* (6 vols., London) vol. III

Cicero, Marcus Tullius *De Officiis*

De Finibus Bonorum et Malorum

De Natura Deorum

Hyde, Edward, first earl of Clarendon (1676), *A Brief View and Survey of the Dangerous and Pernicious Errors To Church and State in Mr Hobbes's Book, Entituled Leviathan* (Oxford)

Clarke, Samuel (ed.) (1662), *A Collection of the Lives of Ten Eminent Divines* (London)

Cockburn, J.S. (ed.) (1971), *Somerset Assize Orders, 1640–1659* (SRS)

(1976), *Western Circuit Assize Orders, 1629–1648* (London)

Coke, Sir Edward (1658), *The Reports of Sir Edward Coke* (London)

Coke, Roger (1660), *Justice Vindicated From the False Fucus put upon it, by Thomas White Gent., Mr Thomas Hobbs, and Hugo Grotius* (London)

Cole, Nathanael (1618), *Preservatives against Sinne* (London)

Cooper, Thomas (1850), *An Answer in defence of the Truth against the Apology of Private Mass,* ed.W.Goodie (Cambridge)

Corbet, John (1660a), *The Interest of England in the Matter of Religion* (London)

(1660b), *The Second Part of the Interest of England, in the Matter of Religion, Unfolded in a Deliberative Discourse* (London)

(1667), *A Discourse of the Religion of England* (London)

(1668) *A Second Discourse of the Religion of England Further Asserting, That Reformed Christianity, Setled in its due Latitude, is the Stability and Advancement of this Kingdom* (London)

Cosin, John (1869–72), *The Correspondence of John Cosin,* ed.G.Ornsby (2 vols.)

Cowell, John (1607), *The Interpreter* (Cambridge)

Cranmer, Thomas (1844), *Writings and Disputations. . .relating to the sacrament of the Lord's Supper*, vol.I of (1844–6)

(1846), *Miscellaneous Writings and Letters*, vol. II of (1844–6).

(1844–6), *The Works of. . .Thomas Cranmer*, ed. J.E.Cox (2 vols., Cambridge)

Crooke, Samuel (1613), *The Discoverie of the Heart Traced By His Treasure* in *Three Sermons* (London, 1615).

(1614a), *The Guide unto True Blessednesse, Or a Body of the Doctrine of the Scriptures directing Man to a saving knowledge of God* (second edn, London).

(1614b), *A Briefe Direction to true happiness abridged out of the larger Treatise, for the more convenient use of private Families and instruction of the younger sort* (London, 1613; second edn)

(1615), *Three Sermons* (London, 1615).

(1658), τα Δια φερσντα, Or Divine Characters in Two Parts, ed. C.B. and W.G. [William Grigge?] (London)

Cudworth, Ralph (1647), *A Sermon preached. . .at Westminster* (Cambridge).

(1678) *The True Intellectual System of the Universe*, pt.i [no more published] (London, preface dated 1671).

Culverwell, Nathaniel (1654) *An Elegant and Learned Discourse of the Light of Nature*, ed.R.A.Greene and H.Macallum (Toronto 1971).

Cumberland, Richard (1672), *De Legibus Naturae Disquisitio Philosophica* (London).

Maxwell, J. [a translation of the *Disquisitio*] (Dublin).

(1727), *A Treatise of the Laws of Nature* trans.

Davis, Sir John (1628), *Le Primer Report des Cases et Matters en ley* (London).

Dering, Edward (1940), *The Parliamentary Diary of Sir Edward Dering, 1670–73*, ed B.D.Henning (New Haven).

Descartes, René (1641), *Meditations on First Philosophy*, vol. II in J.Cottingham, R.Stoothoff and D.Murdoch (trans.), *The Philosophical Writings of Descartes* (3 vols., Cambridge)

Descartes, René *et al.* (1647), 'Third Set of Objections [by Thomas Hobbes] with the Author's Replies', Descartes *et al.*, *Objections and Replies*, vol. II in *The Philosophical Writings of Descartes*

Dodwell Henry (1683), *A Discourse concerning the one Altar and one Priesthood* (London).

Donne, John (1953–62), *Sermons*, ed.E M.Simpson and G.R.Potter (10 vols., Berkeley)

Dryden, John (1661), *To His Sacred Majesty, A panegyrick on his Coronation* (London)

Edwards, John (1699), *The Eternal and Intrinsick Reasons of Good and Evil* (Cambridge)

Elyot, Sir Thomas (1907), *The Boke named the Gouernor* (London)

Farmer, Ralph (1654), *The Great Mysteries of Godlinesse and Ungodlinesse* (London)

(1656), *Sathan Inthron'd in his Chair of Pestilence. Or, Quakerism in its Exaltation* (London)

[Farmer, Ralph] (1660), *A plain-dealing, and Plain-meaning Sermon. . .April 6, 1660* (Bristol).

[Fell, John] (1659), *The Interest of England Stated: Or a faithful and just Account of the Aims of all Parties now pretending* (n.p.)

Filmer, Robert (1991), *Patriarcha and other Writings*, ed.J.P.Sommerville (Cambridge), including:

The Free-Holders Grand Inquest

The Anarchy of a Limited or Mixed Monarchy

The Necessity of the Absolute Power of all Kings

Observations Concerning the Originall of Government

Observations upon Aristotles Politiques

Patriarcha

Fitzralph, Richard (1890), *De Pauperie Salvatoris* in R.L.Poole (ed.), *Wycliffe De Dominio Divino* (London)

Floyd, Thomas (1600), *The Picture of a perfit Common wealth* (London)

Forset, Edward (1606), *A Comparative Discourse of the Bodies, Natural and Politique* (London)

Fortescue, Sir John (1869), 'Declaration upon certayn Wrytinges' in Fortescue (1869)

> (1869) *De Natura Legis Naturae* in *The Works of Sir John Fortescue* ed. Thomas Fortescue, Lord Clermont, vol. I of *Sir John Fortescue and his descendants* (privately printed, London)

> (1885), *The Governance of England*, ed. Charles Plummer (Oxford)

> (1949), *De Laudibus Legum Angliae*, ed. S.B.Chrimes (Cambridge)

Fox, George (1657) *The Throne of truth Exalted over the Powers of Darkness* (London) [under the alias George Bishop]

> (1952), *The Journal of George Fox*, ed.J.L.Nickalls (Cambridge)

Fox, George et al. (1654), *Saul's Errand to Damascus*

Fuller, Thomas (1642), *The Holy State and the Prophane State* (Cambridge)

W.G. [Grigge? William] (1660), *The Life of...Samuel Crooke* in Samuel Clarke, *A Collection of the Lives of Ten Eminent Divines*

Gauden, Edward (1660), *Antisacrilegus* (London)

Gee, Edward (1658), *The Divine Right and Originall of the Civill Magistrate from God Illustrated and Vindicated* (London)

Glanvill, Joseph (1661), *The Vanity of Dogmatizing: Or Confidence in Opinions Manifested in a Discourse of the Shortness and Uncertainty of Our Knowledge, And its Causes, with some Reflexions on Peripateticism; And An Apology for Philosophy* (London)

> (1667), *A Loyal Tear Dropt on the Vault of our late Martyred Sovereign* (London)

> (1668), *Plus Ultra: Or, The Progress and Advancement of Knowledge Since the Days of Aristotle. In an Account of some of the most Remarkable Late Improvements of Practical Useful Learning* (London)

> (1670), *Logos oreskeia or, A Seasonable Recommendation, and Defence of Reason; In the Affairs of Religion* [bound & continuously paginated with *Philosophia Pia*] (London)

> (1671a), *Philosophia Pia; Or, A Discourse of the Religious Temper, and Tendencies of the Experimental Philosophy, Which is profest By the Royal Society* (London)

> (1671b) *A Further Discovery of M.Stubbe, in a Brief Reply To his last Pamphlet against Jos.Glanvill* (London)

Gouge William (1622), *Of domesticall duties* (London)

Grenville, Denis (1861), *A Discourse concerning Christian Resignation and Resolution* in *The Works and Letters of Dennis Granville* (Surtees Society vol. 37, 1860: Durham)

Grey, Anitchel (1769), *Debates of the House of Commons* (15 vols., London)

Grigge, William (1658), *The Quaker's Jesus: Or, The unswadling of that Child James Nailor, which a wicked Toleration hath midwiv'd into the World. Discovering The Principles of the Quaker in general*

Grotius, Hugo (1616), *De Veritate Religionis Christianae* trans. anon. as *The Truth of the Christian Religion* (London)

   (1625), *De Jure Belli ac Pacis* (Paris) (see esp. trans anon. intro. Jean Barbeyrac as *The Rights of War and Peace*, London, 1738).

Gunther R.T. *et al.* (*eds.*) (1923–67), *Early Science in Oxford* (15 vols., Oxford)

Hale, Sir Matthew (1971), *A History of the Common Law of England* ed. C.M.Gray (Chicago)

Saville, George marquess of Halifax (1688), *The Lady's New Year's Gift, Or, Advice to a Daughter*

   (1699), *The Character of a Trimmer*

   (1969), *Halifax: Complete Works* ed. J.P.Kenyon (Harmondsworth)

Herbert, Edward (1937), *De Veritate*, ed and trans. M.H.Carre (Bristol)

Herbert, George (1974), *The Temple* in C.A.Patrides (ed.) *The English Poems of George Herbert* (London)

   (1986), *A Priest to the Temple* in L.L.Martz (ed.) *George Herbert and Henry Vaughan* (Oxford)

Herle, Charles (1642), *An Answer to Doctor Ferne's Reply* (London)

   (1643), *A Fuller Answer to a Treatise written by Doctor Ferne* (London)

Hobbes, Thomas (1651), *Leviathan* (London)

   (1839–45a), *De Corpore* in Hobbes' *Opera Latina*, ed. W.molesworth (5 vols.) (vol. I).

   (1839–45b), *Elements of Philosophy concerning Body* in Hobbes' *English Works*, ed. W.Molesworth (11 vols.) vol. I.

   (1969a), *Elements of Law*, ed. F.Toennies, second (edn., 1928; new intro. by M.M.Goldsmith (London)

   (1969b), *Behemoth*, ed. F. Toennies; second edn, with new intro. by M.M.Goldsmith (London)

   (1971) *Dialogue between a Philosopher and a student of the Common Law*, ed. Joseph Cropsey (Chicago)

   (1983) *Philosophicall Rudiments concerning Government* (London, 1651), ed. by H.Warrender as *De Cive. The English Version* (Oxford) 1983)

Hooker, Richard (1888), *The Works of . . . Richard Hooker* ed.J.Keble, rev. R.W.Church & F.Paget (3 vols, Oxford, 1888)

   (1977–82), *Of the Lawes of Ecclesiastical Politie* ed. W.Speed Hill *et al.* (4 vols., Harvard)

Hooker, Thomas (1656), *The Application of Redemption* (London)

Howard, A.J. and Stoate, T.L. (eds.) (1975), *Somerset Protestation Returns and Lay Subsidy Rolls 1641–2* (SRS)

Howell, T.B. (ed.) (1809–14) *State Trials* (21 vols., London)

[Humfrey, John] (1667), *A Proposition for ye Safety and Happiness of ye King and Kingdome* (London)

(1672), *The Authority of the Magistrate About Religion* (London)

Hutcheson, Francis (1897), *An Enquiry concerning the Original of our Ideas of Virtue and Moral Good*, Vol. I in L.A.Selby-Bigge (ed.) *British Moralists*

Hutchison, Lucy (1968), *Memoirs of the Life of Colonel Hutchison* (edn. London)

James I, (1918) *Political works of James I* ed.C.H.McIlwain, (Harvard), including: *Basilikon Doron*

The Trew Law of Free Monarchies

A Speach in the Starre-Chamber (20 June, 1616)

James, II (1685), *His Majesties Most Gracious Speech To both Houses of Parliament, On Friday the 24th of May, 1685* (London)

Jewel, John (1845–50), *Works*, ed. J.Ayre (4 vols., Cambridge)

Josselin, Ralph (1976), *The Diary of Ralph Josselin, 1616–1683*, ed. Alan Macfarlane (London)

Journals of the House of Lords

Keckermann, Bartholomew (1614), *Opera Omnia* (2 vols., Geneva) including:

(1607), *Systema Ethicae* (London)

Praecognitorum Philosophicorum, Vol. I in Keckermann (1614)

Systema Physicae vol. I in Keckermann (1614)

Systema Logicae vol. I in Keckermann (1614)

Kellison, Matthew (1621), *The Right and Jurisdiction of the Prelate and the Prince* (second edn., Douai)

Kennett, White (1728), *A Register and Chronicle Ecclesiasticall and Civil*, vol. I [no more published] (London)

King, Henry (1621), *A Sermon Preached at Pauls Crosse, The 25, of November, 1621* (London)

Knox, John (1649), *History of the Reformation in Scotland*, ed. Dickinson, W.C. (2 vols., Edinburgh)

(1846–64), *Works*, ed. David Laing (6 vols., Edinburgh)

Lake, Arthur (1629), *Sermons, with some religious and divine meditations* (London)

Lawson, George (1657), *An Examination of the Political Part of Mr Hobs his Leviathan* (London)

(1659), *Theo-politica: Or A Body of Divinity* (London)

(1660), *Politica Sacra et Civilis* (London)

L'Estrange, Roger (1662), *Truth and Loyalty Vindicated, from the Reproches and Clamours of Mr Edward Bagshawe. Together with a Further Discovery of the Libeller Himself, and his seditious Confederates* (London)

[L'Estrange, Roger] (1681–2), *Heraclitus Ridens* (London)

(1681–4), *The Observator* (London)

[Lingard, Richard] (1670), *A Letter of Advice To a Young Gentleman Leaving the University Concerning His Behaviour and Conversation in the World* (Dublin, 1670), ed. F.C.Erb (New York, 1907)

[Lloyd, William] (1673), *A seasonable Discourse shewing the Necessity of Maintaining the Established Religion, In opposition to Popery* (London)

[Long, Thomas] (1689), *The Letter for Toleration Decipher'd and the Absurdity and Impiety of an Absolute Toleration Demonstrated, by the Judgment of Presbyterians, Indedependents, and by Mr Calvin, Mr Baxter, and the Parliament, 1662* (London)

Lonsdale, Sir John Viscount Lonsdale (1808), *Memoir of the Reign of James II* (York)

G. de F.Lord *et al.* (eds.) (1963–75), *Poems on Affairs of State* (7 vols., New Haven)

Journal of the House of Lords

Lowde, James (1694), *A Discourse upon the Nature of MAN* (London)
(1699), *Moral Essays* (York and London)

Lucy, William (1663), *Observations, Censures and Confutations of Notorious Errours in Mr Hobbs His Leviathan, and his other Bookes* (London)

Macaulay, T.B. (1974–81), *The Correspondence of Thomas Babington Macaulay*, ed. T.Pinney (6 vols., Cambridge)

[Mackenzie, Sir George] (1663), *Religio Stoici* (Edinburgh)

Magirus, Johannes (1642), *Physiologae Peripateticae Librae Sex* (Cambridge)

Masham, Damaris Cudworth (1955–6), 'Lady Masham's Letter to Jean Le Clerc', ed. R.L.Colie, *The History of Ideas Newsletter*, I, iv (1955–6) 13–18, II (1956) 9–11, 35–7, 81–8

Marvell, Andrew (1963), 'The Last Instructions to a Painter', in Lord (ed.) (1963–75), vol. I.

Maynwaring, Roger (1627), *Religion and Alegiance in Two Sermons* (London)

Merbury, Charles (1581), *A Briefe Discourse of Royall Monarchie, as of the Best Common Weale* (London)

Merrill, Thomas F. (ed.) (1966), *William Perkins 1558–1602, English Puritan: His Pioneer Works on Casuistry* (The Hague)

Migne, J.P. (ed.) (1843–66), *Patrologia Latina* (Paris)

Milton, John (1642), *The Reason of Church Government urg'd against Prelacy* in Patterson *et al* (eds.), *Works of John Milton*
(1931–8), *The Works of John Milton*, ed. F.A.Patterson *et al*, (20 vols., New York)
(1952–5), *Poetical Works*, ed. Helen Darbishire (2 vols., Oxford), including: *Paradise Lost*, (vol.I)
(1974), *Selected Prose* ed.C.A.Patrides (Harmondsworth), including: *Of Education*

More, Henry (1655), *An Antidote against Atheism* (second ed, London)
(1668), *Enchiridion Ethicum* (London)

[Nalson, John] (1681), *The Complaint of Liberty & Property against Arbitrary Government* (London)

Nicole, Pierre (1828), *Discourses*, trans. John Locke (London)
(1670), *De L'Education d'un Prince* (Paris)

North, John (1671), *A Sermon Preached before the King at Newmarket* (Cambridge)

Novell, John (1662), *The Seditious Principle* (London)

Nowell, Alexander (1570), *Catechism*, ed.G.E.Corrie (Cambridge)

Nye, Stephen (1696), *A Discourse Concerning Natural and Revealed Religion* (London)

404

Oldenberg, Henry (1965–), *The Correspondence of Henry Oldenberg*, ed. A.R and M.B.Hall (Madison and London)

Overall, John (1606), *Convocation Book* (written c.1606, publ.1690, edn. Oxford, 1844)

Ovidius Naso, P. *Metamorphoses*

Owen, John (1674), Πνευματολογία : *Or, A Discourse Concerning the Holy Spirit* (London)

(1971), *The Oxford Orations of Dr John Owen*, ed. Peter Toon (Callington)

[Owen, John] (1667a), *A Peace-Offering in an Apology and humble Plea for Indulgence and Liberty of Conscience* (London)

(1667b), *Indulgence and Toleration Considered: In a Letter to a Person of Honour* (London)

(1850–5), *Works*, ed. W.H.Gould (24 vols., repr. Edinburgh, 1965–8)

[Parker, Henry] (1644), *Jus Populi* (London)

(1645), *Jus Regium* (London)

[Parker, Samuel] (1666), *A Free and Impartial Censure of the Plantonick Philosophie* (Oxford)

(1667), *An Account of the Nature and Extent of the Divine Dominion and Goodnesse* in Parker *A Free and Impartial Censure of the Platonick Philosophie* (second edn, Oxford)

(1670), *A Discourse of Ecclesiastical Politie* (London, really 1669)

(1672), *A Defence and Continuation of the Discourse of Ecclesiastical Politie* (London)

(1681a), *The Case of the Church of England* (London)

(1681b), *A Demonstration of the Divine Authority of the Law of Nature, And of the Christian Religion* (London)

(1684–5) *Religion and Loyalty*, (2 vols., London)

Parry, John (1670), *Nehemiah, or the excellent Governour* (Oxford)

[Parry, John] (1660), *A Resolution of a Seasonable Case of Conscience...* (Oxford)

[Patrick, Symon] (1668), *A Friendly Debate between a Churchman and a Dissenter* (London)

(1669), *A Continuation of the Friendly Debate* (London)

(1670a), *A Further Continuation and Defence, Or, A Third Part of the Friendly Debate* (London)

(1670b), *An Appendix to the Third Part of the Friendly Debate, Being a Letter of the Conformist to the Non-conformist. Together with a Postscript* (London)

Peacham, Henry (1962), *The Complete Gentleman, The Truth of our Times and The Art of Living in London*, ed. V.B.Heltzel (Ithaca), including:

The Complete Gentleman

The Truth of our Times:

Pearson, John (1658), *The Patriarchal Funeral* (London)

(1660a), *No Necessity of Reformation of the Publick Doctrine of the Church of England* (London)

(1660b), *An Answer to Dr Burges His Word by way of postscript in Vindication of No Necessity...* (London)

[Pearson, John] (1668), *Promiscuous Ordinations Are Destructive to the Honour and Safety of the Church of England* (London, really 1667)

[Penton, Stephen] (1688), *The Guardian's Instruction, or The Gentleman's Romance* (London)

(1694), *New Instructions to the Guardian* (London)

Pepys, Samuel (1970–83) *Diary*, ed. R.Latham and W.Matthews 11 vols., London

Perkins, William (1591), *A Golden Chaine*, tr. anon (London)

(1596), *A Discourse of Conscience* in Thomas F. Merrill (ed.), *William Perkins 1558–1602, English Puritan: His Pioneer Works on Casuistry* (The Hague, 1966)

(1970), *The Works of William Perkins*, ed. Ian Breward (Abingdon)

[Perrinchief, Robert] (1668a), *A Discourse of Toleration: In Answer to a late Book Intituled, A Discourse of the Religion of England* (London, really 1667)

(1668b), *Indulgence not Justified: Being a Continuation of the Discourse of Toleration* (London)

(n.d), *Samaratanism Or, a Treatise of Comprehending, Compounding, and Tolerating* (London)

Petto, Samuel (1654), *The Voyce of the Spirit*

Petty, Sir William (1927), *The Petty Papers*, ed. sixth marquess of Lansdowne (2 vols., London)

(1928), *The Petty-Southwell Correspondence*, ed. sixth marquess of Lansdowne (2 vols., London)

Plato, *Republic*

Preston, John (1634), *The Breast-Plate of Faith and Love* (fifth edn, London)

(1639), *The New Covenant* (ninth edn, London)

Price, Richard (1948), *A Review of the Principal Questions in Morals*, ed. D.D.Raphael (Oxford)

[Proast, Jonas] (1690a), *The Argument of the Letter concerning Toleration Briefly Considered and Answered* (Oxford)

(1690b), *A Third Letter concerning Toleration* (Oxford)

Prynne, William (1668), *A Seasonable Vindication of the Supream Authority & Jurisdiction of Christian Kings, Lords, Parliaments, As well over the Possessions, as Persons of Delinquent Prelates & Church-men* (London)

Pufendorf, Samuel (1660), *Elementorum Jurisprudentiae Universalis Libri Duo* (edn, Cambridge, 1672)

(1672), *De Jure Naturali ac Gentium* (edn. Amsterdam, 1688)

(1973), *De Officio Hominis et Civis* (edn, Cambridge, 1682)

Quarles, Francis (1640), *Enchyridion* (London)

Ralegh, Sir Walter (1614), *The History of the World*, ed. C.A.Patrides (London, 1971)

[Ramesey, William] (1672), *The Gentleman's Companion: Or, A Character of True Nobility, and Gentility: In the way of Essay* (London)

Rawlinson, John (1619), *Vivat Rex* (Oxford)

Reresby, Sir John (1936), *The Memoirs of Sir John Reresby*, ed. Andrew Browning, (Glasgow)

Reynolds, Edward (1631), *Three Treatises* (London)

(1660), *The Author and Subject of Healing in the Church* (London)

Robertson, C.G. (1947), *Select Statutes, Cases and Documents* (eighth ed, London)

Rutherford, Samuel (1648), *A Survey of the Spiritual Antichrist opening the Secrets of Familisme and Antinomianisme* (London)

(1726), *Testimony left by Samuel Rutherford*

St. German, Christopher (1751), *Doctor and Student: or Dialogues Between a Doctor of Divinity, and a Student of the Laws of England* (fifteenth ed, London)

Eustachius of St Paul (1649), *Summa Philosophiae Quadripartita* (Cambridge)

Sancroft, William (1660), *A Sermon Preached at St. Peter's, Westminister* (London)

[Sancroft, William] (1652), *Modern Policies, taken from Machiavel, Borgia, and other choise Authors, by an eyewitnesse* (London)

Sanderson, Robert

(1618), *Artis Logicae Compendium* (Oxford)

(1627), *Ten Sermons* (London)

(1660), *De Obligatione Conscientiae: Praelectiones Decem Oxonii in Schola Theologica Habitae...M.DC.XLVII*, ed. William Whewell (Cambridge, 1851)

Sandys, Edwin (1841), *Sermons*, ed. John Ayre (Cambridge)

Savage, Henry (1660), *Reasons shewing That there is no need of such a Reformation of the publique Doctrine...As is pretended by Reasons offered...* (London)

Selby-Bigge, L.A. (ed.) (1897), *British Moralists* (2 vols., Oxford)

Selden, John (1614), *Titles of Honor* (London)

(1927), *The Table-Talk of John Selden*, ed. Frederick Pollock (London)

Seneca, L. Annaeus, *De Beneficiis*

[Elkanah Settle] (1681) *The Character of a Popish Successor* (London, 1681)

Sennert, Daniel (1664), *Epitome Naturalis Scientiae* (Oxford)

[Sexby, Edward] (1657), *Killing No Murder briefly discourst in three Questions* in A.C.Ward (ed.), *A Miscellany of Tracts and Pamphlets* (Oxford, 1927), pp.261–310

Cooper, Anthony Ashley Earl of Shaftesbury (1675), *Two Speeches. I. The Earl of Shaftesbury's Speech in the House of Lords...* (Amsterdam [really London])

Sharrock, Robert (1660), *ʹποθεσις ἠθικη* (Oxford)

(1673), *De Finibus Virtutis Christianae* (Oxford)

Shepard, Thomas (1972), *God's Plot: The Paradoxes of Puritan Piety, Being the Autobiography and Journal of Thomas Shepard*, ed. Michael McGiffert (Amherst)

Sherlock, William (1684), *The Case of Resistance of the Supreme Powers Stated and Resolved* (London)

Sibbes, Richard (1638), *Light from Heaven* (London)

(1639), *The Christians End* (London)

(1853–62), *Works* (7 vols., Edinburgh)

Sidney, Algernon (1698), *Discourses concerning Government* (London)

Smith, Adam (1976), *The Theory of Moral Sentiments*, ed. A.L.Macfie and D.D.Raphael (Oxford)

Smith Sir Thomas (1982), *De Republica Anglorum*, ed. Mary Dewar (Cambridge)

[Somers, John] (1681a), *A Brief History of the Succession, Collected out of the Records, and the most Authenick Histories* (n.p. [but probably London])

(1681b), *Vox Populi: or the Peoples Claim to their Parliaments sitting, To Redress Crievances, and Provide for he COMMON SAFETY* (London)

South, Robert (1660), *Interest Deposed, and Truth Restored. Or, A word in Season, delivered in Two Sermons* (Oxford) [includes *Ecclesiastical Policy the Best Policy: or Religion the best Reason of State*]

(1665), *A Sermon Preached before the Court at Christ-Church Chappel in Oxford* (Oxford)

(1842), *Sermons* (5 vols., Oxford)

Spenser, Edmund (1596), *The Faerie Queen* (London)

Sprat, Thomas (1667), *The History of the Royal-Society of London, For the Improving of Natural Knowledge* (London)

(1682), *A Sermon Preached before the Artillery Company of London at St Mary Le Bow April 20. 1682* (London)

Starkey, Thomas (1948), *A Dialogue between Reginald Pole and Thomas Lupset*, ed. Kathleen M.Burton (London)

Stillingfleet, Edward (1658), *Origines Sacrae* (London)

(1662), *Irenicum. A Weapon-Salve for the Churches Wounds, or the Divine Right of Particular forms of Church-Government: Discus'd and examin'd* (second edn, London)

(1680), *The Mischief of Separation* (edn, London, 1687)

(1681), *The Unreasonableness of Separation* (third edn, 1682)

Stubbe, Henry jr (1659a), *A Light Shining out of Darknes: Or Occasional Queries. . .with A brief Apologie for the Quakers, that they are not inconsistent with a Magistracy* (London)

(1659b), *An Essay in Defence of the Good Old Cause* (London)

(1670a), *Legends no Histories: or, A Specimen of some Animadversions upon the History of the Royal Society* (London)

(1670b), *A Specimen of some Animadversions upon a Book, Entituled, Plus Ultra* (London)

(1670c), *Campanella Revived, or an Enquiry into the History of the Royal Society* (London)

(1671a) *A Censure upon Certain Passages contained in the History of the Royal Society, As being destructive to the Established Religion and Church of England* (second edn, Oxford)

(1671b), *A Letter to Dr Henry More*

(1671c) *A reply to A Letter of Dr Henry More* [bound with *The Letter to Mr Henry Stubs* and *A defence of the Censure of the History of the Royal Society*] (Oxford)

Sydenham, Humphrey (1637), *Moses and Aaron, or the affinity of Civill and Ecclesiasticke power, in Five Sermons* (London)

Sydenham, Thomas (1966), *Original Writings* in Kenneth Dewhurst, *Dr Thomas Sydenham (1624–1689). His Life and Original Writings*, including 'De Arte Medica', 'Anatomie' and 'Theologia Rationalis' (London)

(1991), *Observationes Medicae. . .and. . .Medical Observations*, ed. G.G.Meynell (Folkestone)

Tawney, R.H. and Eileen Power (eds.) (1924), *Tudor Economic Documents* (3 vols., London)

Taylor, Jeremy (1660), *Ductor Dubitantium* (third edn, London, 1676)

(1656), *Answer to the Bishop of Rochester*, in Taylor (1847–54) vol. 7.

(1647), *A Discourse on the Liberty of Prophesying* in Taylor (1847–54) vol. 5

(1847–54), *The Whole Works of Jeremy Taylor*, ed. R.Heber, rev.C.P.Eden (10 vols., London)

Thomas, William et al. (1653), *The Dead Speaking, or, The Living Names of Two Deceased Ministers of Christ* (*contemporary, And eminently usefull in the West of England*) *viz. Mr Sam. Oliver and Mr Samuel Crook* (London)

Thompson, N. (ed.) (1685), *A Collection of Eighty-Six Loyal Poems* (London)

Thorndike, Herbert (c.1659), *The Right of the Christian State in Church-Matters, According to the Scriptures*, in *The Theological Works of Herbert Thorndike* (Vol. VI)

(1662), *Just Weights and Measures: That is, The present State of Religion Weighed in the Balance, and Measured by the Standard of the Sanctuary* (London)

(1667), *The True Principle of Christian Comprehension: Or a Petition against the Presbyterian Request for a Comprehensive Act in 1667*, in *Theological Works* vol.v

(c. 1667–8), *The Plea of Weakness and Tender Consciences Discussed and Answered* in *Theological Works* vol.v

(1851–5), *Theological Works* (6 vols., Oxford)

John Tillotson (1666), *The Rule of Faith* (London)

(1704), *The Works of . . . John Tillotson* (fourth edn., London)

Timpler, Clemens (1605–7), *Physicae seu Philosophicae Naturalis Systema Methodicum* (3 vols., Hannover)

Toletus, Francis (1579), *Commentarium, una cum quaestionibus in octo libros Aristotelis seu Physica auscultatione* (Cologne)

[Tompkins, Thomas] (1667), *The Inconveniences of Toleration* (London)

Towerson, Gabriel (1676), *An Exposition of the Catechism of the Church of England* (third ed, London, 1685)

Tuke, Thomas (1609), *The high-uuay to Heaven* (London)

[Tyrrell, James] (1681), *Patriarcha non Monarcha* (London)

Ussher, James (1661), *The power Communicated to the Prince by God* (London)

(1677), *A body of Divinity: or, the Sum and Substance of Christian Religion* (seventh ed, London : see *DNB*).

(1702), *The Principles of Christian Religion: or, a Short Catechism* (London 1st edn. 1644)

(1964), *The Reduction of Episcopacy unto the form of synodical government received in the Ancient Church*, as printed in R.B.Knox 'Archbishop Ussher and English Presbyterianism', *Journal of the Presbyterian Historical Society of England*, 13, 26–35

Van, Limborch Philip (1686), *Theologia Christiana* (Amsterdam)

Walker, Obadiah (1673), *Of Education* (Oxford)

Wallis, John (1662), *Hobbius Heauton-timorumenos. Or a Consideration of Mr. Hobbes his Dialogus In an Epistolary Discourse, Addressed, To the Honourable Robert Boyle, esq.* (Oxford)

(1791), *Sermons* (London)

[Wallis, John] (1643), *Truth Tried* (London)

Ward, Seth (1661), *Against Resistance of Lawful Powers* (London)

Wendelin, Mark (1648), *Contemplationum Physicarum* (Cambridge)

Whately, William (1618), *The Neuu Birth* (London)

Whichcote, Benjamin (1930), *Moral and Religious Aphorisms*, ed. W.R.Inge (London)

Whitgift, John (1851–3), *Works*, ed. John Ayre (3 vols., Cambridge)

Wilkins, John (1675), *Of the Principles and Duties of Natural Religion: Two Books*, ed. with preface by John Tillotson (London)

Willis, Thomas (1980a), *Thomas Willis' Casebook*, ed. Kenneth Dewhurst (London)

  (1980b), *Thomas Willis' Oxford Lectures*, ed. Kenneth Dewhurst (London)

Winthrop, John (1963), *A Modell of Christian Charity*, in Perry Miller and T.H.Johnson (eds.), *The Puritans* vol. I (revised ed, 2 vols., New York)

[Wolseley, Sir Charles] (1668), *Liberty of Conscience, The Magistrates Interest* (London)

Wood, Anthony (1891–1900), *The Life and Times of Anthony Wood, antiquary of Oxford, 1632–1695, as described by himself*, ed. Andrew Clark (5 vols., Oxford)

Worthington, John (1847–86), *The Diary and Correspondence of John Worthington*, ed R.Crossley and R.C.Christie (3 vols. in 2, Manchester)

Wycliffe, John (1890), *Johnannis Wycliffe De Dominio Divinio*, ed. R.L.Poole (London)

SECONDARY WORKS

Abbreviations

BIHR   *Bulletin of the Institute of Historical Research*

Ec.H.R.   *Economic History Review*

EHR   *English Historical Review*

HJ   *Historical Journal*

HLQ   *Huntington Library Quarterly*

JEH   *Journal of Ecclesiastical History*

JHI   *Journal of the History of Ideas*

LN   *Locke Newsletter*

N & Q   *Notes and Queries*

PP   *Past and Present*

P   *Philosophy*

PBA   *Proceedings of the British Academy*

PR   *Philosophical Review*

PS   *Political Studies*

SCH   *Studies in Church History*

SRS   *Somerset Record Society*

TRHS   *Transactions of the Royal Historical Society*

Aaron, R.I. (1971), *John Locke* (London, 1937; third edn, Oxford).
Aarsleff, Hans (1964), 'Leibniz on Locke on Language', *American Philosophical Quarterly*, 1
    (1982), *From Locke to Saussure* (Minneapolis)
Abernathy, G.R. (1965), *The English Presbyterians and the Stuart Restoration, 1648–1663* (Philadelphia).
Alexander, Peter (1985), *Ideas, Qualities and Corpuscules* (Cambridge).
Ashcraft, Richard (1986), *Revolutionary Politics and Locke's Two Treatises of Government* (Princeton)
    (1987), *Locke's Two Treatises of Government* (London).
    (1992), 'Simple Objections and Complex Reality', *PS*, 40, 99–115
Ashcraft, Richard (ed.) (1991), *John Locke: Critical Assessments* (4 vols., London)
Ashton, Robert (1960), *The Crown and the Money Market* (Oxford)
Ayers, Michael (1991), *Locke* (2 vols., London)
    (1981), 'Locke's Logical Atomism', PBA, 67, 209–25
Aylmer, G.E. (1974), *The King's Servants* (second edn, London)
Aylmer, G.E. (ed.) (1972), *The Interregnum* (London)
Barnes, T.G. (1959), 'County Politics and a Puritan Cause Celebre: Somerset Churchales', TRHS, fifth series, 9.
    (1961a), *Somerset 1625–40: a county's government under the personal rule* (London)
    (1961b), *The Clerk of the Peace in Caroline Somerset* (Leicester)
Bate, Frank (1908), *The Declaration of Indulgence, 1672* (London)
Bauman, Richard (1983), *Let Your Words be Few* (Cambridge)
Beddard, R.A. (1979), 'The Restoration Church' in Jones (ed.), *The Restored Monarchy*, ch. 7
    (1991) 'The Unexpected Whig Revolution of 1688', ch.1 of Beddard (ed.)
Beddard, R.A. (ed.) (1988), *A Kingdom Without a King* (Oxford).
    (ed.). (1991), *The Revolutions of 1688* (Oxford)
Behrens, C.B.A. (1941), 'The Whig Theory of the Constitution in the Reign of Charles II', *Cambridge Historical Journal*, 7, 42–71
Beier. A.L. (1986), *Masterless Men* (London)
    (1988), '"Utter Strangers to Industry, Morality and Religion": John Locke on the Poor', *Eighteenth-Century Life*, 12, 28–41
Berdahl, Robert M. (1988), *The Politics of the Prussian Nobility: the development of a conservative ideology, 1770–1848* (Princeton)

Berlin, Isaiah (1969), *Four Essays on Liberty* (Oxford)

(1976), *Vico and Herder* (London)

(1979), *Against the Current* (London)

(1991), *The Crooked Timber of Humanity* (London)

Berman, David (1988), *A History of Atheism in Great Britain* (London)

Bill, E.G.W. (1988), *Education at ChristChurch, Oxford, 1650–1800* (Oxford)

Bonney, Richard (1991), *The European Dynastic States* (Oxford)

Bosher, R.S. (1951), *The Making of the Resoration Settlement: the influence of the Laudians, 1649–1662* (London)

Bowden, P.J. (1956), 'Wool Supply and the Woollen Industry', Ec.H.R., second series, 9

(1962), *The Wool Trade in Tudor and Stuart England* (London)

Brandt, Reinhard (ed.) (1981), *John Locke: Symposium Wolfenbuettel, 1979* (Berlin)

Braithwaite, W.C. (1979), *The Beginnings of Quakerism* (second ed, York)

Burns, J.H. (1983), '*Jus Gladii* and *Jurisdictio*: Jacques Almain and John Locke', *HJ*, 26, 369–74

(1986), *Absolutism: the history of an idea* (London)

Burns, J.H. (ed.) (1991), *The Cambridge History of Political Thought, 1450–1700* (Cambridge)

Capp, Bernard (1972), *The Fifth Monarchy Men* (London)

Carter, Jennifer (1969), 'The Revolution and the Constitution' in Geoffrey Holmes (ed.), *Britain after the Glorious Revolution*, ch.1.

Chandaman, C.D. (1975), *The English Public Revenue, 1660–88* (Oxford)

Christie, W.D. (1871), *A Life of Anthony Ashley Cooper, First Earl of Shaftesbury* (2 vols., London)

Church, R.W. (1891), *The Oxford Movement, 1833–45* (London)

Clark, Peter (1972) 'The Migrant in Kentish Towns, 1580–1640' in Clark and Slack (eds.)

Clark, Peter (1974), 'Migration in England during the late seventeenth and early eighteenth centuries', PP, no.83

(1983), *The English Alehouse* (Brighton)

Clark, Peter and Slack, Paul (eds) (1972), *Crisis and Order in English Towns, 1500–1700* (London)

Clark, Stuart (1980), 'Inversion, Misrule and the Meaning of Witchcraft', *PP*, no.87, 98–127

Clifton, Robin (1973), 'The Fear of Popery' in Russell (ed.), *Origins of the English Civil War*, ch.3

(1984), 'The Popular Fear of Catholics during the English Revolution' in Slack (ed.), pp.129–61

(1985), *The Last Popular Rebellion: The Western Rising of 1685* (London)

Cockburn, J.S. (1977), 'The Nature and Incidence of Crime in England, 1559–1625' in Cockburn (ed.), pp.49–71

Cockburn, J.S. (ed.), *Crime in England, 1500–1800* (London)

Cohen, G. A. (1985) 'Marx and Locke on Land and Labour', *PBA* 71 pp. 357–88

Coleman, D.C. (1960), *The Domestic System in Industry* (London)

(1971), 'Textile Growth' in N.B.Harte and K.G.Ponting (eds.), pp.1–20

(1975), *Industry in Tudor and Stuart England* (London)

Collinson, Patrick (1982), *The Religion of Protestants* (Oxford)

(1988) *The Birthpangs of Protestant England* (London)

Colman, John (1983), *Locke's Moral Philosophy* (Edinburgh)

Condren, Conal (1990), *George Lawson's Politica and the English Revolution* (Cambridge)

Cook, Harold J. (1986), *The Decline of the Old Medical Regime in Stuart London* (New York)

Cooper, J.P. (1972), 'Social and Economic Policies under the Commonwealth' in Aylmer (ed.), *The Interregnum*

Cornwall, Julian (1967), 'Evidence of Population Mobility in the seventeenth century', BIHR, 40

Cranston, Maurice (1957), *John Locke: a biography* (London)

Cust, Richard and Lake, Peter (1981), 'Sir Richard Grosvenor and the Rhetoric of Magistracy', BIHR, 54

Daly, J.W. (1979), *Sir Robert Filmer and English Royalist Thought* (Toronto)

Davies, Godfrey (1952), 'The general election of 1660', HLQ, 15, 211–35

Dewhurst, Kenneth (1963), *John Locke, Physician and Philosopher* (London)

(1966), *Dr Thomas Sydenham [1624–1689]: His Life and Original Writings* (London)

Duncan, Howard (1985), 'Locke, a Mechanical Philosopher?', *LN*, 16, 11–22

Dunn, John (1969), *The Political Thought of John Locke* (Cambridge)

(1984), *Locke* (Oxford)

(1985), *Rethinking Modern Political Theory* (Cambridge)

(1990), *Interpreting Political Responsibility* (Oxford)

(1991), 'The Claim to Freedom of Conscience: Freedom of Speech, Freedom of Thought, Freedom of Worship', in Grell *et al.* (eds), pp.171–94

Fagiani, Francesco (1983), *Nel crepusculo della probabilità: ragione ed esperienza nella filosofia sociale di John Locke* (Naples)

Feiling, Keith (1924), *History of the Tory Party, 1640–1714* (Oxford)

(1930), *British Foreign Policy, 1660–1672* (London)

Feingold, Mordechai (1984), *The Mathematicians' Apprenticeship* (Cambridge)

Fiering, Norman (1981), *Moral Philosophy at Seventeenth Century Harvard* (Chapel Hill)

Fincham, Kenneth (1990), *Prelate as Pastor: The Episcopate of James I* (Oxford)

Finlayson, M.G. (1983), *Historians, Puritanism and the English Revolution: The Religious Factor in English Politics Before and After the Interregnum* (London)

Fletcher, Anthony (1986), *Reform in the Provinces; the Government of Stuart England* (London)

Bourne, H.R. Fox (1876), *The Life of John Locke* (2 vols., London 1876)

Frank, Robert G. jr (1980), *Harvey and the Oxford Physiologists* (Berkeley, Ca.)

Franklin, Julian (1978), *John Locke and the Theory of Sovereignty* (Cambridge)

Friedman, Jeffrey (1988), 'Locke as Politician', *Critical Review*, 2, 64–101.

Gibson, James (1917), *Locke's Theory of Knowledge and its historical relations* (Cambridge)

413

(1933), 'John Locke', *PBA*, 19, 29–51

Gleason, J.H. (1969), *The Justices of the Peace in England, 1570–1640* (Oxford)

Gobietti, D. (1992), *Public and Private* (London)

Goldie, M. (1983), 'John Locke and Anglican Royalism', PS, 31

(1991), 'The Theory of Religious Intolerance in Restoration England' in Grell *et al.* (eds.)

Gore, Charles (1922), *Belief in Christ* (London)

Grant, Ruth W. (1987), *John Locke's Liberalism* (Chicago)

Grave, S.A. (c.1981), *Locke and Burnet* (n.p.)

Greaves, R.L. (1981), *Society and Religion in Elizabethan England* (London)

Green, I.M. (1978), *The Re-establishment of the Church of England, 1660–63* (Oxford)

(1979), 'The Persecution of "scandalous" and "malignant" clergy during the English Civil War', EHR, 94.

Grell, O.P. Israel, J.I. and Tyacke, N. (eds.) (1991), *From Persecution to Toleration* (Oxford)

Haley, K.H.D. (1953), *William of Orange and the English Opposition, 1672–74* (Oxford)

(1968), *The first earl of Shaftesbury* (Oxford)

(1975), '"No Popery" in the Reign of Charles II' in J.S.Bromley and E.H.Kossman (eds.), *Britain and the Netherlands*, 5, 102–19

(1985), *Politics in the Reign of Charles II* (Oxford)

(1986), *An English Diplomat in the Low Countries* (Oxford)

Hall, Roland and Woolhouse, Roger (1983), *Eighty Years of Locke Scholarship* (Edinburgh)

Hampton, Jean (1986), *Hobbes and the Social Contract Tradition* (Cambridge)

Harris, Ian (1993), 'The Politics of Christianity', in *Locke's Philosophy: Content and Context*, ed. G.A.J.Rogers (Oxford)

(1994), 'Locke on Justice', *Oxford Studies in the History of Philosophy: II*, ed. M.A.Stewart (Oxford)

Harris, Tim (1987), *London Crowds in the Reign of Charles II* (Cambridge)

Harte, N.B. and Ponting, K.G. (eds.) (1971), *Textile History and Economic History* (London)

Hill, Christopher (1956), *The Economic Problems of the Church* (Oxford)

(1972), *The World Turned Upside Down* (London)

(1984), *The Experience of Defeat* (London)

Holmes, Geoffrey (ed.) (1969), *Britain after the Glorious Revolution* (London)

Horton, John and Mendus, Susan (eds.) (1991), *John Locke: A Letter concerning Toleration in focus* (London)

Horwitz, Henry (1964) 'Protestant Reconciliation in the Exclusion Crisis', *JEH*, pp.201–17

(1969), 'The Structure of Parliamentary Politics' in Holmes (ed.) (1969), ch.4

Houlbrooke, Ralph (1979), *Church Courts and the people during the English Reformation, 1520–1570* (Oxford)

Huehns, Gertrude (1951), *Antinomianism in English History* (London)

Hughes, Ann (1991), *The Causes of the English Civil War* (London)

Hunter, Michael (1981), *Science and Society in Restoration England* (Cambridge)

(1988), *Establishing the New Science* (Woodbridge)

Hunter, Michael and Wootton, David (eds.) (1992), *Atheism from the Reformation to Enlightenment* (Oxford)

Hurstfield, Joel (1958), *The Queen's Wards* (London)

Hutton, Ronald (1983), *The Restoration* (Oxford)

Ingram, Martin (1981), 'Le charivari dans l'angleterre du XVIe et du XVIIe siecle' in Jacques Le Goff and J-C Schmitt (eds.), *Le Charivari* (Paris), pp.251–64

(1987), *Church Courts, Sex and Marriage in England, 1570–1640* (Cambridge)

Johnson, M.S. (1977), *Locke on Freedom* (Austin, Texas)

Jolley, Nicholas (1984), *Locke and Leibniz* (Oxford)

Jones, D.W. (1972), 'The "Hallage" Receipts of the London Cloth Markets, 1562–c.1720', second series, Ec.H.R., 25, 567–87

Jones, J.R. (1961), *The First Whigs* (Oxford)

(1963) 'Political groups and tactics in the convention of 1660', HJ, 6, 159–77

(1966), *Britain and Europe in the Seventeenth Century* (London)

Jones, J.R. (ed.) (1979), *The Restored Monarchy* (London)

Jordan, W.K. (1932–40), *The Development of Religious Toleration in England* (4 vols., London)

Judson, M.A. (1949), *The Crisis of the Constitution* (New Brunswick)

Kelly, Patrick (1988), '"All Things Richly to Enjoy"', PS, 36, 277–91

Kenyon, J.P. (1972), *The Popish Plot* (London)

Kerridge, Eric (1985), *Textile Manufactures in Early Modern England* (Manchester)

Kilcullen, John (1988), *Sincerity and Truth* (Oxford)

Knox, R.B. (1967), *Jam̀es Ussher* (Cardiff)

Kors, A.C. (1990), *Atheism in France, 1650–1729: volume i: The Orthodox Sources of Disbelief* (Princeton)

Korshin, P.J. (ed.) (1972), *Studies in Change and Revolution: Aspects of English Intellectual History, 1640–1800* (Menston)

Krailshamer, Alban (1962), *Studies in Self-Interest* (Oxford)

Labrousse, Elisabeth (1983), *Bayle* (Oxford)

Larner, Christine (1981), *The Enemies of God* (London)

Laslett, Peter (1964), 'Market Society and Political Theory', HJ, 7, 150–4

Laslett, Peter, Oosterveen, K. and Smith, R.M. (eds.) (1980), *Bastardy and its Comparative History* (Cambridge)

Lovejoy, A.O. (1961), *Reflections on Human Nature* (Baltimore)

Lyon, T. (1937), *The Theory of Religious Liberty in England* (Cambridge)

McGee, J.S. (1976), *The Godly Man in Stuart England* (New Haven)

McGregor, J.F. and Reay B. (eds.) (1984), *Radical Religion in the English Revolution* (Oxford)

Maclear, J.F. (1950),'Quakerism and the End of the Interregnum', CH, 19, 240–70

Macpherson, C.B. (1962), *The Theory of Possessive Individualism: Hobbes to Locke* (Oxford)

Maddison, R.E.W. (1969), *The Life of the Honourable Robert Boyle* (London)

Malcolm, Noel (1988), 'Hobbes and the Royal Society' in Ryan and Rogers (eds.)

de Lacey Mann, Julia (1971), *The Cloth Industry in the West of England from 1640 to 1880* (Oxford)

Marchant, R.A. (1972), *Church under the Law* (Cambridge)

Mason, M.G. (1961), 'How Locke wrote *Some Thoughts concerning Education*', *Paedagogica Historica*, 1, 244–90

Matthews, A.G. (1934), *Calamy Revised, being a revision of Edmund Calamy's account of the ministers and others ejected and silenced, 1660–62* (Oxford)

Mendus, Susan (ed.) (1988), *Justifying Toleration* (Cambridge)

Michael, F.S. and E. (1989), 'Locke's relation to Gassendi', JHI, 50

Miller, John (1973), *Popery and Politics in England, 1660–1688* (Cambridge)
    (1991), *Charles II* (London)

Miller, John (ed.) (1990), *Absolutism in Seventeenth-century Europe* (London.)

Milne, D.J. (1951), 'The Results of the Rye House Plot and their Influence upon the Revolution of 1688', fifth series, TRHS, 2, 91–108

Mintz, S.I. (1962), *The Hunting of Leviathan* (Cambridge)

Molyneux, W.E. (1957), 'The Development of John Locke's View of Toleration', Oxford University unpublished B.Litt thesis

Morgan, E.S. (1958), *The Puritan Dilemma* (New York)

Mukerjee, H.W. (1934), 'Elections for the Convention and Cavalier Parliaments', N & Q, 166, 398–403, 417–21

Nicholson, Peter (1991), 'John Locke's Later Letters on Toleration' in Horton and Mendus (eds.), pp.163–87

Nobbs, Douglas (1935), 'Philip Nye on Church and State', *Cambridge Historical Journal*, 5, 41–59

Nozick, Robert (1974), *Anarchy, State and Utopia* (Oxford)

Nuttall, G.F. (1946), *The Holy Spirit in Puritan Faith and Experience* (Oxford)

Nuttall, G.F. and Chadwick, Owen (eds.) (1962), *From Uniformity to Unity* (London)

Ogg, David (1955a), *England in the Reign of Charles II* (2 vols., second ed., Oxford)

Olivecrona, Karl (1974), 'Appropriation in the State of Nature', JHI, 35, 211–30
    (1955b), *England in the Reigns of James II and William III* (Oxford)

Pagden, Anthony (ed.) (1987), *The Languages of Political Theory in Early-Modern Europe* (Cambridge)

Parry, Geraint (1978), *Locke* (London)

Passmore, J.A. (1951), *Ralph Cudworth: An Interpretation* (Cambridge)

Patrides, C.A. (1966), *Milton and the Christian Tradition* (Oxford)

Patten, John (1973), *Rural-Urban Migration in Pre-Industrial England* (Oxford)

Pocock, J.G.A. (1987), *The Ancient Constitution and the Feudal Law* (Cambridge, 1957; second edn., 1987)

Polin, Raymond (1960), *La politique morale de John Locke* (Paris)

Ponting, K.G. (1957), *A History of the West of England Cloth Industry* (London)

Popkin, R.H. (1979), *The History of Scepticism, Erasmus to Spinoza* (new edn., London)

Price, J.L. (1979), 'Restoration England and Europe' in Jones (ed.), ch.5

Priestley, Margaret (1951), 'Anglo-French Trade and the Unfavourable Balance Controversy, 1660–1685', second series, Ec.H.R., 4

Quaife, G.R. (1979), *Wanton Wenches and Wayward Wives: Peasants and Illicit Sex in Early Seventeenth Century England* (London)

Rahn, B.J. (1972), 'A Rar-ee Show – A Rare Cartoon: Revolutionary Propaganda in the Treason Trial of Stephen College' in P.J.Korshin (ed.), pp.77–98

Ramsay, G.D. (1943), *The Wiltshire Woollen Industry in the Sixteenth and Seventeenth Centuries* (Oxford)

Reay, Barry (1985), *The Quakers and the English Revolution* (London)

Riley, Patrick (1982), *Will and Political Legitimacy* (Harvard)

Roberts, Clayton (1966), *The Growth of Responsible Government in Stuart England* (Cambridge)

Resnick, David (1984), 'Locke and the Ancient Constitution', *Political Theory*, 12, 97–114

Rogers, G.A.J. (1981), 'Locke, Law and the Law of Nature' in Brandt (ed.), pp.146–62

Rodis-Lewis, G. (1957), *La morale de Descartes* (Paris)

Ronalds, F.S. (1937), *The Attempted Whig Revolution of 1678–1681* (Urbana)

Roy, Ian (1978), 'England Turned Germany?', fifth series, TRHS, 28

Russell, Conrad (ed.) (1973), *The Origins of the English Civil War* (London)

Russell, Conrad (1973), 'Parliament and the King's Finances' in Russell (ed.), ch.3

Russell, Conrad (1990) *The Causes of the English Civil War* (Oxford)

Ryan, Alan (1965), 'Locke and the Dictatorship of the Bourgeoisie', *PS*, 13, 219–30

(1984), *Property and Political Theory* (Oxford)

Ryan, Alan and Rogers, G.A.J. (eds.) (1988), *Perspectives on Thomas Hobbes* (Oxford)

Schaffer, Simon and Shapin, Steven (1985), *Leviathan and the Air Pump* (Princeton)

Schlatter, Richard (1940), *The Social Ideas of Religious Leaders, 1660–1688* (Oxford)

Schochet, Gordon (1975), *Patriachalism in Political Thought* (Oxford)

Scott, Jonathan (1991), *Algernon Sidney and the Restoration Crisis, 1677–83* (Cambridge)

Seaward, Paul (1989), *The Cavalier Parliament and the Reconstruction of the Old Regime, 1661–1667* (Cambridge)

Seaver, Paul S. (1985), *Wallington's World: a Puritan Artisan in Seventeenth-Century London* (London)

Barbara J. Shapiro (1969) *John Wilkins* (Berkeley, C. A. 1969)

Simmons, A. John (1992), *The Lockean Theory of Rights* (Princeton)

Skinner, Quentin (1978), *The Foundations of Modern Political Thought* (2 vols., Cambridge)

Slack, Paul (1972), 'Poverty and Politics in Salisbury, 1597–1666' in Clark and Slack (eds.), pp.164–203

(1974), 'Vagrants and Vagrancy in England, 1598–1664', second series, Ec.H.R., 27, 360–79

417

Slack, Paul (ed.) (1984), *Rebellion, Popular Protest and the Social Order in Early Modern England* (Cambridge)

Snow, V.F. (1962), 'The Concept of Revolution in Seventeenth-Century England', *HJ*, 5, 175–87

Smith, A.G.R. (ed.) (1973), *The Reign of James VI & I* (London)

Sommerville, C.J. (1992), *The Secularization of Early Modern England* (New York)

Sommerville, J.P. (1986), *Politics & Ideology in England 1603–1640* (London)

Spellman, W.M. (1988), *John Locke and the Problem of Depravity* (Oxford)

Spiller, Michael (1980), *'Concerning Natural Experimental Philosophie'* (The Hague)

Spufford, Peter (1973–4), 'Population Mobility in Pre-Industrial England', *Genealogists' Magazine*, 17

Spurr, John (1985), 'Anglican Apologetic and the Restoration Church', Oxford University. D.Phil

(1988a), '"Latitudinarianism" in the Restoration Church', *HJ*, 31

(1988b), '"Rational Religion" in Restoration England', *JHI*, 49, 563–85

(1990), 'Schism and the Restoration Church', *JEH* 41

(1991), *The Restoration Church of England* (New Haven)

Stewart, M.A. (1981), 'Locke's Professional Contacts with Robert Boyle', *LN*, 12, 19–44

Stieg, Margaret (1982), *Laud's Laboratory: The Diocese of Bath and Wells in the Early Seventeenth Century* (Lewisburg, Pa.)

Strauss, Leo (1953), *Natural Right and History* (Chicago)

(1959), Locke's Doctrine of Natural Law' in Strauss, *What is Political Philosophy? and other studies* (Glencoe), pp.197–220

Supple, Barry (1959), *Commercial Crisis and Change in England, 1600–1642* (Cambridge)

Tarcov, Nathan (1984), *Locke's Education for Liberty* (Chicago)

Tarlton, C.D. (1978), 'A Rope of Sand: Interpreting Locke's *First Treatise of Government*', HJ, 21, 43–73

(1981), 'The Exclusion Controversy, Pamphleteering and Locke's *Two Treatises*', HJ, 24, 49–68

Taylor, Charles (1989), *Sources of the Self* (Cambridge)

Thirsk, Joan (1978), *Economic Policy and Projects* (London)

Thirsk, Joan (ed.) (1967), *The Agrarian History of England and Wales* (vol. IV, Cambridge)

(ed.) (1985), *The Agrarian History of England and Wales*, (vol. V, Cambridge)

Thomas, Roger (1962), 'Comprehension and Indulgence', G.F.Nuttall and Owen Chadwick (eds.), pp.191–253

Thompson, M.P. (1987), 'Significant Silences', *Historical Journal*, 31 pp.275–94

Toon, Peter (ed.) (1970), *Puritans, the Millenium and the Future of Israel* (Cambridge and London)

Trench, C.C. (1969), *The Western Rising* (London)

Trevelyan, G.M. (1932), *England under Queen Anne: Ramilies* (London)

Trow-Smith, Robert (1957), *British Livestock Husbandry to 1700* (London)

Tuck, Richard (1979), *Natural Rights Theories: their origin and development* (Cambridge)

(1987), 'The "Modern" Theory of Natural Law' in Anthony Pagden (ed.), pp.99–119

(1988), 'Scepticism and Toleration in the Seventeenth Century' in Mendus (ed.), ch.1

(1989), *Hobbes* (Oxford)

(1992), 'The "Christian Atheism" of Thomas Hobbes' in Hunter and Wootton, pp.111–30

Tully, James (1980), *A Discourse of Property: John Locke and his Adversaries* (Cambridge)

(1991), 'Locke' in J.H.Burns (ed.), ch.21

Tyacke, Nicholas (1987), *The Anti-Calvinists* (Oxford)

(1991), 'The Rise of Puritanism and the Legalizing of Dissent, 1571–1719' in Grell *et al.* (eds.), pp.17–50

Underdown, David (1963), 'A Case Concerning Bishops' Lands: Cornelius Burges and the Corporation of Wells', EHR, 78, 18–48

(1973), *Somerset in the Civil War and Interregnum* (Newton Abbot)

(1985), *Revel, Riot and Rebellion: Popular Politics and Culture in England, 1603–1660* (Oxford)

Underwood, T.L. (1970), 'Early Quaker Eschatology' in Peter Toon (ed.)

Viano, C.A. (1961), 'L'Abbozzo Originario e gli stadi di composizione di "An Essay concerning Toleration" e la nascita delle teorie politico-religiose di John Locke', *Rivista di Filosofia*, 52, 285–311

Von Leyden, Wolfgang (1981), 'Locke's Strange Doctrine of Punishment' in R.Brandt (ed.)

Von Ranke, Leopold (1875), *A History of England, principally in the Seventeenth Century* (6 vols, Oxford)

Waldron, Jeremy (1988a), *The Right to Private Property* (Oxford)

(1988b),'Locke:tolerationandtherationalityofpersecution'inMendus(ed.),ch.3

Wallace, J.M. (1968), *Destiny His Choice* (Cambridge)

Walsh, W.H. (1947), *Reason and Experience* (Oxford)

Ward, W.G. (1953), *The English Land Tax in the Eighteenth Century* (Oxford)

Watts, M.R. (1973), *The Dissenters* (vol.I, Oxford)

Webster, Charles (1975), *The Great Instauration* (London)

Weston, C.C. and Greenberg, J.R. (1981), *Subjects and Sovereigns: The Grand Controversy over Legal Sovereigty in Stuart England* (Cambridge)

White, P. (1983), 'The Rise of Arminianism reconsidered', PP, no.101, 35–54

Williams, Arnold (1948), *The Common Expositor. An Account of the Commentaries in Genesis, 1527–1633* (Chapel Hill)

Willian, T.S. (1938), *The English Coastal Trade 1600–1750* (London)

Wilson, Charles (1957), *Profit and Power* (London)

Wood, F.A. (1903), *Collections for a Parochial History of Chew Magna* (Bristol)

Woolrych, Austin (1982), *Commonwealth to Protectorate* (Oxford)

Wootton, David (1992), 'John Locke and Richard Ashcraft's *Revolutionary Politics*', PS, 40, 79–98

Worden, Blair (1984), 'Toleration and the Cromwellian Protectorate', SCH, 21, 199–233

Wrightson, Keith (1981), 'Alehouses, Order and Reformation in Rural England, 1590–1660' in Eileen and Stephen Yeo (eds.), ch.1

(1982), *English Society 1580–1680* (London)

Wrightson, Keith and Levine, David (1979), *Poverty and Piety in an English Village* (London)

Eileen and Stephen Yeo (eds.) *Popular Culture and Class Conflict 1590–1914* (London)

Yolton, John W. (1956), *John Locke and the Way of Ideas* (Oxford)

(1958), 'Locke on the Law of Nature', *Philosophical Review*, 67, 477–98

(1970), *Locke and the Compass of Human Understanding* (Cambridge)

(1985) *Locke* (Oxford)

Zuckert, M.P. (1979), 'An Introduction to Locke's *First Treatise*', *Interpretation*, 8, 58–74

Index of persons

Abernathy, John 358
Abraham 313, 389
Adam 5, 33, 34, 35, 36, 37, 41, 153, 159, 198, 207, 212, 215, 217, 233–9, 291, 293, 295–7, 299–306, 312, 320–1, 325, 388
Ainsworth, Henry 237, 376
Alexander, Sir William 140, 358
Allestree, Richard 343
Alsop, Nathanial 367
Alsted, John 134, 357
Ames, William 150–1, 153, 347, 361, 362, 390
Andrewes, Launcelot, bishop 299, 388
Aquinas, Thomas, St 368
Aristotle 35, 91, 95, 134, 139, 141, 147, 154, 171, 198, 284, 349, 357, 360, 368, 372, 385
Argyll, Archibald Campbell, ninth earl of 181
Ascham, Roger 284, 385
Ashley, Lord, see Shaftesbury
Assembly of Divines 332
Atterbury, Francis, Bishop 220, 222, 251
Aubrey, John 28, 47, 336, 340, 351, 383, 386
Augustine, St, of Hippo 233, 282, 286, 293, 319–75
Austin, John 269–70, 346, 382

Bacon, Sir Francis, Viscount St Albans 147, 360
Bagehot, Walter 175
Bagshawe, Edward, jr 61–2, 65, 66, 67, 69, 71, 73, 118, 123, 203, 342–5, 354, 355
Barclay, Robert 341
Barlow, Thomas, bishop 121, 139
Baxter, Richard 63, 64, 113, 121, 138, 146, 195, 261, 270, 276, 287, 342–4, 347, 353, 360, 363, 367, 380, 382, 384
Bayle, Pierre 190–1, 280–2, 286, 300, 366

Bentham, Jeremy 6, 327, 346
Berlin, Sir I. 6
Birch, John 121
Blackstone, Sir William 6, 346
Bodin, Jean 195, 197–9, 202, 239, 245, 338, 367, 368, 369, 373, 376, 377
Boyle, Hon. Robert 84–6, 137, 141–2, 143, 348–9, 353, 358, 359, 361
Bradford, John 363
Brady, Robert 370
Bramhall, John, archbishop 84, 107, 348, 350
Brerewood, Edward 357
Bridgeman, Sir Orlando 121, 355
Browne, Sir Thomas 32, 337
Buckeridge, John 342
Buckingham, George Villiers, second duke of 204, 370
Bunny, Edmund 363
Burgersdijck, F.P. 134, 357
Burges, Cornelius 343
Burke, Edmund 5, 175
Burnet, Gilbert 212, 234, 284, 296, 299, 364, 369, 370, 371, 372, 375, 385, 386, 387
Burnet, Thomas 272, 276, 315–16, 384, 389, 390
Burns, Robert 304
Butler, E. 341

Cain 31
Calamy, Edmund 344, 366
Calvin, Jean 53, 234, 340, 375
Campanella, Tommaso 358
Casaubon, Meric 137–9
Chamberlayne, Edward 204, 370
Charles I, King 47, 49, 52, 58, 194–5
Charles II, King 46, 58–9, 63–5, 70, 135, 161–4, 169, 180–1, 237, 244, 377
Charleton, Walter 390
Cheke, Sir John 19, 332
Church, R.W. 332

Cicero, Marcus Tullius 100, 351, 379
Clarendon, Edward Hyde, first earl of 64,
  118, 162, 343, 361
Clarke, Edward 283, 299, 386
Clarke, Samuel 349
Clifford of Chudleigh, Thomas, Baron
  162
Coke, Sir Edward, Viscount 369
Coke, Roger 84, 274, 348, 383
Cole, Nathanael 337
Cooper, Anthony Ashley, *see* Shaftesbury
Cooper, Thomas 363
Corbet, John 62–4, 71, 123, 343–4, 354,
  355
Corneille, Pierre 282
Cosin, John, bishop 61, 342
Cowell, John 373
Cranmer, Thomas 165, 363
Cromwell, Oliver 58, 63
Crooke, Samuel 18, 25, 26, 27, 28–33, 35,
  37–40, 43, 54, 61, 90, 103, 105, 218,
  335–8, 349, 387
Cudworth, Ralph 32, 33, 276, 337, 382,
  384
Cudworth, Damaris, *see* Masham
Culverwell, Nathaniel 345
Cumberland, Richard, bishop 352, 374

Darwin, Charles 6, 328
David 349
Davis, Sir John 369
Denham, Sir John, 49
Dering, Sir Edward 363
Descartes, René 94, 96, 97, 282, 350
Devil 34
Dodwell, Henry 166, 363
Donne, John 33, 85, 348
Dorset, Edward Sackville earl of 49
Dryden, John 237, 376
Durkheim, Emile 7

Edwards, John 390
Elyot, Sir Thomas 173
Epicurus 136, 141, 147
Eustachius of St Paul 357
Eve 33, 34, 37, 41, 297, 306
Evelyn, John 358

Farmer, Ralph 58, 64, 341–2
Fairfax, Sir Thomas (later Lord Fairfax),
  52
Fell, John, bishop 58, 62, 95, 342, 377
Field, Richard 72
Filmer, Sir Robert 27, 159, 192, 198–201,
  203, 205, 206–8, 210–14, 217, 221,
  223, 226, 228, 230, 233, 235–9, 333,
  337, 368, 369, 370, 371, 372, 373, 374,
  375
Fitzralph, Richard 196, 367, 368
Flavel, John 81, 346
Floyd, Thomas 368
Forset, Edward 364
Fortescue, Sir John 18, 196–8, 367–8
Fox, George 54, 341
Fuller, Thomas 55, 341, 374

Gailhard, Jean 284
Gassendi, Pierre 350
Gauden, Edward 340
Gee, Edward 47, 48, 226, 340, 373
Gladstone, W.E. 249
Glanvill, Joseph 140, 143, 359
God 2, 6, 11–14, 17–20, 28–43, 44, 48, 53,
  55–7, 60–8, 71–5, 78–107, 109–10,
  114, 125–7, 130, 132, 135, 136, 138,
  141–2, 145–59, 170–4, 176–9, 187–91,
  193–9, 203, 205–8, 210–25, 228–41,
  243, 246–51, 252–74, 277–9, 280–3,
  288–9, 290–317, 319–24, 327–9, 346–
  7, 349, 350, 363, 380
Gouge, William 283, 385
Gregory of Nyassa, St 296
Grenville, Denis 250, 274, 378
Grey, Anitchel 374
Grigge, William 55, 57, 341–3
Grotius, Hugo 6, 83, 91, 100, 202, 223,
  225, 226–8, 251, 345, 347, 349, 350,
  351, 356, 360, 373, 374, 375, 384

Hale, Sir Matthew 121, 245, 377
Halifax, George Savile, first marquess of
  170, 276, 361, 364, 384
Hamann, Johann George 6
Hancock, Thomas 385
Harrington, James 374
Hegel, G.W.F. 7
Henry, Prince of Wales 19
Henson, H.H. 363
Herbert, Edward, Lord Herbert of
  Cherbury 96, 351
Herbert, George 25, 36, 335
Herder, Johann Gottfried 6
Herle, Charles 369
Hobbes, Thomas 4, 7, 13, 41, 83, 91, 93–5,
  98–9, 101–2, 104–7, 108, 116, 135, 136,
  141, 146, 147, 163, 171, 191, 199–200,
  202, 205, 223, 225, 229, 230, 239, 241,
  245, 247, 251, 274–6, 306, 328–9, 338,
  348, 350, 352, 356, 358, 360, 363, 367,
  368, 373, 376, 377, 378, 388, 389, 390
Holy Spirit (see also God, Jesus Christ)
  38, 53, 72, 75, 76

Hooker, Richard 83, 91–2, 97, 115, 165–6, 219, 251, 349, 350, 353, 363, 367, 369
Hooker, Thomas 31, 220, 337
Hotman, François 368
Hume, David 13, 328–9, 360
Humfrey, John 121–2, 354, 355, 363
Hutcheson, Francis 271, 382, 384
Hutchison, Lucy 58

Jacob 237
James I, King (James VI of Scotland) 19, 163, 170, 172, 173, 198–9, 248, 332–3, 338, 353, 363, 364, 368, 378
James, II, King 180–1, 205, 209, 244, 377
Jerome, St 296
Jesus Christ (see also God, Holy Spirit) 37, 54–5, 66, 186–8, 291, 305–15, 390
Jewel, John, bishop 115, 353
Joseph 237
Josselin, Ralph 58
Kant, Immannuel 6, 13, 327
Keckermann, Bartholomew 134, 353, 357
Keene, Edmund 23
Kennett, White 354
Kellison, Matthew 198
King, Henry 18
King, Richard 375, 389
Knox, John 114, 353

La Rochefoucauld, François, duc de 282
Lake, Arthur 34, 337
Laud, William, archbishop 49–52
Lawson, George 235, 301, 347, 373, 375, 388
Le Clerc, John 404
L'Estrange, Sir Roger 354, 371, 377
Leland, John 21
Leucippus 141
Limborch, Philippus Van 346, 388
Lingard, Richard 386
Lloyd, William, bishop 363
Locke, Agnes (neé Keene) 23, 130
Locke, Edward 23, 26
Locke, John, sr 23, 24, 42, 50, 52, 130, 335, 339–40, 359
Locke, John (for Locke's views, see under appropriate entries in index of subjects) xi, 1–5, 7, 11–15, 17–18, 20–43, 44, 47–9, 51–2, 55–9, 62, 65–83, 86–120, 123–34, 140, 142–59, 160–79, 183–91, 192–4, 197–8, 201–3, 207–51, 252–79, 280–8, 289–94, 297–317, 319–29, 332–90
Locke, Nicholas, 21, 39
Locke, Peter 23, 334
Locke, Peter, jr 130

Locke, Thomas 130
Long, Thomas 366
Lonsdale, Sir John, Viscount 385
Louis XIV, king of France 162, 365
Lowde, James 277, 384
Lower, Richard 130, 137
Lucifer, see Devil
Lucy, William, bishop 84, 348

Macaulay,Thomas Babington, Baron 370
Machiavelli, Niccolo 6
Magirus, Johnnannes 134, 357
Malthus, Thomas Robert 6
Marvell, Andrew 248, 354
Masham, Damaris, Lady 286, 359, 385
Matthew, St 219
Maynwaring, Roger 353
Merbury, Charles 195, 197, 367, 368
Mill, James 282
Mill, John Stuart 7, 175, 282
Milton, John 33, 41, 284, 287, 337–8, 386
Molyneux, William 275, 349, 383, 387
Monmouth, James Scott, duke of 181, 365
Montaigne, Michel de 13, 284
Montesquieu, Charles le Secondat, Baron de 6
Moore, Sir John 244, 377
More, Henry 97, 147, 276, 352, 357, 360
Morley, George, bishop 61, 164
Moses 31, 36, 237, 312

Nalson, John 204, 209, 370, 371
Nayler, James 55–6, 58, 341–2
Nelson, Peter 358
Nicole, Pierre 282–4, 287–8, 384–7
Noah 215
North, John 135, 357
Novell, John 347, 364
Nowell, Alexander 165, 363
Nye, Stephen 347

Oldenberg, Henry 358
Overall, John, bishop 165, 363
Ovid (Publius Ovidius Naso) 298, 379
Owen, John 53, 61–2, 122–3, 135, 191, 340, 342, 344, 354, 355, 357, 367

Pareto, Vilfredo 7
Parker, Henry 374
Parker, Samuel, bishop 70, 183, 226, 238, 269, 353, 361, 374, 376, 382
Parry, John 67
Pascal, Blaise 269
Patrick, Symon 366
Paul, St 69, 74, 208, 211, 233, 346, 371, 373

Peacham, Henry 284, 287, 386
Pearson, John, bishop, 62, 64, 237, 342, 376
Peirs, William, bishop, 50–1, 340, 354
Penton, Stephen 385, 386
Pepys, Samuel 119, 374
Perkins, William 61, 66, 85, 234, 349, 375
Perrinchief, Robert 122, 354–5
Peter, St 371
Petto, Samuel 53, 340
Petty, Sir William 22, 33, 337, 382
Philips, Ambrose 204
Popham, Alexander 51–2
Plato 171, 385
Preston, John 31, 337
Price, Richard 383
Proast, Jonas 112, 188, 191, 293–4, 299, 353, 366, 367, 381, 387
Prynne, William 354
Pufendorf, Samuel von 147, 202, 225, 227, 349, 356, 360, 373, 374

Quarles, Francis 337

Ralegh, Sir Walter 92, 350
Ramesay, William 386
Rawlinson, John 195, 367
Rawls, John 7
Reid Thomas 360
Reresby, Sir John 365
Retz, Paul de Gondi Cardinal de 283
Reynolds, Edward, bishop 61, 64, 234–5, 239, 343, 375, 376
Richardson, Sir Thomas 49
Robins, John 54
Rous, Francis 361
Rousseau, Jean-Jacques 5, 7
Rutherford, Samuel 59, 72, 342, 345

St German, Christopher 136, 358
Sancroft, William, archbishop 64, 340, 343
Sandys, Edwin, archbishop 165, 363
Sanderson, Robert, bishop 68–9, 147, 211, 217, 302–3, 343, 367, 371, 374, 382, 388
Savage, Henry 343
Savile, see Halifax
Selden, Sir John 198, 273, 383, 390
Seneca, Lucius Annaeus 197, 273
Sennert, Daniel 134, 357
Sergeant, John 388
Settle, Elkanah 377
Sexby, Edward 356
Shaftesbury, Anthony Ashley Cooper, first earl of 23, 117–18, 128, 142, 168, 169, 180–1, 184, 193, 205, 209–10, 244, 354, 356, 367, 370, 371
Shaftesbury, Anthony Ashley Cooper, third earl of, 384
Sharrock, Robert 348, 390
Sheldon, Gilbert, archbishop 118, 167
Shepard, Thomas 31, 337
Sherlock, William 205, 370, 371
Sibbes, Richard 33, 337, 341
Sibthorp, Robert 367
Sidney, Algernon 171, 200, 204, 207, 211, 226, 364, 370, 371
Smith, Adam 6, 382
Smith, Sir Thomas 369
Somers, John, Baron 243, 370, 377
South, Robert 138, 147, 345, 361
Spenser, Edmund 338
Sprat, Thomas, bishop 135–8, 141, 143, 209, 357, 358, 371
Stahl, Peter 348
Starkey, Thomas 136, 358
Stillingfleet, Edward, bishop 181–3, 226, 240, 261, 274, 276, 310, 365, 366, 373, 374, 380, 383, 384, 388
Stringer, Thomas 365
Stubbe, Henry, jr 67, 75, 139–40, 342–3, 345, 358
Sydenham, Humphrey 332
Sydenham, Thomas 136–7, 143, 269, 357, 359, 361, 362, 382
Sydenham, William 53

Taylor, Jeremy, bishop 34, 273, 338, 356, 383
Temple, Sir W. 364
Thomas, David 359
Thomas, William 336
Thompson, Nathaniel 377
Thorndike, Herbert 63, 343
Tillotson, John, archbishop 103, 147, 273, 277, 347, 348, 352, 360, 361, 383, 384, 390
Timpler, Clemens 134, 357
Tocqueville, Alexis, Comte de 282
Toinard, Nicholas 390
Toletus, Francis 357
Tompkins, Thomas 122, 355
Towerson, Gabriel 18, 75, 153, 235, 261, 345, 375, 380
Tuke, Thomas 238, 375
Tyrrell, James 144, 183–4, 200, 202, 274, 359, 366, 369, 383

Uriah 349
Ussher, James, archbishop 63, 211, 346, 371, 374, 390

Venner, J. 57
Vico, Giambattista 6

Walker, Obadiah 284, 386
Wallis, John 277, 348, 385, 390
Ward, Seth 209–10, 249, 371, 378
Weber, Max 8
Wendelin, Mark 357
Westrowe, Tom 350
Whately, William 296, 387
Whichcote, Benjamin 32, 337

Whitgift, John, archbishop 114, 353, 363
Wilkins, John, bishop 121, 352, 355, 360
William III, King. 292
Willis, Thomas 130, 137, 142, 359
Winthrop, John 31, 337
Wolseley, Sir Charles 355
Wood, Anthony à 341, 344, 348
Worthington, John 136, 237, 357, 376
Wycliffe, John 367

York, duke of, *see* James II

Index of subjects

Absolutism 87–91, 105–7, 124–7, 168–74, 192–201, 205–12, 223–51
Accommodation (*see* Comprehension)
Acts of Parliament (*see* also Bills)
  Conventicle (1664) 118, 162
  Conventicle (1670) 162
  Corporation (1662) 118
  Test (1673) 180, 182
  Toleration (1689) 182
  Uniformity (1662) 70, 118
Adultery 30, 328
Afterlife 89, 187, 302
Alehouse 42
America 24
Analogy 94
Anatomy 143
Animals (*see* also Image of God) 127, 173, 177
Apostolic Succession 166, 188
Approbativeness 26, 280–7, 289
Appropriation 228–9
Arbitrary Power 209, 223–4, 245
Arts and Sciences 138, 215–16
Atheism 135, 140–1, 158, 188–91
Atomic Theory 141–2
Authority 11, 47–8, 79, 201–2, 213, 241, 261, 291, 320–5, (see also *Superiority*)
Autonomy 224, 241, 247, 321–4

Baptists 53, 54, 58
Belief (*see* also Knowledge, Revelation) 89, 147–9, 278–9, 311–12, 313–14
Bible (*see* also Old Testament, New Testament) 34, 39
Bills, parliamentary 121, 164–5
Book of Sports 49
Bristol 21, 52, 55, 57

Carolina 129
Certainty 95–6, 269
Charity 30

Children (*see* also, education) 25–6, 210, 217, ch. 9 *passim*
Christian doctrine (*see* also Creeds, Fall of Man, theory of Church) 28–40, 114–17, 135, 305–9, ch. 10 *passim*
Church of England 46–7, 50–1, 62–6, 70–1, 120–3, 160–9, 179–84, 250
Church, theory of 47–8, 114–17, 165–7, 186–91
Church ales 26, 49–50
Civil government 40–3, 93, 108, 124–7, ch. 7 *passim*
Civil Magistrate 40–3, 44 ff, 74, 105, 111–12, 124–6, 188–91, 232–3
Civil order, Civil Society (*see* also, social order) 40–3, 55, 60, 67, 71, 75, 105, chs. 6–7 *passim*
Civility 286, 385
Coercion 40–1
Colonies 129
Commerce 128–30
Comprehension (*see* also Toleration) 62–3, 121–3, 167, 181–3
Concupiscence 297–8
Conquest 199, 200, 245–6
Consent 91–2, 103, 310–11
  Express 241–2
  Tacit 241–2
Consequentialism 265–6
Conscience 44, 48, 57–61, 65–77, 104, 108–26
Constitution, English 44–8
Constitutionalism 52
Conveniences of Life 215, 258–9
Copulation 298
Corpuscularianism 142
Covenant
  New 36–9, 310–14, 389ff
  Old 36–9, 304
Creation 79–80
Creeds, Credal Christianity 171, 188
Criticism, Historiographical 10

Decalogue (*see* also golden rule) 29, 36, 39, 103
  First Table 29, 72, 188
  Second Table 29, 72, 188, 345
Declaration of Indulgence 162–4
Demonstration 146–7, 192, 212, 217, 262, 264, 267–8
Despotism 196–7, 198–9, 245
Dissent *see* Nonconformity
Dominion 33, 34, 150–9, 176, 195–200, 225–9, 236, 261

Earth 20–1, 34, 229, 372
Economy, English 24–8
Education (*see* also Children) 230–1, 280–9
Epicureanism 135, 141
Epistemology chs. 5 and 8, *passim*
Equality 173–7, 220
Ethics 28–40, 78–107
Evil (*see* also Good) 31
Excursion Crisis 179–81, 205–6
Executive 243–4
Experiment 260
Explanation, Theological 12–15, 17–20, 28–40, 78–107, 187, ch. 10 *passim*

Fall of Man (*see* also Christian doctrine) 33–4, 37, 39, 61, 233–40, 295–308, 310
Families of Ideas 1–11, 193, 251, 321, 322, 325
Fathers (*see* also Patriarchalism) 17, 26, 201, 213
Fifth Monarchists 53, 57
Force 293–4
Forfeiture 246–8
France 282
Freedom, *see* Liberty
Fundamental Law 195, 199, 201, 206

Gentry, Gentlemen ch. 9 *passim*
Golden Rule (*see* also Decalogue, Love, Natural Law Neighbour, Reason) 219–23, 344
Good, Goodness (*see* also Happiness, Pleasure and Pain) 91, 255, 257, 269–72, 313–14
Grace 36–9, 166, 177, 320
Gratitude 273
Great Design of God 34, 214–16, 224, 226–31

Happiness (*see* also Pleasure and Pain) 33, 35, 127, 259, 265, 314
History 201–2

Holland 184
Human Nature 173, 254, 294, 299
Human Understanding (*see* also Ideas) 80–3, 127–59, 170–9, 252–77, 321
Husbands 232–3

Ideas (*see* also modes, relations, substance) 80–3, 95–8, 130–55, 262–4
  Complex 81–2, 259, 263
  Innate 30–2, 95–7, 153
  Reflection 81
  Sensation 82, 98, 135–7, 144
  Simple 259
Image of God (*see* also Reason) 151–5, 174–5
Immortality (*see* also Afterlife) 304–5
Incest 328
Independents, Independency 57–8
Industry, the Industrious 15–19, 128, 226–30, 253
Infallibility 73–4, 183

Justice 189

Kingship, *see* Absolutism, Monarchy
Knowledge (*see* also Demonstration, Ideas, Probability)
  Demonstrative 89, 146–7, 259, 264
  Intuitive 259
  Sensitive 259

Labour 20–4, 227–9
Labourer 129, 291–2
Land (*see* also, Earth) 20–1, 229
Language 153
Law 86, 88, 92–3, 170–1
Laziness 128–9, 153, 177, 293
Legislative (*see* also Executive) 243–4
Liberty (*see* also right)
  Civil 52, 58, 204, 209
  Natural 217, 220–1
  from arbitrary power 223–4, 228–30
  of the will 176, 298, 300–1
Love 29, 32–4, 219–22, 309
Luxury 129

Magna Carta 125
Marriage 232–3
Mechanism 142
Medicine 130, 142
Modes 258
  Mixed 262–6
Monarchy 169, 172, 202, 369
  jure divino 168–9, 205, 206
Money 128–30, 229
Mothers 17, 210, 230–1

Natural Law (*see* also Obligation, Preservation, Property, Self-preservation) 31, 36, 78–107, 130, 133, 201, 208, 264–77, 309
Natural Philosophy 83–6, 132–44, 147–9, 155–6
Natural Theology 12–14
Nature 5, 20–1, 23–4, 36–7, 60, 133
Neighbour (*see* also Love) 29, 30, 39, 219–22, 309
New Testament ch. 10 *passim*
Nonconformity 70, 118, 165, 183

Oaths 27, 30, 55, 187–9
Obligation, moral 101–3, 104, 133, 145, 261–77, 308–10
of necessity 273, 351, 383
Old Testament ch. 10 *passim*
Omnipotence 79–80, 85
Original Corruption (*see* also Original Sin) 295–6
Original Sin 295–9
Oxford 48, 53, 58, 61, 130
Christ Church 53, 61, 71, 75, 95, 117–18

Parents 17, 25–6, 230–1
Parliament 70, 117–18, 121, 162, 205, 238, 243
Particulars 133, 259
Patriarchalism 27, 159, 206
Political 27, 192, 206–7, 211–13, 233–40
Social 20–7
Pensford 21, 24, 25, 28, 52
Personal Identity 235–6, 301–3
Pleasure and Pain 285, 314
Political Economy 6, 128–30
Political Theory (*see* also Absolutism, Constitutionalism, Despotism, Fundamental Law, Locke, Patriarchalism) Introduction, chs. 2, 4, 6–7, Conclusion
Poor, Poverty 27, 30
Popish Plot 179–81
Population 26, 129–30
Power (*see* also Authority, Superiority)
Ecclesiastical 47–8, chs. 2, 4 and 6 *passim*
God's 12–13, ch. 3 *passim*, ch. 7 *passim*, 315–16
Parental 217, 230–1
Political 170–9 ch. 7 *passim*, esp 217
Preservation (*see* also Self-preservation) 155, 218–23, 257–8
Presbyterianism, Presbyterians 50–1, 57–8, 59, 63, 64–5, 121

Pride 33–4
Principles, Speculative and Practical 109
Probability (*see* also, Knowledge, Revelation) 148–9, 253, 278–9, 310
Property 58, 197, 204, 209, 212–15, 224–30
Private 52, 227–30
Protection 241–2
Promises 315
Psychology 256–8
Punishment (*see* also rights) 106

Quakers 53–7, 58

Ranters 53
Reason 26–7, 30–2, 35–6, 39, 72, 76, 82, 103, 170–5, 221, 228–31, 253, 274, 290, 308, 309
Relations 147, 216–18, 249, 258, 259
Representation
Political 233, 238, 242–4, 248–9
Theological 233–40, 293–6, 303–5
Resistance (*see* also Dissolution of Government, Rights) 193, 249–50
Revealed Theology 12 ch. 10 *passim*
Revelation 81, 103, 148, 228, ch. 10 *passim*
Reward and Punishment 81, 106, 258, 264–5, 315
Righteousness 308–10
Rights 125–6, 246–8
self-preservation 218
execute natural law 218, 250
to property 224–30
to liberty 246
of resistance 249–50
to toleration 68, 125–6
Roman catholicism (*see* also Infallibility, Popish Plot, Transubstantiation) 72–4, 123–4, 139, 179–81
Royal Society 135–40
Rules 145, 263
Rye House Plot 181

Sacraments 38, 166
Salvation, Soteriology ch. 10 *passim*
Scepticism 95–7
Schism 166
Secularity, Secular Society 4, 68, 111–13, 209
Self-direction (*see* Autonomy)
Self-preservation (*see* also natural law, preservation, rights) 38–9, 99, 100, 101, 106, 110, 155, 215, 217–18, 218–23, 247, 257

Servants 210, 217, 232–3
Slaves, Slavery 171–2, 210, 216–17
Sociability 99–101, 351
Sodomy 328
Soldania Bay 97
Somerset 18, 20, 21, 22, 23, 24, 26, 27, 29, 42, 43, 48, 49, 51, 54, 58
Sovereign 87–90
State of Nature 87, 242, 274
State of War 248–50
Substance 131, 147, 258–9
Substance, Natural 258–9
Superiority 11–12, 17–20, 30, 34, 54, 67, 79, 86, 94–5, 104–5, 131, 151–9, 170–9, 203, 210–15, 246, 249–50, 261, 264–6, 306
Supremacy, Royal 62, 120, 125, 162–4
Syllogism 133, 146–7

Taxation 51–2, 200
Technique, Intellectual (see also Families of Ideas) 1–2, 7–11
Teleology (see also Great Design of God) 4, 149–55, 209, 252–7
    Aristotelian 154–5, 362
Things Indifferent 60–1, 62, 107, 108, 163
Theology 12–15

Toleration (see also Comprehension, Church, theory of) 63, 69–70, 76, 108–26, 160–9, 183–91
Tories 179–81
Trade 128–30
Tradition 83, 95, 97
Transubstantiation 72
Tyranny 246, 248

Uniformity, Ecclesiastical 65, 122
Unity Ecclesiastical 61–5, 69, 122
Usurpation 247

Virtue 115–16, 264–6
Vision, Intellectual (see also Families of Ideas, Technique) 1–2, 5–11, 14, 126, 158–9, 319, 323

Westminster School 52
Whigs 179–81
Will (see also Liberty) 31, 300–1
Will of God 380
    Secret and Revealed 315–16
Wisdom 79–81, 170–9, 255
Woollens
    manufacture 21–2, 23
    trade 21, 23
Wrington 25, 28, 51